Love & Death in the Ancient Near East

Love & Death in the Ancient Near East

Essays in Honor of Marvin H. Pope

Edited by

John H. Marks and Robert M. Good

FOUR QUARTERS PUBLISHING COMPANY

Published by
Four Quarters Publishing Company
P.O. Box 195
Guilford, Connecticut

Library of Congress Cataloging-in-Publication Data

Love & death in the ancient Near East.

Bibliography: p.
1. Death—Biblical teaching. 2. Love—Biblical teaching. 3. Near East—Social life and customs. 4. Bible. O.T.—Criticism, interpretation, etc. 5. Pope, Marvin H. I. Pope, Marvin H. II. Marks, John H. (John Henry) III. Good, Robert McClive. IV. Title: Love and death in the ancient Near East.
BS1199.D34L68 1987 291.2′3 86-29441
ISBN 0-931500-06-0

Printed in the United States of America

TABLE OF CONTENTS

PREFACE

The happy inspiration for a festival volume to celebrate the sixty-fifth birthday of Marvin Pope came to his graduate students in New Haven during the winter of 1977. That was the year in which Marvin Pope published his magisterial commentary on the Song of Songs, and it seemed fitting to let one of the commentary's central insights provide broad motifs to guide this collection of essays.

The scope of concerns displayed in the articles published here nicely suits the breadth and depth of Marvin Pope's own interests. His publications touch on matters ranging from the smallest particles in Ugaritic and Hebrew to some of the longest and most complex poetry of the Bible and Ras Shamra; from the gory goddess of India to the black madonnas of Europe. His writings reveal encyclopedic learning and display a rare poetic gift—a talent not only for understanding ancient verse, but also for capturing it in English. Marvin Pope has provided standard works on major topics for students of the Bible and the ancient Near East, and, we trust, will continue to do so for years to come.

We had intended to surprise our honored colleague, but unforseen delays in production frustrated our purpose. All of the articles collected here were completed in time for publication in 1981; uncertainty about the eventual date of publication made it impractical for authors to update their contributions.

The authors of papers in this volume represent the larger group who celebrate Marvin Pope's achievements. Many, whom the press of duty prevented from doing so, intended to contribute a study. All of those represented here—and many others as well—wish to join in saluting a stimulating teacher, a scholar of impressive learning, a colleague of unfailing generosity and kindness, and a cheering friend.

R.M.G.
J.H.M.

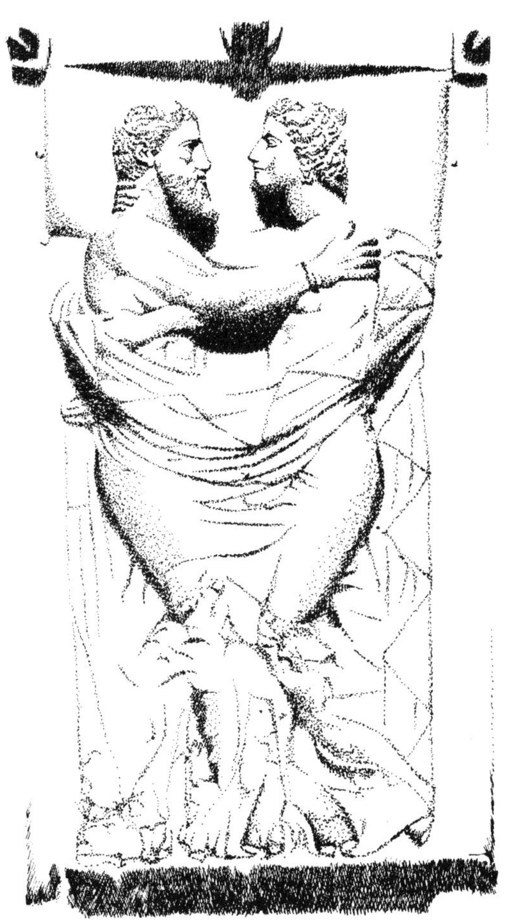

Love & Death in the Ancient Near East

MLK ‘LM: “ETERNAL KING” OR “KING OF ETERNITY”?

ALAN COOPER

A major stumbling block for the student of Ugaritic literature is the incoherence of the pantheon.[1] Fundamental questions—for example, the distinction between divine names and epithets, and the relationship between the gods of the myths and those venerated in the cult—are vexed by the paucity or complexity of the material. Marvin Pope has been in the forefront of the effort to make some sense out of the welter of gods. His *El in the Ugaritic Texts*[2] and his contribution to the *Wörterbuch der Mythologie*[3] remain basic studies of the Ugaritic deities. It is a pleasure, therefore, to dedicate this study of one of the gods to him.

The divine title *rpu mlk ᶜlm* first came to the attention of scholars with the publication of RS 24.252 as *Ugaritica* 5, Text 2.The translation offered by the editor, Charles Virolleaud, was “*Rpu*, le roi du monde,” alternately “le roi éternel.”[4] *Rpu*, he averred, was an appellative of El “sans doute.” The identification of *Rpu* with El has gained wide, although not universal, acceptance.[5]

Subsequent discussion has dwelt on the nature of *Rpu* and the *rpum*,[6] with abundant reference to biblical parallels, but almost no attention has been devoted to the epithet *mlk ᶜlm*. Yet a comparative study of this epithet reveals that *Rpu* should be identified with a god other than El. Furthermore, the correct identification discloses some of the impact of Egypt and Mesopotamia on Ugaritic religious conceptions.

Commentators on *Ugaritica* 5, Text 2 immediately rejected Virolleaud’s “roi du monde” as an anachronistic translation—one suited only to the later Jewish expression *melek hāᶜōlām* so well-known from the blessing formulary.[7] The generally accepted sense of the epithet is now “eternal king,” with temporal signification. A. Caquot[8] (who also provides a bibliography on the subject) has endeavored to be more precise: the epithet *mlk ᶜlm* does not mean “roi éternel,” but “roi d’antan,” *ᶜlm* “indiquant par priorité un temps très lointain . . . .”

It cannot be denied that divine “eternity”—in some sense—is attested in the Ugaritic mythological texts. Foremost among the relevant texts is *UT* 76.3.5-7, as restored and emended by H. L. Ginsberg:[9]

wyᶜny aliyn [bᶜl]	Mighty Baal responds:
lm kqnyn ᶜl[m]	? as our creator is eternal,
kdrd<r> dyknn [ ]	As forever he who fashioned us.

Two other passages speak of the eternity of divine attributes. First, *UT* 51.4.41-43//*ᶜnt* VI.5.38-39:[10]

tḥmk il ḥkm	Your word, O El, is wise,
ḥkmt (ᶜnt: ḥkmk)	You are wise (Your wisdom)
ᶜm ᶜlm	unto eternity.
ḥyt ḥẓt tḥmk	Lucky life by your word.

And *UT* 68.10 mentions the kingship of Baal:[11]

tqḥ mlk ᶜlmk	May you take your eternal kingship,
drkt dt drdrk	Your dominion forever.

1 See the lists of J. de Moor, *UF* 2 (1970): 187-228.

2 M. Pope, *El in the Ugaritic Texts* (Vetus Testamentum Supplements 2, Leiden, 1955); henceforth *EUT*.

3 “Syrien: Die Mythologie der Ugariter und Phönizer” in *Wörterbuch der Mythologie* I/1, “Götter und Mythen im vorderen Orient” (H. W. Haussig, ed.; Stuttgart, 1965): 217-312 (in collaboration with W. Röllig).

4 *Ugaritica* 5, p. 553.

5 For bibliographical details, see my “Divine Names and Epithets” (with contributions by Marvin Pope), in *Ras Shamra Parallels* 3, *s.v. rpu*.

6 See *RSP* 3, as above; also the survey article of M. Dietrich *et al.*, *UF* 8 (1976): 45-52.

7 See, *i.a.*, J. Blau and J. Greenfield, *BASOR* 200 (1970): 12. For the later formula, see J. G. Weiss, *JJS* 10 (1959): 169-71; E. J. Wiesenberg, *JJS* 15 (1964): 1-56; J. Heinemann, *JJS* 16 (1965): 149-54.

8 *Syria* 53 (1976): 299.

9 See *Or* 7 (1938): 9. The sense of the passage is elusive, since most of the preceding context is broken. An invocation to El at this point ought to emphasize his sexual potency rather than his longevity. So A. Caquot, *et al.*, *Textes Ougaritiques* 1 (Paris, 1974): 286 note v. M. Pope had already pointed out that the verbs *q-n-y* and *k-w-n* here and elsewhere denote creation through procreation; see *EUT*, 49-54.

10 It is not clear whether the second colon describes El himself as eternal or not. If we prefer the reading of *ᶜnt* (and possibly also in *UT* 51; see Pope, *EUT*, 42-43), the subject of that colon is the “word of El.” In other words, it is not the god, but his decree that is eternal, in the sense that it is irrevocable once promulgated (cf. Hebrew *bĕrīt ᶜōlām; ḥōq ᶜōlām*).

11 Cf. also *UT* 67.2.10-12; 1 *Aqht* 167-69. As H. Donner has observed (*ZAW* 79 [1967]: 345; see also P. Van Zijl, *Baal* [AOAT 10; Neukirchen/Vluyn, 1972]: 34 n. 2), **tiqqaḥ* is jussive. The passage reflects Kothar’s wish (vain, as it turns out)

Despite these few references, it should be emphasized that there is no god in the Ugaritic pantheon whose power or domain is defined in strictly temporal terms.[12] The concrete sense of the Ugaritic concept of "eternity" is hinted at by another text, *UT* 67.2.12, 20, where Baal surrenders to Mot with these words: *ᶜbdk ank wdᶜlmk*. As E. Jenni notes [13] the literal translation of the sentence is "dein Sklave bin ich und der deiner Ewigkeit." He glosses the latter phrase "und dein für immer." But the literal rendering might actually be preferable. "Ewigkeit" (*ᶜlm*) would then be a substantive denoting the domain of Mot, the netherworld.[14] In any case, since *ᶜlm*, regardless of its grammatical function, is always a substantive in Ugaritic,[15] the epithet *mlk ᶜlm* ought to be translated "King of 'Eternity' " pending a detailed investigation of its nuances.

One attempt to provide a comparative basis for the understanding of *mlk ᶜlm* is J. de Moor's suggestion that the title is probably a translation of Akkadian *šarru dārû*.[16] That suggestion, however, only clouds the issue, because *šarru dārû* is as yet unattested as a divine epithet in Mesopotamia. In fact, it occurs only once—with reference to Nabonidus—as a royal epithet.[17] And even in this case, the context is optative:[18] *anāku lu šarru dārû zānin* [*x-x*]*-uš*, "May I be an everlasting king, who takes care [of the sanctuary]." It is doubtful, then, that *šarru dārû* was ever a royal or divine epithet.[19]

More striking comparative evidence has been brought to light by E. Gaál.[20] Gaál, like most commentators, noticed the occurrence of *mlk ᶜlm* in Ugaritic as an epithet of *Nmry (Ni-im-mu-a-ri-ia* [or the like] = *Nb-m3ᶜt-Rᶜ*, i.e., Amenophis III)[21] in *PRU* 5, Text 8, vs. 9. The fact that an Egyptian Pharaoh bears the epithet suggested to Gaál that the epithet itself had an Egyptian background. He asserts that *mlk ᶜlm* "is the accurate literal translation of the Egyptian [title] *ḥk3 ḏ.t* ('Lord of Eternity')," which is used most frequently in connection with Osiris. He also points to an Egyptian stele, probably to be dated early in the reign of Amenophis V, which depicts the dead Amenophis III adored as Osiris.[22] In front of what remains of the god's image, the signs of the epithet *ḥk3 ḏ.t* are legible. Gaál concludes that the epithet *mlk ᶜlm* refers "to an Osiris-type god, a god of eternity and of the netherworld." *Rpu* might have been the Ugaritic Osiris, god of the dead.

More to the point is the apparent connection between Ugaritic *ᶜlm* and Egyptian *ḏ.t*.[23] This connection not only clarifies the meaning of the Ugaritic term, but it also contains the key to the identity of *Rpu mlk ᶜlm*. An equation other than *Rpu* = Osiris will suggest itself when the evidence is examined in detail, with careful attention to the complex of Egyptian and Mesopotamian deities to which *Rpu* belongs.

It must also be recognized that the Egyptian concept of "Eternity" is both temporal and spatial. The title "Lord of Eternity" (*ḥk3 ḏ.t* or *nb nḥḥ*)—which is, as we shall see, borne by other gods than Osiris—has two distinct nuances. It denotes great duration of reign and it names the god's domain—the realm of the dead.[24]

The penetration of Egyptian notions of divine eternity into Canaanite thought is marked during the Amarna period, particularly in the correspondence of Abimilki of

---

that Baal might exercise eternal kingship. There is no suggestion, either here or elsewhere in the myth, that Baal's dominion was regarded as eternal in fact.

12 The only exception would be El's epithet *ab šnm*, if it meant "Father of Years." But cf. *RSP* 3, s.v. *šnm* and, lately, C. H. Gordon, *JNES* 35 (1976): 261-62, for the correct translation: Father of [the god] *Šnm*." As for *špš ᶜlm*, see below.

13 *ZAW* 64 (1952): 204.

14 Comparative evidence for such an understanding of *ᶜlm* will be presented below. In any case, as Jenni notes (also J. Barr, *Biblical Words for Time*, SBT I:33, 1969², 73-74; Van Zijl, *Baal*, 170), *ᶜlm* here, as in the biblical expression *ᶜebed ᶜôlām*, does not denote "eternity" in the sense of timelessness or the unlimited duration of time.

15 See Jenni, *ZAW* 64 (1952): 202-6.

16 *ZAW* 88 (1976): 325 with n. 18.

17 See conveniently M. -J. Seux, *Epithètes royales akkadiennes et sumériennes* (Paris, 1967): 297. The text is cited in *CAD* D, 116b. The dictionary also mentions a *bēlu dārû in Lugale ix:9, but this text has not been accessible to me. On ᵈ*šamaš dārītum*, see below.

18 And cf. the personal name *šarru-lu-da-ri*, cited in CAD D, 116b.

19 Perhaps the *šarru dārû* of the Nabonidus inscription should be regarded as a variant of the more common *šarrūtam dārītam, zēru dārû*, and *zēr šarrūti dārû*, all of which denote eternal/enduring kingship or dynasty.

20 *Studia Aegyptiaca* 1 (V. Wessetzky Festschrift; Budapest, 1974): 97-99.

21 W. F. Albright, *JEA* 23 (1937): 195; *idem*, *JNES* 5 (1946): 17, no. 36.

22 Aeg. Mus. Berlin 7769, published by A. Radwan, *MDAIK* 29 (1973): 71-76 and pl. xxviib.

23 The two principal terms for "eternity" in Egyptian are *ḏ.t.* and *nḥḥ*. For efforts to explicate them and differentiate between them, see the survey of L. Žabkar, *JNES* 24 (1965): 77-83; E. Hornung, *FuF* 39 (1965): 334-36; also J. Assmann, *Zeit und Ewigkeit im alten Aegypten*, (Heidelberg, 1975): esp. 41-48; *idem*, "Ewigkeit," in *Lexikon der Aegyptologie* 2 (Wiesbaden, 1977): 47-54.

24 On the ambivalence of Osiris' titles (*ḥk3 ḏt* and *nb nḥḥ*, both "Lord of Eternity"), E. Hornung makes the following important remarks (*ZAeS* 81 [1956]: 31-32): "Die beiden Begriffe [*ḏ.t* and *nḥḥ*] meinen nicht nur ungeheuer lange Zeitspannen, sondern ebenso bestimmte räumliche Weltbereiche, die aufs engste mit den anderen chaotischen Weltsphären, vor allem mit Grab und Totenwelt zusammenhängen. . . . " Similarly, Assmann (*Zeit und Ewigkeit*, 48) suggests that when Osiris is specifically associated with the netherworld, his title ought to be

Tyre, which is replete with Egyptianisms.[25] The hymn of EA 147:5-15 (cf. 149:6-7) identifies the Pharaoh with the sun, in keeping with Akhenaten's official theology. This identification finds succinct expression in EA 155:6, 47: *šarru* ᵈ*šamaš dārītum*, "The king [of Egypt] is the Eternal Sun."[26] The epithet of *Šamaš* occurs nowhere else in Akkadian, but it cannot be separated from Ugaritic *špš ʿlm*,[27] and perhaps the later Phoenician *šmš ʿlm*.[28]

The Akkadian epithet recalls the official title of both Akhenaten and his divine father, the Aten—the manifestation of the Sun he venerates:[29] *dy ʿnḫ ḏ.t nḥḥ*, "Who gives/is given life eternally."[30] The same idea is beautifully expressed (in one of many texts which could be cited) in these lines from the Hymn of the High Priest Mairia:[31]

ms.tw.k my msw ytn	You [Akhenaten] were born, as Aten was born;
ʿḥʿw.k m ḏ.t	Your lifetime is Eternity,
ʿḥʿw rʿ m nysw.t t3wy	The lifetime of Re as King of the Two Lands,
rnpw.t ytn m p.t	The years of Aten in the heavens.

A common epithet of the Aten is *nb nḥḥ*,[32] "Lord of Eternity," which is also used for Osiris[33]—and is as likely a retroversion of *mlk ʿlm* as *ḥḳ3 ḏ.t*. In the two hymns on the east wall of the tomb of Ay,[34] the Aten is extolled as "Lord of Eternity" (*nb nḥḥ*), who dawns to grant the king "eternity" (*nḥḥ*) and sets to give him "eternity" (*ḏ.t*). Akhenaten is described as the "son of eternity" (*nḥḥ*) who came from Aten, and he is blessed with "eternity (*nḥḥ*) as king like the Aten." Finally: "O son of Aten, you are eternal" (*nḥḥ*).

The conclusion that the divine name *špš ʿlm* (= *šamaš dārītum*) is a product of the influence of Amarna theology on Canaan seems inevitable. We can extend that conclusion to cover *mlk ʿlm* = *ḥḳ3 ḏ.t/nb nḥḥ*. But an identification of *Rpu mlk ʿlm* with the Aten or *Špš* seems out of the question, and Osiris, too, is problematic: although his cult was widespread in Phoenicia beginning in the fourth century B.C.,[35] there is no evidence that would place him in Ugarit. Even F. Hvidberg,[36] who discusses the possibility of early symbiosis between the cult dramas of Baal and Osiris, also allows for independent, parallel development.

Since it can reasonably be assumed that *mlk ʿlm* represents an Egyptian epithet, we should search for a god who bears the same epithets as Osiris, but who is known in both Egypt and Ugarit. This god must also possess the known characteristics of *Rpu* as described in *Ugaritica* 5, 2. The first such characteristic is an association with "healing," which is suggested by the etymology of *rpu*.[37] Divine healers are typically chthonic deities,[38] and *Rpu*—the eponymous patron of the *Rpum*

translated "Herr der Ewigkeit," but when the god represents the moon or the Nile deluge, the same title is best rendered "Herr der Zeit." For the analogous ambivalence (spatial/temporal) of *ʿōlām* in Jewish thought, see Weiss (N 7): 2-13, but note the rejoinder of Heinemann (N 7). Weiss' evidence for the biblical use of *ʿōlām* in a spatial sense is not persuasive.

25 See W. F. Albright, *JEA* 23 (1937): 190-203. According to Albright, EA 155 dates from the years immediately following the reign of Akhenaten (Amenophis IV).

26 The feminine form of *dārītu* is unexceptionable, in view of the sex of *Špš* at Ugarit. See esp. M. Weippert, *ZDMG Supplementa* 1, xvii. Deutscher Orientalistentag (Wiesbaden, 1969): Vol. 1, 204-5. Weippert also raises the interesting possibility (204 n. 57) that the last sign of *da-ri-tu*$_4$ might be read *tìm*. The substantive *dārītum* would then be an attributive genitive, and the title would be "Šamaš of Eternity," as if it were **šamaš ša dārīti*. This substantive *dārītum* might be an exact semantic parallel for Ugaritic/Phoenician *ʿlm*, while the verbal adjective form is not. See also H. Gese, in *Die Religionen Altsyriens Altarabiens und der Mandäer* (Stuttgart, 1970): 167 with n. 506.

27 *PRU* 5, Text 8, vs 7 (two lines before *nmry mlk ʿlm*).

28 In the Azzitawadda Inscription, *KAI* 26.III.19. For possible biblical reflexes of *šmš ʿlm*, see Y. Avishur, *Phoenician Inscriptions and the Bible* (Hebrew) (Jerusalem, 1979): 138.

29 On the relationship between Akhenaten and the Aten—he is at once the son of the Aten and identified with it—see J. Bennett, *JEA* 51 (1965): 208-9; J. Assmann, "Aton," in *Lexikon der Aegyptologie* 1 (Wiesbaden, 1975): 531.

30 See B. Gunn, *JEA* 9 (1923): 168; G. Fecht, *ZAeS* 85 (1960): 110-16. The epithet of the king is later changed to *ʿ3 m ʿḥʿw.f*, "Great in his Lifespan"; see Assmann, *Zeit und Ewigkeit*, 56.

31 M. Sandman, *Texts from the Time of Akhenaten* (*Bibl. Aeg.* 8; Brussels, 1938): 17.3-4.

32 E.g., Sandman, 28.5; 39.19; 53.4; 90.17; 95.7; 97.15; 101.11; 135.1; 170.5. On the changing conceptions of time and eternity in Amarna theology, see Assmann, *Zeit und Ewigkeit*, 54-61; *idem*, *MDAIK* 27 (1971): 27-28.

33 See *WAeS* II, 299, and *WAeS* Belegstellen 2, 436 for references. Also Assmann, *MDAIK* 27 (1971): 27 n. 63.

34 Sandman, 90-92; English translation by M. Lichtheim, *Ancient Egyptian Religious Literature* 2 (Berkeley, 1976): 93-94.

35 See W. W. Baudissin, *Adonis und Esmun*, (Leipzig, 1911): 185-202; R. de Vaux, *RB* 42 (1933): 31-56; C. Colpe, *lišan mitḫurti* (Von Soden Festschrift; K. Bergerhof, *et al.*, eds.; AOAT 1; Neukirchen/Vluyn, 1969): 23-44.

36 *Weeping and Laughter in the Old Testament* (Copenhagen, 1962): 72.

37 See M. Astour, *Hellenosemitica* (Leiden, 1967²): 225-322, esp. 226-27; 233-40. This work (which predates the appearance of *Ugaritica* 5) must be consulted with caution, but I fully agree with Astour that *rpu* and related terms can only be derived from *r-p-ʾ*, "to heal." See also *RSP* 3, *s.v. rpu*.

38 See Astour on this point (*Hellenosemitica*, 234): "Those who are amazed by the etymology of Rephaim from *rāphâʾ*, 'to heal,' simply do not understand the organic association between the notions of the Nether World—the chthonic cycle—and of healing, i.e., granting health, strength, fertility, and fecundity."

(*"manes"*)[39]—is certainly connected with the netherworld.

Rpu's affinities with the realm of the dead have been stressed by Marvin Pope,[40] who has shown that the god must be closely related to *Mlk* (= the notorious biblical *Mōlek*). The snake bite text in *Ugaritica* 5[41] locates the abode of *Mlk* in Ashtaroth, and *Rpu* shares that address according to the opening lines of *Ugaritica* 5, Text 2:[42]

yšt rpu mlk ʿlm	Let drink *Rpu*, King of Eternity,
wyšt gṯr wyqr	Drink the Mighty and Glorious One
il yṯb bʿṯtrt	The god who dwells in Ashtaroth
il ṯpṭ bhdrʿy	The god who rules in Edrei.

Pope concludes by identifying *Mlk* with *Rpu*, but we have reasons for proposing a different identification.[43]

Other attributes of *Rpu* are listed in *Ugaritica* 5, Text 2, obv. 6ff. as follows:[44]

[ ] rpi mlk ʿlm	[ ] of *Rpu*, King of Eternity
bʿz [rpi m]lk ʿlm	By the strength of *Rpu*, King of Eternity
bḏmrh bl[anh]	By his power, by his might
bḥtkh bnmrth	By his rule, by his goodness
lr[mm b]arṣ ʿzk	To exalt in the land your strength
ḏmrk l[a]nk	Your power, your might
ḥtkk nmrtk	Your rule, your goodness
btk ugrt	In the midst of Ugarit
lymt špš wyrḫ	For the days of Sun and Moon
wnʿmt šnt il	And the pleasant years of El.

Rpu is apparently the patron of the king of Ugarit. Characterized by power, might, and goodness, the god is invoked to grant the king strength and length of reign.

Summing up, we can postulate three leading characteristics of *Rpu mlk ʿlm*:

1. Healer
2. Associated with the Netherworld
3. Mighty Patron of the King

Now there is a Canaanite god who shares these characteristics and is called "Lord of Eternity," and it is *Ršp* (conventionally Resheph).[45] The relationship between *Rpu mlk ʿlm* and *Ršp* might have been signalled by the occurrence of *ršp mlk* in an offering text,[46] but it is the Egyptian and Akkadian evidence that cements the identification.

1. *Resheph as Healer*. The Aberdeen Stele[47] depicts Resheph in his typical warlike pose, but identifies the god as *ršp š3rmʿn3*, that is, Resheph/Shulman (Eshmun),[48] thus identifying Resheph with the best-known of the Canaanite healer-deities.

Resheph is also invoked on a number of steles to bring life, health, and prosperity. He is a giver and protector of life, the opposite side of his well-attested character as a god of pestilence and disease.[49] For example, on a stele in the Oriental Institute in Chicago[50]

39 See *RSP* 3, *s.v. rpu*. The important study of J. F. Healey, *UF* 7 (1975): 235-38, shows that the Ugaritic *mlkm* = Akkadian *malkū* (the Anunnaki as infernal deities). The syllogism *mlk* [*Mōlek*]:*mlkm*::*rpu*:*rpum* suggests itself. See also *RSP* 3, *s.v. mlk*; M. Pope, *Finkelstein Mem. Vol*., 171-72; J. F. Healey, *UF* 10 (1978): 89-91 (esp. 91 n. 23).

40 *Finkelstein Mem Vol.*, 169-72, 181-82.

41 *Ugaritica* 5, 7.41; 8.1.17.

42 For this parsing of the lines (against the *editio princeps*) see B. Margulis, *JBL* 89 (1970): 293-94; also A. F. Rainey, *JAOS* 94 (1974): 187; M. Pope, *Finkelstein Mem. Vol.*, 169-70; *RSP* 3, *s.v. rpu*.

43 It is possible to bring *mlk* and *rpu* even closer together if we follow Pope's discovery of the god *mlk* in UT 124.9-10 (*Finkelstein Mem. Vol.*, 167):

ṯm yḥpn ḥyly	There comes the Mighty One,
zbl mlk ʿllmy	Prince MLK the wise.

Pope's translation of *ʿllmy* as "wise" (cf. also *UT* 123.12; *ʿllmn* in *UT ʿnt* 4.5 and RS 34.126, 1. 7) is hard to accept. As F. Rosenthal has shown (*Knowledge Triumphant* [Leiden, 1970]: 6-12), the meaning "wisdom" for the root *ʿ-l-m* is an inner-Arabic development. More evidence would be needed to assert that a similar development occurred in Ugaritic. (The same argument invalidates all of the purported examples of *ʿ-l-m* = "wise" advanced by J. A. Thompson, *A Tribute to Arthur Vööbus* [R. H. Fischer, ed.; Chicago, 1977]: 159-66.) Without making a forced effort to explain the form, we should either relate *ʿllmy* to *ʿlm* in its normal Ugaritic sense, or seek another derivation entirely. See lately J. F. Healey, *UF* 10 (1978): 86.

44 Reading with Pope, *Finkelstein Mem. Vol.*, 181-82. The case for this parsing of the lines has been made by G. A. Tuttle, "Case Vowels on Masculine Singular Nouns in Construct in Ugaritic," in Biblical and Near Eastern Studies: Essays Presented to William Sanford LaSor (G. A. Tuttle, ed.; Grand Rapids, 1978): 258-60.

45 The data concerning Resheph have been collected by W. J. Fulco, *The Canaanite God Rešep* (American Oriental Series Essay 8; New Haven, 1976). *N.b.* the critical review by A. Spalinger, *JAOS* 98 (1978): 515-17. See also M. L. Barré, *JAOS* 98 (1978): 465-67; *RSP* 3, *s.v. ršp*. On the vocalization of the divine name, see Fulco, 63-65.

46 *Ugaritica* 5, 12.B.7. Surely "Resheph the King," rather than "Resheph *of* the King." See *Ugaritica* 5, 592, but also Herdner in *Ugaritica* 7, 15.

47 Published by W. Spiegelberg, *ZA* 20 (1898): 120-22; Fulco (E 13), 6-7.

48 See Fulco, 25-27; also R. Stadelmann, *Syrisch-palästinensische Gottheiten in Ägypten* (Leiden, 1967): 69, n. 2. Fulco asserts that Albright's equation of Shulman with Eshmun (*AfO* 7 [1931/32]: 164-69) "is probably to be discarded," but without giving any reason. See now *RSP* 3, *s.v. šlm*. Whether the identification stands or not, Shulman is probably a chthonic healer of the Eshmun type. See E. Lipiński, *AION* 33 (1973): 161-83, and note his discussion of the use of *r-p-ʾ* in connection with Eshmun, 181.

49 In the Bible, for example. See Fulco, 56-62.

50 W. K. Simpson, *BMMA* 10;6 (1952): 184 and pl.; *ANEP*, no. 476; Fulco (E 29), 14-15. On the translation, see Spalinger, *JAOS* 98 (1978): 516.

ršpw k3bf nṯr ˁ3 dyf nk ˁnḫ snb rˁ nb

Resheph . ? . great god; may he bring you all life and health every day.

2. *Resheph, Death and the Netherworld.* In *UT* Keret 18-20, Resheph brings about the death of one-fifth of Keret's offspring:[51] *mḫmšt yitsp ršp*, "One-fifth Resheph gathered unto himself." The verb *yitsp* conjures up an image of Resheph as a sort of Ugaritic "grim reaper."

A new ritual text published by Herdner describes an offering to *ršp ḥgb*.[52] The ritual also includes sacrifices for "the gods of the netherworld" (*ilm arṣ*, line 30), and the placement of a throne for Lilū the night demon[53] (*wlll tˁr[k] ksu*, lines 27f.). Most striking is the group of offerings at the beginning of the text, to characters named *ydbil*, *yaršil* and *ˁmtr* (lines 3-5). As Herdner points out,[54] these names, which also occur in the list of RS 24.246,[55] are not divine names, but have the form of theophorous personal names. Nevertheless, as she notes, they do not occur as ordinary personal names in the Ugaritic onomastica. I would suggest that these figures, who are neither gods nor men, are demons, subalterns of Resheph—perhaps the *bny ršp* of Job 5:7.[56] Their bizarre names recall the lists of angels and demons who are invoked, for example, in Jewish magical texts.[57] This ritual text, then, describes a series of propitiatory offerings to the powers of the netherworld, and Resheph is foremost among them.

RS 12.61[58] contains a problematic reference to Resheph. The obverse of the text reads as follows:

bṯṯ ym ḥdṯ	For six days during the month of
ḫyr ˁrbt	Ḫyr, when the sun
špš ṯǵrh	sets, her gatekeeper
ršp	is Resheph.

Regardless of the specific astronomical phenomenon described,[59] it is the mythological content of the text that is important here. W. Fulco correctly apprehends the imagery as a description of Resheph "acting as host/attendant to Šapš in her descent or sudden disappearance into the underworld."[60] The designation of Resheph as *ṯǵr*, "gatekeeper," is well in keeping with the widespread notion that the netherworld is entered through a gate or a series of gates.[61]

51 See the discussion and bibliography in Fulco, 37.

52 RS 24.250 + 259, published by Herdner in *Ugaritica* 7, 26-30. The new text confirms the restoration of *r[š]p ḥgb* in RS 19.13 (*PRU* 5, 5.2). It is hard to give up the attractive "Resheph Sauterelle" (Hebrew *ḥāgāb*, Lev 11:22). Both Fulco, 44, and Herdner, 28, retain it, although they cite an alternate derivation from Arabic *ḥājib*, "gardien de l'entrée," which would relate nicely to Resheph's role as *ṯǵr*, "gatekeeper," in RS 12.61 (see below). Preferable to both might be the Syriac cognate *ḥwgbʾ*, "fana, sacella idolorum" (Payne-Smith, *Thesaurus* 1, 1190b-1191a); hence, "Resheph of the Sanctuary" or the like. Incidentally, the ritual takes place in a garden (*gn*, lines 22, 23). Might this shed new light on the divine title *Ršp gn*? See lately Barré, *JAOS* 98 (1978): 467; also Fulco, 43-44. But note also M. Dahood and G. Pettinato, *Or* 46 (1977): 230-32.

53 Lilū is the male counterpart of Lilītu (Lilith). See, e.g., G. Meier, *AfO* 14 (1941-44): 144, line 84; further references in *CAD* L, 190.

54 *Ugaritica* 7, 6.

55 *Ugaritica* 5, 14.B.4, 6, 7.

56 See Fulco, 58-59, and *RSP* 3, *s.v. ršp, ad* Job 5:7.

57 For such names in rabbinic literature, see R. Margaliot, *Malʾăkē ˁElyōn* (Jerusalem, 1945). Most of the names are of the theophorous type, ending with *ʾl*.

58 *PRU* 2, Text 162 (= *UT* 143).

59 I agree with the assertion of Sawyer and Stephenson (*BSOAS* 33 [1970]: 467-89) that the text contains some special astronomical observation, but their theory that it describes a solar eclipse is hard to accept. First, their analysis of *bṯṯ* as a hitherto unattested L-stem of *b-w-ṯ* (Hebrew *b-w-š*) is forced. If the form is a verb—which I doubt—it would be more reasonable to relate it to Hebrew *b-š-š* (Exod 32:1; Judg 5:28—mistakenly derived from *b-w-š* by early commentators; see Ben-Yehudah, *Thesaurus* 2, 648, n. 1), "to delay, tarry." Isa 24:23 offers scanty support for understanding *b-w-š* in relation to a solar eclipse. Second, the claim that *ˁrbt špš* (= Akkadian *ereb* ᵈ*Šamši*, "sunset"—also perhaps the entrance into the netherworld; see the following note)—is a non-technical term for a solar eclipse is entirely hypothetical. Third, having identified Resheph with Mars, Sawyer and Stephenson then concede that Mars would not have been visible on the date of their proposed eclipse. Their theory depends on the Ugaritians having mistaken Aldebaran for Mars! In sum, the argument that the text describes a solar eclipse seems too contrived. Without claiming the slightest expertise in astronomy, ancient or modern, I would suggest that the text describes the fact that, for a six-day period during the month of Ḫyr, the sun sets in a section of the sky which is known as the "Gate of Resheph." The term "gate," as my friend Prof. Bernard Goldstein kindly informs me, designates a section of the horizon through which the sun and moon rise and set. The setting through a gate refers to the portion of the sky where the sun or moon disappears. See O. Neugebauer, *Ethiopic Astronomy and Computus*, (Vienna, 1979): 156-61. In mythological terms, the sun is perceived to enter the netherworld through the gate.

60 Fulco, 40. He also cites the well-known mythological idea that the sun descends into the netherworld each evening and spends the night there. Cf., for Mesopotamia: K. Tallqvist, *Sumerisch-akkadische Namen der Totenwelt* (Stud. Or. 5/4; Helsinki, 1934): 24-25; for Egypt: K. Sethe, *Übersetzung und Kommentar zu den altägyptischen Pyramidentexten* I (Glückstadt, 1962): 386. For this notion in Ugaritic, see esp. *UT* 62.41-52. Note the divergent interpretations of that text by E. Lipiński. *OLP* 3 (1972): 108-9, and Pope, *Finkelstein Mem. Vol.*, 172. Similarly, the winter sun is subject to the powers of the netherworld. See *UT* 51.8.22 // 49.2.25 // *ˁnt* VI.5.26, and the discussion of Pope, *Finkelstein Mem. Vol.*, 172.

61 I intend to discuss the "gates of the netherworld" in a subsequent article. For comparative material, see *i.a.*, for Egypt: J. Zandee, *Death as an Enemy According to Ancient Egyptian Conceptions* (Suppl. to *Numen* 5; Leiden, 1960): 96-97; 114-25; for Mesopotamia: W. Sladek, "Inanna's Descent to the Netherworld" (Ph.D. dissertation, Johns Hopkins Univ., 1974):

The association of Resheph with the netherworld is clarified by his identification with the Babylonian god Nergal in the bilingual god lists.[62] Building on the hypothesis that *Rpu* = Resheph/Nergal, we may use the Babylonian material to add precision to our understanding of the epithet *mlk* ʿ*lm*.

Nergal, like Resheph, is a mighty god of war and death, but also a life-giver.[63] His status in the netherworld is made explicit in the myth of Nergal and Ereshkigal. Ereshkigal is pleading for her life; she begs Nergal to spare her, and makes him the following offer:[64]

> *atta lu mutima anāku lu aššatka lušeṣbitka šarrūta ina erṣeti rapašti luškun ṭuppa ša nēmeqi ana qātika atta lu bēlu anāku lu bēltu*
>
> You would be my husband, and I would be your wife. I would let you exercise kingship over the Wide Earth [Netherworld]. I would place the tablets of wisdom in your hand. You would be Lord, and I would be Lady.

Nergal naturally accepts the offer. His dominion over the netherworld is expressed succinctly in the famous "Vision of the Netherworld." The narrator of the vision beholds the fearful image of Nergal on his throne, the Annunaki arrayed to his left and right. Nergal is furious at the human interloper for some offense committed against Ereshkigal. But the divine counselor Išum intercedes in behalf of the hapless hero:[65]

> *eṭlum la tušmata šar erṣeti*^{tim} *d*[*a?-n*]*u*?
> Don't kill the man, Mi[ght]y King of the Netherworld . . . .

Nergal's title *šar erṣeti*[66] is, I submit, the nearest thing to an Akkadian equivalent of Egyptian *ḥḳ3 ḏ.t/nb nḥḥ* and Ugaritic *mlk* ʿ*lm*, but it has a more restricted semantic range. While the Egyptian and Ugaritic epithets could have either temporal or spatial signification, the Babylonian one has only the latter. It is clear, then, that *mlk* ʿ*lm* should have the sense of "King of the Netherworld," for this is the point of agreement between the Egyptian and Akkadian parallels. That need not, however, be its only connotation.

3. *Resheph as Mighty Patron of the King*. Amenophis II apparently adopted Resheph as one of his patron deities.[67] In a seal impression, the Pharaoh is called *mry ršp*, "Beloved of Resheph."[68] The Pharaoh's military prowess is elsewhere compared with that of the mighty Resheph.[69]

After the reign of Amenophis II (especially in the Nineteenth Dynasty), when Resheph was more closely associated with popular cults than with royal patronage, he was extolled as a powerful high god.[70] Here his affinity with *Rpu mlk* ʿ*lm* is absolutely explicit:[71]

> *ršpw nṯr* ʿ*3 nb n nḥḥ ḥḳ3 ḏ.t nb pḥty m ḫnw psḏ.t*
> Resheph, Great God, Lord of Eternity [*nb nḥḥ* = *mlk* ʿ*lm*], Lord of Eternity [*ḥḳ3 ḏ.t* = *mlk* ʿ*lm*], Lord of Might in the Divine Ennead.

And similarly:[72]

> *ršpw nṯr* ʿ*3 nb p.t ḥḳ3 nḥtw nṯr nḥḥ*
> Resheph, Great God, Lord of Heaven, Lord of the Ennead, God of Eternity.

The following conclusions may be drawn from the evidence presented above:

1) The appearance of *nmry mlk* ʿ*lm* as a title of Amenophis III in Ugaritic suggests that *mlk* ʿ*lm* represents an Egyptian epithet.

2) The Egyptian notion of eternity (*ḏ.t/nḥḥ*), expressed by the term ʿ*lm*, is independently attested at Ugarit by the divine title *špš* ʿ*lm* (= *šamaš dārītum* [*dārītim*?]), which may well denote the Aten.

3) The divine titles *ḥḳ3 ḏ.t/nb nḥḥ* (= *mlk* ʿ*lm*) are well-attested in Egyptian, but there is only one *Canaanite*

59-60, 67-70; for West Semitic: E. Dhorme, *RB* 16 (1907): 65-71; N. Tromp, *Primitive Conceptions of Death and the Nether World in the Old Testament* (Bib. et Or. 21; Rome, 1969): 152-54.

62 RS 1929, No. 17 = RS 20.24, *Ugaritica* 5, p. 45, line 26; also, RS 24.264 + 280, *Ugaritica* 7, p. 3, line 26. For details of the comparison, see D. Conrad, *ZAW* 83 (1971): 158-64; F. Vattioni, *AION* 15 (1965): 54-55; E. von Weiher, *Der babylonische Gott Nergal* (AOAT 11; Neukirchen-Vluyn, 1971): 90-92.

63 See von Weiher, *Nergal, passim*; also the epithets listed in K. Tallqvist, *Akkadische Götterepitheta* (Stud. Or. 7; Helsinki, 1938): 389-96.

64 EA 357:82ff.; see also von Weiher, *Nergal*, 53.

65 VAT 10057, first published by E. Ebeling, *Tod und Leben nach der Vorstellungen der Babylonier* 1 (Berlin/Leipzig, 1931): 1-9; re-edited by W. von Soden, *ZA* NF 9 (1936): 1-31. The citation is from von Soden, p. 17, line 56. Cf. Ebeling, p. 7, line 16, and also the French translation by R. Labat, in *Les religions du proche-orient asiatique*, (Paris, 1970): 96.

66 And cf. Nergal's related titles, Tallqvist, *Götterepitheta*, 394; *idem, Namen der Totenwelt*, 8-11, 14; von Weiher, *Nergal*, 14-15, 68-70.

67 Fulco, 30-32 and the bibliography cited there.

68 B. Grdseloff, *Les débuts du culte de Rechef en Égypte* (Cairo, 1942): 1-2 and pl. 1; Fulco (E 6), 4.

69 Fulco (E 3; E 5), 3-4, 31. Fulco's interpretation of (E 5) is wrong, see Spalinger, *JAOS* 98 (1978): 516.

70 Fulco, 31-32. Note also Spalinger's collection of Resheph's epithets, *JAOS* 98 (1978): 517.

71 Stela Louvre C86, published by C. Boreux, *Mélanges syriens offerts à M. René Dussaud* 2 (Paris, 1939): pl. facing p. 674; *ANEP* no. 474; Fulco (E 34), 15-16 with n. 71; also R. Stadelmann (N 44): 120; W. Helck, *Die Beziehungen Ägyptens zu Vorderasien im 3. und 2. Jahrtausend v. Chr.* (Äg. Abh. 5; Wiesbaden, 1962): 487, no. 14. [Helck's 1971 revision was inaccessible to me.]

72 Turin 50066 (formerly 1601), in Boreux, p. 682, fig. 3; J. Leibovitch, *Syria* 38 (1961): 28 and pl. II/1 (facing p. 25); Helck, p. 487, no. 28; Fulco (E 36), 16; Tosi-Roccati, *Stele e altere epigraffi di Deir el Medina* (Turin, 1972): 290 pl.

god who bears them: Resheph. The affinities that Gaál noticed between Osiris and *Rpu* are valid insofar as Egyptian Resheph assimilated the character and titles of Osiris.

4) Resheph—along with his Babylonian counterpart Nergal, whose epithet *šar erṣeti* is the Akkadian equivalent of *mlk ʿlm*—fits all the known characteristics of *Rpu mlk ʿlm*.

The equation of *Rpu mlk ʿlm* with Resheph may thus be said to be established to the extent that the evidence allows. In the figure of *Rpu* we can see the confluence of independent and divergent Egyptian and Mesopotamian conceptions of eternity. During the second millennium, a radical change occurred in the Egyptian view of the relationship between time and the gods. Above all, the religious ferment of the Amarna period had far-reaching consequences for Egyptian ideas of divinity, and a notion of time developed "... als Werden und Vergehen, Vergangenheit und Zukunft die zur Vielheit entfaltete innerweltliche Manifestation des göttlichen Willens, der sie in unteilbar Einheit als Ewigkeit in seinem Bewusstein umspannt."[73]

The idea of divine eternity did not flower in Mesopotamia as it did in Egypt during this period. Babylonian divine epithets are typically concrete expressions of the hegemony of a god—the territory he rules, the qualities (wisdom, justice, *et al.*) he bestows. Nergal is associated with specific cult places, he is identified with fire, light, the moon, and the planet Mars. He is a mighty warrior, judge, and ruler, the wise and far-seeing lord of nature and human life, the king of the netherworld.[74] But Nergal's epithets, like those of Mesopotamian gods in general, do not extol him in terms of his dominion over time. This aspect of divinity seems to be relatively unimportant in Mesopotamia.[75] As we have seen, the one extraordinary use of *dārū* in an Akkadian divine epithet is the result of direct Egyptian influence.

The concrete Mesopotamian perception of Eternity (*erṣetu*) and the complex, more abstract Egyptian concepts (*ḏt/nḥḥ*) come together at Ugarit in the figure of *Rpu*:

Resheph	*Rpu*	*Nergal*
nb nḥḥ/ḥḳ3 ḏt	*mlk ʿlm*	*šar erṣeti*
"Lord of 'Eternity' "	"King of Eternity/ the Netherworld"	"King of the Netherworld"

We may now speak of *Rpu mlk ʿlm* as a title of Resheph/Nergal: "The Healer, Eternal King of the Netherworld." He is a patron deity of the king of Ugarit and, as *Ršp*, he is venerated in the Ugaritic cult.

The rich nuances of the term *ʿlm* in the epithet *mlk ʿlm* ought, perhaps, to be borne in mind in connection with first-millennium usage of the term. It may be possible to speak of an Egypto-Canaanite conception of "eternity" that is *both* temporal and spatial; and the point of contact between those two aspects of *ʿlm* is the eternal realm of death. The substantive *ʿlm* never entirely loses its connection with death and the netherworld; it clearly survives, for example, in the idiom *bēt ʿōlām*,[76] and perhaps in other first-millennium expressions as well.[77] With the sources of and parallels to the Ugaritic epithet *mlk ʿlm* exposed, a new perspective may be gained on the complex of ideas associated with "eternity" in West Semitic religious thought.

Jerusalem
26 December 1979*

Additional Note

Since completing this article, I have had the opportunity to study the ritual texts from Ebla published by G. Pettinato in *Or Ant* 18 (1979): 85-215 + 12 pl. In these texts, Resheph ([d]*Ra-sa-ap*, either alone or with modifiers; see pp. 98-100) figures as an important patron of the royal family and the city of Ebla during the reign of King Ibbi-Sipiš. Of all the gods, he is the most prominent recipient of offerings from the royal family, and most of the offerings are made by the king himself (Table 12, p. 201). A sacrifice is also offered to Resheph—and to no other god—on behalf of the "city" (e.g., Text 1, p. 137, v. II, 8-14). These ritual texts, unfortunately, do not permit a characterization of Eblaite Resheph. But his exalted position there might support the claim advanced in this paper that the status of Resheph (= *Rpu*) at Ugarit was higher than the meagre evidence suggests.

73 Assmann, *Zeit und Ewigkeit*, 69.

74 Cf. the source cited above, n. 58.

75 This statement is based on a study of divine *epithets*; it is not an interpretation of the activities of the gods in Mesopotamian literature. For example, on the divine control of history, see B. Albrektson, *History and the Gods* (Coniectanea biblica, OT Series 1; Lund, 1967); W. G. Lambert, *Or* 39 (1970): 170-77.

76 Qoh 12:5, with many parallels. See lately J. Hoftijzer and G. van der Kooij, *Aramaic Texts from Deir ʿAllā*, (Leiden, 1976): 224 with n. 113.

77 This topic will be treated in a sequel to the present paper. Of particular interest are the use of *melek ʿōlām* as a divine title in Jer 10:10, and the *pitḥē ʿōlām* of Ps 24:7, 9.

* I wrote this paper while on a Hebrew University Postdoctoral Fellowship. Thanks are due to Professors Baruch Levine and Moshe Weinfeld, Dr. Tamar Frank, and Mr. Mark Brettler, who read the manuscript and offered many constructive suggestions.

FUNERARY PRACTICES IN EB IV (MB I) PALESTINE: A STUDY IN CULTURAL DISCONTINUITY

WILLIAM G. DEVER

Introduction

The archaeologist need not look far to find material bearing on *one* of the twin themes in this volume honoring Marvin Pope—"Love and Death"—for he or she deals constantly with dead civilizations, particularly with tombs and their rather morbid reflections on life and death in the human past. In this brief tribute to a mentor, colleague, and friend for many years, I wish to focus attention on the unique funerary customs of the Early Bronze IV ("Middle Bronze I") period in Palestine, *ca.* 2200–2000 B.C.[1] Burials of this period have often been treated descriptively in the archaeological literature, but rarely have they been placed in overall cultural context, much less studied from an anthropological perspective.[2] Specifically, what can tombs of this period tell us about those who dug them, used them, and were buried in them? And to what degree do these tombs reflect cultural continuity in an elusive and mysterious period that has often been regarded as "intrusive" in the archaeological sequence of Bronze Age Palestine?[3] To attempt answers to these questions, let us first summarize the evidence available to date and then suggest new interpretations.

I. *Evidence for Funerary Customs in EB IV.*

It will be convenient to summarize the data in terms of the tombs themselves, the manner of interment, and finally the grave goods.

A. *Tomb types.* As far as structural elements are concerned, the distinctive tombs of EB IV Syria–Palestine can be classified according to four descriptive, or "morphological," types.

1. The built-chamber tomb (fig. 1a) is a large, rectangular subterranean chamber, lined and roofed with stone slabs, usually accessible by a square shaft. The best-known example of this tomb type is the *hypogéum* at Til Barsip, now supplemented by many more examples from Tell Hadidi and other sites on the Euphrates recently excavated in connection with the Tabqa Dam Project.[4] This tomb type, which appears to be confined to Upper Syria and is especially characteristic of the Ḫabur region, may be basically of Early Bronze origin.

2. The enigmatic "dolmens" of Syria–Palestine (fig. 1b) consist of several varieties, but all are essentially above-ground chamber tombs, either elliptical or rectangular, constructed of megalithic uprights and roof slabs. Dolmens are typical only of areas such as the Hauran, the Golan heights, and both rims of the Jordan Valley, probably because these regions are characterized by basaltic outcrops rather than softer chalk formations. The location of dolmens in marginal regions also suggests that they are associated more with semi-nomadic than with settled populations. The dolmens have never been dated conclusively, but recent excavations indicate that although they have a very long history many of them were either first built or reused in the EB IV period.[5]

3. Cairns or tumuli (fig. 1c) are similar to the dolmens, though much smaller, consisting of a slab-built, rectangular chamber above ground level, mounded over by a heap of smaller stones. Like dolmens, cairns occur only in rocky, marginal regions, but they are typically found farther south in Transjordan, the Negev, and the Sinai. Though long observed, cairns have been systematically investigated only recently, when excavations have

1 "EB IV" is used here and throughout for the former "MB I" of Albright; for rationale and general orientation to the period, see William G. Dever, "The Early Bronze IV–MB I Horizon in Transjordan and Southern Palestine," *BASOR* 210 (1973): 37–63; *idem*, "New Vistas on the EB IV (MB I) Horizon in Syria-Palestine," *BASOR* 237 (1980): 35-64; Suzanne Richard, "Toward a Consensus of Opinion on the End of the Early Bronze Age in Palestine and Transjordan," *BASOR* 237 (1980): 5-34.

2 This is true even of the most sophisticated interpreters of the period, such as Albright, Wright, Kenyon, Amiran, Lapp, Oren, Prag and others whose works are cited below; cf. nn. 22, 28.

3 So especially Kathleen M. Kenyon; see, for instance, Kenyon *et al.*, "Syria and Palestine c. 2160–1780 B.C.," *The Cambridge Ancient History* 1/2 (3rd.ed.; Cambridge: Cambridge University, 1971): 532–94; and contrast Dever, "Early Bronze IV Horizon" (N 1): 56–60, and "New Vistas" (N 1).

4 F. Thureau-Dangin and M. Dunand, *Til-Barsip* (Paris: Paul Geuthner, 1936): 96–119; Rudolph H. Dornemann, "Tell Hadidi: A Millennium of Bronze Age City Occupation," in *Excavation Reports From the Tabqa Dam Project—Euphrates Valley, Syria* (D. N. Freedman and J. M. Lundquist, eds.; Cambridge, MA: American Schools of Oriental Research, 1979): 113–51.

5 Claire Epstein, "The Dolmen Problem in the Light of Recent Excavations," *Eretz-Israel* 12 (1975; the Nelson Glueck Volume): 1–8 (Hebrew; English summary, p. 117).

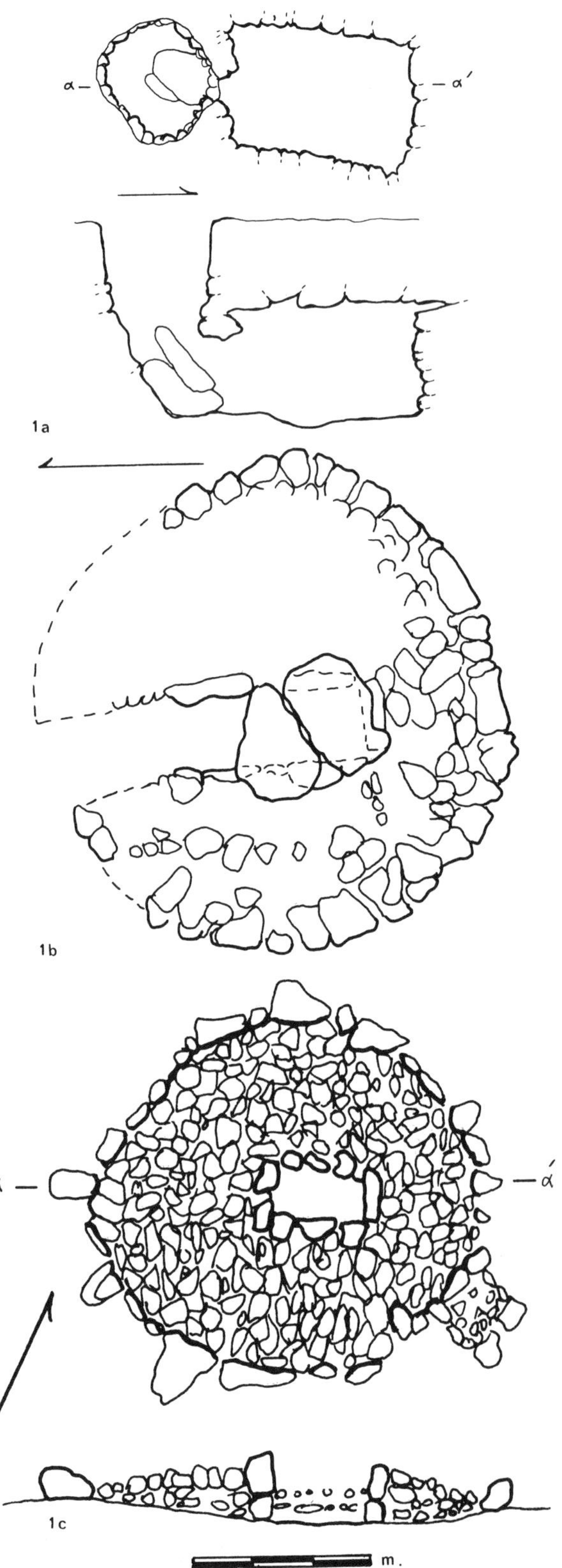

Fig. 1a Area L I chamber-tomb, Tell Hadidi, upper Euphrates;
Fig. 1b Dolmen I, Shamir, lower Golan;
Fig. 1c Cairn/Tumulus T59, Har Yeruḥam, northern Negev.

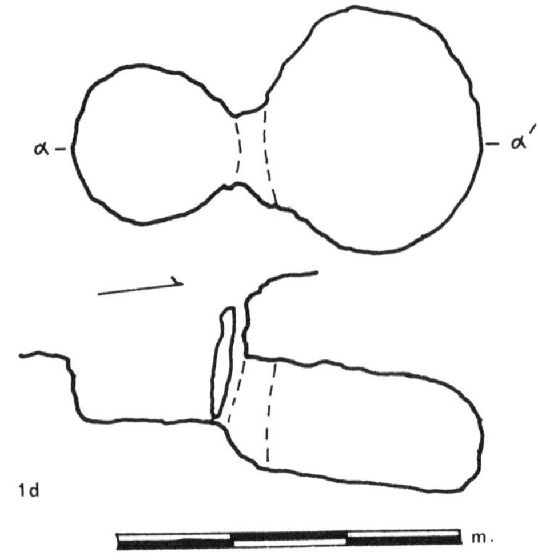

Fig. 1d Single-chamber shaft-tomb B59, Jebel Qaʿaqīr, southern Judaean hills.

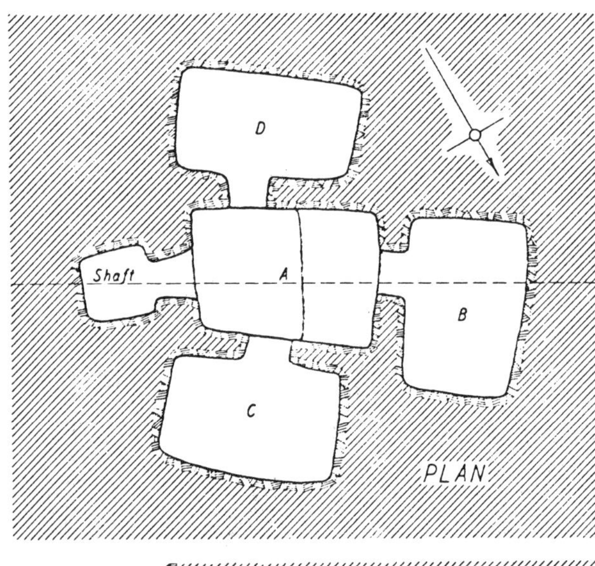

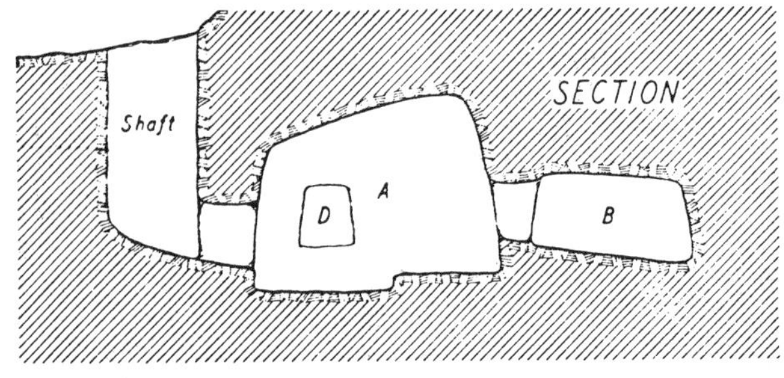

Fig. 1e Multiple-chamber Tomb 878, Megiddo, Jezreel Valley.

indicated that they are more exclusively EB IV in date than the dolmens.[6]

4. By far the most common EB IV tomb type is the shaft tomb, consisting of a rock-cut vertical shaft, normally leading through a small stone-blocked doorway to a single lateral chamber but occasionally to two or four chambers (figs. 1d,e). These tombs vary somewhat in basic form, but the round or elliptical shaft and chamber predominate. They are distributed throughout southern Syria, central Palestine, and even parts of Transjordan, but they scarcely overlap with the regions of the dolmens and cairns, being much more characteristic of the Senonian and Cenomanian limestone regions. Shaft tombs are exclusively EB IV in Western Palestine, but in Transjordan they have recently been shown to belong to a tradition reaching back a millennium to EB I.[7]

Although four basic EB IV tomb types may be distinguished, we would argue that all combine the same salient characteristics. Moreover, they reflect a single cultural tradition, simply adapted to local circumstances (the principal factors being terrain and degree of sedentism). The diagnostic features are, first of all, the location of EB IV tombs: they are not only typically extramural but in fact show no deliberate relation to tell sites—even when they appear nearby, as at Megiddo, Jericho, Lachish, and elsewhere. Indeed, one of the unique phenomena of EB IV is the enormous, isolated cemetary with no neighboring settlements, contemporary or earlier, as for instance the cemeteries at ᶜAin es-Sâmiyeh and many other sites in the central hills, or at Khirbet Kirmil on the edge of the Judean wilderness.[8]

The second diagnostic feature of EB IV tombs is their tendency to occur in large homogeneous contemporary groups, although they overwhelmingly contain individual burials, in sharp contrast to the tradition of multiple burials in both the Early Bronze and Middle Bronze periods (fig. 2, and below).

The third significant characteristic of EB IV tombs, of whatever type, is the enormous expenditure of labor invested in them, far greater than that of any preceding or following period, and certainly in contrast to the otherwise ephemeral aspects of the EB IV material culture (below).[9]

Finally, these tombs are striking in their architectural character, which is particularly noteworthy in a period in which both domestic and monumental architecture by contrast are poorly attested.

B. *Interments.* Two aspects of EB IV burials are unique.

1. One of the most distinctive features of EB IV tombs is the great effort that was expended in preparing tombs that were normally used for a single individual. Because of either inadequate excavation and recording or the poor state of skeletal preservation, information regarding bones has often been indeterminative, but wherever data are sufficient they indicate that single burials were the norm in EB IV. Only occasionally do tombs contain two or more individuals.[10]

2. A second feature of the interments is that the bones are normally disarticulated, indicating a predominant custom of secondary burial in this period (fig. 2). This feature is especially significant, since true secondary burials (in contrast to the custom of *ossilegium*) are relatively rare in Palestine after the Neolithic-Chalcolithic period.[11] They are not normative for any other period, except in EB I in the unique shaft tomb tradition at Bâb edh-Dhrâᶜ in Transjordan, where they may be connected with a semi-nomadic population.[12]

In passing, we should note that the overwhelming majority of these individual and often disarticulated EB IV burials are of adults.[13] This may of course be due to

6 Rudolph Cohen and William G. Dever, "Preliminary Report of the Second Season of the 'Central Negev Highlands Project,' " *BASOR* 236 (1980): 41-60.

7 Paul W. Lapp, "Bâb edh-Dhrâᶜ Tomb A76 and Early Bronze I in Palestine, " *BASOR* 189 (1968): 12–41; *idem*, "Palestine in the Early Bronze Age," in *Near Eastern Archaeology in the Twentieth Century* (J. A. Sanders, ed.; Garden City, NY: Doubleday, 1970; the Nelson Glueck *Festschrift*): 108, 114, 117.

8 Cf. William G. Dever, "Middle Bronze I Age Cemeteries at Mirzbâneh and ᶜAin es-Sâmiya," *IEJ* 22 (1972): 95–112; *idem*, "A Middle Bronze I Cemetery at Khirbet el-Kirmil," *Eretz-Israel* 12 (1975; the Nelson Glueck volume): 18–33.

9 Kenyon points to one of the "outsize" shaft tombs at Jericho from which 155 tons of rock were quarried and removed through a small doorway; see Kathleen M. Kenyon, *Digging Up Jericho* (London: Ernest Benn, 1957): 205.

10 Cf. the comprehensive summary of EB IV human remains in Paul W. Lapp, *The Dhahr Mirzbâneh Tombs: Three Intermediate Bronze Age Cemeteries in Jordan* (New Haven: American Schools of Oriental Research, 1966): 42–49.

11 Cf. Eric M. Meyers, "Secondary Burials in Palestine," *BA* 33 (1970): 2–29. Meyers, however, regards all collected bones, even those deposited in the same tomb in which they were originally buried, as examples of secondary burial. We prefer to regard the latter as *ossilegium* and reserve the term "secondary burial" for the removal of bones to a second and final resting place. See also *idem*, *Jewish Ossuaries: Burial and Rebirth, Secondary Burials in Their Near Eastern Settings* (Rome: Pontifical Biblical Press, 1971).

12 See Paul W. Lapp, "Tomb A76" (N 7); *idem*, *Dhahr Mirzbâneh Tombs* (N 10): 94, 95 (see also pp. 40–49 for an excellent summary of the evidence elsewhere for secondary burials); *idem*, "Bâb edh-Dhrâᶜ: Perizzites and Emim," in *Jerusalem Through the Ages* (J. Aviram, ed.: Jerusalem: Israel Exploration Society, 1968): 108–17.

13 Children's burials are reported only at Tell el-ᶜAjjûl (two); Jericho, (fairly frequent, but only in the "Dagger" tombs); and Jebel Qaᶜaqīr. Cf. Kathleen M. Kenyon, "Tombs of the

Fig. 2 Tomb B59, Jebel Qaᶜaqīr, southern Judaean hills; secondary burial with disarticulated remains of four adults. Photo: Theodore A. Rosen.

the custom of secondary interment, for in the process of exhuming (?) and transporting bodies for burial elsewhere the more fragile bones of children and infants would tend to be fragmented or lost (below).

3. Recent evidence from the writer's excavation at Jebel Qaᶜaqīr suggests a third important EB IV burial feature, the fact that at least in the Hebron hills certain groups of shaft tombs were simultaneously dug and then used for secondary burials in the short summer season.[14] Elsewhere this may also have been the case, although our present evidence is inconclusive.

4. Finally, it should be noted that there is a striking contrast between the care with which many tombs are prepared and the carelessness with which the human remains are deposited. Not only is there little attempt to arrange the bones in the chamber (or to "reconstitute" the skeleton, in the case of disarticulated burials), but many features of the tombs, such as body recesses and lamp niches, remain unused.[15]

Thus in the interments, as with tomb types, there is an apparently random occurrence of various details. Despite this, there is a consistency of basic diagnostic features that points to a uniform cultural background.

C. *Grave goods.* At first glance EB IV burials appear to be characterized by an extreme poverty of objects interred with the dead. The typical burial is accompanied by a few items at best; many burials contain only

Intermediate Early Bronze–Middle Bronze Age at Tell ᶜAjjûl," *ADAJ* 3 (1956): 44; *idem*, *Digging Up Jericho* (N 9): 197; W. G. Dever, "A Middle Bronze I Cemetery on the West Bank of the Jordan," *Archaeology* 25 (1972): 232.

14 The evidence consists of observations that the tombs are systematically laid out in groups, and that the soft chalk of the shafts has never been exposed to winter rain; see William G. Dever, "The Peoples of Palestine in the Middle Bronze I Period," *HTR* 64 (1971): 208, n. 25.

15 The latter is particularly striking at Jebel Qaᶜaqīr; in *no* case in the several tombs where body and lamp niches existed were they actually used. On the incomplete and and dissarrayed skeletons, see n. 42 below.

scattered bones; some are mere cenotaphs, with no contents whatsoever.[16]

Those grave goods that do occur, however, form a consistent pattern. They include principally pottery, especially of certain common types such as the ovoid storejars, smaller amphoriskoi, "teapots" and cups, small bowls, and (frequently) lamps. Although these are all utilitarian vessels, other common types are conspicuously absent, such as cooking pots, large bowls, and many other forms now increasingly attested at the more recently excavated domestic sites. On the other hand, a few forms, such as the squat handleless ovoid jar, are almost exclusively confined to tombs, and it appears that these were especially manufactured as funerary offerings.[17]

In addition to pottery, copper objects appear, including fenestrated axeheads, javelins, pikes, daggers, tanged arrowheads, toggle-pins, awls, and a few miscellaneous items. Beyond these objects, EB IV tomb deposits have yielded only a number of beads. Lithic artifacts are extremely rare.

1. Several observations may be significant. First is the limited range of the repertoire. The grave goods are without exception utilitarian: there are no finds to date that could by any stretch of the imagination be classed as *objets d'art* or "cultic" items. Yet despite this apparent poverty, there are objects that in proportion to the overall material culture represent relatively costly deposits, such as the copper weapons.[18] It must be concluded that the EB IV grave goods with rare exceptions (the small jars above), were chosen precisely because they did represent the culture generally, rather than being especially "funerary" in character. If so, then in these burials we possess a valuable clue for comprehending the EB IV milieu as a whole.

2. Second, we may observe that in the burials there is little, if any, evidence of social stratification, which we should anticipate if indeed it existed. To be sure, scholars have attempted classifications of EB IV tombs on several bases, resulting for instance in Kenyon's "Dagger," "Pottery," "Square-shaft," "Outsize," "Bead," "Multiple," and "Composite" groups at Jericho.[19] But these distinctions are formal and typological, and as such they may be artificial, even arbitrary. In any case, whatever differences are implied they are probably chronological and only secondarily cultural. Also, the tomb groupings observable at Jericho and a number of other sites may reflect varying ethnic backgrounds, or perhaps patterns of political organization. Within each single typological group there is really no artifactual evidence of degrees of wealth or social status: the tombs are entirely homogeneous. What we do encounter is rather more prosaic yet quite expected, that is, sex differentiation. Apart from the universal use of pottery, males are buried with weapons, females with beads or awls (the rare children's burials have no grave goods).

II. *An Interpretation of EB IV Funerary Customs: Cultural Implications.*

As we turn to possible interpretations of the above data, we shall ask first what tombs may tell us theoretically, and then see what the EB IV tombs of Palestine actually do imply.

A. *Theoretical considerations.* It has been thought that burial practices are among the most conservative and thus most revealing aspects of any culture,[20] which, if true, would mean in archaeology that the excavation of tombs would be often especially productive. At the most

16 As, for instance, Cairn 101 at Beer Resisim; see Cohen and Dever, "Second Season, Central Negev" (N 6). At other EB IV cemeteries, the absence of bones has also been noticed; see, conveniently, Lapp, *Dhahr Mirzbâneh Tombs* (N 10): 40–49.

17 So, Kenyon, *Digging Up Jericho* (N 9): 201; Lapp, *Dhahr Mirzbâneh Tombs* (N10): 76, 77.

18 No studies of the EB IV economy have been done, but it seems reasonable to suggest that a copper dagger or javelin may have represented an individual's "cost-of-living" for several weeks or even months. See, provisionally, James D. Muhly, *Copper and Tin. The Distribution of Mineral Resources and the Nature of the Metals Trade in the Bronze Age* (New Haven: Archon Books, 1973).

19 Kathleen M. Kenyon, *Excavations at Jericho, Volume I. The Tombs Excavated in 1952–4* (London: British School of Archaeology in Jerusalem, 1960): 180–202; *idem, Volume II: The Tombs Excavated in 1955–8* (1965): 81–166; see also Kenyon's convenient summary in "Syria and Palestine" (N 3): 570–75; and *Digging Up Jericho* (N 9): 195–207.

20 On the Eastern Mediterranean in the 3rd–2nd millennia B.C., see Saul S. Weinberg, "Ceramics and the Supernatural: Cult and Burial Evidence in the Aegean World" in *Ceramics and Man* (F. R. Matson, ed.; New York: Aldine, 1965): 187–201. Contrast, however, the cautions on the difficulty of correlating burial practices with a culture in Peter J. Ucko, "Ethnography and Archaeological Interpretation of Funerary Remains," *World Archaeology* 1 (1969 / 70): 262–80; and especially Lewis R. Binford, "Mortuary Practices: Their Study and Their Potential" in *Approaches to the Social Dimensions of Mortuary Practices* (J. A. Brown, ed.; Washington: Society for American Archaeology, 1971): 6–20. In this pioneering article Binford surveys previous anthropological and ethnographic literature, updates A. L. Kroeber's earlier study ("The Disposal of the Dead," *American Anthropologist* 29 [1927]: 308–15), and presents arguments drawn from some 40 cultures to argue the wide variability of mortuary practices and their insufficiency in themselves to characterize a culture. See also Arthur Saxe, *Social Dimensions of Mortuary Practice* (unpublished Ph.D. dissertation, University of Michigan, 1970). For general orientation to the problem and to methodology, see W. L. Rathje, "Socio-political Implications of Lowland Maya Burials: Methodology and Tentative Hypotheses," *World Archaeology* 1 (1969 / 70): 359–74; also important is the entire issue of *World Archaeology* (1975) on burials.

elementary level, the chances for recovery of quantities of intact (and sometimes of precious) artifacts are enhanced by comparison with the excavation of disturbed and frequently looted domestic levels. The numerous, well-preserved artifacts recovered from tombs may aid us in reconstructing more representative assemblages of the local material culture, in fixing chronological horizons, and in establishing trade and international relations. And the skeletal evidence, though rarely as well preserved as desirable, may yield data on diet, disease, life expectancy, or (less likely) kinship patterns and possibly even ethnic affinities.[21]

In all these regards, our numerous EB IV tombs, so disproportionate in comparison with the meager domestic remains of the period, could potentially be most revealing. Yet they have not been so, largely for two reasons. On the one hand scholars have tended to minimize the value of evidence from cemeteries as "unrepresentative" of the overall EB IV culture. On the other they have been content with comparative typological and chronological classification of tombs and their contents, failing to recognize that this is but the beginning of archaeological interpretation—more reportage than adequate "explanation" of either historical or cultural processes. It is a sad commentary on the current state of Syro–Palestinian (much less "Biblical") archaeology that analyses to date have either ignored burial practices, or else have failed to proceed beyond the elementary descriptive level.[22] How may we break out of this impasse?

One procedure is to formulate hypotheses (or "models") and then to test them against the available archaeological data. Nearly all previous theories relating to EB IV burials (and indeed for the culture as a whole) have to some degree involved a variation of the "Amorite" hypothesis, which sees the culture as intrusive and attributable to new-comers who supposedly overran Palestine at the end of the urban Early Bronze Age. Thus Kenyon, for example, focuses on the feature of disarticulation in the Jericho tombs as evidence for "nomadic invaders" and on typological distinctions between tomb types as a reflection of "tribal" organization. Or Lapp interprets similar evidence from Dhahr Mirzbâneh to refute the "Amorite hypothesis," substituting for it his theory of trans-Caucasian migrations into Palestine.[23] But these and similar earlier studies (including this writer's) suffer from several serious deficiencies. More recent studies, based both on current archaeological investigation and ethnographic analogy, have rendered all "invasion hypotheses" untenable.[24] Furthermore, traditional studies had concentrated on one or two aspects of EB IV burials, such as artifact groups or secondary interments, but had failed to focus on burial practices as a whole, as we now deem necessary.

B. *An explanatory model: pastoral nomadism.* The analogy of pastoral nomadism has recently been utilized by this writer to explicate the overall culture of EB IV, particularly the Negev complex of settlements currently being excavated in the "Central Negev Highlands" project. On this analogy, the Negev settlements may be interpreted as winter campsites and the Hebron hills cemeteries and cave-dwellings as the summer pasturage and burying grounds of pastoral nomads who migrated along an annual circuit.[25] This analogy draws upon a considerable recent bibliography on pastoral nomadism both in Ancient Near Eastern studies and in modern ethnography. It takes as its point of departure the definition of D. L. Johnson's authoritative study *The Nature of Nomadism: A Comparative Study of Pastoral Migrations in Southwestern Asia and Northern Africa* (1969). Johnson analyzes the general phenomenon of pastoral nomadism (not "full nomadism" or "semi-nomadism," both ill-defined) as a particular form of economic and social adaptation to semi-arid zones, a highly specialized offshoot of agriculture that developed historically along the drier margins of rainfall cultivation. The essential, constant features that distinguish all pastoral nomadism from urban life are: (1) lack of permanent dwellings during part or all of the year, i.e., a high degree of mobility; (2) dependence primarily on some form of animal husbandry (usually sheep / goats in the Middle East); and (3) regular patterns of movement adjusted to seasonal availability of pasture and water.[26] The type of nomadism we shall utilize as a model for

21 The forthcoming publication of the 25 more or less complete, well-preserved skeletons form Jebel Qaᶜaqīr by Dr. Patricia Smith should be the most advanced analysis of EB IV skeletal material to date. Here it will be possible even to document the non-urban nature of this particular population sample; ethnic affinity, however, is much more difficult, perhaps even impossible, to determine.

22 Again, this is true even of the leading specialists in the field; cf. n. 2.

23 See Kenyon, "Syria and Palestine" (N 3); *Jericho* I, II (N 19); contrast Lapp, *Dhahr Mirzbâneh Tombs* (N 10); and for critique, cf. Dever, "Peoples of Palestine" (N 14) and "Second Season, Central Negev" (N 6).

24 For full references, see William G. Dever, "Palestine in the Second Millennium B.C.E.: The Archaeological Picture" in *Israelite and Judean History* (J. H. Hayes and J. M. Miller, eds.; Philadelphia: Westminster, 1977): 70–120; *idem*, "New Vistas" (N 1).

25 See the full bibliography on nomadism in William G. Dever, "Palestine in the Second Millennium" (N 24); and the first full application of the model of pastoral nomadism to EB IV in Palestine in "New Vistas" (N 1).

26 Douglas L. Johnson, *The Nature of Nomadism: A Comparative Study of Pastoral Migrations in Southwestern Asia and Northern Africa* (Chicago: University of Chicago, 1969): 15–19.

understanding EB IV burial practices is Johnson's "horizontal" (in contrast to vertical or transhumance) nomadism, specifically of the "elliptical" pattern, one that characterizes for instance the modern Rwala Bedouin of southern Syria and northern Transjordan.[27] The Rwala, however, are camel-herders who traverse an annual circuit of some 300 miles one way, so that even more suitable for comparison are other pastoral nomadic groups of the area who herd sheep or goats and are therefore somewhat more restricted and may even be partly sedentarized and may engage in some dry-farming and trade. It may be persuasively argued that this model of pastoral nomadism, although experimental at present, is capable of comprehending most if not all our known data on the EB IV culture of Eastern and Western Palestine.

Let us now apply this model of pastoral nomadism specifically to EB IV burial practices as outlined above, feature by feature—something not previously attempted, except in a perfunctory manner.[28]

1. Temporary dwellings. This fundamental aspect of pastoral nomadism goes far toward explaining first the fact that EB IV is an overwhelmingly non-urban period, characterized by the complete absence of any monumental structures such as fortifications and public or cultic buildings, or even domestic architecture. There are no known cities of the period, most of the EB tell-sites of central Palestine being deserted throughout EB IV; few towns or villages exist, except in Transjordan; the Judean hills exhibit mostly isolated cemeteries and scattered cave-dwellings; and even the more numerous domestic sites of the Negev consist largely of a few hamlets with a conglomeration of primitive round stone huts, surrounded by smaller open-country clusters or individual structures of similiar kind. The settlement pattern throughout EB IV is non-nucleated, and the sites themselves are marked by impermanence.[29] It is the numerous cemeteries that conspicuously dominate the period and produce the bulk of our evidence to characterize it. It can no longer be supposed that this "imbalanced" picture is the result of inadequate excavation; rather, it accurately reflects what is basically a pastoral nomadic culture.

How then does the model of pastoral nomadism explain the vast cemeteries, the great care lavished upon burials, and the "architectural" character of tombs—all of which we have noted—especially when we are dealing with a society characterized by an insubstantial material culture? It does so by allowing us to grasp the conception behind the unique EB IV cemeteries: they are "camps for the dead." Indeed, the great preoccupation with elaborately-prepared, individual burials in this society is inexplicable otherwise. Precisely because pastoral nomads have no permanent dwelling in life, they may seek a secure abode for their dead whom they must leave behind. And that is perhaps why similar cemeteries are not found in the urban EB or MB periods preceding and following EB IV, both of which are characterized rather by multiple burials in extramural caves (the latter sometimes in reused shaft tombs), which require neither great investment not efforts at concealment.

Not only is the existence of these unique EB IV cemeteries thereby explained, but their location and layout now become comprehensible. First, as concerns the location of cemeteries, the governing notion of tombs as "houses for the dead" requires that they be constructed as "architecturally" as possible, that is, built of underground stone slab construction (as in Syria) or excavated as deep chambers accessible by vertical shafts. For this reason the major cemeteries are not located in the Hauran, the Transjordan plateau, or the Negev highlands, even though these may have been the primary winter camping grounds. Here the hard limestone cover which cannot be worked with flint or soft copper tools prohibits construction of anything but exposed and ephemeral cairns (or occasional dolmens). Instead, the principal cemeteries are found in the Jordan Valley and the hill country of central Palestine, particularly in areas of soft Senonian chalk where one can easily excavate shaft tombs, i.e., fitting and secure abodes for the dead.[30] Furthermore, these shaft tombs, as we have seen, are systematically laid out in large groups, dug simultaneously and regularly spaced—deliberately, it seems, to form a "camp" for the dead, just as pastoral nomads lay out their camp on trek.

Individual features of EB IV tombs, even details otherwise insignificant or apparently inexplicable, become meaningful on the above model. Only by seeing these tombs as "houses for the dead" can we understand, for instance, the cemeteries at Jebel Qaᶜaqīr, with their frequent stepped shafts; doorways carefully finished then sealed with plastered blocking stones; unique "miniature" doorways cut into the shafts; domed chambers beautifully cut, fashioned, and adze-smoothed; prepared lamp and body niches; the effort involved in preserving and transporting bones for secondary burials; a layer of soft chalk chips beneath the deposited bones; the absence of cultic offerings or artistic objects and the typical

27 Cf. Johnson, *Nature of Nomadism* (N 26): 38–46; Alois Musil, *The Manners and Customs of the Rwala Bedouins* (New York: American Geographical Society, 1928).

28 Kenyon has suggested that the disarticulated burials at Jericho imply pastoral nomadism, but she did not employ anthropological or ethnographic data to document her case; cf. *Digging Up Jericho* (N 9): 200; *idem*, "Syria and Palestine" (N 3): 574, 75. Similarly, Epstein has interpreted the dolmens on the Golan (N 5) in terms of pastoral nomadism, but largely on the basis of the tomb types.

29 Cf. Dever, "Peoples of Palestine" (N 14): 206, 207; *idem*, "New Vistas" (N 1).

30 This above explanation does not seem to have been suggested previously, except by Epstein (N 5), but it makes both geological and cultural sense.

occurrence of grave goods such as pots, weapons, and other utilitarian equipment.[31] Despite the elaborateness of burial practice, there is no evidence here of either sophisticated ritual or profound belief in an afterlife; on the contrary, these EB IV tombs are merely "houses for the dead." Close ethnographic parallels are difficult to cite, but that may be due to the paucity of modern systematic study of nomadic populations in general, as well as to the failure of many observers to pay adequate attention to burial customs in highly mobile societies.[32] However that may be, we believe that the concept sketched above is suggestive, if not definitive.

2. Animal husbandry. The second diagnostic feature of pastoral nomadism—animal husbandry—helps us to grasp still other aspects of EB IV burial practice. If the characterization above is basically accurate, then agriculture (in the form of dry farming) would have played a subsidiary role, and the tending of sheep and goats would have been the mainstay of the economy of this culture. Pastoral nomadism results fundamentally from an ecological compulsion, but the unique form of this adaptation embraces every aspect of society and requires the resources and energies of the entire tribal unit to be focused in a dramatic way on herding and migration. As Barth has shown in his perceptive and eloquent study of the Basseri of south Persia, all other cultural forms—economic, social, and political—derive from this primary fact of existence and can be understood only in relation to it (below).

With the application of this model we may now understand both what is and is not found in EB IV tombs. The inclusion of *objets d'art* and artifacts of ritual or cultic nature with inhumations, so characteristic of burials in nearly all other periods in Palestine, is rare here. Yet that does not necessarily mean that these items were rare in the material culture—only rarely invested with any significant meaning. Thus their absence in burials is explicable not on the assumption that this culture is necessarily poverty-stricken or "primitive," but by noting that many pastoral nomadic societies are characterized by a certain pragmatic and unritualistic attitude, relating to the centrality of migration that we have discussed above. As Barth notes of the activities relating to breaking and setting up camp:

> These meanings, or symbolic aspects, of the activities are of the same logical order and partly of the same form as many of the rituals idioms of a religious ceremony, as these have been analyzed by anthropologists elsewhere.... The context of these meanings is the cycle of migrations, which dominates the life and organizes most of the activities of the Basseri.[33]

The fact that the herds and their maintenance are so crucial would explain, for instance, the curious EB IV custom (hitherto unnoticed) of burying with the dead as the sole tomb offering a sheep or goat carcass, frequently

31 See preliminary reports in William G. Dever, "The 'Middle Bronze I' Period in Syria and Palestine" in *Near Eastern Archaeology in the Twentieth Century* (J. A. Sanders, ed.; Garden City, NY: Doubleday, 1970; the Nelson Glueck *Festchrift*): 132–63; *idem*, "Middle Bronze I Cemetery" (N 13).

32 The usable traveller's accounts and ethnographic studies for our purposes are so few that they may be cited *in toto*: Aref el-Araf, The *Bedouin Tribes of the Beersheba District* (Tel-Aviv, 1935; Hebrew); T. Ashkenazi, *Tribus sémi-nomades de la Palèstine du Nord* (Paris: Paul Geuthner, 1938); F. Barth, *Nomads of South Persia: The Basseri Tribe of the Khamseh Confederacy* (Boston: Little, Brown, 1961); J. Burchardt, *Notes on the Bedouins and the Wahabys* (2 vols.; London: Colburn and Bentley, 1931); H. Charles, *Les tribus moutonnières du Moyen-Euphrate* (Damascus: Institut Français de Damas, 1939); C. S. Jarvis, *Yesterday and Today in Sinai* (Edinburgh, 1931); T. E. Lawrence and C. L. Woolley, *The Wilderness of Zin* (London: Palestine Exploration Fund, 1915); E. Marx, *Bedouin of the Negev* (Manchester: Manchester University, 1967); A. Musil, *Rwala Bedouins* (N 27).

Of general importance for ethnoarchaeology, see Frank Hole, *Studies in the Archaeological History of the Deh Luran Plain. The Excavation of Chagha Sefid* (Ann Arbor: University of Michigan, 1977); Patty Jo Watson, *Archaeological Ethnography in Western Iran* (Tuscon: University of Arizona, 1979); *Ethnoarchaeology: The Implications of Ethnography for Archaeology* (Carol Kramer, ed.; New York: Columbia University, 1979).

Specifically concerning secondary burials among nomads, Burchardt (*Notes on the Bedouins*, 280) in the early 19th century records the practice of Syrian Bedouin of bringing back to the tribal territory the bodies of those who have died on trek outside the district. A century later Musil ([N 27]: 418) notes that among the Syrian Rwala dead are buried where they die, but he does not mention whether or not they were later reburied. Barth notes (*Nomads of South Persia*, 142) of the Basseri of Persia that the corpse is always taken to the nearest village cemetery, never buried out in the hills. Other than these, ethnographic references are difficult to cite, but personal observation of modern Middle Eastern Bedouin populations suggests analogies, some of which could undoubtedly be multiplied through a persistent search of the literature. For instance, I am informed by Professor Benson Saler of Brandeis University that a number of South American nomadic populations on trek regularly bury their dead in shallow graves, then exhume them later, clean the bones completely, and transport them on donkey back for secondary burial at collective cemeteries. Of the Charrúa of Uraguay, who followed the same custom, the early Jesuit Pedro Lozano said: "They carry the bones of their deceased relatives wherever they wander, for love makes this stinking cargo very light"; quoted in C. Beals, *Nomads and Empire Builders: Native Peoples and Cultures of South America* (New York: Citadel, 1965): 118.

33 Barth, *Nomads of South Persia* (N 32): 148.

recorded at Jebel Qaᶜaqīr.[34] Or, similarly, in these tombs we encounter vessels with a skim inside, indicating that a full jar of milk or *leben* was left as an offering. These would have been deemed more suitable than either ritual objects or agricultural products, if the analogy we suggest is accepted. Thus we may see why, apart from these peculiar offerings, there are few specific "tomb offerings" in EB IV tombs, and the pottery and other objects that are found are strictly utilitarian (above). The austerity of the tomb assemblage reflects the simplicity of pastoral existence. The preparation of the tomb itself and the simple deposit of the bones in a "house for the dead" seem to have held adequate symbolic meaning for this culture. (This is also suggested by the lack of order in the deposit of the bones and objects, discussed above.)

3. Seasonal migration. This final and most significant aspect of pastoral nomadism constitutes an even more powerful explanatory model, for it—and it alone—makes sense of many of the most characteristic yet most mysterious features of EB IV burial practice.

First, the assumption of seasonal migration would account for one of the puzzling aspects of EB IV, at least in the Hebron hills: the pattern of widespread shaft tomb cemeteries with no accompanying evidence for contemporary town sites or even permanent settlements of any size. This phenomenon had previously gone unrecognized or had been obscured by what were thought to be inadequate excavations; it was assumed that urban sites to accompany the cemeteries, many discovered in illicit digging, would be found in time with more deliberate excavation. But now the recent excavations at Jebel Qaᶜaqīr, Khirbet Kirmil, and elsewhere make it possible to reinterpret the older evidence from Tell el-ᶜAjjûl, Tell Beit Mirsim, Lachish, and many other southern sites. And it becomes clear that while cemeteries are encountered literally everywhere in the hill country, the Shephelah, and the coastal plain, town sites are conspicuous by their absence.[35] Further excavations can scarcely change the picture of the basic pattern, which is one of temporary, open-country settlements, many of which appear to be little more than campsites. Even though, to judge from the number of EB IV tombs, there may have been a sizable population, it was clearly non-nucleated. This is explicable only if we are dealing with a society that was mostly pastoral nomadic.

This leads us to the concomitant phenomenon in the hills, the shaft-tomb cemeteries themselves. Here the model of pastoral nomadism is even more helpful. First it accounts for the existence of these vast, isolated cemeteries by regarding them as "tribal burying grounds," that is, traditional places of interment to which groups of pastoral nomads return on their annual trek. Although nomadic peoples do not usually own lands, since they are neither sedentary nor primarily agriculturists, both ancient Near Eastern specialists and modern ethnographers point to the persistence of pastoralists' claims to land rights in both their winter and summer encampments. Furthermore, pastoralists are inclined not to wander aimlessly, as "nomads" are thought to do, but rather to return season after season to the same lands to which the tribe lays claim.[36] Thus EB IV cemeteries like Khirbet Kirmil, with at least a thousand tombs in a marginal agricultural region far from any contemporary settlements, have a rationale on the assumption that they were periodically visited by pastoral nomads who migrated to the cooler hills in the summer.

Some of the basic features of these cemeteries are also explicable on the model of pastoral nomadism—especially if we suppose that several related but differing tribal groups, with slightly variant customs, frequented the same summer pasturages. Among these characteristic features, all of which have become clear only recently, are: the existence of several distinct groups of homogeneous tombs and burials in different areas of EB IV cemeteries;[37] the evidence that most of the shaft tombs within each group were prepared simultaneously in advance, and then used and concealed within the brief spring–summer months;[38] and the fact that many of the features in the tombs were not actually used, suggesting the possibility that the people who prepared the tombs were not necessarily the same as those who used them.[39]

The most striking feature of EB IV tombs throughout Palestine is, of course, the nearly universal evidence of secondary, disarticulated burials.[40] These burials, which scholars have puzzled over, are readily understandable on the model of pastoral nomadism—especially if the predominant conception of the tomb as the "house of the dead" required the cutting of deep shaft tombs, which was possible only in the chalk regions of the Shephelah and the hill country (above) to which pastoral groups returned annually in the spring.

34 Jericho may provide similar evidence, although the evidence of sheep / goat bones is simply noted without comment; cf. Kenyon, *Jericho* I (N 19): 260–62 (T. G46; H22); *Jericho* II (N 19): 145 (T. L2). See also Lapp, *Dhahr Mirzbâneh Tombs* (N 10): 22.

35 Cf. n. 29.

36 See especially Johnson, *Nature of Nomadism* (N 27): 1–6.

37 The evidence of grouping is clearest at Jericho (cf. n. 19 above), but is also seen at Megiddo in the distinction between Tomb 1101–02B and the multiple-chamber shaft tombs; in the distinction between the "100–200" and "1500" cemeteries at Tell el-ᶜAjjûl; and in cemeteries A, B, C and D at Qaᶜaqīr. See further K. M. Kenyon, "Syria and Palestine" (N 3): 509–81; Dever, "Middle Bronze I Period" (N 31): 146; *idem*, "Middle Bronze I Cemetery" (N 13): 231, 232.

38 Cf. n. 14.

39 Cf. n. 15.

40 Cf. Lapp, *Dhahr Mirzbâneh Tombs* (N 10): 40–49, for a convenient summary; and on Jebel Qaᶜaqīr, where the evidence for disarticulation is definitive, see Dever, "Middle Bronze I" (N 31): 147; *idem*, "Middle Bronze I Cemetery" (N 13): 232.

It is evident that the bodies in these burials have either been: (1) exposed at the cemetery site until the bones are decarnate; (2) buried elsewhere and exhumed for secondary burial at the cemetery site; or (3) transported for some time before primary burial at the cemetery site. The first possibility is ruled out by the absence of substantial settlements at most of the cemetery sites; certainly there is no indication of permanent, urban establishments with a population of the size necessary to account for the large numbers of individuals buried in the tombs. The second possibility is rendered unlikely by the relative lack of tombs that could have been the primary burials at the Negev or winter sites,[41] and still more by the excellent preservation of delicate skull and other bones that would hardly have survived burial and exhumation. Indeed the bones that usually are included in the burials, chiefly skulls and long bones, point to the custom of transporting previously decarnate bodies.[42] This is further corroborated by preserved evidence of the bags or baskets in which the bones were probably carried and later deposited.[43]

Such disarticulated secondary burials are inexplicable on any model other than one which assumes a migratory population, in this case surely pastoral nomadism, which is indeed implied for the period as a whole. Certainly no known urban society in ancient Syria–Palestine practiced secondary burial. Furthermore, modern ethnographic parallels suggest that such burials are more typical of nomadic than sedentary societies.[44] Finally, one striking ancient confirmation may be found in the well-known Sumerian text which describes the roughly contemporary "Amorites" (often associated with EB IV in Palestine) as uncivilized peoples "knowing neither cereals nor house, feeding themselves on wild truffles and undressed meat, possessing no fixed abode in all the course of their life nor a tomb after their death." That would be almost exactly the description of our EB IV peoples that we should expect from the point of view of the urban writers of the text.[45]

Finally, an explanation of what items typically are and are not encountered with the burials is found in the assumption that we are dealing with pastoral nomads. Such societies can be expected to be much more egalitarian than urban societies, which would account for the general lack of any evidence of socio-economic stratification that we have noted in EB IV tombs. The characteristic "poverty of ritual" among nomads, commented upon by Barth in his study of the Basseri,[46] similarly explains the total absence of any cultic objects in these tombs. And the fact that nomadic populations, because of their simple economy and high degree of mobility, tend to produce little in the way of artistic objects explains our tombs' lack of any objects indicating wealth or developed aesthetic standards. We can now understand, however, the presence of a relatively high proportion of copper implements in these tombs, since nomads in the ancient and modern Middle East are often associated with metallurgy, including copper production, trade, and repair of tools and utensils. Metallurgy is an ideal alternate economic strategy, because the nomadic way of life restricts pastoralists to simple "industries" that are highly portable, and at the same time gives them access both to remote copper sources and to ready markets in the town along their route of migration.[47]

Finally, both the Syrian-Transjordan background and provenance of the distinctive shaft tombs of EB IV, as well as the presence of a few actual imports of Syrian pottery and metals, are explicable on the basis of the fact that pastoral nomads normally move considerable distances and frequently engage in trade as a supplementary economic strategy since animal herding is rarely sufficient in itself.[48]

Conclusion

We began with the question of tombs as a reflection of cultural discontinuity in EB IV. It is now clear from our analysis that the best model for comprehending EB IV funerary practices is pastoral nomadism. This would indeed imply a sharp cultural contrast with the long urban Early Bronze and Middle Bronze cultures preceding and following the brief EB IV interlude. However, on this basis there is no reason to posit the intrusion of a new material culture, much less new peoples in Palestine, as most scholars have done. The EB IV funerary practices are indeed strikingly different, even unique; yet the innovations are more indicative of economic than of ethnic change. Behind that change there lay, of course, even more radical social and political upheavals than those perhaps accompanying the large-scale intrusion of

41 It is significant that nowhere in the vast complex of Negev settlements has a shaft tomb cemetery been discovered. The cairns which are found instead are relatively few; and both their scattered location and the likelihood that some are earlier than the settlements (n. 6 above) makes it unlikely that they were the primary burial places related to the EB IV habitation sites.

42 Cf. Kenyon, *Digging Up Jericho* (N 9): 199, 200; Lapp, *Dhahr Mirzbâneh Tombs* (N 10): 40–49.

43 Cf. Kenyon, *Digging Up Jericho* (N 9): 199, 200.

44 Cf. n. 32.

45 Cf. Dever, "Peoples of Palestine" (N 14): 218–25, for references and discussion.

46 Barth, *Nomads of South Persia* (N 33): 135–53.

47 For full discussion of the unique EB IV copper ingots known from Lachish, Har Yeruḥam, and the Hebron hills, as well as the evidence for nomadism and metallurgy, see William G. Dever and Miriam Tadmor, "A Copper Hoard of the Middle Bronze I," *IEJ* 26 (1976): 163–69. Add now the new hoard from Beer Resisim, Cohen and Dever, "Second Season, Central Negev" (N 6).

48 Cf. Barth, *Nomads of South Persia* (N 33): 90–100; Johnson, *Nature of Nomadism* (N 26): 11, 12, 164, 165.

new people, changes that eclipsed urban life in Palestine for several centuries. The ultimate causes of this revolution still elude us, but thousands of anonymous individual EB IV tombs remain a silent witness to this revolution's devastating effect for generations, before people reverted to town life about 2000 B.C.

GILGAMESH: SEX, LOVE AND THE ASCENT OF KNOWLEDGE

BENJAMIN FOSTER

The Nineveh Gilgamesh epic, a complex Akkadian poem of about 3600 lines, offers a splendor of language, imagery, themes, and ideas to the modern reader.[1] Since the discovery and first interpretation of its contents in the nineteenth century, Assyriologists and other interested critics have read from this text, fragmentary though it remains, an appealing antiphony of analyses and interpretations.[2] Death, heroism, divine disposition, and friendship are but a few of the themes that have aroused the interest of the poet's readers.[3] The Nineveh poet lavished particular care on thematics of love in his poem, and it is these thematics that I will discuss in this essay. It is offered to Marvin Pope, master of the love poetry of the western Semites, as a token that their poet cousins from east of the Euphrates had eloquent thoughts too about love.

The Old Babylonian Gilgamesh epic is not so well preserved as the later version.[4] It treats some of the episodes found in the Nineveh version and preserves others that were presumably in the Nineveh version and which are now lost. The language, poetics, and thematics

1 The Akkadian text is cited from R. Campbell Thompson, *The Epic of Gilgamish* (Oxford, 1930), hereafter referred to as *GETh* or "Nineveh." For some passages reference has been made to P. Haupt, *Das Babylonische Nimrodepos* (Leipzig, 1891). I am grateful to E. Sollberger, Keeper of the Department of Western Asiatic Antiquities of the British Museum, for the opportunity to collate a number of passages. Because of an employees' strike, I was not able to see all of the relevant British Museum tablets at the time of my visit there, so have relied upon the kindness of P. Machinist and C. B. F. Walker for further collations. Portions of col i are quoted using the Nimrud version published by D. J. Wiseman, *Iraq* 37 (1975): 157–63; for collation of that tablet, see W. G. Lambert, *RA* 73 (1979): 89. The Middle Babylonian Ur tablet was published by C. J. Gadd as *UET* VI 394 and edited by him in *Iraq* 28 (1966): 105–21 (collated). For the Assur version I have used Frankena's edition, *CRRAI* 7 (1958): 113ff. For the Sultantepe version, see O. R. Gurney, *The Sultantepe Tablets* I (London, 1957): 14 and 15, edited in *JCS* 8 (1954): 87ff. Neo-Babylonian fragments were copied by W. G. Lambert in *CT* 46. The best translation is that by A. Schott and W. von Soden, *Das Gilgamesch-Epos* (Stuttgart, 1970). The best English translation is that of E. A. Speiser in J. Pritchard, ed., *Ancient Near Eastern Texts Relating to the Old Testament* (2nd ed.; Princeton, 1969), with revisions by A. K. Grayson. I have also profited from the treatment of I. M. Diakonoff, *Ėpos o Gil'gameše* (Moscow / Leningrad, 1961). The most important commentaries on all or part of the poem are those of P. Jensen, *Keilschriftbibliothek* 6/I (Berlin, 1901): 421–531; A. Schott, *ZA* 42 (1934): 92–143; W. von Soden, *ZA* 53 (1959): 209–33, to all of which I am indebted for many insights. My special thanks go to Karen Polinger Foster for her careful reading and comments on this essay, and to the many students who have furthered my understanding of the poem.

2 For a bibliography, see de Mayer, *CRRAI* 7 (1958): 1ff.; Matouš, *BiOr* 21 (1964): 3ff. More recent studies include Komoróczy, *Acta Antiqua Acad. Scien. Hung.* 23 (1975): 41ff.; Thorkild Jacobsen, *The Treasures of Darkness* (New Haven, 1976): 193ff. For a collection of interpretive essays on the poem, see K. Oberhuber, ed., *Das Gilgamesch-Epos* (Darmstadt, 1977).

3 For summary and discussion, see Foster, review of Oberhuber, *Gilgamesch-Epos*, *BiOr* 36 (1979): 185–88, as well as Oberhuber's forward to his volume.

4 The Pennsylvania Tablet ("OB Pa") was copied by Langdon, *UM* 10/3, and re-edited by Jastrow and Clay in their publication of the Yale tablet, *YOS* 4/3. All passages quoted here were collated by the writer with the kind permission of A. W. Sjöberg, Curator of Tablets in the University Museum, University of Pennsylvania, and William W. Hallo, Curator of the Yale Babylonian Collection. In addition to my own collations, I have used a copy of *UM* 10/3 annotated by A. T. Clay and collations of the Yale tablet by J. J. Finkelstein. Parts of an Old Babylonian tablet corresponding to Nineveh Tablet X have been copied by Meissner, *MVAG* 7/I (1902): 14f. and recopied by Pinches, *PSBA* 25 (1903): plates after p. 122; Millard, *Iraq* 26 (1964): 99ff. = *CT* 46 16. Other Old Babylonian material has been published by van Dijk, *TIM* IX 43, 45, 46; Bauer, *JNES* 16 (1957): 254ff. For the unity of the material, see J. Tigay, "Was there an Integrated Gilgamesh Epic in the Old Babylonian Period?" *Essays on the Ancient Near East in Memory of Jacob Joel Finkelstein* (Memoirs of the Connecticut Academy of Sciences 19; New Haven, 1977): 215–18. Jastrow, *YOS* 4/3, 18 already noted that more than one edition of the Old Babylonian epic existed, but dated both the Meissner tablet and the Yale and Pennsylvania tablets to the Hammurabi period. For a somewhat different opinion, see W. G. Lambert, *ZDMG* Supplement 3/1, 68, who suggests, however, that a single person was responsible for his "expanded" Old Babylonian epic that included what is now Nineveh X "weil diese so viel literarische und dramatische Genialität offenbart."

of the Old Babylonian poet are quite different from those of his Nineveh successor.[5] How the two poets treat the same episodes points the reader to the themes developed by each. Among other things, the Nineveh poet added certain thematics of love. He had before him a version of the Old Babylonian poem, though not necessarily the identical one that has survived to the present.[6]

By his use of thematics, the Nineveh poet portrays sex and love as types of human knowledge. The import of his thematic of sex is that sex belongs to the lowest common level of human knowledge—what everyone must know and experience to become human. Once this knowledge is attained, continued non-productive sex is no longer acquisition of knowledge or affirmation of humanity but characteristic of the street, or, at worst, reversion to the animal state. The import of his thematic on love is that love of another person is the next higher order of knowledge and makes a human into a social being. Knowledge of another leads to unity, which need not be based on sexual union. This unity is only apparent, for higher knowledge shows that it is doomed to disintegrate. Such disintegration need not be terminal for the self. The survivor has acquired the next highest human knowledge—of the self that suffering has served at last to delineate. But survival of the self is a matter of chance and following a rational course of action based on the accumulated experience of others.[7] Therefore knowledge itself is the highest knowledge and goal for man and one achieved only after all else has been discarded, even the self. When at last the self perishes, knowledge remains, but only if the self has taken responsibility for making that knowledge available to those who seek it.

This essay will show in detail how the Nineveh poet elaborated his ideas on love, and what themes and devices he chose to make his import clear. These themes are in the first place matters of content. The poet unites, for example, an independent motif of the baseness of the street with the baseness of unproductive sex. In the second place they are matters of technique, in which, for instance, the poet sets up a series of oppositions that he unites and then dissolves, all as a type for his notions on love—its attraction, false unity, and ultimate disintegration. In the third place, they are matters of language, such as artificing and distorting of speech.

This essay proposes that the emphasis on knowledge and on love and sex as intermediary stages to perfect knowledge was primarily the work of the Nineveh poet. This emphasis adds weight and density to the text rather at the expense of freshness, feeling, and spontaneity. Yet over-all, one may judge the effort as successful and appealing, for one has in the Nineveh Gilgamesh epic an interpretation of humanity worked out with a highly interesting and often moving aesthetic.

For the purposes of exposition, I have divided the relevant portions of the poem into five "episodes," each of which corresponds to a stage in Gilgamesh's ascent to knowledge.[8] These episodes may be summarized as follows.

Episode 1: Definition of Opposites (Knowledge of Humanity). Gilgamesh is king, but irresponsible as shepherd, the metaphor for kingship, and is violator of social relationships in some as yet unspecified way. His opposite is created—Enkidu, a man without humanity or society. Enkidu begins the ascent of human knowledge first through sexual awareness and second through use of his rational faculties. When Enkidu attains knowledge of his humanity, he becomes a true shepherd and emerges as a champion of human institutions, especially marriage, which, it is at last revealed, is what Gilgamesh is violating. Within this episode the poet sets up numerous secondary opposites to develop this theme.

Episode 2: Apparent Unity (Knowledge of Another). Gilgamesh and Enkidu fight in the street and become friends. This unity is apparently sanctioned by the city elders and by initiation of Enkidu into an order that consists primarily of prostitutes. This initiation reverses the unity of marriage and attraction to the opposite sex that the poet seemed to be preparing for in the first episode. He shows us thereby that opposites remain so, despite their apparent unity. Enkidu's tragedy begins with his attraction to the opposite sex, is joined by jealousy and revulsion for another of his own sex, and is now sealed by his friendship with Gilgamesh, which has no sexual basis at all. This union seems the closer for being asexual and of near equals, but hints of its falseness abound. One is the adoption or initiation of Enkidu. Others will be provided by Gilgamesh's selfishness.

Episode 3: Antithesis and Rejection (Beginnings of Self Knowledge). Gilgamesh rejects the sexual advances of Ishtar, here personification of unproductive attraction to the opposite sex. Enkidu rejects the prostitute by

5 See B. Groneberg, *Untersuchungen zum Hymnisch-epischen Dialekt der altbabylonischen literarischen Texte* (Dissertation, Münster, 1972). This built on the foundations laid by von Soden in his study of the "Hymnic-Epic Dialect" in *ZA* 40 (1931): 163ff. and *ZA* 41 (1933): 90ff.

6 For a survey of the text history of the poem, see Oberhuber, *Gilgamesch-Epos*, 1ff. I use the term "Nineveh poet" as a convenient name for the author of the text found in the Nineveh recension Tablets I to XI. Mesopotamian scholars believed that the author's name was Sin-liqi-unninni (W. G. Lambert, *JCS* 16 [1962]: 66 VI 10). When or where he lived is uncertain; one usually proposes Uruk and the latter half of the second millennium.

7 This is the import of much Mesopotamian wisdom literature, where the concept called here 'chance' corresponds in varying degrees to 'luck,' 'genius,' or 'divine favor.'

8 These episodes do not necessarily correspond to actual episodes in the story as the poet tells it, but rather to episodes in the development of the particular themes studied here. Many other themes are interwoven with those of sex and love, each with its own dynamics of development.

consigning her to her fate, the street, by a curse and reversal of a curse, both with the same effect. Ishtar descends to the street and becomes just another prostitute.

Episode 4: Disintegration of Unity (Knowledge of the Self). Enkidu dies as a consequence of a vainglorious expedition to secure Gilgamesh fame. Gilgamesh tries first to maintain his unity with Enkidu and then to separate himself from it. Each attempt fails.

Episode 5: Redefinition of Unity (Transcendence of Knowledge beyond the Self). Gilgamesh at last achieves full human knowledge, from lowest (humanity) to highest (the self). The perfection of his knowledge is attained when at last he discards his self, the death of which is inevitable, and perceives that only his accomplishments will remain. Gilgamesh refers to the city walls he had built, but the reader is to understand that his knowledge, as expressed in the text of the poem, is what really remains.

Episode 1: Definition of Opposites (Knowledge of Humanity)

This episode is built upon a series of oppositions and reversals: king versus wild man, shepherd versus exploiter, prostitution versus legitimate marriage and family, male versus female, sexual role reversal, attraction and repulsion, narrative voice versus character voice, dignity versus the street, arousal versus sleep.

The Nineveh poet opens his work with a retrospective portrayal of Gilgamesh as a Mesopotamian wiseman, in the first place endowed with superior knowledge that hard experience and suffering had brought him, and in the second place endowed with the foresight to write down his experiences for the admonition of those who came after him.[9] With considerable skill the Nineveh poet moves into the Old Babylonian poet's beginning, which evidently consisted of conventional terms of praise for Gilgamesh as king.[10] After an account of Gilgamesh's birth or creation, the praise becomes ironic, as Gilgamesh is shown to have a bully's valor.[11]

Nineveh I ii 8–18 (= *GETh* Plate 1, *CT* 46 19)

8. *ug-da-áš-šá-ár ri-ma-niš šá-qú-ú ri-[ši-šú]*
9. *ul i-šu šá-ni-nam-ma te-bu-ú kakkē-[šú]*
10. *ina pu-uq-qi-šú te-bu-ú ru-ʾù-š[u]*
11. *[it?]-ta-ad-da-RI eṭlē šá* Uruk^{ki} *ina ku-u[m-mi-šú-nu?]*
12. *ul ú-maš-[šar* ^{d}]Gilgameš *māru ana abī-[šú]*
13. *[ur-r]a ù [mūš]i i-kad-dir še-[e]-[ret-su]*
14. [^{d}Gilga]meš *š[u-ú rēʾ]-ú šá* Uruk^{ki} *su-[pu-ri]*
15. *šu-ú rēʾu [gaš-ru šu-pu-ú mu-du-ú]*
16. *ul ú-maš-š[ar* ^{d}Gilgameš *batulta ana ummīša]*
17. *ma-rat qur[ādi ḫi-rat eṭli]*
18. *ta-zi-im-ta-ši-na [iš-te-nim-me ilāni rabûti]*

8. He lords it like a wild bull with his head held high,
9. The onslaught of his weapons has no equal.
10. At his *puqqu* his fellows are aroused
11. While the young men of Uruk (stay) fearful in their ch[ambers(?)].
12. Gilgamesh does not release the son to [his] father!
13. [Da]y and [nig]ht grows worse his e[vil way].
14. [Gilga]mesh is shep[herd] indeed of Uruk-su[puri]—
15. Shepherd indeed—[brave, outstanding, and wise].
16. [Gilgamesh] does not re[lease the girl to her mother!]
17. The [warrior's] daughter, [the young man's bride]—
18. Their plaints [the great gods] heard from afar . . .

Commentary[12]

Lines 8–9 can still be understood as positive attributes, for 'proud wild bull' and 'unrivaled weaponry' belong to the conventional inventory of terms of praise for kings.[13]

Line 10 offers three problems. The first is the word *puqqu*. From a Sumerian Gilgamesh story,[14] a version of which was used in the twelfth tablet by the final redactor of the Nineveh version, one can deduce that the *puqqu* was a wooden object, evidently used in a strenuous athletic context at which Gilgamesh excelled.[15] Whether or not the Nineveh poet understood the word in that sense is not clear, as the second problem, the form of the verb, shows. On the basis of the parallel passage, I ii 22, which reads *šu-ut-bu-ú*, von Soden (*ZA* 53 [1959]: 221) suggested an emendation to a causative form 'his fellows are called up' (?), but the fragment BM 34248 (*CT* 46 19 ii 10), which reads *pu-uq-qi-šú te-bu-ú*, favors the translation 'his fellows are aroused,' as now in *AHw* 998b. Arousal is a prominent theme of the first part of the poem, as opposed to sleep in the latter part. The third problem is who is referred to as Gilgamesh's "fellows."

9 I i 1–8 (= *GETh* Plate 1, *CT* 46 17, 19), 39 (= *Iraq* 37 [1975]: pl. xxvii). For recent discussion of the opening lines of the poem, see Wilcke, *ZA* 67 (1977): 200ff.; Moran, *RA* 71 (1977): 190f.; W. G. Lambert, *RA* 73 (1979): 89.

10 I i 27 (cf. Shaffer apud Wiseman, *Iraq* 37 [1975]: 158 note 22).

11 Bullying violence as opposed to valor is an important theme of the Agušaja poem, see Foster, *Studies . . .Finkelstein*, 79ff.

12 This passage (I ii 1–41) has been treated in detail by J. Tigay, "Literary-Critical Studies in the Gilgamesh Epic: An Assyriological Contribution to Biblical Scholarship" (Dissertation, Yale University, 1971): 132ff.

13 Thus Hammurabi was called *rīmum kadrum* 'goring bull,' cf. M.-J. Seux, *Épithètes royales akkadiennes et sumériennes* (Paris, 1967): 250.

14 A. Shaffer, "Sumerian Sources of Tablet XII of the Epic of Gilgameš" (Dissertation, University of Pennsylvania, 1963).

15 I follow here a more cautiously worded suggestion of Shaffer, "Sumerian Sources" (N 14): 31f.; cf. Tigay, "Studies" (N 12): 204ff.

This word seems to be used in a slightly negative sense by the Nineveh poet; in any case, the "fellows" are distinguished from the young men who are citizens of Uruk. Compare the use of *ruʾu* in Ludlul I 88 (= *BWL*, 34) in the progression *aḫu* 'intimate,' *ibru* 'friend,' *tappu* 'companion,' *kinātu* 'associate,' *rūʾu ṭābu* 'good buddy,' *ardu* 'slave.' For further discussion of this word, see F. R. Kraus, *Vom mesopotamischen Menschen der altbabylonischen Zeit und seiner Welt, MKNAW NR* Deel 36 No. 6 (1973): 61.

Lines 12 and 16 are presumably parallels,[16] and need not be taken as reference to Gilgamesh's abuse of marital rights. The description of Gilgamesh's wrong-doing here seems deliberately vague, and does not go beyond asserting that Gilgamesh was not exercising his responsibilities as shepherd of his people.[17]

Line 14 introduces the first of the opposites that the poet wishes to exploit. Gilgamesh is not a proper shepherd, whereas in his portrayal of Enkidu, as will be shown below, he goes to some pains to show that Enkidu would become a true shepherd.

Line 18: The tan-form, normally used for repetitive or continual action, seems to have been favored by the Nineveh poet as a device to represent speaking or perception over a great distance, especially between heaven and earth. Compare VII ii 34: *ul-tu ul-la-nu-um* [*tuk-ku*] *ul-tu šame il-ta-na-sa-áš-šú*[18] "of a sudden a warning shout cried out to him from heaven" and below, I v 28. Could this be a poetic representation of the perceptible time sound takes to travel over a wide space?

The main theme of this passage, a familiar one to Mesopotamian poets, is that valor carried to excess becomes vicious. Within this theme the poet introduces two thematics: violation of family (touched on only lightly), and violation of shepherdship (touched on with heavy irony). The reason for this difference in emphasis between the two thematic motifs seems clear. The poet will dispose of the shepherd motif shortly, so he sets up the opposition in a single bold stroke, but he wishes to explore violation of family at greater length and with greater subtlety, so here he brings it forward with the vaguest of hints, artfully vitiated by the probable parallelism of lines 12 and 16 on the one side and by the false cadence of line 16 to line 17 on the other.[19]

The Nineveh poet moves on to his second theme, seduction. He tells the story of Enkidu's entrapment by the hunter and the harlot with relish, passing lightly over the important point that it is Gilgamesh who provides the harlot (I iii 41). This turn to the story is cast somewhat in the shadow by the ponderous four-fold repetition of the seduction passage by three direct and one narrative speaker: the hunter's father, I iii 19ff.; Gilgamesh, I iii 42ff.; hunter, I iv 8ff.; narrative voice, I iv 16ff. When the actual seduction takes place, the poet conveys excitement by dropping the conventional poetic formulae introducing direct speech.[20] He describes the union of Enkidu and the harlot as follows:

Nineveh I iv 16–21 (= *GETh* Plate 5; *CT* 46 19)

16. *ur-tam-mi* ^mi^*Šam-ḫat di-da-šá úr-šá ip-te-e-ma ku-zu-ub-šá il-qi*
17. *ul iš-ḫu-ut il-ti-qi na-pis-su*
18. *lu-bu-ši-šá ú-ma-ṣi-ma elī-šá iṣ-lal*
19. *i-pu-us-su-ma lul-la-a ši-pir sin-niš-te*
20. *da-du-šú iḫ-pu-pu eli ṣērī-šá*
21. 6 *ur-ri* 7 *mušāti* ^d^*En-ki-dù te-bi-ma* ^mi^*Šam-ḫat ir-ḫi*

16. Šamhat unloosed her attire, opened her vulva, and he took her charms.
17. She was not bashful, she took to herself his vitality.
18. She stripped off her clothes and he lay upon her,
19. She indeed treated him, man, to woman's work.
20. His passionate feelings caressed her.
21. Six days and seven nights was Enkidu aroused and made love to Šamhat.

Commentary

Line 16: The poet replaces *kirimmū* of I iv 8 with *dīdū*, presumably to prepare for a play on *dādu* in line 20. This is rather lamely represented in the translation by attire/desire.

Line 17: *napīšu* 'breath of life' is a significant choice of words here, for in fact, as Enkidu recognized himself (VII iii 6ff.), her seduction led to his death. A rendering 'she took his breath away,' while perhaps not too far from the original, has a tone that the Akkadian poet, so far as I can see, did not intend.

Line 18: The contrast of 'sleep' in this line with 'arousal' in line 21 is one of numerous instances in which vitality and wakefulness are contrasted in different ways with sleep and death.[21] This polarity is particularly exploited in Tablet X when the false vitality of Gilgamesh's sleeplessness is exposed by Ut-napištim.

---

16 Tigay, "Studies" (N 12): 216 note 76.

17 For the Old Babylonian king as shepherd, see F. R. Kraus, *CRRAI* 19 (1971): 253.

18 *GETh* Plate 27, 34; *UET* VI 394 41 (variant: *i-ša-as-sa-šum-ma*); similarly perhaps IV v 5′ (= K 13525, *GETh* Plate 15, note 13).

19 The grammar of this has caused some perplexity; see Tigay, "Studies" (N 12): 137 h–h.

20 There are numerous instances of this device in the Nineveh poem. Compare for example XI 173ff., in which the angry Enlil speaks without a formula of speech, but Ea's conciliatory reply, 176ff., is introduced by the usual formulae. See also below, comments to III ii 10 (emotional prayer), VI 6ff. (seduction attempt), VI 84 (angry Ishtar versus father's conciliatory reply), VII iv 25 (cry for help).

21 Wakefulness: I i 11 13, 23; iv 21; v 12, 19. Sleep is first developed throughout Tablet IV as a vehicle for the numerous dreams portending the unsuccessful outcome of their expedition, then as a vehicle for the ominous dream of Enkidu, portending his

Line 20: For *ḫapāpu* see Moran, *Biblica* 50 (1969): 31 note 3; Cooper, *Essays... Finkelstein*, 43 note 22 ("embrace"). Grayson (*Papyrus and Tablet* [Spectrum Books: 1973]: 142) has proposed 'undulate.'

Line 21: Despite Grayson, *ANET*, 503, I follow Diakonoff, *BiOr* 18 (1960): 62 in assuming that Šamhat is a personal name. It is difficult otherwise to account for the *status absolutus* of the noun; use of the word as a noun in the poem (I v 9 etc.) is no bar to this interpretation. In either case, the stative 'aroused' makes clear that this was a single, heroic act of intercourse extending over six days and seven nights. This prepares us for its opposite: the heroic slumber of Gilgamesh in XI 199ff.

The seduction of Enkidu permits the poet to develop one of the main themes of his poem: vitality and wakefulness. As will be shown below, in the description of Enkidu's shepherdship, his wakefulness is a positive attribute, while Gilgamesh's, as seen in I ii and iv, is mere rowdyism. Both Enkidu and Gilgamesh are to lose their vitality and wakefulness: Enkidu his vitality and his life, Gilgamesh his wakefulness to sleeplessness and eventually to knowledge. At this point in the poem, the motif is introduced almost imperceptibly, as *tēbi* 'aroused' and *ṣalālu* 'sleep (with),' 'lie down (with)' have not yet been enriched with the connotation that the poet wishes to assign them. The artistic principle at work here is evidently the same as that used in introducing the motif of violation of family in I ii; its first appearance is ambiguous and rather lost in the rush of events. This episode draws attention to Enkidu's first loss of vitality. No longer a virgin, he lacks his pristine physical strength. For this the poet has no particular regrets, as he ends on a positive note.

Enkidu has entered the first stage of knowledge, sexual awareness, and now moves to the second, represented by the ability to hear and understand language:

Nineveh I iv 28–32

28. *um-ta-aṭ-ṭu* ^{d}En-ki-[dù *u*]*l ki-i šá pa-ni la-sa-an-šú*
29. *ù šu-ú i-ši-i*[*ḫ*   *r*]*a-pa-áš ḫa-si-sa*
30. *i-tu-ram-mu* [*it-t*]*a-šab ina šá-pal* ^{mí}*ḫa-rim-ti*
31. ^{mí}*ḫa-rim-tum i-na-aṭ-ṭa-la pa-ni-šú*
32. *ù* x̣ x̣ ⌈*ti*⌉ *i-qab-bu-ú i-šem-ma-a-a uznā-šú*

28. Less was Enkidu become, he could not run as he had before,
29. But he gr[ew in . . .   and] broader understanding.
30. He turned back and sat himself down at the harlot's feet.
31. The harlot looked into his face
32. And to [the words(?)] that she was speaking did his ears give hearing.

---

death (e.g., VII ii 13 etc, as the typos for his death), later (IX i 13) as the vehicle for the dream portending Gilgamesh's last expedition, and ultimately as the typos for death itself, XI 199ff.

Commentary

Lines 31ff: Note the inventory of the rational faculties given here: sight, speech, and hearing. Enkidu's ascent to knowledge begins with hearing. Sight, hearing, and speech are developed into a more elaborate conceit in *Enuma Eliš* I 94ff:

ḫa-sa-siš la na-da-a a-ma-riš pa-áš-qa
4 IGI^{II}-*šú* 4 GEŠTUG^{II}-*šú*
šap-ti-šú ina šu-ta-bu-li ^{d}Girra *it-tan-paḫ*
ir-ti-bu-ú 4-ta-àm *ḫa-si-sa*
ù IGI^{II} *ki-ma šu-a-tu i-bar-ra-a gim-re-e*

Unheard of, hard to perceive!
Fourfold his eyesight, fourfold his hearing,
His lips in discourse a fire breaking out.
Formidable his power of fourfold hearing
And his eyesight just as much sees everything.

Line 32: Collation of the second sign in this line (K 2756^{d} = Haupt Nr. 2 p. 7) by P. Machinist: "not A, probably not ḪA." According to C. B. F. Walker, the present trace is as follows: [illegible]. Von Soden, *ZA* 53 (1959): 222 proposes: *ù šá*! $^{m[í}$*ḫa-rim*]*-ti* "and what the harlot was speaking . . . "

The poet has established his two principal opposites, Enkidu and Gilgamesh. He will now pair them off with opposites, Enkidu with the harlot, Gilgamesh with his mother. Here, to keep matters in balance, the negative tone disappears from the portrayal of Gilgamesh, and, in fact, justification is offered for his behavior. Gilgamesh's mother explains to him his dreams of Enkidu (Dreams I and II below), while the harlot explains the real Gilgamesh to Enkidu. The Nineveh poet executes a complicated reversal of the narrative as well, beginning by placing Gilgamesh's speech to his mother in the words of the harlot's speech to Enkidu. With the opposites established, both the Nineveh and Old Babylonian poets introduce the theme of attraction. Each does this, however, in a different way.

OB Pa I 3–14 (Old Babylonian Dream I, Gilgamesh speaks)

3. *um-mi i-na ša-at mu-ši-ti-ia*
4. *ša-am-ḫa-ku-ma at-ta-na-al-la-ak*
5. *i-na bi-ri-it eṭ-lu-tim*
6. *ib-*[*ba*?]-⌈*šu*⌉?*-nim-ma ka-ka-bu ša-ma-i*
7. [x]-*e*?*-rum ša A-nim im-qú-ut a-na ṣe-ri-ia*
8. *aš-ši-šu-ma ik-ta-bi-it e-li-ia*
9. *ú-ni-iš-šu-ma nu-uš-ša-šu ú-ul el-ti-*ʾ*i*
10. Uruk^{ki} *ma-tum pa-ḫi-ir e-li-šu*
11. *eṭ-lu-tum ú-na-ša-qu ši-pi-šu*
12. *ú-um-mi-id-ma pu-ti*
13. *i-mi-du ia-ti*
14. *aš-ši-a-šu-ma at-ba-la-aš-šu a-na ṣe-ri-ki*

3. Mother, in my nighttime
4. I felt proud and was walking about
5. Among young men.

6. Then there ca[me out] around me the stars of heaven,
7. [ ] of Anu fell right upon me.
8. I tried to bear it but it was too heavy for me,
9. I strained but I could not move it.
10. While the land of Uruk was gathered around it,
11. The young men did it homage,
12. I even bent my brow—
13. They loaded me.
14. At last I could raise it and brought it off to you.

Nineveh I v 23–38 (Nineveh Dream I, harlot speaks)

23. *la-am tal-li-ka ul-tu šá-di-ma*
24. ^{d}Gilgameš *ina libbi* Uruk^{ki} *i-na-aṭ-ṭa-lu šu-na-tu-ka*
25. *it-be-ma* ^{d}Gilgameš *šu-na-ta ipaššar*^{ár} *izzakkar*^{ár} *ana ummi-šú*
26. *um-mi šutta aṭ-ṭu-lu mu-ši-ti-ia*
27. *ib-šu-nim-ma kakkabū šamê*
28. *kima ki-iṣ-ru ša* ^{d}*A-nim im-ta-naq-qu-ut e-li ṣēri-ia*
29. *áš-ši-šu-ma da-an e-li-ia*
30. *ul-tab-lak-ki-is-su-ma ul e-li-ʾi-ia nu-us-su*
31. Uruk^{ki} *ma-a-tum iz-za-az elī-*[*šu*]
32. [*ma-a-tum pu-uḫ-ḫu-rat ina muḫ-ḫi-šú*]
33. [*i-ṭàp-pi-ir um-ma*]*-nu el*[*ī*] *ṣēr*[*ī-šú*]
34. [*eṭlē uk-t*]*am-ma-ru eli-šu*
35. [*ki-i šer-ri la*]*-ʾi-i ú-na-šá-qu šēpē-šu*
36. [*a-na-ku ki-m*]*a áš-šá-te elī-šu aḫ-pu-up*
37. [*ù a*]*t-ta-di-šú ina šap-li-*[*ki*]
38. [*aš-šu*? *tul-t*]*a-maḫ-ri-šu it-ti-ia*

23. "Before you came from the steppe,
24. Gilgamesh was having dreams of you in Uruk.
25. Gilgamesh went to tell the dreams to his mother.
26. 'Mother, the dream I saw of my night!
27. Stars of heaven were there around me,
28. Like a concentration of Anu it was falling upon me from afar!
29. I tried to bear it but it was too powerful for me,
30. I tried to bring it over but I could not move it.
31. The land of Uruk was standing around it,
32. [The land made a crowd around it],
33. [A mob jostled towards it],
34. [Young men pi]led up around it,
35. [Like infantile urchins] they did it homage.
36. [As for me, li]ke a woman I caressed it
37. [Then I] threw it down before [you]
38. [That you] might confront it with me.' "

Commentary[22]

Old Babylonian 3 = Nineveh 26: Rewritten in the Nineveh version to be more specific, but hardly improved. For a compromise to this difficult expression, compare VII iv 14: *še-*[*e*?]*-mu ib-ri šu-na-ta aṭ-ṭul* (var. *ša*) *mu-ši-ti-ia* "Li[st]en, my friend, a dream I had of my night. . . ."

Old Babylonian 6 = Nineveh 27: von Soden's latest suggestion in *ZA* 69 (1979): 156: *ip-ḫ*[*u-r*]*u*!*-nim-ma*, while not excluded by collation, has not been followed here. What remains of the badly broken second sign in fact resembles ḪU more than BA, but the better preserved third sign does not look like RU but fits ŠU well, as written, for example, at the end of line 2. Clay's manuscript emendations of Langdon's copy, which do not spare him harsh criticism, find no difficulty with either BA or ŠU. Therefore Langdon and Clay's readings should be maintained in this case until proof turns up for a change.

Old Babylonian 7 is rewritten in Nineveh 28 so as to be more vivid. The Nineveh poet prefers to narrate dreams by introducing subjects abruptly, thus conveying the excitement of the narrator and the bizarre course of events in dreams. In Nineveh 28 therefore one has no clear idea of what (or who) was falling upon Gilgamesh, as he is caught up in the sensation of being fallen upon. For similar abrupt narration of a dream, compare below, VII iv 17ff. Note the Nineveh poet's conversion of G punctive to a tan (of distance?); compare above to I ii 18. Collation does not favor reading [*ki*]*-iṣ-rum* at the beginning of Old Babylonian 7. The second sign looks most like E, and is not a good IṢ. Von Soden's *ar*!*-rum* (*ZA* 69[1979]: 156) is excluded.

Old Babylonian 8 = Nineveh 29: Note the loss of specific 'heavy' for a vaguer 'powerful,' no doubt by analogy with I vi 22 and similar contexts. The word plays back and forth between descriptions of Gilgamesh and Enkidu; compare, for example, I v 1 to I v 18.

Old Babylonian 9 = Nineveh 30: This line was entirely rewritten, perhaps with an eye to desonance of *nuššu*/*niššu*, yet with a new alliteration created between *elīja* and *eleʾa*.

Old Babylonian 12: I understand here a false cadence. Gilgamesh bends down his brow while the others prostrate themselves, but the poet unexpectedly turns the image into one of loading a porter. Note the enclitic *-ma* of emphasis, the presence of which seems to support this interpretation. This is represented in the translation by "even."

Old Babylonian 14 = Nineveh 29: Note the loss of the "ventive" in the later version. The "ventive" seems in many instances to express the interest of the speaker or the subject in the goal or consequence of an action, as opposed to the t-forms, which in many instances seem to express the interest or participation of the speaker or subject in the time or course of the action. For this interpretation of the "ventive" as primarily ethical rather than directional I follow Gelb, *BiOr* 12 (1955): 109 (cf. also Hirsch, *OrNS* 44 [1975]: 313) and Poebel, *AJSL* 50 (1934): 160 rather than Landsberger, *ZA* 35 (1924): 113ff.; von Soden, *GAG*, 107f. and Edzard, *OrNS* 42 (1973): 127.

Nineveh 31–35: This is a further development of the

22 For detailed discussion of the dreams in both versions, see J. Cooper, "Gilgamesh Dreams of Enkidu: The Evolution and Dilution of Narrative," *Studies . . . Finkelstein*, 39–44.

street motif, in which the Nineveh poet unmasks his contempt for the gawking crowd. He implicitly compares the shoving throng to animals jostling at a watering place, cf. I i 40: *it-ti bu-lim maš-qa-a i-ṭàp-pir* "with the wild animals does he (Enkidu) jostle at the watering place." One may note that a similar play on *ummânu* and animals of the steppe is found in the difficult line XI 85: *bûl ṣēri ú-ma-am ṣēri, mārē um-ma-a-ni ka-li-šú-nu ú-še-li* "animals of the steppe, creatures of the steppe, all types of craftsmen(?) did I bring in." Von Soden, *Gilgamesch-Epos*, 89 preferred to translate *um-ma-a-ni* as 'Meistersöhne,' *ú-ma-am* as 'Getier.' So also Diakonoff, *Epos*, 74, understood 'craftsmen,' and this of course finds support in the use of *mārē ummāni* in VI v 21.[23] For another slightly derogatory reference to *ummānu* as the 'masses,' compare Ludlul I 90 (= *BWL*, 34 + Leichty, *Studies Finkelstein*, 145)

šu-piš ina puḫri i-ru-ra-ni ar-di
ardati ina pānī um-ma-nu ṭa-pil-tum iq-bi

"Openly in the assembly (of dignataries) did my slave curse me,
My slave girl voiced contempt of me before the mob."

Nineveh 36: The Nineveh poet introduces the notion of caressing the fallen object here, while the Old Babylonian poet saved this motif until the second dream (Old Babylonian Dream II 33). Furthermore, the Nineveh poet makes Gilgamesh's caressing the object the reason that he is able to move it (note Nineveh 37: *ù* 'and then'). In the Old Babylonian version he is strong enough to move it when the young men help him to get a grip on it.

Nineveh 38: The Nineveh poet introduces the adoption of Enkidu already in this dream. He thus prepares for another of his reversals, for Enkidu is apparently adopted as a *širqu*, or devotee of Gilgamesh, and thus joins the ranks of prostitutes and temple women (III iii 17ff., see below).

OB Pa i 29–36 (Old Babylonian Dream II, Gilgamesh speaks)

29. *ḫa-aṣ-ṣi-nu na-di-i-ma*
30. *e-li-šu pa-aḫ-ru*
31. *ḫa-aṣ-ṣi-nu-um-ma ša-ni bu-nu-šu*
32. *a-mur-šu-ma aḫ-ta-du a-na-ku*
33. *a-ra-am-šu-ma ki-ma aš-ša-tim*
34. *a-ḫa-ap-pu-up el-šu*
35. *el-qí-šu-ma aš-ta-ka-an-šu*
36. *a-na a-ḫi-ia*

29. "An axe was thrown down,
30. Around it they were gathered.
31. An axe it was, but strange its form!
32. When I saw it I felt such delight,
33. I even loved it like a woman,
34. I set to caressing it,
35. I took it and placed it (brother-like) at my side."

Nineveh I vi 8–15 (Nineveh Dream II, harlot narrates Gilgamesh's speech)

8. [*um-mi a-t*]*a-mar šá-ni-ta šu-ut-ta*
9. [*ina* Uruk^{ki} *su-pu-r*]*i ḫa-ṣi-nu na-di-ma elī-šú paḫ-ru*
10. [Uruk *ma*]*-tum izzaz^{az} elī-šú*
11. [*mātum pu-uḫ-ḫu*]*-rat ina muḫ-ḫi-šú*
12. [*i-ṭàp-pir um-ma*]*-nu elī ṣerī-šú*
13. [*a-na-ku*] *at-ta-di-šu ina šap-li-ki*
14. [*ù*?] *ki-i aš-šá-te elī-šú aḫ-pu-up*
15. [*aš-šu*?] ⌜*tuš*⌝*-ta-maḫ-ḫa-ri-šu it-ti-ia*

8. " '[Mother, I']ve had a second dream.
9. [In Uruk-supur]i an axe was thrown down, around it they were gathered,
10. The la[nd of Uruk] was standing around it,
11. [The land was forming a cr]owd above it
12. [The mob was jostling] towards it.
13. [As for me], I threw it down before you,
14. [Then(?)] like a woman I caressed it
15. [That] you might confront it with me.' "

Commentary

Old Babylonian 31: Note that this fine line was deleted by the Nineveh poet in order to make the narrative more consistent internally. This is replaced in Nineveh 10–13 by the crowding sequence ("street motif").

Old Babylonian 34ff. is mangled by Nineveh 14–15.

Old Babylonian 36: As pointed out by Cooper, "Dreams," there is a pun here on 'side' and 'brother'—but it seems unrenderable; cf. Schott, *ZA* 42 (1934): 103.

The narrative frame in which these two dreams are related reads as follows:

OB Pa ii 2–4

2. ^{d}GIŠ *šu-na-tam i-pa-šar*
3. ^{d}En-ki-[du$_{10}$ *wa*]*-ši-ib ma-ḫar ḫa-ri-im-tim*
4. *úr-*[*ta*]*-ʾa$_4$-mu ki-la-al-lu-un*

2. While Gilgamesh was relating the dream,
3. Enki[du was sea]ted before the harlot.
4. The pair made love [together].

Nineveh I vi 28–30 (=*GETh* Plate 8, *CT* 46 18)

28. [*i-pa-š*]*ar šu-na-a-ti-šu*
29. [^{mi}Šam]-ḫat *šu-na-ti* ^{d}Gilgameš *i-ta-ma-a a-na* ^{d}En-ki-dù

23 Only a hint of the role of the crowd is provided by the Old Babylonian version i 22, which seems to read *te-ed-di-ra-aš*?-[*šu*]⌜*ni-šu-ú-ma* "the people will embrace him," evidently the explanation of 13: *i-mi-du ia-ti* "they loaded me." The remains of NI are unambiguous, though the remains after RA are not very good for AŠ (perhaps ÁŠ?). Von Soden's proposal, *ZA* 69 (1979): 156 has to be declined; there is no sign of an erasure. Incidentally, ⌜*it*⌝-⌜*be*⌝ in 25 is correct; *e-mi-a* in 27 is clear on the tablet. Is the latter a reference *pars pro toto* to a wedding party in the streets of Uruk?

30. *[ur-ta-a]-mu ki-lá-la-an*

28. [While he was re]lating his dreams
29. [Šam]hat was telling the dreams of Gilgamesh to Enkidu.
30. The pair [made lo]ve [together].

Here the Nineveh poet plays on his thematics of love, although his material causes him some difficulty. The Old Babylonian poet was content to have Gilgamesh relate his dreams to his mother while Enkidu was dallying with the harlot, but the Nineveh poet decided to sharpen the contrast by introducing a pretty reversal. While Gilgamesh was relating his dreams to his mother, the harlot was relating the same dreams to Enkidu, and, in fact, only one narration took place. To make this possible, the Nineveh poet compressed the dream sequence into a single narrative while the Old Babylonian poet had the dreams occur on two successive nights (OB Pa i 24: *it-ti-lam-ma i-ta-mar ša-ni-tam* "he went to bed and had a second [dream]").

Not satisfied with this, the Nineveh poet added a reversal on yet another dimension. One has at first no way of knowing who is talking in I v 23 ff. (in the Old Babylonian version it is clearly the poet who is speaking the corresponding lines), but in 29 the ambiguity is removed by a specific statement that in fact the harlot spoke all of the preceding. The ambiguity between the voice of the narrator and the voice of his character is a daring self-reference of a confident poet.[24] Similar self-reference is made in I iv 16ff., in which the author addresses directly his own character; but it is here made more piquant by ambiguity. While this ornate device creaks a bit under its own weight, one may still respect it as a poetic tour-de-force.

The loss of the Nineveh poet's treatment of Tablet II leaves us uncertain as to how he handled the motivation for Enkidu's entry in Uruk. Once Enkidu had been seduced into sexual relations with the harlot, he was next seduced to leave his place of birth by glowing accounts of good times and friendship to be had. Here again the Old Babylonian and Nineveh poets treat the same material differently.

OB Pa ii 11–26

11. *a-na-ṭal-ka* ^{d}En-ki-du$_{10}$ *ki-ma* DINGIR *ta-ba-aš-ši*
12. *am-mi-nim it-ti na-ma-aš-te-e*
13. *ta-at-ta-[na]-la-ak ṣe-ra-am*
14. *al-kam lu-úr-di-ka*
15. *a-na libbī* [Uruk]^{ki} *ri-bi-tim*
16. *a-na- bi*t*(im?)* [*el*]*-lim mu-ša-bi ša A-nim*
17. ^{d}En-ki-du$_{10}$ *ti-bi lu-ru-ka*
18. *a-na* É-[an]-na *mu-ša-bi ša A-nim*
19. *a-šar* [^{d}GIŠ *gi*]*-it-*⸢*ma*⸣*-lu ne-pi-ši-tim*
20. *ù at-*[*ta ru*ʾ*tam*?] ⸢*te*⸣*-pu-*⸢*uš*⸣*-ma*
21. *ta-[ra-am-šu*? *ki-ma*?] *ra-ma-an-ka*
22. *al-ka ti-ba i-*[*na*] *qá-aq-qá-ri*
23. *ma-a-ak ri-i-im*
24. *iš-me a-wa-as-sà im-ta-gàr qá-ba-ša*
25. *mi-il-*[*ku*]*m ša sinništim*
26. *im-ta-qú-ut a-na libbī-šu*

11. "As I look at you, Enkidu, your are become like God.
12. Why with animals
13. Would you be roaming the steppe?
14. Come on, let me lead you
15. to Uruk-ribitim
16. To a holy house, dwelling of Anu.
17. Enkidu, arise, let me lead you
18. To Eanna, dwelling of Anu
19. Where is Gilgamesh, most perfect of creatures,
20. And you, having made [friends?]
21. [Will love him like] yourself.
22. Come on, get up from the ground
23. Where no shepherd is."
24. He heard her words, her speech he accepted,
25. The woman's advice fell upon his heart.

Commentary

Line 11: "God" renders the idea of a specific deity of primary importance to the individual, a usage apparently reflected graphically by DINGIR (ii 32?, iv 35), as opposed to *i-li-im* (v 26).

Line 16: The Old Babylonian poet proudly mentions Eanna here as the first attraction of Uruk. Thus one is struck by the fact that the Nineveh poet, XI 306, ends his final glance at Uruk and its walls by mentioning only the Ishtar temple, and not the Eanna temple.

The Nineveh poet expands this incident, as he wishes to develop a polarity of Enkidu's harlot-like relationship to Gilgamesh, a notion only touched on by the Old Babylonian poet. Here the harlot makes a speech to Enkidu that is carefully worked out rhetorically. This point is significant also, for when Ishtar, the harlot's counterpart, speaks, her speech is uncouth. The first part of the harlot's speech, lines 4–11, paints a glowing picture of Gilgamesh's surroundings: proud people dressed in fine clothes, festivities, music, attractive prostitutes, and clamor of merry-making all night long. The second part, lines 12–18, focuses on Gilgamesh himself with increasing ardor. Note for example the rhetorical flourish by which the verb of line 5 is repeated with emphasis in line 13, the urgent imperatives, and the description of Gilgamesh as if he too were a prostitute. This reversal of line 10 in 16 is brought neatly home by reversing the first two words of the line and converting the feminine plural into a poetic a-form, perhaps a form of the "ventive."[25] The harlot now

24 My particular thanks go to Rebecca Comay for sharing with me her researches on the self-reference of Mesopotamian 'anonymous' authors.

25 For this problem, see Hirsch, *OrNS* 44 (1975): 314 note 263.

lets herself be so carried away by her praise of Gilgamesh that she turns on her auditor and points to his inferiority. Gilgamesh is stronger than he is (line 17)—but this she softens with another bit of allure parallel to line 11. In lines 19ff., with another urgent imperative, she rhetorically abjures Enkidu not to go after all, as Gilgamesh is favored of the great gods.[26]

Nineveh I v 4–22

4. *[al-ka i ni]-li-[ka li-mu]-ra pa-ni-ka*
5. *u-kal-lim-ka* ^{d}Gilgameš *a-šar i-ba-aš-šu-ú a-na-ku lu i-di*
6. *a-[lik-ma]* ^{d}En-ki-dù *a-[ba* Uruk]^{ki} *su-pu-ri*
7. *a-šar nišē? us-[sa-ar-r]a-ḫu nēbiḫī*
8. u_4*-mi-šam-ma* u_4*-[mu iš]-šá-kin i-sin-nu*
9. *a-šar it-⌈ta⌉-az-[za-ma-ru pit]-nu a-lu-ú*
10. *ù [šam]-ḫa-a-ti [šu?]-su-ma bi-nu-tú*
11. *kuzba zu-ʾu-na ma-la ri-šá-ti*
12. *i-na ma-a-al mu-ši ú-še-ṣú-ú ra-bu-tum*

13. ^{d}En-ki-dù *[ša la ti]-du-ú ba-la-ṭa*
14. *lu-kal-lim-ka* ^{d}Gilgameš *ḫa-di-ʾu-u-a amēlu*
15. *a-mur ša-a-šú ú-ṭul pa-ni-šu*
16. *eṭ-lu-ta ba-ni bal-ta i-ši*
17. *zu-ʾu-na ku-uz-ba ka-lu zumrī-šú*
18. *dan-na e-mu-qu e-li-ka i-ši*
19. *la ṣa-li-lu[?] ša ur-ra u mūšī*

20. ^{d}En-ki-dù *nu-uk-ki-ra še-ret-ka*
21. ^{d}Gilgameš ^{d}Šamaš *i-ram-šú-ma*
22. ^{d}A-nu-um ^{d}En-líl *u* ^{d}É-a *u-rap-pi-šú ú-zu-un-šu*

4. "Come, let us go, let him see your face,
5. I would show you Gilgamesh, where he is know I full well.
6. Come then, Enkidu, to Uruk-Supuri
7. Where the people(?) are made pr[oud] in sashes,
8. Daily a festival day is held,
9. Where strings and percussion are pla[yed]
10. And [har]lots [fair?] of form,
11. With charm are adorned, full of pleasures,
12. They drive the Great Ones from their beds!

13. Enkidu, [you who know not] how to live,
14. O let me show you Gilgamesh, the joy-woe man.
15. See him, look into his face.
16. Beautiful in youthful vigor, manly pride he has.
17. Adorned with charm is his whole body,
18. Mighty strength, greater than yours, he has.
19. He rests not[. . . ?] by day or night!

20. Enkidu, forswear your evil way!
21. Gilgamesh is one whom Shamash loves,
22. Anu, Enlil, and Ea have made him wise."

26 The identical rhetorical device was used by Ea to spur on Ṣaltu against Ishtar; cf. Foster, *Studies . . . Finkelstein*, 81f.

Commentary

Line 12: The sense of this line seems to have eluded translators. The reference is to a well-known topos in Mesopotamian poetry wherein the "Great Ones" retiring for the night is used as an image for the silence and loneliness of deep night. Compare for instance the Old Babylonian passages AO 6769 1: *bu-ul-lu-lu ra!?-bu-ú* "the Great One(s) are numb(?) (with sleep)," parallel to *bu-ul-lu-lu ru-bu-ú* "the Princes are numb (?) (with sleep)," Dossin, *RA* 32 (1935): 179ff.;[27] compare also below to OB Pa iii 33. Here the image, perhaps humorously, is reversed; the clamor of the merry-makers shatters the sleep of the "Great Ones." The parallel line 19 supports this interpretation.

So far the poets have been attracting opposites and making extremes meet, though the Nineveh poet introduces early a note of jealousy that passes without reaction so far as one can see. In the Old Babylonian version the reversal of shepherdship is now carried out, and one may suppose that this was also the case with the Nineveh version.

Enkidu dresses in a piece of the harlot's clothing[28] and the harlot leads him off to the place of the shepherds. There he is introduced to food and drink, has his hair cut, his body anointed, and finally becomes a human being.[29] He looks like a bridegroom, a motif that the Old Babylonian poet will develop later, and serves, unlike Gilgamesh, as a true shepherd:

OB Pa iii 28–35

28. *il-qi ka-ak-ka-šu*
29. *la-bi ú-gi-ir-ri*
30. *is-sa-ak-pu rēʾū mu-ši-a-ti*
31. *ut-tap-pi-iṣ bar-ba-ri*
32. *la-bi uk-ta-ši-id*
33. *it-ti-[lu] na-qi-[du* x?]*ra-bu-tum*

27 The line offers many difficulties, however; compare the treatments by von Soden, *ZA* 43 (1936): 306 and Oppenheim, *Analecta Biblica* 12 (1959): 295.

28 Note the fine sigmatism of OB Pa ii 27f:

išḫuṭ libšam ištīnam ulabbiššu
lib[šam] šāniam šī ittalbaš

She stripped off her clothing, with one she dressed him
With a second one did she dress herself.

The cumulative effect of nine sibilants in two lines conveys well the rustling or perhaps tearing of the cloth. The effect of her handing over her own garment is carried through well by the chiastic structure of the verse.

29 The first characteristics of "people" are to wear clothes, cut their hair, eat bread and drink beer; cf. OB Pa ii 13f. and 22ff., reading *ultappit* [. . . ?] ŠU.I *šuʾuram pagaršu / šamnam iptašašma awiliš iwe* "the barber treated . . . his hair, his body with oil he (Enkidu) anointed, so he turned into a man."

34. ^{d}En-ki-du$_{10}$ *ma-aṣ-ṣa-ar-šu-nu*
35. *a-wi-lum e-ru-um*

28. He took his weapons
29. Went out hunting for lions.
30. The shepherds laid themselves down at night.
31. Many wolves he slew him,
32. He felled him many lions.
33. The herdsmen, the Great Ones, (all) went to bed.
34. Enkidu was their watchman,
35. A wakeful man

Commentary

Lines 31–32: I assume that the D-stem here reflects plurality of objects and that the t is ethical rather than perfect.

Line 33: Do we have here another reference to the "Great Ones" who go to bed at night? If so, Enkidu's actions are the opposite of the situation alluded to in Nineveh I v 11 (above), whereby Gilgamesh's uproar kept the Great Ones up at night, but Enkidu's conscientiousness allowed them to sleep.[30]

Lines 34–35: The motif of watchfulness and staying up all night is a virtue of Enkidu's, but a vice of Gilgamesh's; compare I ii 13 and I v 12.

The theme of attraction is now dropped, and rivalry introduced. One can only speculate as to what thematics the Nineveh poet used here. The Old Babylonian poet has developed a thematic of marriage. After his grooming at the shepherds' pens, Enkidu is become like a groom; he feasts, and makes merry with the harlot. A man passes with a tray of food, and in response to the harlot's inquiry as to where he is going, he announces that he is off to a wedding. He explains to her, rather pointedly it seems, that the custom of "people" is to get married. His utterance is not directed towards the harlot, it turns out, but leads to a highly charged revelation that Gilgamesh is violating marriage custom by taking brides before the grooms can. Enkidu, who is after all now a real person, becomes champion of lawful marriage, and sets off for Uruk. Such a reversal must have appealed to the Nineveh poet, but we do not know how he treated it.

OB Pa iv 22ff.

[='14'] 22. *bi-ti-iš e-mu-tim* ⌈*iq*⌉-[*ru-ni-in-ni*]
23. *ši-ma-a-at ni-ši-i-ma*
24. *tu*?-*ṣa-ar kal-lu-tim*
25. *a-na paššūri šak-ki-i e-ṣe-en*
26. *uk-la-at bīt e-mi ṣa-a-a-ḫa-tim*
27. *a-na šarri ša* Uruk^{ki} *ri-bi-tim*
[='20'] 28. *pi-ti pu-ug ni-ši a-na ḫa-a-a-ri*
29. *a-na* ^{d}GIŠ *šarri ša* Uruk^{ki} ri-bi-tim
30. *pi-ti pu-ug ni-ši*
31. *a-na ḫa-a-a-ri*

32. *aš-ša-at ši-ma-tim i-ra-aḫ-ḫi*
[='25'] 33. *šu-ú pa-na-nu-um-ma*
34. *mu-tum wa-ar-ka-nu*
35. *i-na mi-il-ki ša* DINGIR *qá-bi-ma*
36. *i-na bi-ti-iq a-bu-un-na-ti-šu*
37. *ši-ma-as-su*

22. "They invited me to a wedding—
23. The custom of people
24. Is seclusion(?) of a bride—
25. On the splendid tray I've heaped
26. Delightful foods for the wedding.

27. For the king of Uruk-ribitim
28. The people's curtains(?) open for taking of a mate!
29. For Gilgamesh, king of Uruk-ribitim
30. The people's curtains(?) open
31. For taking of a mate!

32. The lawful wife he makes love to,
33. He first,
34. The husband after.
35. By God's counsel is it ordained,
36. From the cutting of his cord
37. Is that his fate.

Commentary[31]

Lines 23f.: Here the education of Enkidu, begun with sex, clothes, and food (customs and characteristics of people) continues. Unfortunately the reading of the first word in 24 is unknown. The first sign is much as drawn by Langdon, so also the collation of Finkelstein, *JAOS* 90 (1970): 251 note 41. Does the plene spelling of *šimāt* indicate a rhetorical question?

Line 27: The Old Babylonian poet reserves perfect or near perfect parallelism for moments of highest drama. Compare below, OB Pa iv 27ff.

Line 28: I follow here von Soden's proposal, *ZA* 53 (1959): 211. For a different opinion, see Ravn, *BiOr* 10 (1953): 12ff.

Line 35: Note the contrast here to the "woman's counsel" in OB Pa ii 25.

The end of this episode offers many difficulties. Enkidu arrives at Uruk when a wedding is in progress. The joyous scene similar to that described by the harlot is being enacted. One may wonder whether or not the poet has presented us with another reversal. Is this ceremony in fact a "sacred marriage," where, for once, Gilgamesh was supposed to act as groom, and thus Enkidu was

30 For this topos elsewhere in Akkadian literature, see Foster, *Or NS* 43 (1974): 345 note 5, though contrast, for the Adapa passage, Schramm, *Or NS* 43 (1974): 162. Collation of the Adapa line is indecisive.

31 Note the discussion of this passage, with collation, by Finkelstein, *JAOS* 90 (1970): 250ff., which I have followed here in its essentials.

interrupting a legitimate ceremony, or, was Gilgamesh treating an ordinary wedding as if it were a "sacred marriage"?[32] The latter interpretation is favored by the simile *kima ilim* 'as for a god' (though he was not one),[33] and the invocation of Išhara, the term used for the first nine days of sex following the wedding.[34]

OB Pa v 22ff.

[='16'] 22. *ka-a-na ina [libbi]* Uruk^{ki} *ni-qí-a-tum*
23. *eṭ-lu-tum ú-te-el-li-lu*
24. *ša-ki-in lu-ša-nu*
25. *a-na eṭli ša i-ša-ru zi-mu-šu*
[='20'] 26. *a-na* ^{d}GIŠ *ki-ma i-li-im*
27. *ša-ki-iš-šum me-eḫ-rum*
28. *a-na* ^{d}*Iš-ḫa-ra ma-a-a-lum*
29. *na-di-i-ma*
30. ^{d}GIŠ *it-ti wa-a[r]-[d]a-[ti]m*
31. *i-na mu-ši in-né-⌈mi⌉-id*

22. In Uruk all the while were sacrifices in progress,
23. The young men were making merry.
24. The musical instrument was struck up
25. For the young man straightest(?) of feature,
26. For Gilgamesh, as for a god,
27. Struck up for him was the antiphon.
28. For the Virgin Bride the bed
29. was laid.
30. Gilgameš with the young woman
31. In the night was to come together.

Commentary

For discussion of this passage, see Finkelstein, *JAOS* 90 (1970): 252.

Lines 30–31: Clay's copy happily confirms von Soden's reading, *ZA* 71 (1981): 104 note 2.

Lines 24–27: I understand these to be parallels in reverse, though the meaning of *lušānu* is not certain.

With the confrontation of Enkidu, the type of the true bridegroom, but mated to a harlot, and of Gilgamesh, type of the false bridegroom, to be mated to a real bride, the first Episode draws to a close.

Episode 2: Apparent Unity (Knowledge of Another)

This episode begins with the fight between Enkidu and Gilgamesh. It ends with their union, first as friends, then as companions sanctioned by community and family.

32 For discussion of the "sacred marriage," see *Reallexikon der Assyriologie, s.v.* "Heilige Hochzeit." For recent discussion of this passage, see von Soden, *ZA* 71 (1981), 103ff.

33 Enkidu too was god-like; cf. above, OB Pa ii 11. The names of both were regularly written with the determinative for divinity, but that does not affect this argument.

34 *Atrahasis* I 303f.

OB Pa vi 11ff.

11. *iṣ-ṣa-ab-tu-ma ki-ma le-i-im*
12. *i-lu-du*
13. *sí-ip-pa-am iḫ-bu-tu*
14. *i-ga-rum ir-tu-ud*
15. ^{d}GIŠ *ù* ^{d}En-ki-du$_{10}$
16. *iṣ-ṣa-ab-tu-ú-ma*
17. *ki-ma le-i-im i-lu-du*
18. *sí-ip-pa-am iḫ-bu-tu*
19. *i-ga-rum ir-tu-ud*
20. *ik-mi-is-ma* ^{d}GIŠ
21. *ina qá-aq-qá-ri ši-ip-šu*
22. *ip-ši-iḫ uz-za-sú-ma*
23. *i-ni-iʾ i-ra-as-su*
24. *iš-tu i-ra-as-su i-ni-ʾu$_{5}$*
25. ^{d}En-ki-du$_{10}$ *a-na ša-ši-im*
26. *is-sa-qàr-am a-na* ^{d}GIŠ
27. *ki-ma iš-te-en-ma um-ma-ka*
28. *ú-li-id-ka*
29. *ri-im-tum ša su-pu-ri*
30. ^{d}Nin-sún-na
31. *ul-lu e-lu mu-ti re-eš-ka*
32. *šar-ru-tam ša ni-ši*
33. *i-šim-kum* ^{d}En-líl
(gap of about 10 lines)

Yale i 11ff.

11. [ ]*-bu ša úr-ba-ri*
12. [ ]*-ku-tam wa-aq-rum*
13. *a[m-me-ni]m ta-aḫ-ši-iḫ*
14. *a[n-n]i-a-am [e-pe]-ša-am*
15. *x-ši mi-im-ma* x x x *am-ma-di-iš*
16. [ ]*-iḫ [ta-aḫ]-ši-iḫ*
17. *lu-uš-šu-ú* x x *tam-tim*
18. *ši-ip-ra-am ša* [ ]*-ú i-na nišē*
19. *it-ta-aš-qú-ú-ma*
20. *i-pu-šu ru-ʾu$_{5}$-tam*
21. *[it-ta-aš-bu] uš-ta-di-nu*

11. They seized each other like wrestlers,
12. They bent over,
13. They destroyed the door sill,
14. The wall shook.
15. Gilgamesh and Enkidu
16. Seized each other,
17. Like wrestlers they bent over,
18. They destroyed the door sill,
19. The wall shook!
20. Gilgamesh it was who bent
21. His leg to the ground (for the pin)!
22. His rage was spent,
23. He turned chest away.
24. After he had turned his chest away,
25. Enkidu to him
26. To Gilgamesh did say:
27. "As the one and only did your mother
28. Bear you,
29. The Wild Cow of the stall,

30. Ninsun it was
31. Who has raised your head above those of (valiant) men,
32. Kingship of people
33. Enlil it was who ordained you . . ."
(gap of about twelve lines)

13′. "W[h]y have you wanted
14′. To do such a thing?
15′. [ ] very much
16′. [ ] have you wanted?
17′. Let me . . .
18′. The task that you [ ] from the people."
19′. They kissed each other,
20′. They made friends.
21′. [They sat themselves down] to consult together.

The rest of the passage is lost, and repeated collation yields nothing usable.[35]

Commentary

Lines 11ff: For the Old Babylonian poet's use of perfect or near perfect parallelism for moments of high drama, compare above, OB Pa iv 27ff. For possible phonetic ambiguity in this passage, see Renger in F. J. Oinas, ed., *Heroic Epic and Saga* (Bloomington, 1978), 40f. Contra Renger and others, I take the simile with the preceding line and assume a caesura in 12; note the fuller spelling of *iṣṣabtūma* in 16. This conveys metrically the fluctuations of the struggle.

Line 21: Gilgamesh won the match by grasping Enkidu, throwing him off balance, and holding him aloft. For illustration and discussion, see C. Gordon, *JNES* 7 (1948): 264.

Line 23: This expression indicates unwillingness to continue hostilities, cf. Seux, *Épithètes*, 205.

Line 24: The pronoun 'his' is a surprise anticipation for Enkidu.

Lines 27ff.: Enkidu's lyrical praise of Gilgamesh acknowledges his legitimate superiority, a theme that the Nineveh poet will resume with quite different emphasis.

Lines 13′ff.: Enkidu seems to be remonstrating with Gilgamesh, and in these crucial lines, now lost to us, apparently defined the relationship of the two. The task of Enkidu, reminiscent of the "woman's work" of Nineveh I iv 19 etc., was apparently to serve as the object of Gilgamesh's restlessness, from which the people can now be relieved. Compare the lines from Nineveh I ii 30ff. (the gods are speaking):

. . . *at-ti* ^{d}A-ru-ru *tab-ni-*[*i* ^{d}Gilgameš]
e-nin-na bi-ni-i zi-kir-šú
a-na u_4*-um lìb-bi-šú lu-u ma-*[*ḫir/šil*]
liš-ta-an-na-nu-ma Uruk^{ki} *liš-tap-*[*šiḫ*]

". . . You, Mother Goddess, created [Gilgamesh]
Now then, create his evocation,
To the storminess of his heart let it be [opposite/equal],
Let the two be doubles to each other that Uruk may have peace."

Commentary

Line 19′: For remarks on kissing in the ancient Near East, see Meissner, *Sitzungsberichte der Ber. Akademie der Wissenschaften, P/h Klasse* (1934): 917; Sperling, *JANES* 10 (1978): 114 note 12.

The Nineveh version, II ii 38ff., inserts the "crowd" sequence here (see above, to Nineveh I v 31ff.), ending with "like infantile urchins they did homage to him." After mentioning the wedding preparations, the Nineveh poets describes the fight as follows:

Nineveh II ii 48ff.

48. *iṣ-ṣab-tu-ma ina bāb bīt e-mu-ti*
49. *ina sūqi it-te-eg-ru-ú ri-bit ma-a-tu*
50. [*s*]*ip-*[*p*]*u*? *ir-ú*!*-bu i-ga-ra i-tú-uš*

48. They seized each other in the door of the wedding,
49. They assailed each other in the street, the public crossroad.
50. The doorsills shook, the wall heaved.

Commentary

Line 50: I follow von Soden / Lambert, *ZA* 53 (1959): 223.

It seems clear that what for the Old Babylonian poet was a moment of high drama was for the Nineveh poet a disgusting street brawl. This is shown most clearly by line 49, which emphasizes where the fight was going on, in a public thoroughfare, right outside the house where the wedding was taking place. The intent of the poet is to sneer at the vulgarity of the fight, a view that the reader has already been prepared for by the "crowd" scene that he interpolated immediately before.

Little else is known of this part of the story. After a long gap in the text, Enkidu is found complaining that he has

---

35 25′ [ ] *gi im* x̣ x̣
26′ [*i*?]*-na*? *šu-na-tim* (clear)
27′ [ ] x̣ x̣ x̣
28′ [ ]*-šu*
29′ [ ] x̣
40′ [x] *nam* [ ] x̣
41′ [ ]x̣ *ib-*[*ra-a*]*m* (more space in break!)
42′ [*ša*] *ú-na-i-du* [*at-t*]*i* (")
43′ [*zi-i*]*k-ra-am ú-t*[*e-er*]*-ru*
44′ [*a-na*] *ḫa-ri-*[*im*]*-tim* (")
45′ [*iš-tu i-ru*]*-bu a-na bīt* [*ši*?]*-bu-ti* (BU clear!)

41′ "[a fri]end
42′ [whom] I esteem you (fem. sing.) are."
43′ An answer they returned
44′ [to] the harlot.
45′ [After they ent]ered the elder's house . . .

Is *zikram uterru* a pun on *zikaru*? The sense is most difficult.

become weak and flaccid (OB Yale ii 40ff.), whereupon Gilgamesh proposes an expedition to the cedar country to kill its monstrous guardian and establish eternal fame for Gilgamesh. Enkidu reacts with horror to this scheme (OB Yale iii 14ff.), but, stung by taunts of cowardice, gives in. At the insistence of the city elders, who formally entrust him with the king's safety (Nineveh III i 11f.), Enkidu agrees to walk first. The two go together to Ninsun, to whom Gilgamesh pours out his fears. The unhappy mother goes up on the roof of her house, and prays movingly to Shamash for the safety of her child:

Nineveh III ii 9ff.

9. *iš-kun sur-*[*qí-ni a-na m*]*a-ḫar* ^{d}Šamaš *i-di-šú iš-ši*
10. *am-me-ni taš-kun ana ma-*[*ri*] ^{d}Gilgameš *lib-bi la ṣa-li-la te-mid-su*
11. ⌜*e*⌝*-nin-na-ma tal-pu-us-su-ma il-lak*
12. *ur-ḫa ru-qa-ta a-šar* ^{d}Hum-ba-ba
13. *qab-la šá la i-du-ú i-maḫ-ḫar*
14. *gi-ir-ru šá la i-du-ú i-rak-kab*
15. *a-di* u_4*-mu il-la-ku ù i-tu-ra*
16. *a-di i-kaš-ša-du a-na qīšti erēni*
17. *a-di* ^{d}Hum-ba-ba *da-pi-nu i-na-ru*
18. *u mim-ma lem-nu šá ta-zi-ru ú-ḫal-laq ina māti*
19. *ina* u_4*-mi šá at-ta i-tu-ú* [ ]
20. *ši ia-a i-dur-ka* ^{d}A-a *kal-la-tum li-ḫa-sis-ka*
21. [*šá*]*-a-šu a-na maṣṣarāti šá mūši* [ ]
(at least sixteen more lines missing, perhaps as many as thirty)

9. She set up the offering [stand be]fore Shamash and prayed
10. "Why did you impose on my son Gilgamesh the burden of a restless heart?
11. Now you have moved him to go
12. A distant road where is Humbaba
13. To face what battle he does not know!
14. To ride what campaign he does not know!
15. Until the day he goes and returns,
16. Until he reaches the forest of cedars,
17. Until he slays fierce Humbaba,
18. And wipes out from the world something evil you loathe,
19. In the daytime, for which you're the sign, [ ]
20. She, Aya, (your) bride, may she not fear to remind you
21. Him to the watch of the night [ ]
22. [. . . to commend . . .]"

Commentary

Lines 9f.: Note the omission of the formulae of speech, suggesting the speaker's strong feeling.

Line 10: I take this line to include a highly emotive hendiadys, proceeding from a colorless *šakānu ana* 'set upon' to a stronger *emēdu* 'impose.' The verb: object:verb construction (ABA) was a favorite one with Akkadian poets; cf. Hecker, *Untersuchungen zur akkadischen Epik*, *AOAT* Sonderreihe 8 (1974): 121f. Von Soden's "Warum verliehest du zum Sohn mir Gilgamesch/Erteiltest du ihm ein Herze ohne Ruh" (p. 39); and Speiser's (p. 81) "Why, having given me Gilgamesh for a son, with a restless heart didst thou endow him?"; similarly Diakonoff, p. 28, all seem to me wide of the mark.

The legitimation of the relationship between Gilgamesh and Enkidu, begun by the city elders, is continued by Ninsun, but unfortunately the context is broken and none too clear.

Nineveh III iv 17ff.

17. ^{d}En-ki-dù *dan-nu ul ṣi-it ú-ri-ia at-ta*
18. *e-nin-na at-mu-ka*
19. *it-ti ši-ir-qi šá* ^{d}Gilgameš
20. *ugbabāti qa-áš-da-a-ti* [*ù ku*]*l-ma-šá-a-ti*
21. *in-di it-ta-di a-na ti-ik-k*[*i šá* ^{d}]En-ki-dù
22. *ugbabāti il-qa-a* [ ]*-ta*
23. *ù mārāt ilāni u-rab-b*[*a*] x
24. *a-na-ku* ^{d}En-ki-dù*-m*[*a*]
25. *el-te-qé a-na* [ ]
26. ^{d}En-ki-dù *a-na* [ ] ^{d}Gilgameš

17. "Mighty Enkidu, you are no offspring of my womb.
18. Now I have bespoken you
19. With the devotees of Gilgamesh,
20. The priestesses, holy women, and prostitutes."
21. She placed a tag around Enkidu['s ne]ck.
22. The priestesses took the [ ]
23. And the daughters of the gods made great [ ]
24. "I [have] Enkidu [ ]
25. [Him] have I taken as [ ]
26. Enkidu as the [ ] of Gilgamesh."

For discussion of this passage, see Oppenheim, *OrNS* 17 (1948): 33f. Apparently Enkidu is adopted into the cult of Gilgamesh by the various temple women and prostitutes in a solemn ceremony presided over by Gilgamesh's mother. The apparent unity between the two, begun by attraction and cemented by a violent physical struggle before a wedding, is now made legitimate by the city elders and the mother of Gilgamesh. Would the poet have us believe that this complete reversal of the natural way of things that he had so carefully constructed results in a firmer unity than a mere marriage of opposites, or does he mean to say that all such unity is a dignified hoax?

The poet seems to suggest that the unity now created between the two appears the stronger because it is not based on sexual attraction of opposites but on near perfect similarity. Gilgamesh is superior in birth, physique, and status, and has besides a heart restless for something more than the normal human lot, a restlessness which the loving mother exclaims has its origins in justice and righteousness. Gilgamesh's injustices and extreme behavior are now portrayed in a new light—they were rightly motivated, if wrongly expressed. The prayers of Uruk now go up that justice remain with the king. Here the poet begins a new, highly complex theme: justice and Gilgamesh's right to do as he did, first to the citizens of

Uruk, then to Enkidu, and at last to himself. Interwoven with this theme is the role of Shamash in the story. The only aspect of this theme that concerns us here is the relationship of justice to Enkidu's fate. This will be touched on in Episode 4.

The thematic of sex now passes from the theme of two friends' relationship. Indeed, the poet will turn now to showing that sexual attraction cannot result in a permanent unity. Sexual attraction, as personified by Ishtar and the harlot, will now be portrayed as an outside threat to the unity that the poet has created.

EPISODE 3: Antithesis and Rejection (Beginnings of Self-Knowledge)

The episode consists of two sexual rejections, one anticipatory (Gilgamesh and Ishtar), the other retrospective (Enkidu and the harlot). Both of these incidents are known only from the Nineveh version. The rejection of Ishtar is told in seventy-nine lines of text, only portions of which are quoted here. After killing Humbaba, cutting cedars, and putting the wood on the Euphrates for the journey to Nippur, Gilgamesh undresses and washes himself.

Nineveh VI 6ff.

6. *a-na du-un-qí šá* ^{d}Gilgameš *i-na it-ta-ši ru-bu-tu* ^{d}Ištar
7. *al-kam-ma* ^{d}Gilgameš *lu-ú ḫa-ᵓi-ir at-ta*
8. *in-bi-ka ia-a-ši qa-a-šu qí-šam-ma*
9. *at-ta lu-ú mu-te-ma ana-ku lu-ú áš-ša-at-ka*

6. Ishtar the princess looked covetously on the beauty of Gilgamesh.
7. "Come to me, Gilgamesh, you should be a lover,
8. Give, O give me freely of your fruits of love!
9. You should be my husband and I should be your wife."

Commentary

Line 6: The term "princess" recurs throughout this section, and is appparently used ironically by the poet for reasons that will become clear below.

Line 7: Note omission of the formulae of speech, emphasizing the abruptness and excitement of the speaker. Note also the simple declarative statement in the second person.

Line 8: Ishtar continues in the second person ("your fruits") but gives way to an agitated first person, expressed here by the independent pronoun and the "ventive" on the one hand, and the cognate accusative (here: "freely") on the other.

I have emphasized the use of person in this passage because in this and the parallel passage (below, VI 68f.) the fluctuation of person emerges as a minor thematic of this poet.[36] Represented schematically, the distribution of persons in these three lines is as follows:

2+1	2	2
alkamma	Gilgameš	*atta*
2	1	2+1
inbīka	*iāši*	*qīšamma*
2+1	1	2
atta mūtē	*anāku*	*aššatka*

By exploiting a full range of grammatical possibilities: imperative, ventive, vocative, possessive suffixes, subjective and objective independent pronouns, the poet aptly portrays the intensity of her desire. The poet's intention is clear: Gilgamesh is first urged to be a lover, then her husband. By this device the poet undermines the legitimacy of her proposal, as not only is a woman here proposing to a man, but she is proposing intercourse before marriage.

In the following eleven lines Ishtar offers him a splendid chariot, a magnificent dwelling, abundant income, fertility and energy to his flocks, steeds, and beasts of burden. That she omits all reference to her own, personal attractions is striking, especially, so one assumes, to an audience well-versed in poetic praises of Ishtar and her loveliness. The poet prepares us, subtly still, for his ultimate revelation that Ishtar is not attractive at all, but only a harlot. This is so far only hinted at by the necessity of her bribing her lover rather than seducing him with her charms. Even the harlot was not reduced to that.

Gilgamesh replies at length in a speech, coolly introduced by the conventional formulae. In the first eight lines or more he demands of her what he is to give her if he took her: food, clothing, oil—all perhaps in false humility in the face of her splendid offerings. He then abuses her ornately:

Nineveh VI 34ff.[37]

34. ^{giš}*daltu ár-ka-b[i-in-nu šá la ú]-kal-lu-ú šara u zi-i-qa*
35. *ekallu mu-nap-pi-[ṣa-at mārē?] qàr-ra-di*
36. *pi-i-ru [x̣ mu]-ak-ki-lat ku-tùm-mi-šá*
37. *it-tu-ú mu-[ṭàp-pi-lat] na-ši-šá*
38. ^{kuš}*na-a-da mu-[na-ki-sa-at] na-ši-šá*
39. *pi-i-lu mu-[nap-pi-ṣa-at] dūr abni*
40 *ia-šu-pu-ú [mu-ab-bit dūri? ina?] māt nu-kúr-ti*
41. ^{kuš}*šēnu mu-na-[aš-si-kàt šēp] be-lí-šá*

34. "A flimsy door which does not keep out the wind nor blast,
35. A palace which crushes the hero['s son](?),
36. An elephant which [de]vours its own covering,
37. Pitch which d[irties] its bearer,
38. Waterskin which l[eaks on] its bearer,

36 I am indebted to Rebecca Comay for this observation.

37 The composite text is based on *GETh* and the Assur version, as edited by Frankena, *CRRAI* 7 (1958): 113ff.

39. Limestone which [undermines] a stone wall,
40. Battering ram which [destroys the wall(?) against(?)] an enemy land,
41. Sandal which pinches the foot of its owner. . . ."

This passage may shock modern readers, but not perhaps always for the reasons intended by the poet. The language used here may have been familiar to its hearers in quite another context: school days, when abuse of this type, like debating, was a cultivated school-boy art.[38] Gilgamesh is not hysterically rejecting Ishtar, but rather is talking to her as if she were a girl still in school.

The poet abandons this thematic for a moment (though it will reappear later in VI 159), and now turns to Ishtar's lovers. Her childhood sweetheart was Dumuzi, and he was left to mourning. Her next three lovers were all animals, and the next two were men whom she turned into animals: the shepherd and the orchardman. She is thus the opposite of the harlot, who made Enkidu from an animal to a human being. With stunning effect Gilgamesh mimics Ishtar's attempted seduction of the orchardman:

Nineveh VI 64ff.

64. *ta-ra-mi-ma I-šu-ul-la-nu* ^{lú}*nukarribu abī-ka*
65. *ša ka-a-a-nam-ma šu-gu-ra-a na-šak-ki*
66. u_4*-mi-šam-ma ú-nam-ma-ru pa-áš-šur-ki*
67. *i-na ta-at-ta-ši-šum-ma ta-tal-kiš-šu*
68. *I-šu-ul-la-ni-ia kiš-šu-ta-ki i ni-kul*
69. *u qāt-ka liš!-te-ṣa-am-ma lu-pu-ut ḫur-da-at-ni*
70. *I-šu-ul-la-nu i-qab-bi-ki*
71. *ia-a-ši mi-na-a ter-re-ši-in-ni*
72. *um-mi la te-pa-a a-na-ku la a-kul*
73. *ša ak-ka-lu uklūt pi-šá-a-ti u er-re-e-ti*
74. *šá ku-uṣ-ṣi el-pe-tu ku-tùm-mu-ú-[ia?]*
75. *at-ti taš-mi-ma an-na-a [qa-be-šu]*
76. *tam-ḫa-ṣi-šu a-na dal-la-li tu-ut-[ter-re-šu]*
77. *tu-še-ši-bi-šu-ma ina qa-bal ma-na-[ḫa-ti]*
78. *ul e-lu-ú mi-iḫ-ḫa ul a-rid da-l[u-u]*
79. *u ia-a-ši ta-ram-mìn-ni-ma ki-i ša-šu-nu tu-[ši-mìn-ni]*

64. "You even fell in love with Ishullanu, your father's orchardman,
65. Who always brought you offerings of date clusters—
66. Every day he made your table splendid.
67. You looked at him covetously and went up to him,
68. 'My Ishullanu, let us have a taste of your manliness!
69. So let your hand be stretched forth to me and—touch our vulva!'
70. Ishullanu says to you:
71. 'Me? What do you want of me?
72. Hath my mother not baked and I not eaten?
73. Shall what I eat be breads of obscenities and curses?
74. Shall [my] covering from cold be a reed?'
75. You, when you heard what [he said],
76. Struck him and tu[rned him] into a toad(?).
77. You made him live in the gard[en patch](?).
78. He can't get over a conduit or out of a bucket(?).
79. As for me, when you love me, you'll fate me like them."

Commentary

For discussion of this passage, see Oppenheim, *OrNS* 17 (1948): 37ff.

Line 68: Note once again omission of the formulae of direct address. The poet continues here his thematic of personal confusion. As a term of endearment, Ishtar begins with a first person singular, but in an effort to preserve her dignity, she turns to the first plural cohortative at the end. The second pronoun used, curiously, is feminine. While such fluctuation of pronouns is well known in this period of Akkadian and in this text, this particular instance of it is nonetheless striking.

Line 69: For the reading LIŠ, I follow von Soden, *ZA* 53 (1959): 226. Collation by Machinist and C. B. F. Walker favors the reading *šú*, which is otherwise so unexpected in such a context that, even if it is correct, one may wonder if it is a pseudo-correction. Ishtar's dignity is maintained in the first half of the line by using a passive of the causative, but she ends in a simple imperative—finished off, however, by another royal plural! Her surrender of dignity is complete: cohortative to precative to direct command.

Line 72: The archaic verb form suggests a proverbial expression, here used perhaps with the obstinate recourse to clichés often thought characteristic of the peasant in literature, cf. B. Alster, *Studies in Sumerian Proverbs* (Copenhagen, 1975): 13.

Line 78: This line, by analogy with 61ff., seems to refer to the gardener's fate, so I assume that he is the subject of *elu* and *arid* (contra *CAD* D, 56b and Oppenheim, *loc. cit.* although I have adopted his translation 'conduit' for *miḫḫu*). Although his fate is not clear, it was presumably appropriate for an orchardman, just as the shepherd was doomed to be chased off by his own dogs (VI 62f.).

The tension of person discussed above in lines 7ff. has been heightened by the poet by means of a *stretto*-effect. The proposition is condensed into two lines, with the following distribution of persons:

2+1	2	1 pl.
Išullānia	*kiššūtaki*	*i nīkul*
2	3+1	2+1 pl.
qātka	*lišteṣamma*	*luput ḫurdatni*

The use of the "royal plural" seems to satirize the epithet "princess" applied to Ishtar throughout this episode. Comparing this passage with that studied above, 7ff., one sees that the poet intensified his portrayal of Ishtar's desire by condensing her proposition, scrambling her use of person, and causing the dignity of her speech to

38 For literature, see Foster, *JANES* 6 (1974): 80; Hirsch, *Kinlers Literaturlexikon s.v.* "Akkadische Streitgespräche"; Wilcke, *ibid, s.v.* "Sumerische Streitgedichte."

collapse, despite her use of a royal plural at the end of each line. Thus in two lines the Nineveh poet sets out the discordant counterpoint of her lust and pride.

The fall of Ishtar continues with her furious ascent to her parents:

Nineveh VI 82ff.

82. *il-lik-ma* ^{d}Iš-tar *ana pānī* ^{d}*A-nim [abī-šá i-bak-ki]*
83. *ana pānī An-tum ummī-šá il-la-[ka di-ma-a-šá]*
84. *a-bi* ^{d}Gilgameš *it-ta-az-za-ra-an-ni*
85. ^{d}Gilgameš *un-den-na-a* ⌜*pi*⌝*-šá-ti-ia*
86. *pi-šá-ti-ia u er-r[e-e-ti]-ia*
87. ^{d}*A-núm pa-a-šá īpuš*^{uš}*-ma iqabbī*
88. *izzakkar ana ru-bu-[ti]* ^{d}Ištar
89. *a-ba la at-ti te-eg-re-e ša[rri* ^{d}Gilgameš]
90. *u* ^{d}Gilgameš *ú-man-na-a pi-šá-ti-ki*
91. *pi-šá-ti-ki u er-[re-e-ti-ki]*

82. There went Ishtar, [weeping], before Anu [her father],
83. Before Antu her mother were [her tears flowing down].
84. "Father, Gilgamesh keeps insulting me!
85. Gilgamesh has been recounting obscenities about me,
86. Obscenities about me and cu[rses about me!]"
87. Anu opened his mouth and spoke,
88. Said to the prince[ss] Ishtar:
89. "Well now, did you not incite the ki[ng Gilgamesh],
90. And then Gilgamesh recounted obscenities about you,
91. Obscenities about you and curses about you?"

Commentary

Line 85: The unique form *un-den-na-a* looks like an example of distorted or colloquial speech, used by the poet to make Ishtar look childish. Note that her father in answering uses the same verb but in a regular form.

Line 89: Note the word play between *a-bi* (line 84) and *a-ba* (line 89), as well as the abruptness of Ishtar's address to her parents in contrast to her father's deliberate reply (formula/no formula). Anu refers to Gilgamesh as "king" (if the restoration is correct), apparently another satirization by the poet of Ishtar's epithet "princess" used in the preceding line.

The contrast between the harlot and Ishtar is unmistakable: the harlot is eloquent, attractive, and successful in what she tries to do. The poet favors strongly the sexual initiation that she represents. Ishtar speaks badly, is not attractive, and fails. The poet rejects the sexual apostasy that she represents. Through manipulation of person and number in speech, satire, and outright contempt, the Nineveh poet pictures the kind of sexual attraction represented by Ishtar first as a fundamental distortion of personal relationships and second as a surrender of dignity leading at once to childishness and ultimately to debasement (Tablet X). Gilgamesh's rejection of personal confusion and loss of pride is an important step in his acquisition of knowledge.

Ishtar's fall is complete with the episode of the "Bull of Anu." She borrows her father's totemic symbol, a bull, and sends it Uruk to destroy the two friends.[39] Gilgamesh and Enkidu kill it in a heroic struggle.

Nineveh VI 157ff.

157. *i-li-ma* ^{d}Iš-tar *ana elī dūri šá* Uruk^{ki} *su-[pu]-ri*
158. *iš-ḫi-iṭ ḫup-pa it-ta-di a-ru-ru-ta*
159. *al-lu-u* ^{d}Gilgameš *šá ú-ṭap-pil-an-ni alu id-duk*

157. There went Ishtar up onto the walls of Uruk-supuri,
158. She stamped her feet(?) and cast a curse:
159. "That (bully) Gilgamesh who treated me like a child, he's killed the bull!"

Commentary

Line 158: For this translation of *ḫuppu*, see Kilmer, *Studies . . . Finkelstein*, 133.

Line 159: Literally, 'That there Gilgamesh.' This translation attempts to catch the play on words between *allû* and *alû*. As pointed out by the *CAD* A/1, 377b, *allû* seems to be a colloquialism, in our terms, street language.

Enkidu tears off the bull's leg and throws it before her with an insult. Ishtar convenes the harlots and prostitutes and sets up a wailing over the bull's leg. This final act consigns her majesty to the domain of whoredom, where the poet would have her remain. The unity of the two friends remains unbroken.

To Gilgamesh's rejection of Ishtar the Nineveh poet provides a counterpart, Enkidu's rejection of the harlot. While Gilgamesh's rejection affirmed the apparent unity of his relationship with Enkidu and his own self-identity, Enkidu's was symptomatic of his fall. He curses the person who gave him knowledge and led him to the unity that Gilgamesh's rejection of Ishtar had so roundly asserted. Not satisfied with this, the Nineveh poet brings in another theme that he had developed previously, beginning with Ninsun's prayer: justice, as personified by Shamash.

From Ninsun's prayer the theme was developed throughout the search for Humbaba, to climax with Shamash's direct intervention in the expedition to ensure its success. Although the subsequent development of this theme is lost for the most part, it appears that Enkidu dreamt of the gods convening and decreeing that one of the two must die. Thus the unity portended by Gilgamesh's dream found its end portended in Enkidu's. Enlil apparently insisted that Gilgamesh be spared, perhaps, one suspects, on account of the splendid cedar door that was sent to his city Nippur. Enkidu awakes and curses his fate.

39 For the separation, even hostility of emblems and the deities they represented, see Jacobsen in *Towards the Image of Tammuz and Other Essays on Mesopotamian History and Culture* (W. L. Moran, ed.; Cambridge, MA: 1970): 4f.

He begins by cursing the cedar door. The poet takes pains to point out that Enkidu is losing his senses, windows of his hard-won knowledge.

Nineveh VII i 37ff. (= K 3588, *GETh* Plate 14)

37. *it-ti dalti [i-t]a-ma-a ki-i [amēlūti]*
38. *dalti ḫal-bi la ḫa-[sis-tu]*
39. *ba-šat uz-ni šá la i-ba-áš-šu-[ú]*

37. He talked to the door as if it were [human],
38. A bosky door, insen[sate].
39. It lent an ear that wasn't there!

He furiously reverses the curse formula normally put on door stones to guarantee perpetuation of the builder's name and wishes that someone would erase his name and write another. This may well have sounded humorous to an audience familiar with the genre. Gilgamesh comforts his friend by saying that he should be happy to die; those who live on must mourn. Besides, he will provide a splendid funerary cult for his dead companion.

Unmoved, Enkidu resumes his crying and cursing the following morning (note the time gap, perhaps another humorous touch). He disposes of the hunter:

Nineveh VII ii 39ff. (= *UET* VI 394, 5f.; *CT* 46 23, 5′f.)

39. *ša la ú-šam-ṣa-an-nu ma-la ib-ri-i[a]*
40. *ṣa-a-a-du a-a in-ṣa-a ma-la ip-ri-šu*

39. He who did not let me attain what my friend did,
40. The hunter, may he not attain what will feed him.

A pun may lurk at the end of line 40, on *ibru* 'friend' and *epr* 'provide with food.' After further curses, he turns to the prostitute.

The curse of the prostitute is one of the most problematic sections of the poem. The two basic discussions of the text are those of Gadd, *Iraq* 28 (1966): 105ff. and Landsberger, *RA* 62 (1968): 123ff. Collation of the Middle Babylonian tablet treated by Gadd in most cases supports his readings and copy against emendation. The following transliteration is "in score" because of the great number of significant variants found for this passage.

A = K 8590, Haupt, *Nimrodepos* No. 6 p. 18, 6ff.
B = K 2589, Haupt, *Nimrodepos* No. 5 p. 16, 3ff.
C = *CT* 46 25, 14ff.
D = *UET* VI 394, 11ff. (collated)
E = *CT* 46 23, III 1 6ff.
F = K 3389, Haupt, *Nimrodepos* No. 4 p. 15, 25f.
G = K 11659, Haupt, *Nimrodepos* No. 55 p. 94 (collated)

Nineveh VII iii 6ff.
Numeration of lines follows that of *GETh*, 27f.

6. A [ ]*-tu lu-šim-ki*
B [ ]*-ki* ^mi^Šam-hat x̣ [ ]-⸢*šim*⸣*-ki*
D *al-ki Šam-*⸢*ḫa*⸣-⸢*at*⸣ *ši*-ma-ta *lu*-⸢*šim*⸣-[*k*]*i*
E [*Š*]*am-ḫat ši-ma-at lu-šim-ka*

7. A [ ]-⸢*ur*⸣ *da-a-ár*
B [ ]*-mat la i-qat-tu-ú ana d*[*u*] x [ ]*-a-ár*
D omits
E [ ]-⸢*tu*⸣*-ú a-du-ru da-a-ri*

8. A [ ] x GAL-*a*
B [ ]*uz-zur-ki iz-ra* [ ] GAL-*a*
D *lu-uz-zur-ki iz-zi-ra ra-ba-*⸢*a*⸣*
E [ ] ⸢*iz*⸣*-ri ra-ba-a*

9. A [ ]*-ki ka-a-ši*
B [ ] x *ḫar-piš iz-ru-ú-*[ ] *liṭ-ḫu-ki ka-a-ši*
D *ḫa-an-ṭi-iš ḫar-piš iz-zi-ru-ú-a l*[*i-i*]*ṭ-ḫu-*[ ] x̣[ ]*-ši*
E [ ] x̣ x̣ x̣ *-ḫu-ka* [ ]

10. A [ ]*-le-e-ki*
B [ ] ⸢*te*⸣*-pu-ši* É *la-le-ki*
D *e te-pu-ši* É *la-*[ ]*-ki*

11. A [ ]-⸢*ḫu*⸣*-ti*(!)*-ki*
B [ ]-⸢*ram*⸣*-mi i-*x̣[ ] *šá ta-ḫu-ti-ki*
D omits

12. A [ ] *šá* KI.SIKIL.MEŠ
B [ ]*-ri*?*-bi* [ ] x *šá* KI.SIKIL.MEŠ
D *e tu*-ri-bi i-na* É [x x x?] *ša* KI.SIKIL.MEŠ
* no room on tablet for *še*

13. A [ ] *li-šaḫ-ḫi*
B [ ] *ma*? [ ] x̣ [ ]*-šaḫ-ḫi*
D *su-nu-ki dam-qa qa-du*?-⸢*tu*⸣? [ ] *še*?*-ḫe*?*-e*

14. A [ ]*-bal-lil*
B [ ] x̣ [*ba*]*l-lil*
C [ ] *ú*? *l*[*i-ba*]*l-lil*
D *lub*?*-ši**? *i-si-in-na-ti-ki šak-ru i-na tu-*[*re*?]*-e*? li-bal-lil
*second sign has horizontal after it that is too highly placed for BAR.

15. A omits
B [ ]*-*x̣*-te*
C [ ] *u-ba-na-a-tú*
D (= D.18?) [ ] x̣ x̣ *ir-*x̣[ ]-⸢*ti*⸣?

16. A [*e*]*n-nu šá pa-ḫa-re*
B [ ]*-re*
C omits?
D (= D.19?) *ša*? *lu-*x̣*-tum* x̣ [ ] x̣

17. A [*ta*]*r-ši-i*
B [ ]*-i*
C [ ]x̣*-ri pu-rim mim-ma e tar-ši-i*
D (= D.20?) x̣ x̣ *pa-ni*? *bu*?*-ri*?*-ti*? x̣?x̣ LÚ *da-a-a-ni ši* x̣ x̣ x̣ [ ]

18. A [ ] *i*?*-na-di ina* É*-ki*
B omits
C [ ] KÙ.BABBAR SIKIL *šá-muḫ* UN.MEŠ *a-a in-na-di ina* É*-ka*

D [ ] KÙ.BABBAR *šu-mu-uḫ ni-ši bal-tum a-a* RU
[ ]

19. A [ ] KASKAL *lu-u mu-šá-bu-ki*
B omits
C adds one line
[ ]x̣*-li-ma*(!) *lu-ú dak-kan-nu*
[ ] *šá* KASKAL *lu-ú mu-šá-bu-ka*
D [ ] *in* x̣ *la-le-ki lu-ú* ⸢*dak*⸣-⸢*kan*⸣-x̣
iš-pal-lu-ur-ti pa-ḫa-re lu-ú mu-ša-bu-ki

20. A [ ] *lu-u man-za-zu-ki*
B omits
C [ ] x̣*-ṣal-lu-ka* GIŠ.GI$_6$ BÀD *lu-ú man-za-zu-ka*
D adds one line:
ḫur-ba-tum lu-ú ma-a-a-la-k[*i*]
ṣi-il-li BÀD *lu-ú man-za-zu-k*[i]

21. A [ ] x̣ GÌR.MEŠ*-ki*
B omits
C [ ]*-qi li-qal-li-pu* GÌR^{II}*-ka*
D [*š*]*e-gu bal-tu li-qal-li-pi* G[ÌR]

22. A [ ] *lit-ki*
B omits
C [ ] x̣*-mu-ú li-im-ḫaṣ la-ka*
D [ ]*-ru ù ṣa-mu-ú li-im-ḫa-ṣu li-i*[*t*]
D adds here two lines:
(a) [ ]*-ru**? *ina su-qí al-ki* [ ]*ši*?*-ib-*x̣
(b) [ ] x̣ *iš-ša-ki-in qa*?*-al-*[ ]

23. A [ ] x̣*-ki lil-si*
B [ ]*-*x̣*-si*?
C [ ]*-*⸢*na*⸣*-*⸢*ti*⸣*-ka ni-šu e-li-ka li-is-su*?
D [ ]*-na-ti-ki né-e-*[ ]*-si*

24. A [ ] *i-tin-nu*
B [ ]*-nu*
C [ ] *a-a i-ṣi-ir i-tin-nu*
D [ ] x̣ *i* [ ]

25. A [ ]*-du-ú*
B [ ] x̣
C [ ] x̣ *ir-bi-ṣi qa-du-*⸢*ú*⸣
D [*i*]*r-bi-ṣu* UR? [ ]

26. A [ ]*-*⸢*e*⸣*-tum*
C [ ]*-kin qé-*⸢*re*⸣*-*⸢*e*⸣*-*[ ]
D [*š*]*a-kin qé-*[ ]

27. D [ ] x̣ [ ]
G [ ]*e* x̣[ ]

28. D [ ]*-*x̣*-ti-i* x x *ta-ri-im-*[ ]
G [ ]x̣ ⸢*šá*⸣ *ta-rim-an-*[ ]

29. D [ ] ⸢*šaḫ*⸣*-ti* ⸢*lu*⸣*-ú taš-ḫi-tum*
G [ ]*-reb su-ni šaḫ-*[ ]

30. D [ ] x̣ x̣ *el-lu-ú lu-ú ni-di-in* x̣ [ ]
F (here?) [ ] in-ni
G *šá su-un-ki** *šaḫ-*x̣ [ ]
* KI is certain, against Landsberger's ŠU

31. D [ ] ⸢*ši*⸣ x [ ] EGIR *ḫi-ir-*[ ]
G *áš-šú ia-a-ši* [ ]

32. D [ ] *te*? [ ]x̣*-id-din-ni i-na* EDIN*-ia*
F [ ]*-ni ina* EDIN*-ia*
G *u ia-a-a-ši* KÙ [ ]

6. "Come, Šamhat, let me ordain you a fate,
7. A fate never ending for ever and ever.
8. I'll lay on you a mighty curse,
9. Swiftly and soon may my curses draw nigh to you.
10. May you never make a home you delight in,
11. May you never love a c[hild] of your womb(?),
12. May you never [be admitted to(?)] the . . . homes of (decent) women,
13. May beer dregs impregnate your lovely womb,
14. And the drunkard bespatter your best clothes with vo[mit(?)],
15. [ ] fingers
[ ] may the judges . . . [ ].
16. [ ] of earthenware,
17. May you never have any shining alabaster at all,
18. May silver, people's (variant: pride and) joy, never be kept in your home.
19. May the [abode] of your delight be a doorway,
The crossroad of the potters' quarter be your dwelling,
20. May a vacant lot be your sleeping place,
The shadow of a wall be your station.
21. May thorn and bramble gouge your feet,
22. Drunk and thirsty slap your cheek,
[ ] in the street [ ] 'Come . . . '
[ ] let there be set [ ]
23. [On your jour]neys may lions roar at you.
24. [Your house] may no builder [des]ign.
25. May the screech owl (variant: dog?) lurk [in your]
26. No meals be served [in your]
27. [ ]
28. [ ] which you love [ ]
29. The [entr]ance to your . . . womb, may it be impregnating (?),
30. The one who impregnates your womb, may . . . be his? (wedding?) gift,
31. Because you [killed me] after marrying [me],
32. You should have given me, yes me, the silver!"

Commentary

For detailed discussion of the philological problems of this passage, see the works of Landsberger and Gadd cited above.

Line 9: I follow the suggestion of Schramm, *RA* 64 (1970): 94.

Line 23: Restoring [*ina ḫar-ra*]*-na-at* with von Soden, *Gilgamesch-Epos*, 61.

Lines 29f.: Evidently an elaborate play on words of the root *šḫ*ʾ is developed here, but the meaning of the passage is obscure.

In the first part of his curse, Enkidu would deny the harlot a home, children, and the society of decent women.

The only thing to impregnate her is beer, and drunkenness is her only celebration. She shall have neither money nor fine belongings. Her home will be public places, where she is subject to abuse by all. The latter part of Enkidu's curse is broken and obscure, but seems to refer bitterly to marriage. Gadd (p. 108, note 11) and Landsberger (p. 127), restoring *ḫi-ir-[ti-ia]* at the end of line 31, reached the conclusion that Enkidu had been married before he encountered the harlot. This most implausible notion is not supported by the text. Even if the restoration is correct, the intent of the line, to judge from the parallel blessing (below, iv 10), probably was that the harlot had denied him the chance for a normal marriage.

At this juncture Shamash cries out abruptly from heaven that Enkidu is being unfair:

Nineveh VII iii 35ff.

35. *am-me-ni* ^{d}En-ki-dù *ḫa-rim-[t]i* ^{mi}Šam-ḫat *ta-na-an-za-ár*
36. *šá ú-šá-ki-lu-ka uklāt si-mat il-ú-ti*
37. *ku-ru-un-na iš-qu-ka si-mat šàr-ú-ti*
38. *ú-lab-bi-šu-ka lu-ub-ši ra-ba-a*
39. *u dam-qu* ^{d}Gilgameš *tap-pa-a ú-šar-šu-ka ka-a-šá*
40. *[e]-nin-na-a-ma* ^{d}Gilgameš *ib-ri ta-li-me-ka*
41. *[uš-na]-a-al-ka-a-ma ina ma-a-a-li rabi*^{i}
42. *[i-na] ma-a-a-al taq-ni-i uš-na-al-ka-ma*
43. *[u-š]e-šib-ka šub-ta ni-iḫ-ta šu-bat šu-me-li*
44. *[ma-al]-ka šá qaq-qa-ri ú-na-áš-šá-qu šēpē-ka*
45. *[ú-šab]-kak-ka nīše šá* Uruk^{ki} *ú-šad-ma-ma-ak-ka*
46. *[šam-ḫa-a-ti] nišē ú-ma-al-lak-ka dul-la*
47. *[ù šu]-⌈ú⌉ ar-ki-ka ú-ša-áš-šá-a ma-la-a pa-gar-[šú]*
48. *[il-tab-bi]-⌈iš⌉ maš-ki lab-bi-im-ma i-rap-pu-ud ṣē[ri]*

35. "Why, O Enkidu, would you curse the harlot Šamhat,
36. Who fed you bread fit for divinity,
37. Gave you wine to drink, fit for a king?
38. Garbed you in a princely garment,
39. And let you get fair Gilgamesh for your very own friend?
40. Now then, Gilgamesh is your best friend, is he not?
41. Will he not lay you down in a princely sleeping place?
42. In a suitable sleeping place he will lay you down!
43. He'll make you(r cult image) sit comfortably in a seat at his left,
44. And the kings of the earth will do you homage,
45. The people in Uruk he'll make weep and cry for you!
46. [Prostitutes] and people will he fill with misery for you!
47. As for him, after you die he'll make his hair unkempt,
48. Put on a lion skin, and run through the steppe."

Commentary

Lines 36f.: The parallelism is now ironic, as Enkidu is not a god (he has to die) and not a king (Gilgamesh is the king). Shamash is in effect saying that Enkidu had already had more than he could reasonably have expected, in that he had been almost as good as Gilgamesh, so should take his death in good part. Cf VI 27f.

Line 39: 'very own' = *kāša*. The absurdity of this speech is emphasized by the hyperbole of lines 36 and 37, the pompous parallelism of lines 41–42, the anticlimax of line 43, the pairing of prostitutes and people in 46 (restored from VIII iii), even using the word *šamḫatu*, the name of the person being cursed, and the final absurdity of lines 47–48 in which Gilgamesh is supposed to replace Enkidu as the hairy man of the steppe. That a god should attempt to calm the rage of a man is strange enough, but the terms and language used leave little doubt as to the poet's satiric, if bitter, intent. This is brought home by Enkidu's reply, in which he elaborately undoes his 'perpetual' curse.

Nineveh VII iv 1ff. = D, 47ff.; F, 1ff.

(line x, not in F)
D *al-ki* Šam-[ ]

1. D ⌈*pi*⌉*-ia ša iz-*[ ]⌈*ub*⌉*-ki*
F [ ]*-ru-ki li-tur lik-*[ ]

2. D *ša-ak-ka-na-ak-*[ ] x̣ *li-ra-[mu]-ki*
F [ ]*-ki ù* NUN.MEŠ *li-ir-a-*⌈*mu*⌉*-*⌈*ki*⌉

3. D [ ] 1 DANNA *li-i[m š]a-par-šu*
F [ ]*-ḫaṣ šá-par-šu*

4. D *šá* 2 DANNA ⌈*li*⌉*-*⌈*na*⌉*-*⌈*si*⌉*-*⌈*sa*⌉*qi-*⌈*im*⌉*-ma-at-*⌈*su*⌉
F [*l*]*i-na-as-si-sa qim-mat-su*

5. D *a-a ik-la-ak-ki* [ ] *sír***-ra-šu* [ ]
F [ ] *re-du-ú mi-sír-ra-šú líp-ṭur-ki*

6. D *li-din-ki ṣum-mur-ra* x̣ x̣ x̣ x̣ x̣*
F [^{n}]^{a_4} ZÚ ^{na_4}ZA.GÌN u GUŠKIN
*Landsberger's emendation of D does not fit the traces

7. D *an-ṣa-ab-tu tur-tu-ri li-mil-la-a* x̣ x̣ x̣
F [ ] x̣ x̣ *tur-ru-ú lu-u ni-din-ki*

8. D *ana*-KU*?[ ] x *zu-un-*[ ] *iz?**-nu-nu-šu iš-pik-*[ ]
F [ ] x̣***-nu-nu-šú iš-pik-ki-šú šap-ku*
* The second sign in D does not look like ŠA.
** This sign does not look much like IZ in either exemplar.

9. D MAŠ.MAŠ [ ] KÙ x x? DINGIR.MEŠ li-še-ri-[ ]
F [ ] DINGIR.MEŠ *lu-še-rib-ki ka-a-ši*

10. D *áš-šu-mi-ka li-ir*-*[ ] *um-mi* 7 *ḫi?-ir?-tum*
F [ ]*-in-né-zib* AMA 7 *ḫi-ir-tum*

a. "Come, Šam[ḫat]
1. My mouth which cursed you, let it bless you again.
2. May generals and dignitaries fall in love with you,
3. May [one] a league away slap his thigh (in frustration),
4. May one two leagues away (already) be letting down his hair,
5. Nor let the underling hold back from you, let him

open his drawers for you.
6. May he give you obsidian, lapis, and gold,
7. Earrings of . . . gold may your ("wedding") gift be (variant: may he fill . . .)
8. . . . plentiful rain? may they? give him, his yield be garnered.
9. May exorcists . . . (into?) the holy . . . (of the?) gods bring you in.
10. For you may the wife and mother of seven be abandoned (variant: be . . .)."

Commentary

Lines 3–4: I understand these to mean that her lovers will be so eager for her that one league away they slap their thighs in frustration, and two leagues away are already beginning to undress. For slapping the thigh, see Gurney, *AnSt* 5 (1955): 110; van Dijk, *CRRAI* 7 (1958): 81. For letting down the hair as a sign of undressing, compare VI 2 (Gilgamesh) [*u-na-si*]*s qim-mat-su e-lu ṣi-ri-šu* "[He let] his hair [down] over his back."

In the passages quoted in this episode, the Nineveh poet has rejected non-productive sex. For Enkidu, the knowledge with which he became human was also the beginning of his suffering and downfall. For Gilgamesh, the knowledge was not needed. The rejection of Ishtar is framed in such a way that the reader is compelled to agree with its necessity; she is treacherous and degrading. The rejection of the prostitute is a blessing and a curse with the same effect. Ishtar and the prostitute share a common fate, relegation to the street. Yet of the two, the prostitute is given an ironic reprieve: having done her work well, she is blessed with a distinguished, eager, and generous, perhaps marriageable clientele. A somewhat similar destiny was the fond hope of a real prostitute, who implored Ishtar in the following words:

May my lips be honey, my hands charm
May the lip(s) of my vulva (?) be lip(s) of honey!
As birds twitter over a snake which comes out of a hole,
May these people fight over me![40]

Episode 4: Distintegration of Unity (Knowledge of the Self)

With this episode, the Nineveh poet turns from exploration of love and sex to the theme of separation, the new "unity" of Gilgamesh. The poet introduces this theme by stressing the impending separation of the two friends. Enkidu has a frightful dream:

Nineveh VII iv 15ff. (composite text)[41]

15. *il-su-ú šame^e qaq-qa-ru i-pul*
16. *ina bi-ri-su-nu az-za-zi a-na-ku*
17. *ša 1-en eṭ-lu uk-ku-lu pa-nu-šú*
18. *a-na ša an-ze-e pa-nu-šu maš-lu*
19. *ri-it-ti nēši rit-ta-a-šu su-pur a-re-e su-pur-a-šú*
20. *iṣ-bat qim-ma-ti ú-dan-ni-na-an-ni ia-a-ši*
21. *am-ḫa-su-ma kima kip-pe-e i-šaḫ-ḫi-iṭ*
22. *im-ḫaṣ-an-ni-ma ki-ma [a ?]-mu uṭ-ṭib-ba-an-ni*
23. *ki-ma ri-i-mi ú-[kab]-bi-is elī-ia*
24. *ni-tam il-ta-ma-a [ka]l pag-ri-ia*
25. *šu-zib-an-ni eb-ri [ul tu-še-zi]-ib-[an-ni]*
26. *tap-laḫ-ma ul [ ]*
27. *at-ta [ ]*

15. "Heaven cried out, earth made reply,
16. Between them I was standing.
17. The first man's face was darkness,
18. Like a stormcloud bird was his face,
19. The claws of a lion were his claws, the talons of an eagle his talons.
20. He seized my hair and tried to overpower me.
21. I hit him but like a jump rope he bounced back.
22. He hit me and capsized me like a [ra]ft,
23. Like a bull he trampled over me.
24. My whole body he held in his clench!
25. 'Save me, my friend!' [But you sa]ved [me not].
26. You were too afraid and did not [save me]
27. You [ ]."

Commentary:

Line 21: One can also understand "like a trap he sprung." For the connection of the jump rope, plaything of Ishtar, with battle, see Landsberger, *WZKM* 56 (1960): 121ff.

Line 22: The raft appears in a difficult simile in Atrahasis III iv 8f.: *ki-ma a-mi-im i-mi-da a-na s*[*a-pa*]*n-*[*ni*] / *ki-ma a-mi-im i-na ṣe-ri i-mi-da a-na ki-ib-ri* (Nintu speaks of the people drowned in the flood): "Like a raft they drift against the shore / Like a raft overturned they drift against the bank."

Line 25: Note the utterance without a formula of speech, indicating Enkidu's excitement, echoing the abrupt narrative of line 17.

Enkidu became a spirit and was vouchsafed a vision of the netherworld, where he saw, among others, those who had served and honored the great gods. After a long illness, Enkidu dies, and Gilgamesh is left alone.

At first Gilgamesh refuses to acknowledge the physical separation (cf. X v 15), circling the corpse like an eagle or a lioness deprived of her whelps (VIII ii 18f.). He commissions a statue of lapis and gold and dedicates Enkidu's sword and whetstone (VIII iv 48ff.). He gives a funeral oration in which he describes his friend's valor.

Gradually the separation becomes wider. In his subsequent speeches Gilgamesh moves more and more from consideration of his friend to consideration of his own situation. One example will suffice. The Old Babylonian version and the Nineveh version show this change in different ways:

40 Caplice, *SANE* 1/1, 23.

41 *GETh* Plate 27, 79–7–8, 320 ii 4ff.; *UET* VI 394, 61ff.; *CT* 46 24, 15ff.

OB Meissner ii l'ff.

1′. *it-ti-ia it-ta-al-la-ku ka-lu mar-ṣ[a-a-tim]*
2′. ^{d}En-ki-du$_{10}$ *ša a-ra-am-mu-šu da-an-ni-iš*
3′. *it-ti-ia it-ta-al-la-ku ka-lu mar-ṣa-a-tim*
4′. *il-li-ik-ma a-na ši-ma-tú a-wi-lu-tim*

1′. "Who with me suffered every misfortune,
2′. Enkidu, whom I love so much,
3′. Who with me suffered every misfortune,
4′. Gone is he to the fate of mankind!"

Nineveh X v 8ff.

8. [*šá nin-nen-du-ma ni-lu*]-*ú šá-da-a*
9. [*ni-iṣ-ba-tu-ma a-l*]*a-a ni-na-ru*
10. [*nu-šal-pi-tu* ^{d}Hum-ba-ba *šá ina qī*]*šti erēni áš-bu*
11. [*ina ne-re-bi-ti šá šadī^{i} ni-du*]-*ku nēšē*
12. *ib-ri šá a-ram-mu dan-niš it-ti-ia ittallaku^{ku} ka-lu mar-ṣa-a-ti*
13. [^{d}En-ki-du$_{10}$ *šá a-ram-mu dan-niš*] *ittallaku^{ku} ka-lu mar-ṣa-a-ti*
14. [6 *ur-ri u* 7 *mu-ša-a-ti*] *elī-šú ab-ki*

8. "It was we who were together and crossed the mountains,
9. We who caught and killed the Bull of Anu,
10. We who felled Humbaba who dwelt in the cedar forest,
11. [At the crossings of the mountains it was we who kil]led lions!
12. My friend whom I love so much, who suffered every misfortune with me,
13. [Enkidu whom I love so much, who] suffered [with me] every misfortune,
14. [Six days and seven nights] did I weep for him!"

In the Old Babylonian version, Gilgamesh stresses his friend's participation[42] and ends with a statement of his friend's death, whereas in the Nineveh version he stresses their joint participation and ends with a description of his own mourning. The gap widens as he seeks desperately to avoid sharing his friend's fate. His new-found unity consists of himself alone. His ascent to knowledge begins again, but, like Enkidu, he begins now on the steppe.

In fact, Gilgamesh is become Enkidu in reverse. He runs the steppe, but he kills animals, rather than living with them, and he seeks the remotest corner of the earth to begin his ascent, rather than the urban delights of Uruk, as Enkidu had been led to. Most important, unlike Enkidu, he knows that he is a human being. Gilgamesh's ascent will come about in each case through the intervention of a woman:[43] his mother, whose prayer assures the intercession of Shamash; the wife of the scorpion man, who evidently persuades her husband to admit Gilgameš to the passes; the tavern keeper, who tells him of Ur-Šanabi; and Ut-napištim's wife, who persuades her husband to give Gilgamesh something to show for his long journey.

In his first adventure, the killing of Humbaba, Gilgamesh relied on his valor, and, in increasingly violent acts, seems to be gaining his goal. He approaches the scorpion man with courage, though politely. He threatens the tavern keeper, though makes no assault. He attacks Ur-Šanabi outright, and forces him to take him across the waters of death. For his final battle he is well prepared, and is astonished to find his prospective opponent languid and indifferent.

Nineveh XI 5f.

5. *gu-um-mur-ka lib-bi ana e-piš tu-qu-un-ti*
6. [ ] *a-ḫi na-da-at-ta e-lu ṣe-ri-ka*

5. "My heart imagined you a maker of battle,
6. [But you do] nothing, and lie on your back."

This "no contest" disposes of Gilgamesh's valor, and Ut-napištim thereupon disposes of his great show of mourning, the trappings of his new-found independence. The village idiot, he points out, wears wretched clothes and eats bad food, but no one accords him merit for that—he is just a fool. Gilgamesh is now not only separated from his friend by death, he is separated from the new, independent self that this separation seems to have created. His lonely valor and ostentatious mourning do not make him a self that will survive. The last touch is put on this destruction by the test of whether or not he can stay awake for seven days and nights. He falls asleep at once, and thereby passes from the scene the all-night rowdy that was introduced to the reader in the first tablet. Knowledge of one's separate self is not the end of the journey.

Episode 5: Redefinition of Unity (Transcendence of Knowledge beyond the Self)

The denouement is swift. Gilgamesh's last hope is that his new-found and newly lost self can be preserved by the artificial means of a magical plant of eternal rejuvenation.

42 This is in sharp contrast to Gilgamesh's original conception of the expedition and his role in it. The clearest example of Gilgamesh's egocentricity is afforded by an Old Babylonian "Dream of Gilgamesh" from Tell Harmal (*TIM* 9 43, edited by von Soden, *ZA* 53 [1959]: 215ff.). Note, for example, line 4: *a-na-ku rīmī ṣé-ri-im aṣ-ṣa-ab-ta-nim* "I captured for myself wild bulls" in which one line contains an independent first person pronoun, a first person verb in the (ethical?) t-form with (plural? or singular? see Jacobsen, *JNES* 22 [1963]: 2) "ventive" ending—perhaps the ultimate in self-predication. Enkidu, by contrast, explains the dream in the first person plural (13, 16).

43 I am grateful to P. Michalowski for making available to me his essay entitled "Gilgamesh: History and the Structure of Desire," which treats this aspect of the poem.

Because of his unwillingness to eat the plant at once, he loses it on the return journey. The final lines of the text find him speaking the poet's lines at the outset, describing the walls of Uruk, almost as if they were all that he had salvaged from his life and journey. Is this how the poet expects his reader to interpret his poem? Such an interpretation seems to find support in the parallelism of the poet's early invocation of his reader to look at the wall, and Gilgamesh's final invocation of Ur-Šanabi to do the same.[44] This interpretation, moreover, echoes a belief common enough in Mesopotamia, at least in royal ideology.

Yet the Nineveh poem is not really about royal ideology, though that was a theme useful to both poets and the Old Babylonian poet even opened with it. The Nineveh poet, by contrast, opened with an invocation of Gilgamesh's knowledge, and it is Gilgamesh's knowledge and how he acquired it that is the subject of the poem. The reader must ask, therefore, what Gilgamesh knew that set him apart from other men. Of course Gilgamesh knew from the beginning what every king knows, that if his works survive, the king's name survives. This the poet's narrative voice grants, but vitiates in a strange way. The poet transfers the words from his own narrative voice to that of his character, and reduces the poet's audience to one, another character, and a minor one at that. This reduction can be seen as a subtle denigration not only of the opening speech but of the walls themselves. Gilgamesh knew more than what he said to Ur-Šanabi, and what he knew must be what the narrative voice tells the reader in the end, the poem itself.

Mesopotamian poets were wont to refer to the circumstances of the poem's conception or composition at the end of their work.[45] The Epic of Gilgamesh is no exception, save that it employs the device at one remove—implicitly in the poet's rhetorical silence. Gilgamesh knew that knowledge was his self that transcended him, uniquely his, but, like a poem, independent of him at the moment of its fulfillment, and no longer needing his continued existence. His mortal self and the walls he built were his, but limited by immutable laws of physical existence. His inscription was more important than the walls it commemorated, for the walls without it communicated nothing beyond their existence. His knowledge was more important than the self that acquired it, but was limited to that self until he gave it independent existence, in Greek terms, "did" something with it.

Near the beginning the poet asks the reader to read well Gilgamesh's inscription,[46] a well known literary cachet, the metaphor for the text at hand.[47] At the conclusion, by his final silence, the poet asks the reader to read well his poem, and know too. Therewith the poem begins over again.

---

44 This character seems a curious choice, but the reason may lie in a hermeneutic on his name "Servant-of-Two-Thirds" and the fabulous genealogy of Gilgamesh whereby he was one third human and two thirds divine. This proportion is treated playfully by the poet in IX ii 19ff., in which the scorpion man's wife pedantically corrects her spouse and a paranomasia is developed on *zikaru* 'man' and *zakāru* 'say.'

45 E.g., *Erra* V 42ff.; Nin-me-ŝár-ra 136ff. (= *YNER* 3, 33); Agušaja = Foster, *Studies . . . Finkelstein*, 84 note 38; *Atrahasis* III viii 11ff; *Enuma Eliš* VII.158.

46 I i 25 (= *Iraq* 37 [1975]: 160): *ṭup-pi* ^{na_4}ZA.GÌN *ši-tas-si* "read well the lapis tablet."

47 Güterbock, *ZA* 42 (1934): 19ff.

THE MARRIAGE AND DEATH OF SINUHE

CYRUS H. GORDON

Modern westerners stress the need to live well while tending to neglect the desirability of dying well. The wise men of the East knew that it is impossible to judge a life as a whole until death has terminated it. It is only after the game is over that we know the score. This is what Ecclesiastes (7:1) means by: "A good name is better than precious ointment, and the day of one's death than the day of his birth." The sage Solon similarly maintained that no man should be called fortunate until he is dead (Herodotus 1:30-32, 86).

The Egyptian romance of Sinuhe is a diverting tale with a happy ending: a blessed death prepared to crown a full life. The text has survived in a number of exemplars because it remained popular from Middle to Late Egyptian times.[1] It was placed in tombs so that the deceased would have good reading matter in the world beyond the grave. The Egyptians were a civilized people who sensed that man does not live by bread alone; and the upper classes, at least, required diverting literature in the next world as well as is this.

The story goes that Sinuhe was a courtier in the entourage of Sesostris I: son, coregent and successor of Amenemmes I who founded the Twelfth Dynasty early in the second millennium B.C. Sinuhe was with the army of Sesostris on a victorious campaign against the Libyans in the Delta, when news was secretly delivered to Sesostris that his father had died in the Capital, near Thebes. Sinuhe got wind of it and took fright as Sesostris clandestinely raced to the Capital to secure the reins of government. Apprehensive of intrigue and shake-ups, Sinuhe panicked and fled across Suez into Palestine and Syria, called Retenu[2] in Egyptian. For an Egyptian, Retenu was a *ḫ3st* ("barbarous land") outside the civilized ecumene which was limited to Egypt.[3] But Egypt was known and respected in Retenu, where there was a significant though sparse stratum of diplomats, administrators and traders from Egypt so that one could speak Egyptian and establish contacts with the Nile Valley, even at the Pharaonic level.

Sinuhe wandered from *ḫ3st* to *ḫ3st* until he came to a fertile principality called Yaa. It was a natural paradise, full of orchards and vineyards, where "wine was more abundant than water." The Prince of the realm took a liking to Sinuhe and initiated him into his household with the formulae: " 'Lo, you are here; you shall stay with me. What I am doing for you is good.' He made me chief of his children. He married me to his oldest daughter. He let me choose for myself of his land, of the best he had."[4]

Each of the above utterances is sociologically meaningful. "Lo, you are here" indicates that Sinuhe is part of the Prince's household. "You shall stay with me" makes the relationship enduring. "What I am doing for you is good" signifies that the Prince is conferring a singularly great boon on Sinuhe; to wit, "He made me chief of his children." Thus Sinuhe is not only adopted but is made the fratriarch.[5] Simultaneously, Sinuhe is given the hand of the Prince's oldest daughter. Finally, as chief heir-apparent[6] Sinuhe gets the choicest part of the Prince's land as his domain.

The expression *rdi.n.f wi m ḥ3t ẖrdw.f* could by itself be translated "he put me over his children" (with *m ḥ3t* = prepositional "over") as well "he made me chief of his children" (with *m* of predication or equivalence);[7] that the latter is correct is supported by the MAN determinative that follows *ḥ3t* when Sinuhe's new title (= "fratriarch") is repeated.[8]

Parallels, even when they cogently elucidate each other, should not be equated. The Nuzi parallel we shall examine is highly suggestive but it differs from the Sinuhe episode mainly (but not only) in that Sinuhe is a foreigner, whereas in the Nuzi tablet, as far as we can tell, the man initiated into the family is a native. The Nuzi

---

1 The Egyptian versions are aligned in Aylward M. Blackman's edition of *Middle-Egyptian Stories* (Brussels: Édition de la Fondation Égyptologique Reine Elizabeth, 1932). For bibliography, etc., see the annotated translation of Miriam Lichtheim, *Ancient Egyptian Literature: A Book of Readings* (Berkeley: Univ. of Cal. Press, 1973): 222–35.

2 From older "Reṯenu" (with ṯ).

3 Egypt was called Kemet (*Kmt*) "The Black (Country)" or *T3-mri* "The Beloved Land" or *T3wy* "The Two Lands" (= Upper and Lower Egypt).

4 The Egyptian text (see Blackman, pp. 22–23) is: *m.k tw ꜥ3 wn.n.k. ḥnꜥ.i nfr irt.i n.k rdi.n.f wi n ḥ3t ẖrdw.f mni.n.f. wi s3t.f wrt rdi.n.f stp.i n.i. m stpw n wnt ḥnꜥ.f.*

5 "Fratriarch" is a useful term to designate the offical leader of a group of siblings. See Cyrus H. Gordon, "Fratriarchy in the Old Testament," *JBL* 54 (1935): 223–31.

6 From what we know of ancient Near East sociology, such an adopted son remains chief heir (and fratriarch) only as long as no real son is begotten by the adopting father (note the Nuzi tablet translated below).

7 The different usages are listed by Raymond O. Faulkner, *A Concise Dictionary of Middle Egyptian* (Oxford: Griffith Institute, 1962; rpt. 1964): 162.

8 In text B:108 (Blackman, p. 25). The fact that Blackman writes "sic" over the MAN determinative reflects the general failure to grasp the social connotation.

parallel has it that a father of daughters, but not of sons, first adopts a man as his son. Then, in the same document, he marries off a daughter to him. This provides filial support for the father, and keeps the inheritance in the family. The Nuzi tablet runs as follows:[9]

> The adoption tablet of Našwi son of Aršenni. He adopted Wullu son of Puhišenni. As long as Našwi lives, Wullu shall give (him) food and clothing. When Našwi dies, Wullu shall inherit. Should Našwi beget a son, (the latter) shall divide equally with Wullu but (only) Našwi's son shall take Našwi's gods. But if there be no son of Našwi's then Wullu shall take Našwi's gods. And (Našwi) has given his daughter Nuhuya as wife to Wullu. And if Wullu takes another wife, he forfeits Našwi's land and buildings. Whoever breaks the contract shall pay (as damages) one mina of silver (and) one mina of gold.

Although there is no blood relationship between the Nuzi bride and groom, they are legally brother and sister. It is interesting that in ancient Egypt (and in other countries such as Ceylon), marriages between real brothers and sisters took place often enough.[10]

It was not uncommon to welcome desirable foreigners (like Sinuhe) as sons-in-law.[11] But in such cases, the husband joined the bride's family; and, if he eventually returned to his homeland, he could not force his wife to leave her father's domain. Such a marriage gave the groom practical opportunities, but socially the wife was protected; for she, her children and property could not be removed.[12] Come what might, she remained the native lady, and could not be transported against her will to her husband's land where she would be an alien laboring under the opprobrious disabilities of a "foreign woman."[13]

When Sinuhe, after a long and successful career in Yaa, earnestly sought and gratefully accepted the Pharaoh's invitation to return to Egypt for good, he set his Retenu house in order. He did not take his wife, children or property with him, for everything had to be left behind. So he turned over his possessions to his children. His oldest son assumed the command of Sinuhe's tribe, and took possession of Sinuhe's retainers, cattle and orchards. This is the standard arrangment for a man who enters what Assyriologists call an "*erêbu* marriage" whereby he joins the bride and lives with her in her father's domain. Should he decide to return to his native land, he leaves alone, without family and property.

It might at first appear strange that the text records not a word of sadness or tender good-byes on leaving wife and children forever. To be sure, family and inheritance are important and the narrative records that Sinuhe put his Retenu house in order before departing for the Nile. However, our story is Egyptian, and in the land of the Pharaohs there was something more important than one's love for wife, children and possessions; namely, proper burial in Egypt. When the Pharaoh recalled Sinuhe, he did not promise him the pleasures of a harem and other amenities of this world. Instead he admonished him to think of the day of burial with its ointments and wrappings, the funeral procession, a mummy case of gold with a head of lapis lazuli. The inside of the lid will depict the sky, over him for eternity. Musicians will precede the ox-drawn hearse. Dancers will perform at the entrance of his tomb. The tomb pillars are of white stone near the tombs of royal princes.

Far more precious to an Egyptian than "life, liberty and the pursuit of happiness" in this vale of tears, is a stone pyramid, well located, well constructed and well carved with the right scenes and hieroglyphic texts; endowed with mortuary priests; furnished with Sinuhe's statue overlaid with gold and sporting a skirt of electrum.

The marriage of Sinuhe was a great triumph in this world. But the climactic happy ending was the first-class funeral sponsored by the Pharaoh. "There is no commoner for whom the like has been done. I was in the favor of the king until the day of landing came."

No man should be called blessed until his life is over. We, on earth, are like mariners sailing the hazardous sea. We can be considered fortunate only when the voyage has ended successfully. It is lucky to live favorably until the day of landing. But it is only after the landing that reality began for an Egyptian.[14]

---

9 C. J. Gadd, "Tablets from Kirkuk," *Revue d'Assyriologie* 23 (1926): 49–161. The text translated below is number 51, on pp. 126–27.

10 In Ceylon there is an institution called "*beena* marriage" whereby the groom lives in the house of the bride's father. Not infrequently the groom is the bride's own brother. James G. Frazer (*The Golden Bough* [3rd ed.; New York: Macmillan, 1935]: part IV, vol. 2, pp. 215–16) maintains that brother–sister marriages in Egypt and Ceylon aimed essentially at keeping the property within the family.

11 For one Homeric and a number of biblical cases, see Cyrus H. Gordon, "*Erêbu* Marriage," to appear in the E. R. Lachman *Festschrift*. Somewhat different is the Arabic *ṣadîqa* "marriage." The man visits his *ṣadîqa* "girl friend." Whether we should call such arrangements "marriage" is questionable. They seem to be something like what our younger generation calls "a meaningful relationship" (which is neither holy wedlock nor outright promiscuity). Marriage, being a contractual relationship, can be terminated only by a counter-contract (a bill of divorcement). A "meaningful relationship" is not contractual and can therefore be ended simply by "splitting up." For a discussion of marriage, cf. R. de Vaux, *Les Institutions de l'Ancient Testament* (Paris: Cerf, 1958): 1. 45–65 (*ṣadîqa* is covered briefly on p. 52).

12 I.e., without the consent of her family. Such consent could change the marriage into a more usual arrangement whereby she and the children would live in her husband's domain (Genesis 31:27).

13 Note Exodus 21:8–9. The Book of Proverbs repeatedly refers to foreign women pejoratively (2:12–21; 5:3–5; 7:5–23; etc.).

14 For the spread of such Egyptian concepts, see Meir Lubetski, "The Early Bronze Age Origin of Greek and Hebrew *Limen* 'Harbor,' " *Jewish Quarterly Review* 69 (1978): 158–80.

THE BIRTH OF KINGS*

WILLIAM W. HALLO

"Love is strong as death." This defiant challenge from the Song of Songs, which Marvin Pope made the motto and *Leitmotif* of his monumental commentary, was also the starting-point of Franz Rosenzweig's essay on "Revelation, or the Ever-Renewed Birth of the Soul," the center-piece of his programmatic synthesis of religious philosophy, with its "grammatical analysis of the Song of Songs" according to which "the analogue of love permeates as analogue all of revelation."[1] For an Assyriologist who has spent many profitable hours studying both authors, it would therefore be intriguing and rewarding to trace the theme of love and death in the cuneiform sources. But this would have to be done in terms of kings (or gods), the preferred focus of cuneiform literature.

The reason for these preferences is not far to seek. Palaces and temples were the chief patrons of both arts and letters in Sumer and Akkad—and then as now, he who pays the piper calls the tune. As a result we unfortunately know less than we would like about the common man: his concerns, his aspirations, his reactions to life. These matters figure in literature only or chiefly in proverbs and other types of so-called wisdom texts, numerically a relatively small literary genre. And in the plastic and other representational arts, Mesopotamia preserves little to rival the revealing vignettes of the lot of the average man or woman provided in Egypt by funerary deposits and tomb paintings. By contrast we know almost too much about the king—too much at any rate to convey in the span of a brief article. I will not attempt to do so here, nor even to summarize the lifetime of a typical Mesopotamian king by constructing a kind of biographical collage derived from all the abundant documentation of the third and second millennia B.C. Such a composite portrait would properly begin with a study of the mystique surrounding the royal birth, and grappling with this question has convinced me that it deserves, all by itself, all the time at my disposal. It has the advantage of highlighting the differences between royalty and commoners and whatever (if anything) lies in between. Then too, it involves also the royal parents, so that it covers much of the royal lifetime anyway. And finally, it touches on a basic problem of any political system, namely the mechanics of transferring power from one administration to the next. Even in our day, the presidential succession continues to be the subject of constitutional amendments—how much more acute the problem is in authoritarian governments around the world. This is obvious from a look at the headlines: China yesterday, Yugoslavia today, Russia tomorrow—all confront problems of succession, and so did early Mesopotamian monarchy. I will therefore reject Shakespeare's invitation "For God's sake let us sit upon the ground and tell sad stories of the death of kings"[2] and focus instead on the generally happier tales of their birth and accession.

The birth of the royal heir, "la naissance du dauphin" as it is put in a recent French treatment,[3] has an elemental importantce in the whole ideology of kingship whenever and wherever that office is hereditary. It was not always so. At the dawn of Mesopotamian history lies what archaeologists call the Jemdet Nasr period—one of the most fruitful and inventive cultural phases of all. I equate it with what native historiographic traditions call the antediluvian period, that legendary time when eight shadowy kings ruled five ancient cities until all were swept away by the Great Flood.[4] In the various Babylonian versions of this tale, the kings in question were not connected to each other as father and son; they were not even necessarily consecutive. That view of the matter was injected into the antediluvian traditions, perhaps under Amorite influence, in their biblical recasting in Genesis 4 (Adam to Naama) and Genesis 5 (Enosh to Noah).

---

* The substance of these remarks was delivered to the symposium on Kingship in the Ancient Near East, Brooklyn Museum, October 24, 1976, organized by Madeline I. Noveck and chaired by Edith Porada. The full version, including a transcript of the ensuing discussion, will appear in the forthcoming proceedings of the Symposium. The footnotes incorporate references to the illustrations included as slides in the original presentation.

1 Franz Rosenzweig, *The Star of Redemption* (William W. Hallo, trans.; Boston, Beacon Press, 1972): Part Two, Book Two, esp. pp. 156, 199, 201-204.

2 *Richard II*, Act III, Scene 2, line 155.

3 Herbert Sauren *apud* Paul Garelli, ed., *Le Palais et la Royauté* (= Rencontre Assyriologique Internationale 19 [1971], 1974): 457-71. This volume is an excellent survey of the current state of studies on Mesopotamian kingship. (Hereinafter cited as RAI 19.)

4 For a convenient if schematic chart of the literary evidence, see W. W. Hallo and W. K. Simpson, *The Ancient Near East: a History* (New York: Harcourt Brace Jovanovitch, 1971): 32 (fig. 6). (Hereinafter cited as ANEH.)

After the flood mankind was vouchsafed a second chance. Once more, according to native Mesopotamian historiography, "kingship was lowered from heaven" and this time it was entrusted to a single city, Kish. We may therefore call the period after the first dynasty of Kish, and I equate it, in archaeological terms, with the First Early Dynastic Period (ca. 2900-2700).[5] A dozen names of kings are recorded in one form of the native traditions but they are of no importance—mere names without associations (other than those—e.g., animals or totems—conjured up by the meanings of the names themselves) and without family connections to each other. But another tradition is more significant: it begins kingship with a certain Etana of Kish, and weaves a long legend around his lengthy efforts to secure an heir. This legend is known in fragments of neo-Assyrian, Middle Assyrian and Old Akkadian date. Thus it represents one of the most persistent, not to say perennial concerns of Mesopotamian arts and letters: how to insure male issue.[6]

Recent discoveries of new fragments have made a somewhat better understanding of the epic or legend of Etana possible. As interpreted by an Assyriologist who is also a historian of medicine, the new fragments are said to show that Etana married a certain Mu-dam, whose very name is pregnant with meaning—to wit: she is the one who gives birth (mud-àm)![7] But her first pregnancy ended badly, almost disastrously.[8] Fortunately, the queen had a dream which revealed the means needed to overcome her obstetrical problems: Etana had to get her the plant of life. Unfortunately that was easier said than done and the next three chapters (or tablets) concern Etana's complicated and adventurous quest for this rare pharmaceutical, including one or more flights to heaven on the wings of an eagle, the theme most often illustrated in the Old Akkadian "Etana seals."[9] But despite at least one crash landing, his efforts were crowned with success, or so we may surmise. For one thing the Sumerian King List preserves the name of Balih, Etana's son and successor, together with the royal descendants of *his* successor. For another the newly identified fragments of the legend describe just how a shoot from the plant of life was used, like a poultice, to relax the uterus at the first signs of labor-pains; and a painless delivery followed.[10]

The legend I have just excerpted has many other interesting features and can be understood on many levels. A recent interpretation, for instance, regards it as an elaborate astral allegory.[11] The portions I have quoted might lead one to consider the tale as a paradigm for obstetrical complications—indeed, it may owe its long survival and apparent popularity to the fact (demonstratable in other myths and epics, though not here) that its recitation was prescribed as a prophylactic measure against the illness or other evil narrated in it. And the device of attaching the paradigm to the figure of a king would be of a piece with the vast majority of Sumerian and Akkadian belles-lettres generally.

That still entitles us to ask why this particular legend was attached to this particular king, the first king of all (after the Flood) according to its own version of history. My answer would be that the ancient author was deliberately trying to explain the origin of royal succession, and in the process to give it the highest possible antiquity and therefore also authority. Even heaven was not too far to go when it came to facilitating the birth of the royal heir, and this was established by the very first king. Nor was it possible to substitute a concubine for the proper queen (although admittedly the passage in question is very fragmentary). Much the same theme inspired the Ugaritic epic of Keret, sometimes thought to be the Kirta who was regarded as the founder or eponymous ancestor of the royal house of Mitanni. Depending on how the text is interpreted, Keret's difficulties began when a succession of disasters wiped out either all his children[12] or all his intended brides.[13] Here the main quest is for a new wife of royal blood, but the birth of the heir is again the goal of the exercise.[14]

But for all assurances of the legend, neither hereditary kingship nor Mesopotamian unity was securely established by Etana's alleged precedent. For as we move into the Second Early Dynastic Period (ca. 2700-2500 B.C.), we see the rule of the country divided between several competing city-states, and the succession passing from

5 ANEH 41 (fig. 7).

6 *Ibid.* 40, note 29, for literary allusions to Etana, to which add M. E. Cohen, *ZA* 65 (1977): 3, note 6 (*ad* 14, line 78); G. Komoróczy, *Acta Antiqua* 23 (1975): 46f. and notes 27-34.

7 J. V. Kinnier Wilson, "Some Contributions to the Legend of Etana," *Iraq* 31 (1969): 8-17; *idem*, "Further Contributions to the Legend of Etana," *JNES* 33 (1974): 240. This reading and interpretation is, however, far from certain in any of the three fragmentary passages involved (Sm 157+, first and last lines; K9610, last line), nor is the attribution of either of the fragments to Etana conclusively proven, according to W. G. Lambert, *JNES* 39 (1980): 74, n. 1.

8 Kinnier Wilson's restorations and translations of the fragmentary passage (*JNES* 33:239) are, however, quite problematical and it is not even clear that the two fragments on which they are based belong either to each other or to Etana; cf. Lambert, *ibid.*

9 For one of many examples, see André Parrot, *Sumer: the Dawn of Art* (New York: Golden Press, 1961): 188 (fig. 226).

10 *Iraq* 31 (1969): 15f.

11 Sauren (N 3).

12 So most persuasively, not to say ingeniously, Joshua Finkel, "A Mathematical Conundrum in the Ugaritic Keret Poem," *HUCA* 26 (1955): 109-49.

13 So most recently B. Margalit, "The Ill-fated Wives of King Krt (*CTA* 14:14-21a)" *UF* 8 (1976): 137-45.

14 Herbert Sauren and Guy Kestemont, "Keret, roi de Hubur" *UF* 3 (1971): 181-221; M. C. Astour, "A North Mesopotamian Locale for the Keret Epic?" *UF* 5 (1973): 29-39.

father to son only intermittently.[15] In fact, this is the heroic age of Mesopotamia's early history, enshrined forever in the Sumerian epics about Gilgamesh[16] and the other lords of Uruk in the south and their antagonists at Kish in the north and in Aratta far to the east. The charismatic leader, chosen for his prowess in battle or his skill in diplomacy, characterized this age, and immortality (if we credit "Gilgamesh and the land of the living" as well as the later Akkadian epic of Gilgamesh) was sought not through progeny but by heroic and memorable exploits leading to lasting fame (*zikir šumi*). Election to kingship was by vote of an assembly of arms-bearing citizens, and royal birth was evidently neither necessary nor sufficient to secure that election.

This pattern changed by the middle of the 3rd millennium, in what archaeology likes to describe as the 3rd (and last) of the Early Dynastic periods (ca. 2500-2300).[17] Actually it is only now that we are really entitled to speak of true dynasties—at least if we mean by that term a succession of kings who claimed the right to rule by virtue of birth (or, occasionally, of marriage) into a given family. This was achieved by a new alliance of royal and ecclesiastical interests: the king endowing ever more lavish temples and their growing complements of priests and tenants, and in return having his claims to the reins of government legitimized by the priesthood. Already in the heroic age, some rulers had claimed divine descent: Meskiaggashir and Enmerkar of Uruk from Utu according to the Sumerian King List and the epics respectively, Mesilim of Kish from the mother-goddess Ninhursaga according to his own inscription. Beginning with the great Eannatum of Lagash, every ruler now explicitly proclaimed his divine descent. In the famous Stele of Vultures,[18] Eannatum even calls himself "the seed-implanted-in-the-womb of Ningirsu" or, again, says that "Ningirsu implanted the seed of Eannatum in the womb and [Ninhursage or Baʾu] bore him."[19] His two immediate successors were regarded as sons of Lugal-uru(b) and, presumably, of Inanna, his divine spouse.[20] The last Lagash rulers in this period (Lugalanda and Urukagina) were respectively sons of the goddesses Nanshe and Baʾu, while their contemporary and conqueror, Lugalzagesi of Umma, had Nisaba for a divine mother.

The new ideology did not content itself with the impregnation and gestation by a divine father and mother respectively. Throughout the pre-natal and post-natal period, the gods attended the pre-ordained successor. This is stated most explicitly in the royal epithets. To illustrate, we may revert to the stele of Eannatum, which describes him as "king of Lagash, endowed with strength by the god Enlil, nourished with life-giving milk by the goddess Ninhursaga, named with a good name (throne-name?)[21] by the goddess Inanna, endowed with understanding by the god Enki, heart's choice of the goddess Nanshe," and so on and so forth.

Of course, not all Mesopotamian kings were "born to the purple." New dynasties were founded, and old ones toppled, when usurpers seized the throne. In such cases, legitimation came of necessity after the fact, not before—in part, for example, by the very name assumed on accession, which defied all challenges, as in the instance of the most celebrated usurper of all, Sargon of Akkad,[22] whose Akkadian name has been interpreted to mean "the king is legitimate." As if to make up for his lack of divine parentage and innate endowments, posterity surrounded Sargon's birth with an extraordinary profusion of legends, the most famous of which is no doubt that according to which his mother was a high-priestess (and thus either not free to bear children or possibly specializing in the procreation of royalty!)[23] who therefore exposed him in a basket of rushes in the Euphrates where, like Moses, he was rescued and raised by a foster-parent. This tale recurs in one form or another all over the world; the general tendency is to regard the Moses tale as modelled on the Sargon legend, or both as derived from a common original. A third possibility is too often overlooked—namely that the tale of Sargon is modelled on that of Moses! For its earliest textual witnesses date from the seventh century, and there are no internal indices requiring us to suppose a date of composition appreciably closer to the events of the late 24th century which it describes.

The considerable family of Sargon managed to extend its sway over all the high political and priestly offices of Mesopotamia, a land which thus experienced its first

15 ANEH 47 (fig. 8).

16 See Parrot, *Sumer* (N 9): 186f. (figs. 223-225), for what are generally taken to be Old Akkadian representations of Gilgamesh.

17 ANEH 52f. (fig. 9).

18 Parrot, *Sumer* (N 9): 135 (fig. 164).

19 Åke W. Sjöberg, "Die göttliche Abstammung der sumerisch-babylonischen Herrscher," *Orientalia Suecana* 21 (1973): 87-89; T. Jacobsen, *Kramer Anniversary Volume* (= AOAT 25, 1976; hereinafter abbreviated as *Kramer AV*): 251 and note 13, now favors Baʾu.

20 See below, note 66.

21 Literally "sweet name," as in Hittite myths of Hurrian derivation; see H. A. Hoffner, *JNES* 27 (1968): 201f. Is a loan-translation involved? Cf. Hittite "sweet sleep" (*ibid.*, notes 36 and 39) with Sumerian *ù-du*$_{10}$*-ku-ku*. I hinted at the sense "throne-name" in my *Early Mesopotamian Royal Titles* (= AOS 43, 1957): 133f. Sjöberg, however, sees *mu-nam-en-na* as the throne-name; "Abstammung" (N 19): 112.

22 Parrot, *Sumer* (N 9): 171 (fig. 206). But the head may equally well picture his grandson Naram-Sin.

23 On a possible son of Enheduanna and on the question whether the en-priestess was allowed to have children (inside or outside the sacred marriage), see the discussion by J. Renger, *ZA* 58 (1967): 131 and H. Hirsch, *AfO* 20 (1963): 9 and note 79.

truly imperial unification.[24] But Sargon's two oldest sons and first successors were (in my reconstruction) born before this unification had been achieved, and they too could not claim divine parentage. Indeed, their birth may have been complicated by a statistical rarity. Although it is only, so far, a learned guess, they may in fact have been twins. This is indicated on the one hand by the tradition that the succession passed first to the younger of the two, and on the other by the very name of the elder brother, Man-ishtushu,[25] which means "who (is) with him?" and may be an abbreviation (to judge by parallel Sumerian names) of either "who compares with him?" or "who comes out with him?"[26]

It was only with the son of this Manishtushu that the "dynastic ideology" could be fully applied to the Sargonic kings. Naram-Sin the great, in my opinion really the greatest member of the dynasty, actually claimed divine status for himself (the first Mesopotamian king to do so),[27] as did his son Shar-kali-sharri after him. The latter in addition claimed divine parentage again after the manner of the Early Dynastic rulers.[28]

But the empire forged by the great Sargonic kings collapsed in anarchy after the death of Sharkalisharri, and the country reverted to its characteristic pattern of small to medium-sized city-states.[29] Culturally, the pendulum swung back to the south, where Lagash enjoyed a renaissance under the house of Ur-Baʾu. But a curious phenomenon characterized the succession here. Ur-Baʾu was blessed with a large number of daughters, and presumably no sons. So it appears that the throne passed successively to no less than three of his sons-in-law.[30] Of these the most famous was certainly Gudea,[31] whose own humble origins are only lightly concealed behind his telling autobiographical note: "I have no mother: you (oh goddess Gatumdug) are my mother; I have no father: you (oh Gatumdug) are my father."[32]

With the accession of Gudea begins what I like to designate as the classical phase of Mesopotamian civilization, a half millennium (ca. 2100-1600), roughly coterminous with the Middle Bronze Age in the rest of Western Asia, when the cultural traditions crystallized into their most typical form. I will therefore spare you a detailed history of the separate stages in the evolution of the ideology of royal birth and present instead an overview of the legacy which this entire age bequeathed to posterity. This is the easier because the period as a whole is amply documented and, in particular, a new literary vehicle, the royal hymn (and to a lesser extent the royal correspondence) emerged now to give formal expression to the details of the royal ideology. Combined with the older but intimately related genres of royal date formulas and royal inscriptions, the testimony of the hymns allows us to generalize with some assurance.

Perhaps the most significant new development is a "solution" of the mechanics of divine birth. It may have occurred to you to wonder how the concept of divine parentage was reconciled with a basic reluctance to regard the royal offspring himself as a deity—a reluctance the more conspicuous by contrast with Old Kingdom Egypt.[33] Though two of the Sargonic kings and (after Ur-Nammu) all those of Ur and Isin in the classical phase claimed divinity of sorts, only one king (Shu-Sin of Ur) actually permitted himself to be worshipped like a "real" god in temples dedicated to his worship in his own lifetime,[34] a practice which was apparently particularly abhorrent to the many Amorite dynasties which divided the rule of Mesopotamia among themselves about 1900 B.C., a century after the fall of Ur. I would like to propose here a new solution to the paradox: that the divine parentage of the future king was achieved or symbolized in the cultic rite of the so-called sacred marriage or, in other words, that the (or at least an) object of that rite was to produce a royal heir and to establish his divine descent.

In all the recent spate of discussions on the sacred marriage, this point of view has barely been considered.[35]

24 ANEH 58 (fig. 10).

25 Parrot, *Sumer* (N 9): 178 (figs. 214 f.).

26 ANEH 59; previously T. Jacobsen, *AS* 11 (1939): 112n. 249. The nearest Sumerian equivalent is *a-ba-an-da-è or a-ba-i(in)-da-(an)-è*, for which cf., e.g., MSL 13:87:40 and NRVN I 14, and which C. Wilcke *apud* D. O. Edzard, *BiOr* 28 (1971): 165 n. 8, regards as a possible twin-name.

27 Parrot, *Sumer* (N 9): 175-77 (figs. 211-13).

28 Sjöberg, "Abstammung" (N 19): 91f. and note 1.

29 ANEH 66 (fig. 12).

30 Renger, "The Daughters of Urbaba: Some Thoughts on the Succession to the Throne During the 2. Dynasty of Lagash," *Kramer AV* (1976): 367-69.

31 Parrot, *Sumer* (N 9): 204-17 (figs. 251-66).

32 Cylinder A iii 6f. and the related passage in "The rulers of Lagaš," for which see E. Sollberger, *JCS* 21 (1967) [publ. 1969]): 286 and note 80. At the same time the physical description in the next line of the Cylinder implies divine birth; cf. Jacobsen, *Kramer AV* (1976): 251, note 15; A. Falkenstein, *Die Inscriften Gudeas von Lagaš* (AnOr 30, 1966): 2f.

33 Cf. Henri Frankfort, *Kingship and the Gods* (Chicago: Chicago Univ. Press, 1948): 301, who grapples with the Eannatum pasages (above, note 19) in this connection.

34 ANEH 84 and Hallo, "The Royal Inscriptions of Ur: a Typology," *HUCA* 33 (1962): 18. For other possible indications of "emperor-worship" in Ur III times, see Claus Wilcke, RAI 19 (1974): 179f. with notes 30-58 (pp. 188-92).

35 J. van Dijk, *BiOr* 11 (1954): 84, note 9, at least raised the question: "It is not at all certain that the sacred marriage had any relation to procreation" (translation mine). Cf. also Renger's reference to "children of an en-priestess who (at least in part) sprang from the union in the sacred marriage," *ZA* 58 (1967): 131 (translation mine). Sjöberg ponders whether the royal offspring could have been engendered in the sacred marriage, and Inanna thus regarded as divine mother as specified (only) in the case of Anam of Uruk; see *Or* 35 (1966):289f.

Let me therefore give you first a brief description of the institution as now known. It was a ceremony in the temple precincts in which a king and what is generally taken to be a priestess[36] consummated a sexual union to the accompaniment of offerings and hymns or prayers by the clergy. The prayers make it abundantly clear that the union was, at least on one level, a symbolic one. The king symbolized a god and his partner a goddess. Most often the divine couple were perceived as Dumuzi and Inanna respectively, but other pairs were possible depending on local circumstances.[37] The prayers also suggest a variety of symbolic meanings for the act: as the basis for the royal partner's own claim to divinity,[38] as a guarantee of fertility for the country as a whole,[39] as a ritual enactment of an astral myth, as proof (or refutation) of the belief in a seasonal resurrection of Dumuzi, as a possible part of the annual new year's ritual[40] or, alternatively, as a unique element in the coronation ritual once at, or near, the beginning of each reign.[41]

Apart from the obvious lack of clarity in the sources themselves reflected in these partly divergent interpretations as to the significance of the sacred marriage, it must be emphasized that they all confine themselves to its symbolic level. They ignore the real act and its reality level. If we stop to consider what actually transpired, it was, after all, the consummation of a sexual union. This is explicitly stated in the texts, and may be deduced also from innumerable artistic representations, if not in quite the measure that earlier interpretations suggested.[42] I would like therefore to propose that on the real, as against the symbolic level, the sacred marriage in the classical phase served to engender the crown prince, thus bridging the gap between the cosmic and the earthly which had been left open by the earlier ideology. For the king, this is expressed tellingly by substituting for his name the name of Dumuzi (or another god) in certain sacred marriage texts;[43] for the priestess—if the feminine partner *was* a priestess—it is explicit in her very title (or one of them: nin-dingir) which means "the lady who is a deity" (*not* the lady of the god),[44] a point underlined by the statue of a high priestess of the moon-god at Ur which has attachments for the horned cap symbolizing divinity—with this attachment (now lost), the statue represents the moon-god's heavenly consort (Ningal), without it the priestess who dedicated the inscription to her.[45] And just as mortal king and human priestess are god and goddess in the rite, so the product of their union emerges as divinely born without forfeiting his essential humanity. A solution has been found for uniting a transcendent conception of divinity with an immanent conception of kingship, and the solution is congenial to the Mesopotamian world-view.

But if this solution is so genial, it may be asked why it has not been proposed before. One reason may be the ambivalent role of Inanna, whose multifarious roles conspicuously minimize the maternal one,[46] another the relative silence of the sources. They seem to dwell in loving detail on the physical aspects of the sacred marriage on the one hand, and on the divine birth of the

36 Cf., e.g., S. N. Kramer, RAI 17 (1970): 140: "And who, finally, played the role of the goddess throughout the ceremony? It must have been some specially selected votary of the goddess, but this is never stated . . . ."

37 A novel illustration of such local variations comes from Emar, where the sacred marriage was consummated in an annual (?) seven-day ritual between the high priestess (*entu*) and the storm-god (Baal); see for now D. Arnaud, *Annuaire de l'École Pratique des Hautes Études* (Ve section) 84 (1975-6): 223f.

38 So especially Frankfort, *Kingship* (N 33): 295-99.

39 Here as elsewhere (see below, note 41), one interpretation is not necessarily mutually exclusive with another. According to Kramer, the very purpose of Ninsun's giving birth to Shulgi was to assure the fertility of the country; see RAI 19 (1974): 165.

40 See especially van Dijk, "La fête du nouvel an dans un texte de Šulgi," *BiOr* 11 (1954): 83-88; W. H. Ph. Römer, *Sumerische "Königshymnen" der Isin-Zeit* (= DMOA 13, 1965): cf. IV.

41 Renger, *RLA* 4 (1975): 257. In fact, the coronation may have been scheduled to coincide with the New Year's ritual, but previous commentators seem to have overlooked this possibility.

42 Frankfort, *Sculpture of the Third Millennium B.C. from Tell Asmar and Khafajah* (= Oriental Institute Publications 44, 1939): pl. 112, fig. 199. Line drawing by Johannes Boese, *Altmesopotamische Weihplatten* (= Untersuchungen zur Assyriologie . . . [ZA Suppl.] 6, 1971): pl. IV, fig. 1 (AS 4). This, together with some half dozen seals, is the only representation of an erotic scene considered a remotely possible candidate for a sacred marriage depiction by J. S. Cooper, "Heilige Hochzeit. B. Archäologisch," *RLA* 4 (1975): 259-69, esp. p. 266.

43 Hallo, *BiOr* 23 (1966): 244f.

44 Falkenstein, *Inschriften Gudeas* (N32): 2, note 8; cf. Renger, *ZA* 58 (1967): 134f., 144.

45 L. Legrain, *Museum Journal* 18 (1927): 223-29. Hallo, "Women of Sumer," *apud* D. Schmandt-Besserat, ed., *The Legacy of Sumer* (Bibliotheca Mesopotamica 4, 1976): 32f. and fig. 16.

46 F. R. Kraus, *WZKM* 52 (1953): 53f. She is invoked as mother only by two or three minor deities, notably Lulal (Kramer, *JCS* 18 [1964]: 38, note 13; but elsewhere Lulal seems to be regarded as son of Ninsun: Sjöberg, *Or. Suec.* 21 [1972]: 100 and note 1), Šara (Šu-Sin 9; otherwise only in Anzu I iii 77, for which see Hallo and Moran, *JCS* 31 [1979]: 84f.), and Sutitu (BRM 4:25:44; but in An-Anum IV 135, Sutitu is herself a manifestation of Inanna), and only by one king (above, note 35). In the "Descent of Inanna," Shara and Lulal are both spared by Inanna but not identified as her sons; Kramer, *JCS* 5 (1951): 13:312-30. Curiously, the logogram for mother-goddess (protective goddess) is AMA.^{d}INANNA, but here ^{d}INANNA has its generic sense of "(any) goddess"; cf. *CAD* s.vv. *amalītu, ištarītu*; J. Krecher, *HSAO* (1967): 89, note 2. The frequent reference to Inanna as kiskil (*ardatu*) refers to her youthfulness and (relative) childlessness, not to her virginity.

royal heir on the other, without ever linking the two events explicitly. It would not be difficult to account for the silence: marriage and birth were sacraments of the royal lifetime which were celebrated in an elaborate liturgy, but the gestation period which intervened was not. It therefore was not the cultic stimulus for commissioning a textual genre. Moreover, the silence of the texts is more apparent than real. Besides the frequent references in hymns and elsewhere to the paternity of Mesopotamian kings in the royal epithet "seed of kingship" or "seed of the gods,"[47] at least one of these kings, Ur-Nammu of Ur,[48] seems to refer to his maternal descent with the epithet "seed of the high-priestess" or "high-priesthood."[49] And, indeed, the very solution proposed here had been adumbrated by Thorkild Jacobsen.[50] Writing on early Mesopotamian political development in 1957, he analyzed the liturgical abab-hymn[51] now known as Shulgi Hymn G. Jacobsen concluded "one is led to interpret (it) as meaning that Shulgir was engendered on an *entu* priestess of Nanna in Nippur, presumably during the celebration of the 'sacred marriage' between Nanna and the *entu*, in which Ur-Nammuk as king embodied the divine bridegroom, Nanna."[52] But except for a single and somewhat ambiguous remark in my own history of the Ancient Near East,[53] and a generally negative critique by Sjöberg,[54] this suggestive insight has not been followed up, even by Jacobsen himself. In his "Religious Drama in Ancient Mesopotamia"[55] and even more fully in his recently published history of Mesopotamian religion,[56] Jacobsen returned to the problem of the sacred marriage with never a hint of the engendering of the crown-prince. S. N. Kramer came up with a different analysis of the Shulgi hymn,[57] which he entitled "Šulgi, Provider of the Ekur: His Divine Birth and Investiture." He has also contributed an entire monograph on the sacred marriage rite[58] as well as numerous editions of new sacred marriage texts;[59] nowhere does he mention any human birth resulting from it. Wilcke interprets the same Shulgi-hymn to mean that immediately upon his birth in the Ekur, the temple of Enlil at Nippur, Shulgi was recognized as crown-prince by Enlil in the lifetime of his father Ur-Nammu, but without suggesting a sacred marriage in this connection.[60] Renger, who summed up the textual evidence on the institution for the authoritative *Reallexikon der Assyriologie* in 1975, mentions Jacobsen's suggestion in passing only to reject it.[61] For good measure he attributes a similar opinion to Adam Falkenstein,[62] but it is not true that Gudea is said by the latter to have sprung from a union of priestess and male partner "anlässlich einer H[eiligen] H[ochzeit]." On the contrary, Falkenstein twice emphasizes that the nature of the cultic setting to which Gudea alludes is unknown![63]

The new conception of divine birth as here proposed involves of necessity also a clarification of the royal father's role. He had now for the first time to be regarded as the husband of the goddess, and the royal titulary duly reflects this. Beginning with Amar-Sin of Ur, and consistently with nearly all the kings of Isin, he is styled "the (beloved) spouse of Inanna."[64] The attempt to trace

47 W. G. Lambert, "The Seed of Kingship," RAI 19 (1974): 427-40.

48 Parrot, *Sumer* (N 9): 228, fig. 281.

49 Claus Wilcke, RAI 19 (1974): 180 and 194, note 72. Lambert, however, translates one of the two passages involved "seed of lordship" ("Seed" [N 47]: 428). (Note that en can mean either lord or priest[ess].)

50 Previously, Adam Falkenstein spoke obliquely of the "Gotteskindschaft des Königs, die aus der Stellvertretung eines Gottes . . . durch den König bei der Götterhochzeit erwachsen ist" in *BiOr* 7 (1950): 58.

51 Published by Gadd as CT 36:26f.

52 Thorkild Jacobsen, *ZA* 52 (1957): 126f., note 80; reprinted in his *Towards the Image of Tammuz* (= Harvard Semitic Series 21, 1970): 387f., note 80.

53 ANEH, 49: "The crown prince, born of the sacred marriage between the king and the priestess of a given god, was considered the son of that god and subsequently invoked him as his personal patron." Whether or not this state of affairs can be projected back into the Early Dynastic III period as proposed there, it is here maintained that, by the classical phase, the crown-prince became, rather, the son of the god represented by the king and the goddess represented by the priestess.

54 *Or* 35 (1966): 287-90.

55 *Apud* Hans Goedicke and J. J. Roberts, eds., *Unity and Diversity* (= The Johns Hopkins Near Eastern Studies 7, 1975): 65-97.

56 *The Treasurers of Darkness* (New Haven: Yale Univ. Press, 1976): esp. 32-37. At the same time Jacobsen returned to the theme of the "birth of the hero" (i.e., king) without explicitly referring to the sacred marriage; see *Kramer AV* (N 19); previously: *JNES* 2 (1943): 119-21.

57 S. N. Kramer, "CT *XXXVI*. Corrigenda and Addenda," *Iraq* 36 (1974): 93-95; *idem*, RAI 19 (1974): 165f.

58 Kramer, *The Sacred Marriage Rite* (Indiana University Press, 1969). Cf. *idem*, "The Dumuzi-Inanna Sacred Marriage-Rite: Origin, Development, Character," RAI 17 (1970): 135-41.

59 Kramer, "Cuneiform Studies and the History of Literature: the Sumerian Sacred Marriage Texts," *Proceedings of the American Philosophical Society* 107 (1963): 485-527; *idem apud* J. B. Pritchard, *Ancient Near Eastern Texts* (3rd ed.; Princeton: Princeton Univ. Press, 1968): 637-45.

60 Wilcke, RAI 19 (1974): 181 and 195, note 76.

61 Renger, "Heilige Hochzeit. A. Philologisch," RLA 4 (1975): 258.

62 *Ibid.*; cf. *idem*, "Daughters" (N 30): note 16.

63 Falkenstein, *Inschriften Gudeas* (N 32).

64 Hallo, *Royal Titles* (N 21): 140f.; cf. *idem*, *JNES* 31 (1972): 88.

this usage back to Eannatum of Lagash[65] was already rejected by me in 1957[66] and the alleged reference to it under Naram-Sin of Akkad[67] is from a late copy where its authenticity must be at least questioned.

Somewhat more ambiguous is the role of the female partner in the new conception of the sacred marriage. Was she exempt from the interdiction of childbirth such as we posited in the case of Sargon's mother? Could she have been the high-priestess of the moon-god as Jacobsen suggested, given the fact that this office was, during the classical phase, regularly filled by the daughter of the king himself? Or was she some other member of the royal family, as in the case of many other highly placed priestesses? Was she, or did she become, the wife of the king?[68] Or was she, at least sometimes, the sister of the king, as has been suggested in the case of the last king of Ur, Ibbi-Sin?[69] If the woman did not prove to yield a male heir, was she allowed to try again, or not? In other words, was the sacred marriage performed only one time or as many times as proved necessary? Was it performed in only one place, or were a number of cities privileged to have their temples conduct the ceremony—as seems indicated by the fact that the new king later regarded different deities as his parents in different cities of his kingdom. Did a consistent ideology emerge which defined a dynasty as a succession of kings sharing the same divine parents, and identified a change of dynasty as a change of divine parents?[70] What about sons born to the king before his accession, i.e., presumably outside the framework of the sacred marriage? Were they excluded from the succession? These and other intricacies involved in the intertwining of heavenly and dynastic relationships remain to be resolved by further study of the royal hymns and other relevant sources.

Such studies will also yield significant new data on the further career of the crown-prince after his birth—the solicitude of his mother or wet-nurse as expressed in royal lullabies,[71] the education of the prince in such diverse fields as scribal skills, music, athletics, hunting and warfare,[72] his service in the administration as viceroy of the ancestral domains,[73] his own (earthly) marriage, his coronation,[74] his actual reign,[75] his death,[76] and his afterlife in the cult[77] and memory[78] of the people.

Here there is time only for a short look at what became of the concepts I have already discussed after the classical phase. The phase I have described included (in one sense indeed climaxed in) the reign of Hammurapi of Babylon.[79] For after him a period of decline set in terminating with the sack of Babylon about 1600 and the ushering in of the Babylonian Dark Ages or Middle Ages. One often characterizes the period beginning with Hammurapi as marked by a gradual break-down of the older religious values, more specifically as a time of secularization.[80] But that is not entirely fair. More to the point may be again Jacobsen's characterization of the late second millennium in terms of the rise of a personal religion, as a period, that is, in which the individual turned directly toward his own personal deity rather than, through the mediation of priests and kings, to the

65 Renger, "Heilige Hochzeit" (N 61): 258f.; Wilcke, RLA 5 (1976): 80f., even wants to extend the usage back to Mesannepada.

66 Hallo, *Royal Titles* (N 64); similarly Sjöberg, *Abstammung* (N 19): 90, and Sollberger and Kupper, *Inscriptions Royales Sumériennes et Akkadiennes* (= Littératures Anciennes du Proche-Orient 3, 1971): 55.

67 Renger, "Heilige Hochzeit" (N 65), based on F. Thureau-Dangin, *RA* 9 (1912): 34f. Cf. also Wilcke (N 65): 80f.

68 Cf. notes 84-91 to the Discussion (above, note *).

69 Jacobsen, "The Reign of Ibbi-Suen," *JCS* 7 (1953): 37 n. 6; cf. N. Schneider, "Die 'Königskinder' des Herrscherhauses von Ur III," *Or* 12 (1943): 190, who suggests rather that Ibbi-Suen's queen and (his!) daughter may have been namesakes. Jacobsen's reference to Schneider, *Götternamen* (AnOr 19): 202, appears to be in error.

70 So most explicitly, it would seem, according to "The Rulers of Lagaš"; see Sollberger (N 32): 275-91, esp. 279, note 5.

71 Kramer *apud* Pritchard *ANET*, 651f. For additional literature, see my "Women of Sumer" (N 45): 32, note 68.

72 See especially G. R. Castellino, *Two Šulgi Hymns (BC)* (= Studi Semitici 42, 1972).

73 See my "The Princess and the Plea," (forthcoming).

74 Hallo, "The Coronation of Ur-Nammu," *JCS* 20 (1966): 13-41. For parallels to the text edited there, see now Wilcke, *Kollationen . . . Jena* (= Abhandlungen der Sächsischen Akademie . . . 65/4, 1976): 47f. On the coronation ceremony, see now A. K. Grayson, *Babylonian Historical-Literary Texts* (1975): ch. 7, with literature cited, 78 n. 2.

75 See especially Kramer, "Kingship in Sumer and Akkad: the Ideal King," RAI 19 (1974): 163-76.

76 Kramer, "The death of Ur-Nammu and His Descent to the Netherworld," *JCS* 21 (1967 [publ. 1969]; 104-22; Wilcke, RAI 17 (1970): 81-92; Kramer (N 71): 659; Piotr Michalowski, "The Death of Šulgi," *Or* 46 (1977): 220-25.

77 See, e.g., Josef Bauer, *Zeitschrift der Deutschen Morgenländischen Gesellschaft* Suppl. 1 (1969): 107-14; Ph. Tallon, *RA* 68 (1974): 167f.

78 As expressed particularly in the onomasticon. Cf. on this point already Hallo, *JNES* (1956): 220n. 4 and now H. Klengel, "Hammurapi und seine Nachfolger im altbabylonischen Onomastikon," *JCS* 28 (1976): 156-60 (ref. courtesy R. Kutscher). For Shulgi as private name see R. Frankena *AbB* (1966): 65 (LIH 2:83) 24.

79 Parrot, *Sumer* (N 9): 305-7 (figs. 373-75).

80 Rivkah Harris, "On the Process of Secularization under Hammurapi," *JCS* 15 (1961): 117-20; *eadem*, "Some Aspects of the Centralization of the realm . . . ," *JAOS* 88 (1968): 727-32, esp. 727f. For the emergence of seals dedicated to the king instead of the deity of his temple (*ibid.*) see more specifically Hallo, "Royal Inscriptions of Ur" (N 34): 18-20.

awesome great gods of the older pantheon.[81] And he approached them, not as subject to ruler, but as child to parent—capricious still like all the Mesopotamina gods, but potentially at least loving and caring like a parent.[82] In so doing, however, he was merely following in the footsteps of royalty: the kings of the earlier era had already discovered the divine parent in the ideology of kingship. Now the common man claimed the same privilege for himself. Perhaps, then, we should characterize the Late Bronze Age not so much in terms of secularization as of democratization. Whether this prepared the Mesopotamian citizen adequately to cope with the emerging ideology of Assyrian kingship I will leave for others to decide.[83]

81 Jacobsen, *Treasures* (N 56): ch. 5: "Second millennium metaphors. The Gods as parents: rise of personal religion."

82 On some of the problems involved, such as the number, gender, and character of the personal deities, see Achsa Belind *apud* Yvonne Rosengarten, *Trois Aspects de la Pensée Religieuse Sumérienne* (Paris: de Boccard, 1971): 156-59. See now in detail H. Vorländer, *Mein Gott* (= AOAT 23, 1975).

83 For Middle Assyrian notions of divine parentage (of the king) see Peter Machinist, "Literature as Politics: the Tukulti-Ninurta Epic and the Bible." *CBQ* 38 (1976): 455-82, esp. 465-68. For the sacred marriage in the first millennium, see *CAD* and *AHw s. v. hašādu*; differently Renger, *RLA* 4 (1975): 258 §24.

HITTITE TERMS FOR THE LIFE SPAN

HARRY A. HOFFNER, JR.

One of the most common expressions which in Hittite corresponds to our English "long life" is *dalugaeš witteš* "long years."[2] The purpose of this study is to assemble the various expressions involving the word "year" or "years" which connote aspects of the human life span and its characteristics. It is fair to say that the Hittites like other peoples contemplated life in terms of its probable duration. Life was in a sense defined by death, which set limits upon it. To quote a Hittite writer: "Life is bound up with death, and death is bound up with life. Mortal man doesn't live forever. The days of his life are numbered."[3]

I have left out of consideration here the many uses of the word "year" or "years" which have no reference to the life span. Most of the uses pertaining to the life span employ the plural "years" rather than the singular.

1. Expressions Denoting Long Life Span

The first of these is "long years." In promising votive offerings to the deity for keeping her ailing husband alive Queen Puduhepa wrote: "If, O goddess my lady, you shall have kept His Majesty alive and healthy for long years, so that he shall walk before and behind you for long years, (I will give you thus-and-so)."[4] "Long years" is clearly the most frequent notation for longevity in the lists of good things requested from the gods. In the vanishing god myths the blessings of the god's reconciliation and return include "long years and offspring."[5] At the end of one such myth and ritual the practitioner beseeches the deity: "Calm down. Be appealed to. Evermore give to the king, and to (Queen) Ašmunikal sons, daughters, descendants and long years."[6] In the lists of good things we find the following grouped items: long years, vigor (*innarauwatar, innaraḫḫuar*), life (*ḫuišwatar* or TI-*tar*), fruitfulness (*miyatar* often adding: of crops and livestock), youth (*mayandatar*),[7] heroism (*tarḫuilatar*), health (*ḫaddulatar*), brightness of mind or mood (ZI-*aš lalukkimaš*), joy (*dušgaraz*), gentle or mild treatment at the hands of the gods (*šiunaš miummar/minumar*), the love of the gods (*šiunaš aššiyawar*), and lordliness (*išḫaššarwatar*).[8]

Along with the qualification "long" one sometimes finds the added expression "wide," i.e., "long and wide years." This seems to be an Old Hittite expression, which is found in prayers and solicitations for the well-being of the king. "Let the Labarna's years be long and wide."[9] Longevity is also indicated by the expression "many years" (*mekkuš wettuš*). In an Old Hittite ritual the king says: "In my capacity as king the gods have granted to me many years (of life and reign). There is no limit to the years."[10] A similar sentiment found elsewhere in the same ritual is: "The Sungod and Stormgod have looked after the king. They have rejuvenated him. They have set no limit on his years."[11]

Reminiscent of the biblical expression "Thy youth is renewed like the eagle's" (Ps 103:5) is a phrase from the same Old Hittite ritual: "The Sungod and the Stormgod have renewed (the king's) years."[12]

Picturesque is the description of longevity in terms relating to the shaggy fleece of the sheep. "As the sheep is

1 Dedicated affectionately to Marvin Pope, remembering our happy years together on the Yale faculty, 1969–1974.

2 J. Friedrich, *HW* 206 sub *daluki-*, 255 sub *witt-*; H. Hoffner, English-Hittite Glossary 55 sub "longevity."

3 *ḫuišwatarmapa anda ḫingani ḫaminkan ḫinganamapa anda ḫuišwanniya ḫaminkan dandukišnaša* DUMU-*aš ukturi natta ḫuišwanza ḫuišwannaš* UD.ḪI.A-*ši kappuwanteš* KUB 30.10 obv. 20–21 (Kantuzili prayer, MH/MS).

4 Vow of Puduhepa, col. I, lines 3 ff., edited Otten, StBoT 1:16f. Transl. follows Otten, *loc. cit.* against Laroche, RA 43:67, cited *HW* 206.

5 *našta anda* MU. KAM. GÍD. DA. DUMU. MEŠ-*latar kitta* KUB 17.10 iv 30–31; cf. KUB 33.12 iv 16.

6 KUB 33.21 iii 18-21 (Laroche, *Textes mythologiques*, 121); cf. KUB 33.31:1-5 (Laroche, 63).

7 Belonging to the female as well (KBo 15.10 +20.42 i 35–36, edited Szabo, THeth 1:18–19), *mayandatar* can hardly be only "young manhood"! The word means young adulthood viewed as the prime of life and opposed both to childhood and senility. Often it is best translated simply as "youth."

8 KBo 14.91:9ff.; KBo 11.72 + ii 33f.; KUB 36.89 obv. 16f.; KUB 33.38 iv 6–10; KBo 17.60 rev. 10f.; KUB 24.3++ iii 17ff.; KUB 24.2 rev. 12–18; KUB 33.68 ii 15f.; KUB 24.1 iii 4–15; KUB 33.62 ii 8–10, 19–20; KUB 27.67 iii 28f.; KBo 2.32 rev. 2.

9 *nu La-ba-*[*ar-na-aš* MU.HI.A-*še-eš*] *talugaeš palḫaeš aš*[*andu*] KBo 17.22 iii 6–7, cf. 8–9. Note also KBo 22.133:6-7 "[long] years, wide [years . . .] like the sea."

10 LUGAL-*emu* DINGIR.MEŠ *mekkuš* MU.KAM.HI.A-*uš maniyaḫḫir wittanna kutrešmet* NU.GÁL KUB 29.1 i 21–22.

11 ^{d}UTU-*ušza* ^{d}IM-*ašša* LUGAL-*un* EGIR-*an kappuer nan dān mayandaḫḫir* MU.KAM.ḪI.A-*šaššan kutriš UL ier* KUB 29.1 iii 6-8.

12 MU.ḪI.A-*ašši* EGIR *newaḫḫir ibid.* ii 50.

shaggy, so also may the years of the king, queen and (their) children be 'shaggy.' "[13]

Drawn from the familiar imagery of spinning wool is the figure of the deities spinning the years of an individual's life. Parallels from other cultures are too numerous to mention. "(The mentioned deities) are spinning the king's years. Neither the limit nor the number of (these) years is prescribed."[14]

In a fragment which seems archaic in language it appears that the gods might be besought to "guard" or "keep" the years of the Labarna King: "Keep ye his years."[15]

2. Expressions Denoting Short Life Span

Many of the expressions which indicate a curtailed life span are merely the adjectival antonyms of the formulas found in section 1 above.

The antonym, for example, of "long years" (*dalugaeš watteš*) seems to be "short years" (*maninkuwanteš wetteš*).[16] This expression can occur in the singular, "short year," in the same sense of a short life span.[17] The genitive construction "a person of a short 'year' (life span)" is also attested. Puduhepa relates in a prayer how it was said of her husband, Ḫattušili, during the reign of his predecessor, Urḫitešup: "He is a person of short life span."[18] A magical expert called the Old Woman in the performance of her ritual to ensure health and continued life pronounces her client's name before the gods and says: "Let not the evil day, the short year, the anger of the gods, or the tongue of the multitude see this person anywhere."[19] Another incantation put is so: "As the door turns on its hinge, let the short life span and the anger of the gods turn back by the common road."[20] An equivalent expression utilizing the verb *maninkuwaḫ*—"to make short, shorten" is: "If you gods . . . have shortened my days, months and years, let this living substitute stand in my place."[21] Another incantation groups several causes of woe for the patient: "If (it is) death by violent means (lit., oppression), or if it is the shortening of the life span (lit., years) by [. . .], if it be any kind of judgments, if I have committed any kind of sin."[22]

The antonym of "many years" (**mekkeš wetteš*) is "few (lit., counted) years" (**wetteš kappuwanteš*),[23] which occurs once in the myth Kingship in Heaven: "For only a few years Anu was king in heaven."[24] This adjectival expression is but a grammatical transformation of the related phrase "limit and counting / numbering of the years."[25] The collocation "count the years (of life)" together with the other evidence about spinning years and promising years points to the fates' predetermining the number of years of a person's life.

A final expression for short life span is "called-in (recalled) years" (*wetteš nininkanteš*).[26] The verb *ninink-* means "to call up (troops)" among related meanings.[27] It would appear that a foreshortened life involved the fates' recalling from the mortal some of the years which they had once allotted to him. A colophon indicates that a ritual was performed "If years belonging to a person, whether man or woman, have been recalled."[28] A library or archive shelf list mentions a similar ritual for the case "if [. . .] or if [he gets] into some kind of impurity, [or if] his years have been recalled, or if . . . [he sees] an evil [dream], or if he has committed perjury, or if his father and mother have cursed him before the gods, or if . . . , etc."[29]

3. The Fixing or Determining of the Life Span

The above expressions for long and short life span have included several which presuppose the action of the fates in setting the number of years of a person's life. That the Hittites conceived of such activity on behalf of the fates has been known by scholars for a long time.[30] It is even possible that one of the two words for "death," *ḫinkan*, is derived from the verb *ḫink-* which means "to give, present, allot(?)." Thus death is "that which has been granted to all men as their lot." A number of years ago

13 UDU-*ma maḫḫan wa*[*rḫ*]*uešzi Ù ŠA* LUGAL SAL. LUGAL *ŠA* DUMU.MEŠ MU.ḪI.A-*ŠUNU* [x x] *warḫueštu* KBo 20.82 ii 22–23.

14 *nu* LUGAL-*waš* MU.KAM.ḪI.A-*uš malkiyanzi wittanna kutrešmit kappuwawaršamet UL duqqari* KUB 29.1 ii 8–10.

15 MU.ḪI.A-*šu paḫḫaššanu*[*tten*] KBo 12.18 iv 10, cf. Labarna in 6.

16 On *maninkuwant-* "short, deficient" see *Chicago Hittite Dictionary* 3/2 (1983): 173–74.

17 *maninkuwand/tan* MU-*an* KUB 9.34 i 29, iv 7, KUB 9.4 ii 7, Tunnawi iii 42.

18 *ma-ni-in-ku-wa-an-ta-aš-wa* [MU.KAM-*aš-apāš*] KUB 21.27+ iii 16.

19 *kūnnawa antuḫšan idualuš* UD-*az maninkuwanza* MU.ḪI.A(sic)-*za* [DIN]GIR.MEŠ-*aš karpiš pa*[*ng*]*auwaš* EME-*aš le kuwapikki aušzi* HT 6 + KBo 9.125 obv. 25ff.

20 KBo 25.193 obv.? 8–10 with duplicate KBo 21.6 obv. 6–8. My translation assumes that *pangawaz* KASKAL-*az* does not mean "by the entire road," but is equivalent to a genitive construction *pangawaš* KASKAL-*az* "road of the multitude," i.e., "common road," and that the ablative doesn't mean "(turn back) *from* the road" but "(turn back) *by means of* the road."

21 *numu* UD.ḪI.A ITU.ḪI.A MU.ḪI.A-*ya maninkuwaḫten* KUB 17.4 obv.! 18, edited Kümmel. StBoT 3:58f.

22 KUB 43.72 ii 9–14, cf. [M]U.KAM.MEŠ-*aš māninku-waḫḫuwar* in 10.

23 Since *kappuwant-* is a participle, it follows its noun when used attributively; cf. Friedrich, *Hethitisches Elementarbuch*, p. 115; cf. also *Chicago Hittite Dictionary* 3/2 (1980): 61–62, *sub liliwant-*.

24 KUB 33.120+ i 8, cf. MU.ḪI.A-*aš kappuwantaš*.

25 See note 14.

26 Although all attestations are predicates, the participial attribute would also follow *wetteš*; cf. note 23.

27 Cf. Friedrich, *HW* 151 with literature cited there.

28 KBo 11.14 ib 24f. and duplicate KUB 43.57 iv 24f.

29 KUB 30.51 + 30.45 + ii 19–24.

30 E. von Schuler in H. W. Haussig, *Wörterbuch der Mythologie* 168f., 192f.; H. Kümmel, StBoT 3:3f., 91f.

Einar von Schuler pointed out that an expression in the Hittite instructions texts "If the day of one's father and one's mother is long" must mean "If someone lives a long time (and thus outlives the king under whom he has taken an oath of loyalty)."[31] And the much more abbreviated expression "the day" is also attested meaning the appointed day of death.[32]

In fact the full sweep from "year" to "day" to "hour" seems to have been employed by the Hittites to denote the time of death, if our interpretation of the Hittite word *lamarḫandattašši-* is correct. In our article on this word in the *Chicago Hittite Dictionary* we proposed a translation "pertaining to the setting or fixing of an hour or moment."[33] The term is one of several which describe activities of the goddess Aalaš and of the tutelary deity ^{d}LAMMA. Given the context of other activities, it is quite possible that this expression alludes to the setting of the hour of death.

31 E. von Schuler, "Hethitische Dienstanweisungen" (*Archiv für Orientforschung*, Beiheft 10) 13, 18–19 sub iii 14ff.; note *:ḫalliya* in iii 17ff.

32 In the same instructions text the servant wishing to avoid responsibility for his oath says: "He who made me swear (loyalty to himself) has already gone to his 'day' (i.e., death)" (*:ḫalliya weḫtat*) von Schuler, "Dienstanw." 13, lines 17–18. Speaking of the fate of his opponents after he assumed the throne, Hattušili III wrote: "Some of them died by the weapon," *kuiešma* UD.KAM-*za* (var. UD-*azza*) *ekir* "others died on(?) the day (of fate, i.e., natural death)" KUB 1.8 iv 26 with dupl. KUB 1.1 iv 46 (Apology of Ḫatt.). The translation "on the day" presupposes that UD.KAM-*za* and UD-*azza* represent the nominative in a local sense. Parallelism with *IŠTU* ^{GIŠ}TUKUL in the preceding clause might suggest an ablative here. But implied opposition here of violent death with a natural one seems to favor our interpretation.

4. Conclusion

In a Festschrift article so short it was obviously impossible to undertake a survey of all aspects of the subject of death as reflected in Hittite texts. What has been attempted rather is an examination of the terminology for "life span" as it affects the broader subject of death and fate. More particularly, the use of time words such as "hour," "day," and especially "year" or "years" have been studied in order to show how the Hittites used them to express the duration and termination of life as predetermined, measured out, foreshortened, or terminated.

Although it often appears from his writings that Marvin Pope has a certain fascination with the subjects of love and death, it is the fond wish of this friend and admirer that he will accept this essay as tribute to his ability to celebrate life in all his doings. As the Hittites were fond of wishing one another, "May the gods ever guard and keep you in life!"

33 *Chicago Hittite Dictionary*, 3/1:37.

TWO *BAL-BAL-E* DIALOGUES

THORKILD JACOBSEN

The Kubātim Dialogue

Dies diem docet! Some time ago, in 1954, we treated briefly of the difficult text published by Chiera as no. 23 of his *Sumerian Religious Texts* (Upland Pa. 1924).[1] We suggested that it was a dialogue between Shu-Suen and his vestal lukur[2] Kubātum, who thanked him for gifts he had given her because she broke into jubilation when Shu-Suen's consort Abī-simtī gave birth to a child. Recently, however, a seal inscription of Abī-simtī's brother Babāti, has come to light;[3] and it establishes beyond any possibility of doubt that she was Shu-Suen's mother, and not, as we had conjectured, his wife. Reconsideration of the problems of the text in the light of this new fact is thus indicated.

A significant step in the right direction has been taken, we believe, by Sollberger, who in a recent article in the *Journal of Cuneiform Studies* proposes that the text was occasioned by Kubātum having borne Shu-Suen a child. He supports this with evidence that a lukur was not necessarily vestal, but could have children, and he can even point specifically to the mention of a "daughter of

1 *Journal of Cuneiform Studies* 7 (1953): 45–47 = *Toward the Image of Tammuz* (W. L. Moran, ed.; Cambridge, MA, 1970): 182–86. Earlier studies were Falkenstein, *Die Welt des Orients* 1/2 (1947): 43–50 (cf. Falkenstein and von Soden, *Sumerische und Akkadische Hymnen und Gebete* [Zürich, 1953]: 119–20 and p. 370); Kramer, *Ancient Near Eastern Texts* (Princeton, 1950, 1969): 496; *From the Tablets of Sumer* (Indian Hills, CO, 1956): 251–52, and *The Sacred Marriage Rite* (Bloomington, IN, 1969): 93–95. Kramer closely follows Falkenstein.

Abbreviations used in the following are: ANET: *Ancient Near Eastern Texts* (J. B. Pritchard, ed.; Princeton, 1950, 1969); AS: The Oriental Institute of the University of Chicago, *Assyriological Studies; Atrahasīs*: W. G. Lambert and A. R. Millard, *Atra-hasīs* (Oxford, 1969); *GSG*: A. Poebel, *Grundzüge der Sumerischen Grammatik* (Rostock, 1923); *CAD*: I. Gelb, L. Oppenheim *et al., The Chicago Assyrian Dictionary*; *ISET*: *Istanbul... Sumer Edebê Tablet ve Parçalari*; *JCS*: *Journal of Cuneiform Studies*; *JRAS*: *Journal of the Royal Asiatic Society*; *MAD*: I. Gelb, *Materials for the Assyrian Dictionary* (Chicago, 1952–); *MSL*: B. Landsberger *et al., Materialien zum sumerischen Lexikon*; PSBA: Proceedings of the Society for Biblical Archaeology; R: H. C. Rawlinson, *A Selection from the Miscellaneous Inscriptions of Assyria; Šaziga: R. D. Biggs šà.zi.ga Ancient Mesopotamian Potency Incantations* (Locust Valley, NY, 1967); *SRT*: Chiera, *Sumerian Religious Texts* (Upland, PA, 1924); *TCL: Musée du Louvre, Département des Antiquités Orientales, Textes Cunéiformes; TIT: Toward the Image of Tammuz* (W. L. Moran, ed.; Cambridge, MA, 1970); *UET: Ur Excavations Texts; ZA: Zeitschrift für Assyriologie; WdO: Die Welt des Orients.*

2 On this term see Renger, *ZA* 58 (1967): 149–79. Its precise meaning is difficult to delineate. Basically, as suggested by the traditional orthography *munus-me(.ak)* "woman (in charge) of an office," it probably denoted a priestess of kinds. The later reading of the sign group, lukur, seems a variant of lagar "servant" but also "attendant" (šukkallum) and a term for a high ranking priest.

In the sense of "attendant," "maid in waiting," it occurs as a term describing the status of Ningirsu's seven daughters at his court (Gudea, Cyl. B xi.; cf. Uru-inim-gi-na, Oval Plaque V.16′). Related meanings are *batultum* "young girl" and *nadītum* "spinster," "nun," given for it in the lexical texts. (*MSL* XII, p. 42. 263–265. For *qadištum* in line 264 see Renger [N 2]: 179ff. The precise sense which made it natural for the scribe to list it here is not clear). The meaning "concubine" seems to belong properly to lukur when qualified as lukur-kaskal(.la), which is translated as *šugitum* (*MSL* XII 129.28) a class of priestesses typically chosen as concubines (Renger [N 2]: 176ff.), and is listed between munus-šu-gi_4: "*šugitum*" (i.e. šugi.ī *(a) tum* = "woman of an old man," "old man's darling," and dam-$banda_3^{da}$: "concubine" in *MSL* XII, p. 58f. 710–11. The term suggests a "handmaiden" (lukur) who accompanied a man on journeys (kaskal) away from home to look after his comforts, or possibly who had her own establishment at often visited points of the journey. As a parallel for such an arrangement may be mentioned that according to my late teacher, Oestrup, caravan leaders around the turn of the century usually had a wife at either end of their route. In the case of the rulers of the Third Dynasty of Ur, who travelled extensively around the realm, such an arrangement may well have existed, Kubātum being Shu-Suen's wife in Uruk; with others, perhaps, in Ur and Nippur. The long title lukur kaskal(.ak) could presumably be shortened to lukur at will.

Falkenstein in his treatment of the text, cited in note 1 above, suggested that the lukur in Uruk might have been the one who took the goddess' part in the yearly ritual of the sacred marriage. That is an attractive idea, but so far it remains conjectural only.

3 R. Whiting, "Tiš-atal and Babati, Uncle of Šu-Sin," *JCS* 28 (1976): 173–82, esp. pp. 178ff.

Kubātum" in a Drehem text dated to Shu-Suen's fourth year, almost certainly the child with whose birth SRT 23 deals.[4]

Left is thus only a question about the rôle of Abī-simtī, whose name occurs in lines three and five of the beginning section. Sollberger translates this section as follows:

She is holy – she has given birth! She is holy –
  she has given birth!
The lady: she is holy – she has given birth!
(My) 'Abī-simtī': she is holy – she has given birth!
The lady: she is holy – she has given birth!
My cloth-beam of the cloth of good fortune, my 'Abī-simtī'!
My warp-beam of the . . . -woven cloth, my lady Kubātum!

Basing himself on the fact that in the parallel lines five and six "my Abī-simtī" corresponds to "my lady, Kubātum" he argues that the two names here mean the same thing, "My Abī-simtī" is not to be taken as referring to the actual Abī-simtī but is used, rather, as a metaphor for Kubātum: as Shulgi(r) had his Abī-simtī, so Shu-Suen has Kubātum, who is *his* Abī-simtī. Unquestionably an ingenious and bold solution, which, for all we know, may turn out to be the correct one.

A few things, though, tend to give us pause. First of all: while of course possible, it does not seem to us altogether natural to use one's mother's name as a metaphor for one's wife—or concubine—as Shu-Suen is supposed to do here. Secondly, it would seem that if "my Abī-simtī" in line five is intended to contrast with an understood "Shulgi(r)'s Abī-simtī," then the possessive pronoun ought to have been stressed more, e.g. by the use of g̃u$_{10}$-me-en "you who are my . . ." or of ní-g̃u$_{10}$ "my own. . . ." Such stress, however, is not there. Line five uses the simple possessive suffix -g̃u$_{10}$ "my," in which, because of its frequent use for caritative in texts of this nature, the possessive force can not have been felt as very strong; and line three leaves it out altogether. Thirdly, one will ask oneself whether in actual fact the parallelism of "my Abī-simtī" with "my lady, Kubātum" in lines five and six *does* imply identity since it may just as well have followed from the natural placing over against each other of two entities compared. In favor of this latter interpretation of it is clearly the contrasting natures of the metaphors used in lines five and six. Abī-simtī is "my cloth-beam," Kubātum "my warp-beam." The former is thus characterized by an accomplished task, the finished cloth, the latter by a promising beginning only, the warp. Accordingly, if these metaphors were meant to apply to one person only, they would begin with the end and end with the beginning, and to praise someone for mere warp after having praised her for superb finished cloth would surely be anticlimactic. It may therefore be worthwhile—even though these points are of course moot—to look at the text afresh to see whether perhaps there might be other possible ways of understanding it.

Tentatively we would read and translate as follows:[5]

kù-ga-àm in-dú-ud kù-ga-àm in-dú-ud
nin-e kù-ga-àm in-dú-ud
A-bi-sí-im-ti kù-ga-àm in-dú-ud
nin-e kù-ga-àm in-dú-ud
g̃iš-ge-na túg nam-sa$_6$-ga-g̃u$_{10}$
g̃iš-sag̃-DU túg-⟨dun⟩-dun na-g̃ál-[la]-g̃u$_{10}$
  nin-g̃u$_{10}$ Ku-ba-tum
suhur-e-d[u$_7$i-b]é-gub-ba-mu ù-mu-un
  ^{d}Šu-^{d}Sú-en-mu
inim-ma-[sì-ga-^{d}Mu-ul]-⸢líl⸣-l[á]-mu
  ṭu-mu ^{d}Šul-gi-ra-mu
bí-du$_{11}$-ga-ke$_4$-eš bí-du$_{11}$-ga-ke$_4$-eš
  ù-mu-un-e ém ma-an-ba
me-e a-al-la-ri bí-du$_{11}$-ga-ke$_4$-eš ù-mu-un-e
  ém ma-an-ba
bulug̃-guškin na$_4$-kišib-za-gìn-na
  ù-mu-un-e ém-ma-an-ba
HAR guškin HAR kù-babbar-ra
  ù-mu-un-e ém-ma-an-ba
ù-mu-un ém-ba-zu na-⸢ám⸣-[hi-l]i sù-ga-an
  ibi$_x$ (IGI)-zu ha-ma-[ra-íl-en]
^{d}Šu-^{d}Sú-en ém-ba-zu n[a-ám-hi-li sù-ga-an]
  ibi$_x$(IGI)-zu ha-ma-[ra-íl-en]
[. .] ⸢ù⸣-mu-un X [ ]
  [ù]-mu-u[n]
[. . . .] X sa$_6$ m[à-]
  [ ] mu taškarin-dím mu-[ ]
urú-zu ku$_5$-da-dím šu hé-íb-[íl]i
  ù-mu-un ^{d}Šu-^{d}Sú.en
ur-⸢nim⸣-dím mèr-zu-šè hé-nú
  ṭu-mu ^{d}Šul-gi-ra-kam
Ìl-um(?)-mi(?)-ia X-mu

4 Edmond Sollberger, "A Note on the Lyrical Dialogue SRT 23," *JCS* 30 (1978): 99–100. The identification of Abī-simtī as Shu-Suen's mother, and Kubātum as his wife vindicates Falkenstein, who assigned these rôles to them in his study cited above in note 1. Falkenstein—and Kramer following him—further assumed, however, that the whole composition was laid in the mouth of a singer, presumably the tapstress of line 19, who was perhaps herself a lukur. This seems excluded by the interchange of Eme-gir$_x$(ŠÈ) and Eme-sal for male and female speakers which the text exhibits. See generally Sollberger's reasoned critique of previous work, p. 99f.

5 We have incorporated Kramer's collations in *ZA* 52 (1957): 76ff. For our transliteration ṭu-mu rather than du$_5$-mu in lines 7 and 18 we refer to Roman Jakobson's observation that emphatic (pharyngealized) consonants are heard as rounded by speakers of languages which do not have them and vice versa. (Roman Jakobson, C. Gunnar Fant and Morris Halle, *Preliminaries to Speech Analysis* [Cambridge, MA, 1969]: 31). Apparently the Akkadian-speaking scribes heard Sumerian consonants rounded because between *u*'s as the emphatics with which they were familiar.

sà-bi-tum-ma kaš-a-ni zé-ba-àm
kaš-a-ni-dím sal-la-ni zé-ba-àm
du$_{11}$-du$_{11}$-a-ni-dím sal-la-ni zé-ba-àm
kaš-a-ni zé-ba-àm
kašbir-a-ni kaš-a-ni zé-ba-àm
^{d}Šu-^{d}Sú.en ba-sa$_{6}$-ge-na-ĝu$_{10}$
ba-sa$_{6}$-ge-na-ĝu$_{10}$ ba-zil-⸢zil⸣-i-na-ĝu$_{10}$
^{d}Šu-^{d}Sú.en ba-sa$_{6}$-ge-na-ĝu$_{10}$
ki-áĝ-^{d}En-líl-lá ^{d}Šu-^{d}Sú.en-ĝu$_{10}$
lugal-ĝu$_{10}$ dinĝir kalam-ma-na
bal-bal-e ^{d}Ba-ba$_{6}$-kam

(*Shu-Suen:*)
She is clear:[6] she has given birth! She is clear:
she has given birth!
The lady is clear: she has given birth!
Abī-simtī is clear: she has given birth!
The lady is clear: she has given birth!
My cloth-beam which, as in it is,[7] made
(a) good (job of) the cloth, my Abī-simtī,
and my warp-beam which, as in it is, got
warp[8] on, my lady Kubātum!

(*Kubātum:*)
O my one (so) seemly of locks, my one
on whom my eyes are riveted,[9] my lord, Shu-Suen
my one *planned by Enlil,*[10] my
Shulgi(r)-son!
Because I hailed it,[11] because I hailed it
the lord gave me things!
Because I hailed it with a cry of
exultation[12] the lord gave me things!
a gold pin and a cylinder seal of
lapis-lazuli!—The lord gave me things!
a gold ring and a ring silver inwrought![13]
The lord gave me things!
O lord! Make your gifts full of allure
that you may lift your eyes to me!
..... lord ....
lord ....
.... *pleasing* ....
my .... *like a boxwood tree* ......
May your city crablike raise its hand in greeting.
O lord Shu-Suen!
May it, like a lion cub lie down at
your feet (saying:) "It is Shulgi(r)'s son!"

6 The precise meaning of kug in this context calls for reflection. Falkenstein (N 1) translated "den Reinen," applying it to Shu-Suen and was followed by Kramer. That reference of the term becomes unlikely, however, if Shu-Suen himself is the speaker. Sollberger (N 4) translates "she is holy" and applies it to both Abī-Simtī and Kubātum. However, while the deified rulers of Ur III may have been able to claim sanctity for themselves, though we know of no clear such use of kug for them, there is no indication that such exceptional status was ever extended to their mothers, consorts, or concubines. Even a modified translation "(ritually) pure" is open to doubt, at least in the case of Kubātum, for a woman in confinement after having given birth was considered still taboo. *MSL* X, p. 136:307. [túg-níĝ-dara$_{2}$-úš-a]: MIN (= *kan-nu*) *šá ha-riš-ti* "bloodied bandage": "bandage of a woman in confinement" and Nabnîtu XXII 47 [túg]-niĝ-dara$_{2}$-úš-a : *kan-nu šá ha-riš-ti* = *ša* NU KUG-ti "bloodied bandage": "bandage of a woman in confinement" = "of an unclean woman." The bandage in question (*kannu*) refers, we assume, to the swathing of the abdomen of women after childbirth, a custom prevalent until quite recently. It is reflected also in the term for a woman in confinement *harištum*: the tied or swathed one.

We have therefore looked to the meanings of kug that have to do with purification and making clear of noxious outside influences; specifically we assume that as its Akkadian equivalent *elēlu* it can denote "clear of claims or obligations." Such a meaning fits the context well.

7 An analysis in terms of nam-sa$_{6}$-ga: *du-um-qum* (Nabnîtu R 189) such as proposed by Sollberger [N 4]: 100): "My cloth beam of cloth of good fortune" seems to us difficult, because it presupposes a double genitive ĝis-gi-na túg nam-sa$_{6}$-ga-ka-ĝu$_{10}$ when the text has only nam-sa$_{6}$-ga-ĝu$_{10}$. We accordingly consider nam- as representing the profix na- followed by infix -m- verbal stem sa$_{6}$-g and clausal -a. This analysis has the added advantage of bringing out the close parallel in form with na-ĝál-[la]-ĝu$_{10}$, the verb in the following and parallel line 6. For the force of na- as indicating inner urge to the action in the subject (agent) see AS 16 p. 73f., note 4.

8 The expected form is túg-dun-dun; see *MSL* 10, p. 133. 199 túg-dun-dun: MIN (= *ka-an-du*) "warp," and the spacing in *SRT* 23.6 suggests that one sign dun is missing. The tablet from which the scribe of *SRT* 23 copied may therefore have had a lacuna here.

9 For igi-gub "to stay the eye," i.e., "to rivet the eyes," "stare"; cf. Gudea Cyl A. V.8 a-am-zi-da igi-ĝu$_{10}$ gub-ba "over a fine white poplar on which my eyes steadily were."

10 For inim-ma sí-ga "to put into words," "to think of," "to plan" see my remarks in "Early Political Development in Mesopotamia," *ZA* 52 (1957): 91-140, note 80 = *TIT*, p. 387, note 80.

11 In bi-dug$_{4}$ the prefix bí-, as taught by Poebel, refers to the thing remarked on, the "dazu" of German "Ich sagte dazu." We have rendered this nuance by translating "I hailed it."

12 For a-al-la-ri see IV R 20 no. 1 12–13 kaskal a-li-ri translated as *har-ra-an šu-lu-lu* and cf. *CAD* A, p. 331 "*alālu* B. lex. sect. The form a-li-ri seems derived form a-al-la-ri by vowel assimilation, shortening of l and loss of inital aleph.

13 Poebel pointed out orally—we have been unable to find this in print—that Sumerian construes form and material as an apposition. A genitive denotes a less close relationship e.g. of ornamentation, produce (e.g., udu-siki(.ak) "woolproducing sheep") or similar.

The beer of my . . . . . , Il-ummiya,[14] the tapstress
is sweet!
and her private parts are sweet like her beer
—and her beer *is* sweet!
and her private parts are sweet like her chatter
—and her beer *is* sweet!

(*Lord in Waiting:*)
O Shu-Suen, my one with whom I am pleased
my one with whom I am pleased, my one
by whom I am made cheerful ever!
Shu-Suen, my one with whom I am pleased,
my Shu-Suen, beloved of Enlil,
my king, god of his country!

A dialogue pertaining to Baba

The first six lines of the text we have assigned—as in our earlier treatment—to Shu-Suen, since they are in Eme-gir_x (ŠÈ) and so presuppose a male speaker, and since the following answer to them in Eme-sal is addressed to him (see lines 7 and 8).

Also, it will be noted, we see as unifying theme for his praise of his mother and Kubātum the prevailing notion that a wife was under obligation to provide her husband with offspring. His mother has fulfilled that obligation—comparing her to the cloth-beam of the loom with the finished cloth celebrates her as mother of a family. Kubātum, who has just produced a child, presumably her first, is compared to the warp-beam; that is to say, she is praised for having started a family.[15] That Shu-Suen's mother Abī-simtī figures so prominently—almost as a model of perfection—may well be because she was actually present and within earshot, and so could not be ignored. It would be natural for her to have served as birth-helper at the birth of her son's child.

Shu-Suen is answered by a woman (the section lines 7–22 is in Eme-sal), obviously the one he has just praised for having given birth, Kubātum; they will therefore have been within earshot of one another, and one will assume that Shu-Suen had anxiously awaited the birth in an adjoining room, perhaps kept company by an attendant, a close relative or friend.

Kubātum thanks Shu-Suen for gifts of personal jewelry given to her when he heard the cry of exultation with which she greeted her newborn baby. Such gifts from a husband on the occasion of the birth of a child are attested also elsewhere.[16] She deftly suggests that the finery is so that she will please him by her looks, and that he should therefore give her alluring things. Then she hails him as king and ends up recommending her tapstress Il-ummiya (the reading of the name is unfortunately not certain) as companion and bedfellow for him. It was customary to celebrate the birth of a child with a feast in the house, so one may conjecture that Il-ummiya would be the one who would serve the beer on that occasion. Since the mother of the newborn child was still taboo and in confinement, she was not allowed to join in the festivities, nor would she resume, until later, normal marital relations.[17] It would thus seem that Il-ummiya was meant to substitute for her in both functions, as dinner and as bed companion.

The composition ends with four lines of praise of Shu-Suen in first person singular in Eme-gir_x (ŠÈ) conceivably spoken by the attendant who—we surmised—kept Shu-Suen company on his lonely watch.

Tavern Dialogue

The prominence given to describing the various attractions of the tapstress Il-ummiya, her bodily charms, her conversational charms, and the excellence of the kinds of beer she had on tap, seems rather odd in the context and sounds suspiciously like self advertising. One cannot but wonder, therefore, whether she may not have been the "poet" who composed the dialogue and so saw an opportunity to put in a plea *pro domo* as it were.

---

14 We follow the tentative reading of S. N. Kramer in his collation of the text *ZA* 52 (1957): 76ff.: AN(?)-um(?)-mi(?)-ia-a-?-mu reading the first four signs as an abbreviated Akkadian name *Ìl-um-mi-ia*, i.e., *Il-ummiya* "The (tutelary) god of my mother did / does . . . ." In the cryptic -a-? before -mu we surmise a word giving her title.

15 Falkenstein (N 1) read her name as Dab_5-ba-tum. The reading Ku-ba-tum was proposed by us in 1954 on the grounds that dab_5 occurs only as a determined, not as a free, phonetic value in Ur III and Isin-Larsa ([N 1]: note 75). We still consider this the most probable reading at our present stage of knowledge, but realize that new materials could alter the picture. If Falkenstein's reading should prove correct, Shu-Suen's use of imagery taken from the loom and weaving may well have been prompted by the similarity of the name Dabbatum to the word da-ba-tum, a term for a special kind of cloth. See Waetzoldt, *Untersuchungen zur neusumerischen Textilindustrie* (Rome, 1972): index on p. 291.

16 An early example is apparently Thureau-Dangin, *Recueil de Tablettes Chaldéennes* (Paris, 1903): no. 12, gift of a house and lot and a slave, witnessed to in "the bedroom" (ki-ná iv.6) by one man and five women, four of whom will have assisted at the birth and one of whom was the midwife ($šag_4$-zu. iv.4).

17 Cf. the feast given by Enki after the birth of man in the myth "Enki and Ninmah" and the rules given in the story of Atrahasīs (*Atra-hasīs*, 62, lines 17–19 *šab-su-tu-um-ma ina bīt ha-riš-ti li-ih-du ak-ki a-li-it-tu ú-la-du-ma um-mi šèr-ri lu-har-ri-šá ra-ma-an-[šá]* "The midwife may make merry in the house of the woman in confinement; / as soon as the woman giving birth gives birth / the mother of the baby may swathe herself," and see W. L. Moran, "Atrahasis: The Babylonian Story of the Flood," *Biblica* 52 [1971]: 58, n. 3 on the rules for resumption of marital relations and the accompanying festival). In line 302 we would restore *i-na bi-it [ha-re]-e* "in the storeroom." The sexual congress was intended magically to increase wealth.

The idea of a tapstress "poet" in the circle around Kubātum and Shu-Suen can of course be conjectural only. It would help, though, to make another oddity somewhat more understandable, the crude low-life piece beginning "O my lushest one!" which also features a tapstress, and which somehow has managed to make its way into the Isin-Larsa school curriculum.[18]

In this latter dialogue a stranger, after an evening in the alehouse, makes a play for the tapstress, a plea full of beery sentimentality. She proves an easy mark but does pretend that, since she does not know him, he must swear that he lives in an outlying village and is not an enemy spy. The oath she proposes, the kind taken while touching the genitals of the person to whom one swears, is here clearly a mere erotic ploy.[19] The remainder of the dialogue is given over to her pleasure in watching him as he is getting more and more sexually excited.

The text reads

lu-bi-ğu$_{10}$ [lu]-bi-ğu$_{10}$ lu-bi-ğu$_{10}$
la-bi-ğu$_{10}$ la-b[i-ğu] ⸢ka⸣-⸢làl⸣-ama-na-ğu$_{10}$
⸢gú⸣-duru$_{5}$-ğu$_{10}$ làl-ab-⸢ba⸣-ğu$_{10}$ ka-làl-ama-na-ğu$_{10}$
igi-za igi-dug$_{8}$-ru-na-bi ma-dùg ğen-nin$_{9}$-ki-áğa-ğu$_{10}$
ka-za inim-di-di-bi ma-dùg ka-làl-ama-na-ğu$_{10}$
šudu-za gaba-⸢su-ub⸣-bi ma-dùg ğen-nin$_{9}$-ki-áğa-ğu$_{10}$
nin-ğu$_{10}$ še-za kaš-⸢bi⸣ in-dùg ⸢ka⸣-làl-⸢ama⸣-na-ğu$_{10}$
šim-za ⸢gú-me⸣-⸢lám⸣-[b]i in-dùg ğen-nin$_{9}$-ki áğa-ğu$_{10}$
é-⸢a⸣ la-la-zu t[ukun mu-gu$_{8}$-e] ka-⸢làl⸣-ama-na-ğu$_{10}$
nin$_{9}$-ğu$_{10}$ la-la-zu [tukun mu-gu$_{8}$-e ğen-nin]-ki-áğa-ğu$_{10}$
é-zu é-ge-na-[àm sağ-si-sá hé]-ak
  ka-[làl-ama-na-ğu$_{10}$]
za-e dumu-lugal-la-[me-en ğen-nin$_{9}$-ki-áğa]-ğu$_{10}$
mu-un-⸢ti⸣-⸢le⸣-na mu-un-ti-le-na
  na-ám-erím ma-ku$_{5}$-[dè]-en
šeš urú-bar-ra mu-un-ti-le-nam
  na-ám-erím ma-ku$_{5}$-[dè]-en
lú-kúr-ra šu nu-mu-ni-in-du$_{11}$-ga
  na-ám-erím ma-ku$_{5}$-dè-en
lú-kúr-ra ka nu-[um-mi-in-t]e-ma-a
  na-ám-erím ma-ku$_{8}$-dè-en
túg-ém-lám-sal-la ma-⸢ra⸣-[ab-si-ge-na]-mu
ki-ig-ga-áma-mu mu-lu [hi-li-mu ba-te]-⸢a⸣
[za-ra n]a-ám-erím-ma [ṭu-mu-ra-an-m]ar-mar
  šeš i(!?)-b[í-sa$_{6}$-sa$_{6}$-m]u
šeš-mu na-ám-erím-ma ṭu-mu-ra-an-mar-mar
  šeš i-bí-sa$_{6}$-sa$_{6}$-mu
šu-zi-da-zu sal-la-mà dè-em-mar
gab-bu-zu sa$_{12}$(m)-mu-uš im-ši-ri
ka-zu ka-mà um-me-te
šu-um-du-um-mu ka(?)-za ù-ba-e-ni-dab$_{5}$
za-e ur$_{5}$-ta na-ám-erím ma-ku$_{8}$-dè-en
ur$_{8}$-ra-àm ušum-munus-e-ne-kam
  šeš i-bí-sa$_{6}$-sa$_{6}$-mu
ul-gùr-ru-mu ul-gùr-ru-mu
  hi-lizu zé-ba-àm
kiri$_{6}$ ^{ğiš}hašhur-a ul-gùr-ru-mu
  hi-li-zu zé-ba-àm
kiri$_{6}$ ^{ğiš}hašhuru-a gurun íl-la-mu
  hi-li-zu zé-ba-àm
Ṭu-mu-zi-ab.zu ní-te-na-ni
  hi-li-zu zé-ba-àm
dìm-kù-ga-mu dìm-kù-ga-mu
  hi-li-zu zé-ba-àm
dìm mu$_{9}$-nu$_{4}$-gal n⸢a$_{4}$⸣-za-gìn KESDA
  hi-li-zu zé-ba-àm
bal-bal-e ^{d}Inanna-kam

(*The Amorous Tavern Guest:*)
O my lushest one![20] My lushest one!
  my lushest one!
My most alluring one![21] My most alluring one!
  mother's little honeybun![22]

18 Chiera, *SRT* no. 31. For a most valuable collation of the text see Kramer in *ZA* 52 (1957): 85f. A translation and interpretation of it was given by him in his *The Sacred Marriage Rite* (Bloomington, IN, 1969): 104–106. It differs radically from the one here suggested.

19 For this type of oath cf. Gen 24:2–9 where Abraham has his servant thus swear to him. As a mere brazen invitation to sexual congress, with no mitigating pretense that it is sanction for an oath, the gesture is asked of Ishullānu by Ishtar in the Gilgamesh Epic Tablet VI 69 *u qat-ka ut-te-ṣa-am-ma lu-pu-ut hur-da-at-ni.*

20 We take lu-bi to represent a superlative in -bi (Poebel *GSG* 656 § 174) of lu: *dešû* (*CAD* D, p. 129 *dešû* lex. sect.), "to be lush, abundant."

21 Like lu-bi a superlative in -bi of la: *lalû* (*CAD* L, p. 49 *lalû* lex. sect.) "allure."

22 The translation is free but does, we hope, render both basic meaning and diction reasonably well. Literally the phrase means "My (one who is the) honeyed mouth of (i.e. 'to') her mother." The precise reference of ka-làl is unfortunately not clear. One may compare Ká-gal D sect. 4.9.′ (*MSL* 13, p. 245) [ka-l]àl-la: . . . *pu-u d*[*i-iš-pi*] "mouth of honey" listed between "grand(iloquent) mouth" (ká-mah:*pu-*[*u ṣi-ru*] and "fierce mouth" [ka-d]ù-dù:*pu-u al-d*[*u*] which presumably denotes "sweet-spoken," "honeyed" mouth. Other occurrences are Hh. XXIII iii 25′ (*MSL* 11, p. 72) sún ka-làl-munu$_{4}$ = *šá pi* RIK-*ti* "wort from 'honey mouth' of malt" and *ibid* iv. 15 (*MSL* 11, p. 73) ka-làl munu$_{4}$:*pi* RI[K-*tim*] "honey mouth of malt." The reading and meaning of the Akkadian translation is not clear to us. Generally, though, judging from the Sumerian, the term would seem to refer to the sweetness of the gaping germinated grains of malt, and it may well be this sense of the term that underlies its use as a term of endearment.

My juicy chick pea! My one who is father's "honey,"
mother's little honeybun!
The glance[23] from your eyes is sweet to me,
Quickly *say yes*,[24] my beloved sister!
The holding forth[25] of your mouth is sweet to me,
mother's little honeybun!
The *kiss on the chest*[26] of your greeting is sweet to me,
—Quickly *say yes*, my beloved sister!
My sister! The beer from your grain does one good,
mother's little honeybun,
The *strength and glow* from your wort does one good,
Quickly, *say yes*, my beloved sister!
In the house, desire for you *soon began to consume me*[27]
Quickly *say yes*, my beloved sister!
My sister, desire for you *soon began to consume me*
Quickly *say yes*, my beloved sister!
Your house is an honest house, *may it prosper*,
mother's little honeybun!
You are a (very) princess—quickly *say yes*,
my beloved sister!

(*Tapstress*:)
"You must swear to me that you live,
that you live . . . . . .
Brother, you must swear to me,
that it is just that you live in an outlying town!
You must swear to me that no enemy
has put the hand in them,
you must swear to me that no enemy
has brought the mouth near to it!
My letting down for you
the *thin*, exquisite gown,
—o my beloved one, man I am enraptured by—
will set the (manner of) oath for you,
o my brother (so) fair of face,
will set, my brother the (manner of) oath for you
o my brother (so) fair of face!
Your right hand be placed in my private parts,
your left shall support my head,
and when you have neared your mouth
to my mouth,
when you hold my lip
in *your mouth*,[28]
(then), thus you must swear me the oath!
Thus only, o you, the one (and only one) to (all) women,
my brother (so) fair of face!

O my budding one, my budding one,
sweet are your charms!
My budding garden of the apple tree,
sweet are your charms!
My fruiting garden of the apple tree,
sweet are your charms!
Dumuzi-Apsû himself,
sweet are your charms!
O my clear pillar, my clear pillar
sweet are your charms!
Pillar of alabaster set in lapis-lazuli
sweet are your charms![29]

A dialogue pertaining to Inanna

23 Note the full form igi . . . durun of the phrase igi . . . . dug_8/dug_8-ru "to look," on which see Falkenstein *MSL* 4, p. 29, note to line 25.

24 The reading presents difficulties. We have tentatively read ğen, taking it in its meaning "agree," "say yes" (Akkadian *magāru*), assuming that an original suffixed -u may have been elided between the two *n*'s in the sequence ğen(u)nin, perhaps deliberately in imitation of the slurred speech of the guest, fuddled after indulging in the highly praised beer. On u "without delay," "quickly" see AS 16, p. 75f.

25 Literally: "speaking words." For inim-di-di: *a-ma-a-tum qa-bu-u* Nabnitu IV 33. See *CAD* A/2, p. 29 *amātu* A lex. sect.

26 Kramer in *ZA* 52 (1957): 85f. reads gaba-su-ub-ub for Chiera's gaba-su-ub-bi. We have, however, kept the latter reading as the grammatically more likely one. As for the meaning, one might think of a greeting by shoulder kiss such as is still practiced in the Near East. We have, however, been unable to find either literary or pictorial support for such a custom in the ancient materials.

27 The restoration of this and the following line is based on tukun = *sur-ru* = *za-mar* in Hg. I 6 (*MSL* 5, p. 43) and on CT XV 25, 27=Pinches *PSBA* 17, pl. 2 iii. 14–15 na-an-ni (var. na)-ku_4-ku_4-dè (var.+-en) um(var. im)-mi-dug_4 a-la-bi mu(var.+un)-gu_8-e:*la er-ru-ub-šú aq-bi-ma la-lu-šú ik-kal-an-ni* "when I have said about it: 'I may not enter it!' desire for it will consume me."

28 The sign, which in Chiera's copy looks like SAĞ is clearly a defective KA, as shown by *ISET* pl. 61 (=119) Ni 4569 iii. 5′ which has the same expression with a clear KA; šu-um-du-um-mu KA-na ba-a[n-dab_5]. The nature of the caress in question is not clear. Perhaps it is simply holding the girl's lips in one's own. To read zú "teeth" rather than ka "mouth" seems to inject a sadistic note not called for.

29 Lines 27–32 raptly contemplate, as noted, the growing sexual excitement of the customer. The imagery employed is fairly stereotypical and is frequently met with in Sumerian and Akkadian erotic poetry. Metaphor for the male member is here the apple tree (lines 28–29) with the pubic hair the garden in which it stands. Another metaphor is that of a pillar of alabaster set in dark blue lapis-lazuli (lines 31–32). The apple tree metaphor occurs also in the text *TCL* XV no. 20 and *UET* VI no. 121 edited by Kramer in *PAPS* 107 (1963): 508, line 4: ^{ğiš}hašhur-àm sa_{12}-mà gurun il-la-mu $kiri_6$-àm a ba-an-dug_4 "did my (darling) apple tree bearing fruit at the top flood the garden." Here "garden" stands for the pudenda of the woman speaker, "flooding" for the emission of semen. Not only the apple tree (hašhur) but any tall tree can be used as metaphor. In the Shulgi(r) text *SET* pl. 24 (–82) Ni 4171 the planting of trees in the garden (among them the apple tree) in rev. 10-21 serves as a metaphor for sexual congress, and going to the garden (*ibid.*,

As will be seen, this dialogue, as it stands, is hardly uplifting, either as poetry or in other ways, so one may well wonder why such a scene of low life would be considered worthy of inclusion in the school curriculum as clearly it was. Here obviously, one can only conjecture, but if one could assume that it came in as part of the total body of Shu-Suen lovesongs and was accepted there because it was written by Il-ummiya as a joke, some of the apparent crudeness would be mitigated. The Ur III kings were regularly travelling through their realm; and waiting faithfully for Shu-Suen to arrive and blessing him at departure is a well-known motif in the lovesongs. Thus the tavern dialogue can have been a joking pretense—not, perhaps, in the best of taste—that the visiting king was but an unknown stranger who had dropped in at Il-ummiya's imagined lowly alehouse and was making a pass at her, successfully of course.

10f. and 20f.) has the same connotation. So does, in that text, going to the field and attending to the various early and later irrigations of it (*ibid.*, obv. 10ff.). Cf. also *SET* pl. 61 (=119) Ni 4569 iii. 11–12 (We read the third sign in line 11 as ĝiš [!?]).

Akkadian examples are the incantation Biggs, *Šaziga*, no. 15, where the swaying of the orchard in the wind before rain symbolizes the involuntary movement of the male organ in erection before emission of semen; the Old Akkadian myth, Gelb *MAD* 5 no. 8 lines 8 and 17–18, where *ki-rè-šum* "into the garden" and *ki-rì-iš* ᵈ*Sú-en* "to the garden of Suen" have reference to the crescent shaped female pubic triangle; and the Nabû and Tašmêtum Text, van Dijk *Sumer* 13 p. 119 rev. 15′–32′, where *kirû* is similarly used.

"AS STRONG AS DEATH"

DENNIS PARDEE

Marvin H. Pope has made the funerary cult in the ancient world one of his main areas of study. The link between the phrase *kmtm ʿz mʾid* of the Ugaritic letter studied here[1] and the phrase *ʿazzāh kammāwet ʾahăbāh* of Song of Songs 8:6, with the latter verse an important element in Pope's presentation of the funerary cult in the ancient world, has been explicitly pointed out over the years[2] and is a specific part of Pope's most recent treatment of the verse from the Song.[3]

During a recent trip to Syria, I not only had the privilege of traveling with Prof. Pope and of learning from him, but was also able to spend three days in the museums of Aleppo and Damascus collating Ugaritic tablets. One of these texts was the letter studied here; a new study based on first-hand examination of the tablet seemed particularly appropriate as a tribute to Prof. Pope. Though the readings of the tablet are quite clear, there has over the years been some disagreement on details[4] and my text will vary in some small points from previous editions (including *KTU*, though here the differences are minimal).[5] I wish to express here my gratitude to Dr. Adnan Joundi, Curator of the National Museum of Damascus, and to Dr. Wahid Khayata, Director of the National Museum of Aleppo, and to their assistants, for permission to study the tablets and for the facilities which were accorded me for study.

TEXT

1) *ṯḥm . ʾiwrḏr*
2) *l . plsy*
3) *rgm*

---

4) *yšlm . lk*

---

5) *l . trǵds*
6) *w . l. klby*
7) *šmʿt . ḫtʾi*
8) *nḫtʾu . ht*
9) *hm . ʾin mm*
10) *nḫtʾu . w . lʾak*
11) *ʿmy . w . yd*
12) *ʾilm . p . kmtm*

Lower edge

13) *ʿz . mʾid*
14) *hm . nṯkp*
15) *mʿnk*

Reverse

16) *w . mnm*
17) *rgm . d . tšmʿ*
18) *ṯmt . w . št*
19) *b . spr . ʿmy*

---

1 RS 4.475 = *CTA* 53 = *UT* 54 =*KTU* 2.10. The French registration number is AO 17316 and the old Aleppo museum number is A2709. The latter is given in *KTU*. The artifacts in the Aleppo museum are being re-catalogued and the new number is M3330. The *editio princeps* was by E. Dhorme, "Deux tablettes de Ras Shamra de la campagne de 1932," *Syria* 14 (1933): 229–37, esp. 235–37. Important early studies were offered by W. F. Albright ("Two Letters from Ugarit (Ras Shamra)," *BASOR* 82 [1941]: 43–9, esp. 46–9; cf. also the brief note in *BASOR* 54 [1934]: 26) and H. L. Ginsberg with B. Maisler ("Semitized Ḫurrians in Syria and Palestine," *JPOS* 14 [1934]: 243–65). For a further note on the find spot, see C. Virolleaud in *La légende phénicienne de Danel* (MRS 1; Paris: Geuthner, 1936): 54–56.

2 Cf. U. Cassuto, *The Goddess Anath* (Jerusalem: Magnes, 1971 [Hebrew original, 1951]): 32; M. Dahood, *Biblica* 39 (1958): 309.

3 *Song of Songs* (Anchor Bible 7C; Garden City, NY: Doubleday, 1977): 668.

4 There are five photographs of this tablet in *CTA*, vol. 2 (pls. 45, 47) which allow most readings to be checked. The sides of the tablet, onto which writing has extended in several cases, are not included, however, in these photographs. Moreover, the basically squared edges of this tablet are slightly rounded (i.e., though the edges are squared off, the surface of the tablet is convex), making photography of those portions of the edges which are visible from a frontal view difficult because of problems of depth of field and light balance.

5 The philological study of this text by M. Dietrich, O. Loretz, and J. Sanmartín ("Der Brief RS 4.475 = CTA 53," *UF* 7 [1975]: 529–30) does not include remarks on minor textual matters. The most recent philological study of this text (but without benefit of *KTU*) is by W. H. Ph. Römer, "Zur Deutung zweier Briefe aus Ugarit in alphabetischer Keilschrift," in *Übersetzung und Deutung. Studien zu dem Alten Testament und seiner Umwelt Alexander Reinhard Hulst gewidmet von Freunden und Kollegen* (Nijkerk: Callenbach, 1977): 135–153.

Vocalized Text[6]

1) *taḥmu ʾewariḏarri*
2) *lê pilsiya*
3) *rugum*

---

4) *yišlam lêka*

---

5) *lê tarǵudassi*
6) *walê kalbiya*
7) *šamaʿtu ḫataʾī*
8) *naḫtaʾū hitta*
9) *him ʾêna mimma*
10) *naḫtaʾū walaʾak*
11) *ʿimmiya wayadu*
12) *ʾilima pā kī môtuma*

Lower Edge

13) *ʿazzu maʾda*
14) *him naṯkapū*

Reverse

15) *maʿnûka*
16) *waminummê*
17) *rigmu dū tišmaʿu*
18) *ṯammata wašīt*
19) *bisipri ʿimmiya*

Translation

1) Message of Ewari-šarri
2) to Pilsiyu,
3) Say:

---

4) May it be well with you!

---

5) Concerning Tarǵudassi
6) and Kalbiyu,
7) I have heard of the blows (with which)
8) they have been stricken. Now
9) if they have not
10) been stricken, then send (word)
11) to me. Also, the "hand of
12) a god" is here, for Death

Lower edge

13) (here) is very strong.
14) If they have been overcome,

Reverse

15) your reply
16) and whatever (else)
17) you may hear
18) there, put
19) in a letter to me.

Philological Notes

Lines 1–3. A. L. Kristensen considers the relationship of correspondents here uncertain because of the unique formulation (*UF* 9 [1977]: 145 and n. 10).

Line 1 *tḥm*. The vocalization *taḥmu* (i.e., with case vowel included) is preferred over Römer's *taḥam* (*Hulst* [1977] 135, 137). The retention of the case vowel in the construct state seems to me to have been proven definitively by Gary A. Tuttle: "Case Vowels on Masculine Singular Nouns in Construct in Ugaritic," in *Biblical and Near Eastern Studies: Essays in Honor of William Sanford LaSor* (ed. Gary A. Tuttle; Grand Rapids: Eerdmans, 1978): 253–68.

Line 1 *ʾiwrḏr*. *KTU* gives *iw*rḏ*r*, but the asterisks (indicating partially effaced signs in *KTU*) are unnecessary as the signs are perfectly clear on the tablet (though not clear in the published photographs). The *ḏ* and the *r* are written on the right edge of the tablet and thus are not visible in the published photographs though they were drawn correctly in the *editio princeps* (Dhorme, *Syria* 14 [1933] pl. 25 accompanying pp. 235–37; reproduced in *CTA*, vol. 2, fig. 105).

Line 2 *l*. Though slightly damaged, the first letter of line 2 is certainly *l* and not *d* (as read by *KTU*).

plsy. Vocalization not certain; see Gröndahl, *PTU*, pp. 172–173; H. B. Huffmon, *Amorite Personal Names in the Mari Texts* (Baltimore: Johns Hopkins, 1965) 255.

Line 4 *yšlm lk*. For the greeting formula *yšlm l*, see Pardee, *BO* 34 (1977) 4–5, and for the difficulties entailed in vocalizing the verb form, see Römer, *Hulst* (1977) 137–38. The vocalization *lê* for the preposition, on the other hand, appears to me to be beyond doubt (against Römer's *le*, *ibid.*, p. 136). The writing of the particle in the polygot text *Ugaritica* V_N 130 III 5′ as *le-e* appears to indicate that we are not dealing with the simple preposition *l*(*a*) well known from the other West Semitic languages, but with a monosyllabic form of the preposition *ʾilay* → *ʾilê* (cf. Hebrew *ʾĕlê*) → *lê* (see Pardee, *UF* 8 [1976]: 288 and n. 2).

Lines 5–7. For the syntax of *l . . . l . . . šmʿt* as translated here, see E. Lipiński, *Syria* 50 (1973): 47; Pardee, *UF* 7 (1975): 371; *idem*, *UF* 8 (1976): 270; Dietrich, Loretz,

6 Though Prof. Pope prefers not to vocalize ("Notes on the Rephaim Texts from Ugarit," in *Essays on the Ancient Near East in Memory of Jacob Finkelstein* [Connecticut Academy of Arts and Sciences: Memoires 19, 1977]: 163–82, see especially p. 182, n. 90), I persist in finding vocalization a useful concise form of grammatical statement (cf. my remarks in *BO* 34 [1977]: 3; *JANES* 10 [1978]: 75, n.5). See Römer's Vocalization in *Hulst* (1977): 146. This is the only complete vocalization of which I am aware and several of my remarks below will be addressed to points of agreement or disagreement with Römer on matters of grammar and interpretation which are made explicit in the vocalized text.

and Sanmartín, *UF* 7 (1975): 529–30.

Line 5 *trǵds*. According to Gröndahl (*PTU*, p. 297), this personal name is derived from the place name *Tar-ḫu-da-aš-ši* (*PRU IV*, p. 169 = RS 17.158:2, *et passim*; *ibid*., p. 171 = RS 17.42:1, *et passim*).

Line 6 *klby* is vocalized following Ugaritic syllabic cuneiform *kál-bi/be-ya* (*PTU*, pp. 150, 339; cf. P. R. Berger, *WO* 5 [1969–1970[: 273) rather than Hebrew *k*^{e}*lûbāy* (1 Chron. 2:9).

Line 7 *ḫataʾī* is taken as a noun, accusative (oblique) plural, construct state. It was perceived early on (cf. Ginsberg and Maisler, *JPOS* 14 [1934]: 245–46; Albright, *BASOR* 82 [1941]: 47 and n. 27) that the form in question is probably not an infinitive absolute, because of the *ʾi*. Since the early years of Ugaritic studies it has become clear that in the "infinitive absolute" construction, the infinitive is vocalized as a nominative or adverbial (see E. Hammershaimb, "On the So-Called *Infinitivus Absolutus* in Hebrew," in *Hebrew and Semitic Studies Presented to Godfrey Rolles Driver* [D. W. Thomas, W. D. McHardy, eds.: Oxford: Clarendon, 1963]: 85–94). Unless *ḫtʾi* is an anomalous "infinitive absolute" form (such as the *qutāli* form of the infinitive absolute isolated by W. L. Moran in the el-Amarna texts: *JCS* 4 [1950]: 169–72), the analysis as a common noun remains the most plausible explanation (see Römer, *Hulst* [1977]: 149–50).

Line 7 *ht*. See Aartun, AOAT 21/1 (1974): 67, 68, 71.

Lines 8–9. Dietrich, Loretz, and Sanmartín translate lines 8–11 as follows: "Nun, wenn nichts ist, (oder) sie niedergeschlagen wurden, so sende zu mir" (*UF* 7 [1975]: 529). The "oder" appears to me to be taking too much for granted and I prefer to see *ʾin mm* as an emphatic negative, with both elements modifying *nḫtʾu* (literally: " . . . if they have in no way at all been smitten . . . "; cf. Römer, *Hulst* [1977]: 150).

Line 9 *ʾin*. Comparing with Hebrew *ʾayin/ʾên*, this form must be vocalized *ʾên-* (< *ʾayn-*) rather than *ʾin* (Römer, *Hulst* [1977]: 146).

Line 10 *ľak*. The *ʾa* is partially visible on the photographs; the *k* is completely on the right edge (but well preserved).

Lines 11–12 *yd ʾilm*. There is very little doubt that *yd ʾilm* denotes some form of catastrophic illness, as the following texts indicate:

EA 35:13–14 *šum-ma i-na KUR-ia ŠU-ti* [d]*MAŠ-MAŠ EN-li-ia gab-ba LU.MEŠ ša KUR-ia i-du-uk* "I swear that pestilence, the disease of my lord Nergal, was in the land, and has killed all the people of my land" (A. L. Oppenheim *Letters from Mesopotamia* [Chicago: University of Chicago, 1967]: 120).

EA 35:37–39 *aš-šum ŠU-ti* [d]*MAŠ.MAŠ i-ba-aš-ši i-na KUR-ia ù i-na É-ia DAM-ia TUR i-ba-aš-ši ša-a mi-it* " . . . (it was) because the 'hand' of Nergal (i.e., pestilence) was in my country; even in my family, there was a child of my wife's who died" (Oppenheim, ibid., p. 123).

ARM X 87:10–23 [*i-na*]*-an-na a-na Sa-ga-ra-tim*[KI] (*11*) [*at-ta-a*]*l-kam-ma* (*12*) [*i*]*š-*[*t*]*u* u_4*-mi-im* (*13*) [*ša a*]*t-ta-al-kam (14)* [*ma*]*-ar-ṣa-ku (15)* [*ù*] *1-šu 2-šu da-*[*n*]*a*[!]*-ku*[?] *(16)* [*ù*] *qa-at Ištar-ra-da-na-ma (17) ù be-lí i-de* (*18*) *ki-ma qa-at Ištar-ra-da-na* (*19*) *e-li-a da-an-na-at* (*20*) *i-na-na šum-ma li-ib-bi* (*21*) *be-lí-ia wa-ar-ka-at* (*22*) *mu-ur-ṣí-im an-ni-im* (*23*) *li-ip-ru-us* "Maintenant, pour Sagarātum [je suis par]tie et, [de]puis le jour [où je] suis partie, je suis [ma]lade, (15) [et] 1 fois, 2 fois, j'ai été très atteinte (?). C'est bien la 'main' d'Ištar-radana. Or, mon seigneur sait que la 'main' d'Istar-radana est plus forte que moi![7] (20) Maintenant, s'il plaît à mon seigneur, qu'il enquête sur ce mal!"

Ludlul Bēl Nēmeqi III 1 *kab-ta-at qāt-šu ul a-liʾ-i na-šá-ša* "His hand was heavy upon me, I could not bear it" (W. G. Lambert, *Babylonian Wisdom Literature* [Oxford: Clarendon, 1960]: 48).[8]

Exod. 9:3 *hinnēh yad-YHWH hôyāh b*^{e}*miqn*^{e}*kā ʾăšer baśśādeh bassûsîm baḥămōrîm bagg*^{e}*mallîm babbāqār ûbaṣṣōʾn deber kābēd m*^{e}*ʾōd* 'The "hand" of YHWH will be among your cattle out in the fields, among your horses, your donkeys, your camels, your cattle, and your flocks—a severe pestilence.'[9]

These various texts from several milieux of the ancient Near East make it quite clear that the word 'hand,' when associated with a deity, denoted illness, either individual (*ARM* 10:87) or of plague proportions (Exod. 9:3). Because of the severely restricted context of the Ugaritic letter we are studying, it is impossible to say whether the reference there is to illness limited to a few persons or whether it is to a more general epidemic. If the "blows" with which *trǵds* and *klby* have been struck (lines 7–8) refer to blows from the hand of the god(s), then one would

7 It appears to me that the alternative translation given in a note to line 19 in *ARMT* (with a reference to the following text cited here, Ludlul Bēl Nēmeqi III 1) is to be preferred: "est lourde sur moi."

8 Lambert notes the ancient commentary *kab-tu dan-nu* ('heavy [here means] strong'). We might note here that D. Marcus has compared the Ugaritic *yd ʾilm* to the Akkadian phrase *lipit ili* 'the touch of a / the god,' also used to denote disease (*Biblica* 55 [1974]: 406).

9 Perhaps the best passage from the Bible for comparison with Exod. 9:3 is 1 Sam. 5:6–11 where the phrases *yd-YHWH* and *yd hʾlhym*, modified by *kbd* 'heavy, severe,' *qšh* 'hard, harsh,' and *mhwmh* 'panic, destruction,' are used to describe the plague which accompanied the ark into Philistine territory. For a previous treatment of Exod. 9:3 in the light of the comparative material from the Akkadian literature, and for the light this throws on the use of the phrase 'the hand of YHWH' in the prophetic literature, see J. J. M. Roberts, "The Hand of YHWH," *VT* 21 (1971): 244–51.

be tempted to adopt the second hypothesis—ʾ*iwrḏr* is writing from one place besieged by disease to learn news of others in another place in the same condition.

A further point in need of elucidation is that of the form and meaning of ʾ*ilm*. Several semantic / syntactic analyses are possible:

yadu ʾ*ilima* 'the hand of a god / the hand of the god' (common noun singular, with specific or non-specific referent, 'enclitic' *m*)
yadu ʾ*ilīma* 'the hand of (the) gods' (common noun, plural)
yadu ʾ*ilima* 'the hand of Il' (proper noun, 'enclitic' *m*)

The last analysis is perhaps the least likely, since Il is not known as a god of pestilence. The plural form seems unlikely because of the many forms cited above which refer to a single deity (*contra* Römer, *Hulst* [1977]: 150). Among those forms cited, however, the reference can be either definite ('hand of X-deity'; in the case at hand 'the hand of *the* god' could refer to Rashap[10]) or indefinite (*qāt/lipit ili*, with *ili* used generically). Now, there is little doubt that in *formulation* the Ugaritic phrase follows the latter type, i.e., it is *yd* ʾ*ilm*, rather than *yd DN*. It appears safest, then, to translate literally, 'the hand of a god,' less literally 'a divine hand,' or idiomatically 'disease / plague / pestilence.' By this translation we are recognizing that *yd* ʾ*ilm* is a frozen phrase which refers to calamitous disease and that it exists alongside the specific formulation 'hand of DN,' the latter being used to express the intervention of a specific deity. Thus I agree with one aspect of Pope's interpretation of these lines (*mtm* = "Mot"—*Song of Songs* [1977]: 668[11]) while disagreeing with another (*yd* ʾ*ilm* = 'hand of an [unnamed] god' rather than "hand of the gods," though we agree that the reference is to disease).

One final point on *yd* ʾ*ilm*: As one would expect in Northwest Semitic, *yd* takes feminine modifiers in all the Hebrew texts cited above. Moreover, *yd* is regularly feminine in Ugaritic (the only exception of which I am aware is in *UT* 52 = *CTA* 23:33–35, where a feminine form, *t*ʾ*irkm*, is paralleled by an unmarked form of the same verb, ʾ*ark*, probably an infinitive). It is this consideration which renders unlikely the translation "the hand of the gods . . . is here, like Death, exceeding strong" (Pope, *ibid.*; cf. also, e.g., Dhorme, *Syria* 14 [1933]: 235; Dahood, *Biblica* 39 [1958]: 309; *idem, Psalms I* [Anchor Bible 16; 1965]: 194; *idem, Biblica* 48 [1967]: 436). It was undoubtedly the feminine gender of *yd* which has led many scholars over the years to a syntactic analysis comparable to the one adopted here (e.g., Albright, *BASOR* 54 [1934]: 26; *idem, BASOR* 82 [1941]: 47; Cassuto, *Anath* [1971]: 32; Römer, *Hulst* [1977]: 150). S. Ahl's appeal to Arabic to explain a masculine modifier (ʿ*z*) for a feminine noun (*yd*) can hardly stand without extensive defense (*Epistolary Texts from Ugarit* [dissertation Brandeis; Ann Arbor: University Microfilms, 1973]: 406).

Line 12 *kmtm*. The final *m* is written on the edge of the tablet. The analysis of *k* as a conjunction rather than as a preposition is tied directly to the relationship of *yd* and ʿ*z* (see preceding note).

Line 13 *m*ʾ*id*. See Marcus, *Biblica* 55 (1974): 404–07; Rainey, *IEJ* 19 (1969): 108; cf. also Loretz, *UF* 6 (1974): 481–84, primarily dealing with Hebrew. I have vocalized the form as an 'adverbial accusative.'

Line 13 *nṯkp*. This form was much debated in the early years of the discussion of this text, with much emphasis on a link with Akkadian *sakāpu* 'repel' (Dhorme, *Syria* 14 [1933]: 237; Albright, *BASOR* 82 [1941]: 48, n. 32; Aistleitner, *WUS* § 2868). Albright also cited Jewish Aramaic *tkp* 'join,' while Ginsberg and Maisler (*JPOS* 14 [1934]: 250) compared Arabic *ṯqf* 'overcome.' As there is at least one difficulty with each of these comparisons (Akk. *sakāpu* rather than *šakāpu*; Aram. *tkp* has a Hebrew counterpart *tkp* rather than *škp*, Arab. is *ṯqf* rather than *ṯkf*[12]), my translation is based on contextual rather than etymological considerations.

Lines 15–16 syntax. It is uncertain whether the *w* in line 16 links two verbs ("If your reply is *nṯkp*, then . . . ") or two noun phrases (*m*ʿ*nk wmnm rgm*); or, to put it another way, whether the protasis marked by *hm* ends with *nṯkp* (as I have taken it) or with *m*ʿ*nk* ("If your reply is *nṯkp*, then . . . "). For an interpretation based on the latter

10 On the destructive aspect of Rashap's nature, see M. Pope and W. Röllig, "Syrien: Die Mythologie der Ugariter und Phönizier," in *Götter und Mythen im vorderen Orient* (Wörterbuch der Mythologie, vol. 1; H. W. Haussig, ed.; Klett: Stuttgart, 1965): 217–312, see especially pp. 305–06; A. Caquot and M. Sznycer, *Textes ougaritiques, Tome 1 Mythes et Légendes* (Littératures anciennes du Proche-Orient 7; Paris: Cerf, 1974): 51–52 (who doubt the uniquely destructive character of Rashap); and W. J. Fulco, *The Canaanite God Rešep* (American Oriental Series, Essays 8; New Haven, CT: American Oriental Society, 1976) see especially the summary pp. 69–71.

11 Thus the final *m* in *mtm* is 'enclitic' on a singular noun as it is in my analysis of ʾ*ilm*. See Aartun, AOAT 21/1 (1974): 54, for this analysis of *mtm* (he takes ʾ*ilm*, however, as plural: AOAT 21/2 [1978]: 28). This analysis of *mtm* avoids recourse to Akkadian etymologies (Römer, *Hulst* [1977]: 150) by seeing the reference as regarding the well-known West Semitic deity *mt*. It appears to me quite possible that *yd* ʾ*ilm* originally referred to a specific god of pestilence (euphemistically?) and that the comparison in the text under discussion with the action of Mot reveals a loss of specificity in the perception of the phrase, i.e., that it had come to be perceived idiomatically as a phrase for pestilence without specificity as to the deity in question.

12 Each of the anomalies has a potential explanation (cf. Albright on the Akkadian: *BASOR* 82 [1941]: 48, n. 32), but so many anomalies render one cautious.

analysis, see Römer, *Hulst* (1977): 146. Since *mʿn* 'reply' is not attested elsewhere in letters, the formulaic nature that one would expect it to have in letters is as yet unclear. (The usual formula of reply, *rgm ṯṯb*, is quite different syntactically, e.g., *mnm šlm (w)rgm ṯṯb l* "return word to (someone) of how things are" [1013:11; 2009 I 9; 2115 II 11, etc.])

Line 17 *tšmʿ*. The *ʿayin* is written on the edge of the tablet.

Line 18 *št*. For *št* as an imperative rather than a *waw*-consecutive (Gordon, *UT* §9.50; Dahood in *The Claremont Ras Shamra Tablets* [ed. L. R. Fisher; AnOr 48; Rome: Pontifical Biblical Institute, 1971]: 52), see Rainey, *UF* 3 (1971): 160–61; *idem*, *IOS* 3 (1973): 38. For caution with respect to the specific translation 'write' for *št*, see Pardee, *UF* 8 (1976): 271.

Line 19 *ʿmy*. Only the beginning of the *y* is visible on the photograph in *CTA* (vol. 2, pl. 45), though it is complete on the tablet.

Horizontal line after line 19. Though the practice is not universal, the use of a horizontal line to mark the end of a letter is very frequent and should be indicated in modern editions, for, if present on the tablet, it may indicate to the student without a photograph at hand that the letter is complete as preserved.

General Interpretation

The relationship of the correspondents in this letter is unsure. Because of the brevity of the formulae, however, I would suggest that the letter is probably not from an inferior to a superior.[13] The purpose of the letter is to inquire about the situation of two further persons, named *trǵds* and *klby*, who have been "stricken," perhaps by the "hand of a god," i.e., by disease. The writer says specifically that the "hand of a god" is in his locality, that death is very strong. He closes with a request for a reply (*mʿn*) which is more specific than the usual stereotyped formula, apparently further underscoring the gravity of the situation.

With reference to Pope's use of this text for the elucidation of the funerary cult in the ancient world, it remains to be said that the link with Song of Songs 8:6 is almost uniquely lexical, as the two texts are different in genre, originate in different situations, and have entirely different points of reference (love vs. pestilence) in different syntactic constructions. Thus Pope's modest use of the comparison between the two texts[14] is entirely appropriate.

13 Cf. my remarks on Hebrew letter formulae in *JBL* 97 (1978): 332–333 (in collaboration with P.–E. Dion and J. D. Whitehead).

14 *Song of Songs* (1977): 668.

DEATH AND DEVOTION: THE COMPOSITION AND THEME OF *AQHT**

SIMON B. PARKER

The history of the interpretation of *Aqht*, like that of most of the Ugaritic poetic texts, is largely the history of the study of Ugaritic language and religion. Philological studies have generally treated the texts atomistically, taking them a line, or at most a few dozen lines at a time. Religious studies have treated them in terms of larger issues and themes—sacral kingship, the dying and rising god, astronomical phenomena—relating the alleged subject matter of the poem to comparable subjects treated elsewhere in the ancient world.[1]

There has not yet been any adequate study of the whole poem as literature, that is, of the form and character in which it presents itself to us. The problem with any treatment of the whole is of course that we do not have the whole.[2] First, there are sizable gaps in that portion of the story which the three tablets cover: in each of the first and second tablets the two middle columns are completely missing. Second, as appears from an analysis of the narrative, the story is truncated—the last column of the third tablet records only the beginning of a narrative section which must have been continued on a subsequent tablet.

Given these lacunae, a literary analysis of *Aqht* can best proceed as follows. First, recognizing that it is largely composed of traditional forms and motifs, we must identify the stereotypes at each level—from the lowest level of formulaic lines and pairs of parallel words or phrases—to the highest level of complete episodes or narratives. For the purposes of the present paper I shall give some indication of the smaller stereotypes out of which the larger are constructed—the bricks and mortar, as it were, of the edifice—but will concentrate on the larger stereotypes—the rooms of the building. These can be identified by internal structural analysis and by comparison with similar structures elsewhere. When the text is complete and relatively well understood, comparison not only allows identification of the stereotype but may also illumine common features that had previously been obscure in one text or the other, and bring into relief the individual characteristics and aims of each example.[3] Where the text is incomplete or damaged, identification of the stereotype allows the general outlines of only partially preserved structures to be provisionally completed.

Finally it will be possible to look for a consistent emphasis running through the particular characteristics of all the episodes in which the evidence is sufficient to permit the isolation of distinctive features. Hypothetically any consistent thrust uniting those peculiarities may be treated as the theme of the whole—pending wider attestation and investigation of the identified stereotypes, recognition of further stereotypes in the preserved part of the poem, and discovery of further material belonging to the same poem.

Aqht, as we know it, consists of one six-column tablet followed by two four-column tablets. The general structure of the work is as follows. It consists of five main

* Scholars now refer to the Ugaritic texts variously by their numbering in *UT, CTA* or *KTU*. To refer to all three for every text reference would make for clumsy reading. I have limited myself to *CTA*, which contains a table giving the corresponding text numbers in *UT* (*CTA*, pp. XIX-XXX), and to whose numbers *KTU* provides an index giving the corresponding *KTU* numbers (*KTU*, pp. 499-500).

1 For a summary of older interpretations see A. Caquot and M. Sznycer, *Textes ougaritiques* (Paris: Editions du Cerf, 1974): I, 401-15. A major new interpretation since 1974 is that of P. Xella, "Una 'rilettura' del poem di Aqhat," in *Problemi del mito nel Vicino Oriente Antico* (Suppl. 7 of *Annali dell'Istituto Orientale di Napoli* [1976]: 61-91). Xella sees the poem as an old hunting myth, modified by an agrarian culture, and finally serving to represent the ideology of the Ugaritic monarchy. Other recent studies treat only portions of the poem, and will be referred to in the final discussion of the theme of *Aqht*. I have refrained from citing the abundant literature on grammatical and lexical matters except where it impinges directly and significantly on the definition of the literary units in the poem.

2 Hence "no satisfactory comprehensive interpretation is possible" according to J. C. L. Gibson, *Canaanite Myths and Legends* (Edinburgh: Clark, 1978): 27. K. H. Bernhard notes that the difficulty in interpreting *Aqht* arises not only from the damaged state of the text, but also from the difficulty in establishing its genre and setting: "Anmerkungen zum 'Sitz im Leben' des *Aqht*-Textes von Ras-Schamra (Ugarit)," in *Proceedings of the 25th International Congress of Orientalists* (Moscow: 1962): I, 328-29.

3 Cf. D. Irvin, *Mytharion. The Comparison of Tales from the Old Testament and the Ancient Near East* (AOAT 32; Kevelaer: Butzon und Bercker, and Neukirchen-Vluyn: Neukirchener Verlag, 1978): xv. I differ from Irvin in focusing on the *structure* of discrete units of narrative, structure being the least variable aspect of a story (as compared with setting and theme, which are unstable and so more readily altered). See J. Vansina, *Oral Tradition. A Study in Historical Methodology* (Chicago: Aldine, 1965): 57-65.

sections which I shall call A, B, C, D and E. The first concerns the birth of Aqhat (*CTA* 17.1-2). It opens with the formulaic bicolon introducing Aqhat, and concludes soon after the text breaks off in column 2. The narrative is initiated by Danel undertaking an incubation rite, the reason for which is given in Baal's following intercession with El: Danel needs a son. Section A concludes with the birth of Aqhat, which is imminent in the last preserved lines of column 2, in which Danel is counting the months of his wife's pregnancy.

What follows immediately after Aquat's birth we do not know, since the next two columns are completely missing. It is not immediately apparent whether col. 5, which describes Kothar's delivery of the bow to Danel, belongs with the missing preceding material or with what follows, though I shall argue that the balance of probability lies with the former suggestion. There is no observable tension or necessity for the story to continue after Danel passes the bow to Aqhat at the end of col. 5. Therefore I provisionally refer to cols. 3-5 as section B.

Certainly there is a discrete narrative unit in *CTA* 17.6-19.1.19. Section C begins when Anat catches sight of Aqhat with his bow, and is stirred with envy. This new turn in the plot is not resolved until 19.1.19 when Anat has accomplished the death of Aqhat and the loss of the bow. The absence of a further two columns in the middle of section C is less significant precisely because they come in the middle of a narrative with a well preserved beginning (of approximately one and a half columns) and end (of a little more than one column) and with clear cognate structures elsewhere in Ancient Near Eastern literature.

The next section (D) portrays Danel's ritual acts and words as he responds to the new conditions. Its beginning is marked by the group of three bicola reintroducing Danel at his traditional judicial duties (19.1.19-25). The first part of this section is concerned with the drought that has afflicted the land (19.1.34-2.74). In a badly damaged passage (19.2.75-104) two messengers arrive and announce to Danel that Aqhat has been killed. Danel now turns his attention from the symptoms to the cause of the drought, so that his following acts and words deal directly with the murder (19.2.105-4.184).

The final section (E) continues the response to the news of the murder, but shifts from ritualistic acts and pronouncements to the mission of vengeance undertaken by Aqhat's sister, who now for the first time moves to the center of the action. The extent of this section and of any further sections is unknown, but the poem presumably covered at least another four-column tablet.

Further justification for this division will appear in the course of the following discussion of the structure and composition of each section, and comparison of other examples of the same genre. Whenever comparison with other examples of the same structure allows, I shall attempt to identify the peculiar thrust of the form it takes in *Aqht*. The conclusion will offer some tentative remarks about the poem as a whole. Where the text is lacunose or obscure I shall raise questions—and perhaps leave the reader with more questions than answers. But that seems appropriate in a tribute to a scholar who, rather than claiming to settle all questions, has sought to extend their boundaries and open up new fields for a younger generation to develop. I hope that this focus on the larger literary units of *Aqht* will provide a fresh perspective both for those working primarily in the fields of lexicography and grammar and for those working on the history of ancient Syrian society or religion.

A. The Birth of Aqhat

"Your prayer has been heard: your wife . . . will bear you a son"

Luke 1:13.

The first lines introduce the hero engaged in an incubation rite. In response Baal intercedes with El, asking him to bless Danel and grant him a son to perform the traditional filial duties. El accedes and blesses Danel as requested. Danel is told of El's blessing, is overjoyed at the news, and returns home. The Katharat also arrive at his home and he gives them food and drink. After their departure he goes to bed with his wife, who conceives. As the months of her pregnancy pass, so do the last traces of text on this column.

This may be described more formally. The poem opens with the stereotyped full introduction of the hero (17.1.1-3, cf. 2.27-29; 5.4-5; 13-15; 33-35; 19.1.19-21). The brief description of the incubation rite (3-6) is extended through the framework of a seven-day sequence (6-16). The seventh day marks the transition to Baal's intercessory speech (16-17: *mk. bšbᶜ. ymm/[w]yqrb. bᶜl. bḥnth.* "Then on the seventh day/Baal drew near in his compassion"). Baal's speech (17-34) consists of an account of Danel's plight (17-23), which includes a reprise of the first bicolon describing his incubation (22-23); an appeal for blessing (24-26)—including the general appeal for blessing (24-25; cf. 15.2.14-16) and the specific wish for the supplicant to have a son (26-27; cf. 43-44); and a list of the duties performed by a son (27-34).[4] The introduction to El's blessing (35-37; cf. 15.2.16-20) is followed by El's speech (37ff.), consisting of a general blessing (37-39; cf. 19.4.198-201), specific instructions for Danel (39-42), announcement that he will have a son (43-44; cf. 26-27), and the list of filial duties (45ff.).

The letters and words of the first lines preserved in the second column are clearly remains of the list of filial duties, with the former third person singular suffixes now

4 O. Eissfeldt, "Sohnespflicten im Alten Orient," *Syria* 43 (1966): 39-47 = Eissfeldt, *Kleine Schriften* (ed. R. Sellheim and F. Maass; Tübingen: Mohr, 1968): IV, 264-70; and K. Koch, "Die Sohnesverheissung an den ugaritischen Daniel," *ZA* N.F. 24 (1967): 211-21.

replaced by the second person singular (1-8). Someone is announcing El's blessing to Danel. The missing lines must have contained an account of Baal's coming from El back to Danel, or possibly of the sending of some other messenger with the good news.[5] The announcement may have begun with a version of the earlier part of El's speech, including the specific instructions (17.1.39-42), and possibly the announcement that Danel will have a son (43-44; cf. 26-27) or that a son would be born to him like his kin, as in Danel's following speech (14-15; cf. 17.1.19-20, 21-22). Danel responds to the announcement in language commonly used in describing the reaction to good news (8-11; cf. 4.4.28-30; 6.3.14-16).[6] Lines 11-12 introduce Danel's speech (12-23), consisting of a statement of his relief (12-14), the reason for this—the birth of a son like his kin (14-15; cf. 17.1.19-20, 21-22), and the duties of such a son—now with first person singular suffixes (16-23).

Up to this point there is a symmetry in the narrative: the movement is from Danel through Baal to El and from El back through Baal (?) to Danel. Danel's need leads to El's blessing, and the blessing leads back to the relief of Danel's need. The section is further bound together by the recurrence in each of the speeches of the list of filial duties.

The divine word already assures Danel that his need has been met. He now returns home (26-27; cf. 19.4.170-171). The cult of the Katharat follows, framed by reference to their arrival (26-27) and departure (39-40). After their arrival the full introduction of Danel recurs (27-29) and the brief notice of the cult (29-31) is extended through a seven-day sequence (32-39), the seventh day introducing the departure of the Katharat (39-40). The text breaks off with words such as *ʿrš* "bed," *yrḫ* "month," and numerals—presumably an account of the execution and fulfillment of El's specific instructions and predictions in 17.1.39-42.

Thus the section has a central core consisting of an appeal to the gods and the divine answer, but also a more extended form in which the hero acts upon the divine answer, following the cultic and natural procedures necessary for the fulfillment of the blessing. That final fulfillment would have come with the birth of the desired son around the end of column 2. Thus the tension set up by the opening incubation scene expressing Danel's need is relaxed in a series of stages: first, by Baal's intercession on his behalf, then by El's blessing, then by the announcement to Danel, by the favorable visit of the Katharat and Danel's proper treatment of them, and finally by the conception and birth of Aqhat.

The course of this section of the poem is a familiar one in ancient Near Eastern literature. Its main structural elements are as follows: 1) the introduction of the hero as childless; 2) the appeal to the god; 3) the god's response; and 4) its natural outworking: conception and birth. The essence of the genre is distilled at the beginning of the Egyptian tale of *The Doomed Prince*.[7] This version is short enough to quote in its entirety:

> It is said, there once was a king to whom no son had been born. [After a time his majesty] begged a son for himself from the gods of his domain, and they decreed that one should be born to him. That night he slept with his wife and she[became] pregnant. When she had completed the months of childbearing, a son was born.[8]

The preserved part of the Hurrian tale of *Appu* uses the same genre.[9] 1) Appu is portrayed as childless (col. I:16-37). 2) He presents a white lamb to the Sun-god (I:38-40), 3) who turns himself into a youth, approaches Appu, and asks him what is the matter (I:41-45). 2) Appu tells him (II:1-4), and 3) the Sun-god says: "Sleep with your wife and the gods will give you a son" (II:4-9), 4) at which Appu goes home (II:10) and (after a damaged passage concerning the Storm-god's reception of the Sun-god when he returns) presumably slept with his wife (in what is now a gap in the text), who became pregnant. Nine months pass and a son is born.

Here are the same four essential structural elements. But *Appu* also shares with *Aqht* certain details, beyond even those given in the above summary: the hero's childlessness is what distinguishes him from his community, and it is a ritual act that elicits the divine response. It is noteworthy that the god comes directly to the supplicant and grants his request, and only later consults the Storm-god (?).[10] In another version of *Aqht* it is likely that Baal first asked Danel what he wanted (as El does in *Krt*) and only then took the message to El—17.1.17 is suspiciously elliptical.

The same genre appears in the first chapter of 1 Samuel. 1) Hannah is introduced as barren. 2) In the

5 The communication does not take place in a dream, as in *Krt*: there is no reference to Danel's falling asleep or waking up. Cf. A. Caquot, "Les songes et leur interprétation selon Canaan et Israel," in *Les songes et leur interprétation*, *Sources orientales* (Paris: Editions du Seuil, 1959): II, 99-124, esp. 105 and 123, n. 1.

6 *šmḫ* DN is more common: 4.2.20; 4.5.97-98; 4.6.35-36; 5.2.20. Cf. especially 10.3.38: *yšmḫ. aliyn. bʿl* "Aliyan Baal rejoiced" after hearing the announcement of the birth of his bovine offspring.

7 Irvin, *Mytharion*, 86.

8 *Ancient Egyptian Literature. A Book of Readings* (trans. M. Lichtheim; Berkeley and Los Angeles: Univ. of California, 1976): II, 200. Cf. the translation of E. F. Wente in *The Literature of Ancient Egypt. An Anthology of Stories, Instructions and Poetry* (ed. W. K. Simpson, 2nd ed.; New Haven: Yale, 1973): 85-86.

9 J. Friedrich, "Churritische Märchen und Sagen in hethitischer Sprache," *ZA* 49 (1950): 213-55, esp. 214-25.

10 Is the purpose of this encounter in fact to recount the Sun-god's presentation of Appu's request to the Storm-god for his approval, as Baal presents Danel's request to El for approval?

sanctuary at Shiloh she expresses her need through a standard cultic form, in this case a vow (1:11). 3) The priest of Shiloh blesses her (1:17), and Yahweh "remembers" her when she goes to bed with her husband (1:19). 4) She conceives and bears a son (1:20).

Another example is found in the same culture as *Aqht*, somewhat modified as it is absorbed into a larger and more complex form. In the first section of *Krt* we see 1) Keret's plight (childlessness). 2) He cries himself to sleep, which 3) prompts El to appear to him in a dream. El asks him what he wants, and when 2) Keret tells him, 3) responds with instructions on how to get a wife. 4) Keret executes the instructions, and immediately after the marriage children are born.

All four stories, from four different literatures, share with *Aqhat* the same generic features: the hero's sonlessness, his appeal to the god(s), the god's/s' response, and its natural outworking: conception and birth. Other briefer references to the same sequence of events in Gen 25:21 and 30:22-23 suggest that the genre represents a standard interpretation of a birth to a childless couple following an appeal to the deity.[11] It is possible that stories developed around this interpretation of experience had an independent existence in the communities of ancient East Mediterranean societies. Their purpose would have been to give hope to the childless by showing that the gods have granted offspring to those who have turned to them.

In all the above cases, however, the story is found at the beginning of a much larger and more complex narrative. In the tale of *The Doomed Prince* it merely introduces the hero whose real story begins with the subsequent pronouncement of his fate by the Hathors. In 1 Samuel it also introduces the hero, and through the vow explains how Samuel came to be living in the temple from his childhood. In both these cases, as in *Aqht*, it essentially serves to introduce the hero as one whose birth was already an extraordinary event, the result of divine favor. In *Krt* it has been integrated with other genres—the expedition for a wife, the account of a military campaign—and the resulting complex genre serves not so much to introduce the hero (Keret himself is the hero of the story), as to show how El reversed the king's wretched state through Keret's careful execution of El's detailed instructions. Keret's obedience results in his producing a large number of children. Only later and gradually are some of these individually distinguished. We can say nothing about the function of the genre in the larger story of Appu, as so little of the sequence is preserved.

What distinguishes *Aqht* from these other cases is (1) the carefully patterned cycle of speeches, including the list of filial duties repeated four times as a refrain; and (2) the repetitive accounts of ritual acts: incubation and the cult of the Katharat.

B. The Bow of Aqhat

"Pandaros, with the bow that was the actual gift of Apollo."

Iliad II 827 (Lattimore)

Between the end of the text preserved in column 2 and the beginning of that preserved in column 5 there is a gap of some 150 lines: 10 lines at the end of column 2, two complete columns and then about 12 lines at the beginning of column 5. Since the story of Aqhat's birth must conclude in the first lines of this lacuna, some new episode must have been introduced near the beginning of column 3. Given the schematic nature of this literature, there would not have been a lengthy account of how Aqhat grew up. The story may have continued with some section of which we can see no trace in the surviving text, but in view of the centrality of the death of Aqhat in everything that follows, and the role of the bow in precipitating his death, it seems more likely that there was a lengthy account of the origins of the bow, which is then concluded in column 5 with its delivery to Danel.

The text resumes in column 5 with the conclusion of a speech, evidently by Kothar, in which he says: "I will bring the bow there" (17.5.2-3; cf. the fulfillment of his announced intention in lines 12-13: "he brings the bow here"). Perhaps, as many have supposed, the bow had been requested by Danel, who may have gone, or sent his son—perhaps directed by Kothar—in search of the materials listed by Aqhat in 17.6.20-23. These would then have been presented to Kothar, whose construction of the bow may have been described. Be that as it may, the fifth column begins with Kothar's announcement of his intention to deliver the bow.

The bulk of column 5 is a discrete episode concerning Kothar's visit to Danel. It is introduced immediately after the end of Kothar's speech by what is usually the climactic line of a seven day sequence.[12] The text proceeds by means of a number of stereotyped lines: the full introduction of the hero (4-5), the description of his judicial activity on the threshing floor at the city gate (6-8; cf. 19.1.21-25), and the interruption of that activity at his sight of Kothar approaching with the bow (9-13). The recurrence of the full introduction of the hero at this point (13-15) divides the episode neatly in half. Danel now addresses his wife, bidding her prepare food for the visitor and give him food, drink and honor (15-21). Her

11 Contrast those biblical narratives in which the childless couple is approached by divine initiative. Such stories, issuing in the birth of, e.g., Isaac, Samson, John the Baptist, use many of the same motifs, but for a different purpose: to introduce one who has a significant divine mission.

12 The rest of the sequence is lacking, unless the two lines of Kothar's speech are part of the body of such a sequence. Since the form of the line is unique, it seems more likely that the line is used independently without explicit reference to the repetition or protraction of any particular action, to indicate the passage of time between Kothar's departure and his arrival at Danel's gate.

execution of his instructions (21-31) is interrupted by Kothar's presentation of the bow to Danel (25-28). This comes after she has prepared the food, but before she has served it. The episode then concludes with Kothar's departure (31-33).

This episode is comparable to the visitation of Abraham in Gen 18:1-16.[13] Abraham is portrayed resting at the door of his tent during the heat of the day. Three men suddenly appear before him. Abraham eagerly greets them and prevails upon them to stay and enjoy his hospitality. He then instructs his wife to bake for them, while he himself fetches some meat, which he has a servant prepare. When the food is ready he serves it, and stands by while his guests eat. In a postprandial conversation the visitors promise him a divine gift—progeny. A conversation between the visitors and Abraham's wife introduces some material bound up with the larger context. Finally the visitors depart.

Another instance of the same genre appears in the next chapter, where two of the same visitors come to the gate of the city at which Lot is sitting. He too goes to meet them, prevails upon them to stay with him, and feeds them. In a special development he protects them from a gang. They reward him by warning him of the city's imminent destruction, and then depart, helping him to escape with them (Gen 19:1-16).

Both stories share a common structure: 1) the central character is portrayed at rest or engaged in his daily task; 2) he is approached by strangers (actually divine envoys, but not initially recognized as such); 3) he offers them lavish hospitality; 4) the strangers reward their host; and 5) they depart. The two Genesis stories are but adaptations of a widely found tale,[14] which probably was circulated independently with the purpose of encouraging hospitality to strangers. In Genesis, though the basic structure has been conserved, this purpose has been overshadowed by the larger themes and purposes of the patriarchal stories.

Two other biblical examples are found in a different context. In 2 Kgs 4:8-17 a woman presses her hospitality on Elisha. He then stops at her house regularly, and she, recognizing that he is a holy man, furnishes a small room which is reserved for him. He enquires what it is she most desires, and, learning that she is childless and that her husband is an old man, promises her a son—which duly arrives as promised. Again, hospitality, voluntarily given, is rewarded. Even though the woman recognizes her visitor early on as an *ʾyš ʾlhym qdwš* (v. 9), she does not anticipate by far the reward she gets (not even believing him when he promises it to her). The story teaches both the virtue of hospitality and the power of the man of God and his word. Although it lacks both the first and the last structural elements in its present setting, it clearly draws on the same genre as the two Genesis stories.

A more radical adaptation of the genre appears in 1 Kgs 17:9-16. A woman is gathering wood. Elijah approaches her and asks for hospitality, announcing in a divine oracle what her reward will be. She gives him the requested hospitality, and receives the promised reward. The relation of this story to the preceding ones is vouched for by the appearance of the same structural elements (except the last), and by the underlying motif of hospitality rewarded. But here the prophet *requests* the hospitality, and offers the reward for it *before* receiving it. Like the last story this adaptation of the genre emphasizes the power of the prophet, but it also introduces the test of the woman's faith. It encourages respect for the former and emulation of the latter more than the practice of hospitality to strangers. In both these stories the interests of the prophetic stories in Kings have prevailed over the original purpose of the genre.

In the *Aqhat* version, while all the structural elements of the genre are there, a number of modifications have obscured the original purpose of the genre. The identity of the visitor and the purpose of his visit are known from the start.[15] Danel first sees Kothar coming with the bow, and then gives directions for his entertainment. Further, Kothar presents the gift *before* Dinatiya's hospitality, not after it. Thus his visit cannot be seen as a *test* of hospitality. The traditional materials have been completely adapted to the present narrative, in which they serve as a simple transitional episode describing Kothar's delivery of the promised bow (17.5.2-3).

After Kothar's departure the full introduction of Danel reappears. As the text deteriorates, we learn that he gives the bow to Aqhat, whom he then addresses, apparently giving him directions concerning the etiquette of the hunt (references to *prʿm ṣdk* "the first of your game" and *ṣd bhklh* "game in his/her residence": 17.5.37-39).

It was suggested above that the bulk of the missing material of cols. 3 and 4 may have been concerned with the bow, and that Kothar's bestowal of it on Danel and Danel's transmission of it to Aqhat concluded a second major section of the poem. That section B in fact ends near the missing end of col. 5 is confirmed by the fact that a new section begins near the beginning of col. 6, as will be argued below.

---

13 First noted by E. M. Good, "Two Notes on Aqhat," *JBL* 77 (1958): 72-74, esp. 72, n. 4; and further explored by P. Xella, "L'Episode de Dnil et Kothar (*KTU* 1.17 [= *CTA* 17] v 1-31 et Gen XVIII 1-16," *VT* 28 (1978): 483-86.

14 In classical literature see Ovid, *Fasti* V 493-536; *Metamorphoses* VIII 611-724. For other instances from farther afield see *Motif-Index of Folk Literature* (ed. S. Thompson; Bloomington: Indiana, 1955): V, Q45.1. Cf. T. H. Gaster, *Myth, Legend and Custom in the Old Testament* (New York: Harper, 1969): 156-57.

15 Xella appears not to recognize this: "Una 'rilettura'," 67; "L'Episode de Dnil et Kothar."

C. The Death of Aqhat

" . . . that man who fights the immortals lives for no long time"

Iliad V 407 (Lattimore)

With col. 6 we are at the beginning of a section that is not in any sense concluded until the death of Aqhat in 18.4. The general course of that section is as follows. Anat makes various offers to Aqhat in exhange for his bow, and is repulsed. She goes off to El, whom she bullies into letting her have her way with Aqhat. She then returns to Aqhat, apparently making up to him with conciliatory proposals. It is at this point that the second two-column gap occurs. When the narrative resumes, Anat is journeying to Yutpan, with whom she has a brief dialogue, concluding with her plan for killing Aqhat. The plan is carried out, and as the text once again becomes damaged and badly understood, Anat is evidently regretting her action.

A more detailed analysis of the construction of this section follows. The broken lines at the beginning of column 6 disclose that a meal is in progress (lines 4-6 are formulaic; cf. 4.6.57-59 and 5.6.14-16), and odd words in the following three lines confirm that drinks are being served. In line 10 the formula of recognition appears: *bnši. ʿnh. wtphn* "she (Anat, from the sequel) looks up and sees." The next few lines, still only partially preserved, seem to describe Anat's reaction to the approach of Aqhat carrying his new bow, which is probably what prompts her proposals in the following dialogue.[16] This is more likely than the supposition of others that Aqhat had failed to present the first-fruits of the hunt to the temple (cf. 17.5.37-39).[17] There is scarcely enough space in the damaged section for the recounting of such a development. More certainly, the preserved part of the sequel gives no hint of Aqhat having committed such a cultic *faux pas*, and his fate is adequately accounted for by his rejection of Anat's requests (especially in light of the Gilgamesh passage to be compared below).

There ensues a dialogue consisting of two pairs of speeches—each comprised of an offer by Anat[18] and a rejection by Aqhat—and a final threat by Anat. Anat first offers Aqhat silver and gold in exchange for his bow (17.6.16-19). Anat's *tn* "give" is countered by the *tn* "give" of Aqhat, who tells her to give the materials of which the bow is made to Kothar, who would make one for her (20-25). Anat then offers Aqhat immortality (26-33). This offer is expanded with a promise (28-29), and a motivating clause, describing the celebration that takes place when Baal gives life (32-33). (This time she does not mention the condition: Aqhat's yielding his bow to her.) Aqhat's second speech is a much more direct rejection of Anat (34-40/41). He rebukes her as a liar; quotes what appear to be proverbial questions and their answers that directly contradict the claim that immortality can be conferred on mortals; asserts his own mortality; and finally in a numerical saying declares that bows and hunting are man's affairs and not woman's. Anat now drops her winning tone, and utters a threat, couched in a conditional sentence (42-45).

Formulaic lines now convey Anat to the residence of El. There follows a dialogue between the two deities (17.6.51-18.1.20). Only the beginning of Anat's first speech is preserved at the end of tablet 17, but it is introduced as a slander on Aqhat. Some 12 lines on tablet 17 and some 5 at the beginning of tablet 18 must have been occupied by Anat's first speech and El's first response, because in 18.1.6 appears the word *tʿn* "she spoke up," which must introduce Anat's second speech. This is badly preserved, though the remains of 6-12 recall 3.E.27-33. In particular, in lines 11-12 Anat threatens El's person, as she does in 3.E.32-33 (and proposes to do in 3.E.10-11), and then ironically suggests that Aqhat will protect him from her (12-14). In his second speech (16-20) El acknowledges Anat's character (as he does in 3.E.35-36), bids her do what is on her mind, and pronounces the fate of those who would oppose her.

Further formulaic lines bring Anat back to Aqhat, as she begins her strategy for dealing with the uncooperative and insolent youth. It is appropriate to stop at this point to consider a comparable unit in another major work of ancient Near Eastern literature.

The dialogue between Anat and Aqhat, the goddess' journey to El and her conversation with him have rather close analogues in the sixth tablet of the Gilgamesh Epic. Ishtar, aroused by the sight of the newly washed and dressed Gilgamesh (1-6), accosts him, proposing they become lovers, and offering him rich gifts, greatness and prosperity (7-21). Gilgamesh rejects the offer, asking what he is to give in return, graphically asserting that Ishtar is a treacherous object on which to rely, and citing her betrayal of various lovers—to which he would be added (24-78). Ishtar then hurries off to Anu (79-82). She complains that Gilgamesh has insulted her (83-85). Anu responds that she got what she deserved (89-91). (This suggests the purport of El's missing reply to Anat's first speech.) Ishtar then makes her demand—the gift of a monster to destroy Gilgamesh—and threatens Anu with the release of the dead (94-100). Anu warns her that a drought will ensue (103-106), but Ishtar says she is ready for such an eventuality (109-113). Anu then cedes the Bull of Heaven (117ff.).

The structure and the motifs are the same: 1) First

16 J. Aistleitner, *Die mythologischen und kultischen Texte aus Ras Schamra* (2nd ed.; Budapest: Akadémiai Kiadó, 1964): 66.

17 As surmised by, for example, J. C. L. Gibson, "Myth, Legend and Folktale in the Ugaritic Keret and Aqhat Texts," in *Congress Volume Edinburgh* (VTS 28: Leiden: Brill, 1975): 65; *Canaanite Myths and Legends*, 27.

18 In the form: *irš . . . watnk//wašlḥk* "ask . . . and I will give you//and I will bestow upon you" 17.6.17-18, 26-28.

dialogue: a goddess is excited by the hero or his appurtenances, tries to entice him to yield what she desires, but is rebuffed.[19] 2) She hurries off to the high god. 3) Second dialogue: (a) she maligns the hero, and gets an unsympathetic response; (b) she threatens the high god directly, thus finally gaining his authorization to have her revenge on the hero. 4) She proceeds to execute her plan to punish the hero. The divergence of the two versions at this point betrays the particular larger literary purposes of their present contexts.

The common structure of the two passages suggests that both draw on a common genre. (The differences in wording, style and content are sufficient to my mind to eliminate the possibility that either text is directly dependent on the other.) The purpose of the generic story would have been to warn males against male pride and female treachery. The latter knows no bounds, even in the divine sphere. *Gilgamesh* uses the genre to depict another of the death-defying exploits of Gilgamesh and Enkidu—in fact their last, so that tablet 6 becomes the turning point in the epic.

The *Aqht* material is distinctive in several respects. First, in the gradual growth of the conflict between Anat and Aqhat through the five speeches of the first dialogue (contrasted with the two of Gilgamesh): the goddess' offer first of wealth,[20] then of immortality; the hero's rejection of her, first indirectly by the instructions on how to get a bow made, and then directly by denunciation of Anat as a liar and cheat; and finally Anat's parting threat. Unlike Gilgamesh, Aqhat is not immediately scornful of the goddess. His death is thus rendered more tragic than Gilgamesh's would have been (had he died).[21] The distinctive content lies in Anat's aspiration to a role of the opposite sex, and in Aqhat's detailed account of the composition of the bow and his assertion of the reality of death and of the normativeness of standard sex roles.

In the following passage the verbal correspondences between *Aqhat* and *Bʿl* suggest a relationship that must be investigated alongside any comparison with *Gilgamesh* 6. The correspondences are found in 17.6.42-3 and 3.E.7-8; 17.6.46-9 and 3.E.12-16; 18.1.6-12 and 3.E.27-33; and 18.1.16-17; and 3.E.35-6. In 18.4.7-8 and 16-17 Anat uses similar language to that of the first pair of correspondences, which suggests that these are four instances of a commonly used formulaic system. The second pair are but two examples of a widely attested cluster of formulaic lines. Thus neither of the first two pairs of correspondences can be regarded as indicative of a specific, significant relationship between the two Ugaritic contexts. The other correspondences may have been more common than we now see—may have been part of the mythological language characteristic of Anat and her relationship to El. It is remarkable that this language does not recur anywhere else among the various visits that gods and goddesses pay to El. It is also clear that Anat's threats and El's acknowledgement of her character appear to fit their context in *Bʿl* much less satisfactorily than their present position in *Aqhat*. Their position and function in *Aqhat*, on the other hand, are strikingly analogous to the position and function of the similar material in *Gilgamesh*. While the Akkadian and Ugaritic text each uses its own language, I conclude that the close structural relationship between the two is more significant than the verbal correspondences between the two Ugaritic texts. The latter are better explained as illustrating the degree to which particular lines and clusters of lines have become formulaic in Ugaritic poetry.[22]

The comparison with *Gilgamesh* 6:1-119 supports the claim that 17.6 begins a new section of the poem. Each section is joined to the preceding material in a similar way. Gilgamesh's washing and dressing in the first lines of tablet 6 conclude his defeat of Huwawa in tablet 5, but then also make him the object of Ishtar's desire and so initiate the next episode in his and Enkidu's exploits. Similarly Aqhat's sporting the bow concludes the section concerned with the fashioning and delivery of that object, but then also makes it the object of Anat's desire, so initiating the next section of *Aqhat*.

Ishtar's revenge takes quite a different course from Anat's, so it will not be fruitful to compare the two sequels.[23] I continue with the analysis of *Aqhat*. Anat returns directly to Aqhat, and another dialogue begins. In her first speech Anat proposes a reconciliation, offering to teach Aqhat how to use the bow, apparently near Ablm. It is at this point that the text breaks off for rather more than two columns (some 20 lines are missing at the end of column 1 and at the beginning of column 4).

19 In the words of P. Considine: "Ishtar and Anath are both angered by the way in which a mortal hero contemptuously exposes a specious offer of glory." P. Considine, "The Theme of Divine Wrath in Ancient East Mediterranean Literature," *Studi Micenei ed Egeo-anatolici* 8 (1969): 85-159, esp. 90.

20 It was a commonplace that a mortal would want riches from a deity—and even that he would reject the offer. Besides *Gilgamesh* and *Aqht* cf. 1 Kgs 3:11 and Keret's rejection of gold, silver, etc. in *CTA* 14, *passim.*

21 What Aistleitner says of the poem as a whole is true of this section (and of this section only): "Seine Einstellung wirkt geradezu tragisch"—Aistleitner, 70; and similarly H. Gese, "Die Religionen Altsyriens," in H. Gese, M. Höfner, and K. Rudolph, *Die Religionen Altsyriens, Altarabiens und der Mandäer* (Stuttgart: Kohlhammer, 1970): 90.

22 Similarly some of the Akkadian material is formulaic, and found in other quite different contexts. For example, the threat to release the dead also appears in *Nergal and Ereshkigal*: STT I, No. 28, col. V, 11-12 and 26-27; O. R. Gurney in *An. St.* 10 (1960): 105-31, esp. 122-23; *ANET*³, 511; and in the *Descent of Ishtar* obv. 19-20; *ANET*³, 107.

23 Further exploration of the alleged genre used by both *Gilgamesh* and *Aqht* would involve attention to the remains of the Sumeriam antecedents of *Gilgamesh* 6.

The preserved part of column 4 begins with Anat en route to Yutpan, and continues with a dialogue between the two. The text is broken, but it is clear that an initial speech by Anat (7-11, introduced in 6-7) is followed by a speech by Yutpan (12-15, introduced in 11), which in turn is followed by a second speech by Anat (16-27, introduced in 16). In her first speech Anat refers first to Ablm, and then to the moon (*yrḫ*):

ik . al . yḥdṯ . yrḫ	How will the moon (not) be renewed?
b[ ]/bqrn . ymnh .	In [,]/in its right horn
banšt[ ]/qdqdh .	In waning(?) [ ]/its head.

Ablm is of course the *qrt zbl yrḫ* "Town of Prince Moon." Is Anat suggesting that the renewal of the moon is threatened by Aqhat and his bow? Or is she reassuring Yutpan that the moon will be renewed, that Yarikh will not react unfavorably to having Aqhat dispatched in the territory of his city Ablm?[24] The latter suggestion has the merit of treating the speech as a unit. Yutpan now refers to Anat's striking Aqhat for his bow (*at. . . tmḫṣh*). Clearly he knows what is in the air without having to be told in this conversation. Is this a statement of approval ("you may strike him"), or is he insisting that *she* do the deed ("*you* strike him")? Or is he still demurring ("will you strike him?")? He concludes by saying that the lad has laid food. Was he responsible for seeing that Aqhat had kept the assignment at Ablm?

The damage to these lines raises several questions. But since we know from the sequel that Anat in fact had Aqhat killed near Ablm, where she was proposing that they go in 18.1.27-31, we may presume that most of the missing material between columns 1 and 4 was concerned with her preparations for that coup. First, perhaps in a lengthy dialogue involving some thrusting and parrying comparable to that in 17.6, she would have persuaded Aqhat to go to Ablm to meet her there. Then she would have set about acquiring an assistant. She may have tried unsuccessfully to persuade others to assist her before turning to Yutpan (cf. *Inanna's Descent*, 179 ff.); or, since the dialogue with Yutpan in the preserved part of column 4 suggests that he was by then already familiar with the situation, and that she was dealing with objections he had raised, the missing section may have included an initial proposal to Yutpan and some subsequent investigation or action designed to overcome his objections. She may, for example, have cleared things with Yarikh (in the same way that she "cleared things" with El?).

In any case, Anat now tells Yutpan how she will use him in the murder of Aqhat. Her predictions and instructions of 17-26 reappear in the account of their fulfillment and execution in 27-37. The broken last lines of the column disclose Anat weeping (*wtbk*) and speaking of restoration (*abn . ank*). Her further reactions appear to be recounted in the first 19 lines of tablet 19. Unfortunately only the formulaic parts of these lines have been satisfactorily construed.

Anat's use of Yutpan in order to dispose of her enemy is comparable with Inaras' use of a mortal to dispose of the dragon in the Hattian story preserved in the words of a priest giving an account of the *purulli* festival of the Storm-god of Heaven.[25] In that lapidary account, Inaras prepares a rich banquet, meets a mortal, and proposes that he help her to capture the dragon. The mortal, Hupasiyas, agrees, on condition that he can sleep with her, to which she consents. Inaras then dresses up attractively and invites the dragon to a banquet, having hidden Hupasiyas nearby. When the dragon has drunk every vessel dry, Hupasiyas emerges and trusses up the helpless beast.[26]

In both *Illuyankas* (as the Hattian story is usually called) and *Aqht* 1) a goddess meets a mortal and 2) by some means prevails upon him to assist her. 3) Somehow it is arranged for the victim to partake of a meal. 4) When the goddess has victim and helper where she wants them, the helper overcomes the victim. We can only speculate whether Anat like Inaras used her sexual charms to bargain for the mortal's aid, or to attract her victim to the banquet; and whether Aqhat like the dragon had succumbed to drink by the time the goddess's henchman fell on him.

The specific characteristics of this *Aqhat* material can scarcely be stated with confidence. Too much of the text is missing or not understood, and there is too little with which to compare it.[27]

---

24 Kapelrud thinks that Anat warns Yutpan "that the moon must not be renewed"—A. S. Kapelrud, *The Violent Goddess. Anat in the Ras Shamra Texts* (Oslo: Universitetsforlaget, 1969): 76. Gibson surmises that Anat is afraid that the new moon will bring a change of luck, and Aqhat will escape them: *Canaanite Myths and Legends*, 25.

25 *ANET*^{3}, pp. 125-26; Vieyra in *Les Religions du Proche-Orient asiatique*; Le trésor spirituel de l'humanité (Paris: Fayard-Denoel, 1970): 526-27, esp. 527.

26 Either he or the goddess may have killed the dragon in another version of this story, but it has now been framed by references to the Storm-god, who is first defeated by the dragon and orders Inaras to prepare a feast for it, and who at the end reappears to kill his already captured enemy. It is only this *frame* which allows the narrative to be compared to myths telling of the killing and reviving of storm-gods.

27 Gibson also considers "the patently fantastic and supernatural scenes, especially the exciting ones from an ideological or theological standpoint," namely 17.6–18.4, as a discrete unit, which he even designates "secondary"—"a mere backcloth against which Danel's piety is put to the test," and so comparable to the opening scenes of the book of Job: Gibson, "Myth, legend and folktale," 67. But while both the prose

D. The Consequences of Aqhat's Death

"... all true rites and lawful ceremonies."

Julius Caesar III.1.241

Lines 19.1.19—4.184 or 189 consist largely of a succession of ritual acts and pronouncements undertaken by Danel. The first group (19.1.19—2.74) follows his recognition of a natural calamity, but precedes his realization that Aqhat has been killed. A middle section, badly damaged, introduces messengers who announce the fate of Aqhat (from 19.2.75 to the broken end of the column). There follows a second group of ritual acts and pronouncements in which Danel deals directly with the loss of Aqhat (19.3.105—4.184 or 189). Throughout this section the narrative seems to the modern reader to be practically at a standstill. Only with Pughat's request that she be blessed for a mission of vengeance does the narrative pick up again.

The effects of the murder are the withering of the vegetation (1.29-31) and the hovering of the birds of prey (32-33).[28] At these sights Pughat weeps and Danel rends his garment. Since neither Pughat nor Danel is aware that Aqhat has been killed, these responses are not to be interpreted as acts of mourning for Aqhat. Rather they are the appropriate reaction to the natural calamity that father and daughter see before them. Danel then adjures rain,[29] and directs Pughat to prepare his riding beast. Weeping, she executes his instructions,[30] and in a passage repeated twice with some substitutions[31] he proceeds on a tour of the cultivated fields, kissing what vegetation there is, and expressing the wish that it may sprout up and that the hand of Aqhat might gather it in. All these acts and words are directed toward bringing the drought to an end. They are now followed by the broken and obscure visit of the messengers and their account of the murder.

The rest of the poem, as far as it is preserved, is concerned with the bereaved family's responsibilities to their murdered kin. The lengthy next episode is a description of a ritual that is repeated three times, only the third performance being successful. Each account begins with a speech in which Danel calls on Baal to break the wings of the hovering birds of prey (their mother and father in the second and third accounts respectively), so that he can look for Aqhat's remains in their insides, and, if he finds them, weep over them and bury them.[32] Each time Baal accedes.[33] In the first two versions Danel finds nothing and calls on Baal to restore the birds. In the final version he finds Aqhat's remains in the father of the birds, removes them, weeps over them and buries them.[34] The passage concludes with what is this time a conditional curse: May Baal break the wings of the birds of prey if they fly over my son's grave and disturb his sleep.

The next ritual is a cursing of three towns close to (*ʿl*) which Aqhat was killed, the third being *Ablm*.[35] The threefold repetition of this action is presumably again intended to imply two failures and a final success. In a passage reminiscent of the cult of the Katharat in 17.2.

framework and the poetic body of Job can each be read and understood on their own, *Aqht* would be far less coherent than it is now if section C were omitted. Though that section could stand on its own, *Aqht* would fall apart without it. I therefore conclude that it is an established part of the poem in the version in which it has come down to us.

28 Danel as yet sees only the effects without knowing the cause. So in 2 Sam 21:1 David did not recognize the connection between a three-year drought and the murder of the Gibeonites by Saul, until he enquired of Yahweh concerning the reason for the drought. It was finally only by the killing of those who bore the blood-guilt that the drought was stopped (2 Sam 21:8-10; cf. Num 35:33). So in *Aqht* it will be only with the execution of vengeance on Aqhat's behalf that this drought will cease. Cf. T. Fenton, "Ugaritica—Biblica," *UF* 1 (1969): 65-70, esp. 68.

29 Aistleitner, 66, 76; M. Pope, in *Götter und Mythen im Vorderen Orient* (ed. H. W. Haussig; Stuttgart: Klett, 1965): 243; T. Fenton, 68; Caquot and Sznycer, 444; Gibson, *Canaanite Myths*, 25, but cf. 115.

30 The instructions and their execution use formulae that appear in 4.4.2-15, where Asherat has Qdš-w-Amrr harness her riding beast in preparation for her visit to El. The *Aqht* version is distinguished by the reference to the weeping of Pughat.

31 Indicative of dialectical variations according to A. Jirku, "Doppelte Überlieferungen im Mythus und im Epos von Ugarit?" *ZDMG* 110 (1960): 20-25, esp. 23-24; "to indicate persistence in ritual" according to J. Gray, *The Legacy of Canaan* (2nd ed., VTS 5; Leiden: Brill, 1965): 301. But cf. 17.6.17-18 and 26-28 where two successive attempts both end in failure, and contrast 19.3.151-55, 156-62 and 163-69 where, as often, the third attempt after two failures is successful. Is the repetition of an act two times a conventional device for emphasizing failure?

32 The language recalls that used of Mot's proposed, and Anat's actual, burial of Baal in 5.5.5-6 and 6.1.16-18.

33 There is a structural analogy in the story of *Adapa*: "'Let me break your wing.' No sooner were the words out of his mouth than its wing was broken" (EA 356:3-5). Cf. W. G. E. Watson, "Puzzling Passages in the Tale of Aqhat," *UF* 8 (1976): 371-78, esp. 372.

34 The language now varies from the formulaic words used by Danel above and by Mot and Anat.

35 The situation is similar to that presupposed by Deut 21:1-9, particularly in its pre-Israelite form (see Z. Zevit, "The *ʿeglâ* Ritual of Deuteronomy 21:1-9," *JBL* 95 [1976]: 377-90). Both texts presuppose that any town was accounted liable, in the absence of a known criminal, for crimes committed in the country around—as also in the laws of Hammurapi (pars. 23 and 24) and in international agreements found in the Ugaritic archives. The curses of Danel are directed against the towns he thinks closest to the scene of the crime (consistently represented by the circling birds of prey). The elders of the town would ward off such curses by a ritual in which they deny their guilt (as in Deuteronomy).

Danel now returns home and is there visited by mourners. The visit is framed by references to their arrival and departure, and is extended over seven years through a formula that speaks of days becoming months and months years (cf. 6.5.7-9).[36] Danel finally offers up a sacrifice, whose function is not immediately clear.

I know of no narrative in ancient Near Eastern literature which describes at such length and in such elaborate, carefully patterned forms the activities engaged in by a bereaved family, or a community of which a member has been murdered. In the absence of adequate comparative material we cannot say to what extent Danel's individual acts conform to traditional rituals or traditional descriptions of such rituals or are elaborations of normal practice with particular relevance to the purposes of the present work. It seems likely, given the role of the vultures in section C, that the description of Danel's retrieval of Aqhat's body will be peculiar to this poem, but the striking similarity of a key part of that activity to a small but significant passage in *Adapa* advises caution even here. Without fuller accounts of the same rituals in other narratives we cannot lay great stress on particular aspects of this material, but only on the length at which it expatiates on such acts. Given this state of our knowledge, the purpose of this long section would seem to be to portray Danel as a pious father, carrying out to the letter all the duties and responsibilities that fall upon him in this most dire situation.

E. Pughat's Mission of Vengeance

"Revenge triumphs over death;"

Francis Bacon, "Of Death"

It is not clear whether Danel's sacrifice in 19.4.184-87, as well as the broken passage in 187-89, is the sequel to the visit of the mourners, or the initiation of the mission of vengeance. That Pughat's speech begins by referring to Danel's sacrificing (191-93) in terms corresponding to those of 184-87 may indicate a narrator's technique for attaching the next section, or it may indicate Pughat's appropriate response to what we should understand as an initiatory move by the father. A third alternative will be suggested below.

After referring to Danel's sacrifice, Pughat requests his blessing, and proposes to avenge the death of Aqhat (194-97). Danel responds with a general blessing (198-201; cf. El's general blessing of Danel at Baal's request in 17.1.37-39), and the specific commission to avenge Aqhat's death (201-2, corresponding to 196-97). Pughat then prepares for her mission by taking care first of her toilet (202-5) and then of her wardrobe (206-8). In her toilet Pughat washes and rouges herself, as Keret did in preparing for his campaign (14.2.62; 3.156). Her dressing here involves putting on male garments and weapons under female attire. She then journeys to the tent of Yutpan (208-12), who is informed that *agrtn* has come (213-14). Yutpan bids her drink his wine (215-16), which she does (216-18). Yutpan then begins a speech which is only fragmentarily preserved (218 ff.).

Does Pughat know who Yutpan is? Does Yutpan know who Pughat is? The context and the comparison to be made below suggest that the first question is to be answered in the affirmative. The second question is more difficult. Yutpan and his entourage identify Pughat as *agrtn*. The word may mean "she who hires us" or "she whom we hire."[37] Assuming the former meaning, several scholars have suggested that the reference is to Anat, implying that Pughat is disguised as the goddess. Unfortunately the preserved part of *CTA* 18 does not indicate whether Yutpan was hired, or prevailed upon in some other way, to assist Anat (cf. the discussion of the latter half of section C above). Further, there is nothing in the description of Pughat's toilet and dressing to suggest that she is making herself look like Anat. Yet the form *agrtn* strongly suggests that Yutpan and his retinue recognize Pughat in *some* way—though they have not as far as we know seen her before. Does the second meaning make any more sense in the context? If the word *agrtn* means "our hired woman" (so Ginsberg, *ANET* 155 b), the reference could be to one hired for her sexual favors. In that case, Yutpan's retinue would recognize Pughat not for who she is, but as belonging to a class, i. e. prostitutes. One point of the description of Pughat's dressing is that under her woman's clothes she had concealed male garments and weapons—the motif of the hidden weapon (see below). But a second reason for both the toilet and dressing might be that she was making herself sexually attractive. Comparative study tends to bear this out.

Several scholars have compared this final section with the story of Judith[38] and some with that of Jael and Sisera,[39] in each case using the comparison to suggest the conclusion of the Pughat episode. But the Jael episode has nothing in common with the material here preserved. Even if it is already granted that Pughat went on to kill Yutpan, there is then only one common motif shared by the two episodes: that of a man being killed by a woman (cf. the fate of Abimelech in Judg 9:53-54). The

36 Cf. Ashertu's reaction to the news that 77//88 sons of hers have been killed: "She appointed wailing-women and began to wail for 7 years" in the Hittite fragment entitled by Hoffner, "El, Ashertu and the Storm-god," in *ANET*[3], 519. Note that in *Aqht* the drought apparently lasts 7//8 years (19.1.42-44; so Caquot and Sznycer, 455, n. r).

37 Cf. Akk. *āgirtu* "mistress, employer," and *agirtu* "hired woman, hireling." *CAD* A/1, 151.

38 Pope, in *Götter und Mythen*, 243-44; Watson, "Puzzling Passages," 375-76.

39 T. H. Gaster, *Thespis. Ritual, Myth and Drama in the Ancient Near East* (2nd ed.; New York: Doubleday, 1961): 320; Watson, "Puzzling Passages," 375.

comparison with Judith is much more significant. And it is worth analysing that part of both stories which is preserved, in order to discover the possible peculiarities of the Pughat episode, as well as to lay a foundation for claims about the sequel to the Ugaritic tablet.

Judith promises that God will deliver Israel by her, and prays to God to that effect (8:32–9:14)— a promise and prayer that correspond roughly to Pughat's proposal and request for blessing. Judith then sees to her toilet and wardrobe (10:1-5), journeys to her destination (10:6-10), and is introduced to her victim by his attendants (10:11-18). After some developments peculiar to the more elaborate narrative of Judith, the victim prevails upon the heroine to come and drink with him (12:10-20).[40] Each of these elements has its exact counterpart in the story of Pughat. It is on the basis of such a common sequence of narrative elements that one may suppose that Pughat went on, like Judith, to wait until her host was overcome with an excess of alcohol, and then killed him.

But it is more important and sound to pursue the comparison of the preserved part of the two narratives. Contrasting with the monotheistic piety of Judith, who trusts her life to God in a bold and clever plan to save his people from a foreign invader, is the patriarchal religion of Pughat, who demands of her father the blessing and commission for an errand of family vengeance. It seems likely that Pughat, like Judith, exploited her sex appeal in her relationship with Yutpan. Both women employ a special ruse, Judith pretending to be a traitor to her people, and Pughat concealing weapons under her clothing. Pughat's ruse is echoed in that of Ehud (Judg 3:12-30), who conceals a sword under his clothing, and then, having been received in Eglon's private suite and, like Judith, contrived to be left alone with the victim, kills him, and makes his escape. In all three passages the guest has plotted in advance the means of killing the host; is welcomed by the host as a *bona fide* visitor; and in the two Hebrew stories accomplishes his end after seeing that they are alone. It seems likely on this evidence that in *Aqht* Pughat killed Yutpan. The Pughat material would then include the motifs of the concealed weapon (as in the case of Ehud), of the use of sex appeal enhanced by toilet and wardrobe (as in the case of Judith; cf. Inaras in the role of hostess in *Illuyankas*), of the killing of a warrior by a woman (as in the cases of Holophernes, Sisera, and Abimelech), and of the vulnerability of the victim through drunkenness (as in the cases of Holophernes and the dragon in *Illuyankas*). A quite different reason for thinking that Pughat killed Yutpan is that blood vengeance is the means of stopping a famine incurred by unpaid blood-guilt— see 2 Sam 21:1.[41]

But there are some further details that bear comparison. The inhabitants of Bethulia had humiliated themselves at the national calamity they faced (4:9-12, 14-15). (Judith is introduced as in mourning garb [8:5], but that is because she still mourns her late husband.) Thus in both literary compositions the woman's mission is preceded by a notice of a state of mourning for a general calamity which the woman's mission is designed to end. Second it is noteworthy that Judith utters her prayer at the time the evening incense is offered (9:1). "Incense" is precisely the meaning which has been reasonably claimed for the Ugaritic word *dġṯ*— that which Danel offers up in conjunction with his sacrifice, and to which Pughat refers when she asks his blessing on her mission (9.4.184-87; 191-93).[42] The offering of incense as the occasion for both Pughat and Judith to appeal for the blessing of their respective missions is striking, and confirms that Danel's sacrifice marks the beginning of this last episode, rather than the conclusion of the preceding rites.[43]

The Theme of Aqhat

The conclusion of the poem would have involved at least the vengeance of Aqhat's family on his murderer and

40 Note that it is Judith's drinking that is referred to first (12:19). Though we may expect that it is Yutpan who eventually succumbs to an excess of alcohol, that is not sufficient reason for violating the grammar and making Pughat ply him with drink (as do, e.g., H. L. Ginsberg in *ANET*, 155; Watson, "Puzzling Passages," 375). According to the text Pughat, like Judith, is served drink, and proceeds to drink, as translated by Gaster, *Thespis*, 374; Caquot and Sznycer, 457; Gibson, *Canaanite Myths*, 121.

41 See above, n. 28; Gibson, "Myth, Legend and Folktale," 66.

42 H. A. Hoffner, "An Anatolian Cult Term in Ugaritic," *JNES* 23 (1964): 66-68; J. C. de Moor, "Frustula Ugaritica," *JNES* 24 (1965): 355-64, esp. 355; Hoffner, "Hittite *tarpiš* and Hebrew *tĕrāphîm*," *JNES* 27 (1968): 61-68, esp. 66, n. 40.

43 It is worth remarking at this point on the construction of the book of *Judith*. The book's initial broad focus on the West is narrowed in stages— from the West in general (chapters 1-4), to Israel (chapters 4-7), and finally to Judith (chapters 8-13). Chapters 1-7 provide a historical setting, as well as introducing Judean themes. But the heart of the book is in chapters 8-13, precisely that part whose structure we have observed to be remarkably analogous to that of *Aqht*, section E. None of the reminiscences of biblical passages that Dubarle finds in *Judith* is of the scope of this narrative structure (A. M. Dubarle, *Judith. Formes et sens des diverses traditions* [An. Bib. 24; Rome: Pontifical Biblical Institute, 1966]: 137-60); hence his characterization of the book is inadequate: "le genre littéraire de *Judith* se caractérise comme une broderie d'épisodes à couleur biblique sur un canevas de faits traditionnels beaucoup plus sobre" (164).

It seems that the central narrative of the present book uses a literary structure that goes back to the second millennium. The question whether the essential structure of 8-13 was expanded into the more epic proportions the book now exhibits, or the larger national account adopted the account of the individual mission as its more personal climax, is beyond the scope of this essay.

the return of rain and fertility to the land. I do not find in an internal analysis of the poem, nor in the structural analogues to its major components, any grounds for concluding that the sequel would have told of the resurrection of Aqhat,[44] though the name of Danel's patron deity, Rāpiʾu, "Healer," may point in that direction.[45] Possibly there were other versions of the tale in which Aqhat did return to life. The so-called Rephaim texts may preserve fragments of such a version. But I do not see any compelling reason for accepting them as the sequel to *this* version.

What emerges as the distinctive common theme that unites the several traditional narratives adopted and adapted by the composers of *Aqht*? Social roles seem to be a recurrent concern.[46] Though the purpose of the genre has been entirely displaced, a tale exhibiting the generous hospitality of a host has been used to portray Kothar's delivery of the bow to Danel. Kinship roles are emphasized in the refrain on the dutiful son in section A, in the elaborate account of the conscientious actions of the dutiful father in section D, and in the promptness to act on behalf of her family that we see in the dutiful daughter of section E. Sex roles are an issue: in section C the female Anat seeks the male weapon used by Aqhat, and is repudiated by him for her confusion of roles. Her aggressiveness and penchant for violence, which appear in her attitude toward El, as well as in her final treatment of Aqhat, are heightened by comparison with the role of Ishtar in *Gilgamesh* VI and even more with that of Inaras in *Illuyankas*. In section C Anat wears a *ḥbš//tʿrt* in which she puts Yutpan as her weapon. In section C Pughat dons a male garment in whose *nšg//tʿrt* she puts her *ḫ[ṯr]//ḥrb*. The innate and blatant masculinity of Anat, which leads to the death of Aqhat, is balanced by the assumed and concealed masculinity of Pughat, which apparently leads to her avenging the death of Aqhat. Finally, cultic rules are prominent in the poem: Danel's incubation and cult of the Katharat in section A, his rituals for the blighted land and the murdered son in section D.

This emphasis on the prominence of social roles and duties in *Aqhat* contrasts with the mythological interpretation of the poem preferred by most commentators.[47] It is worthwhile reconsidering briefly some of the bases for the mythological constructions. Again, I wish to emphasize that I am here attending not to the meaning of the narrative units, motifs or symbols *in general*, but to their use in the particular poem before us, and hence to the meaning of that poem for those involved in its composition and recital.

The bow, of which in different ways several recent interpreters have made much,[48] is a distinct feature of sections B and C. But it appears in only 4 of the 10 preserved columns (17.5, 6; 18.4 and 19.1). It is not anticipated in section A, and is not heard of again after section C. In contrast Aqhat himself is the main subject even of those sections in which he is not alive: section A and sections D and E—the former anticipating his birth almost from the first line, the latter being preoccupied with his murder and its effects, and disregarding completely the bow and its loss. This suggests that whatever its significance for the two sections in which it appears, the bow is not of crucial significance for the interpretation of the poem as a whole. It may be thought that as a *divine gift* it is worthy of more attention; but its divine origin is explained by the need to justify Anat's envy and Aqhat's presumption in refusing her offers. Divine bows are part of the mythological baggage the poets were heir to—as indicated by the passing reference in the line of Homer quoted at the beginning of section B above. This traditional trait is here used simply to precipitate the unjust murder of Aqhat. It is the latter that is the significant point for the present poem. What is distinctive about the bow is the fact that it is a composite bow, a relatively new piece of technology, and one that allows Aqhat to exhibit his modern analytic knowledge in his response to Anat's first offer.

The vultures also are a distinctive feature of the poem.[49] But their appearance too is limited to two of the

44 As believed by S. Spiegel, "Noah, Danel and Job," in *Louis Ginzberg Jubilee Volume* (English Section; New York: Academy for Jewish Research, 1945): 305-55; Gaster, *Thespis*, 320-26; Pope in *Götter und Mythen*, 244; Gibson, "Myth, Legend and Folklore," 68; *Canaanite Myths*, 27. Doubts were expressed by Gese, *Die religionen Altsyriens*, 89-90; and arguments against some of these interpretations have now been presented by H. H. P. Dressler, "The Identification of the Ugaritic Dnil with the Daniel of Ezekiel," *VT* 29 (1979): 152-61, esp. 152-55.

45 S. B. Parker, "The Ugaritic Deity Rāpiʾu," *UF* 4 (1972): 97-104, esp. 103.

46 Contrast the comment of Aistleitner: "Die menschlichen Relationen der Familie *Dnil*'s sind nur ein Hintergrund und haben keine besondere Bedeutung." Aistleitner, 65.

47 But contrast the interpretations of Bernhard, "Anmerkungen"; Liverani, "L'epica ugaritica nel suo contesto storico e letterario," *Accademia nazionale dei Lincei, Atti* (del Convegno Internazionale sul tema "La poesia epica e la sua formazione"), Quaderno N 139 (1970): 859-69; Gibson, "Myth, Epic and Folktale," 68; *Canaanite Myths*, 27; H. H. P. Dressler, "Is the Bow of Aqhat a Symbol of Virility?" *UF* 7 (1975): 217-20, esp. 219; Caquot and Sznycer, *Textes ougaritiques*, 413-14.

48 Earlier, Gaster, *Thespis*, 316-26. More recently, D. R. Hillers, "The Bow of Aqhat: The Meaning of a Mythological Theme," in *Orient and Occident, Essays . . . Cyrus H. Gordon*, (ed. H. A. Hoffner: AOAT 22; Neukirchen-Vluyn: Neukirchener Verlag, 1973): 71-80; Dressler, "Is the Bow of Aqhat a Symbol of Virility?"; Liverani, "L'epica ugaritica," 866 and 868-69; Xella, "Una 'rilettura'." Contrast Gibson, "Myth, legend and folklore."

49 And exploited as mythologically significant by Xella, "Una 'rilettura'."

five sections of the poem (C and D). Even there their role is quite traditional. Hovering over Aqhat before the murder, serving Anat's ends in the actual murder, consuming Aqhat's remains, contributing to Danel's and Pughat's anguish as they see the effects of the drought, making a protracted appearance in Danel's ritualistic search for his son's remains, and finally being threatened by a perpetual curse if they ever disturb the remains of Aqhat, they clearly bear their widespread symbolic value of death, and thus reinforce the centrality of death in the poem. The vultures themselves cannot be taken to be the key to the meaning of the whole.

The death of Aqhat is clearly central. Section A serves as a conventional introduction to stories about personages with remarkable fortunes. 17.5, whatever leads up to it, leads directly into 17.6, and everything from Anat's first sight of Aqhat and his bow tends toward his death in 18.4; and that is the cause of all the action that follows. But we must be more specific. This is not the threatened death of the king, as in *Krt*, nor the mysterious death of a god, as in *Bʿl* (*CTA* 5-6). We have to do clearly and concretely with murder. Is this some kind of mythological or ritual murder, as of Adonis or Osiris? Clearly not. Admittedly the murder is recounted with mythological trappings. But so is Ishtar's conflict with Gilgamesh in *Gilgamesh* 6, and yet it is undisputed that that episode serves as yet another daring exploit of the two heroes, whom it brings finally to face the reality of death. As in *Gilgamesh* so here a traditional mythological narrative is used for a larger literary purpose. The divine initiatives, responses and conflicts of 17-18 produce the catastrophe to which the social (cultic, familial) rituals of 19 are seen to be the appropriate and adequate response. The solution to the murder of Aqhat is no more mythological than it is bureaucratic.

Aqhat rejects Anat's offers with his knowledge of the materials from which the composite bow is made, and his acceptance of the inevitability of death. (Note that there is here no question of the special status of the king, as in *Krt*.[50]) He is familiar with "modern" technology and exhibits a secular view of human mortality. Whether the realism of Aqhat was deprecated or not it is difficult to say, as in consequence it is difficult to know whether his death was partly deserved or purely an irony of fate— that a gift of a god became the cause of a goddess killing him. In contrast with this brash modern wisdom and morality, Danel retrieves Aqhat's remains and indeed proceeds to remedy all the consequences of his murder with a more traditional wisdom and morality: those of sacred deed and word. Pughat assists, and continues in the same vein, as she seeks to avenge the murder. This is not a myth in any esoteric sense, but a story of human life and death and of a society's traditional response to murder. While the rituals of 19.1-4 may seem to us to be a lull in the story, an interlude, to their ancient audience they may well have been the climax of the story. As we have seen, much of the rest of the narrative is quite conventional, familiar stuff. It is precisely the social customs and rituals— referred to, described or repeated— that are its distinctive features.

A final question concerns the place of such a strong emphasis on traditional, familial responsibilities in a poem used by the central institutions of the state of Ugarit. Do they not militate against the legal institutions of the Ugaritic monarchy?[51] Is there here an indirect criticism of the more rational aspects of the Ugaritic administration? Or was the poem used innocently by the priesthood simply to reinforce its own faith in the power of sacred word and act? Or was the main function of the poem purely aesthetic? Certainly the careful structuring and patterning of, for example, the whole of section A, 17.6 in section C, and 19.3.105—4.184 in section D betray a strong interest in aesthetic form, and therefore by definition an artistic motivation. Perhaps the poem was enjoyed because it portrayed an idealised past era, and the order, power and beauty of man's institutions in the olden days. It is not impossible that the poem served several of these purposes, either on the same occasion or on different occasions.

---

50 As maintained recently by Liverani and Xella. But contrast Caquot and Sznycer, 414; Gibson, "Myth," 66, who compares Danel with the village chief of Job 29 and with the patriarchs of Genesis; Dressler, "Identification," 152-54.

51 Cf. Liverani, 869; Xella, "Una 'rilettura'," 483.

ON THE BITE OF A DOG

MARCEL SIGRIST

In the course of reading cuneiform tablets in the Archaeological Museum of Andrews University I have discovered this amusing little tablet.[1] I offer it with pleasure to Professor Marvin Pope.

A. Text

Palaeography suggests the Old Babylonian period.

Division into paragraphs or units of signification is facilitated by the presence on the tablet of horizontal lines. It is therefore possible to delimit clearly the first two paragraphs (§§ i, ii) despite the erasure at the beginning of the tablet. Actually, the loss of the beginning of the tablet results partly from the tablet's poor state of preservation but also from the fact that the scribe or someone else has deliberately erased the opening lines.

B. Text Commentary

Lines 1–2: These two lines repeat *šim*, which is considered to be the imperative or stative form of the verb *šiāmu*. The other words: *x-hu/ri-it* and *pa-ra-ʾī* are the direct objects of this verb. Unfortunately it is not possible to present any translation of these lines.

Line 3: This second paragraph constitutes an entity in itself separated from what precedes and follows by lines traced in the clay: "A dog bit a man." The meaning of the sentence is limpid; it establishes or reports a fact.

The *anumma* of the following line introduces the response to this fact. However, no conjunction joins the first and second paragraphs—that which would have permitted reading this as the announcement of a remedy to extirpate the evil "when" a dog bit a man. Since it is preferable not to make the scribe say what he did not write, the latter paragraph must be kept independent of the former without offering a line of thought leading from one to the other. Had it been the case of a letter one could have believed that at the beginning of this new paragraph the author repeats an unrelated fact that had been communicated to him: "You tell me that a dog has bitten a man." But since it is impossible that a letter is in question, this suggestion cannot be retained.

Cuneiform literature mentions dog bites only rarely. The following are a few pertinent references:

A. A letter from Nippur speaks of a dog bite and the treatment that must be given.[3]

b. A lexical text mentions a "dog-mouth" herb in a

i obv	1	*x-hu/ri-it ma-ṭi-im ši-im*	determine . . .
	2	*ù pa-ra-ʾi ši-im*	and . . .
ii	3	*ka-al-bu-um a-wi-lam iš-šu-uk*	A dog bit a man;
iii	4	*a-nu-um-ma a-na ša-ri-im*	"now, to the passing
	5	*a-li-ki-im qí-bi-a-ma*	wind, say:
iv rev	6	*ni-ši-ik ka-al-bi-im*	'May the bite of the dog
	7	*me-ra-ni e*[2] *ib-ni*	not produce puppies.'
v	8	*šu-ri-ma ka-al-ba-am*	take the dog away
	9	*a-na ṣí-bi-it-ti-im*	into custody.
vi	10	*ka-al-bu-um li-mu-ut-ma*	Let the dog die
	11	*a-wi-lum li-ib-lu-uṭ-ma*	(so that) the man may live."

1 I gratefully thank Dr. Lawrence Geraty, Curator of the Archaeological Museum of Andrews University in Berrien Springs, Michigan, for permission to publish this tablet, and Miss Eugenia L. Nitowski, Assistant Curator, for the photographs accompanying this article. I thank also Professors Jean Bottéro, Aaron Shaffer and Barry Eichler for the numerous comments and references they provided me for this article.

2 The photograph indicates clearly the sign e followed by an erased sign of which only two vertical strokes remain before the sign ib. These two verticals, considered the residue of the erased sign, are therefore not entered in the transliteration. It is likely that the scribe started to write a-ai then erased the sign to write e.

3 PBS 7:57. 2 sìla ì-giš *i-na ka-ar-pa-tim/ ša-ki-in šu-bi-lam/ a-wi-lum* ! / *ka-al-bu-um i-šu-uk-ma/ ú-ra-ka-àṣ ina* ì-giš/ *šu-bi-lam* (1.12–17) "There are two silas of oil in the container, send (it) to me; a dog bit the master; send (it) to me so that I may make a bandage with the oil."

series of herbs, for use against snake and dog bites.[4]

c. An incantation text mentions a dog bite, parallel to the teeth of men.[5]

d. An extispicy text announces in its apodosis that a dog will bite a man in the street.[6]

e. Finally, the laws of Eshnunna contain a legal provision concerning the bite of a rabid dog (*šegû*).[7] There are few other references to rabid dogs in cuneiform literature. Nevertheless it is curious that an occurrence such as the bite of a dog, which cannot have been particularly rare in Mesopotamia, finds so little place in the literature.

Lines 4–11: Once the fact is indicated, the author of this text introduces the message *anumma*: "Here is what must now be done." The purport of the message is twofold: a magic or apotropaic act, and a practical or prophylactic action, followed by a final wish for the death of the dog.

1. *Apotropaic measure*

"Now, to the passing wind say: 'May the bite of the dog not produce puppies.' " (lines 4–7, §§iii and iv)

If the literal translation of this sentence seems to transmit an apparently bizarre message, the appearance vanishes once it is read in the light of the two following texts:

Text 1[8]

i-na ši-in-ni-šu	in his teeth (those of the dog)
eʾi-il ni-il-šu	hangs his semen;
a-šar iš-šu-ku	wherever he bites
ma-ra-šu e-zi-ib	he leaves his progeny.

Text 2[9]

[*wa-ru*]-*úḫ bi-ir-ki-in* *da-an la-sà-ma-am*	it (the dog) is fleet-footed, fierce in running,
[*pa-g*]*i*(?)-*il ka-ab-ba-ar-ti-in* *ma-li i-ir-*[*tim*]	strong(?)-legged, powerful chested;
[*ṣi*]-*il-li du-ri-im* *mu-uz-za-zu-ú-šu*	the shadow of the wall is his station
as-ku-pa-tum na-ar-ba-ṣu-šu	the threshold (of the house) is his resting-place
i-na pi-i-šu na-ši-i ni-il-šu	in his (the dog's) mouth is carried his semen
a-šar iš-šu-ku ma-ra-šu i-zi-ib	there where he bites he leaves his progeny
inim-inim-ma ur-gi$_7$ ti-la-kam	incantation for resurrecting a thoroughbred dog.

Another text[10] also mentions a dog, but it has been impossible to connect its few legible elements with the two texts mentioned above.

These two texts transmit what was apparently a popular belief that a dog's saliva is or carries its semen, perhaps accounting for the great fertility of the canine species and the fact that dogs often rip each other while fighting. Of course it is difficult to harmonize or explain this belief in light of other physiological knowledge possessed by the Sumerians and Akkadians.

As an apotropaic measure this belief must be articulated and expressed in the passing wind. One notes that the verb is plural: *qibiā*, "say (2nd pl.)." It is not simply the man who has been bitten who is invited to say this to the passing wind; but undoubtedly this plurality refers to all members of the community of the bitten individual or to the witnesses of the incident. What is important is not to know the identity of those who perform this magic act, but rather to note that an incantation specialist is not summoned. This could therefore be a magic act in a primitive, rudimentary stage.

It remains to say a word about the wind called to receive and carry off this declaration. Wind is a purifying element which carries the evil far away.[11] This attribution is based on the common experience that the wind sweeps through a place, picking at debris, acting as a purifying agent. In identical fashion the passing wind will carry off the spoken word, i.e., will annihilate the reality this expression intends to convey. The element which is important to underscore here, if this interpretation of the action of the wind is correct, is the relationship established between word and reality. Speech calls a thing into being. Thus, to pronounce an evil is to bring that evil into existence, to give it a reality, but also to enable the wind to carry it off.

2. *Prophylactic measure* (lines 8–9; §v)

In the final two paragraphs the author addresses only one person: *šūrima*[12] (2nd sg.). The dog must be recalled from circulation because of the danger he represents, and

4 *CT* XIV 23 1–3: ú-KA-ur-gi$_7$

5 MSL IX p. 83, no. 56. *mar-tam pa-ši-tam* ^{d}DÌM+ME *ek-ki-im-tam ni-ši-ik* ur-ge$_7$-ra *ši-in-ni a-wi-lu-tim* (cf. *CT* 42 41:10, *BiOr* 18, pp. 71–72 and *CAD* M, p. 304^{a} 3′). Despite a check of a large number of texts relating to magic or magical practices, it has not been possible to find a text similar to this in its formal structure. In effect, the magic act recounted in this "ritual" consists of taking up a simple formula recited to bring back the order of things destroyed by the bite of the dog. Such forms, which by their simplicity are close to this type, but not exact parallels, may be found in *JNES* 14 (1960), 14 and *JNES* 17 (1963), 56.

6 *CT* 20 49:31.

7 *AASOR* 31 §§56 / 57.

8 *BiOr* 9 (1954), 81–84, LB 2001.

9 VS 17:8.

10 *Sumer* 13, p. 107 p. 20 B.

11 BWL 114:50; *Iraq* 6, 184.

12 As normalized the verb is *šūrû* 'to lead.' However, in context the reading *šūrimma* seems preferable. But then the scribe should have written *šu-ri-im-ma* or *šu-ri-ib-ma* (cf. *ARM* 2 106).

Fig. 1: AUAM 73 2416

Obverse

Reverse

Fig. 2: Autograph

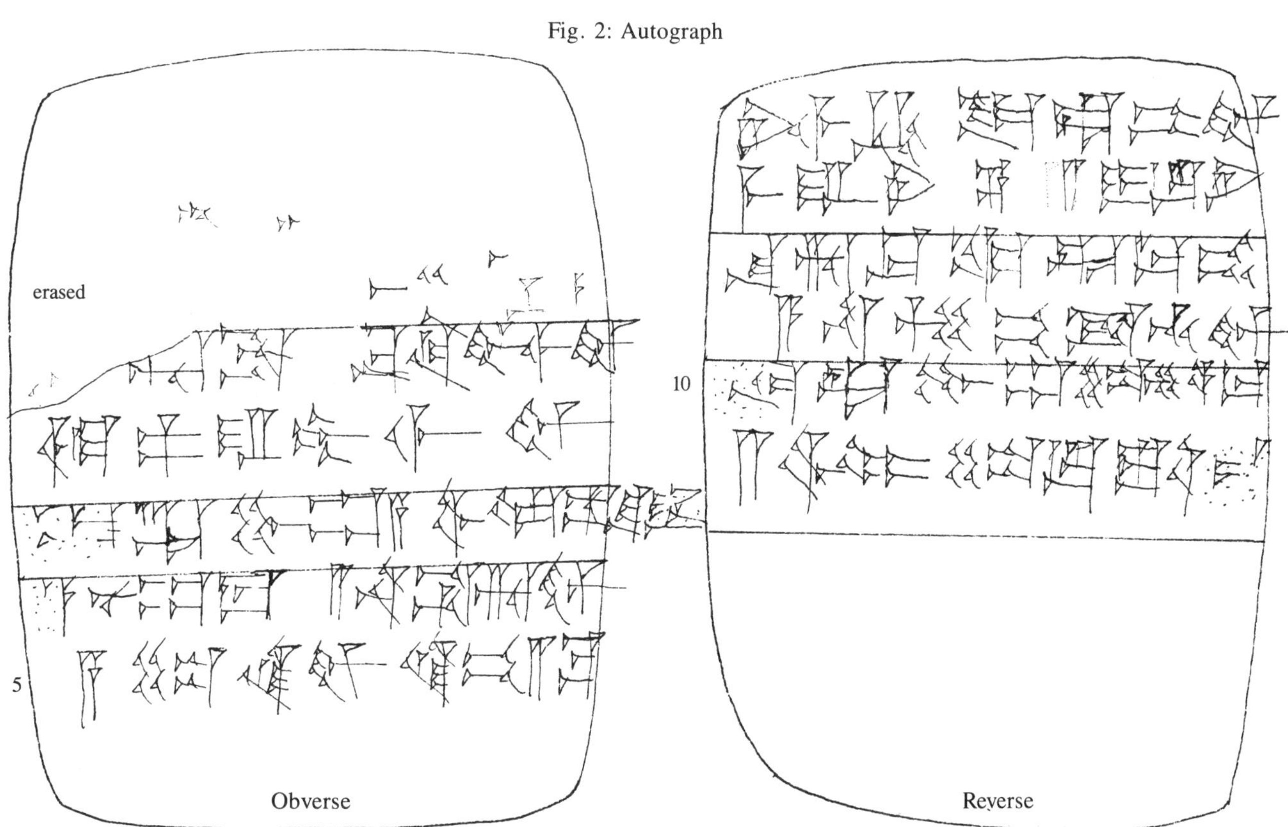

as though speaking of a man the author orders the dog to be placed in confinement. This text probably gives the only attestation of the use of *ṣibittu* for an animal, even if the author of the text actually was thinking of a cage.

3. *Final wish* (lines 10–11; § vi)

The text ends with a double wish governing the fate of the two protagonists: death for the dog and life for the man.[13] The author seems to establish a link between the dog's death and the well-being of the bitten man. The disappearance of the dog annuls in some manner the evil of which he was the carrier and thus guarantees the health of the man. It would of course be tempting further to develop this antithesis of death and life, but because of the slender basis for speculation on this point it would also be imprudent.

A prophylactic act and the execution of the dog are in fact two related elements. It seems proper to get rid of an animal that is a proven hazard. In this respect the case of the dog-that-bites is merely one of many parallels to the typical case of the ox-that-gores.[14] That the death of the dog is demanded is therefore not at all surprising. However, the fact that this death seems to permit the reestablishment of the man's health remains somewhat unexpected.

Nevertheless, the death of the dog does independently guarantee the proper recovery of the dog's victim. Based on Mesopotamian beliefs concerning dog saliva, a kind of magical practice of rudimentary nature is to be executed. This is not connected with the victim but is designed to remove from the immediate environment nefarious potentialities engendered by the bite.

The two actions mentioned in the tablet, the magic action and the killing of the dog, should not be viewed as alternative measures, although the first may be interpreted as a means of ridding the environment of evil; both may be necessary to ensure the recovery of the victim.

C. Letter or Ritual?

The direct character of the address *qibiūma*, *šūrima* could suggest the epistolary style. But more probably it is a magic ritual against a dog bite. Other rituals are frequently expressed in direct addresses.

13 Similar parallelism in *Maqlu* I 19: *ši-i li-mut-ma a-na-ku lu-ub-luṭ*.

14 See similar juxtaposition in the laws of Ešnunna.

DEATH AND DYING IN OLD TESTAMENT THEOLOGY

BREVARD S. CHILDS

It should come as no surprise that the treatment of the subject of death and dying has varied greatly within the discipline of Old Testament theology. Few topics mirror more dramatically the effect of changing perspectives on theological reflection.

By the beginning of the 19th century the older, post-Reformation manner of treating the biblical material as a unified system of doctrine[1] had already been seriously modified. Only occasionally did essays of the older type persist. Rather, the great variety within the material was perceived and an effort was made to register widely differing concepts. Even the conservative Hävernick characterized the Old Testament's understanding of the afterlife, not as a fixed doctrine, but as a "shadowy, movable picture" into whose darkness occasionally a stream of light fell.[2] Increasingly a history of development within Israel's religion was depicted, usually under the venerable rubric of "progressive revelation."[3] Other scholars spoke of the "germ of truth"[4] found in the Mosaic law and in Job's confessions which began to transcend Israel's this-worldly focus and to grow towards a fuller understanding of life beyond the grave.

The effect of early literary criticism and the redating of the Old Testament sources only increased the dependence upon a developmental scheme by which to accommodate the diversity. In an impressive survey Schultz[5] emphasized that the Old Testament horizon during most of its history lay wholly on this side of the grave. Continued existence, such as that of Sheol, provided no element of consolation, but was as bitter to the pious as to the ungodly. Only toward the close of the exile did prophets begin to see, at first, a collective resurrection, and, finally, one also for the individual.

The introduction into the discussion of comparative material brought a surge of new monographs which focused on aspects of the subject which had largely been overlooked up to then. Tylor's famous book in 1871[6] which mounted the theory that animism undergirded the beliefs of all primitive cultures had an immediate effect on Old Testament studies. Similarly, the impact of James Frazer,[7] especially in the English-speaking world, who drew parallels from every conceivable culture, was all-pervasive. The studies of Schwally,[8] Bertholet,[9] and Lods[10] applied the new insights of comparative religions specifically to the problem of the afterlife in the Old Testament.

The growth of knowledge of the literature of the ancient Near East brought an increased support for the study of the Bible from a comparative perspective, now enriched by innumerable cuneiform parallels. Although the similarity of the *rephaim* of the Old Testament to the "shades" of Hades in Homer had been long noticed, the impact of the Babylonian parallels added a great stimulus to the study of death and the underworld. Now for the first time the exact topography and geography of the netherworld began to be sketched with aids from parallels

---

1 Cf. the classic formulations of J. Gerhard, *Loci communes theologici* (Tübingen: Cotta, 1777): Tom. XVII, Loci XXVII and XXVIII; Charles Hodge, "The Old Testament Doctrine of the Future State," *Systematic Theology* (New York: Scribner, 1873): 716-723. Consult in addition the bibliography on this older approach offered by R. Kübel, "Tod," *Real-Encyklopädie*, herausg. Hauch, 2 Aufl. 1885, vol. 15, 696f. H.-J. Kraus' treatment of Calvin's understanding of life and death in the Psalms demonstrates the Reformer's exegetical skill, "Vom Leben und Tod in den Psalmen," *Biblisch-theologische Aufsätze* (Neukirchen-Vluyn: Neukirchener Verlag, 1972): 258-277.

2 H. A. C. Hävernick, *Vorlesungen über die Theologie des Alten Testaments* (Erlangen: Heyder, 1848): 107.

3 G. F. Oehler, *Theology of the Old Testament* (English translation, New York: Funk and Wagnalls, 1884): 169ff., 511ff., 558ff.

4 E. H. Plumptre, *The Spirits in Prison and Other Studies after Death* (London: Pitman, 1884; rpt. 1905): 47. The growth of a moral consciousness which transcends death is an approach also used by A. B. Davidson, *Theology of the Old Testament* (Edinburgh: T. and T. Clark, 1904): 432ff.

5 H. Schultz, *Old Testament Theology* (English translation, Edinburgh: T. and T. Clark): vol. 2, 327f. Cf. also B. W. Stade, *Über die alttestamentlichen Vorstellungen vom Zustand nach dem Tode* (Leipzig: Vogel, 1877); K. Marti, *Geschichte des israelitischen Religion* (Strassburg: Bull, 1903): 117. The classic, popular formulation of this position in English remains Harry E. Fosdick, "The Idea of Immortality," *A Guide to Understanding the Bible* (New York: Harper, 1938): 257ff. W. Eichrodt's treatment offers a sober corrective to some of these extravagances, *Theology of the Old Testament* (2 vols.; English translation, Philadelphia: Westminster, 1967): 2.210ff.

6 E. B. Tylor, *Primitive Culture* (2nd ed.; London: John Murray, 1893): 1.210ff., 2.1ff.

7 J. G. Frazer, *The Golden Bough* (Abridged Edition; London: Macmillan, 1923): 296ff., 691ff.

8 F. Schwally, *Das Leben nach dem Tode* (Giessen, 1892).

9 A. Bertholet, *Die israelitischen Vorstellungen vom Zustand nach dem Tode* (Freiburg: Mohr, 1899).

10 A Lods, *La croyance à la vie future et le culte des morts dans l'antiquité israélite* (Paris: Fischbacher, 1906).

in vocabulary and concepts.[11] The stress fell on the similarity of mythopoetic images regarding the descent into the underworld, of the cheerless melancholy of Sheol, and of the many threats of non-existence.[12]

The reaction which set in against the hegemony of the comparative method came from scholars who had been fully trained in this approach, but who sought to make important modifications. Pedersen's fascinating chapter on "The World of Life and Death"[13] shared much from the earlier comparative approach. He set the Israelite understanding of death in the context of primitive religion in which both earth and stones were given life. He saw the parallels with the Babylonian world of the dead and pursued closely the similarity in imagery between Israel and ancient Near Eastern culture.

However, Pedersen's main contribution was in trying to formulate a holistic understanding of Israel's beliefs which would do justice to their dynamic quality. For Pedersen the key lay in his understanding of a psychic whole which arose from a view of the soul. In spite of this somewhat idiosyncratic perspective which has not been widely accepted, Pedersen saw, as no one before him, the peculiar features of the Hebrew view of death as a power and as a place. "Sheol is the entirety into which all graves are merged" (p. 462). "Where there is grave, there is Sheol, and where there is Sheol, there is grave" (*ibid.*).

Pedersen did a masterful job in tracing the realms of death, which he called "non-worlds," and which were manifested in Sheol, desert, and ocean. Pedersen did not actually formulate a theory of a special Hebrew mentality, but his dynamic view set Israel apart from its neighbors and from the earlier portrayals of a piecemeal borrowing from the cultures of the ancient Near East.

The credit for working out the implications of some of Pedersen's theories with more philological refinement and theological depth goes to Christoph Barth.[14] As a student of Walter Baumgartner, he exploits to the fullest the use of comparative materials with emphasis on the cuneiform parallels. Barth's main approach, however, is exegetical. He addresses his central question: should one understand all the references to death in the Psalter metaphorically or "realistically"? Exactly what is meant by realistic is not fully explained, but it appears to be the opposite of metaphorical, and not quite the same as literal.

Barth comes down forcefully in rejecting a metaphorical interpretation of the terminology referring to death. Such a reading fails to do justice to the peculiar dynamic of the Old Testament which conceived of life and death in different categories. "Die Grenzen zwischen Leben und Tod verlaufen für sie anderswo als in unserem Denken" (p. 22). Although neither Pedersen nor Barth explicitly develops the concept of a special Hebrew mentality, one can easily see how such a theory would find warrants in their work. Indeed it is unclear whether the unique character of the Hebrew understanding of death lay in the assigning of peculiar semantic ranges to clusters of words or whether a different structuring of reality is being claimed. Barth has not pursued the issue, but left it unresolved with the word "realistic." When James Barr[15] launched his formidable attack on the whole notion of a special Hebrew mentality, he found much to criticize in Pedersen, but left C. Barth untouched. Whether this omission was accidental or intentional is unknown. Interestingly enough, the latest Old Testament theology to appear, which is that of C. Westermann,[16] simply summarizes the results of Barth's work with no basic criticism.

Finally, and perhaps the last major theological contribution to the discussion[17] is the important article of G. von Rad.[18] Von Rad stands fully on the shoulders of Gunkel's cultic interpretation of the Psalter, indeed agreeing with Mowinckel that Gunkel has not been fully consistent in still retaining vestiges of an older romantic interpretation. He argues that the "ultimate decision between life and death was for Israel a cultic matter, and only with the cultus did the individual receive assurance that he would have life" (p. 254). He then offers an important corrective to the work of Barth. Barth had concluded that none of the statements about God's saving a person from death actually involved a future life. Von

11 Cf. the summary and bibliography in O. C. Whitehouse, "Cosmogony," *Dictionary of Bible* (ed. J. Hastings; New York: Scribner, 1903): 1.503ff.

12 Fr. Delitzsch, *Das Land ohne Heimkehr. Die Gedanken der Babylonier-Assyrer über Tod und Jenseits* (Stuttgart: Deutsche Verlags-Anstalt, 1911); E. Ebeling, *Tod und Leben nach den Vorstellungen der Babylonier* (Berlin: Gruyter, 1931). For a more recent critical evaluation of this comparative material, cf. L. Wächter, *Der Tod im Alten Testament* (Stuttgart: Calwer, 1967). The use of Ugaritic is especially emphasized in N. J. Tromp, *Primitive Conceptions of Death and the Nether World in the Old Testament* (Rome: Pontifical Biblical Institute, 1969).

13 J. Pedersen, *Israel. Its Life and Culture* (2 vols.; Copenhagen, 1926; rpt. London: Oxford, 1946): 453-496. Some of Pedersen's conclusions appear to have been arrived at independently by A. R. Johnson, *The Vitality of the Individual in the Thought of Ancient Israel* (Cardiff: University of Wales, 1949).

14 C. Barth, *Die Erretung vom Tode* (Zürich: Zollikon, 1947).

15 J. Barr, *The Semantics of Biblical Language* (London: Oxford: 1961).

16 C. Westermann, *Theologie des Alten Testaments in Grundzügen* (Göttingen: Vandenhoeck, 1978).

17 This statement is not to suggest that no further work has been done on the subject. Cf. the bibliography in *RGG*[3] under "Tod und Totenreich im AT" and "Höhle." Further, H. Gese, "Der Tod im Alten Testament," *Zur biblischen Theologie* (Munich: Kaiser, 1977): 31-54.

18 G. von Rad, "'Righteousness' and 'Life' in the Cultic Language of the Psalms," *The Problem of the Hexateuch and Other Essays* (English translation, New York: McGraw Hill, 1966): 243-266.

Rad feels that this issue has been obscured by Barth's statistical method and his isolating of certain elements of the Psalmist's thought. He then suggests in classic form-critical style that one should attempt to shed light on the problem by investigating the peculiar cultic traditions which underlie the statements rather than seeing them apart from a setting. Moreover, he is able to show that the effect of such traditions as Yahweh's being Israel's portion provided a continuity of trust in God's presence which defied death.

However, equally important in von Rad's article is his insight regarding the new function of language—I would have said Scripture—which does not stem directly from his application of the form-critical method. Von Rad recognizes that an old cultic expression gives rise to a variety of different meanings which in time alter one's hearing of the older formulae. He speaks of a wealth of new meanings which were drawn from the older language. In my judgment, this insight goes far beyond the practice of the classic form-critical method which anchored a formula to its cultic function, and begins to pursue the effect of the language itself in creating new and fresh levels of meaning from older conventions.

A new avenue into the literature opens up when one begins to inquire how was it possible for later Jewish and Christian interpreters to hear, for example, in Ps 130, the promise of resurrection from the dead when originally this note was unexpressed. In my judgment, a most fruitful avenue for the theological reflection on death and dying in the Old Testament would be one which would reckon, not only with the original sociological setting of a biblical text, but with the later audiences who received, transmitted, and transformed the ancient literature to serve a new religious function.

LOVE AND DEATH AT EBLA AND THEIR BIBLICAL REFLECTIONS

MITCHELL DAHOOD

Browsing through the Ebla personal and place names that have been published, one comes to the conclusion that one reason why so many biblical names remain unexplained is the paucity of material in Canaanite to work with. For example, the name of the coastal city *ʾašdôd* has traditionally been derived from the root *šdd*, "to devastate," and the *aleph* explained as prothetic, an explanation that does not compel assent.[1] But now the thousands of tablets and fragments from Tell Mardikh-Ebla dating to circa 2500 BC in a Paleo-Canaanite language with thousands of personal and place names are putting an end to the paucity of material at the disposal of the biblical scholar.

The Eblaite personal name (hereinafter PN) *i-i-da-du*, "May he live long, O Love (*Dadu*)" (TM.75.G.336 obv. VII 3),[2] reveals the existence of the Canaanite god of love. Not recognizing that the language of Ebla is Canaanite, I. J. Gelb[3] analyzed the name as *ʾIjji-dādu*, "Where is the beloved?" but comparison with Ugaritic PNN *yḥṣdq*, "May he live long, O Justice," *yḥšr*, "May he live long, O Prince," and Hebrew PNN *yᵉḥîʾēl*, "May he live long, O El," and *yᵉḥîyāh*, "May he live long. O Yah," shows that syllabic *i-i* is an attempt to realize *yiḥî*, "May he live long." Of course, the root *ḥyh*, "to live" does not exist in Akkadian but is found only in Canaanite and Arabic languages; Akkadian employs *balāṭu* instead, a verb thus far not attested in the more than hundred published tablets from Ebla. Returning to *ʾašdôd*, the philologist now prefers to interpret it "Love has donated," wherein *ʾaš* parses as qal perfect of *ʾwš*, "to donate," a root widely documented at Ebla and witnessed in Ugaritic as *ušn*, "donation" (//*ytnt*, "gift"). The energic imperative of this root can be seen in the PN *u-ša-il*, "Donate, O Il" (*MEE* 1,760) whose juxtaposition of roots recalls *UT*, Krt:135–136, *udm.ytnt.il wušn ab.adm*, "Udum is the gift of El and the donation of the Father of mankind." Compare also *áš-ba-ni*, "the Builder has donated" (TM.75.G.336 rev. I 1), and *áš-má-sí-piš*, "Sun has donated" (TM.75.G.2238 rev. VI 9), with enclitic *-má-* inserted between the verb and the subject.[4] When compared with the Heb. PN *ḥur*, the PN *ʾašḥûr* in 1 Chron 2:24; 4:5 may be interpreted "(the god) Ḥûr has donated."

The semantic equivalent of *ʾašdôd*, "Love has donated," is represented by the toponym *šè-da-du*[ki], "Legacy of Love" (*MEE* 1,6536), whose initial element identifies with Ugar. *ṯy*, Heb. *šay*, "gift offered as homage," an isogloss uniting Hebrew, Ugaritic and Eblaite. It recurs in *šè-la-ṭù*[ki], "Legacy of Ladanum"[5] (*MEE* 1,6522), *ar-šè-a-ḫu*, "Light, Legacy is Brother" (TM.75.G.336 rev. IV 14), *ìl-šè* (AN.ŠÈ), "El is a Legacy" (*MEE* 2,7 obv. II 5), and *ší-a-um* "Legacy of the Terrible (TM.76.G.523 rev. XI 6).[6]

Another reference to the god of love is found in the toponym *šu-da-du*[ki], "Lamb of Love" (TM.75.G.6030, obv.III)[7] Though some would prefer to understand *šu* as the determinative pronoun, "the one of," the frequency in the Eblaite onomasticon of animal plus divine name favors the interpretation of *šu* as "lamb, small head of

* Please note the following abbreviations: MEE = *Materiali Epigrafici di Ebla. MEE* 1 = G. Pettinato, *Catalogo dei Testi Cuneiformi di Tell Mardikh-Ebla* (Istituto Univeritario Orientale di Napoli; Seminario di Studi Asiatici, Series Maior; Napoli, 1979); *MEE* 2 = G. Pettinato, *Testi amministrativi della Biblioteca L. 2769* (Napoli, 1980); *UT* = C. H. Gordon, *Ugaritic Textbook*.

1 See F. M. Cross, Jr. and D. N. Freedman, "The Name of Ashdod," *BASOR* 175 (1964) 48–50, who correctly argue that the name *ʾašdōd* is Canaanite, but their derivation from an unattested *ṯdd*, with prothetic *aleph*, is fraught with difficulties. Nor does their statement "The city was founded probably in the sixteenth century B.C." (p. 48) bear up in the face of evidence from Ebla where the city is mentioned; see G. Pettinato, *Ebla: Un impero inciso nell'argilla* (Milano: Mondadori, 1979): 206. See also M. C. Astour in *Ras Shamra Parallels* II (ed. L. Fisher; AnOr 50; Rome: 1975):/8 255-257, for a full discussion of Ugaritic *aḏdd*. A derivation from *ʾāšēd*, "slope," proposed by A. Bongini, *Annali dell'Istituto Universitario Orientale di Napoli* 19 (1969): 182–84, seems less likely.

2 Published by G. Pettinato, *Rivista degli studi orientali* 50 (1976): 5.

For the nuance "live long" in *ḥāyāh*, see Job 21:7, for example, or *UT*, 76:II:20, *ḥwt aḫt wnar*[*k*, "May you live long, O my sister, and prolong your days!"

3 *Thoughts about Ibla: A Preliminary Evaluation*, March 1977 (Syro-Mesopotamian Studies 1/1; Undena Publications, Malibu, CA, May, 1977): 24.

4 Another convincing example is provided by *i-ti-ma-il*, "With me indeed is El" (*MEE* 2,7 obv. XI 5), which may be compared with Gen 10:28, *ʾăbîmāʾēl*, "My father indeed is El."

5 The name of this deity is apparently borne by *lôṭ*, the nephew of Abraham.

6 Published by G. Pettinato in *State and Temple Economy in the Ancient Near East* I (ed. E. Lipiński; Orientalia Lovaniensia Analecta 5; Leuven, 1979): 171–233; see p. 232.

7 Consult G. Pettinato, *Ebla* (N 1): 91.

cattle."[8] Similar formations recur in *šu-ra-um* "Lamb of the Merciful" (*MEE* 1,760); *šu-ma-lik*, "Lamb of Malik" (*MEE* 2,19 obv. I 9); *šu-ma-ni*, "Lamb of Destiny" (*MEE* 2,7 rev. VI 8); *šu-ra-an*, "Lamb of the Verdant" (*MEE* 1,2150-2214, 6522), and *šu-ì-lum*, "Lamb of God" (TM.75.G.336 obv. V 8).

In the Index of toponyms in *MEE* 1, one recognizes some place names beginning with the sumerogram é "house, temple" that will surely prove relevant to biblical theology. The most striking is é-*da-bar*[ki], "Temple of the Word," where the theologian immediately recognizes the divinized Word. Since *dābār*, "word," has been till now exclusively Hebraic, its appearance in third-millennium Ebla may reveal something of Hebrew origins. Then there is é-*šu-mu*[ki], "Temple of the Name," but the divinized Name has already been identified in Eblaite PNN such as *ṭù-bí-šum*, "My good is the Name," and *iš-má-šum*, "the Name has heard."[9] In é-*za-an*[ki] is recognizable biblical Beth-Shan "Temple of Shan," the god of repose and tranquility, and é-*da-du*[ki], "Temple of Love," which further manifests the popularity of this god among the Canaanites. The same holds true for the frequently mentioned place name which Pettinato reads *NI-da-tum*[ki] (*MEE* 1,782,1268 etc.) but which is preferably read *ì-da-dum*[ki], "Island of Love," whose preformative *ì* equates with Heb. *ʾî*, "island, coast," a geographical term found till now only in Hebrew and Phoenician.[10]

Till now unattested, the qal perfect of the root *dwd* appears in the PNN *da-da-ar*, "Light loves" (*MEE* 1,860); *da₅-da-ar*, "Light loves" (*MEE* 1,760,5010):[11] *da-da-yà*, "Ya loves" (*MEE* 1,1671). The last name possibly provides the vocalization for the Ugaritic PN *ddy* (*UT*, 2014:44).

An exclusively Canaanite[12] root till now witnessed in Hebrew, Punic, and Ugaritic, *ʾhb* appears in two different conjugations in Eblaite PNN. The qal active participle occurs in the hypocoristic name *a-i-bù* / *ʾahibu*, "Lover," (*MEE* 1,1603) and the passive qal participle in *a-ù-bù* / *ʾahubu*, "Beloved" (*MEE* 2,43, rev. VII 6). The piel conjugation is represented by *i-ib-ma-lik* / *ʾihhib-malik*, "Malik loves" (*MEE* 2,3 obv. IV 13; 19 rev. VIII 1). In Biblical Hebrew the piel conjugation occurs only in the participial form.

How one classifies Eblaite will influence one's interpretation of personal names whose limited syntax allows for considerable ambiguity. In a conference given at the 25th Rencontre d'Assyriologie in Berlin 3–7 July, 1978, Pelio Fronzaroli interpreted the Ebla PN *ré-ì-ma-lik* as "ND est (mon) berger" (*MEE* 1,833; *MEE* 2,12 rev. IV 4), a defensible translation in the light of Akkadian *rēʾû*, "shepherd." Even G. Pettinato, who considers Eblaite a Paleo-Canaanite language, translates *ré-ì-na-*[d]*IM* = *ré-ì-na-im* "il mio pastore è (il dio) Na'im,"[13] overlooking the fact that in Northwest Semitic *rēʿū* signifies "friend," so that the proper rendition of these names would be "My friend is Malik" and "My friend is *Naʿim*." In other terms, both components should be treated consistently; since *malik*, "King" is Canaanite and not Akkadian, sound method requires the translation of *ré-ì* as "my friend"; in Canaanite "my shepherd" would be *rāʿî*, Heb. *rōʿî*, and is probably witnessed in the PN *gú-ra-u₉*, "Voice is shepherd" (*MEE* 2,22 rev. IV 10). Ugaritic carefully distinguishes between *rʿy*, "shepherd," and *rʿ*, "friend."[14] Other names containing *ré*, "friend," include *ré-ì-ḫa-lam*, "My friend is Health" (*MEE* 2,11 rev.III 7); *ga-du-rí*, "Fortune is my friend" (*MEE* 2,30 obv. X 4); *gú-rí-ì*[ki], "Voice is my friend" (*MEE* 1, 1671); and *ré-dì*, "A friend is Abundance" (*MEE* 2,19 obv. VI 2).[15] Compare the biblical PNN *rēʿû* (Gen 11:18); *rēʿûʾēl*, "El is a friend" (Exod 2:18); *rēʿî*, "My friend" (1 Kgs 1:8), a hypocoristic name whose divine component is omitted.

Friendship is also expressed by the term *wa-lu*, "companion, kinsman," Ugar. *yly* (// *aḫ*, "brother"), in the toponyms *gú-wa-lu*[ki], "Voice is a companion" (TM.75.G.188 obv. III 4; rev. II 10),[16] and *wa-lí-ni-um*[ki], "My companion is the Oracle" (*MEE* 2,32 obv. VI 6). In the second name *ni-um* is to be identified with Heb. *nēʾūm*, "oracle," another Hebrew-Eblaite isogloss relating these two Canaanite languages, whereas *wa-lu*, "companion," may be recognized in Ps 139:17, *wēlî mah-yyāqērû rēʿêkā*, "O my companion, how precious are your friends!" Ugaritic PN *yly* may now be interpreted "My companion is Ya."

The bilingual vocabulary from Ebla which defines Sumerian sal, "female," by *ì-ma-tum*[17] furnishes the

8 Hebrew *śeh* does not argue against this; compare Eblaite *pù*, "mouth," with Hebrew absolute *peh*, "mouth."

9 Consult my article "The Ebla Tablets and Old Testament Theology," *Theology Digest* 27, (1979): 303-11.

10 See my study "Some Preformatives in Eblaite Place Names" in *Mélanges Henri Cazelles* (AOAT; Neukirchen-Vluyn, 1982).

11 Compare *da-du-sipiš* (UD), "Love is Sun" (*MEE* 1,4932).

12 Its occurrence in Aramaic is doubtful according to C. F. Jean – J. Hoftijzer, *Dictionnaire des inscriptions sémitiques de l'ouest*, p. 6.

13 *Oriens Antiquus* 19 (1980): 70.

14 Accordingly, Phoenician-Punic PN *rʿmlk* should be understood in the light of Eblaite *ré-ì-ma-lik*, "My friend is Malik." H. Donner's speculations (*ZAW* 73 [1961]: 274, n. 34) that *rʿmlk* is a late, no longer understood remnant of the name of an office, *rēʿe(h) hammelek* (in Heb.) ultimately of Egyptian origin, has no further claim on our attention.

15 Identifying the important Eblaite god *dì* with Heb. *day*, "sufficiency, abundance," predicated of Yahweh in Mal 3:10, *ʿad bᵉlî-dāy*, "until my abundance is exhausted" (cf. Ps 72:7). Many of the names of the Canaanite gods at Ebla have ended up in Hebrew poetry as attributes of Yahweh.

16 Published by G. Pettinato, *Ebla* (N 1): 207–08, 211. Of course, *gú-wa-lu*[ki] recalls *gú-rí-ù*, "Voice is a friend," discussed above.

17 See G. Pettinato, *Ebla* (N 1): 262.

solution to a text describing love and envy in Prov. 6:34–35:

kî qinʾēʾāh ḥămat gāber
wĕlōʾ-yaḥmôl bĕyôm nāqām
lōʾ yiśśāʾ pĕnê kol-kōper
wĕlōʾ yōʾbeh kî tarbeh-šōḥad

If a wife incites her husband to jealousy,
he will not be sparing on the day of revenge;
no payment will placate his fury,
nor will he accept though she make the bribe enormous.

For piel *qinnēʾ*, "to incite to jealousy," see Deut 32:21 and 1 Kings 14:22. In Eblaite the qal is preserved in the PN *iq-na-da-mu*, "Damu is jealous" (*MEE* 1,866,1009, etc.). The chief problem in vs.34 has been *ḥămat*, usually taken as "wrath"; the identification of *ḥămat* with Eblaite *ì-ma-tum* clears up the difficulty. Cf. Ugaritic *ḥmḥmt*, "impregnation," Egyptian *ḥm.t*, "woman, wife," and Punic *bt ḥm*, "vulva," the last discussed by G. Garbini, *Rivista degli studi orientali* 46 (1971) 138–39. The absolute form *ḥămat*, "wife," would be another example of feminine nouns ending in *-t* instead of *-āh*, in the absolute state.[18] The root of *yaḥmôl* occurs in the Eblaite PN *a-mu-lu*, "spared" (TM.75.G.1764 rev.X 5),[19] which may be compared with the biblical name *ḥāmûl*, the grandson of Judah mentioned in Gen 46:12.[20] The suffix of *pĕnê* "his fury," parses as third person masculine singular, as in Phoenician,[21] while the sense of *pānîm*, "fury," is quite evident from this as well as other contexts.[22] The bilingual vocabulary which renders Sumerian URUDU, "copper," by Eblaite *kà-pá-lu*[23] sheds lights on *kōper*, "payment, gift."[24] Since the scribes at Ebla sometimes write *lu* for *ru*,[25] the equivalence of *kà-pá-lu* and *kōper* is quickly established, and the etymology of Cyprus, a chief source of copper in antiquity, discovered. This definition also elucidates *kōper*, "henna," a reddish-orange (hence the color of copper) dye made from the leaves of henna, and *kĕpîr* frequently rendered "young lion," but now preferably to be understood as "tawny lion." Ezek 38:13, *sōḥărê taršîš wĕkol-kĕpîrêhā*, may now be translated "the traders of Tarshish and all her copper goods."[26]

In a recent study[27] I proposed that *kî tarbeh-šōḥad* be rendered, "however large the bribe," with *tarbeh* parsed as a masculine whose subject is *šōḥad*, but now with the recognition that *ḥămat* means "wife," I prefer the version "though she make the bribe enormous," with *tarbeh* parsed as third feminine singular. The chiastic sequence of the verb genders in Prov 6:34–35 now comes into focus: *qinʾēʾāh* : *yaḥmôl* :: *yiśśāʾ* : *yōʾbeh* : *tarbeh*.

In this new information from Ebla may lie the solution of the problems besetting a verse usually considered corrupt, Ps 76:11:

kî – ḥămat ʾādām tôdekkā
šĕʾērît ḥēmōt taḥgōr

Indeed women, men praise you,
with the descendants of women you surround yourself.

In Prov 6:34 *ḥămat* and *gāber* are juxtaposed; here the juxtaposition *ḥămat ʾādām* is strikingly similar. The MT vocalization *ḥēmōt* in the second colon reflects the initial vowel of Eblaite *ì-ma-tum*, "female," and this suggests that first-colon *ḥămat* should probably be repointed to *ḥēmat*, but both here and in Prov 6:34 I have retained the MT vowels for the time being. The reflexive rendition of *taḥgōr*, "you surround yourself," is based on context and the usage in Ps 65:13, *wĕgîl gĕbāʿôt taḥgōrnāh*, "and

18 Consult Gesenius-Kautzsch, *Grammatik*, § 80e-g.

19 Published by G. Pettinato, *Oriens Antiquus* 18 (1979): 142.

20 The suggestion in W. Baumgartner, *Hebräisches und aramäisches Lexikon zum Alten Testament* (Leiden: Brill, 1967): I, 313b, that *ḥāmûl* stems from *ḥāmûʾēl* (*ḥām* + *ʾēl*) can be safely dismissed.

21 For Job 41:2 *lpny* "before him," see M. Dahood in *The Role of the Phoenicians in the Interaction of Mediterranean Civilizations* (ed. W. A. Ward; Beirut: American University, 1968): 133. Cf. also Jer. 6:7, *ḥāmās wāšōd yiššāmaʿ bāh* / *ʿal pānēy* (MT *pānay*) *tāmîd ḥōlî ûmakkāh*, "Violence and destruction resound in her / upon her face never-ending sickness and wounds." Since the suffix of *bāh* refers to feminine city, the suffix of *pny* should also be construed as feminine, as in Phoenician. For the parallelism of the prepositions *bāh* // *ʿal pny*, see *UT*, *ʿnt*:III:29–31, *bh.pʿnm tṭṭ.* / *bʿdn.ksl.ṯṯbr* / *ʿln. pnh.tdʿ*, "In her, her feet become like clay / behind, her loins are shattered / above, her face sweats."

22 To the examples cited in *Biblica* 51 (1970): 399–400, I would add Jer 3:12, *lōʾ – ʾappîl pānay bākem kî-ḥāsîd ʾănî*, "I will not drop my fury upon you since I am merciful."

23 See G. Pettinato, *Ebla* (N 1): 206, 248, n. 31, and 262. The tablet number is TM.75.G. 1678 obv. III 6. Since Sumerian-Akkadian bilinguals equate URUDU, "bronze," with *erû*, it becomes obvious from URUDU = *kà-pá-lu* at Ebla that Eblaite is not early Akkadian but rather a Canaanite tongue.

24 For a recent study of *kōper*, see H. C. Brichto, *HUCA* 47 (1976): 19–55, esp. 26–27, 35. Brichto correctly points out that etymological derivations of *kipper*, "to compose a difference," from putative cognates in Arabic with the meaning "to cover" or in Akkadian with the sense "to rub, wipe" are without support in biblical Hebrew; derivation from Eblaite *kà-pá-ru*, "copper," now offers a Canaanite commercial explanation for an important theological term, as well as upsetting the Egyptian etymology of biblical *kappōret*, "cover, lid," recently proposed by M. Görg, *Biblische Notizen* 5 (Bamburg 8, 1978): 12.

25 Consult G. Pettinato, *Ebla* (N 1): 68.

26 Contrast the most recent English translation of the Bible, the *New International Version of the Holy Bible* (Abbr. *NIV*; Grand Rapids: Zondervan, 1978), which renders, "the merchants of Tarshish and all her villages," with the alternate version or "her strong lions." If the latter is correct, *kĕpîrêhā*, "her tawny lions," may have a metaphorical sense of "tycoons," the metaphor suggesting the color common to the copper currency and to the lions. Consult my comments on Ps 34:11, *kĕpîrîm*, in *Psalms I* (AB 16; Garden City: Doubleday, 1966): 206.

27 "Third Masculine Singular with Preformative *t-* in Northwest Semitic" in *Orientalia* 48 (1979) 97–106, esp. 105.

with exultation may the hills gird themselves." The nuance "descendants" of *šĕʾērît* is suggested by Gen 45:7; 2 Sam 14:7, and Isa 14:22 where masucline *šĕʾār* also bears this connotation. That *šĕʾār* must not be emended to feminine *šĕʾērît* with IQIs[a] appears from the comparison of Ps 76:11 *šĕʾērît ḥēmōt*, "the descendants of women," with *UT*, Krt:15, *ṯar um*, "the offspring / descendants of a mother."

In Song of Songs 1:12 where the beloved describes the effect of her perfume, she employs the phrase *ʿad šĕhammelek bimĕsibbô*, "while the king was on his cushion," where the hapax legomenon *mĕsibbô* has been interpreted in various ways.[28] The more common renditions "table" or "couch" may be inexact in the light of the economic text *MEE* 2,11 rev.IV 4–6: 20 KIN_x-síg UNKEN-aka 10 *ma-sà-bù*, "20 skeins of wool to make 10 round cushions." One can scarcely dissociate *ma-sà-bù* from Heb. *mĕsibbô*; made of wool and round, this hapax should mean something like a round cushion or rug, hardly a table or divan.

The bilingual vocabulary TM.75.G.1302 obv. IV 12-V 1, which equates Sumerian šà-gal, "stout heart" and Eblaite *da-gi-lu*, suggests that biblical lexicographers would be well advised to distinguish now between *dgl* I, "to be visible," and *dgl* II, "to be stout-hearted." To *dgl* II would be assigned the following four texts.

Ps 20:6

nĕranĕnāh bîšûʿātekā
ûbĕšēm ʾĕlōhênû nidgōl

That we might exult in your victory,
and in the Name of our God be stout-hearted.

On this hypothesis, the second colon translated thus becomes synonymous with 8b, *waʾănaḥnû bĕšēm-yhwh ʾĕlōhênû nazkîr*, "But we through the Name of Yahweh our God are strong," when *nazkîr* is explained as a denominative verb from *zākār*, "male."[29] The Ebla equivalence enables us to dispense with the emendation of *nidgōl* to *nĕgaddel* or *nagdîl*, as some on the basis of the LXX would prefer.

Equally attractive is the sense that this new root brings to Song of Songs 5:10:

dôdî ṣaḥ wĕʾādôm
dāgûl mērĕbābāh

My beloved is radiant and ruddy,
more stout-hearted than ten thousand.

This combination of beauty and courage recalls the description of David in 1 Sam 16:12, *wĕhûʾ ʾadmônî ʿām* (MT *ʿim*) *yĕpēh ʿênayim wĕṭôb rōʾî*, "He was ruddy, robust, bright-eyed, and handsome."[30] The latest translation of Song of Songs 5:10 by *NIV*, "outstanding among ten thousand," makes free with the preposition of *mērĕbābāh*, whereas the new definition ascribes to it a comparative function.

Beauty and strength also combine in Song of Songs 6:4:

yāpāh ʾatt raʿyātî kĕtirṣāh
nāʾwāh kîrûšalāim
ʾāyummāh kannidgālôt

You are beautiful, my darling, as Tirzah,
lovely as Jerusalem,
awesome as the fortified cities.

Balancing the cities Tirzah and Jerusalem, which are feminine, the niphal feminine participle *nidgālôt* should express a substantive belonging to the same category. The new root from Ebla renders this possible. Whether the poet intended *nidgālôt* to stand in apposition with Tirzah and Jersalem or indicate fortified cities in general cannot be securely established. On the basis of Akk. *dagālu*, "look with astonishment," R. Gordis renders our phrase "awe-inspiring as these great sights,"[31] but this version does not compel assent. Cf. also Song of Songs 6:10, where "as the fortified cities" yields satisfactory sense, though not as convincing as in the context of 6:4.

In his detailed commentary on Song of Songs 2:4, M. H. Pope[32] observes that *degel* in the present context has occasioned no little difficulty and discussion; he rightly notes that while the consonants of *dglw* should not be changed, this has no bearing on the question whether in the present instance the word should be read as noun or verb. The Eblaite definition permits its reading as a verb

28 See the most recent discussion by M. . Pope, *The Song of Songs* (AB 7c; Garden City: Doubleday, 1977): 347–348, who translates it "couch" with the comment "a low couch or divan on which participants in a banquet reclined." The root is *sbb*, "to go around, surround."

29 As proposed by me in *Psalms I* (N 26): 129.

30 On numerous occasions I have argued that Ugaritic and Hebrew possessed the root *ʿmm*, "to be robust, strong"; e.g., see *Psalms III*, XXXI, 68, 116.

In the light of biblical *yĕpēh ʿênayim*, the personal name *ypʿn* in text 78 / 19 from Ras Ibn Hani may be translated "Bright-eyed. This tablet has been published along with several others by A. Caquot in *L'Annuaire du Collège de France 79e Année*: Resumé de cours et travaux année scolaire 1978–1979, p. 482. In this preliminary publication Caquot does not attempt an analysis of the name.

31 "The Root *dgl* in the Song of Songs," *JBL* 88 (1969): 203–04. It would appear that the Ebla finds are going to call for a reassessment of our priorities when seeking solutions to textual problems in the OT. When the Ebla bilinguals translate Sumerian en by *ma-li-ku*, "king," and not by Akk. *šarru*, and urudu, "copper," is rendered by *kà-pá-lu* and not by Akk. *erû*, and eme-bala, "translator," by *tá-da-bì-lu* (*tadabbiru*), a root unknown in Akkadian, it becomes rather evident that the language of Canaan was distinct from that of Mesopotamia, so that today the biblical philologist will have to exercise greater caution when invoking Akkadian etymologies.

32 *Song of Songs* (N 28): 375–77. Appealing to Akk. *diglu*, "wish," he renders vs. 4, "He brought me into the wine house / His intent toward me Love" (p. 364).

and the tentative translation of 2:4:

hĕbî ʾanî ʾel-bêt hayyayin
wĕdigĕlô ʿālay ʾahăbāh

He brought me into the house of wine,
which fortified in him his love for me.

Though scholars usually parse MT *diglô* as the noun "his banner," it can also be pointed *digĕlô*, the piel preterit without the doubling of the *ghimel* because of the following vocal *shewa*, and analyzed as the intensive of *dāgal*, "to be stout-hearted," followed by the dative suffix. Since the aphrodisiac effects of wine are well known, the verse needs no further commentary.

DEATH AT EBLA

Since no literary texts in Eblaite have yet been published, the philologist must, as in the discourse about love, content himself with personal and place names and the information yielded by the bilinguals. To judge from these sources alone, though, one concludes that the Eblaite conception of death was not unlike that of the Israelites who borrowed many of their terms describing the realm of the dead from their Canaanite predecessors.[33] For example, Israel's principal name for the netherworld, *šĕʾôl*, has never been identified outside the Bible, but now Ebla witnesses the toponym *ši-a-la*^{ki} (*MEE* 1,1027) which phonetically answers to biblical *šĕʾôl*. What is more, *ši-a-la*^{ki} preserves the feminine ending which has been lost in *šĕʾôl*, but which is nonetheless feminine in Hebrew. Another exclusively Hebrew designation for the abode of the dead is *ʾăbaddôn*, a term recurring six times in the poetic books but which now appears in an economic tablet from Ebla (*MEE* 2,40 rev. III 12–14): 11 *é-da-um*-túg-2 11 aktum-túg 11 ib 3-túg-ša$_6$-dar *mi-ti a-ba-da-nu*, "11 Edaum fabrics of second quality, 11 Aktum fabric, 11 top-quality Ib fabrics for the dead in Abaddan." From the objects and furnishings found in the stone tombs of Ras Shamra, it is clear that the Canaanites considered the dead in need of food and drink, and now we learn from this Ebla document that garments as well were provided for the denizens of Abaddan. The construct chain *mi-ti a-ba-da-nu*[34] juxtaposes two roots that are also juxtaposed in Job 28:22, *ʾăbaddôn wāmāwet*, "Abaddon and Death," and Job 26:6 balances *šĕʾôl* and *ʾăbaddôn*, both of which are found in Ebla if the equation *ši-a-la*^{ki} equals *šĕʾôl* proves correct.

Another frequent biblical designation for the underworld is *šaḥat*, "Pit," cognate with *šûḥāh*, "pit." Among the gods receiving offerings from the royal family of Ebla is a certain ^{d}*šu-ḫa*, a name that Pettinato[35] reads as Sumerian, "il dio pescatore," but since these texts reflect an aspect of Eblaite culture which is "puramente semitico-occidentale"—to use Pettinato's description[36]—the name should be interpreted as Canaanite *šu-ḫa*, "Pit," an infernal deity who can scarcely be dissociated from Heb. *šaḥat*, "Pit." Compare Prov 2:18, *kî šāḥāh ʾel-māwet bêtāh*, "For her house sinks down to Death." It might also be noted in the discussion concerning the links between Ebla and Genesis that one of the sons of Abraham and Keturah was named *šûaḥ* from the same root as ^{d}*šu-ḫa* (Gen 25:1). This identification may bear upon the interpretation of the divine name ^{d}*gú-bí*, who receives offerings from the royal family in the sixth and eleventh months.[37] Hebrew preserves the noun *gēb*, "pit, ditch, trench," from the verb *gûb*, "to dig," and Syriac *gûbâ*, "cistern," may prove even more relevant because of its vocalization.

But the most important of the infernal deities receiving offerings is ^{d}*ra-sa-ap*, who is mentioned at least 20 times in the four tablets from which Pettinato has reconstructed the official cult at the time of Ibbi-Sipiš, the last king of the dynasty at Ebla.[38]

The three gods ^{d}*šu-ḫa*, ^{d}*gú-bí*, and ^{d}*ra-sa-ap*, do not, however, exhaust the list of nether deities. The administrative text registering the outlay of loaves for gods and humans (*MEE* 1,238) mentions along with ^{d}*ra-sa-ap* the god ^{d}*sa-mi-ù*. Could this be an epithet of Death, the Thirsty One, who is probably alluded to in the imagery of Isa 5:13b? MT reads *ûkĕbôdô mĕtê rāʿāb wahămônô ṣiḥēh ṣāmāʾ*, "Their men of rank will die of hunger and their masses will be parched with thirst" (*NIV*). This version assumes that MT *mĕtê* "men of" is to be read *mētê*, "dying of," though no note informs of a repointing. If MT *mĕtê* is preserved but *rāʿāb* and *ṣāmāʾ* revocalized *rāʿēb* and *ṣāmēʾ*, respectively, the distich would translate "their men of rank are men for the Hungry One / and for their masses the Thirsty One thirsts."[39] Verse 14 states, "Therefore Sheol opens wide her throat / and distends her mouth without limit," so that the new readings *rāʿēb* and *ṣāmēʾ* fit the context.

In a series of Ebla toponyms beginning with the

---

33 Consult the valuable study by N. J. Tromp, *Primitive Conceptions of Death and the Nether World in the Old Testament* (Biblica et Orientalia 21; Rome: Pontifical Biblical Institute, 1969).

34 From the nominative ending of *a-ba-da-nu*, as well as from other examples, it is clear that Eblaite, unlike Ugaritic, did not observe case endings, a conclusion which will upset some theories about the development of Semitic languages.

35 "Culto ufficiale ad Ebla durante il regno di Ibbi-sipiš," *Oriens Antiquus* 18(1979): 85–215, esp. 110. These four tablets published by Pettinato possess a special significance in that they reveal who were the important gods receiving homage from the royal family.

36 *Ibid.*, 85.

37 Pettinato, *ibid.*, p. 104, n. 116, suggests an identification with Kubi(m) of Paleo-Assyrian texts.

38 *Ibid.*, 108–110, and n. 130, which sends the reader to W. J. Fulco, *The Canaanite God Rešep* (New Haven: American Oriental Society, 1976), for further information.

39 I would parse the hapax legomenon *ṣiḥēh* (or *ṣiḥeh*) as the piel preterit and compare Aram. *ṣeḥaʾ* and *ṣeḥî*, "to be thirsty."

sumerogram é "temple of," such as *é-da-bar*[ki], "Temple of the Word," figures *é-sà-mi*[ki] (*MEE* 1,6536), which may be interpreted "Temple of the Thirsty One"; in the Ebla syllabary the sign sà sometimes reflects the emphatic *ṣa* and the vowels of *sà-mi* answer to Heb. **ṣāmēʾ*, "the Thirsty One."

In recent decades the dispute over child sacrifice among the ancient Canaanites has elicited numerous articles and responses, and sooner or later the Ebla archives will have something to contribute to the ongoing debate. At present the most relevant item seems to be the place name *kùr-tá-pi₅-tù*[ki] (Pettinato *gur-da-bí-tù*[ki] in *MEE* 1,6522) which when interpreted in the light of Heb. *kûr*, "furnace," and *tōpet*, "Topheth," would suggest a place for child sacrifice. There is also the toponym *kàr-tá-pi₅-tù*[ki] (Pettinato *gàr-da-bí-tù* in *MEE* 1,6522), "the Market of Topheth." When compared with *kàr-kà-mi-iš*, "Market of Kamish," it becomes quite clear that *tá-pi₅-tù* was a deity. Just as Molech (Eblaite [d]*ma-li-ku*) was a god to whom children were sacrificed (e.g. 2 Kgs 23:10), so too Topheth appears to have been originally a Canaanite god to whom children were sacrificed and whose name later came to indicate the place of such immolations (e.g. Jer 7:31).

The text of Job 33:22 is clear except for the final congeries of consonants (*lmmtym*) which may be divided and translated in several different ways.

> *wattiqrab laššaḥat napšô*
> *wĕḥayyātô lmmtym* (MT *lamĕmītîm*)

The scholar we honor has correctly seen that the second colon is speaking of the infernal waters and proposed to read *lĕmê-māwet-mô*, "to the waters of Death," wherein the final *-m* of *lm* is taken as *scriptio defectiva* for *mê*, and the final *-m* of *mytm* parsed as enclitic *-mô*.[40] This attractive solution omits the *-y-* of *mtym* on the assumption that the original text read *mtm*. An Ebla bilingual with *ma-wu* expressing the term for "water,"[41] and the phonetic development *ma-wu*>*maw*> *mô* now prompt the reading *wĕḥayyātô lĕmō mĕtîm*, "and his life to the Waters of the dead." The partial balance with *šaḥat*, "Pit," points to *lĕmō*, "to the Waters," as the vocalization of *lm* precisely because these terms concur in Job 9:30–31, *bĕmô-šāleg*, "with water from snow," . . . *ʾāz baššaḥat tiṭbĕlēnî*, "then you would plunge me into the pit."[42]

In fact, this new reading in Job 33:22 recovering the phrase *mō-mĕtîm*, "the waters of the dead," may shed light on the obscure final phrase in Isa 53:8:

> *kî nigzar mēʾereṣ ḥayyîm*
> *mippešaʿ ʿammî nāgaʿ* (MT *negaʿ*) *lāmô*
>
> For he was cut off from the land of the living,
> for the rebellion of his people[43] he reached the Waters.

In antithetic parallelism with "from the land of the living" and followed by *qibrô*, "his grave," in the next vese, *lāmô*, "to the Waters," may be understood as short for Job's *lĕmō mĕtîm*, "to the Waters of the dead." In other terms *nāgaʿ lāmô*, "he reached the Waters," would be semantically close to Job 33:22, *wattiqrab... lĕmō mĕtîm*.[44]

In Ps 66:7 *lāmô*, "into the waters," carries a double meaning: the waters of the Reed Sea and the waters of the dead. The tricolon may now be read:

> *mōšēl bigĕbûrātô ʿôlām*
> *ʿênāyw baggôyīm tiṣpênāh*
> *hassōrĕrîm ʾēl* (MT *ʾal*) *yĕrāyāmô* (MT *yarymû*) *lāmô*
>
> Dominating by his eternal might,
> his eyes keep watch on the nations,
> the stubborn—God hurled them into the waters.

The Ebla PN *il-maš-il* (*MEE* 2,35 rev. II 8) suggests that MT *ʾal* be repointed to *ʾel* so as to recover the composite divine name *ʾēl mōšēl*, whose components are separated in the first and third cola. Compare Ps 59:14, "That they might know that God rules from Jacob to the edges of the earth," where the psalmist uses *ʾĕlōhîm mōšēl*. The mention of *ʾēl* in the third colon would be an instance of delayed identification.[45] The *casus pendens hassōrĕrîm* may be rendered either "the rebellious" or "the stubborn"; since these are the Egyptians who refused to be convinced by the signs worked by God on behalf of the Israelites, "the stubborn" appears to preferable. The unexplained series of consonants *yrymw* makes sense when *yry* is parsed as the archaic form of *yārāh*, with the preservation of the original final *-y* as in Ugaritic *yry*, and *mw* analyzed as the plural resumptive suffix which resumes the *casus pendens*, "the stubborn."[46] The reconstruction of *yrymw lmw*, "He hurled them into

---

40 M. H. Pope, *Job* (3rd. ed.; AB 15; Garden City, NY: Doubleday, 1973): 246, 251.

41 See M. Dahood, " 'A Sea of Troubles': Notes on Psalms 55:3–4 and 140:10–11," *CBQ* 41 (1979): 604–607, esp. 606.

42 The new evidence from Ebla conflicts with the analysis in L. Fisher edit., *Ras Shamra Parallels* I (Analecta Orientalia 49; ed. L. Fisher; Rome: Pontificium Institutum Biblicum, 1972): p. 243, where I proposed to find the parallel pair *l // lm* in *laššaḥat*, "to the Pit," and *lĕmō mĕtîm*, "to the dead," though I incline toward the "Ebla" solution because of the pair *mô*, "water," and *šaḥat*, "pit," in Job 9:30–31. Hence I cannot agree with *NIV* which, following Pope, renders Job 9:30a, "Even if I washed myself with soap."

43 The variant *ʿmw* in IQIs[a] shows that MT *ʿammî* should be rendered "his people," but to emend *ʿammî*, to *ʿammô* is no longer necessary, since the suffix of *ʿmy* can, within the larger paradigm of Northwest Semitic, be parsed as third masculine singular.

44 Compare also Ps. 88:4, *wĕḥayyay lišĕʾôl higgîʿû*, "and my life has reached Sheol."

45 For other instances in Ugaritic and Hebrew, see M. Dahood, *Ugarit Forschungen* 1 (1969): 27, and *Psalms III*, 56.

46 Cf. P. Joüon, *Grammaire de l'Hébreu Biblique*, § 158h–k, who employs the term "rétrospectif" to describe this kind of suffix.

the waters," recalls Exod 15:4, "The chariots of Pharoah and his army he hurled into the sea" (*yārāh bayyām*).

Among modern scholars no one has written more extensively or more penetratingly about the ancient institution called the *marzēaḥ*, than Marvin Pope. He has traced the history of this bacchanalian funeral banquet in art and letters from circa 1500 B.C. down to early Christian centuries. The earliest textual reference to the *mrzḥ* that Pope discussed in 1977[47] came from 14th-century Ugarit, and he will surely be delighted to learn that the term now appears a millennium earlier in *MEE* 2,46 rev. I 1–3, in ud *mar-za-u*₉ itu *i-ši*, "on the day of the Banquet in the month of Man (May)." Pope has also observed that "the 'Marzēaḥ House' is thus virtually synonymous with the 'Banquet House,' *bêt mišteh* literally 'house of drinking'."[48] This too is borne out by an Ebla text that mentions two garments offered to the god Rasap, in ud *maš-da-ù* dumu-nita-*sù*, "on the day of the drinking feast of his son" (*MEE* 2,2 obv. IV 10–17). A comparison of the two contexts and phrases reveals that in Eblaite as well, the two terms *mar-za-u*₉ and *maš-da-ù* are semantically akin.

To the Anchor Bible series Professor Pope has contributed two of the most original commentaries, those on Job and the Song of Songs. What marks them as original and seminal is, among other things, their consistent application of new philological data from Northwest Semitic literature to problems of the Hebrew text. That his is a valid approach finds confirmation in the tablets from third-millennium Ebla; even the limited material published thus far bids fair to clear up some of the remaining textual puzzles in these highly sophisticated poetic compositions,[49] and we pray that Marvin Pope will continue to contribute to this ongoing process in the years to come.

47 *Song of Songs* (N 28): 210–222.

48 *Ibid.*, p. 221.

49 See my comments in this regard in *Congress Volume: Göttingen 1977* (*VTS* XXIX; Leiden: Brill, 1978): 111.

ABRAHAM—LOVER OR BELOVED OF GOD

M. GOSHEN-GOTTSTEIN

1. This paper deals with one specific aspect of love, as a contribution to the theme set for the volume to honor Marvin Pope. This aspect is the love-relationship concerning one particular figure, theologically most significant and perhaps archetypal. At first blush we may seem to be dealing with little more than different reading traditions or rather trivial variants. Yet as we proceed, issues of exegetical traditions and linguistic usages will emerge and the theological implication will become visible. Once we have studied those issues we shall have to make up our minds whether a purely textual solution is methodologically satisfactory.[1]

2. Students of biblical traditions are aware that the major *dramatis personae* of Pentateuchal history are mentioned but sparingly in other sources. The figure of Abraham is no exception. In fact, if we look outside the historical books we are left with very few statements in the Prophets and in Psalms. Little more is predicated of him than that he was God's "servant." This, to be sure, is a general term used with regard to various prophetic figures. But the exact content of this "servanthood" has not been clarified by the considerable amount of writing on the servant-problem. In any event, non-Pentateuchal sources seem to add nothing over and beyond the Pentateuchal epithets of the patriarch.

3. This gets us, then, to our specific case. For Isa 41:8 introduces what seems a new nuance. Abraham is called, according to MT, God's *ʾōhēbh*. To be exact, God speaks of Abraham as *ʾōhabhī*. This may or may not be a succinct summary of the contents expressed by God in Gen 18:18f.; the term itself stands in need of clarification. Formally speaking, *ʾōhēbh* is an active participle and as such conveys the sense of relationship from actor to goal. If man can be commanded to act out the contents of the root *ʾhb* towards God—and this is such a basic command that no prooftexts are necessary—then one can imagine that the archetypal figure of Abraham was conceived as having attained that status:[2] "to love God" leads to the ultimate distinction of being God's "lover."[3] Now, this line of analysis does not presuppose that we know what is implied in our being commanded to act out *ʾhb* towards God. The semantics of transferring a most essential human emotion to the sphere of the divine are a separate issue. All that we are concerned with at this stage is to ask ourselves whether it is legitimate to speak in the man-God relationship of "love" and "hate," emanating from and moving into a certain direction. More forcefully: Exod 20:6 seems a suitable prototype for such an expression: "those who love me and keep my ordinances." The direction is unequivocal. It may be a problem of English that we prefer a circumlocutory relative clause to a *nomen agentis*. But the legitimacy of MT-exegesis cannot be denied: MT uses in Isa 41:8 an active participle with God in the goal-status,[4]—it employs love imagery and names Abraham uniquely as having attained the level of being God's *ʾōhēbh*. It is rather our own sense of language that prevents us from speaking of Abraham as the "lover of God."

4. These considerations may seem quite unnecessary; but we may have to come back to them as we proceed. It may not be coincidental that in the crowded field of the semantics of God-man relations, "love" is the obvious two-directional one. We need not contrast "love" of God with "fear," in order to extract their exact senses. "Fear" is one-directional, for it is predicated only of man; only "love of God" can be understood both ways. Are we, then, justified in stressing the character of *ʾōhēbh* as an active participle, even in its purely nominal usage? Perhaps *ʾōhēbh* was largely neutralized already in biblical Hebrew, meaning little more than "friend," just

1 For my papers inquiring into certain theoretical aspects of such issues cf. *Textus* 3 (1963) and *Mélanges Dominique Barthélemy, OBO* 38 (1981). Case material comes from my work in connection with the edition of the *Hebrew University Bible: The Book of Isaiah* 1 (1975); 2 (1981); cf. also the *Sample Volume and Introduction* (1965). I am indebted to members of the staff at the Hebrew University Bible Project and at the Institute for Lexicography for some details they have checked for me.

2 It is worth noting that the command appears in what is often termed Deuteronomic sources. One could test a theory that makes the command-form developmentally dependent on a participle as in Exod 20:6.

3 Below (§ 11) we shall deal with some Rabbinic traditions in their own right. At present I should like to draw attention to the fact that we can hardly improve on the *derasha* which exemplifies the basic command "You shall love YHWH" (Deut 6:1) by saying: be like Abraham—and goes on to quote our verse in Isaiah. Cf. Sifre (ed. Finkelstein, Berlin [1940]: 58). This kind of juxtaposition can be found in various sources; cf. e.g. *Sota* 31a. Note Maimonides, *Teshūbhā* 10:2.

4 Again, the analysis of Ibn-Ezra *ad loc.* is perfect: "*ʾōhabhī* is not like *ʾahūbhī*, for *ʾahūbhī* refers to the object and

as, say, its synonym *rēᶜa*.[5] A preliminary study of biblical *ᵓōhēbh* (in nominal function) shows that it should generally be construed as a transform of a verb-goal construction, i.e., with its directional meaning intact. Rarely is it neutralized and never can we attribute to it a changed direction. Hence I would reject the rather baffling recent exegetical attempt (by Elliger) to construe *ᵓōhēbh* in 41:8 not just as directionally neutral but as actually indicating love directed by God towards Abraham![6] We just have to face the statement that for the first time in the Bible one particular figure is termed God's *ᵓōhēbh*.[7] It is of no avail to try and get rid of the entire problem by claiming that the tricolon structure of Isa 41:8 is stylistically out of character, hence the last unit including the expression should be omitted altogether.[8] This kind of "metric criticism" solves nothing, and merely shifts the issue to a side-track.

5. We are now ready to take a closer look at Isa 41:8. There is no doubt that the LXX does not quite fit the MT's *ᵓōhēbh*. It almost seems as if the LXX tries to avoid a verbatim rendering, for "Abraham" is followed by a relative clause. Its sense is clear: *hon ēgapēsa*, "whom I have loved." This is precisely what the MT cannot mean, as I have maintained. What is referred to by the LXX is God's love for Abraham. The LXX does not use a neutral expression like "friend" nor a passive participle (see below). In fact, it is the circumlocutory character of the clause that makes us suspect the assumption that the difference between the MT and LXX ought to be solved on textual lines. There would be nothing easier than following the lead of various scholars who suggest that the letters *ᵓhby* represented *ᵓahūbhī*, hence the Greek.[9] However, what we really seem to confront is an exegetical elaboration in line with similar expressions of God's love and choice. Just as God "chooses" Jacob—in the parallel stich—he "loves" Abraham, and the two relative clauses are made to fit. In the entire context God is the agent, not the recipient—and this is repeated in 51:2 (see below). Hence what we are dealing with seems to be a harmonizing exegetical tradition rather than a textual variation. To be sure, that tradition is in line with the basic statement in Deut 4:37, where God is described as the one who loves and chooses the forefathers. And in this light the addition of *ēgapēmenos* in the LXX of 44:2 might be understood.

6. Matters might have rested at this point but for the choice of words of Aquila. For the MT's *ᵓōhābhī* is rendered by A′ *agapētou mou*. Now, this is not a circumlocution as in the LXX and it can be retroverted verbatim to *ᵓahūbhī*, if we so wish. This raises a new question: does A′ represent a textual fact, an actual variant reading? Is the tradition of A′ genetically connected with that of the LXX? Does our evaluation of the facts of A′ make us change our previous evaluation of the LXX? Or is it conceivable that A′ simply expressed the exegetical tradition of the LXX with one word, and coincidentally chose what only appears to reflect a variant reading *ᵓahūbhī*.[10] Contrary to what has been suggested in the past, the facts of LXX and Aquila do not necessarily point in the same direction.[11]

7. In order to try and answer the questions we have posed, it may be useful to ask ourselves whether our case is unique. We have already remarked that Isa 41:8 is the earliest instance of Abraham being referred to as God's *ᵓōhēbh*. The same expression recurs in 2 Chr 20:7, and we are free to speculate whether that verse is proof of an almost freely used fixed epithet or whether there exists a literary connection. In any event, the verse in Chronicles does not provide a parallel expression to *ᵓōhēbh*, and the term as such is contextually unmotivated. A new dimension of our problem now emerges. For, again, the LXX does not render *ᵓōhēbh*, as we would expect, by some active or neutral expression but by *tō ēgapēmenō*

ᵓōhabhī is a transitive action emanating from the *ᵓōhēbh* and cleaving to the *ᵓahūbh*, the object."

5 Juxtaposition of those two nouns seems peculiar to Psalms and Proverbs, but perhaps there is an unnoticed nuance in Hos 3:1. On the other hand, Haman's *ᵓōhabhīm* (Esther 5-6) may reflect the kind of usage often found in post-biblical Hebrew. I need not add that an often described midrashic situation, speaking of a king and his *ᵓōhēbh*, may be of direct relevance to exegetical traditions on Abraham as God's *ᵓōhēbh*; see below. In such sources the sense seems to lie somewhere between friend, well-wisher and retainer. In any event, while later usage (or versional interpretation) may be of interest for our understanding, we should attempt to ascertain the biblical usage itself with as little prejudice as possible.

6 K. Elliger (*Deuterojesaja* [1978]: 138) claims as follows: "JHWH ist 41:8, 48:14 ebenso Subjekt des *ᵓhb* wie an der dritten Stelle, an der das Verbum bei Dtjes vorkommt, 43:4." Now, this is precisely the problem. Given the fact that *ᵓhb* can be predicated in both directions, exegetical connections might develop (see below). But I can see no way that 41:8 MT can be made to yield the sense that it is God who loves Abraham.

7 I would submit that all other usages, in biblical and post-biblical literature, of the "Abraham–*ᵓōhēbh*" picture are lastly dependent on our verse. But this assumption is not material for our argument. In any case, the concept is not expressed before Deutero-Isaiah on an individualized level, in contrast to Exod 20:6 and its derivatives.

8 This was argued by Fohrer, *VT* 5 (1955): 242. Fohrer was not concerned with the expression we are studying.

9 We need not analyse in detail differences of presentation by different scholars. A glance into BHS or Elliger's commentary suffices. I might add that Elliger does not pay attention to the differences between the various Greek (and Latin) renderings. But in contrast to BHS he disallows the assumption of reading *ᵓahūbhī*.

10 The only other versions that are of interest for our problem are T and P, because only they use participles of a root signifying "love." See below.

11 The notation of BHS is more exact than that of Elliger.

sou, "to your beloved (seed)." It does not seem very convincing that an assumed *ʾōhēbh/ʾahūbh* interchange should have happened twice, as a purely textual event. Moreover, the wording is too different for Chr-LXX to be directly dependent on Isa-LXX.[12] Hence the assumption gains weight that there is a tradition that avoids using the *ʾōhēbh*-picture, possibly for exegetical-theological reasons.

8. We can now test our assumption from a different angle. We have seen that twice the MT *ʾōhēbh* is represented as the recipient of love. There exists a third instance which takes us beyond the confines of Hebrew scripture. Again Abraham is being referred to by what seems by now a fixed epithet; again it is God who loves. But, of course, we have no MT and the tradition alone speaks for itself. I refer to the prayer of Azaria in the Greek Daniel 3:35, where the circumlocution leaves no doubt: . . . *ton ēgapēmenon hypo sou* "the one beloved by you."[13]

9. From here we can follow the epithet for Abraham into later literature. But the possibility to check on the active/passive aspect gets lost. It would seem—I did not check all the details—that in later sources *philos* takes over and appears as some kind of fixed epithet as in epic tradition. Thus we find it in Job 19:9, Philo, *de sobrietate* 11,[14] James 2:23, Clemens, Rom 10:1, 17:2 and possibly in quite a number of other sources.

10. The tradition of Abraham being the one loved by God emerges from yet another unexpected Greek source. That source is the Isa-LXX itself, and one is tempted to connect the two instances occurring in Isa-LXX. Again, the tradition of the LXX could not be suspected on the basis of the MT. Isa 51:2 refers to Abraham, but nothing in the MT refers to love, either way. The LXX, however, has three verse-final verbs instead of the MT's two. The additional one is—need I say it—*ēgapēsa auton*.[15] At present I shall not deal with the question whether ואהבהו* is a graphically explicable doublet of the MT's וארבהו, or was omitted by haplography. What matters in the context of our inquiry is the recurrent tradition of love emanating from God towards Abraham.

11. For the purpose of our present inquiry I do not wish to analyse differences beyond those between the Hebrew and Greek traditions. I should point out that what started as a routine check into an alleged simple textual issue must lastly also be viewed in light of possible inner-Hebrew developments or functional equivalences in post-biblical times. An example must suffice here. In *Aboth d'Rabbi Nathan*[16] we find the following statement: "There are five that are termed *ʾahūbh*. Abraham is termed *ʾahūbh* for it is said: the seed of Abraham *ʾōhabhī*." Now, one may suggest that the biblical *ʾōhēbh* is "rendered" by post-biblical *ʾahūbh*. This is not a matter of text but of linguistic usage and interpretation.[17] On the other hand, the sense of direction is expressed very well in a paraphrase of Deut 33:12, the source for the neutral *yədīd YHWH*. The following inner-Hebrew equation is offered by Sifre-Deut (ed. Finkelstein, 1940, p. 409): "A king has many *ʾōhabhīm*, but most dear is the one whose *ʾōhēbh* is the king."[18]

12. To round out our observations, a note on the Aramaic Targum may not be superfluous. We have just noted that in post-biblical usage *ʾōhēbh* is often a general neutral noun for "friend," and only sometimes specifically expresses active-transitive direction. The interdialectal Targumic equivalent for Hebrew *ʾhb* is Aramaic *rḥm*. The preferred Aramaic noun in the neutral sense "friend" is *rəḥīm*, whereas verbatim rendering of a Hebrew active participle sometimes seems to generate the Aramaic active participle *rāḥem*. This, then, may lead to an inner-Aramaic conflict which may find its expression in textual

---

12 It would be very difficult, on purely formal grounds, to construe MT *ʾōhabhxā* as adnominal of *zeraʿ*; but this is what the LXX has done. Hence, for the LXX the picture has shifted and the issue got further complicated: the seed is described as beloved, not Abraham himself. It would go too far to analyse here a text from the Mechilta (ed. Horovitz-Rabin [1930]: 312) which seems to express a similar idea and also has other interesting *derasha*-material on *ʾōhēbh*. Only (later) Antiochian tradition offers the variant *philou* for *philō*, so that according to the tradition it is again Abraham who is adorned by the epithet. But the textual evidence is such that simple inner-Greek *ou/ō* variation may be suspected.

13 I am not maintaining that there exists no *ʾahūbh* in the biblical text in the expected sense and, as it happens, in a roughly contemporary source. Cf. Neh 13:26, rendered *agapōmenos* in Esdras B 23:26. But, altogether, we deal with rare occurrences.

14 The context is that of Gen 18:17. To be sure, it is no coincidence that we encounter the Aramaic equivalent in a Targum on that verse, and finally in Rashi *ad loc.* Cf. also below n. 19.

15 Nothing will be found in BHK or BHS *ad loc.* Since Isaiah 51 was one of the sample chapters of my 1965 Introduction to HUB, the facts are discussed there.

16 I am quoting from the 1945 reissue of the 1887 edition by S. Schechter, recension B:43. I do not reproduce certain MS details.

17 I shall refrain from tackling again the issue of paying attention to Rabbinic sources, emphasized on and off since the days of Frankel and Geiger. Cf. my remarks in *Textus* 3 (1963).

18 "Dear" is my rendering for *ḥabhībh*. It is of interest that a variant reads: the most *ʾāhūbh*. The final clause can be rendered, "whom the king loves." For a similar play on *ʾōhēbh* with regard to a king. cf. *Mechilta ib* 311. All this leads us to the conventional terminology of *Königsgleichnisse* and should be analyzed with regard to the details of the Hebrew text. On the other hand, post-biblical Hebrew offers many examples of *ʾōhēbh* in the general sense of good friend or wellwisher; cf. n. 5 above. Note that also the general-purpose *rēʿa* can be equated with the specific *ʾōhēbh* of Isa 41:8; cf., e.g., *Exod Rabba* 27, 1; *Tanḥūmā* (ed. Buber) II 23b.

variation. Thus, Isa 41:8 has *rāḥmī* (and, similarly, S). Sperber's edition, however, shows a reading *rəḥīmī*. On purely formal grounds this could be interpreted as mirroring *ʾahūbh* vs. *ʾōhēbh*. I shall only indicate at present that such an interpretation is rather unlikely and that, again, a simplistic textual solution would not do justice to the linguistic complexity. A more acceptable, albeit tentative, solution would seem to be the assumption that a preferred lexeme was substituted for the less usual one.[19]

13. Let us return to our basic inquiry and sum up. The picture that emerged from our comparison of the MT and LXX in Isa 41:8 is of interest precisely because the issue as such seems of little consequence. What could be interpreted as a matter of text turned out, more and more, to reflect issues of exegetical tradition and linguistic usage. Whether as a result of separate developments or secondary influences—what we encounter in the LXX is a rather consistent tradition as regards the relationship between God and Abraham. The love referred to in the text is one that emanates from God.[20] However unimportant the detail, there is a lesson as regards the relationship between God and chosen man and there may be, in the final outcome, a lesson as to theological differences between Hebrew and Greek Scriptures.

19 Attention has to be drawn, however, to the fact that the reading *rəḥīmī* is quoted from the Antwerp Polyglot only. In light of what we have learned recently about the Targum text of the Antwerp Polyglot (cf. my remarks in *Biblica* 56 [1975]: 301f.) we had better be careful until MS evidence is clarified. As for *rəḥīmī* as an epithet for Abraham it should be noted that in Isa 46:11 it is substituted by *Biblia Rabb II* for *bəḥīrī* of other sources (no MT). This may, then, be some kind of fixed epithet, just as we found in Greek sources. But the evidence needs strengthening and, in any case, we have nowhere the kind of relative clause circumlocution as in Greek. Perhaps the *locus classicus* for this use of the epithet can be found in the traditions on Gen 18:17; cf. T. Pal MS Neofiti *ad loc.*; but there the form is *rāḥmī*, without variants. Note *rəḥīmā* in Deut 33:12 (cf. above §11).

20 I am aware of the possibility that in light of the later usage of referring to Abraham as God's *philos* we may have to reckon with an aspect of Hellenistic thought that may go back as far as Plato. As an aside I might add that lexicographical explanations in Arabic sources on the meaning of Quranic *khalīl* are most unconvincing and, in any case, add nothing to our discussion.

DUST: SOME ASPECTS OF OLD TESTAMENT IMAGERY

DELBERT R. HILLERS

"The Holy Ghost in penning the Scriptures delights himself, not only with a propriety but with a delicacy and harmony and melody of language, with height of metaphors and other figures . . . ." In his enthusiasm for the imagery of the Bible, where he found "such voyages, such peregrinations to fetch remote and precious metaphors, such extensions, such curtains of allegories, such third heavens of hyperboles," John Donne joined a chorus of 17th and 18th century European writers who remarked on the difference between their own poetic diction and that of the ancient Hebrews, which they found especially "Oriental."[1] By the last adjective they meant bold, vehement, not concerned for correctness, not artificial, vivid, violently agitated, affecting, wild, possessing an "agreeable Rudeness."[2] Voltaire, who found the figures and metaphors of the Bible "presque toujours outrées," referred to the Mediterranean heat to account for this barbarism: "l'imagination était sans cesse exaltée par l'ardeur du climat."[3]

Modern students of Old Testament literature seem overly content to repeat cliches about "Oriental imagery" and uninterested in a fresh examination of the subject.[4] In spite of the prominence given to study of metaphor and simile in modern criticism of literature, a recent biblical handbook with the promising title *Exegese als Literaturwissenschaft*[5] does not even mention "image," "metaphor," "simile" in its index, nor is the classic *Semantics of Biblical Language*[6] interested in these topics, though it would seem that figurative language is more than peripheral to religious discourse. There are works that begin to balance this neglect, but there seems to be room for the present attempt to characterize Old Testament imagery.

I have chosen to treat one set of images, similes and metaphors having to do with "dust" or "dirt," as manageable in a preliminary study and relatively unproblematic. A brief review should suffice to define the set of commonplace associations connected with "dust" in Old Testament literature. Then tentative conclusions can be drawn as to the nature of Old Testament imagery and the implications for the world view of its writers. The principal conclusion that arises is that much Old Testament imagery is what may be called conceptual imagery. This is, in using simile or metaphor involving a given object, Hebrew writers evoke a severely limited range of associated commonplaces—abstract, common qualities belonging to the concept of a class of objects rather than sensuous, particular, or temporary characteristics associated with an individual object. By frequent use of conceptual imagery, Old Testament literature stresses the stability and intelligibility of the physical and moral world. These conclusions are offered for confirmation or modification by study of other sets of Old Testament images, or to serve to identify groups of images or literary compositions which depart from the standard.

The Hebrew terms most prominently involved are the following. The most important is *ʿāpār*, which means "soil, dirt, dust." Another term often linked with *ʿāpār* is *ʾēper*, in many translations of the Bible this is rendered "ashes," but as especially Kutscher has demonstrated, in a great many biblical contexts the sense is "dust, dirt," and in fact the word is probably etymologically connected with *ʿāpār*, by way of Akkadian where the initial laryngeal of the root was changed.[7] Other terms that are partially synonymous with these two, and which figure in the same sort of imagery, are *ʾābāq* "dust, powder"; *ṭîṭ* and *ḥōmer* "clay"; *ḥōl*, "sand"; *ʾădāmāh* "ground" and *ʾereṣ* "earth." In studying these terms I have given some attention to cognates or counterparts in Ugaritic and Akkadian, and have neglected later literatures because I am interested in uses which may be prior to biblical use, not just in parallel phenomena in world literature (*pulvis et umbra sumus*). I have omitted Egyptian from consideration as less accessible to me; it is possible,

1 This is a much altered version of a lecture given as one of the Schaff Lectures at Pittsburgh Theological Seminary in 1970.

2 The phrase is from Husbands, "A Miscellany of Poems . . . Preface," cited in Rolf P. Lessenich, *Dichtungsgeschmack und althebräische Bibelpoesie im 18. Jahrhundert* (Anglistische Studien 4; Cologne, Graz: 1967).

3 Cited in Lessenich, p. 32.

4 V. H. Kooy, "Image, Imagery," *Interpreters' Dictionary of the Bible* repeats 18th century observations to the point of being a caricature.

5 By Wolfgang Richter (Göttingen: Vandenhoek and Ruprecht, 1971). By contrast, note the enormous literature collected in Warren A. Shibles, *Metaphor: An Annotated Bibliography and History* (Whitewater, WI: Language Press, 1971).

6 By James Barr (Oxford: Oxford Univ. Press, 1961).

7 Literature is cited in Koehler-Baumgartner, *Lexikon*³, s.v. *ʾēper.*

however, that the biblical tradition was fed from this stream also.

Dust is plentiful. There is a lot of it, and therefore dirt or dust becomes a way of describing a vast quantity, an uncountable multitude of a substance. Thus God says: "I will make your seed like the dust (*ʿăpar*) of the earth, that is, if anyone can count the dust of the earth, then your seed can be counted" (Gen 13:16; cf. 28:14). This stock image is used also by the Chronicler, 2 Chr 1:9. As is well-known, "sand" (*ḥōl*) is used in this kind of context even more often than "dirt" (*ʿāpār*). Biblical usage of this comparison is not restricted to use of large numbers of persons; anything uncountable can be compared to dirt: God's thoughts (Ps 139:18); the grain in Egypt (Gen 41:49); the intelligence of a king (1 Kgs 5:9); the meat sent to the Israelites in the wilderness (Ps 78:27); clothing a miser can hoard (Job 27:16). In hyperbolic expressions it is said that a man can "heap up silver like dirt" (Job 27:16) and in Zech 9:3 that Tyre has "heaped up silver like dirt, and gold like the mud in the streets." This is very similar to expressions which occur in the Amarna letters, where hopeful kings write to the wealthy Pharaoh: "God is (as common) in your land (as) dust." Very likely there is a direct connection between the idiom of these pre-Israelite letters and the biblical image, especially since other expressions in the Amarna texts are echoed in the Old Testament.

This is such an obvious and common metaphoric usage of "dust" that it needs no further comment, except to point out that as a metaphor for cheapness—"dirt cheap" is idiomatic also with us—dirt enters into a structure of other metaphors for value. At the top, quite obviously, is gold, consistently symbolic for the highest value; next comes silver, then bronze, then iron, then dirt or clay. This is the sequence of the materials in the great statue in Nebuchadnezzar's dream (Dan 2:31-33). The metaphoric or symbolic structure in this case corresponds with the actual monetary system. The structure is itself traditional. Within biblical literature, note Isa 60:17; a description of the glories of the new Jerusalem: "Instead of bronze I will bring gold, and instead of iron I will bring silver; instead of wood, bronze, instead of stones, iron." Every material is moved up a notch. A similar pattern is attested in literary use as early as about 2000 B.C., in the Sumerian text called "The Curse of Agade."[8]

Dirt is useful as a metaphor for vileness and low worth in another way. Not only is it common but it is also that which gets stepped on, and in contrast to the sky the dust, or ground, is the lowest thing. Here the passages are too numerous to cite with anything approaching fullness. The following are typical examples in which dirt is clearly thought of as what is trodden down. "For the king of Aram destroyed them and made them like dirt to trample on" (2 Kgs 13:7). "(The wicked) shall be dust under your feet" (Mal 3:21). Ps 7:6 illustrates that frequently in this kind of use *ʿāpār* ("dirt") may be a B-word to *ʾereṣ* "earth, ground" as A-Word: "And he trampled to earth my life, and put my liver in the dirt." This pair—and the image involved—is attested already in Ugaritic epics, though the verb involved is a bit obscure: "We'll thrust my foes into the earth, To the ground those that rise against my brother" (76 [10].2.24-25). Akkadian also knows this image: "Should I say yes, Shamash would treat me as if I were the dust upon which you have stepped" (see the *Chicago Assyrian Dictionary* s.v. *eperu*, p. 186b). Rather closely allied to this usage but not identical is the use of "dirt" or "earth" as the opposite pole to something higher, especially the sky. A wide variety of verbs is used to assert that someone or other has brought a man down to the dirt: Isaiah (25:12) writes of the fortresses of Moab: "And the high fortifications of his walls (God) has brought low, levelled, made touch the earth, down to the dirt." In this usage also *ʿāpār* is often associated with *ʾereṣ* "earth." Hence "dust" is figurative for what is low, defeated, contemptible, and it is used metaphorically to express those ideas also in passages where the *tertium comparationis* is left unexpressed. Thus Ezek 28:18 "And I made you dust on the ground in the sight of all who beheld you." Note also Zeph 1:17 "And their blood will be poured out like dirt." Job says: "Your maxims are proverbs of dust (*mišlē ʾēper*), and your defenses are defenses of clay." Especially interesting is the use of this image for men. Job says (30:19): "He has brought me down to the clay, and I am made like dirt and dust" (*ʿāpār wāʾēper*). Similarly Abraham says to God, most deferentially, "Here I have dared to speak to my lord, and I am but dirt and dust" (Gen 18:27). "Dust" is used in these cases, especially the latter, of man *coram deo*. Although one might think of creation stories as the source of the imagery, the parallels from the Amarna letters deserve citation. A vassal describes himself to Pharaoh as "a true servant of the king, the dust of the feet of the king" (EA 248:5) or elsewhere as "Your servant and the dust you walk on." In other words, there seems to be an additional dimension in Abraham's description of himself before his "lord" as "dirt"; the image is perhaps not derived directly from the traditional connotations of dirt, but comes by way of political language, the language used by a servant for someone immensely his superior. To put it in terms which have been used above, the "dust" metaphor here is drawn into a larger structure of metaphor, in which the relation of God to man is conceived in terms of the relations between men in society. The metaphor remains clear, but it is not absolutely simple.

A rather uncommon use of "dust" arises from the fact that dust can be light, and powdery, and easily swept away by the wind. Thus Isa 29:5 "But the multitude of your strangers (?) shall be like fine dust (*ʾābāq daq*), and the multitude of the violent like chaff which passes away." In only a couple of other passages (Isa 5:24; Ps 18:43 = 2 Sam 22:43) dust is used in a similar way; more commonly chaff is the symbol in this sort of context. An

8 Lines 241-43, p. 650, *ANET*[3] p. 650.

Akkadian epic, of about 1000 B.C. (Irra Epic I 107) similarly refers to the dust which the storm wind carries away.

The final major metaphoric use of "dust" which we will consider is as a description of the nature of man: "Dust thou art." The significance of this metaphor is two-fold at least. "Dust thou art" refers to, and is derived from, accounts of the creation of man. "Yahweh God made man of dirt from the ground." "Dust thou art" points in the other direction also, to the end of man—"and unto dust shalt thou return." This in its turn is suggestive of, and derived from, the association of dirt and dust with death, the grave, and the world of the dead.

Lines from the Genesis creation story have already been quoted to illustrate use of "dirt" in describing the origin of man. Such a use is not restricted to Genesis, however. In one of his impassioned outbursts Job says "Remember that you made me of clay" (10:9). "All are from the dirt" Ecclesiastes says (3:20), and Ps 103:14-15 echoes Job: "Remember that we are dust; man's days are like grass." Still another passage in Job (33:6) is significant as linking Old Testament imagery to that of Akkadian creation stories; addressing Job, Eliphaz, in a rather obscure sentence, reminds him that he too is a man and adds: "I too was dug out of clay" (*mēḥōmer qôraṣtî gam ʾānî*). The very verb used is identical to that which appears in various Akkadian texts in referring to the creation of man. In the so-called "Babylonian Job," *Ludlul bēl nemēqi*, mankind is called: "Creatures whose clay Aruru took in her fingers" (*ikruṣu kirissin*).[9] Another Akkadian wisdom text, the "Babylonian Theodicy," refers to a pair of gods thus: "Narru, king of the gods, who created mankind, and majestic Zulummar, who dug out (*kariṣ*) their clay."[10] And in the Atra-hasis epic, an Old Babylonian composition best known for its close parallel to the biblical flood account, there is also a story of the creation of man, in which Ea treads clay like a potter, and the creator-goddess recites the proper incantations, then nips off (*karāṣu* is used) fourteen pieces of clay, from which seven human couples are made.[11]

As stated, in biblical usage the idea that man is created out of clay is seldom far removed from the idea that man returns to dust: "Dust thou art" is completed by "and unto dust shalt thou return." The associations which formed the picture of "dusty death" are obvious. The dead are laid in the dirt, and after a time the body becomes one with the soil. Thus it is that Isaiah, addressing in his imagination the dead, called out: "Awake and sing, you that dwell in the dirt" (26:19). Elsewhere the dead are "all who go down to the dirt" (Ps 22:30), or "those who sleep in the dirt" (Dan 12:2). To die is to "lie down in the dirt" (Job 20:11; 21:26). A psalmist compresses the picture into one word. "What profit is there in my death? . . . Can dirt praise you?" (30:10). Especially common is the idea that death is a return to the dirt, a conception that encompasses the whole fleeting life of man. This is found not only in the climax of the Yahwist's creation story, but elsewhere: in the majestic 90th Psalm: "You turn men back to dust (*dakkāʾ*), and say 'Return' O children of men.'" The death of a prince is described thus: "His breath departs, he returns to the ground" (Ps 146:4). Job's "Remember that you made me of clay" is answered by: "and you turn me back to dust" (10:9). Ecclesiastes completes the number of those who use the image: "All came from the dirt, and all return to the dirt" (3:20); "the dirt returns to the ground, as it was" (12:7).

Dust is used as synonymous for the realm of the dead also in a Ugaritic text (17[2 Aqht].I.29), but it is Akkadian literature which provides the closest parallels for the image under discussion. The following phrases are cited under *eperu* in the *Chicago Assyrian Dictionary*. A medical text says of a child with certain symptoms that it "belongs to the soil." A description of the underworld in the famous myth of Ishtar's descent to the Netherworld gives this picture: "Dust is lying on door and lock"; the world of the dead is where "their sustenance is dust, and clay their food." And as a kenning for "to die" the expression "return to dust" (*târu ana ṭiṭṭi*) is well-known and ancient in Mesopotamia, in both wisdom texts and epic literature.

This completes the overview of metaphoric uses of "dirt," but before we turn to an analysis of the kind of language and thought employed, one more aspect deserves notice—that this verbal symbolism was accompanied by a symbolism of gestures, of physical actions, which express in a different medium the same association of dirt with everything lowly and vile, and with death. Sitting on the dirt is a common gesture in times of distress and humiliation, especially as a gesture of mourning. There is reference also to self-abasement in the form of putting the head, or the mouth in the dirt. In time of mourning, one put on sackcloth and dust, or put dust on one's head, or wallowed in the dust. These gestures in turn are used in literary contexts, thus Isaiah (47:1) tells Babylon: "Get down and sit in the dirt, fair virgin Babylon!" and numerous passages incorporate references to actual physical contact with dirt. Akkadian also makes reference to sitting on the dirt, but it is a portion of the Ugaritic epic of Baal which provides the closest parallel to the gestures we are discussing. On hearing of the death of the god Baal, the father-god El "gets down from his throne, and sits on the footstool. Then from the footstool he sits on the ground. He pours dust of mourning on his head, dirt of wallowing on his crown." (5 [67].6.12-16). The phrase "dirt of wallowing" employs the same verb that is found in biblical contexts (Heb. *hitpallēš*).

9 Tablet IV, lines 40, W. G. Lambert, *Babylonian Wisdom Literature* (Oxford: Clarendon Press, 1960): 58-59.

10 Line 277, Lambert, pp. 88-89.

11 Tablet I, line 256; W. G. Lambert and A. R. Millard, *Atra-Ḫasis: The Babylonian Story of the Flood* (Oxford: Clarendon Press, 1969): 60-61.

This survey is not complete, but does give a fairly detailed overview of how the Old Testament uses words referring to dirt and dust in non-literal ways, and we may turn to the question with which we began: if this is typical, what are the essential characteristics of Hebrew poetic imagery?

I would conclude, first of all, that Old Testament imagery is not especially "concrete," or at least that it is misleading to single this out as an especially prominent characteristic. To put it positively, Old Testament poetic imagery is remarkable for its abstractness. So that this may not be a quibble about terms, let me concede at once that in a sense this imagery is concrete. The writers say "Dust thou art," not "Thou art mortal, thou art transitory," or the like. But on the other side, note that the only qualities of dirt singled out for non-literal employment are the properties common to all dirt everywhere: lowness, tendency to blow away, commonness. Never is the word "dirt" qualified by an adjective to tell us that only one particular kind of dirt is referred to. There is absolutely no reflection of what we might call "landscape." The sands beside the Red Sea shore are not like the Mediterranean sands, the Mediterranean sands being white or brown, whereas the Red-Sea sand at Solomon's port of Elath is a beautiful blend of pinks and black and gray. The hill country of Palestine shows, in thin layers over the rock which crops out everywhere, a distinctive red soil, *terra rossa*, quite unlike, for example, the brown loose soil of the Negeb. None of this whatsoever gets into the imagery. In discussing imagery in modern poetry, Wellek and Warren refer to "sensuous particularity" as one of the characteristics of poetic imagery. "Sensuous" is scarcely what comes to mind when one reflects on Old Testament imagery. If "dirt" is a fair sample, Hebrew poetic imagery is far removed from the particular and the sensual, and draws closer to the abstract and intellectual.

It is helpful at this point to quote a modern poet by way of contrast. Theodore Roethke, a 20th century American poet also writes of dust, in a poem called "Dolor." The poem as a whole concerns the sadness, the deadlines, of a life of office-work. This passage ends the poem: "And I have seen dust from the walls of institutions, / Finer than flour, alive, more dangerous than silica, / Soft, almost invisible, through long afternoons of tedium. / Dropping a fine film on nails and delicate eyebrows, / Glazing the pale hair, the duplicate gray standard faces."[12] This is truly concrete, and sensual. As compared to any of the biblical imagery involving dust, it makes a point by compelling us to see a specific kind of dust in a particular setting. It is interesting to see that the associations evoked by the modern poet are not wholly different from some of the ideas biblical poets associated with dust. Even granting that, however, the technique is far different. Many make the point that biblical imagery is foreign to the modern mind. There is some truth in that judgment, but some assert it for the wrong reason. It is often our own poets who stir us into contemplating the concrete and particular, whereas the ancient writers give us images that are far more abstract and general.

Related to this is a second important characteristic: Hebrew poetic imagery is clear and unequivocal. It is not difficult or ambiguous—qualities much admired in modern verse by some critics. It is quite true, of course, that "dirt" is used metaphorically in more than one sense. But the particular context in the overwhelming majority of cases clearly sorts out which sense (or senses) is intended. There is one way in which this is done which is particularly unmodern, but quite characteristic of biblical style. We might call it the explained metaphor. "I will make your seed like the dust of the earth"; in view of the limited number of traditional associations involved, this is already sufficient to make the sense clear, but the text adds: "that is, if anyone can count the dust of the earth, then your seed can be counted." Similarly in the case of "sand" and "locusts," both traditional similes for great number, biblical writers frequently add: *lārōb* "in multitude"; "their armies were like the locusts *in multitude.*" Or take this example from Micah (5:6-7) of the explanation of slightly less obvious metaphor: "And the remainder of Jacob shall become, in the midst of many peoples, like dew from Yahweh, like showers on the grass, which does not wait for man, or tarry for the sons of men. And the remnant of Jacob shall become, . . . in the midst of many peoples, like a lion among the beasts of the forest, like a young lion in the herds of sheep, which when it has come along and trodden down, tears its prey, with none to deliver (from it)." Of course not all the figurative language is thus patiently explained, yet it is correct to say that the intention to be clear rather than obscure is a persistent trait. It is sometimes achieved by a rigorous narrowing down of the associational possibilities of a substance. "Gold" is a striking example. This metal has a number of properties, its color, its gleam, its heaviness, and so on, which conceivably could have been used in simile and metaphor, but as far as I can tell, Old Testament usage is completely consistent in singling out only one characteristic to the exclusion of all others. Gold is symbolic of the highest value among substances, and that is its sense in all contexts. The result is the clarity or consistency to which I referred.

Still another generalization one may make, assuming that "dirt" metaphors guide us in the right direction, is that Hebrew poetic imagery was traditional literary imagery, and hence largely learned by the individual poet as part of his language. Writers about Hebrew imagery have tended to stress the opposite, saying that the imagery is drawn from experience. This is misleading in two ways. The first is that if one says the imagery comes from experience, one is led to think of the experience of the individual poet. Thus Herder paints for us a picture of

12 From *Words for the Wind: the Collected Verse of Theodore Roethke* (1958) used by permission of the publisher, Doubleday and Co., Garden City, NY.

Amos the shepherd on the hills near Tekoa, "where he gathered his flowers of pastoral poetry." It is difficult to maintain that romantic point of view when one can show, as is occasionally possible, that the imagery in question had been current in literature for a thousand or more years before Amos tended sheep in Judah. Occasionally it is difficult to imagine that the Old Testament writer had ever personally witnessed the phenomenon. Had Jeremiah, or Hosea, or the writer of Daniel ever seen a wild ass in its element, that is the wilderness? I doubt it; both in literature and popular speech, the wild ass was traditional from remote antiquity for being, in a word, wild, and a person learned that by hearing about it, just as a character in a P. G. Wodehouse novel learned about aspen trees. "I was trembling like an aspen. I don't know if you've ever seen an aspen—I haven't myself as far as I can remember—but I knew they were noted for trembling like the dickens."

The Old Testament poets, then, seem to have felt little necessity to be creative in the area of inventing new images. Here again we may note the contrast to much modern verse, a contrast which can be illustrated from the same poem by Roethke that was quoted previously. These are the opening lines: "I have known the inexorable sadness of pencils, / Neat in their boxes, dolor of pad and paper-weight, / All the misery of manilla folders and mucilage, / . . . . Ritual of multigraph, paper-clip, comma, / Endless duplication of lives and objects." This is obviously new, and derived from the poét's own observation. The pencil and paper-clip are not, to my knowledge, traditional images for heavy despair in Western literature. Old Testament poetry is different: the poet mostly used inherited images, not fresh creations from his own experience of the world.

A further characteristic of Old Testament imagery is the tendency for an image to stand in fixed relationship to other imagery. This was alluded to above, and so can be recalled quite briefly here. "Dust" thought of as the ground, the earth, is at the opposite pole from the sky. As the most plentiful of materials, it is at the opposite pole from the rarest, gold. "Dirt and dust" used in self-deprecating speech before a superior sets the servant apart from his lord. This tendency to form a network of fixed relationships with other images makes evident the potentiality of biblical imagery as a medium for thought. It would be exaggerating to say that these rather elementary metaphorical structures constitute a system of thought like a scientific or philosophical system, but on the other hand it is perhaps even more mistaken to think of biblical imagery as decorative or primarily a means of expressing emotion.

If some of the above conclusions are true for a substantial portion of Hebrew imagery, it may be further asserted that this would have had the effect, at a level close to the linguistic (lexical), of promoting a view of the world as ultimately morally intelligible and stable—important functions of a religious system. There are many theories of metaphor available to us, beginning with Aristotle's. One that is particularly congenial to the material treated here is that of Max Black, who views metaphor as a "filter."[13] A member of a given society knows the "system of associated commonplaces" attached to a word such as "wolf." If we say "Man is a wolf," the effect is "to evoke the wolf-system of related commonplaces." Elements of the wolf-system that fit "man" emphasize some human characteristics and suppress others: "the wolf-metaphor . . . *organizes* our view of man."[14] Black's view has the advantage of stressing the role of metaphor—we may include biblical metaphor—in *creating* rather than simply observing the similarity between subjects. And the world created by Old Testament imagery is one that is familiar, intelligible, and stable.

The above is meant as a description, not an encomium, of Old Testament imagery. It is well to remember on the one hand that other ancient literature displays similar characteristics, and on the other that the Old Testament contains the Song of Songs, whose imagery is probably animated by a different aesthetic. In evaluating Old Testament conceptual imagery, it may be illuminating to recall C. S. Lewis' reaction to I. A. Richards' disparagement of "Stock Responses." "By a Stock Response Dr. I. A. Richards means a deliberately organized attitude which is substituted for 'the direct free play of experience.' In my opinion such deliberate organization is one of the first necessities of human life, and one of the main functions of art is to assist it. All that we describe as constancy in love or friendship, as loyalty in political life, or, in general, as perseverance—all solid virtue and stable pleasure—depends on organizing chosen attitudes and maintaining them against the eternal flux (or 'direct free play') of mere immediate experience. This Dr. Richards would not perhaps deny. But his school puts the emphasis the other way. They talk as if improvement of our responses were always required in the direction of finer discrimination and greater particularity; never as if men needed responses more normal and more traditional than they now have."[15]

---

13 Max Black, *Models and Metaphors: Studies in Language and Philosophy* (Ithaca: Cornell Univ. Press, 1962): 39.

14 *Ibid.*

15 *A Preface to Paradise Lost* (New York: Oxford Univ. Press, 1961): 54-55.

THE SECOND TABLE OF THE DECALOGUE AND THE IMPLICIT CATEGORIES OF ANCIENT NEAR EASTERN LAW

STEPHEN A. KAUFMAN

Love and death are nowhere more closely connected in biblical literature than in the Decalogue, wherein the prohibition of illicit sexual relations (*lôʾ tinʾāp*) follows immediately upon the prohibition of manslaughter (*lôʾ tirṣāḥ*). Is this concatenation intentional or coincidental? If intentional, does it reflect a recognition of the kind of intimate relationship between these two concepts dealt with by Marvin Pope in his *magnum opus* on the Song of Songs, or is it rather the result of a broader principle of arrangement operating on the Decalogue as a whole? Indeed, can one discern any principles at all lying behind the order and content of the Ten Commandments?

Students of the Decalogue have long distinguished between the two "tables" of Commandments: the first said to regulate relations between Man and God; the second treating of relations among men.[1] This division is based on more than just a need to account for two tablets, however. In terms of form, the terse apodixis of commandments VI-IX stands in marked contrast with the expansive rhetoric of the other commandments. Moreover, the series "murder, adultery, theft and lying" appears by itself elsewhere in the biblical canon (with the order of the elements modified, to be sure).[2] Accordingly, it seems probable that these four laws may have had an independent existence outside of the Decalogue, into which they have been subsequently incorporated—a separate *Sitz im Leben*.[3] The thesis presented here is that such a *Sitz im Leben* is to be sought in the fact that the four rubrics represented by these laws constituted the major classificatory categories of law for ancient Near Eastern jurists. These four commandments are thus, in the ancient Near Eastern mind, a summary of all "civil" law.

If this interpretation is correct, it has obvious ramifications for two arguments that have become almost axiomatic in recent Decalogue "research." The first is that all of the commandments of the Decalogue were originally brief, apodictic statements like VI-IX.[4] This is a neo-fundamentalist dogma that has absolutely no support other than the belief that briefer is older! If VI-IX had an independent existence as a distillation of civil law, the other commandments were from the start "other" in content and probably in form as well. The second "axiom" is that *ḥmd*, "to covet," represents something other than a mental state in the last commandment (and, as a corollary, that "You shall not steal" refers only to mantheft). I have already demonstrated that this theory is absolutely false as far as Deuteronomy is concerned.[5] As for the pre-Deuteronomic stage, if commandments VI-IX represent the entirety of varieties of "action" in ancient Near Eastern civil law, then *lôʾ taḥmōd* must represent a specifically Israelite addition to the list designed to deal with something that was not dealt with elsewhere—state of mind. Moreover, as we shall see, *lôʾ tignōb* is most definitely not limited to mantheft, although it does include it.

Ever since the first discovery of a major ancient Near Eastern compilation of laws, the "Code" of Hammurapi, scholars have attempted to account for the order of its individual laws. Early scholars not surprisingly were wont to "lay upon the code the straight jacket of modern legal terminology,"[6] itself based on Roman Law. D. H. von Müller's classic attempt to demonstrate a relationship among the Code of Hammurapi, the Covenant Code of Exodus, and the Roman Twelve Tables[7] is indicative of some of the more extravagant claims of the earlier writers with regard to relationships of content and structure among western man's earliest attempts to systematize law. Direct ties between ancient western Asia and Rome are usually no longer granted much weight.[8] As for Hammurapi and the Bible, most scholars seem to be content with a general recognition of certain

---

1 See Moshe Greenberg, "Decalogue," *Encyclopedia Judaica* (1971): 5.1444. We follow here the traditional Jewish enumeration. For the various systems of enumerating the Decalogue see Greenberg, "Decalogue," 1442 and Stephen A. Kaufman, "The Structure of the Deuteronomic Law," *MAARAV* 1 (1979): 152 n. 57.

2 Jer 7:9; Hos 4:2.

3 Cf. W. H. Schmidt, "Die Komposition des Dekalogs" (VT Sup 22; Leiden, 1972): 216ff. and references there.

4 Cf. J. J. Stamm with M. E. Andrew, *The Ten Commandments in Recent Research* (London, 1967): 18-22; E. Nielsen, *The Ten Commandments in New Perspective* (Naperville, 1968): 78–93.

5 Kaufman, "Structure" (N 1): 145f.

6 David G. Lyon, "The Structure of the Hammurapi Code," *JAOS* 25 (1904): 249.

7 D. H. von Müller, *Die Gesetze Hammurabis* (Wien, 1903).

8 See Schiller, *Roman Law: Mechanisms of Development* (The Hague, 1978); 158.

well known commonalities of topics of interest and form.[9] Comments on comparative structure have in recent years tended to concentrate on the gross structural elements of the compositions: e.g., historical preamble, body of laws, epilogue and curses; whereas comparisons of the order of the individual laws and the principles governing their arrangement have generally been avoided until recently.[10] This was primarily due to the fact that until recently—no doubt as an overreaction to the excesses of their academic forebears—scholars have generally claimed that, for extra-biblical law at least, there were no observable overriding principles of order.[11] The existence of train-of-thought connections between individual laws has, of course, always been noted. Recently, however, it has increasingly been recognized that ancient Near Eastern law compilations are structured according to their own unique set of organizational principles based on a system of priorities. Elsewhere I have characterized the three major common principles as follows:

> Principle 1: Laws, possibly of many different origins, are grouped together according to general topics.
> Principle 2: Within each topical unit the laws are arranged according to observable principles of priority.
> Principle 3: The individual laws and larger sub-units of each topical unit are arranged according to the ancient Near Eastern method of "concatenation of ideas, key words and phrases, and similar motifs" so as to form what for the ancient eye and ear were smooth *transitions* between sub-units and, frequently, between the various topical units themselves. This feature has frequently been characterized as "free association," but in reality it is a carefully planned procedure which is anything but "free."[12]

But what of the ordering of the topical units (of principle 1) themselves? In the above mentioned article (see note 12) I demonstrated that the units of the Deuteronomic Law (Deuteronomy 12-25) are arranged according to the order of the Decalogue. Further research is needed, however, in order to uncover the principles governing the order of the units of Hammurapi or of the Decalogue itself. But when we begin such research, the first thing we notice is that there is no agreement upon just what constitutes the various topical units; i.e., what are the categories of ancient Near Eastern law?

In order to answer this question it will be necessary to compare the structure of all known ancient Near Eastern legal compilations.[13] A problem immediately arises. To present each text in full would be overwhelming and unenlightening. On the other hand, simply to make parallel lists of their topical divisions alone presupposes the solution we are attempting to achieve. I have chosen a middle ground, grouping separate laws together under a single rubric only when those laws can clearly be seen to deal with the same general subject.

The Laws of Hammurapi[14]

As demonstrated by Petschow, the structure of codex Hammurapi is indeed explicable. The major organizational principles governing its overall arrangement are the priority of socio-economic worth and the primacy of contracted rights over non-contractual relationships.[15] The major topical divisions may be outlined as follows:[16]

1-5	The basic rules of Evidence and Testimony.
6-25	General rules of Theft.[17]
	(including:
	14 Kidnapping.

9 See S. M. Paul, *Studies in the Book of the Covenant in the Light of Cuneiform and Biblical Law* (VT Sup 18; Leiden, 1970): *passim*, and the literature cited there.

10 A notable exception was R. H. Pfeiffer who claimed in an oral paper that "Hebrew Law" has the reverse order of that of Hammurapi; see *Akten des 24. Intern. Orient. Kongress., München 1957* (1959): 148f. As we shall see, his observation was on the right track.

11 Cf. W. F. Leemans' review of Driver and Miles' edition of the Laws of Hammurapi, *AfO* 18 (1957–8): 407f.

12 Kaufman, "Structure" (N 1): 115.

13 We exclude the so-called "Sumerian Laws" (*ANET*[3], 525), now known to be a student's exercise, and the fragmentary Neo-Babylonian laws.

14 For the sake of uniformity and ease of reference, the enumeration of the paragraphs of the various law "codes" used herein follows the treatments by Meek, Kramer, Goetze and Finkelstein in J. B. Pritchard, ed., *ANET*[3], 1969, even though some of those enumerations are often misleading and clearly erroneous (especially in the case of Hammurapi). Basic bibliographies for each of the texts are available there. For additional bibliography on Hammurapi see R. Borger, *Babylonisch-assyrische Lesestücke* (Rome, 1963): 2.2–4 and A. Finet, *Le code de Hammurapi* (Paris, 1973).

15 H. Petschow, "Zur Systematik und Gesetzestechnik im Codex Hammurabi," *ZA* 23 (1965): 146–72.

16 It must be noted that two copies of the "code" on tablets have a few "headings" before selected groups of related rules (see J. J. Finkelstein, "A Late Old Babylonian Copy of the Laws of Hammurapi," *JCS* 21 [1967]: 42ff.) As Finkelstein showed, these provide insight into the drafting procedures and conceptions governing the various small units of related laws. He was especially successful in using them to demonstrate the principle of "transitions" (p. 43); see my principle 3. Unfortunately we have no original headings introducing larger units of the kind that concern us in this study.

17 According to Petschow this section deals with capital crimes (against society)—an interpretation both forced and inaccurate. The common denominator of "theft" is perfectly clear.

	15-20 Slave "napping.")
26-35	Transfers and forfeitures of personal property of a public servant.
36-58	Fields.[18]
	42-52 Tenancy.
	53-58 Damages to another's field.
59-66	Orchards (damages and tenancy).
67-78	Houses (i.e. "estates")—largely damaged, but clearly dealing with the "property" aspect of houses.
79-87	not preserved.
88-126	Loans and Deposits.
127-194	Marriage and Family Law.
195-225	Bodily Injury.
226-227	Removal of "slave marks." (This may properly belong with the preceding.)
228-233	Dangerously built houses.
234-240	Fees and damages regarding boats.
241-260	Oxen and others that work the fields.
	241-256 Oxen.
	257-160 Others.
261-267	Shepherds.
268-277	Various Rates of Hire.
278-282	Slaves.
	278-281 Purchases and Claims.
	282 Insolence.

Let us now simplify the above:

- I (1-5) Evidence.
- II (6-126) Property (its theft, transfer, forfeiture, impairment, loan and safekeeping.)
- III (127-194) Marriage and Family Law.
- IV (195-227) Bodily Injury.[19]
- V (228-277) Miscellaneous Fees and Damages relating to hired objects. (Alternatively it may be argued that 228-252 constitute a sub-category of "Bodily Injury" characterized by dilapidated buildings and "goring" oxen, i.e. public nuisances. See below on Eshnunna.)
- VI (278-282) Slaves.

The parallel with the Second Table of the Decalogue now looms intriguingly. Note:

	Hammurapi		*Decalogue*
I	Evidence	IX	Do not give false witness.
II	Property	VIII	Do not steal.
III	Marriage and Family Law	VII	Do not commit adultery.
IV	Bodily Injury	VI	Do not commit manslaughter.

Two significant observations need to be made here. The four topics paralleled in Hammurapi and the Decalogue are the *first four* in Hammurapi (and thus, according to the principles of ancient Near Eastern law, the most important); and the two groups of four are in the *same sequence,* although the order is reversed.

It is hard to imagine that all of this is mere coincidence. Indeed, this evidence of itself is sufficient to suggest—if not prove—that rubrics I-IV of Hammurapi are the native ancient Near Eastern categorizations of legal material and that commandments VI-IX of the Decalogue represent distillations of the essence of those categories. But let us examine the other law "codes" of the ancient Near East for corroboration and, if possible, a source wherein not only the sequence but also the order is the same as that of the Decalogue.

Lipit-Ishtar[20]

The preserved text of these Sumerian laws is quite fragmentary. The bulk of the available material comes from the second half of the "code." Nevertheless, the similarities with the content and order of Hammurapi's "code" are striking:

	major break	
1-19	Property (including slaves: 12-14).	= II
	major break	
21-33	Family Law	= III
	break[21]	
34-38	Damages to a rented ox	= V

In spite of the fragmentary text, Lipit-Ishtar is seen to follow the same divisions and order as Hammurapi, i.e., as others have noted,[22] Hammurapi may well have been modeled after Lipit-Ishtar and other (as yet unknown) texts like it.

Ur-Nammu

Only a relatively brief section of laws near the beginning of the series is preserved, and much of what is preserved is broken and/or difficult to interpret:

2	Seems to deal with orchards
3	broken
4-5	Seduction and Rape
6-8	Divorce
9	broken
10-11	Accusations of infidelity
12	Law of the rejected fiancé

18 I divide here rather than between 41 and 42 in order to follow the native division as expressed in BM 78944+78979; see Finkelstein, "Babylonian Copy" (N 16): 43.

19 For the transition between these two sections see Kaufman, "Structure" (N 1) 117f.

20 See M. Civil, "New Sumerian Law Fragments," *Assyriological Studies* 16 (Chicago, 1965): 1–12.

21 If UM 55-21-71 is indeed a part of Lipit-Ishtar (Civil [N 20]: 4ff.), then its column iii preserves laws from the section of bodily injury (IV). If so, however, it is very difficult to imagine how and where the text preserved on column ii fits into the "code" as we now have it.

22 See Civil (N 20): 1f.

13	broken
14	Return of an escaped slave
15-19	Bodily Injury
20	break (at least two paragraphs)
21′-23′	Slave (insolence?)
24′	broken
25′-27′	Testimony (27′ involving plowing another's field)
28′-29′	Damaging another's field

It is not surprising that this early "code" does not follow precisely the pattern of the later compilations of Lipit-Ishtar and Hammurapi, even though many of the laws dealt with are the same or similar to those found in the later texts. Nevertheless, upon simplification the outline of the basic pattern is still to be seen. Note that here "testimony" comes at the end:

II	(2+)	Property
III	(4-12)	Marriage and Family Law
	(14)	Escaped Slave
IV	(15-19)	Bodily Injury
	(21′-23′)	Slaves Again
I	(25′-27′)	Testimony
	(28′-29′)	Damaging another's field

The position of 28′–29′ can be explained by attraction to the protasis of 27′. The only other intrusions in the order are laws concerning slaves. Note that in Hammurapi the laws concerning escaped and stolen slaves (15–20) are brought under the larger category of "theft," those dealing with damage to a slave are placed with "bodily injury," and the rest of the slave laws are grouped at the end as a kind of appendix. There thus appears to have been no topical division concerned with slaves *per se* in ancient Near Eastern law. Laws concerning them were merely brought in under other rubrics. Because of the broken contexts, however, the reasons for their various placements here are uncertain.

Eshnunna[23]

The Akkadian law "code" from Eshnunna seems to be "peripheral" in terms of its structure as well as its geographical origin. It differs substantially from the plan of the three texts we have already examined in that it lacks the characteristic prologue and epilogue.[24] Moreover, it begins with an uncharacteristic list of current prices and rates. We are not surprised, then, to find it substantially different in terms of the rest of its structure as well:

1–24	Money: i.e., prices, wages, rates, loans and distrainment
25–35	Family Law
36–37	Deposits
38–39	Redemption of property
40	General rule of legitimate purchase
41	Rights of certain individuals to sell their beer!
42–48	Bodily Injury
49–52	Stolen and escaped slaves
53–58	Public nuisances:
	53–55 The Goring Ox
	56–57 The Vicious Dog
	58 The Dangerous Wall
59	A divorce law
	broken

The topical divisions here are clearly different, especially the first: Laws that are elsewhere found under other rubrics, such as the suspect thief caught in the act (12–13) and the "son-in-law, father-in-law" motif (17–18),[25] are placed here apparently because of their concern with the payment of "money." Except for this additional category of "money" (subsumed under "property" elsewhere), the basic categories remain the same, however, and a certain parallelism of structure with Hammurapi can be demonstrated:

	Eshnunna		*Hammurapi*
I	(1–24) Money	II	Property
II	(25–35) Family Law	III	Family Law
III	(36–41) Property		
IV	(42–48) Bodily Injury	IV	Bodily Injury
V	(49–52) Slaves		(Cf. 226–227!)
VI			First half of Miscellaneous
	(53–58) Public Nuisances	V	(228–252)
	(59) A divorce law		

Once again we note the intrusion of slave law into the pattern.[26]

Middle Assyrian Laws[27]

These laws are at first glance totally different from what has come before. Not only are prologue and epilogue missing, but the overall arrangement is completely new.[28] The laws are preserved on tablets, each of

23 See the recent treatment of Reuben Yaron, *The Laws of Eshnunna* (Jerusalem, 1969).

24 The broken seven-line introduction to the laws can by no means be deemed equivalent to the prologues of the other texts. It appears to be just a date formula (cf. Yaron [N 23]: 20 n.) On the other hand, inasmuch as Hammurapi circulated in later times without a prologue, we cannot exclude the possibility that the Eshnunna tablets are also copies from a stele that contained the requisite monumental style introduction and conclusion.

25 See J. J. Finkelstein, "ana bīt emim šasū," *RA* 61 (1967): 127–36.

26 Yaron ([N 23]: 53ff.) comments on the relative lack of structure in Eshnunna as compared to Hammurapi but fails to note the striking similarities.

27 See now G. Cardascia, *Les lois assyriennes* (Paris, 1969) and bibliography there pp. 13ff.

28 The most complete attempt to uncover the plan of the Middle Assyrian Laws is that of Cardascia (N 27): 37ff.

which was apparently devoted to a single, major subject. For example, the largest of the preserved tablets, A, treats exclusively the subject of women.[29] Nevertheless, our basic pattern is to be found even here!

Tablet A
I (1–6) Theft (2 is a subordinate paragraph on blasphemy.)
II (7–10) Bodily Injury and Murder
III A (11–24) Adultery and sexual crimes
B (25–43) Marriage Laws
I′ (44) Pledges
(45–6) Property of a widowed or abandoned wife
(47) (Magical preparations!)
(48–9) Pledged daughter
II′ (50–53) Miscarriage
(54) broken
III′ (55–6) Rape and seduction
IV (57–9) Judicial procedures

Thus not only do our categories appear here in a group of laws limited to the subject of women, three of them (the only three found in Eshnunna and Lipit-Ishtar) appear in a double series—repeated in the same order.[30] The laws close with some procedural rules which can be deemed to belong to the general category of "evidence / judicial procedures." Here, however, the order of the categories is changed; it is not that of Hammurapi and Lipit-Ishtar. It reminds us more of the Decalogue. In fact it is identical to the order of the basic ethical sins cited in Jer 7:9: theft, murder, adultery, false swearing.

The quadripartite division of ancient Near Eastern law has been established. The sixth through ninth commandments of the Decalogue state those divisions clearly, but we have noted that the usual sequence in the casuistic law collections is precisely the chiastic reverse of the Decalogue order. Whence, then, the sequence found in the Decalogue?[31] For this parallel we turn to the Hittite Laws—not surprisingly, for the cultural fount of much that is Israelite is to be found in the Hittite-ruled Levant of the Late Bronze Age, as more and more studies have demonstrated in recent years.

The Hittite Laws

These laws, too, are not of the "covenant" type of mainstream Mesopotamian law; moreover, internal evidence suggests a long and complex history of development. Nevertheless, our pattern shows up clearly and in a most interesting fashion:

I A (1–6) Murder and death
B (7–18) Bodily Injury
(19–24) Lost slaves
(25) Fouled cistern
II (26–37) Marriage Law
(38) Lawsuit avenger (by attraction to 37)
III A (39–43) Substitutes for property-holding duties
(44) Pushing one into a fire (by attraction to 43)
B (45) Lost property
C (46–56) State service (e.g., responsibilities of property-holding)
D (57–149) Theft and / or Damage to property
(150–162) Rates
(163–169) Violations of property rights
(170–174) Miscellaneous
(175–186) Rates
(187–200) Sexual crimes

Note once again that the three normative topical units begin the collection, while miscellaneous and unusual material is relegated to the end. Of importance with regard to the structure of the Decalogue is the fact that the very first Hittite laws deal with murder, not just bodily injury as elsewhere, and that the order of the three units is the very same as that found in the Decalogue.

For a final confirmation of our thesis we turn to the Rabbinic tradition of "the seven laws of the sons of Noah," that is, those divine laws which ancient Judaism deemed to be binding upon all mankind.[32] They are: (1) not to worship idols; (2) not to blaspheme God's name; (3) to establish courts of justice; (4) not to kill; (5) not to commit adultery; (6) not to rob (*gzl*)[33]; (7) not to eat flesh cut from a living animal. The "civil" laws of this list—those that deal with relations between individuals (3–6)—are precisely our four categories. That this list is a separate witness, independent of the Decalogue, is indicated by the fact that it uses "rob" (*gzl*) instead of "steal" (*gnb*) and that it has the more general rule to establish courts of justice instead of the specific prohibition of false witness in those courts.

Why is the order of the Decalogue (and the Hittite Laws) the reverse of that of the Hammurapi tradition? No doubt the answer lies in the insight long expressed by theologians. It is all a matter of priorities. In Mesopotamia, the temple and state come before the private citizen and contracted rights take precedence over non-contractual

29 Cf. Cardascia (N 27): 37.

30 This observation is somewhat different from, although related to, the recognition of "doublets" in the Assyrian Laws. (Cf. Cardascia [N 27]: 48ff.) The double pattern is puzzling, but I would not go so far as to suggest that it demonstrates the existence of two originally separate texts that have been joined.

31 The sixth through eighth commandments are, of course, attested in other orders in the versions and early Hebrew manuscripts. There is no longer any reason to doubt that the order as found in the Masoretic Text is the most ancient, however, in light of my demonstration that the Law of Deuteronomy follows just that order; Kaufman, "Structure" (N 1): esp. p. 145.

32 See J. H. Greenstone, "Laws, Noachian," *The Jewish Encyclopedia* 7, 648ff.

33 Cf. *Bereshit Rabbah* 16:9.

relationships.[34] Thus the rules for governing the state ("Testimony") and the contractual regulations of the church's or state's property must precede private affairs; and in the private realm the contracted relationships of family formation and maintenance take precedence over the individual's right to life and limb. The underlying priority system reflected in order of the Decalogue needs no elaboration on our part; it speaks eloquently for itself.

34 See Kaufman, "Structure" (N 1): 117.

DANCE AND DEATH IN THE SONG OF SONGS

ROLAND E. MURPHY, O. CARM.

One cannot escape being overwhelmed by the massive erudition displayed by Marvin Pope in his Anchor Bible Commentary on the Song of Songs. The philological comment on individual words and phrases, and the historical-religious background to several themes are exhaustively treated, and it will be a long time before any student of the Song will have something to add on this score. Nonetheless at least two questions persist: Does the woman dance in 7:1ff? In what way is love as strong as death? The exploration of these questions is meant as a tribute to Pope's stimulating commentary.

1. The Dancing Maiden

Turn, turn, Shulammite,
  turn, turn, that we may gaze upon you!
Why do you gaze upon the Shulammite
  as upon the dance of the two camps? (7:1)

The meaning of *šûbî* has been debated back and forth, and Pope remarks that the meanings or emendations proposed "are inevitably dictated by theories of interpretation" (p. 595). Not many will be tempted to follow him in reading *š*^{e}*bî* or *šēbî*, presumably from *yšb* (**wṯb*) which purportedly has the meaning "leap" in Arabic. Obviously, if one translates the verb as "leap," as Pope does, one may be rather well into a dance. Aside from the uncertainty of postulating a meaning from an Arabic cognate here, the invitation itself, which an unidentified plurality addresses to the Shulammite, does not suggest a dance. The intention of their imperative is that they may gaze (*w*^{e}*neḥĕzeh*) upon her, presumably to admire her. Is she told to come back? This would be the most natural meaning of the MT, *šûbî*. But the context leaves this uncertain; 7:1 follows on one of the most obscure (and textually corrupt) verses in the Song. It is to be admitted that sudden changes in scene (such as would be exemplified in 6:12-7:1) are not unusual in this work (e.g., 4:8). Hence "return," or "turn," is possible, and even more natural, in view of the purpose of the invitation. Pope would even be satisfied with retaining *šûbî*, since "it is possible to make a connection with some aspect of dancing" (p. 595) even with the meaning "turn," or "return." But it is still not clear that the girl is dancing (this inference can arise, of course, from her reply in 7:1b). Rather, the speakers simply request a movement on her part that will facilitate their vision of her.

It is the Shulammite (for a discussion of this term, to which nothing can be added, cf. Pope, pp. 595-600; and even he remarks that "the final word has not been written on the term") who answers. However, the NEB attributes these lines (6:13 in English Bible numbering) to the "bridegroom" who continues in the following verses with the description of the woman's physical charms. Doubtless this interpretation is motivated by the reference to the Shulammite in third person address, assuming that she would not speak of herself as the Shulammite. However, it hardly recommends itself; it envisions an abrupt switch in the man's address, from the group to the woman whose physical charms he begins to describe; moreover, it is to be expected that the Shulammite would answer a question addressed to her.

The crux of the problem about dancing lies in the Shulammite's reply (7:1b). She takes up the verb used by the group: *māh teḥĕzû*? *Māh* is ambiguous, and can be variously translated: "what," "why," "how," or as a negative. "Why?" is found in many modern translations and seems less abstruse than the "how?" preferred by Pope. The exact nuance is not essential; it is at least clear that the speaker challenges in some way those who want to gaze on her.

She then describes herself with the words, *kimm*^{e}*ḥōlat hammaḥănayim*. The full discussion of *m*^{e}*ḥōlāh* in Pope (pp. 601-603) ensures the meaning of "dance" for this word, although Pope would not exclude the notion of antiphonal singing urged by J. Sasson. The word *maḥănayim* normally means camps, and is in the dual; it is also the name of a town in Transjordan (2 Sam 2:8; 17:24, 27). It matters little whether one translates "the two camps," or "Mahanayim." The precise allusion escapes us, even if it refers to the method in which the dance was carried out. The difficulty we see is the role of the Shulammite; does she refer to herself as dancing?

The MT has *kimm*^{e}*ḥōlat*, whereas several MSS read *b-* instead of *k-*. Pope remarks (p. 605) that "the *k-* may also be taken as having temporal meaning, on the occasion of the dance, i.e., as she dances. (R.) Dussaud suggested an ellipsis, 'like (in) the dance'." The versions had some difficulty with the phrase, but LXX and Syriac both understood it as a comparison, and the Vulgate also perhaps implicitly (*nisi choros castrorum*) Symmachus testifies to *b- (en)*. I am proposing that it be taken as a simple comparison: why do you gaze upon the Shulammite as you would gaze upon the dance . . . ? Grammatically there is no difficulty with the omission of *b-* (notice the *neḥĕzeh bāk* in v. 1a) before *k-* (Joüon, 133*h*). The import of her reply is to ask why she is the cynosure of all eyes, as one would view a spectacle, in this case referring to a well-known dance. But she does not refer to herself as dancing. She compares the interest of the onlookers to the interest that the "dance of the two camps" would inspire.

The dancing maiden of chap. 7 has received "confirmation" from the *waṣf* that follows, describing the physical charms of the woman, beginning with the feet. *Māh yāpû pᵉʿāmayik* means "how beautiful are your steps." *Paʿam*, while parallel to *regel* in Isa 26:6 (and cf. Ps 68:11), usually designates the feet in motion, but not necessarily in a dance. Indeed, there is no compelling reason to interpret the *waṣf* as the description of a dancing woman. Perhaps the most influential factor in the picture of the dancing maiden of chap. 7 is the famous description of the sword dance which J. G. Wetzstein witnessed in Syria. On the wedding day, the bride danced, wielding a sword, before two groups, men and women (hence the *maḥănayim*). F. Delitzsch made this interpretation very popular, but it is difficult to associate a nineteenth-century wedding custom with this specific event in the Song. There is nothing in the ensuing description of the woman which indicates that she is dancing, and the mention of her "steps" can be understood as merely part of the *waṣf*.

2. Love and Death

Place me as a seal on your heart,
  as a seal on your arm.
Strong as death is love,
  hard as Sheol is ardor;
Its shafts are shafts of fire,
  a flame of Yah.
Deep waters cannot quench love,
  nor rivers sweep it away,
Were one to give all one's patrimony for love,
  one would be thoroughly despised. (8:6-7).

Most translations and commentaries ascribe these lines to the woman, although the NEB attributes them to the man, continuing his words in 8:5b. The words of the woman in 8:6aα concerning the seal are quite clear. The seal could be worn about the neck (Gen 38:18) and thus on the "heart," or else on the hand as a ring (Jer 22:24). It served for identification (Gen 38:18), and signature purposes. "Arm" may be interchangeable here with hand, just as "hand" in 5:14 can be understood as "arm." The practice of wearing something that belongs to one's beloved is widespread, and the close association between apparel and person is reflected in the Cairo love songs:

I wish I were the seal ring,
the guardian of her [fingers],
then [. . . .] (Simpson, p. 311)

The metaphors used in the lines associated with this fragmentary piece (maid, washerman) indicate that the intent is to express inseparability, intimacy, and the attendant advantages of being present to the loved one. Is there an apotropaic practice intended—the wearing of some device such as a charm to ward off any harm to the wearer? This seems to go beyond the wish expressed here, which is a simple memento.

The words about love are introduced by *kî*, which is frequently taken as causal. However, the words do not contain an explanation for her request. They are too "heavy" to be an explanation; the power of love is *not* a reason why he should set her as a seal on his arm. Rather, this is a simple aphorism about the power of love. Hence it seems reasonable to understand the conjunction as the *kî* of affirmation (Joüon, 164*b*), which need not be translated; it underlines an emphatic statement. The statement is that love is as strong as death. It does not state that love and death are locked in battle or that love will overcome death (contrary to Pope, p. 667: "Love's power over against that of death"; p. 673; "Love withstands even Death and the rigors of Hell.") It is simply a comparison concerning the strength of Love, and this strength is compared to one of the most powerful figures that confronted ancient Israel, Death (cf. C. Barth; N. Tromp). The personification of Death as a dynamic power, hostile to humans, but subject to Yahweh, has been documented many times. Hence there is no need to speak of the "mysterious bond between Love and Death" for this verse. It is hard to improve on the words of Robert (pp. 300-302): "Joüon, Miller, Ricciotti, Buzy veulent que la mort soit ici nommée pour son avidité insatiable. Mais dans l'Écriture, on parle tout aussi souvent de ses coups inéluctables: la mort est une puissance à laquelle nul au monde ne peut résister. Dieu seul est capable d'en triompher . . . Dire que l'amour est fort comme la mort, c'est donc souligner l'âpreté qu'il met à réclamer son droit, sa prétention à posséder en entier son objet et a le défendre contre toute emprise étrangère."

A word about the usual English translation of *qinʾāh*, which is parallel to *ʾahăbāh*. It is commonly rendered as "jealousy" (RSV), which does not really suit the confident love that exists between the man and the woman. "Passion" (NEB; Pope) is better, but in modern usage may leave something to be desired; "ardor" (used by Pope, p. 669, in his explanation of the term) seems better. The import of the whole pasage is that love pursues its object, the beloved one, with the same finality and tenacity as Death pursues every human being.

The fires of that love are associated with the flames of Yah, if one may so translate the enigmatic *šalhebetyāh* at the end of the verse. Pope has a succinct summary of the various views advanced concerning this term (pp. 670-71), and he takes it as a gloss to *rᵉšāpehā*. There is no certainty here, but "a flame of Yah" is also possible. If this interpretation of *šalhebetyāh* is correct, an important and new dimension is introduced into the Canticle. It is commonly said that there is no mention of God in the Song, but such a view fails to take *šalhebetyāh* seriously. As it stands, it has to mean that there is somehow a connection between human love and divine love. One might argue to this philosophically, or one might invoke 1 John 4:8, but neither of these moves is necessary. The ending of v 6 makes the connection between the human and divine, even if without further comment.

The comparison between love and death is heightened in 8:7 a, which is not, as Pope (p. 673) claims, "the same as" 8:6 aβ. An important key to the heightening (Gerleman, pp. 217-18) is the juxtaposition of fire (v 6) and water (v 7). If love is fire, its natural enemy is water. But not even the *mayim rabbîm* can quench love. Now, love is *stronger* than death. *Mayim rabbîm* is used frequently in the Bible, and it clearly carries the mythical background of the conflict between Baal and Yam in Ugaritic lore, and between God and the powers of chaos in Gen 1, Isa 51:9-10, Ps 74:12-14, etc. Pope argues for a narrow parallelism, that the waters are identical with Death of the previous verse. Then v 7 simply repeats v 6, somewhat flatly. It is to be admitted that Death/Sheol also have water associated with them. But it is not at all clear that the *mayim rabbîm* is a simple synonym for Sheol and is bereft of its "cosmic connotations" (H. G. May). The appropriateness of the water metaphor is twofold: it contrasts fire, and it represents the powers of chaos which only the Lord can dominate. Love refuses to be conquered even by such strength as the *mayim rabbîm* represent. The "rivers" (*nehārôt*) are interpreted by Pope, as one would expect, as the waters of death, and he points to Jonah 2:4 as a parallel instance. However, the Jonah text has the singular, and is a verse that needs synonyms for water. More apposite for the imagery is that of the waters of chaos as in Ps 93:3 (*nehārôt*, plural as in Cant 8:7; see also Ps 24:2). Robert, as Pope points out, calls attention to the great similarity between 8:6-7 and Isa 43:2; and in 43:2 a the world of chaos is evoked by *mayim* and *nehārôt*. The imagery of water in the Bible is much more far-reaching than as a connotation of Death/Sheol.

The ambiguity of 8:7b in the Hebrew is difficult to resolve. It could mean that a person is despised for attempting to purchase love, or that the possessions one offers are spurned. And it is even possible to understand it as a question implying that no disdain would be shown anyone prepared to make such a sacrifice for love. In any case, the purpose of the line is to enhance the value of love.

A final observation on 8:6-7 is in order. The woman's request in 8:6 is not unusual in itself. She has already expressed her desires for his kisses (1:1), invited him to herself (2:17; 4:16), and more than once suggested a rendez-vous (1:7; 7:12-13). Hence the desire to be as a seal on his arm is in harmony with the mood of the Song. What is unusual is the rather formal pronouncement about love, introduced by the emphatic *kî*. Pope's comment on this line seems uncomfortable, if not obscure: "Love is here personified in that the signet to be set on the heart and hand of the lady's lover represents her essence and power which is here revealed as Love" (p. 668). Rather, there is no intrinsic connection between her request and the statement about love's power. Indeed, this statement stands out from the love language that is typical of the Song. The speakers are usually centered on each other, extolling their delights, describing beauty and mutual possession. But in 8:6 aβ and 8:7 one is confronted with judgments that take a distance from the phenomenon of love in order to render a judgment on it. Any reference to the particular love of the speakers, which has been out front through the entire poem, is now only implicit. This is the kind of observation that one would make of human love in general. Hence it is not surprising that J. -P. Audet (1955: pp. 216-17) remarked that it is not gratuitous to suppose that the preservation of the Canticle is the work of Israelite sages. In particular he pointed to the reflections in 8:6-7 "qui relèvent du genre sapientiel et ne tiennent au *Cantique* que par l'artifice assez précaire de la conjonction *kî*, indice caractéristique de la réflexion de l'éditeur." Such a view was already espoused by Renan for 8:7, as Pope notes (p. 675), and Robert has given the title, "aphorisme d'un sage," to 8:7b.

It should be emphasized that the Canticle is *not* wisdom literature, nor simply written by sages. These are love poems. J. -P. Audet (1955: pp. 215-18) seems to have been the first to ask: who would be the ones responsible for the preservation and editing of this literature? He claimed that Israelite sages would have recognized here a certain resonance to such passages as Prov 5:15-19. This is a thoroughly reasonable hypothesis, much more cautious and solid than that drawn by E. Würthwein in his recent commentary (1969: pp. 30-31), who thinks that this poetry derives from wisdom circles.

BIBLIOGRAPHY

Audet, J. -P., "Le sens du Cantique des Cantiques." *RB* 62 (1955): 197-221.

Barth, C., *Die Errettung vom Tode* (Zollikon: Evangelischer Verlag, 1947).

Delitzsch, F., *Commentary on the Song of Songs and Ecclesiastes* (Edinburgh: Clark, 1891). Cf. esp. pp. 170-76.

Gerleman, G., *Das Hohelied* (BKAT VXIII/2-3. Neukirchen-Vluyn: Neukirchener Verlag, 1965).

Joüon, P., *Grammaire de l'hébreu biblique* (Rome: Pontifical Biblical Institute, 1947).

May, H. G., "Some Cosmic Connotations of Mayim Rabbim, 'Many Waters'." *JBL* 74 (1955): 9-21.

Pope, M., *Song of Songs* (AB 7; New York: Doubleday, 1977).

Robert, A., A. Feuillet and R. Tournay, *Le cantique des cantiques* (EB. Paris: Gabalda, 1963).

Simpson, W. K., *The Literature of Ancient Egypt* (New Haven: Yale University Press, 1972).

Tromp, N., *Primitive Conceptions of Death and the Netherworld in the Old Testament* (AnBib 21; Rome: Pontifical Biblical Institute, 1969).

Wetzstein, J., "Die syrische Dreschtafel." *ZE* 5 (1873): 270-302.

Würthwein, E., "Das Hohelied" in *Die fünf Megilloth* (HAT 18; Tübingen: Mohr (Siebeck), 1969): 25-71.

LOVE AND DEATH IN THE COURT HISTORY OF DAVID

JOHN VAN SETERS

One of the most conspicuous places in the Old Testament where the theme of love as passion is closely conjoined with death is in the Court History of David.[1] For the sake of the present discussion, the Court History may be limited to 2 Sam 2:8–4:12; 9–20; 1 Kgs 1–2.[2] The purpose of the present study is to clarify the nature of this theme and to discuss possible parallels to it in antiquity, especially since some recent treatments of it have tended to obscure rather than carefully to delineate its true character.[3] The Court History contains accounts of four episodes in which the love or passion of a man for a woman leads to a death, either for the lover or the woman's husband. Now, on the face of it, such a story theme would appear to the modern reader as very commonplace, but in fact it is quite rare in the rest of the Old Testament and in early Classical antiquity and virtually non-existent in ancient Near Eastern literature. Let us consider the four examples in the Court History.

In the first instance (2 Sam 3:6ff.), Abner has an affair with Rizpah, a former concubine of Saul. There is nothing to suggest that this was anything more than an act of passion which because of the close family tie was considered indiscrete.[4] The affair leads to a quarrel between Ishbosheth and Abner. The former criticizes the action while the latter regards it as an insult to be rebuked over a woman. The result is an alienation between the two and Abner's subsequent attempt to join forces with David. After considerable negotiation Abner meets with David in private to work out a deal, but Joab learns of it and intercepts Abner after his departure. Already having a grudge against him because of his brother's death at Abner's hands Joab murders him. The defection and death of Abner in turn greatly weaken the position of Ishbosheth and leave him most vulnerable (2 Sam 4:1ff.). This leads to his assassination by two of his own men who thought that they could benefit from it. Thus it is possible to see the death of both Abner and Ishbosheth as related to the one act of passion by Abner.

The second example of love and death together has to do with the well-known episode of David and Bathsheba in 2 Samuel 11. While his faithful troops are off to war David remains behind in Jerusalem. From the roof of his palace one day he sees a woman bathing. Aroused by her beauty, he inquires about her and learns that she is Bathsheba, the wife of his warrior Uriah, the Hittite. Nevertheless, he sends for her and seduces her, after which she becomes pregnant. When David learns of this he attempts to cover up the matter by recalling Uriah from the battlefield in order to have him cohabit with his wife. But Uriah, out of a sense of honor because his fellows are at war, cannot be persuaded to go home. So David sends him back to the front lines with a letter of instructions to Joab which is also Uriah's death warrant. He is to be put in such a vulnerable place in the battle that his death will be assured. In this way Uriah is killed and David is free to marry Bathsheba, after a discrete period of mourning. In a sequel, in chapter 12, the child that is born as a result of the act of adultery also dies as a divine judgment and as a surrogate for David himself.

The third story of love and death follows immediately in 2 Samuel 13 and is the account of the rape of Tamar by Amnon. Tamar is the beautiful sister of Absalom and half-sister of Amnon, royal sons of David. Amnon falls in love with Tamar and, with the aid of a cousin, devises a plan to seduce her. He feigns illness and requests of the king that Tamar be permitted to prepare his food in his private quarters. When she comes to do so he forces her

1 The study that constitutes the basic point of departure for all recent discussion of the Court History or Succession Story is L. Rost, *Die Überlieferung von der Thronnachfolge Davids* (BWANT III/6, 1926; reissued in *Das Kleine Credo und andere Studien zum Alten Testament* [Heidelberg: Quelle & Meyer, 1965]: 119-253). See also G. von Rad, "The Beginnings of History Writing in Ancient Israel" (1944), in *The Problem of the Hexateuch and other Essays* (Edinburgh: Oliver & Boyd, 1966): 166-204; R. N. Gunn, *The Story of King David* (JSOT Supplement Series 6; Sheffield, 1978).

2 I have discussed my reasons for these boundaries in a paper prepared for a faculty seminar at Toronto, 1974, to be published in *Orientalia* 49 (1980) (see already "Oral Patterns or Literary Conventions in Biblical Narrative," *Semeia* 5 [1976]: 147f.). I would also include 2 Sam 1:5-10, 13-16; 6:16, 20-23; cf. Gunn, *King David* (N 1): 65-84.

3 J. Blenkinsopp, "Theme and Motif in the Succession History (2 Sam xi 2ff.) and the Yahwist Corpus," VTSup 15 (1966): 44-57; D. M. Gunn, "Traditional Composition in the 'Succession Narrative,' " *VT* 26 (1976): 222f., and repeated in *King David* (N 1): 43. See my earlier criticism in "Problems in the Literary Analysis of the Court History of David," *JSOT* 1 (1976): 26f.

4 The Greek adds the phrase at the beginning of v. 8, "And Abner took her," which may be original; but there is still no reason on this account to suspect Abner's loyalty. I can find no good example where the marriage to a concubine of a previous ruler gave anyone a claim to the throne. Marriage to a widowed queen or the daughter of a previous ruler is quite another matter.

against her will and rapes her. Then his love turns to hate and he throws her out. She takes her bitter complaint to Absalom, her brother, who bides his time to seek revenge. After two years he holds a special sheepshearing celebration at which the king's sons are all present, and during the festivities Absalom has Amnon murdered.

Finally in 1 Kgs 2:13ff., Adonijah becomes infatuated with Abishag, the former concubine of David, and makes a request for her from Solomon through Bathsheba. In this case, since Abishag was still a virgin (1:4) she was eligible for remarriage. There is no need to think that Adonijah's intentions were in any way treasonable, but Solomon interpreted his request in the worst possible way and used it as a pretext to have him put to death.

Recently D. Gunn has suggested grouping all of these stories under the rubric of "the woman who brings death." In this he is largely following the earlier suggestion of J. Blenkinsopp who classified a number of biblical stories as belonging to this motif.[5] However, the attempt cannot be viewed as very successful. The theme of the woman who brings death is most clearly presented in the instruction texts of Proverbs 1–9,[6] as the seductress or adulterous woman who plays an *active* role in leading men astray. This does not apply to a single case in the Court History for even though sexual passion is involved, the woman is passive, resists the male's advances, or her role is unspecified.

The other examples of parallels to the Court History, with one exception, are too farfetched to be helpful. It is suggested, for instance, that the daughter of Shua who marries Judah (Genesis 38) is a woman who brings death because her first two sons die violently. But these deaths occur after the sons reached maturity and as a direct punishment by God for their wickedness (vv 7, 10). How can their mother be held responsible for their deaths any more than Judah their father? The reason for the suggestion is to force a connection between this daughter of Shua (Bath-Shua) and Bathsheba of the Court History.[7] Incidentally, Judah believes, erroneously, that Tamar is a "woman who brings death" and so withholds his third son; but in the end she is vindicated.[8] It is equally doubtful that the Yahwist, in Genesis 3, regards Eve as "*the* woman who brings death" because at the end of the episode she is specifically called the "mother of all living"; she is not regarded, in the divine judgment, as any more guilty than Adam. The woman is not presented as the seductress in the Story of Eden. Only the snake can be viewed as a seducer of the woman, and even this is open to some doubt.

Instances of the woman who brings death, or at least trouble, are not lacking in the Old Testament but they are of an entirely different order from those in the Court History. One example of the adulterous woman who causes trouble is that of the wife of Potiphar in the Joseph story (Genesis 39). More obvious are the cases of wicked foreign queens, such as Jezebel and Athaliah, but there are examples in which the heroine uses beauty and seduction to destroy an enemy, as in the case of Jael (Judg 4:17–22), Esther and Judith. Yet none of these correspond to the episodes cited from the Court History since there the woman is portrayed as completely *passive* as far as the death of the victim is concerned.

Consequently, one must describe or classify the motif in an entirely different way. It is the *love or passion of a man for a woman resulting in death* that constitutes the basic element of the motif. It is not the character or behavior of the woman herself that is important but that of the man who loves her. The only clear instance of a parallel in the rest of the OT is the story of the rape of Dinah in Genesis 34. Here Dinah is certainly innocent and passive in the affair and it is the initial passion of Shechem and then his continuing love for Dinah that is his undoing. This makes it parallel with the story of the rape of Tamar. In both cases also the brother or brothers of the violated sister take revenge in the face of the rather indulgent attitude of the girl's father. Yet it must be said that Shechem's continuing love for Dinah contrasts with the immediate change to hatred by Amnon and provides less justification for his murder. He was prepared to go through with a formal marriage agreement and remain entirely within the law (see Exod 22:15–16 + English text 16–17) whereas Amnon refused to consider this.

The motive of revenge also plays a role in the story of Abner because his prior slaying of Asahel (2 Sam 2:18ff.) is the stated reason for his own murder by Joab (2 Sam 3:27, 30). Here it is a case of brotherly love that leads to the death of the offender, just as it is the love and concern for a sister in the other two stories. On the other hand, David's love for his son Absalom cannot prevent his death at the hand of Joab.

The notion of love or passion for a beautiful woman that leads to the death of her husband may also lie behind the so-called "Threat to the Ancestress" stories in Gen 12:10–20; 20:1–18; 26:1–11. Because the woman is beautiful the patriarch feels his life is threatened when he enters a foreign realm where there is no "fear of God" so he pretends to be the woman's brother. Again the woman plays an entirely passive role in the whole episode.[9] In addition it should be noted that in these three stories and

5 See above n. 3.

6 Prov 2:16-19; 5:1-23; 7:1-27; 9:13-18.

7 This connection is based entirely upon the identity of Bathsheba with Bathshua which is supported only by 1 Chron 3:5. That the personal name of the daughter of Shua in Genesis 38 would be Bathshua is also most unlikely.

8 See also the case of Sarah in the Book of Tobit. But this is surely an entirely different motif from those in the Court History.

9 For a fuller discussion of these texts see J. Van Seters, *Abraham in History and Tradition* (New Haven & London: Yale Univ. Press, 1976): 167-91.

in that of Genesis 34 the setting is the foreign court and the standard of behavior that one expects in such places.

To sum up, apart from the one direct example of the love and death theme in Genesis 34 and the indirect allusions in the stories mentioned above, the theme is not found in the Old Testament outside of the Court History. But within this work it plays a very dominant role.

The literature of the ancient Near East contains some instances in which the woman as seductress plays an *active* role in the troubles or death of others. The Egyptian tale of the *Two Brothers*, like the Joseph story, tells how an unfaithful wife attempts to destroy either her husband or an unwilling lover. There are also stories in which the goddess tries to avenge unrequited love, as in *Gilgamesh* or the Ugaritic tale of *Aqhat*.[10] However, I have not found any example that is parallel to those of the Court History in which the love of a man for a woman leads to death. It is not an element of the historical epics of Mesopotamia nor of the so-called *Königsnovellen* or other historical novels of Egypt.

If we turn, however, to early Greek literature, and particularly to the epic tradition of Homer, the matter is altogether different. In general there is a certain correspondence in subject matter having to do with love and war and the life of the court; but in the employment of this theme of love and death, the correspondence between the Court History and Greek epic is most striking. The whole of the *Iliad* could be construed as an example of this theme since it deals with the rape and abduction of Helen by Paris from the palace of Menelaus, and the war against Troy that followed. In this war many of the heroes fall, although neither Menelaus, her husband, nor Paris, her abductor, suffer death in this work. But the poem is also, or more directly, about the wrath of Achilles which is brought on by another episode illustrating this theme of love and death. Agamemnon has taken, as a prize of war, Chryseis the daughter of the priest of Apollo, and he refuses to return the girl to her father for ransom. Whereupon the priest invokes a curse of plague upon the camp of the Greeks which causes much death and can be relieved only by the return of the girl. This Agamemnon does, but to restore his honor he takes from Achilles his concubine Briseis. This enrages Achilles who withdraws from battle and allows many among the Greeks to die, returning to the fighting only after the death of his dear friend Patroclus and as vengeance for his death.

The *Odyssey* also is framed by the theme of how Penelope, who waits for Odysseus' return from Troy, must resist the constant advances of a number of suitors. In the end when Odysseus does return he and his son Telemachus kill all the suitors and their accomplices. Within the work, however, one meets with many other women who are anything but passive in the events. In a complete contrast to Penelope is the unfaithful and adulterous Clytemnestra who murders Agamemnon with the aid of her paramour Aigisthus. But this is a very minor motif in comparison with the studied passivity of Penelope.

While Homer is somewhat ambiguous about the role of Helen in the original abduction, she hardly plays an active role in the subsequent events of the *Iliad* and receives a certain vindication in the *Odyssey*. Briseis, who also has an important place in the love and death theme of the *Iliad*, is completely passive in all the scenes where she appears.

Greek tragedy leans heavily upon the epic tradition for its themes; but in the presentation of love and death, which is certainly prominent in many of the plays of Aeschylus, Sophocles, and Euripides, it does not follow the dominant pattern of epic on this subject. In tragedy there is much more interest in the faithless woman who inflicts death out of revenge, such as Clytemnestra—a very minor theme in Homer—or in the woman who is herself the object of abuse and suffering, for example, Electra or Antigone, than in the woman who plays a passive role. One might also compare the role of the captive women and their suffering in the *Trojan Women* with the role of Briseis as simply a prize of war in the *Iliad*. Only rarely in tragedy, and in a secondary role, is it the woman who, through being loved, is the cause of violence not of her own doing.[11]

Herodotus also represents a great source of stories about life in the courts of kings. But while his work contains examples of women involved in a pattern of love and death they do not really follow the simple epic pattern. Thus, in book I, 6-12, Candaules' high regard for his wife's beauty leads ultimately to his own death. Gyges, who commits the deed, is not described as loving or desiring Candaules' wife but acts upon the latter's demand that he either kill himself or Candaules. So she takes an active part in the events. In book III, 1, the cause of war between Egypt and Persia is said to result from an act of deceit played on Cambyses by the Pharaoh Amasis. Cambyses had asked the Pharaoh to give him his daughter, but Amasis, not wishing to lose his daughter nor to provoke Cambyses, sent another in her place. Once Cambyses learned of this deceit, he went to war against Egypt. Yet the whole episode is more a matter of international diplomacy than an example of love and death. In book IV, 43, Sataspes rapes the daughter of Zopyrus and is condemned to death. At this point an appeal of Sataspes' mother wins a reprieve for her son by setting a task for him that could gain his pardon from the king. Sataspes, however, fails in his task and so earns death. Thus the real cause of his death is complicated by

10 All these texts may be found in J. B. Pritchard, ed., *Ancient Near Eastern Texts Relating to the Old Testament* (Princeton, NJ: Princeton Univ. Press, 1950).

11 In *The Trachinae* of Sophocles, Iole plays this passive role which results in Heracles' death. But more central is his wife Deianeira whose action is directly, though inadvertently, responsible for it.

the direct action of a second woman who becomes, at least in part, responsible for it. The intrigues of Xerxes, book IX, 108-13, to gain the love of the wife of his brother Masistes and then of her daughter, does ultimately lead to Masistes' death and the mutilation of his wife. But more in keeping with Greek tragedy is the vengeful activity of Xerxes' wife that leads to the subsequent course of events.

From this brief survey of early Greek literature it would appear that only Greek epic contains this motif of love and death in its simple form. Yet both the Homeric epic and the Court History give to this motif a very prominent place in the course of events that they present. Thus it does not prove that the Court History is merely a prose rendering of an epic tradition, since it has none of those other characteristics associated with the epic form. It is in every respect anti-heroic in outlook. This correspondence between Homer and the Court History cannot be used to suggest an early date for the latter since the Homeric poems in their present form are no earlier than the late eighth century B.C. There are other grounds for considering the Court History and the Yahwist of Genesis as exilic in date.[12] Furthermore, one can safely rule out direct dependence of a Judean author upon the Homeric poems.

It is possible that the Court History and Homer reflect what was, in fact, the real position of women in the oriental court with Clytemnestra or Jezebel being the exceptions. One could then account for the more active place given to women in the literature of fifth century Athens as the consequence of its democracy. This may account for the contrast between the passive and the active roles of women, but it does not really explain the combination as well of the love of such women and death.[13]

Another possibility is that a model or style of court story developed, perhaps, in Phoenicia, in which this motif was a primary element.[14] From there it spread to the Aegean world, on the one hand, and to Israelite literature on the other. It is certainly a royal motif reflecting court mores, but it could be used in a heroic presentation, as in Homer, or in a derogatory portrayal of the men involved, as in the Court History. In the end, however, such suggestions must remain rather speculative.

In this study I have tried to define more precisely the theme of love and death in the Court History. I have also looked for possible parallels in the rest of the Old Testament in which there are one direct and three indirect examples in Genesis. It is not a theme otherwise used in the literature of the Near East but it is quite prominent in the Homeric epic tradition of Greece. Whatever the possible relationship between Israelite and Greek literature at this point, perhaps joined indirectly through Phoenicia, it seems highly advisable to take up again a comparative literary study between the two regions.[15]

12 On the dating of the Court History see my forthcoming article in *Orientalia* 49 (1980). On the dating of the Yahwist see *Abraham in History and Tradition* (N 9): esp. pp. 249ff.

13 Compare the role of Michal (1 Sam 18:20-30; 19:11-17) and Abigail (1 Samuel 25) both of whom save David from death or from killing someone else.

14 The fact that the Genesis stories associate this attitude so strongly with a foreign court may be significant.

15 I wish to express my thanks to my research assistant Ms Teresa Smith for her help in the research and preparation of this manuscript.

ON THE DEATH OF ABINER

DAVID NOEL FREEDMAN

David's dirge over Abiner, the commander-in-chief of the armies of Israel (2 Sam 3:33–34), has been overshadowed by the more famous elegy for Saul and Jonathan (2 Sam 1:19–27), but it is deserving of study and appreciation of its literary merit and artistic features. Thanks to the recent publication of prime textual data from Qumran (4QSam[a] in particular) in the *Biblica Hebraica Stuttgartensia*, it is possible to restore the poem to a more original and complete state than what is preserved in MT or LXX.[1] What has survived in any case is very brief, perhaps only an excerpt or stanza of a much longer work. If we compare it with the Lament over Saul and Jonathan, we note that the latter consists of 110 words, whereas the former has only 16 (MT) or 17 (4Q). The preserved portion, whether the entire elegy or only a fraction of it, is itself a carefully constructed entity, which can be examined and evaluated apart from the question of its completeness.

In what follows, we offer a reconstruction of the text; the vocalization is in accordance with MT except where otherwise indicated. Explanations and arguments will be appended.

hakkĕmôt nābāl yāmût ʾ*ăbînēr*	(Line A)	As the dying of a scoundrel, did Abiner die?
ʾ*ăsūrôt yādêk lōʾ bĕziqqîm*	(Line B)	Bound were your hands not in manacles;
raglêk lōʾ binḥuštaym huggāšû	(Line C)	Your feet not into fetters were thrust;
kinpôl lipnê bĕnê ʿ*awlâ nāpālt*	(Line D)	As a falling before criminals did you fall?!

NOTES

Line A: That the name is correctly vocalized ʾ*ăbînēr* is shown by the spelling in 1 Sam 14:30 (ʾ*bynr*). Throughout MT the older spelling, as here, ʾ*bnr*, is preserved, and it has affected the vocalization, so that MT regularly reads ʾ*abnēr* (cf. P. Kyle McCarter, *1 Samuel: A New Translation with Introduction, Notes & Commentary* [AB 8; Garden City: Doubleday, 1980]: 254).

Line B: MT *ydk*, if correctly interpreted as singular, must be adjusted in the light of the context and sense to the plural, as with many MSS and the versions. For the whole line I have adopted the apparent and reconstructed reading of 4Q, with the changed order of words, and the addition of the phrase *bzqym* 'in manacles.' Whether this word is a plus in 4Q, or a minus in MT and LXX is not easy to determine, but the following arguments may be presented in support of the view that *bzqym* is an integral part of the text, and belongs to an earlier form of the poem than what was preserved in MT and LXX:

1. The phrase *bzqym* is a very suitable parallel for *lnḥštym* (so MT; 4Q has *bnḥš.m*), a noticeable lack in the standard text. Nevertheless, in view of the formidable textual evidence against this expression, along with a normal preference for the shorter text, as well as the absence of a rationale for its omission through scribal error, it could be argued that *bzqym* was added by a conscientious and poetically sensitive editor under the influence of *bnḥštym* in the next colon. That analysis has a certain appeal, but it does seem odd to attribute greater sensitivity to prosodic and rhetorical factors to an editor or scribe, rather than to the poet himself. Furthermore, in spite of the obvious connection between *zqym* and *nḥštym*, they are not found together in any other passage in the Bible; that is a strong indication that the presence of *nḥštym* would not naturally or automatically suggest *zqym* to an inattentive scribe. In other words it is not only not a common word-pair in biblical Hebrew, but until the present discovery not even known to exist in that language. In addition, in this poem practically every word is balanced by a corresponding term. The glaring exception is *nḥštym*, that is, in MT. Please note the following pairs: a. *kmwt* and *ymwt* (A) and *knpwl* and *nplt* (D); the two pairs also balance each other; b. there is a matchup between *nbl* and ʾ*bnr* in A, but there is a more important association between *nbl* (A) and *bny* ʿ*wlh* (D); c. *ydyk* (B) and *rglyk* (C); d. ʾ*srwt* (B) and *hgšw* (C); e. even *l*ʾ (B) is matched with *l*ʾ (C). The only elements without a direct matchup are the interrogative *he* at the beginning of A, and the compound preposition *lpny* in D. The implication of this steadfast pairing is that originally there was a parallel term for *nḥštym*, and that it was lost in the process of transmission. While it would be temerarious to supply one, we may take a more positive view of the one preserved in 4Q.

2. It has been observed that the order of the words in lines B and C is different in 4Q when compared with MT

1 The idea for this paper and the approach were stimulated by the excellent studies of 1 and 2 Samuel by P. Kyle McCarter, Jr. in his published and unpublished works on those books. All the textual information used in this article, however, is to be found in the apparatus of *BHS*.

or LXX; furthermore, the order in 4Q preserves an excellent example of chiasm, which is largely lost in MT, and therefore 4Q may be regarded as more original than MT in this respect. The chiasm in lines B-C is to be seen in the placement of the parallel verb forms: *ʾsrwt* at the beginning of line B is balanced by *hgyš* at the end of line C. This is not the case in MT, where the verb forms are in parallel pattern: *ʾsrwt* at the end of line B, and *hgšw* at the end of line C. This circumstance in 4Q might be regarded as trivial and possibly accidental, but the latter is not likely, especially since there are several other elements in the poem which support the view that the chiasm is deliberate and an integral element in the structure. Lines A and D are closely related in the selection and order of words, as well as in their content. They form an envelope around lines B and C, and provide the basic theme of the dirge: Did Abiner die as a scoundrel dies? On the contrary, he was the innocent victim of people like that, criminals. The envelope construction is an important ingredient in the overall pattern of chiasm. The chiasm or cross-over occurs at the very center of the poem, in this case in lines B-C. This emerges more clearly in 4Q than in MT or LXX, with the placement of the verbs at opposite ends of the bicolon. We infer then that 4Q preserves an earlier form of the text, which includes *bzqym*. Hence that term belongs to the older stratum, while its loss is reflected in a later tradition (i.e., MT and LXX).

Line C: Through a comparison of texts preserved in MT, 4Q, and different versions of LXX, we can recover two variant and competing texts of this line:

1. *raglêk lōʾ linḥuštaym huggāšû*
2. *wĕraglêk binḥuštaym lōʾ higgîš*

The first is based mainly on the existing MT; the initial conjunction is not found in LXX, and may therefore be omitted. The second is based mainly on 4Q; the final Hiphil form of the verb is supported in all likelihood by the major witnesses of LXX. Very likely these two versions are old and derive from the process of oral transmission. Nevertheless it may be possible to establish priority for one rather than the other on the basis of poetic factors. In trying to choose between the Hophal 3rd m. pl. verb, and the Hiphil 3rd m. s., we note that passive verb forms are less common in biblical Hebrew than active ones, and therefore that the Hophal is likely to be more original than the Hiphil. An added point is that when we compare the chiastic verb forms in lines B and C, we note that *ʾăsūrôt* has the vowels "a" and "u" in that order, while *huggāšû* has the same vowels in the opposite order ("u" and "a" from the beginning of the word as in the case of *ʾsrwt*). Needless to say, such refinements vanish from the scene if the Hiphil reading *higgîš* is adopted.

In choosing between the colon with initial *waw* (as conjunction) and the one without, we must consider the general pattern of usage. On the whole, there is a tendency to omit the conjunction at the beginning of opening cola (e.g., line B) and to include it at the beginning of second cola (e.g., line C) in balanced constructions. To what extent the transmission of poetic texts has been influenced by normal prose usage (with its endless proliferation of clause-initial conjunctions) and therefore how many of these conjunctions at the beginning of second cola have been introduced secondarily is difficult to say, but other texts indicate that there has been relatively little contamination of poetic texts. In this case, therefore, we might expect the conjunction before *rglyk* to be original, but the evidence of the LXX, which omits the conjunction, and the syllable count for parallel cola (lines B and C) tips the scale in favor of deletion.

We must still deal with the question of *bzqym*. If it was part of the original poem, then how did it disappear from the mainstream of the textual tradition, i.e., MT and LXX? In order to explain this serious omission, we require evidence pointing to one of the more familiar scribal lapses, namely haplography. An examination of the texts preserved in MT and LXX gives no such indication, and while it is not necessary to explain every vagary of the human actor, especially a scribe, the lack of a rationale may undermine the case for the originality of *bzqym*. So we wish to propose a hypothetical case, an unattested stage in the history of transmission, but which would provide a plausible occasion for the desired scribal error. The existence of this stage can also be defended on grounds other than its suitability for scribal errors. We have already noted the classic instance of chiasm in the 4Q version of lines B-C. That, however, is a single or partial chiasm, the remaining words being in parallel order. Since the three texts, MT, LXX and 4Q reflect a variety in the order of the words in lines B-C, we suggest still another order, more original perhaps than any extant. This would involve complete or perfect chiasm, in which each term balances its correlate in reverse order. For line C that would produce a sequence such as this:

bnḥštym rglyk lʾ hgyš

Thus in addition to the verb pair already matched at the beginning of B and the end of C, we have matching nouns (*ydyk* and *rglyk*) in the middle of each colon, and the prepositional phrases (*bzqym* and *bnḥštym*) at the end of B and the beginning of C. These two words would be in direct sequence, and an explanation of the apparent haplography is at hand: *bzqym bnḥštym*. In this case, the scribe's eye would have skipped from the first *b* to the second *b* and in the process the word *zqym* would have disappeared from the text. While we have disposed of the cumbersome *zqym* we must still explain the shift from the presumed original preposition *b* to *l* before the second term, *nḥštym*. This looks like an example of the substitution of the common or normal preposition *l* with the H-stem of *ngš*, in contrast with the unusual instance of *b* which does not occur anywhere else in the Bible with the H-stem of *ngš*.

Line D: The pattern of verb forms, *knpwl . . . nplt* is deliberate and matches the similar pair in line A: *kmwt . . . ymwt*. In each case the infinitive form of the verb is preceded by the preposition *k*, and followed by the finite form of the verb: imperfect (prefix) in the first case (*ymwt*) and perfect (suffix) in the second case (*nplt*). The alternation of prefix and suffix forms of the finite verb is an important feature of classic Canaanite and Hebrew poetry and should be regarded as part of the basic plan of the poet. As in so many other cases, it is altogether likely that they share the same tense and aspect, and hence should be translated in the same fashion: "Did Abiner die?" and "Did you fall." While the context implies that the last line (D) is a response to the question in the first line (A), I wonder whether the poet may have intended to place both possibilities before the audience, and leave the issues unsettled. In that case the force of the initial interrogative *he* would carry over to the second infinitive (*knpwl*).

In line D there is extensive use of sound effects. We wish to call attention to repeated instances of the consonants n–p–l: *knpwl lpny . . . nplt*, with reversal or chiasm (*npl–lpn–npl*). In addition the consonants *bn* and *l* appear in the compound noun *bĕnê ʿawlâ*; the only difference is the substitution of the sonant stop *b* for the voiceless stop *p*. This last term, however, has a more significant link with *nābāl* in line A, which shares exactly the same consonants. As previously noted, lines A and D balance each other, and the terms *nābāl* and *bĕnê ʿawlâ* perform parallel functions in their respective clauses. In addition, the letters *bn* appear in the name *ʾbnr* (Abiner) in line A. While we may dismiss the last collocation as a coincidence, there is no doubt that the repetition of sounds plays a definite and important role in the art of poetic composition; the association of *nbl* and *ʾbnr* in the mind of the poet may have arisen in part from the similarity of sounds.

Now we wish to turn to the metrical structure of the poem. On the basis of the proposed restoration we secure the following syllable count:

hakkĕmôt nābāl yāmût ʾăbînēr	(A)	3+2+2+3 = 10
ʾăsūrôt yādêk lōʾ bĕziqqîm	(B)	3+2+1+3 = 9
raglêk lōʾ binḥuštaym huggāšû	(C)	2+1+3+3 = 9
kinpôl lipnê bĕnê ʿawlâ nāpālt	(D)	2+2+2+2+2 = 10

I have used the short form of the 2nd m.s. perfect form of the verb (*nāpālt* for *nāpaltā*) and of the 2nd m.s. pronominal suffixes (*yādêk* and *raglêk*), based upon the written text (the Kethib). It is quite possible that the long forms were used by the poet, in which case we must add a syllable to each of the last three lines (10–10–10–11). There is no great difference, but perhaps some weight should be given to the precise symmetry produced by counting the short forms.

This analysis produces a perfectly balanced metrical pattern reflecting the chiastic structure of the poem already described. Thus lines A and D match each other metrically as well as in form and content and sound effects, while the same is true of lines B and C. Needless to say the omission (or loss) of *bzqym* distorts the chiasm and demolishes the metrical symmetry. We can be permanently grateful to the unknown scribe at Qumran for transmitting to us a more exact version of David's elegy for General Abiner, thus confirming to a substantial degree the artistry and reputation of the great royal poet. This dirge is a model of exquisite craftsmanship.

THE PLANTING OF MAN: A STUDY IN BIBLICAL IMAGERY

TIKVA FRYMER-KENSKY

There are two distinct traditions about the creation of man in Sumerian literature. In one, man is created from clay, most probably on analogy to the work of potters and sculptors. This tradition is continued in Akkadian literature, where creation from clay becomes the dominant image of the origin of man, and, of course, in Israel, where creation from clay is the only story preserved of man's creation (Gen 2:6–7). In the other Sumerian tradition, man sprouts up from the earth like grass. This concept did not play a major role in Babylonian religion, possibly because it was associated with An and Enlil rather than with Enki.[1] It is, however, a powerful symbol of the nature of man and survived in biblical literature as a pervasive image of man, and more particularly of the people of Israel.

Creation from clay is certainly the most widespread and best known of the Mesopotamian motifs. The major Sumerian source for this idea is the myth of "Enki and Ninmah."[2] In this text, which describes the labor of the gods before the creation of man and their distress, Enki decides to make man and to bind on to him the corvee of the gods. He creates the Siensišar to assist in the birth[3] and tells his mother Ninsun, "After you knead the heart of the clay above the *apsu*, the Siensišar will nip off pieces of clay; after you have given it form . . . (the various mother- and birth-goddesses) will assist in the giving of birth." This *abzu*-clay, here called "clay above the *abzu*" and elsewhere "clay of the *abzu*"[4] is the material from which Ninmah later fashions her creatures in "Enki and Ninmah," and from which Enki fashions the turtle in "Enki and the Turtle" (UET VI:36). It is known in the later incantation literature as the material from which Enki made the craftsmen gods (R. Acc. 46:6) and from which ritual figurines are fashioned (CT 17 29:30–33). A more oblique reference to this concept is found in Enki's creation of the *kalatur* and *kurgarra* from the dirt under Enki's fingernails in Inanna's Descent[5] and, similarly, the creation of the *dimgi* and *saltu*, also from the dirt under Enki's nails.[6]

Babylonian literature contains numerous references to creation from clay.[7] In the creation of Enkidu in the Gilgamesh epic, a "special creation" paralleling the original creation of man, Aruru washes her hands, takes the clay and casts it onto the steppe (ii 37–38); in the Babylonian Theodicy Zulummar nips off clay in the *abzu* and Mami fashions it (277–278); in a late ritual for the restoration of temples Ea nips off the clay in the *abzu* and fashions man and lesser deities; and in a fire incantation Ea nips off clay in the *apsu* and creates mankind (fire incantation no. 3 25–27).[8] Babylonian religion also introduced a new concept to Mesopotamia, the idea that man was created from the flesh and blood of a slaughtered

1 The relationship between Enlil and Enki is very complex. Much of the mythology known from Babylon is associated with Enki in the Sumerian sources, although in one instance (the Atrahasis Epic) the role played by Enki in the Sumerian is played by Enlil in the Akkadian. The reason for the greater impact of Enki-stories is not fully known. It may have something to do with the role Enlil (i.e. Nippur and its priests) played in the destruction of Sumer. Another possibility, suggested by van Dijk, is that when the Babylonian dynasties could not gain the approval of the Nippur priesthood, they transferred supremacy to the Eridu cult (van Dijk, "Les contacts éthniques dans la Mésopotamie et les syncretismes de la religion Sumérienne" in *Symposium on Cultural Contact, Meeting of Religions, Syncretism Turku, Finland 1966* (ed. Sven Hartman; Stockholm, 1969): 187 and "L'Hymne à Marduk avec intercession pour le roi Abiʾesuh," *MIO* 12 (1966): 57–74.

2 The myth "Enki and Ninmah" has not yet been adequately edited. A preliminary edition was prepared by Carlos Alfredo Benito, "Enki and Ninmah" and "Enki and the World Order" (Ph.D. diss., University of Pennsylvania, 1969). For texts and studies see the entry in Borger, *Handbuch der Keilschriftliteratur*, p. 155 under TCL XVI 71.

3 The word si$_7$-en-si-šár is unknown in Sumerian. It is parallel to the *šassuru* (birthgiver) of the Atrahasis Epic and possibly related to it.

4 For a discussion of the clay of the *abzu* and its role in Sumerian sources see Margaret Green, "Eridu in Sumerian Literature" (Ph.D. diss., University of Chicago, 1975): 169–74.

5 In the edition by William Sladek, *Inanna's Descent to the Nether World* (Ph.D. diss., Johns Hopkins University, 1974), this is 1.219f. See also 1.219–20 in Kramer's earlier and less complete edition in *JCS* 5.

6 See Green, *Eridu* (N 4): 174 for the references.

7 For citation and discussion of some of these passages see Giovanni Pettinato, *Das altorientalische Menschenbild und die sumerischen und akkadischen Schöpfungsmythen* (*Abhandlungen der Heidelberger Akademie der Wissenschaften*; Heidelberg, 1971): 41–42.

8 Published by W. G. Lambert, "Fire incantations," *AfO* 23 (1975): 39–45.

god.[9] In the Babylonian Atrahasis Epic the clay is mixed with the flesh and blood of We-ilu, a god who has rationality, so that man will have a spirit. In Enuma Elish the clay is not mentioned, and it appears that man is created entirely from the blood of Kingu. In KAR 4, a bilingual text which may be a scholastic composition (see below) the Anunnaki decide to slay Lamga gods and create mankind from their blood.

The imagery of creation from clay is two-fold. In its simplest form the image used is that of potting and sculpting: "nipping off" the clay (*ṭiṭam karaṣu*), moistening the clay (in Atrahasis the gods spit on it, in Gilgamesh Aruru washes her hands, and in Genesis 2 the first step in the creation of man is the rising of the *ʾed* to moisten the earth), mixing or kneading the clay, and casting it (Gilgamesh). This craft imagery is also combined, in Enki and Ninmah and Atrahasis, with a sexual idea: birth goddesses, mother goddesses and midwives are called to assist, and in Atrahasis the clay undergoes a gestation of nine months before man is "born." The two images are juxtaposed rather than harmonized, for both the creation of man which is analogous to the creation of a statue, and the birth of the first man which is like the births of all subsequent humans are understood as parallel metaphors.

The second Sumerian tradition about man's creation also draws on a fundamental metaphor of human existence, the parallel between man and plants. This parallel is inherent in language, which speaks of the numun, *zeru*, *zeraʿ*, "seed" of mankind, and is ultimately related to the idea of "mother earth" and to the relationship between human sexuality and the earth's fertility which is so important to pagan religions. The female, like the earth, is "ploughed" by the "farmer" and "planted" with "seed."[10] The birth of man from woman is thus like the emerging of plants from the fructified earth. This is a profound human symbol, and the "vegetal" model for the creation of man is not confined to the ancient Near East.[11] Within the ancient Near East the image is well developed, and the picture emerges of man being "planted" in the ground.

The tradition of the sprouting of man appears in its simplest form in the introduction to the hymn to the E-Engur, the temple of Enki at Eridu:[12]

a-ri-a nam ba-tar-ra-ba
mu hé-gala$_7$ an ù-tu-da
ukù-e ú-šim-gim ki in-dar-ra-ba

when destinies had been established for all engendered things,
when An had engendered the year of abundance
when people had broken through the ground like plants.

From the other Sumerian source for this tradition, the "Creation of the Pickaxe" (en-e ni-du$_7$-e) it is clear that this "sprouting" of man was not an accident, but was intended by the gods, in this case Enlil. The text brings us back to the beginning of finite time, and indicates that the motive force behind the separation of heaven and earth was precisely the creation of man:

^{d}En-líl numun-kalam-ma ki-ta e$_{11}$-dè
an ki-ta bad-du-dè sag na-an-ga-àm-mi-in-si
ki an-ta bad-du-dè sag na-an-ga-àm-mi-in-si
uzu-è sag mú-mú-dè
dur-an-ki-ka búru$^?$ nam-mi-in-lá

9 Creation from blood does not exist in Sumerian. Lambert has suggested that Enki mixed clay with his own blood in "Enki and Ninmah" (Lambert, "Creation of Man in Sumero-Babylonian Myth," *CRRAI* XI [1964]: 102). This rests on an erroneous translation of mud mu-gar-ra-zu, which should better be understood as "the creature you are creating/have created." Because of the non-existence of this idea in Sumerian, and the mystic importance of blood in Israel, I have suggested elsewhere that perhaps this motif was introduced into Mesopotamia by the West Semites (Tikva Frymer-Kensky, "The Atrahasis Epic and its Significance for our Understanding of Genesis 1–9," *BA* 40 [1977]: 154).

10 One famous example is Rib Addi's letter EA 74:17 A.ŠÀ-*ia aššata ša la muta mašil aššum bali errēši* "my field is like a wife without a husband because it is without a tiller" and similarly in other letters of Rib Addi. The relevant material has been collected by Marvin Pope, *Song of Songs* (AB 7c; Garden City, 1977): 323–26.

11 Many cosmological perceptions are found throughout the ancient Near East (in its broadest sense) and should be considered part of a general religious heritage. This is true also of the idea of man growing as a plant. In Greek mythology we have the story of Jason's sowing of the dragon's teeth and the warriors who then arose. Persia also preserves a similar idea in the story of the first pair, Mašya and Mašyanag, who grew from a rhubarb plant which itself had sprung from the seed of Gayomard, the ancestor of man (Greater Bundahišn XIV 5–10; for discussion see Mary Boyce, *A History of Zoroastrianism Vol. I The Early Period* [*Handbuch der Orientalistik*, 1975]: 96–97 and 140). The concept is not confined to the Near East, however, and is referred to by Levi-Strauss as the *authochthonous origin* of mankind (C. Levi-Strauss, "The Structural Study of Myth," *Journal of American Folklore* [1955]: 428–44; reprinted in *The Structuralists: From Marx to Levi-Strauss* [Richard and Fernande de George, eds.; 1972]: 169–94. For authochthonous origin see p. 179.) As can be seen from "the pickaxe," however, in Sumer the origin of man was premeditated rather than authochthonous.

12 This tradition was originally elucidated by Jacobsen, "Sumerian Mythology: a Review Article," *JNES* 5, 135 and n. 4. It was analyzed by van Dijk, "Le motif cosmique dans la pensée sumérienne," *Act.Or.* 28, 23–24, who named it creation by "emersion." For these passages see also Pettinato (N 7): 30–32.

Enlil, in order to cause the seed of the land to arise from the earth,
hastened to separate heaven from earth,
hastened to separate earth from heaven.
In order that the "flesh-producer" might produce the vanguard (of man)
he bound up the gash in Duranki ("the bond of heaven and earth")

The "flesh-producer," uzu-è, is probably the same place as "the place where flesh grew forth," the uzu-mú-a, a well known sacred area of Nippur, "the bond of heaven and earth."[13] Here Enlil planted man, who thereupon grew out of the ground toward him (1.18–20):

uzu-è ^{giš}al-a sag-nu gá-gá-dè
sag nam-lú-u_x-lu ^{giš}ušub-ba mi-ni-gar
^{d}en-líl-šè kalam-ma-ni ki mu-ši-in-dar

placing the "vanguard of man" in the "flesh-producer" with the pickaxe,
he placed the vanguard of mankind into the mold.
towards Enlil (the people) of his land sprouted up through the ground.

Despite the numerous minor difficulties in reading this passage, it is clear that man was placed (or planted) in the womb of the earth to emerge.

Perhaps because of the highly urbanized nature of Mesopotamian civilization, and possibly because the plant-image was associated with Enlil, this view of the creation of man did not have as much force in Babylonian religion as the clay metaphor. A reference is found in the Sumerian version of *mis pi* (CT III 36:20–21)[14] and in the bilingual KAR 4. As mentioned before, KAR 4 shows many earmarks of being a scholastic text: it concludes with an invocation to Nisaba, patron of scribes, and with a prescription that the wise should teach the mystery to the wise; it contains a lengthy (now fragmentary) description of the duties of man, and it has no dramatic impact. It would therefore probably be wrong to call this text a myth, but it contains many ancient mythic elements, and preserves both the idea that man was created from the blood of a slaughtered god (in this case the Lamga gods) and the idea that "skilled worker from skilled worker, unskilled worker from unskilled worker, they sprouted out of the earth like grain" (1.60–61). Unilingual Akkadian texts, however, do not preserve this image.

In Israel, on the other hand, the agricultural metaphor is very important. The only version preserved of the creation of man is creation from clay (Gen 2:6–7), but the vegetal image survives in numerous metaphors and similes, and in the concept of the Israel-plant. The idea of man as a plant is applied in Israel to the people, and the pervasive image of "plant-Israel" is an important metaphor to understand and express the history of the people.

Part of the plant-people imagery is embedded in the Hebrew language. The word *zeraᶜ* 'seed' can also mean 'semen' and 'offspring,'[15] the word *perî* 'fruit' can also mean 'offspring,' both as *perî beṭen* "fruit of the womb" and simply as *perî*, and many of the verbs used in agriculture, *pry*, *prḥ*, *ṣmḥ* can mean literally 'bear fruit,' 'flower,' 'grow' or be used in an extended sense to mean 'increase,' 'flourish' and 'grow.' Such parallels as *ᶜqr* 'to uproot' and *ᶜăqārāʰ* 'barren woman,' *yônēq* 'nursling' and *yôneqet/yônēq*[16] 'sapling,' 'shoot,' 'tender plant' are built into the language, and their use is not consciously metaphorical. In addition to these unconscious metaphors, many images from the plant world are consciously applied to mankind. Many of these rely on the fact that the agricultural world was an immediate referent in Israelite life, and the similes would therefore be immediately understood. Hebrew poetry makes abundant use of similes comparing men to various plants (particularly to grass and trees) and to parts of plants.

The tree, of course, is the image of long life: "for the days of my people will be like the days of the tree" (Isa 65:22) and its verdancy is like the virility of man. A eunuch might consider himself a "dry tree" (but should not, Isa 56:3), and Jeremiah's enemies plot against him "let us destroy the tree in full sap,[17] cut him off from the land of the living, that his name be remembered no more" (Jer 11:19). Grass, on the other hand (*ᶜēśeb* and *ḥāṣîr*), although abundant (for which see below) is noted for its fragility and impermanence. It is therefore a prime image for man who "grows like grass in the morning. In the morning it grows and flourishes, by evening it is cut down and dried" (Ps 90:5–6). This simile relies on two characteristics of grass, the ease with which it is cut, and the rapidity with which it can dry up. So too "evildoers will be cut down quickly like grass and wither like green herb" (Ps 37:1–2). The drying up of grass is likened to man's days and heart (Ps 102:5 [4] and 12 [11]) and

13 So Jacobsen (N 12): 137. The alternative is to understand the term uzu-è as the "flesh-producer," i.e., Enlil (so van Dijk [N 1/12]: 24.

14 Quoted by Pettinato (N 7): 32.

15 The relevant passages have been catalogued by Abraham Even-Shoshan, *A New Concordance of the Bible*, vol. 1, p. 340.

16 The word for 'sapling, shoot' is usually *yôneqet*, generally found in the plural *yônᵉqôt*. However, the parallelism of *yônēq // šōreš* in Isa 53:2 indicates the *yônēq* could also bear the sense of 'shoot, sapling,' or at least that Isaiah was consciously playing on the connection between *yônēq* 'nursling' and *yôneqet*, 'sapling, shoot.'

17 Reading *bilehi-ma* "in (his) sap" or *bilehimō* "in his sap" with possessive suffix following the enclitic *mem*. This last is chosen by Bright, *Jeremiah* (AB 21; Garden City, 1965): 84, following M. Dahood, *Gregorianum* 43, 66. The translation "in full sap" is Bright's.

those who abandon God are like reeds without water which dry up even before grass (Job 8:11–18). Unlike God's compassion (Ps 103:17), word (Isa 40:8) and power (Isa 51:12–13), man is impermanent and as vulnerable as grass and wildflowers before the wind (Ps 103:15–16):

> Man, his days are like grass,
> his flowering like that of a wildflower.
> For a wind passes over it, and it is no more,
> and one cannot find its place.

and the people is like grass in its vulnerability (Isa 40:6–8):

> A voice said "call' and I said "what shall I call?
> All flesh is grass and all its (deeds of) compassion like wildflowers.
> Grass dries, wildflowers wither,
> for the Lord's wind has blown on them:
> just so the people is grass.
> Grass dries, wildflowers wither,
> but the word of the Lord will stand forever.

So too the beauty of Ephraim, unable to withstand the tempest of God's wrath, is like that of wildflowers withering and blowing away in the wind (Isa 28:1–4). And all of us wither like a leaf blown away by the wind (Isa 64:5 [6]).

The only thing even more impermanent than grass is the grass which grows on roofs (*ḥăṣîr gaggôt*) which does not even get a chance to grow fully and reach harvest before it dries up: just so will be those who hate Zion (Ps 129:6–7):

> Let them be like roof grass,
> which dries up before it is fully grown
> that a reaper has not filled his hand with,
> nor the sheave-binder his bosom.

and the inhabitants of the cities destroyed by Sennacherib are like grass and roof grass (2 Kgs 19:26 and Isa 37:27).

The tree similes rely on the fact that Israel is familiar with the world of nature. The characteristics of the differing trees are well known, and both simple metaphors and extended parables rely on this intimate knowledge of nature.[18] Ezekiel's parable of the "vine-tree," particularly suited for firewood and little else, is used as the simile for the inhabitants of Jerusalem (Ezek 15:1–8). The parable of Jotham (Judg 9:7–15) and the parable of Jehoash (2 Kgs 14:9) both rely on the contrast between brambles (Judg 9:15 *ʾāṭād*) and thistles (2 Kgs 14:9 *ḥōaḥ*) and other trees, particularly the cedars of Lebanon. The cedar is noteworthy for its luxuriance, height and strength, and Ezekiel tells an allegory of Assyria as a cedar which grew taller than any other tree, but was ultimately chopped down (Ezekiel 31). The height of the Amorite is compared to a cedar (Amos 2:9), the righteous are to flourish like the palm and the cedar (Ps 92:3) and the tents of Israel seem to Balaam like aloes planted by God, like cedars on the water (Num 24:26). Trees planted by water are the most fortunate, for they can withstand drought. The man who delights in God's law is like a tree planted by streams (Ps 1:3), as is the man who trusts in the Lord (Jer 17:7–8):

> Blessed is the man who trusts in the Lord,
> and the Lord is his mainstay:
> For he is like a tree planted near water,
> that sends its roots towards the stream,
> that does not fear[19] the coming of heat,
> for its leaves remain green.
> It does not worry in years of drought
> and does not fail to bear fruit.

in contrast to the man who trusts in man, who is like a desert scrub that dwells in a salt uninhabited land (Jer 17:5–6). In addition to all these similes using natural aspects of trees, there are four passages in Proverbs that compare wisdom (Prov 3:18), the fruit of the righteous (Prov 11:30), desire (Prov 13:12) and wholesomeness of tongue (Prov 14:14) to the possibly mythical "tree of life."

Man is a plant which comes from seed (*zeraʿ*), grows and bears fruit. The root of the man is therefore his foundation and his stability. The man, woman, family or tribe who turns away from God is a "root bearing gall and wormwood" (Deut 29:17–18); "out of Ephraim came a root against Amalek" (Judg 5:14); "the root of the righteous bear" (Prov 12:12); and the fortunate man (Job in happier times) has his "root opened towards the waters" (Job 29:19). Although Jeremiah complains "you planted them (the wicked) and they took root, they went and bore fruit" (Jer 12:2), in the future the adversaries will not take root (Isa 40:24):

> they (the princes and rulers of the world) will not be planted, will not be sown. Their stock will not take root in the earth, and he will blow on them and they will dry up and the storm will carry them away like straw.

They will not be left "root or branch" (Mal 3:18 [4:1] the evildoers); they will be uprooted (Ps 52:7, Doeg the Edomite; Jer 12:14–15, the evil neighbors of Israel); their roots will become rotten (Isa 5:24, those who call evil good), and the root will be killed (Isa 14:20, all

18 I have omitted the many similes used in the Song of Songs. Considering the idyllic nature of the book, we would expect numerous nature similes even if they were not prevalent elsewhere in the Bible.

19 Reading *yirāʾ* with the *k^etib* and LXX. The *yirʾe^h* of the *q^ere* is influenced by v. 6. See also Bright, *Jeremiah* (N 17): 115.

Pelešet, and cf. the root of the Amorite destroyed, Amos 2:9). Israel's messianic hopes are also expressed with this metaphor, for the future king will be "a branch from the stem of Jesse, a stalk from his roots" (Isa 11:1) and the root of Jesse will be an ensign to the nations (Isa 1:10). God will raise up for David a righteous sprout (*ṣemaḥ*) who will rule and be called "the Lord is our victory" (Jer 23:5–6 and 33:15–16), and the one who will rebuild the temple will be called "sprout" (Zech 6:12). Similarly, the "servant of God" will be "like a 'shoot/sapling'[20] before him, like a root from dry ground" (Isa 53:2).

Above all, it is Israel which is compared to a plant, and the plant image becomes a very important way in which Israel expresses its history, the way that God tended it, planted it, will destroy it, and will then replant it. Israel is a leafy olive tree destroyed by lightning (Jer 11:16):

> leafy olive tree,
> beautiful, lovely to behold—
> so did the Lord name you.
> With a tumultuous noise he sets fire to its leaves[21]
> and its branches are shattered.

The classic image of Israel is that of a vineyard (the land) and a vine (the people). The vineyard is noteworthy for the care given it, the choicest grapes planted there, its indifferent yield and the ease of its destruction. This vineyard image may have originated with Isaiah, who gives it in its most complete form in "the song of my lover about his vineyard," Isa 5:1–7. In this song God

> had a vineyard in a fruitful corner:
> He fenced it and removed its stones
> and planted it with choice grapes (*śôrēq*)
> built a tower in its midst, and also made a winepress in it
> and he expected it to make grapes, but it made wild grapes
> (Isa 5:1–2)

and this song also seems to be the source for Jeremiah's similar statement of frustrated expectations, "I planted you with choice grapes (*śôrēq*), all true seed; how did you become foul for me, a strange wild vine"[22] (Jer 2:21). The result of the improper yield of the vineyard is its destruction (Isa 5:5–6):

> And now I will tell you what I will do to my vineyard:
> I will take away its hedge—and it will be for destruction.
> break its fence—and it will be for trampling.
> And I will lay it waste: it shall not be pruned, or dug,
> and there will come up briars and thorns,
> and I will command the clouds not to rain on it.

The vineyard is an important image in Isaiah and Jeremiah. The vineyard has been corrupted and destroyed by its elders and rulers (Isa 3:14) and is therefore destroyed. The remnant of Israel is gleaned like grapes are plucked (Jer 6:9) and many shepherds devastate it and trample it under foot (Jer 12:10). In the future, however, God will again plant and tend his vineyard and it will be called a "vineyard of red wine" (Isa 27:2–4).[23]

"The vineyard of the Lord of Hosts is the house of Israel, and the man of Judah is his delightful plant" (Isa 5:7), and the image of the vine can describe an Israel without its land. The grapes existed before they were brought into the land, for God "found Israel like grapes in the desert" (Hos 9:10). The allegory of the "vine out of Egypt" (Ps 80:9–16 [8–15]) describes the process (Ps 80:9–11 [8–10]):

> you brought a vine out of Egypt,
> you chased out the nations and planted it.
> you made room before it, and it took deep root and
> filled the land.
> The hills were covered with its shade,
> and its branches were mighty cedars.
> it sent its boughs to the seas and its shoots to the river.

The vine, however, turned into an "empty vine"[24] (Hos 10:1), and the root must therefore dry up (Hos 10:16). The destruction of Israel is depicted as the plucking of the vine in "The vine out of Egypt" (Ps 80:12–13) and in Ezekiel's allegory of the "mother vine" (Ezek 19:10–14). In this poem Israel is conceived as a vine "planted by water, fruitful and branching from the many waters" (Ezek 19:10), but in (Ezek 19:12):[25]

> she was plucked in fury and cast to the ground
> and the east wind dried its fruit
> and her strong limb was broken and dried up,
> fire consumed it.

The vine/vineyard imagery can depict many aspects of God's relationship with Israel because it can express the

---

20 See note 16 above.

21 For the reading (b^e) *ʿălêhû* (to) its leaves rather than *ʿălêhā* "to her" (with masculine referent) see Bright, *Jeremiah* (N 17): 82–83, n. e..e.

22 Reading *lî sōriyyah gepen nōkriyah*. Bright, *Jeremiah* (N 17): 11 reads *l^esoriyyah* "what a foul-smelling thing you've become."

23 For comments on this passage and God as vintner see Pope, *Song of Songs* (N 10): 326.

24 Taking *bôqēq* in the well known sense of 'be empty.' The attempt of *BDB* (p. 132) to attribute this verse to another *bôqēq* meaning 'luxuriant' seems futile, for this other *bôqēq* exists only in Arabic, and is otherwise unattested in the Bible.

25 Eichrodt takes the mother-vine to refer literally to Hamutal, the mother of the king (*Ezekiel.* Old Testament Library, p. 257). However, this interpretation means that he has to take vv. 13–14a "and now she is planted in the desert in a dry and thirsty land. And a fire has gone out from a limb of her

conscious planting, the constant care required, the frustration, the fragility of vineyards and the ease of their destruction. The idea of an Israel planted by God, however, is not confined to these vineyard/vine allegories, but is rather a very ancient image. Israel's entry into its land is depicted as its "planting" in the "Song of the Sea" (Exodus 15), "you brought him and planted him in your 'heritage mountain' " (Exod 15 :17); and in Ps 44:3, "you, your hand drove out the nations and you planted them (Israel)."[26] The destruction of the plant is an important metaphor for the destruction of the people. Israel, found like grapes in the wilderness (Hos 9:10) is smitten, its roots dried up, unable to bear fruit (Hos 9:16). The "Israel-plant" withers, or is uprooted. The image of the "withering" (*nbl*) of the people is Isaian: "for you will be like an oak whose leaves wither and a garden which has no water" (Isa 1:30); "Its (Ephraim's) crown of glory which is on the fruitful valley will be like a withering wildflower" (Isa 28:1); "the land will be emptied, the land will be despoiled, the land will wither..." (Isa 24:3–4); "grass dries up and wildflowers wither for the Lord's wind blows on tthem, just so is the nation grass" (Isa 40:7–8). Uprooting (*ntš*), on the other hand, seems to be primarily Deuteronomic. Thus in Deut 29:27, at the covenant in the plains of Moab, the people are told that if they go and worship other gods they will be destroyed, and the nations will be told that "the Lord uprooted them from their land in anger and wrath and great fury and sent them to another land as this day." In 1 Kgs 14:15 Ahijah tells Jeroboam "the Lord will smite Israel as a reed moves in the water, and he will uproot Israel from this good land which he gave to your fathers, and will scatter them across the river, because they made the Asherahs which anger the Lord." Jeremiah relates the Lord's word to Baruch (Jer 45:4) "behold that which I have built I am destroying and that which I have planted I am uprooting, for the whole land is mine."[27] And in 2 Chr 7:20 Solomon is told that if the Davidic rulers forsake God's commandments, then "I will uproot them (Israel) from my land which I have given to them, and this house which I have sanctified for my name I will cast away from me, and will make it a proverb and byword among all the nations." The concept of uprooting can be extended to other nations, and Jeremiah delivers this message to Israel's enemy neighbors (Jer 12:14–16):

> Behold I am going to uproot them from their land, and root out the house of Judah from their midst. And after I have uprooted them I will once more have compassion on them and return them each to his possession and each to his land, And if they will learn the ways of my people to swear by my name, "by the life of the Lord" (as they taught my people to swear by Baal), then they will be built up in the midst of my people. And if they will not listen, then I will uproot that nation, uprooted and destroyed.

The plant image is particularly important to describe God's actions at the restoration. As the destruction was an uprooting and a razing, the restoration is a planting and a building (Jer 31:27). This concept is already found in Hosea, "and I will sow her for myself in the land, and I will have compassion on 'not mercied' and I will say to 'not my people,' 'my people' and he will say 'my God' " (Hos 2:25); and in Amos 9:15 (if the passage is original), "and I will plant them on their land and they shall no more be uprooted from their land which I gave to them." Jeremiah is particularly fond of the replanting image (and of the uprooting image), and he sees the restoration as the time when "I will sow (*zrʿ*) the house of Israel and the house of Judah with the seed of man and the seed of beast" (Jer 31:26) and when "I will rejoice over them to do good for them, and I will plant them in this land in truth, with all my heart and with all my soul" (Jer 32:41). Furthermore, to Jeremiah this new planting

---

branches and devoured her fruit, and she has no strong rod, a scepter to rule" as later additions. Eichrodt also believes that this spells the end of the Davidic dynasty, since no one can expect a vine that has been so brutally treated to grow again after being replanted. If we realize that the vine is Israel, however, vv. 13–14 fit integrally into the passage referring to exile. Moreover, the idea of replanting fits all the other passages which refer to the replanting of luxurious regrowth of the Israel-plant. Ezekiel uses similar imagery in his "parable of the vine and the eagles," Ezekiel 17. The great eagle (Nebuchadnezzar/God) took a high branch of the cedar and set it in a city of merchants (Babylon/the Land of Canaan, v. 4), took seed of the land and put it into field and it grew and became a spreading vine (17:6). The vine then bent its roots toward another eagle (Egypt/Baal) that it might water it, and therefore God decrees that the vine should wither. The passage has immediate political import and is explained in vv. 11–18 as referring to the alliance made by Nebuchadnezzar with the seed of kingship which he brought to Babylon, but which then looked toward Egypt. However, in v. 19 Ezekiel shifts gears from talking about breaking the covenant with Babylon to breaking Israel's covenant with God, and he continues with a promise of restoration (22–24) in which God will take the highest branch of the cedar and plant it on a high mountain of Israel, and it will grow and bear fruit. It seems likely that Ezekiel intends that his parable be read on two levels, and that this is what he means when he calls it a "riddle parable" (17:1). In both these passages in Ezekiel it is clear that he is alluding to the classic vine/vineyard image.

26 By comparison of this verse with the similar verse in Ps 80:9 it is clear that the referent "them" is to Israel rather than the nations.

27 Bright, following LXX, omits the phrase *wᵉʾet kol-hāʾāreṣ lî hîʾ* believing it to mean "that is, the whole land" and to be therefore a superfluous gloss (Bright, *Jeremiah* [N 17]: 184). However, the phrase is really a justification of God's destruction of the land (for, after all, the whole land is his), and perhaps a reassurance to Baruch that God will after all not abandon his land.

of Israel (unlike the original planting) will not be uprooted: "I will watch over them benevolently and return them to this land, and I will build them and will not destroy, will plant them and not uproot" (Jer 24:6; so too Jer 42:10 and cf. Jer 31:39 for the non-uprooting of new Jerusalem). Isaiah expresses the idea that the replanted Israel will take root: "And the remnant which remains from the house of Judah will take root below and bear fruit above" (Isa 37:31; cf. 2 Kgs 19:30), "Jacob will take root, Israel will flower and bud, and they will fill the world with fruit" (Isa 27:6). In the eschaton envisioned by Deutero-Isaiah, the people will all be righteous, inherit the land forever, and be the "branch of my planting, the work of my hands to glory in" (Isa 60:21) and "righteous oaks, the plant of God to glory in" (Isa 61:3). This idea of "replanted Israel" is not an empty or fossilized metaphor, moreover, and the agricultural image can be extended to express watering and growth (Hos 14:6–8):

> I will be as dew to Israel and it will flourish like a crocus
> and cast forth its roots as Lebanon.
> Its branches will spread and its beauty will be like an olive,
> and it will have a scent like Lebanon.

One of the important aspects of the restoration of Israel is the multiplication of the people, the resettlement of the land with abundant population (e.g., Ezek 36:10–11). This hope may be expressed by comparing the people to grass, a recognized simile for abundance. In Ps 92:8 it is the wicked who flourish like grass, in Ps 72:16 those of the city will flourish like grass at the time of the righteous king's son; in Job 5:25 Job is told "your seed will be numerous and your offspring like the grass of the earth." In Ezek 16:7 Jerusalem is told "I made you abundant like the plants of the field, and you grew many and great." In Isa 43:3–4 this image is applied to the restored Israel:

> I will pour water on the thirsty and liquid on dry ground.
> I will pour my spirit on your seed, and my blessings on your offspring,
> and they shall sprout up as among grass, as willows by waterways.

It is in this context that the somewhat problematical verses of Hos 2:1–2 (1:10–11) become clear:

> And the number of the children of Israel will be like the sands of the sea which cannot be measured and cannot be counted, and instead of it being said to them "not my people" it will be said to them "children of the living god." And the children of Judah and the children of Israel will gather together and appoint themselves a head and "come up from the earth," for great will be the day of Jezreel.

The problem with this passage is the somewhat ambiguous phrase *wᵉʿālāʰ min hāʾāreṣ*, which might conceivably be translated "go up from the land" or "come up from the ground." "Go up from the land" does not seem to fit the context, for the children of Israel and Judah are coming back to, rather than leaving the land, nor does it seem necessary to emend the passage.[28] The phrase also appears in Exod 1:10 "let us outsmart him lest he multiply, and if there should be a war he will join our enemies and fight us *wᵉʿālāʰ min hāʾāreṣ*." The traditional translation "and so get them out of the land" does not make sense, for Pharaoh's worry is not that they should leave, but that they should be numerous and then join the enemies. The new *JPS* translation "gain ascendancy over the land" makes much better sense, but is philologically difficult.[29] The meaning of the phrase is clear from the context in Hosea 2 which, as shown by Cassuto, is a coherent poem with A–Z, B–Y parallelism.[30] Our lines are thus thematically parallel to Hos 2:24–25:

> And the land will answer the grain and the corn and the oil,
> and they will answer Jezreel.
> And I will sow her for me in the land
> and will have compassion on "not pitied"
> and I will say to "not my people" "my people"
> and he will say "my god."

The poem begins and ends with a reference to Lo-Ammi ("not my people"), to Jezreel, and to the planting of man. Jezreel itself is a triple entendre: as palace of Ahab and site of the disaster, the name also means "God sows" and the passage indicates that God will sow the people. Thus in vv 1–2 the people are going to be very numerous, reunite, choose a ruler and "rise up from the earth" because "great is the day of 'god sows.' "[31] Seen in this context it is clear that the phrase "rise up from the earth," like the phrase "sprout up as among grass" in Isa 44:4, is an image of man emerging from the ground, with the

28 For a review of some of the suggested emendations (and rejections of them) see Cassuto, "The Prophet Hosea and the Books of the Pentateuch," 1933; rpt. in *Biblical and Oriental Studies*, p. 87 and Wilhelm Rudolph, *Hosea, Kommentar zum alten Testament*, p. 57.

29 For the justification of this translation see Orlinsky, *Notes on the New Translation*, p. 149. Childs, however, rejects this new translation as philologically weak (Brevard Childs, *Exodus*, Old Testament Library, p. 5).

30 Cassuto, "The Second Chapter of the Book of Hosea," 1927; rpt. in *Biblical and Oriental Studies*, pp. 101–103. Cassuto, however, does not realize the implication of our phrase because of his feeling, expressed elsewhere ("The Prophet Hosea" [N 28]: 87), that the phrase is intended to remind the audience of the Exodus story, and that it means "come up from Egypt" and therefore "come back from Exile."

31 The play on Jezreel was noted already by Rudolph, *Hosea* (N 28): 58, who translates "und sie werden aus dem Boden wachsen." This translation was noted but not accepted by Mays, *Hosea*, Old Testament Library, p. 33, but perhaps the material in this article will give ample background to these verses and make this translation more assured.

implication of the numbers of man. So too in Exodus, the sense of the passage is that Israel, being so numerous, may join the enemies—and he is "popping up all over the place" (to use a somewhat equivalent English idiom).[32] The phrase "rise up from the earth" is thus a continuation of the ancient image, attested in Sumerian literature and so productive in Israelite poetry, of man arising like grass from the earth.

32 The concentration on numbers is a prominent feature in the story of Balak and his fear of Israel, a clear parallel to the story in Exodus. In Num 22:5 and 11, the parallel phrase to *w^{e}ʿalā^{h} min hāʾāreṣ* is *kissā^{h}/way^{e}kas ʾet ʿēn hāʾāreṣ* "covered the face of the ground," again an idiom for sheer numbers.

EXODUS 32:18

ROBERT M. GOOD

In recent years the short poem at Exod 32:18 has attracted the interest of a number of writers. Attention has focused on the enigmatic word *ʿannôt* in the third and final stichos of this deceptively simple piece:

ʾên qôl ʿănôt g^{e}bûrâ — אין קול ענות גבורה
w^{e}ʾên qôl ʿănôt ḥălûšâ — ואין קול ענות חלושה
qôl ʿannôt ʾānōkî šōmē^{a}ʿ — קול ענות אנכי שמע

The poem occupies a central place in the story of the golden calf, and while a number of critics have denied the originality of this setting, most exegetes interpret the poem and the difficult verb *ʿannôt* contextually.

The most recent attempt to explain the poem and the verb is that of Ariella Deem. Deem reports the discovery of a new Hebrew verb *ʿānâ* with the meaning "to make love." That such a verb exists is inferred from the existence of its piel *ʿinnâ*. Deem rejects the conventional understanding whereby *ʿinnâ* means "to humiliate, to rape" and derives from its qal *ʿānâ* "to be humble." She prefers to interpret *ʿinnâ* as an intensive form of *ʿānâ*, the latter meaning "to make love," the former presumably meaning "to make love intensively." Two types of evidence justify postulating the new verb. First, this verb provides the etymology of the divine name ʿAnat. The name of the goddess of love and war is to be explained as a feminine derivative of the verb "to copulate." Second, the assumption of such a verb gives a satisfactory explanation to a number of passages in which *ʿānâ* or related words occur, among which is the poem at Exod 32:18. Deem joins ranks with those exegetes who consider Israel's golden calf apostasy to have been licentious, and in this context and in the light of the new-found verb she translates the poem thus:

> It is not the sound of shouting for victory
> or the sound of the cry of defeat
> but the *sound of an orgy*, that I hear.[1]

This contextually apposite rendering is not contingent on the validity of Deem's lexical discovery. The existence of a verb *ʿinnâ* expressing some kind of forced or otherwise wrongful sex act is not in doubt. However, the derivation of this verb from its qal "to make love" is dubious. To relate ʿAnat's name to a verb "to copulate" is unexceptionable, but the existence of such a verb is nowhere evident among Deem's examples, as a single case will illustrate. Deem has recognized that an ambiance of fertility imbues the truly problematic oracle at Hos 2:23-24. Since the verb *ʿānâ* occurs five times in this passage, she believes that to recognize its meaning "to make love" will elucidate the text. The result, if the text be translated, is cosmic debauchery:

> On that day, I shall copulate, says Yahweh. I shall copulate with the heavens, and they will copulate with the earth, and the earth will copulate with corn, wine, and oil, and they will copulate with Jezreel.

In view of Hosea's stance against fertility cults, this is not a very seductive understanding. We may note in passing that this difficult text begins to yield sense if it is recognized that Hebrew *ʿānâ* may sometimes, like its Arabic cognate,[2] be predicated of the earth and mean "to yield plant growth." The passage therefore may be translated,

> On that day, I shall answer, says Yahweh. I shall answer the heavens, and they will answer the earth, and the earth will give forth corn, wine, and oil, and they will answer Jezreel.

It must be suspected that the answering of heaven and earth signifies a forensic act, a reversing of the covenant lawsuit.[3]

In a certain sense Deem has been anticipated in connecting the Exodus poem and the name ʿAnat. In 1950[4] and again in 1966[5] R. Edelmann proposed to translate the word *ʿannôt* as ʿAnat. The contextual basis for this interpretation is clear. Israel's calf apostasy can be understood as a manifestation of the worship of the great Canaanite goddess. Philologically, this notion seemed at first to require disregarding the Masoretic consonantal text. But on the basis of André Dupont-Sommer's identification of the ʿAnot in the biblical toponym Bet-ʿAnot and the Aramaic vocable *bʿlʿnwt* as

---

1 Ariella Deem, "The Goddess Anath and Some Biblical Hebrew Cruces," *JSS* 23 (1978): 25-30.

2 *ʿanā/yaʿnū*

3 On the call to heaven and earth in association with the covenant lawsuit, see Herbert Huffmon, "The Covenant Lawsuit in the Prophets," *JBL* 78 (1959): 285-95.

4 R. Edelmann, "Exodus 32:18," *JTS* NS 1 (1950): 56.

5 R. Edelmann, "To *ʿannôt* Exodus xxxii 18," *VT* 16 (1966): 355.

the name of the goddess, R. N. Whybray[6] has concluded that the consonantal text may stand. The pronunciation ʿAnot, written *ʿnwt*, can be taken as a dialectal variant of the expected form ʿAnat, *ʿnt.*

F. I. Andersen has also attempted to interpret the poem. He believes the final stichos of the poem to be defectively preserved in the Masoretic text. He uses the witness of the versions to justify appending a noun **ṣĕḥûqâ* to the end of the poem. The verb *ʿannôt* is to be referred to cultic singing.[7] J. Sasson holds a similar opinion, denying that there are indications of sexual irregularities in the narrative of the golden calf. For Sasson, the difficult verb *ʿannôt* means "to sing antiphonally," and the offense of the golden calf affair is located in its pagan thrust.[8]

It seems that no topic escaped the notice and comment of W. F. Albright. In *Yahweh and the Gods of Canaan,* Albright assigns the poem a 13th-century date and translates its closing noun phrase "the sound of music."[9]

These recent studies of the poem provide a background but not a starting point to our investigation of the problem. Our starting point must be the text itself, which is in doubt at precisely the point of controversy. Where the Masoretic text reads *ʿannôt*, the Samaritan tradition offers manuscripts with the variant *ʿăwōnôt*, a reading for which there is support in a major Syriac text. The Septuagint renders the close of the poem *exarchontōn oinou,* a reading which presupposes *ʿănôt yayin.*[10] The reading *ʿăwōnôt* arose through a simple consonantal metathesis of *ʿnwt*. This change effected a differentiation of the word *ʿnwt* of the opening lines of the poem and the originally orthographically identical word in the final line. It appears that the reading **ʿănôt yayin* was calculated to have the same effect. In other words, at an early date it was recognized that the word *ʿnwt* of the third stichos of the piece must have a different meaning from that of the word *ʿnwt* of the preceding stichoi, but the distinction between these two words had been lost. The Masoretic vocalization of *ʿnwt* as a piel represents no more than a third attempt to fashion a difference between the two words *ʿnwt.* In the final line of the poem, *ʿnwt* should be vocalized *ʿănôt*. The purpose of this study is to recover the sense of this word and to situate the poem in its larger context.

To pursue this goal by turning to the Ugaritic literature is fitting in a tribute to Marvin Pope. Having begun with a problematic poem, we may turn to another in search of an understanding of both. At an occasion when certain gods had gathered to dine with El, the god Yamm dispatched messengers to demand from El the surrender of the god Baal. Yamm instructed his messengers not to render homage to the assembled divines who, when they saw the approaching messengers, lowered their heads. Thereupon the god Baal rebuked the assembly with these words:

lm ġltm ilm
  raštkm lẓr brktkm
  wln kḥṯ zblkm
aḥd ilm tʿny
  lḥt mlak ym
  tʿdt ṯpṭ nhr
šu ilm raštkm
  lẓr brktkm
  ln kḥṯ zblkm
wank ʿny
  〈lḥt〈 mlak ym
  tʿdt ṯpṭ nhr *CTA* 2.1.24-28

Baal's words have been divergently understood. There can be no doubt that he offered the assembly of gods reassurance, and there is no controversy surrounding the heart of his message. His call

šu ilm raštkm
lẓr brktkm
ln kḥṯ zblkm

means

Lift up, O gods, your heads,
From the tops of your knees
From your princely thrones.

That which has been disputed is the meaning of the parallel declarations

aḥd ilm tʿny
lḥt mlak ym
tʿdt ṯpṭ nhr

wank ʿny
〈lḥt〉 mlak ym
tʿdt ṯpṭ nhr

Supposing the first verb *ʿny* to be cognate with Hebrew *ʿānâ* "to be humble" and the second to match *ʿānâ* "to answer," H. L. Ginsberg translated

I see the gods are cowed
  With terror of the messengers of Yamm
  Of the envoys of Judge Nahar

6 R. N. Whybray, "*ʿannôt* in Exodus xxxii 18," *VT* 17 (1967): 122.

7 F. I. Andersen, "A Lexicographical Note on Exodus xxxii 18," *VT* 16 (1966): 108-12.

8 J. Sasson, "The Worship of the Golden Calf," in *Orient and Occident, Essays Presented to Cyrus H. Gordon* (AOAT 22; Neukirchen: Neukirchener, 1973): 151-59.

9 W. F. Albright, *Yahweh and the Gods of Canaan* (rpt. Winona Lakes, IN: Eisenbraun, 1968): 43-44.

10 Cf. BH³.

And I'll answer the messengers of Yamm,
The envoys of Judge Nahar.[11]

By Ginsberg's reckoning, *lḥt* must be analyzed into the components *l* and *ḥt*, the former being a preposition and the latter a noun from the verbal root *ḥtt* "to fear." There are major alternatives to this interpretation. Driver relates *ḥt* to Syriac *ḥat(t)ītûtâ*, "severity," and derives a noun signifying harsh demands.[12] This seems to be Jirku's understanding as well.[13] Aistleitner ties *lḥt* to a verb *lḥy* and produces a noun meaning "insult" or the like.[14]

None of these interpretations is compelling. Jirku has demonstrated that when the Ugaritic gods bow heads to knees at the approach of Yamm's messengers, they enact a customary Egyptian posture of mourning.[15] Their response to the approaching messengers is one of grief, not one of terror and humiliation, nor one of outrage, and although "sharp demands" may have summoned this reaction, the basis for this interpretation seems tenuous.

To appreciate the meaning of *lḥt*, it is necessary to consider the broad context in which Baal's utterance occurs. His adversary is a god called Sea and *Judge* River. In what sense this god is called Judge is not directly revealed, but the language of the poem takes seriously his judicial title. His messengers are called *tʿdt*. In the poetic parallelism of the text this word may be substituted for the commonplace *mlakm*, "messengers," but to construe *tʿdt* simply to mean "commission," as the vast majority of commentators do, greatly impairs our understanding of the myth. The fact that this text offers the only instances of the word pair *mlakm-tʿdt* is sufficient indication that *tʿdt* is not an ordinary synonym of *mlakm*. It is in fact a term drawn from the world of jurisprudence meaning "testimony," as its etymology and Hebrew cognates suggest.[16] Yamm's messengers are his testimony because Yamm is *Judge* River. The imagery of the poem is forensic. When this is recognized, the meaning of *lḥt* becomes clear. This is, as many have noted, the common Ugaritic word "tablets," standing metaphorically for, or literally embodying, a judgment of Baal's antagonist. Leaving the verb *ʿny* untranslated for the moment, we may indicate the outlines of Baal's declarations:

One of the gods will *ʿny*
the tablets of Yamm's messengers,
the testimony of Judge River.

I shall *ʿny*
the tablets of Yamm's messengers,
the testimony of Judge River.

On a basic level the myth portrays consistently and coherently an essentially legal collision. But this level does not carry the greater meaning of the confrontation, the earnest of which is nothing less than kingship among the gods. This we learn in part from the Babylonian myth Enuma Elish, whose family resemblance to the Ugaritic Baal-Yamm cycle is well-known. To the god Sea (Yamm) of the latter corresponds the goddess Sea (Tiamat) of the former, while the role played by Baal is filled by Marduk in the Babylonian composition. The similarity between the two myths must not be pressed in excessive detail, but there is an illuminating point of contact between them with relevance to the present context. At the moment in Enuma Elish when Tiamat undertakes the promotion of her consort Kingu to the first rank among the gods, the text reports that she bestowed upon him the Tablets of Destiny:

She gave him the Tablets of Fate, fastened on his breast:
"As for thee, thy command shall be unchangeable,
"[Thy word] shall endure!"[17]

The tablets signify supremacy among the gods, conceived as unalterable speech. The tablets carried by Yamm's messengers seem to have a similar function. They betoken his imperium, as does his "testimony"— the word is cognate with Hebrew *ʿēdût*, used at 2 Kgs 11:12 with reference to a symbol of sovereignty. In effect, the forensic language of this portion of the Baal-Yamm cycle is translatable into terms conveying the cosmic significance of the events which transpire. This is to have been expected.

It is with this understanding that the verb *ʿny* must be interpreted. What is needed is a judicial term capable of carrying a larger meaning appropriate to the central concern of the myth. Such a word is at hand in the Akkadian verb *enû*, etymologically *ʿny*, the meanings of which precisely match the requirements of *CTA* 2. *Enû* means "to reverse," and can be predicated of a judge's decision, as in the Code of Hammurabi:

If a judge renders a verdict but reverses [*iteni*] his verdict

11 H. L. Ginsberg, *ANET*, 130; he does not restore *lḥt*.

12 G. R. Driver, *Canaanite Myths and Legends* (Old Testament Studies 3; Edinburgh: T. & T. Clark, 1956): 138.

13 Anton Jirku, *Kanaanäische Mythen und Epen* (Gütersloh: Gerd Mohn, 1962): 22.

14 J. Aistleitner, *WUS*, no. 1450.

15 Anton Jirku, "Das Haupt auf die Knie legen," *ZDMG* 103 (1953): 372.

16 Cognates include Heb. *ʿēdût*, *tᵉʿûdâ*, etc., evidently from a root *ʿy/wd* ("witness"?), unless Cross (*Canaanite Myth and Hebrew Epic* [Cambridge, MA: Harvard Univ., 1973]: 267) is correct in assuming **ʿhd*.

17 Trans. E. A. Speiser, *ANET*, 63 (tablet 1, lines 156-57).

> afterwards, one will convict this judge of having reversed the verdict which he had given.[18]

At the same time, *enû* is used where the issue is final authority among the gods, as in the previously quoted passage from Enuma Elish. Equipped with the Tablets of Fate, Kingu's word is unchangeable: *la innina.*[19] Similarly, the god Ninurta is one "whose word none of the gods in the divine assembly can reverse."[20]

Enû is the Akkadian cognate of Ugaritic *ʿny*; it is safe to assume that the jural use of Hebrew *ʿānâ* "to answer" represents a further cognate. Baal's avowal

> *aḥd ilm tʿny*
> *lḥt mlak ym*
> *tʿdt ṯpṭ nhr*
>
> *wank ʿny*
> *<lḥt> mlak ym*
> *tʿdt ṯpṭ nhr*

means

> One of the gods will reverse
> the tablets of Yamm's messengers,
> the testimony of Judge River
>
> I shall reverse
> the tablets of Yamm's messengers,
> the testimony of Judge River.

This promise of judical action conveys figuratively a claim to kingship among the gods.

The implication of this understanding of Ugaritic *ʿny* for Exod 32:18 becomes evident when the poem is contextually situated. The piece with which we began represents Moses' assessment of the significance of the din of the Israelite camp. Immediately after he gives utterance to the poem, Moses enters Israel's camp and smashes the two tablets he is carrying from Yahweh and the mountain of God. The word *ʿănnôt* of the third stichos of the poem, Hebrew equivalent of Ugaritic *ʿny*, looks forward to the breaking of the tablets, an act which symbolizes a reversal of Israel's compacted relationship with her God. The logical complement of *ʿănnôt* is thus *lūḥôt*, an arrangement verbally identical to the earlier Ugaritic construction. The ellipsis of the word *lūḥôt* ("tablets") in the poem itself conforms to the possibilities of Akkadian usage, where the verb *enû* may be used without object.[21] Now the text of Exodus 32 refers to the tablets as *lūḥôt ʿēdût* "tablets of testimony" (v 15), and this suggests a more than casual relationship between the story of the golden calf and the Ugaritic myth, for *ʿēdût* corresponds etymologically to Ugaritic *tʿdt.*[22] It can at least be said that the two employ a common forensic vocabulary. That this vocabulary may address cosmic concerns in the Exodus text as in the Ugaritic is possible, but to explore this possibility leads away from our immediate purpose, which is to translate Moses' poem. Adapting the meaning of *ʿny* to *ʿănnôt*, we may render the final line of the piece, "I hear the sound of reversal."

A translation of the opening lines of the poem is more easily achieved. The narrative introduction to the poem (v 17) serves notice that Joshua interpreted the sounds coming from Israel's camp to be the shout of war. Within a military context, the verb *ʿănnôt* of the opening stichoi must be interpreted to mean "to sing," in line with the ancient, ubiquitous Near Eastern custom of punctuating military adventures with a song and dance. The same verb occurs at 1 Sam 18:6-7:

> When they [Saul and his company] arrived, as David returned from killing the Philistines, the women from all Israel's cities came out to sing and for the *mĕḥōlôt*-dances before Saul the king, with timbrel, glad song, and triangle. The revelling women (*mĕśaḥăqôt*) sang [*taʿănênâ*]:
> Saul smote his thousands
> David his myriads.

We may somewhat freely render Moses poem thus:

> It's not the sound of a hero-song,
> nor the sound of a coward's taunt.
> I hear the sound of reversal.

Having arrived at a translation of the poem, we must finally consider its contextual setting. According to the poem, Joshua incorrectly interpreted what he heard emanating from the Israelite camp. Yet so nearly correct was Joshua that the chapter calls attention to what seem to be elements of the battle-day song and dance, revelry (*ṣiḥēq*, v 6) and "war"-dance (*mĕḥōlôt*, v 19). The chapter is subtly, deliberately playing with the life-situation imagined by Joshua. The poem functions as a denial of this military setting and consequently an invitation to reconsider the connotations of revelry and *mĕḥōlôt*-dances. The narrative report of Israel's rise to frolic (v 6) creates a certain ambiguity in the story of the golden calf, for the verb *ṣiḥēq* can imply sexual merriment. The narrator of the story capitalized on this ambiguity, for there is an exactly similar uncertainty infecting the meaning of the noun *mĕḥōlâ*. Whereas this noun regularly

---

18 *CAD*: 174 (1d1').

19 *Ibid.*, 177 (4).

20 *Ibid.*, 175 (id2'), written BAL-ú.

21 *Ibid.*, (1e).

22 Other occurrences of *lūḥôt ʿēdût* are to be found in P, but in Exodus 32 the phrase seems not to belong to a Priestly tradent. It is probably necessary to attribute the shape of the chapter to E, and it is difficult to eliminate v 15a from an early narrative. The literary problems of the chapter are severe.

occurs in contexts like that quoted from 1 Samuel and designates a kind of war-dance, there is one biblical text from which we catch a glimpse of the wider field of associations attaching to the *mĕḥōlâ*. The text in question is Song of Songs 7:1ff., which Marvin Pope has recently translated in his commentary:

> Leap, leap, O Shulamite!
> Leap, leap, and let us gaze upon you.
> How will you gaze on Shulamite
> In the Dance (*mĕḥōlâ*) of the two Camps?
> How beautiful your sandaled feet,
> O prince's daughter!
> Your curvy thighs like ornaments
> Crafted by artist hands.
> Your vulva a rounded crater;
> May it never lack punch![23]

Landsberger's identification of the Akkadian cognate of *mĕḥōlâ* has been a key to understanding the passage. He saw that *melultu* corresponds to the Hebrew word,[24] and W. F. Albright adapted this suggestion to the Song of Songs by noting the association of *melultu* with the goddess Ishtar. Her epithets include *ša melultaša tuquntu*, "she whose dance is battle" and, as Nanaia, *ša melul <ta> ša qablum*, "she whose dance is combat." This association of *melultu* and the Babylonian goddess of love and war led Albright to infer that the Shulamite of Song of Songs is none other than the goddess Shulmanitu, a west Semitic name of the goddess known in the Akkadian literature as Ishtar, in Ugaritic texts as ʿAnat.[25] Pope promotes this suggestion arguing the similarity of the dance of the two camps in Song of Songs and ʿAnat's bloodbath between two camps (*qrtm*) in an Ugaritic text.[26] The proposal is striking. Equally striking is the Song of Song's enclosure of the military character of the *mĕḥōlâ* in the erotic. The martial, erotic equivocation in the *mĕḥōlâ*-dance is of a piece with the ambivalent nature of the goddess of love and war.

The narrative of the golden calf apostasy has made use of this equivocation, and brings matters into focus in the final line of Moses' poem in a clever bit of paronomasia. The words *qôl ʿănnôt* not only mean "the sound of reversal," but also suggest "the voice of ʿAnat." The ability of Moses' words to multiply meanings has become a mechanism for simultaneously characterizing Israel's apostasy as pagan and implying that it involved sexual license. This implication, inherent in the nature of the goddess and the *mĕḥōlâ*, connects with the deliberately chosen verb "to frolic" in a network of innuendo.

It goes without saying that the sexual innuendo of the chapter has a purpose. That purpose is recovered by noting a second bit of word play, introduced at v 9. Cognizant of events unfolding in Israel's camp, Yahweh tells Moses, "I have seen this people, it is a stiff-necked people(*ʿam-qĕšê-ʿōrep*)." The verbal structure of this complaint is deliberately imitated at v 25: "Moses saw the people, that they were wanton (*pārūaʿ*)." "Wanton" (*pārūaʿ*) scrambles the consonants of "neck" (*ʿōrep*"). At v 25, Israel is described by a rare word (*pārūaʿ*) which is defined by means of itself: "Aaron had driven them wild (*pĕrāʿō*)." As Hugo Gressman observed, this creates the impression of a name etiology.[27] The chapter has more to offer in this regard. Moses' vision of the people as *pārūaʿ* corresponds to Aaron's characterization of them as "inclined to evil" (*bĕrāʿ*), v 22. The verbal structure of the verse again resembles that of vv 9, 25. The chain is completed with one additional link. As he returned to Israel's camp, Joshua heard "the sound of the people as they roared (*bĕrēʿō*)," v 17. The phrase *bĕrēʿô* finds its motivation in the full chain of which it is a part: *ʿam-qĕšê-ʿōrep*; *ʿam pārūaʿ*; *ʿam bĕrāʿ*; *ʿam bĕrēʿô*. Gressman believed that the word play in this chain points to a toponym absent from the chapter, Peʿor. This is a striking observation, although the attraction of the Baal Peʿor and golden calf traditions seems not to have resulted, as Gressman thought, from a spatial displacement of the latter. Rather, it should be assumed that the tale of the golden calf has been composed in such a way as to invite comparison with the Baal Peʿor traditions (Num 25:1ff). The narrator of the Exodus story has subtly indicated that the offense at the foot of Sinai was sexual and he has virtually embedded the name Peʿor within his narrative.

The inspiration for this narrative movement is easily located. A central concern of Exodus 32 is, as has often been asserted, rival claims of priestly houses. The argument supporting this assertion is quite simple.[28] The narrative of Exodus 32 portrays Aaron in an unfavorable light, while casting the tribe of Levi in the role of the only faithful remnant of Israel. On the other hand, the traditions of Baal Peʿor assign to Phinehas, presumed eponymous ancestor of the Bethelite, Aaronid priestly house, eternal priesthood for his role in combatting Israel's licentious Baal Peʿor apostasy. Exodus 32 seems to respond to that tradition. It evokes the name Peʿor, and then tells how Phinehas' grandfather was the author of

23 Marvin H. Pope, *Song of Songs* (AB 7c; Garden City, NY: Doubleday, 1977): 593.

24 Benno Landsberger, "Einige unerkannt gebliebene oder verkannte Nomina des Akkadischen," *WZKM* 56 (1960): 119ff.

25 W. F. Albright, "Archaic Survivals in the Text of Canticles," in *Hebrew and Semitic Studies Presented to Godfrey Rolles Driver* (D. Winton Thomas and W. D. McHardy, eds.; Oxford: Clarendon, 1963): 5-6.

26 Pope, *Song of Songs* (N 23): 606 (*CTA* 3.2.3-41).

27 Hugo Gressman, *Mose und seine Zeit* (Göttingen: Vandenhoeck & Ruprecht, 1913): 199-218.

28 Cf. Cross, *Canaanite Myth* (N 16): 198ff. for a version of the argument.

Israel's first national, sexual disgrace. By so doing, the story of the golden calf nullifies the effect of Phinehas' piety.

This is the compositional horizon on which Moses' poem functions. Whereas his words convey in a straightforward manner the results of Israel's apostasy (the breach of Israel's legal relationship with Yahweh), they also operate to indicate a polemical interpretation of the event. We hope in this study to have shed light on the poem at Exod 32:18. The writer counts it a special privilege to offer the study as a tribute to his teacher, Marvin Pope.

EZEKIEL 16: A PANORAMA OF PASSIONS

MOSHE GREENBERG

In Marvin Pope's monumental *Song of Songs*, the chapter of Scripture most often cited is Ezekiel 16 (27 references; runner up 1 Kings 6!). This is not unexpected, in view of the range of passions so vividly described in that lurid diatribe. It seems fitting to salute our learned and curious colleague with a study of one of the most startling effusions of the most learned and curious of Israel's prophets.

Our aim is to describe the workings of this elaborately constructed chapter—its structure and coherence, its particular employment of traditional themes, and its linguistic and rhetorical devices. For detailed commentary and essays at reconstructing the literary history of the chapter, one may consult W. Zimmerli's exhaustive treatment.[1] Here we focus upon the product of that hypothesized history. Our hypothesis is that the product is not haphazard or merely accretional, but an intelligent choice and collocation of elements. Our analysis indicates that they have been skillfully deployed to create a shocking impact, and to describe a movement from extreme conflict to resolution. To the extent that others share our persuasion that the analysis is valid, our hypothesis will tend toward confirmation.

I. Structure, Language and Rhetoric

This longest prophecy of the book—63 verses between one revelation formula (16:1) and another (17:1)—has three thematic divisions. After the command to arraign Jerusalem for her abominations (2), come A. an extended metaphor of the nymphomaniacal adulteress (3-43); B. the invidious comparison of Jerusalem to her sisters Sodom and Samaria (44-58); and C. a coda foretelling the mortification of restored Jerusalem before covenant-true YHWH (59-63). Each division ends with an epitomizing sentence concluding with the formula "declares (the Lord) YHWH." That formula, affirming the divine authorship of a passage and thus appropriately occurring at its terminus, seems to mark the subunits within each division as well (beginnings and ends).

A. consists of a detailed bill of indictment (introduced by "and say, Thus said the Lord YHWH" [3] and running on to 34) and a sentencing ("So harlot, hear the word of YHWH; thus said the Lord YHWH: Because . . . assuredly . . . ." [35-43]). (For a similar structure, see chap. 34: indictment, vv 2-6; consequence, 7ff.) The formula "declares (the Lord) YHWH" further subdivides A. as follows:

A.1 An abandoned baby girl is saved and possessed by YHWH (3-8). The narrative moves in vivid episodes from the birth and exposure of the baby (3-5, abounding in negatives; note the *inclusio* formed by the expression "on the day of your birth"), to God's first notice of the infant, in which he preserves her and lets her grow to nubile ripeness (6-7), to his second notice when he takes her and pledges his troth (8). Forsaken by her natural parents, she is saved alive and covenanted with by her gracious divine savior.

A.2 She is provided for splendidly and becomes a famous beauty (9-14). God lavishes on her the care her parents denied her (9 contrasts with 4), clothes and adorns her (10-12) to indulgence (in 13 she, not God, is the subject), and declares that her renowned beauty is his doing 14).

A.3 She spends her endowment on fornication (15-19). After a general indictment (anticipating A.5; 15b = 25), 16-19 describe how she used her gifts for the making and tending of "male" images." *Watihyî lî* "You became mine" at the end of 8 reverberates in the agitated ejaculations of outrage at the end of 15, 16, 19.

A.4 She sacrifices her children to the images (20-22). Not content with infidelity, she murdered her children to feed her images, forgetful of her bloody plight as a baby, from which she had been saved. Her filicide evokes her own verging on death, naked and bloody, a victim of her own parents' cruelty.

A.5 She fornicates with every passerby (23-29). (Here and in A.6 "declares (the Lord) YHWH" is in the opening line of the section.) Verses 24f. heighten the language of 15f.: instead of a single term (*bāmâ*) come two (*gāb*, *rāmâ*); multiple locations are mentioned, an obscene gesture, and the "extension" of harlotry. A new level of outrage has been reached, with human males, instead of idols, as paramours. Along with "male" partners, "female" enemies appear, thus filling out the register of Jerusalem's international contacts. "You were not satisfied," repeated at the end of the section, underlines the woman's abandoned frenzy and prepares the sequel.

1. Zimmerli, *Ezechiel, Biblischer Kommentar* xiii. (Neukirchen-Vluyn: Neukirchener Verlag, 1955–1969): 331-371 [Eng. trans. by Ronald E. Clements, ed. F. M. Cross, et al., *Ezekiel 1*, in series *Hermeneia* (Philadelphia: Fortress, 1979): 322-353]. See also J. Wevers, *Ezekiel, Century Bible, New Series.* (London: Nelson, 1969): 118-133.

A.6 The contrariety of the nymphomaniacal harlot (30-34): she is now equated with a harlot (*zônâ*)—a grade lower than "one who fornicates" (*tiznî*). The resumption of 24-25a in 30-31a ends by announcing the theme of contrariety: "You were not like other harlots...." Reflecting this, vv 33f. are constructed antithetically; 34 is strongly patterned: two phrases with *hēpek* "contrary" form an *inclusio*, and the two central verb clauses are each chiastic [verb-(obj.)-obj.-verb]. Thematic "Harlot's hire" announced in 31b resounds in the highly alliterative penultimate verb clause of the final sentence (34).

A.7 God sentences her to violent death (35-43). After a summons to the harlot (35), a message formula opens the verdict: a summary of offenses (36) is followed by a list of consequences—public exposure (37), condemnation to punishment for adultery and murder (38), and delivery to the mob for pillage and lynching (39-41). Only then will God's wrath quieten (42). An afterwave, evoking the beginning of the prophecy (the woman's forgetfulness of her youth[ful covenant and its benefits]) rounds off the sentence. In the rhetorical question that follows "declares the Lord YHWH" (43), *zimmâ*, combines with *darkēk* preceding the formula to evoke v 27, in which the shame of the Philistine women at Jerusalem's depraved conduct (*darkēk zimmâ*) is mentioned. The question seeks to bring home to Jerusalem that she has piled wickedness upon wickedness—toward which she is brazenly indifferent. The overtones of 27, with its contrast of more virtuous gentiles and its motif of shame, foreshadow the next division of the prophecy.

B. is dominated by comparisons unfavorable (*scil.* causing shame) to Jerusalem. The thought moves quickly from the opening epigram ("like mother like daughter") through an implicit "like mother like daughters" to the explicit equation of the three sisters, which is the point of departure for the division.

B.1 Jerusalem is the worst of three depraved sisters (44-47). The perfidious family is introduced ("mother" and "mother-father" not only form an *inclusio* [44b-45] but connect B.1 with A.1 [note the inversion of the parents], the sisters are identified (46) and Jerusalem is said to have soon outdone them in wickedness (47).

B.2 Jerusalem must be ashamed for having made her sisters look righteous, and for being restored only as an adjunct to their restoration (48-58). Sodom stands at the beginning and at the end of this section (48-50; 56f.), for as a byword of corruption its "vindication" by Jerusalem is the latter's most stinging humiliation (note the association of "pride" with each). The sequence of 53-55 is: restoration of the three, with Jerusalem "among them" (53), which equalization is their consolation and her disgrace (54); the three will attain to their former states—an implicit curb on Jerusalem's dream of hegemony over the land of Israel—and a preparation for the sequel. Verse 58 echoes 43 (*zimmâ, tôʿēbâ*).

C. Recovenanted and re-endowed beyond her former state (she will eventually attain hegemony!), Jerusalem will feel shamed by remembrance of her past (59-63). Starting with the *kî* plus message formula that serves often to introduce a new turn (see at 14:21), this coda is at once a climax and a resolution: a climax in terms of God's victory over human obduracy, and a resolution in terms of Jerusalem's reformation and acknowledgment of her abominable conduct as shown by her deep shame. Themes of A—covenant of youth—and B—sisters, shame—are tied together in a sublime catharsis.

Though B is evidently a new turn, it is dependent upon A: it assumes the reader knows the identity of the wanton (she is never identified in B), the baseness of her parents, and her abominations (which while referred to are not described). The temporal setting is determined by the equal footing of all three sisters; Jerusalem has joined the others in the limbo of has-beens awaiting restoration. What was threatened in A has occurred. C marks a further advance of the historical horizon, beyond the restoration to a new dispensation in which the two "sisters" will be subject to Jerusalem. C's dependence on B (sister motif) and A (covenant of youth) is manifest. The prophecy thus moves in a cumulative chronological sequence.

The prophecy is united through several continuities, some of which undergo transformation. The family theme runs through all three divisions; an ever-changing aspect is "daughters"—children (20), women (=enemies, 27), dependencies (46 and B *passim*), including the surprise transformation of "sisters" (61). Shame occurs in A only in the Philistine women (27), in B and C in Jerusalem. Common to A and B (where it is more frequent) is the term "abomination"—answering to the charge laid on the prophet in v 2. The wanton does not "remember" her youth in A (22, 43), but God does in C (60), while she, having been reformed, then "remembers" her evil ways (61).

The most pervasive feature of the prophecy is contrast or antithesis. The life-course of the wanton runs from discovery at death's door soon after her birth, rising to the peak of beauty, adornment and fame, then plunging to the depth of loathsome degradation and bloody death (A). B continuously compares and contrasts the wanton's acts and fate with those of her sisters. C foretells Jerusalem's shame at the contrast between her past behavior and God's future graciousness. The brazen adulteress who does not blush at any perversion (A) learns shame (B) and when chastened is mortified by her past (C). God, whose fury unleashes savage retribution (A), appears in B as tempering redemption with humiliation, and finally (in C) as graciously absolving from all sin.

The parts of each division are closely interconnected. Consider division A: What the child's parents withheld from her God gave her without stint. The "field" was to be her death-site; after God's vivifying command it is part of a simile for her flourishing growth ("like the plants of the field"). "Stark naked" describes the woman arrived at nubility, ready to receive God's lavish endowment; "stark naked" describes her stripped of her last bit of clothing on the verge of her execution. In between, the prophet pauses in his account of how she squandered all she had on "male images" to denounce her forgetfulness of her childhood when she was "stark naked," wallowing in her blood.

Contrasts are highlighted by the use of repetition. God "happened by" and preserved her alive; he "happened by" again when she came of age and took her; she on her part pressed her favors on "all who happened by." A series of six (or seven) verb clauses details the gifts God made to the woman ("I clothed . . . , I shod . . . , I bound . . . ," etc.); six corresponding sentences relate how she spent them—and her children—on her "male images" ("you took . . . and made / put . . ."). Her blood, in which she lived through God's word, reverberates in the blood of her children who were slaughtered for her idols. God covered her nakedness, but her nakedness was exposed in her harlotry, so God will deliver her over to executioners who will expose and see all her nakedness.

While the key term in the tale of the harlot's sin and punishment is *zānâ* "to harlot, fornicate" (and derivative *taznût*)—twenty occurrences—her offenses escalate. Fornication with idols was "too little," so she killed her children for them. Idols too, were not enough, so she "extended (increased) her harlotry" (3 times in 25-29) to male neighbors—without ever finding satisfaction (3 times in 28-29). Her nadir of degradation, paying out hire instead of receiving it, is dwelt upon in several antithetical sentences (31b-34). The verdict on her conduct is an outpouring of accumulated rage, heaping up items of indictment and measures of punishment.

Alongside the climactic structure, lurid images and shocking language serve to sustain this long and verbose diatribe: fornicating with male images, slaughtering children for them to eat, spreading legs for every passerby, "your 'juice' was poured out," a bloody object of fury and passion, "hack you with their swords." The prophecy is also interspersed with a good number of rare or unique words and grammatical anomalies:

Unique words (including words found again only in Ezek):

mkrt (3), *lmšʿy* (4), *hmlḥ*, *hḥtl* / *ḥtl* (4), *gʿl* (5), *mtbwsst* (6), *mšy* (10), *tznwt* (passim and in chap. 23 only), *pśq* (25), *mh ʾmlh lbtk* (30), *ndh*, *ndn* (33), *šḥd* (verb, 33), *nḥšt* (obscene, 36), *btq* (40).

Rare words or usages:

mldt (pl.) (3), *rbbh* ("growth," 7), *rbh* ("grow up") *ʿdy ʿdyym*, *ʿrm wʿryh* (7), *ʿgyl* (12), *ṭlʾwt*, *lʾ bʾwt wlʾ yhyh* (16), *gb*, *rmh* (obscene, 24), *gdly bśr* (26), *znh* with accus. (28), *qls* (31), *hpk* (34) *znh* (pass. 34), *rgz l-*, *hʾ* (43).

Grammatical anomalies:

2nd fem. sing. verbal afformative *ty* (ktib)—13, 18, 22, 31 (twice), 43 (twice); pl. suff *-yk* on substantives ending in *ut* (*ot*)—15, etc. 31; doubled *r*—4 (twice); assimilation in noun pair *ššy wmšy* (13).

Some of these rarities are due to topics not otherwise taken up (care of the newborn, the argot of whoring), others may be a colloquial level of language. To the latter we may account exclamations, Akkadianisms (*ndn, btq, nḥšt*—also perhaps argot), and Aramaisms (afformative *ti* [cf. Kutscher, *Isaiah Scroll* (Heb.) 20f., 142f.], *pśq*, *lbt-*, perhaps *qls*). The penchant for plural forms *mldt*, *mkrt*, *dmy*, *rmwt* [39], and 2nd fem. pl. suffix on *-u/ot* nouns) suits the turgid style of the passage.

Choice of language thus combines with climactic structure and antithesis to produce a sensational effect that does not flag despite the length of the passage.

The transition from A to B is made by the quip, "Like mother like daughter," which facilitates the shift in focus to the three "(daughters) / sisters," and to the antithesis Jerusalem–Sodom (and Samaria) that dominates B. The point of this antithesis is its inversion of the traditional evaluation of Sodom relative to Jerusalem, the latter's pride being replaced by the reproach and disgrace of making the other "sisters" look righteous by comparison.

The linguistic features of A continue in B: unique and rare words (*qt, pll, šmwʿh* "byword," *kmw ʿt* "now"), an Aramaism (or Akkadianism, *šwṭ* "despise"), 2nd fem. sing. *ty* verb afformative (51, perhaps 50), morphological assimilation (50) and other irregularity (in the accidence of *ʾḥwt*). Style and linguistic texture confirm the connection of B to A.

The bridge from B to C is *kaʾăšer ʿaśît*,[59] "as you have done," which echoes *kol/ka/ʾăšer ʿăśît* in 48, 51, 54; here the clause is defined as alluding to violation of the covenant, introducing the main theme of the coda (*bᵉrît*, 60 [twice], 61, 62). Around the covenant the prophet constructs his final contrast—the faithfulness of God despite the faithlessness of Jerusalem, expressed in his ultimate eschatological bounty, which will shame her into silence. Even this brief division has its unusual term, *pitḥôn pe* (63).

The coherent structure, the progressive temporal sequence, the homogeneous style and linguistic texture, and the intricate connection of the parts of this prophecy give it an architectural aspect; such flaws as exist are overborne by the great design.

II. Themes and Their Deployment

"Make known to Jerusalem her abominations" embodies the main issue of this complex oracle: Jerusalem is oblivious to her shame (in Jer 2:23 she denies it), hence the prophet must confront her with her appalling record. The passage through time distinguishes this indictment from the preceding ones. It is the first of three surveys of Israel's history (chaps. 16, 20, 23) and the most impressive: its metaphor is worked out more elaborately and in more directions than that of chap. 23 (chap. 20 has no metaphor); it takes in more history than chap. 20; neither of the other two can match its structure and rhetoric. We turn now to its themes.

The figure of Israel as YHWH's wife derives from the cardinal commandment that Israel worship YHWH alone. To that demand of exclusive fidelity, the obligation of a wife to her husband offered a parallel. Certain usages in the Torah already reflect the figure. In the Decalogue and the smaller "Covenant Code" YHWH is called *qannāʾ* "passionate, jealous" toward those who break faith with him (Exod 20:5; 34:14). The related noun (*qinʾâ*) and verb (*qinnēʾ*) describe the agitation of a husband suspicious of his wife's fidelity in Num 5:14, 30 (cf. Prov 6:34). Apostasy is expressed by *zānâ* "go whoring" in Exod 34:14f. and Num 15:39 (whence Ezek 6:9; on the foregoing see the luminous remarks of G. Cohen, "The Song of Songs," in *Samuel Friedland Lectures 1960-1966* [New York, 1966]: 1-22, esp. 4ff.). The prophetic development of this figure built upon this early foundation. Hosea was the first to use it, in his denunciation of the northern kingdom. "Arraign your mother (= the kingdom of Israel)," he cried to her "children" (= citizens), " . . . for she is not my wife, and I am not her husband" (= a formula of divorce; cf. Muffs, *Studies in Biblical Law* IV, 4ff.). "Let her remove her harlotry from her face and her adultery from between her breasts, lest I strip her as on the day of her birth . . . . Their mother has fornicated . . . for she said, 'Let me go after my lovers who give me my bread, my water and my wool, my flax, my oil and my drink . . . . She did not realize that it was I who gave her grain, new wine and oil; the silver I gave her so much of, and the gold they made over to Baal! So I shall take back my grain in its season, and my new wine in its time, and pluck off my wool and flax that it not cover her nakedness. Now will I uncover her shame in the sight of her lovers, and no one will save her from my hand . . . . I will desolate her vines and fig-trees of which she said, 'They are my wages which my lovers paid me.' " (Hos 2:4-14).

All this is a manifest forerunner of the imagery of our prophecy. Israel is an unfaithful wife; having received bounty from her God, she attributed it to others, on whom she spent it (this motif derives ultimately from the story of the golden calf, made out of the gold objects God disposed the Egyptians to give the departing Israelites; cf. also Deut 32:15). God will punish her by stripping her and exposing her naked to her lovers. There is no time perspective in Hosea (how Ezekiel expanded upon the simile "as on the day of your birth"!), no political "harlotry," and no maniacal perversity and insatiability.

Jeremiah took up the image. In 2:20-25 he brands Israel's illicit cults as harlotry and pursuit of "strangers" (see our v 32). But it is in chap. 3 that he speaks in terms familiar from Ezekiel:

> You have fornicated with many "friends." Look around at the hills and see, where have you not been laid? You waited on the roads for them . . . and polluted the land with your fornication and your evil . . . . You have the forehead of a harlot; you refuse to be ashamed . . . . She fornicated with wood and stone . . . . Know your iniquity, for you have rebelled against YHWH your God, and scattered your favors (lit. ways) among strangers under every green tree (v 1-13).

Promiscuity in many places (the shrines to foreign gods), brazen shamelessness, wood and stone, scattering of favors—these features in Jeremiah's figure bring her to within a step of Ezekiel's wanton.

The extension of the figure to alliances with foreign nations came to Ezekiel by the same route. Other prophets denounced reliance on foreign powers as an insult to God (Isaiah 7-8 [Assyria]; 30-31 [Egypt]), but it was Hosea who, after railing at Israel for "straying" from God after Egypt and Assyria ("like a silly dove"; 7:11-13), brands her pursuit of alliances as "offers of love" (8:9). Just over a century later, Jeremiah foretold Judah's disappointment by Egypt as it had been earlier disappointed by Assyria "for YHWH has spurned those you trust" (Jer 2:36f.); then, following Hosea, he calls Judah's allies her "lovers" (22:20, 22 [*rōʿayik* "companions" as in Prov 29:3]; 30:14; cf. Lam 1:19). Ezekiel not only adopted this imagery from his predecessors but spelled out the "sexual attractiveness" of the lovers in characteristic vividness (v 26; cf. 23:6ff.). By seeking its security in alliances with earthly powers, Israel has broken faith with YHWH, "fornicating" with the Gentiles (cf. the nonfigurative language of 29:16).

By extending the metaphor in time Ezekiel provided the adulterous wife of Hosea and Jeremiah with a biography. The impulse to do so came from theodicy. The imminent destruction of the "remnant of Israel" (9:8, 11:13) was a catastrophe that demanded a correspondingly enormous sin to justify it. The doom prophets of the age supplied it by summoning up the accumulated sin of Israel's entire history: Jerusalem and Judah would be eradicated "because they have done what is evil in my sight and have been vexing me from the day that their fathers came out of Egypt to this day" (2 Kgs 22:15—Manasseh's reign); in Jehoiakim's reign Jeremiah denounced the people for having "gone backward, not forward, from the day your fathers left the land of Egypt until today" (7:24f.). In 20:8ff. and 23:3, 19 Ezekiel pushes back Israel's rebellion against YHWH to its Egyptian sojourn. Here he follows a different tack; by starting from the very origins of the people (Hos 2:5 may have suggested this) he heightened the effect of the denunciation.

The infant castaway foundling, known from life and story, serves to represent the weakness verging on death of Israel's natural state at its beginnings (cf. the opening line of the farmer's liturgy, "My father was a fugitive Aramean," Deut 26:5). Her desperate plight throws into relief God's gratuitous kindness. His finding her in the "field" resembles the depiction in the poem of Deut 32:10, in which God finds Israel "in the wilderness, in the empty, howling desert," and the purport is the same: to start the account of God's relation to his people with a situation best designed to enhance his beneficence toward them and illustrate his providential and tender care of them (Driver, *Deuteronomy*, 356)—the blacker to paint their subsequent apostasy. (R. Bach [*TLZ* (1953): 687] thought to find in Hos 9:10, 10:11; Deut 32:10

and in our passage an aberrant tradition of Israel's foundation, which exalted the desert age as a time of harmony between God and Israel, and knew nothing of the patriarchal or Sinai tradition. But this makes too much of a poetic picture, drawn for the sake of antithesis and is justly criticized by Rudolph, *Hosea*, 185 n. 5). The prophet ignores the traditional ancestors of Israel, the patriarchs, precisely because they gave honor and encouragement to the people (cf. the post-fall reliance on Abraham's covenant in 33:23ff.); he chooses instead the pagan antecedents of Jerusalem, thus providing a motive for the cruel abandonment of the infant (necessary to highlight God's kindness) and a hereditary ground for her future dissolute conduct.

Moderns have followed Gunkel in regarding the story of the exposure, preservation, and eventual marriage to royalty of the foundling as too detailed, and too remote from Jerusalem's history, to have been a creation of the prophet.

> The detailed story of the exposure of the girl and her growth amidst [?] the plant of the field defies interpretation in connection with the destiny of Jerusalem. Here one can palpably feel how Ezekiel has adopted material derived from elsewhere. There existed a story about a girl exposed in the wilderness right after her birth; uncared for, she was given over to die. While she weltered in the blood that still covered her from birth, a man came by who granted her life. Ezekiel says in his adaptation that it was YHWH; but since the man granted life to the girl by some act, it must originally have been a magician. The girl grew up, thanks to the magician's word, and became a robust maiden; but no clothes covered her. Again blood appeared on her—the first blood of her puberty. Someone else came by—according to Ezekiel it was YHWH again; but the sequel in which the girl is elevated to royalty indicates that the story meant the man to be a king. But if the two passersby were really from the first identical—and that is not self-evident—we must suppose a magician-king, who now beholds in all her glory the product of his lifegiving word—perhaps to his own surprise. He falls in love with the girl, covers her with his own garment, and takes her in marriage. He brings her home, adorns her with costly garments and sets a crown on her head. Thus the poor rejected girl becomes a queen and her beauty becomes renowned among the nations. All this is evidently a fairytale with strong oriental coloration. We may [with complete certainty] assume it to be a fairytale (H. Gunkel, *Märchen*, 115f.).

Comparison with the basic scheme of exposure stories casts doubt on this assessment. The typical foundling is a *Wunderkind* destined for greatness; indeed the reason for the story is the eventual greatness of its hero(ine), which it enhances. The child's abandonment is forced on the parent(s) by shame or necessity. The child grows up under foster tutelage, betraying unsuspected qualities even before its true identity is revealed (G. Binder, *Enzyk. des Märchens* [Berlin, 1977]: 1.1048-65, s.v. "Aussetzung"). Ezekiel's story is designed to account for and illustrate baseness—an unexampled motive of exposure stories. The parents' abandonment of their child is wanton cruelty (a trait inherited by the child); her remarkable qualities are not hers but YHWH's glory that he has set upon her. She would not be wonderful but for the care and gifts bestowed on her by YHWH. If any relation is to be supposed between Ezekiel's story and the scheme of exposure tales it is one of inversion; on that supposition the relation makes some sense. But it is a question whether, given all the aforementioned ingredients—the metaphor of the adulterous wife, the view of the radical evil of Israel, the practice of exposure—the origin of this story is better explained by inversion of a folk motif than by the free inspiration of the prophet.

A peculiar detail of the story inclines one to the second alternative. The assertion that the tale is remote from Jerusalem's history loses most of its weight when it is realized that Jerusalem stands for Israel; God entered into a covenant only with the people, never with the city (v 8). On the contrary, it would seem that only on the basis of Israelite history can the details of God's passing by the girl twice and the untended interval between be explained. In the scheme of exposure stories, between the foundling's rescue and revelation, it lives under the care of a guardian. Here the girl grows up so untended that her body remains filthy till the time of her marriage. God's abandonment of the girl after he commanded her preservation until her nubility is an artificial adjustment of the narrative to the Exodus tradition. During the long interval of the Egyptian bondage Israel flourished and grew, apparently forsaken by its God, until the time of redemption arrived, when it was taken by God to be his people (the child's abandonment in the "field" and its development "like the plants of the field" recall the Israelites' labor "in the field" and God's wonders worked against Egypt, "the field of Zoan" [Exod 1:14; Ps 78:43]). Hence the inference may be ventured that the rejection of the child and its outcasting by its Canaanite parents somehow refer to the forced emigration of Jacob's family into Egypt because of famine in Canaan, where they were providentially sustained (Gen 45:7; 50:20). Gunkel's puzzlement over the identity of the two passersby indicates a problem in the reconstruction of his hypothetical fairytale that is obviated by taking the plot to reflect, roughly as is Ezekiel's habit in his historical surveys, the outlines of the traditional account of Israel's beginnings as a people.

Having proceeded this far contrary to the fairytale interpretation, one is tempted to match the other details in the story with items in the early historical tradition. Is the concurrence of items used in building the tabernacle and outfitting the priests with the ornaments of the woman accidental? The fantastic lengths to which one may be led in this direction—and an appreciation of the motive of Gunkel's approach if not of its results—emerge from a glance at the Targum to v 3-14:

> Your sojourning and birthplace was of the land of the Canaanite; there I revealed myself to your father Abraham (in the covenant made) between the pieces [Genesis 15] and

informed him that you would go down to Egypt, with an upraised arm I would redeem you, and through the merit of your fathers I would expel the Amorites before you and destroy the Hittites. [4]Moreover, when your fathers went down to Egypt, sojourners in a land not theirs, enslaved and afflicted, the congregation of Israel was like an infant abandoned in the field whose navel cord was not cut, etc. [5]Pharaoh's eye did not pity you to do even one kindness to you, to give you rest from your slavery, to have mercy on you; but he issued against you a decree of annihilation, to throw your males into the river, to make you perish, at the time you were in Egypt. [6]And the memory of the covenant of your fathers came before me, and I revealed myself in order to redeem you, for I saw that you were afflicted in your slavery, and I said to you, 'Because of the blood of circumcision I will pity you,' and I said to you, 'Because of the blood of the paschal sacrifices I will redeem you.' [7]Myriads like the plants of the field I made you, and you grew numerous and powerful, and became generations and tribes; and because of the righteous deeds of your fathers, the time for redeeming your congregation arrived, for you were enslaved and afflicted. [8]Then I revealed myself to Moses in the bush, for I saw that the time for redeeming you had arrived, and I sheltered you with my word and I removed your sins, and I swore by my word to redeem you as I swore to your fathers," said the Lord God, "that you might become a people serving me. [9]And I redeemed you from the slavery of Egypt and removed harsh tyranny from you, and led you to freedom. [10]And I clothed you in embroidered garments of your enemies' valuables, and I put gorgeous shoes on your feet, and consecrated some of you as priests to serve me in turbans of linen, (and) the high priest in many-colored clothes. [11]And I adorned you with the ornament of the words of the Torah written on two tables of stone and given by Moses, and consecrated you with the holiness of my great name. [12]I placed my ark of the covenant among you, with my cloud of glory shading you, and an angel commissioned by me leading you at your head. [13]And I set my tabernacle in your midst, adorned with gold and silver and curtains of linen and many-colored and embroidered stuff, and I fed you manna as good as fine flour and honey and oil; so you grew very very rich and powerful, and you prospered and ruled every kingdom.

The wicked sisters, the theme of B, reappear (i.e., two of them do) in chap. 23; they occur first in Jer 3:6ff., a passage dated to Josiah's reign. Jeremiah extends the Hoseanic figure of the faithless wife (used in the immediately preceding vv 1-5) to Israel and Judah, representing the related kingdoms as sisters.

You saw, did you not, what that apostate Israel did—how she went up onto every high hill and under every spreading tree, and fornicated there . . . . And that faithless one, her sister Judah, saw this. She saw (reading *wtr*ʾ) that it was precisely because Israel . . . had committed adultery that I turned her out and gave her a bill of divorce. Nevertheless her faithless sister Judah was not afraid, but went herself and fornicated too . . . . Apostate Israel has shown herself more in the right than faithless Judah (Jer 3:6-11).

In Ezekiel's adaptation, the sisters represent cities (determined perhaps by his focus on Jerusalem), but their treatment in our passage and in chap. 23 is quite different—in each case, however, showing features directly related to Jeremiah. In chap. 23 two sisters only figure (as in Jeremiah) and they have a history of infidelity that goes back to the sojourn in Egypt (unlike our passage, but cf. 20:7-8). In our passage, there are three sisters—Sodom is added—and while all have "spurned their husbands" none is explicitly YHWH's spouse; this point is muffled in order to accommodate Sodom, which was never "married" to YHWH and whose sin, accordingly, was not infidelity. Over against this major difference from Jeremiah and chap. 23, the central point of our passage—namely, Jerusalem's "justification" of her sisters by her wickedness—is an almost literal adoption of a motif in Jeremiah, elaborated here and ignored in chap. 23. Indeed it was only to heighten the disparaging comparison of Jerusalem that Sodom was adopted as a sister and given precedence over Samaria in the argument. We conclude that our passage and chap. 23 are independent adaptations of Jeremiah's theme, each selecting different aspects for elaboration. We shall soon see why the "justification" motif was chosen here.

The covenant theme of the coda (C) is ambiguous and liable to confusion with other eschatological covenants mentioned later in the book. The covenant enforced by curse-sanctions (v 59) imposed obligations on Israel (mediated by Moses), which she violated. The "covenant of your youth" (v 60) to be remembered by YHWH is his unilateral pledge made to Israel (in Egypt, according to 20:5, but incorporating promises to the patriarchs). Here YHWH avers that despite Israel's violation of its obligation, he will be mindful of his and will (re)establish (*whqmwty*) [it as] an eternal covenant with Israel in the future.

Now in 34:25, Ezekiel mentions a new future "covenant of peace" which God will make (*krt*) with Israel; when this is iterated in 37:26 it is further qualified as an eternal covenant. Critics have noted that elsewhere in Ezekiel *krt* alone is employed for making a covenant (17:13); combining this with the preceding fact, they have concluded that Ezekiel's concept of the eschatological covenant between YHWH and Israel regarded it as a new beginning, not a continuation of the old covenant, and that his term for making it was *krt,* not *hqym.* It follows that our passage is not from Ezekiel. The supposed discord vanishes when the covenant of 34:25 is correctly understood not as the grand bond between God and people, but as a specific assurance of everlasting physical security in the land. In future, the contingent blessing of Lev 26:6—that obedience would be rewarded by God's "granting peace in the land, and you shall lie down untroubled by anyone; I will rid the land of vicious beasts and no sword shall pass through your land"—would be realized forever: "I will make with them a covenant of peace, and I will rid the land of vicious beasts, so that they can dwell secure (even) in the wilderness, and sleep (even) in forests" (Ezek 34:25). That is indeed a new covenant, never before made (*krt*); its subsequent qualification as eternal, if not a borrowing from our passage, is no more significant than the identical qualification of several such specific covenants in the priestly writings: the sabbath (Exod 31:16), the priestly emoluments (Num 18:19), the hereditary privilege of a priestly family (Num 25:13). It does not signify that the "covenant of peace" is the great link between God and Israel, thus repeating in different terms the purport of 16:59, 62. Our passage (with 20:37) contains the only references in the book to the great eschatological covenant using the term *b^{e}rit* (the other references use the double adoption/marriage formula, 11:20; 14:11 etc.); its use of *hqym*, taken with its explicit reference to the ancient covenant, suggests that (whether or not a continuation of it) the eschatological covenant will reaffirm the ancient one. Nothing in this passage indicates a hand other than Ezekiel's.

Critics generally regard B and C as subsequent accretions to the core prophecy in A. The setting of A is clearly pre-fall; the punishment of the city is still to come (= chap. 23). In B, however, the punishment has occurred; the three sisters are compared as being on an equal footing of political dissolution remediable only by a future act of God. Since the implied setting is post-fall, critics suppose that to be the time of composition as well. In C, the mere restoration of Jerusalem (predicted in B) is superseded by its hegemony over its sisters; this (argue the critics) is an even later addition, comparable to the latest prophecies of consolation (e.g., 37:4).

Rhetorical and psychological considerations are advanced in support of the accretional view of the chapter. Would a single creative moment contain so extreme a shift in mood from the furious denunciation of A to the serene reconciliation of C? Furthermore, would not the consolatory aspects of B and C defeat the purpose of the arraignment? From the doom-prophet's viewpoint, the unregenerate audience does not deserve to be comforted; comfort pertains to a broken-hearted, despairing post-fall audience. The analogous sequence of ruthless threats of doom and assurance of God's reconciliation with contrite survivors in Deut 28-30 and (even more closely affinite to Ezekiel) in Lev 26 is no effective check to this reasoning, which simply nullifies this counter-evidence by subjecting it to the same disintegrating analysis (e.g., Eissfeldt, *Introduction*, 237f. on Lev 26:40-45; von Rad, *Deuteronomy*, 183, on Deut 30). The possibility that prophetic (and Torah) covenant theology could not regard the destruction of Israel as YHWH's final word; or that the reversal in mood reflected a catharsis induced by giving voice and vent to rage, allowing the underlying permanent bond of YHWH with Israel to reassert itself; that accordingly there may be a parallel here to the familiar prayer phenomenon of the metamorphosis of anguished lament into serene confidence (Heiler, *Prayer*, 260ff.)—these possibilities await exploration as alternatives to the literary-historical explanation of the sequence of thoughts in our chapter and analogues.

We need not await a decision in this matter in order to appreciate, finally, the unifying function of two alternating themes that converge climactically in the coda: original or secondary, the sense of a single grand movement from start to finish of this long oracle owes much to its permeation by these two themes.

From the latter phases of the oracle it emerges that the terrible arraignment of the wanton aims beyond her sentencing to her reformation; she must come to realize her guilt. "In every criminal trial, the primary object is to elicit a confession of guilt from the culprit. Confession is the best guarantee that the sentence fits the offender, and that the court has not committed a miscarriage of justice" (H. J. Boecker, *Redeformen des Rechtslebens* [1964] 111). For this, two faculties the wanton abnormally lacks must be generated in her: memory and shame. By following the themes of *zākar* "remember" and *bwš / klm* "shame" we may trace the wanton's progress.

Israel's duty always to remember YHWH's redemptive and sustaining deeds (particularly in her prosperity) as the chief motive of obedience to his commandments is a Deuteronomic commonplace (5:15; 8:2-18; 15:15; 16:12; 24:18, 22; 32:7). The priestly writings, on the other hand, extol YHWH's remembrance of his covenant as a feature of his trustiness (Gen 9:15f.; Exod 2:24; 6:5). Especially germane is the epilogue to the covenant curses in Lev 26:42ff. At the sight of the remnant of penitent exiles

> Then I will remember my covenant with Jacob; I will remember also my covenant with Isaac, and also my covenant with Abraham. . . Yes even then when they are in the land of their enemies I will not spurn or reject them so as to destroy them, violating my covenant with them; for I YHWH am their God. I will remember in their favor the covenant with the ancients, whom I freed from the land of Egypt in the sight of the nations to be their God, I YHWH.

Our oracle contrasts human dereliction toward and divine fulfillment of this duty. Wanton Jerusalem did not, in her willfulness, remember her lowly beginnings and all that she owed to God (vv 22, 43), for which she paid the ultimate penalty. But YHWH will remember the "covenant of her youth" (60) and restore the prodigal to a glory greater than her former state. The effect will be to awaken in her a memory of her former abominable behavior, and she will be ashamed.

Jeremiah preceded Ezekiel in deploring the shamelessness of the Judahites; they have "the face (lit. forehead) of a harlot; they will not feel disgrace" (3:3; cf. 6:15; 8:12). The characteristic phrase of confession Jeremiah puts into the mouth of the contrite people is "We feel shame and disgrace" (3:25; 31:19). In the arraignment division of our oracle (A), the shamelessness of the wanton is too amply displayed to need explicit mention; the Philistines' "shame" at her conduct highlights her lack of it (v 27). In B, however, the wanton is repeatedly summoned to feel shame in a situation designed to elicit it even in her: she is unfavorably compared with her siblings, especially to "sister" Sodom, toward whom she had always felt superior. Sibling rivalry gives occasion for her first experience of shame—really humiliation over having made her disdained sisters look righteous by comparison with her. This prepares an organ within her which, in her final stage of restoration, can respond to God's undeserved favor with penitential shame over all her past offenses.

This theme is related to the self-loathing predicted in 6:9. In 36:31f. shame and self-loathing are combined; thereafter only shame and disgrace occur (39:21; 43:10; 44:13). Their appearance in Jeremiah's formulas of confession accounts for their presence in Ezekiel's restoration prohecies: shame and disgrace over the past bespeak the new, impressionable, contrite heart that will animate the future Israel.

With the awakening of wanton Jerusalem's memory of her wicked past and her brokenhearted shame over it foretold in the coda, the purpose and end of the condemnation with which at the start of the oracle the prophet was charged, has been achieved.

SMITTEN BY FAMINE, BATTERED BY PLAGUE (DEUTERONOMY 32:24)

JONAS C. GREENFIELD

Marvin Pope has had occasion to deal with the god Resheph in his commentaries to both *Job* and *Song of Songs*. In the passage from the *Song of Songs* which Pope used in the dedication of his commentary, the word *rešef* in the meaning of "dart" or "spark" occurs (8:6).[1] This slight contribution in his honor will deal with part of another passage (Deut 32:24) in which the same term occurs: *mĕzē raᶜab ūlḥūmē rešef.* If one examines the recent literature on the Song of Moses it becomes clear that the text under consideration has not been the object of serious conjectural emendation.[2] The ancient versions reflect the text as it has come down to us in the Masoretic Text, and what has been published to-date from Qumran also attests to it.[3] Thus the Septuagint's τεκόμενοι λιμῷ καὶ βρώσει ὀρνέων "destroyed (lit. desolved) by famine and the eating of birds" has long since been explained by associating Hebrew *mzh* with either *msh* or *mss*, meaning "to melt," while *lĕḥūmē* was obviously taken from *lḥm* "to eat" and *rešef* was considered a collective noun and explained as "birds."[4] This understanding of *rešef* may have been traditional, but more plausibly, was based on the interpretation of Job 5:7: *bĕnē rešef yagbīhū ᶜūf*. The interpretation of *rešef* as birds is clearly stated in the Midrash, where the word *rĕšāfīm* of Ps 78:40 is interpreted as *ᶜōfōt* "fowl," citing Job 5:7 as the proof text (*Exodus Rabba*, s. 12).

The Targum's *nĕfīḥē kĕfan waᵓăkīlē ᶜūf* "bloated by famine and eaten by birds" is derived by associating *mĕzē* with Aramaic *lĕmēzēᵓ* "to blow up a fire" (cf. Dan 3:19) but the rest of the text is interpreted in the same manner as the Septuagint.[5] The same may be said for the Vulgate's *"consumentur fame et devorabunt eos aves."* It is only the Peshitta which seems to present a different text: *wĕneṭṭarfūn bĕkafnā wĕneštalmān lĕhōn rūḥē bīšāṭā walṭayrā ᵓašlem ᵓenōn*. This is in all likelihood an expansion of an Aramaic text similar to the Targum's.[6] The translation *ṭayrā* "bird" for *rešef* follows the interpretation noted above. This is to be found elsewhere in the Peshitta's rendition of *rešef*.[7] The traditional reading of the Samaritan text basically reflects the same text.[8]

The role of Resheph as the Canaanite god of Pestilence, now familiar to us from a variety of sources, was naturally unknown to the ancients; and they could not draw any insights as to the nature of that god, or from that of the gods with which he was assimilated such as Apollo on Cyprus or at an earlier period Nergal at Ugarit.[9] Modern translators have departed only partially from the ancients. If we examine four modern English translations of this part of the verse under consideration we find essentially the same translation for *mĕzē raᶜab* (except for *NEB* whose translations, although eloquent, are frequently based on fantastic philology).[10] It is in the understanding of *rešef* that they part company:

"wasted with hunger and devoured with burning heat"	(RSV)
"emaciating hunger and consuming fever"	(NAB)
"wasting famine, ravaging plague"	(NJPS)
"pangs of hunger, ravages of plague"	(NEB).

1 M. Pope, *Job* (3rd ed., AB; New York, 1973): 42-43; *Song of Songs* (AB 7c; New York, 1977): 670.

2 The most comprehensive discussion of this passage may be found in S. Carillo Alday, *El Cantico de Moses (Dt 32)* (Madrid, 1970): 20-21. E. Henschke in *ZAW* 52 (1934): 281 proposed reading *mĕṭē* for *mĕzē*. On the other hand, *mĕzē* is often proposed for the *mĕtē raᶜab* of Isa 5:13.

3 D. Barthélemy, J. T. Milik, *Discoveries in the Judaean Desert* I, p. 60.

4 See S. R. Driver, *Deuteronomy* (ICC; Edinburgh, 1902): 367.

5 The other Targums present expanded versions of this translation, cf. *Pseudo-Jonathan* (D. Rieder, ed.; Jerusalem, 1974): 303. Thus by adding *lĕmazzīqē* "for the demons" before *ᵓakīlē ᶜūf* reference is made to the interpretation of this verse in *BT Berakhot* 5a.

6 The treatment of this verse by A. Vööbus, *Peschitta und Targumim des Pentateuch* (Stockholm, 1958): 75-76 is not satisfactory.

7 The Peshitta to Hab 3:5 and Job 5:7 also translates *rešef* as *ṭayrā*. Interestingly enough the traditional Targum to Job 5:7 translates *bĕnē rešef* as *bĕnē mazzīqē* reflecting the tradition noted above.

8 The Samaritan text reads *lḥmw* rather than *lḥmy* and this is read *lĕmu*, cf. Z. Ben-Hayyim, *The Literary and Oral Tradition of Hebrew and Aramaic amongst the Samaritans* III,1 (Jerusalem, 1961): 159. The initial word *mzy* is read *mizzē* and this is reflected in the Samaritan Targum: *mdn kpnh lḥmh ršpw; mizzē* was taken as "from this." Cf. *The Samaritan Targum of the Pentateuch* II (A. Tal, ed.; Tel Aviv, 1981): 390.

9 For Resheph, cf. D. Conrad, "Der Gott Reschef," *ZAW* 83 (1971): 157-83; and W. Fulco, *The Canaanite God Rešep* (American Oriental Series Essay 8; New Haven, 1976). Fulco treats the biblical passages on pp. 56-62.

10 The *Jerusalem Bible* following the *Bible de Jérusalem*, strays from the Masoretic Text.

Thus the *RSV* and *NAB* take *rešef* as "burning heat" or "fever" based it would seem on the "root" meaning of *ršp*, "flames, sparks."[11] But *NJPS* and *NEB* are cognizant of Resheph as the plague and pestilence deity and have translated accordingly.[12] Indeed, it has been proposed that Resheph, along with Dever and Qeṭeb, were the names of demons feared by the Israelites.[13] Others have even been tempted to see in *raᶜab*, the personification of hunger.[14]

This writer has been hesitant for some time as to the correctness of the meaning attributed to *mĕzē* and *lĕḥūmē* by both ancients and moderns. The basis for taking *mĕzē raᶜab* as "wasted, emaciated" on the basis of the putative *mzh* "to suck out" seems very doubtful. The correct meaning was hinted at by the third edition of the Baumgartner *Lexikon*, when the Akkadian *mazāʾu/mazû* was listed among the etymologies. But their interpretation "entkräftet," following the traditional German translation, does not fit this derivation.[15] As a perusal of the usages of this verb in the *CAD* (M/1, 439-40) will show, the G-stem of the verb is used for an action in the making of beer, which the *CAD* translates as "to squeeze," while the D-stem means "to rape." One may assume that it is the pressing and the beating of the grain, on the one hand, and the pressure put on the woman, on the other, that is common to the two usages. This insight may also help us to explain the name of the demon mentioned in the first line of the second Arslan Tash incantation—*MZH*.[16] Some have associated it with the *mĕzē* of our verse and seen in it the name of a blood-sucking demon.[17] It may best be seen as a general name for a demon such as "smiter, beater."[18]

The same reservations hold true for the translations offered for *lĕḥūmē rešef*. If *lĕḥūmē* is derived from *lḥm* "to eat"—an interpretation shared by ancients and moderns alike—and then translated "consumed," "ravaged" by fever or by plague, a semantic development proper to European languages has been imposed on this root, not necessarily proper to the more concrete Semitic usage. In addition, as far as biblical Hebrew is concerned, the verb *lḥm* "to eat" is limited almost exclusively to Proverbs.[19] Understanding *lĕḥūmē* as "eaten" does not fit the nature of Resheph as it emerges from the texts, from the epithets with which the divine name is associated, or with the iconography of Resheph as known from Egyptian sources.[20] Therefore the suggestion made some years ago that *lĕḥūmē* be translated "combattus" seems appropriate to me.[21] I would go one step further and propose that the more basic, concrete etymological meaning of *lḥm* "battered" rather than "battled" be applied in this verse.[22] This would fit both the needs of the verse, if the interpretation of *mĕzē* is correct, and also the nature of Resheph as a combative deity.[23]

---

11 This was already the translation of Saᶜadya Gaon who offered *al-wahj* for *rešef*.

12 The recent French "Traduction oecumenique de la Bible" offers both "foudre" and "fièvre" for *rešef*.

13 So A. Caquot, "Sur quelques démons de l'Ancien Testament," *Semitica* 6 (1956): 58-59.

14 See R. Gordis, *JAOS* 63 (1943): 177-78. N. J. Tromp in *Primitive Conceptions of Death and the Netherworld in the Old Testament* (Rome, 1969): 107-08 has even conceived a *Raᶜeb* "the Hungry One."

15 W. Baumgartner et al., *Hebräisches und aramäisches Lexikon*, Lieferung II, (Leiden, 1974): 535. My interpretation for this verse on the basis of Akkadian *mazû* stems from 1955, after reading B. Landsberger's discussion of the verb *mazû* in the Irishum inscription, *Belleten* 14 (1950): 219-68. [For the possible occurrence of the root *mzh* in a Hebrew inscription from Lachish, see A. Lemaire, *Tel Aviv* 7 (1980): 92-94.]

16 For this inscription, cf. A. Caquot and M. du Mesnil du Buisson, *Syria* 48 (1971): 391-406; T. H. Gaster, *BASOR* 209 (1973): 18-26; F. M. Cross, *CBQ* 36 (1974): 486-90; E. Lipiński, *RSF* 2 (1974): 50-54.

17 So Gaster; cf. note 16, above.

18 Thus the verb *maḫāṣu* is used for gods, demons and diseases striking a person, cf. *CAD* M/1, 75-76.

19 I believe that a good case can be made that *ubal-ʾelḥam* of Ps 141:4 should not be translated "and I will not eat." As is well known the book of Proverbs has a lexicon of its own.

20 The epithets and iconography of Resheph are discussed by Fulco (see above, n. 9).

21 It must be admitted that Nergal is frequently described as "eating," i.e., ᵈ*Nergal māta ikkal*, cf. K. K. Riemschneider, *Babylonische Geburtsomina in Hethitischer Übersetzung* (SBoT 9, 1970): 45-48; E. von Weiher, *Der babylonische Gott Nergal* (AOAT 11; Neukirchen, 1971): 85. But in these passages from omina Nergal seems to be assimilated to Erra. For this function of Erra, cf. J. J. M. Roberts, *The Earliest Semitic Pantheon* (Baltimore, 1972): 21-29.

22 It would also not be amiss to note that *laḫāmu* B (cf. *CAD* L, 38) is also used for making beer.

23 My colleague M. Weinfeld reminds me that along with the association of arrows with Resheph, the phrase *ḥiṣṣē ha-raᶜab* is known to us from Ezek 5, 16; cf. M. Weinfeld, *Eretz-Israel* 14 (1978): 26-27. Weinfeld discusses, *inter alia*, various passages mentioning Resheph in a broader Near Eastern background.

THE DOOR OF LOVE

R. LANSING HICKS

In spite of its apparent simplicity, The Song of Songs has proved from the earliest times to be an unusually complex book to expound. As a guide to the composition itself as well as to the rich and variegated world it mirrors and to the extraordinary range of interpretation it has received, no volume past or present can equal Marvin Pope's commentary in The Anchor Bible series.[1] It is unlikely that any of us will see this work surpassed in the future.

As is also the case with the book of Job, some of the difficulties in Canticles which most resist solution arise from the presence of rare or obscure words. In this area particularly, towering above all others, Pope's contributions to the elucidation of philological and linguistic problems which have troubled readers of both of these beautiful, beloved books will stand as permanent tributes to his scholarship. From his vast knowledge of Near Eastern languages and cultures, Professor Pope has greatly illumined our understanding of many abstruse terms and enigmatic expressions in Job and Canticles.[2]

Another set of difficulties, however, and one especially characteristic of The Song of Songs, arises not from the presence of rare words but from uncertainty over the author's use of terms which in themselves are quite common and well-known but which carry a variety of meanings. Such doubt not only generates but also often compounds our confusion over the proper interpretation of the passage at hand.

Canticles 8:9 offers a notable example of this second type. The Hebrew text of the verse reads plainly enough:

> *ʾim-ḥômāʰ hîʾ nibneʰ ʿālêhā ṭîrat kāsep*
> *wᵉʾim-delet hîʾ nāṣûr ʿālêhā lûᵃḥ ʾārez*

Nevertheless, both it and the small unit to which it belongs (vv. 8–10) are widely acknowledged to be among the darkest in the entire book.[3] Although *ṭîrāʰ* and *nāṣûr* have been the focus of considerable comment, they can hardly be classified as obscure terms.[4] The nouns *ḥômāʰ* and *lûᵃḥ* and the other verb, *bānāʰ*, certainly fall into the standard vocabulary of classical Hebrew and could not support any claim to lexicographical peculiarity. The same must be said of *delet*, for each of the word's usual significations—door, gate, board, tablet, column of writing—points to a simple, easily perceived object. Notwithstanding its lapidary simplicity of meaning, the role of *delet* in this verse has occasioned a protracted debate.

Virtually all commentators agree that as used here in reference to the maiden, *delet* represents 'the door of love.' In Near Eastern literature the metaphorical use of architectural openings for bodily orifices is well-attested. Thus, in his catalogue of afflictions which evil spirits have visited upon him, the righteous sufferer of *Ludlul Bēl Nēmeqi* complains that "A snare is laid on my mouth / And a bolt bars my lips. / My 'gate' is barred, my 'drinking place' blocked."[5] Even closer to Cant 8:9 is the Akkadian expression, "you anoint her navel and the opening [doorway] of her vagina."[6] Both of these citations happen to use KÁ / *bābu* instead of GIŠ.IG / *daltu*, but as figurative expressions they employ the same imagery as our verse.

Most commentators and modern English Versions agree here in accepting *delet* as 'door.' There is no problem of translation. The debate about the term appears at the point of interpretation. Concerning the meaning of v. 9 and consequently the significance of the picturesque couplet in the interpretation of the larger unit, *delet* occupies an axial position. In reference to the structure of the unit, *delet* is associated with *ḥômāʰ* in 9a; and in reference to the exposition of the unit, with *lûᵃḥ* in 9b. Although both pairings are important, neither enjoys a consensus among scholars as to its intended use. Accordingly, this essay will focus principally on the relationship of these two sets.

DELET AND ḤÔMĀʰ

There is first the relation of *delet* to *ḥômāʰ*. Here the question of literary symmetry is raised. Structurally the two stand in a formal parallelism. But is there a complete parallelism of members and does the construction convey synonymous or antithetical concepts? Is the 'door' of v 9b

---

1 Marvin H. Pope, *Song of Songs: A New Translation with Introduction and Commentary* (Garden City, 1977).

2 See also Marvin H. Pope, *Job: Introduction, Translation, and Notes* (3rd. ed.; Garden City, 1973).

3 So, e.g., Helmer Ringgren, *Das Hohe Lied* (*Das Alte Testament Deutsch* 62/2; Göttingen, 1958): 35.

4 Considering the high level of poetic, semantic, and structural artistry in Canticles, it is quite possible that the author is here playing on the similarity of the roots *ṭûr* and *ṣûr*.

5 "*. . . ba-bi e-di-il pi-ḫi maš-qu-u-a*," W. G. Lambert, *Babylonian Wisdom Literature* (Oxford, 1960): 42f.

6 "*abunnassa* KÁ *uriša tapaššaš* (*CAD* B, p. 24b).

to be viewed as open or closed?[7] That is, does the juxtaposition of these two terms express the brothers' confidence that their little sister will remain chaste, as impregnable as a wall, so that they need only give her moral support or does it betray their concern that she could be successfully assaulted[8] before marriage so that they need to protect her by their own measures? The meaning of the MT itself on this issue has always appeared ambiguous, as a survey of translations—ancient and modern—makes clear.

In addition to this problem, both the question of the unity of these verses and the identification of the speakers are much disputed. Concerning the integrity of vv. 8, 9, and 10, Father Krinetzki, for example, argues quite appealingly that they constitute a unity which exhibits a triple parallel structure in an a,b,c / c',a',b' pattern.[9] The weakness of this otherwise attractive schema is that the correspondence between b and b' must be sought in the concepts behind the words whereas the parallelism of the other two sets is found in the words themselves. Nevertheless, he has shown that the unit has formal, structural integrity. Others have focussed upon the thematic unity which not only binds these verses together but also associates them more closely to the following couplet, vv. 11–12, than is indicated by the usual designation of these blocs as "two appendices."

Concerning the question of who is speaking, nearly every possible combination of the *dramatis personae* has been proposed. Some commentators even assign this couplet to the chorus of women heard earlier at 1:8; 3:6–11; 5:9; 6:1; 7 :1; and 8:5a.[10] But since the verbs in vv. 8 and 9 use the first person plural, Gordis, along with Tur-Sinai, assigns both verses to the suitors.[11] To me, this seems an awkward and improbable reading because the line which Gordis renders as "on this day [sic] when she is being spoken for" would not only make the suitors both the speakers and those to whom the question is addressed but it requires further that v. 9 be read as their massive efforts to break down the defenses of a maiden who, by their own admission in v. 8, either appears physically undesirable or is too young for marriage. With the majority of commentators, however, I attribute both verses to the brothers. Whether they speak antiphonally or in concert and whether their words are seen as a direct quote from that time or as being remembered later by the sister is immaterial.

Support for the position that vv. 9a and 9b are synonymous and therefore that both images represent the damsel as unassailable, is marshalled by some commentators by citing Ezek 46:23 where *ṭîrā^h^* stands as a synonym for *ḥômā^h^*; by others, more strongly, by citing Ezek 38:11 where *ḥômā^h^* is parallel to *delet*.[12] Or, from another point within the verse, additional support for this affirmative view seems to be supplied by such renderings of *nāṣûr ʿālêhā* as "we will reinforce it [the door]."[13] That the two lines are completely parallel, not only with *delet* being synonymous with *ḥômā^h^* but also *lû^a^ḥ ʾārez* with *ṭîrat kesep*, is championed by Robert. After lengthy arguments he states categorically, "It is therefore not permitted, as is so commonly done, to see a contrast between the two parts of the verse, the wall arresting the assault of the lovers, the door inviting them to enter."[14]

For the latter position, that the parallelism is antithetical, support is indicated, first of all, by translating *w^e^ʾim* with an adversative force, "but if . . . "[15] Here a concept opposite from 'wall' is implied and thus the virtue of the damsel is viewed by the brothers as uncertain. This position is also substantiated by those Versions which render the clause in v. 9b by "we will enclose her" (*KJV, ASV, JPSV, RSV*), "secure her" (*The Complete Bible*), or "close it [the door] up" (*NEB*). This negative view is conveyed quite pictorially in *The Jerusalem Bible* by "we will board her up." *The Good News Bible* expresses the adversative sense of the parallel member even more forcefully by rendering, "But if she is a gate, we will protect her with panels of cedar." But of all the English Versions consulted, Moffatt's[16] moves farthest from translation to interpretation: "If she holds out like a wall, we will adorn her with silver for dowry; if she gives way to lovers like a door, then we will plank her

---

7 With characteristic perception, Pope states clearly that "the exegesis of this verse is divided by the door . . ." (*Song of Songs* [N 1]: 680).

8 Numerous commentators lay heavy stress on the military overtones which can be heard in most of the key terms in vv. 8–10, including even the final embattled phrase *k^e^môṣ^e^ʾēt šālôm*.

9 a = 8a ("no breasts"), b = 8b ("what shall *we* do?"), c = 9 ("she is a wall"); c' = 10aα ("I was a wall"), a' = 10aβ ("my breasts"), b' = 10 ("then *I* was"). b and b' form a contrast expressing irony on the girl's part: "you do not have to *do* anything; I have already done it myself and (now) surrendered myself to my lover." Leo Krinetzki, *Das Hohe Lied: Kommentar zu Gestalt und Kerygma eines alttestamentlichen Liebesliedes* (Düsseldorf, 1964): 248–51.

10 So T. J. Meek, *The Interpreter's Bible* 5 (New York, 1956): 144f.

11 Robert Gordis, *The Song of Songs: A Study, Modern Translation, and Commentary* (New York, 1954): 75.

12 Gordis, p. 97. Against Gordis's argument, however, I suggest that in Ezek 38:11 the two terms are more properly seen as antithetical, for the verse depicts open villages which have neither "walls" nor "barred gates" (taking *b^e^rîah ûd^e^lātayim* as a case of hendiadys). The fact that gates have to be barred indicates that, in contrast to walls, they are used primarily for access.

13 So the *NAB*.

14 A. Robert and R. Tournay, *Le Cantique des Cantiques* (Paris, 1963): 311.

15 So the *RSV, NEB, The Complete Bible, The Good News Bible*, and *The New American Standard Bible*.

16 James Moffatt, *The Bible: A New Translation* (New York, 1954).

up." Presumably, however, the "planking up" will take place too late to save the girl's virginity!

The concept 'door' cannot reasonably be predicated as synonymous with 'wall' regardless of the specific terms chosen to convey them. To be sure, walls can be breached and walled enclosures are not impregnable. But they *must* be breached, for they are intended without qualification to be solid and to protect what is behind them. Doors, however, are by definition movable. Normally they are set in frames, consist of swinging leaves, and are accompanied by hinges, sockets, grooves, or pivots. That is, they are built to be opened.[17] Robert may be correct in observing, as have others, that *delet* is formally distinguished from *petaḥ*.[18] But he is wrong in concluding on this basis that "*delet* may not, then, as is usually thought, here represent a person who is easy to seduce" and that the "idea is, on the contrary, that of an obstacle and of protection . . . ."[19] One would not expect *petaḥ* to be used here because, even metaphorically, it is inappropriate for a *virgo intacta*. The choice of *delet* was proper, for in contrast to *petaḥ* it is an ambivalent term; it can support either of two opposite interpretations—'opened' or 'closed'—but it does not mandate the one to the exclusion of the other. Since the essence of the concept of 'door' is that by design it is at least capable of being opened, it does not seem a logical reading of v. 9 to construe 'door' as equivalent to 'wall.'

But how is *ṭîrat kesep* to be understood in this unit? There is, of course, adequate justification for regarding it, as some insist, chiefly as an additional defense measure. So viewed, *ṭîrā^h* could indicate the row of turrets which crowned Palestinian public buildings and especially city walls.[20] But two considerations militate against that choice. First, it does not comport well with the clear meaning of 'wall.' The standard interpretation of v. 9a starts with the assumption that the sister will solidly resist all assaults. Further fortification is unnecessary. Second, in contrast to iron or bronze, silver would be chosen for its beauty, not for strength.[21] But for purposes of decoration and display, a silver turret would be a logical addition.[22] And in biblical Hebrew the root *ṭûr* is indeed associated with ornamentation and decoration.[23]

Both 'silver turret' and its opposite member in 9b, 'cedar board,' are legitimate figures for beauty and strength. Both would entail on the part of the brothers a considerable expenditure, whether for defense or display.[24] I suggest that *ṭîrat kesep* portrays here a picture of lavish decoration, whereas in the contrasting line *lû^{a}ḥ ʾārez* conveys primarily the idea of strength.

DELET AND *LÛ^{A}Ḥ*

In the second line of v. 9, *delet* is associated with *lû^{a}ḥ*. Accordingly, each of these two terms is important for an understanding of this parallel construction. But further, since this is the only sentence in the Masoretic Text where the two words appear together, their relationship to each other can prove instructive in several areas.

Whether in this verse *delet* is construed as simply the door to a private house or as the door of a city gate, it does not in either case logically support the claim that it is a synonym for *ḥômā^h*. Pre-eminently the door of a house (*delet habbayit*)[25] is meant to afford access or egress, just as its windows fenestrate the otherwise solid walls to permit light and air to enter. In the case where the doors have been set within the larger gates of a city (*daltôt haššᵉʿārîm*, 1 Chr 22:3, or *daltôt šaʿar hāʿîr*, Jud 16:3),[26] the argument is equally as strong. It is reasonable to regard the gates themselves as normally closed, protecting and minimizing the necessary aperture. But the only reason for including a door within the gate complex is to facilitate traffic. Certainly in Cant 8:9 the brothers are concerned that there be no 'trafficking' with their sister until she is married.

The picture created by this verse conforms quite accurately to what is known about wooden doors and door panels in the ancient Near East. Although at the poorer levels of society mats of reed or cane might have been

17 See the expression "to set (*heʿĕmîd*) a door" in Neh 3:3 and the various references to *mᵉzûzā^h* in the Old Testament. For a detailed linguistic and technical study of doors, gates, and their appurtances in the ancient Near East, see Armas Salonen, *Die Türen des alten Mesopotamien* (Helsinki, 1961), especially Part II for doors and their parts, and Part III for construction materials. See also *daltu* in *CAD*, D, p. 55b, especially § g.

18 Though it is usually asserted that *petaḥ* never means 'door,' the phrase *mᵉzûzôt pᵉtāḥāy* at Prov 8:34 stands in synonymous parallelism with *daltôtāy*. Consult the various English Bible translations of this pair.

19 Robert, *Cantique* (N 14): 310.

20 See the turretted towers on Assyrian reliefs which depict assaults on various Phoenician, Israelite, and Philistine cities (Pauline Albanda, "Syrian-Palestinian Cities on Stone," *BA* 43 [1980]: 222–29).

21 See below, p. 157 and notes 41, 42.

22 As decoration on cultic buildings, see the kind of crenellated copings reconstructed for the Temple of Solomon by Th. A. Busink (*BA* 41 [1978]: front cover and p. 50).

23 Brown, Driver, Briggs, *Hebrew Lexicon*, p. 377a.

24 A recent study of Ugaritic commercial records yielded the following ratios for the value of gold, silver, and copper in Phoenicia at the beginning of the Late Bronze Age—1:4:800 (R. R. Stieglitz, "Commodity Prices at Ugarit," *JAOS* 99 [1979]: 15).

25 Cf. Akkad. *dalat bīti*. Frequently the Hebrew form occurs in the plural, either as masculine *daltê bîtî*, Jud 11:31, or more commonly as feminine *daltôt habbayit*, Jud 19:27. But, as Jud 3:25 makes clear, the plural usage most often implies the door leaves of a single opening, not a number of individual doors.

26 Cf. Akkad. *dalat bābi* or, designating segments of the greater outer gates, *dalat bāb kamī* and *dalat bāb rabī*.

used for doors,[27] at the level implied by Canticles wood was the material of choice. In Akkadian records almost a dozen different woods employed in the construction of doors have been identified[28] and more than half a dozen others appear which are either subspecies of the principal types or whose species have not yet been satisfactorily determined. Of this wide selection cedar emerges as one of the preferred materials.

Lebanese cedar was beautiful and costly. Both of these qualities would be obvious even from Old Testament allusions alone; see, for example, Isa 9:9 and the apparently proverbial status of such passages as 1 Kgs 10:27 (so 2 Chr 9:27; but cf. 1:15, and see also 1 Kgs 10:21 = 2 Chr 9:20). Fortunately we have other data concerning the price of Phoenician lumber. In his study of Ugaritic texts, Stieglitz computed the relative costs of three different woods: *šmn*, which he identifies as an "oil tree" and renders with "pine"; *tišr*, fir or sherbin; and *dprn*, juniper, which appears to be far more expensive than the other two.[29] Elsewhere he argues that *tišr*, which is cognate with Hebrew *tᵉʾaššûr*, is "a type of cedar wood."[30] Unfortunately neither the identification of *tᵉʾaššûr* nor the precise classification of certain other woods is clear from the various Near Eastern texts. Brown, Driver, Briggs give "box-tree" for *tᵉʾaššûr* but add that others prefer "*sherbîn*, a species of cedar," while Köhler-Baumgartner argue that it probably denotes cypress wood. However, since true firs and cedars belong to the same division, class, order, and family (Pinophyta, Pinopsida, Coniferales, Pinaceae), it is possible that we do find here an indication of the commercial value of Phoenician cedar, at least in the period about 1500 B.C.E. The high value set on cedar wood is also attested by Egyptian as well as by Mesopotamian records. The purchase of cedar timbers for Amon-Re's ceremonial barque was the principal purpose of Wen-Amon's trip to Phoenicia; and Tiglath-Pileser I's boast, "I went to the Lebanon. I cut (there) timber of cedars for the temple of Anu and Adad, the great gods, my lords, and carried (them to Ashur)"[31] is a typical feature of Assyrian and Babylonian campaign records.

In this connection, we may observe that by mentioning cedar boards at 8:9, as also by the reference in 5:15, Canticles strengthens its association with Solomon, for the use of cedar for beams, rafters, and, most of all, panelling is a dominant and recurring note in accounts which describe the construction of his Temple.[32]

In reference to the expression "cedar boards" in v. 9b, it is possible that the use of *lûᵃḥ* reflects some external procedure for reinforcing the door—for example, immobilizing it by fastening wooden planks over it and thus 'boarding it up.'[33] In texts mentioning doors and gates in the ancient Near East there is adequate reference to bars and bolts and horizontal struts to allow such an interpretation.[34] But it is much more probable that here *lûᵃḥ* reflects a method of strengthening which is more intrinsic to the door. In fact, on the basis of considerable evidence we may posit that the relation between *delet* and *lûᵃḥ* is closer than that suggested above and signifies a structural reinforcement of the door itself.

In Mesopotamia doors were sometimes strengthened by the addition of metal framing or sheathing. Asshurnaṣirpal II, for instance, records that he "mounted the cedarwood doors in copper sheathings and hung them in its (the palace's) doorways."[35] In this same vein, it would

27 At least, such was the custom in Mesopotamia where there are references to *dalat ḫurdi* (Salonen, *Türen* [N 17]: 101 and also Pls. II.3 and IV.2) and *dalat kišši*, "the door of plaited reeds" (*CAD* D, p. 54b). Goetze reported in detail on the vocabulary and formal structure of previously unpublished texts dealing with reed mats (A. Goetze, "Umma Texts Concerning Reed Mats," *JCS* 2 [1948]: 165–202). Although his study was restricted to the subject of boats, their construction, cargoes, and shipping data, Salonen asserts that generally the pertinent physical data can also supply information about the use of reed mats in the construction of doors. In Old Babylonian *kubusu* signifies a reed that was specially treated for making doors (*dalat kubusi*) and baskets (*CAD* K, p. 490b).

28 Salonen gives specific classifications and the literary sources for boxwood, cedar, cypress, fir, juniper, mulberry, oak, sisso, tamarisk, and willow (*Türen* [N 17]: 96–100). In the short notice at 1 Kgs 6:31–36 which refers to doors and beams used in the Temple, the Masoretic Text mentions *ʿăṣê-šemen*, *ʾărāzîm*, and *ʿăṣê-bᵉrôšîm*. Most English Versions translate the first two with 'olive' and 'cedar' respectively. But considerable disagreement exists concerning the identification of *bᵉrôš*, which has been variously rendered by 'cypress,' 'fir,' 'pine,' and 'juniper.' Since it is cognate with Akk. *burāšu*, it is probably best taken as designating the Phoenician juniper.

29 Stieglitz, "Commodity Prices" (N 24): 17.

30 R. R. Stieglitz, "An Unrecognized Meaning of Ugaritic ŠMN," *JNES* 29 (1970): 56.

31 Pritchard, *ANET*, p. 275a.

32 The individual passages are too numerous to list, but perhaps the late notice in 2 Sam 7:7 preserves for us the single, most lasting impression made on the people when it calls the Temple simply *bêt ʾărāzîm*.

33 So, in fact, *The Jerusalem Bible*. See above.

34 As examples, from *mēdelu/mēdilu* (GIŠ.ŠU.DIŠ) in *CAD* M/2 pp. 2b–3a, *šunu daltú ul ikallūšunūti mēdilu ul utár[šu]nūti*: "The door does not hinder them, the bar does not turn them back; or from *edēlu*, "to lock/bolt a door," in *CAD* E, p. 26b, *Šamaš ina qibītika... edlu ippettû petû in-ni-dil*: "Upon your order, O Šamaš, what is locked [barred/bolted] opens, what is opened becomes locked." For representative Old Testament usage, from early and late periods, see Jud 16:3 (Samson pulled up the doors of the city's gate and its two posts, "bar and all") and Neh 3:3 (in building the Fish Gate, the sons of Hassenaah "laid its beams and set its doors, its bolts, and its bars").

35 *dalāte erēni... ina mēsir siparri urakkis ina* KÁ.MEŠ-*ša* [*bābuša*] *urette* (*CAD* B, p. 16b).

be possible to envisage bracing the wooden crossbars which constitute the outer structure of the door, the *bardû ša dalti.*[36] Possibly the *dalat parzilli*, "iron (reinforced) door," occurring in the annals of Nabonidus,[37] reflects this or a similar technique.

But more commonly doors and door leaves[38] were fortified by covering the existing panels, or replacing them, with stronger materials. At this stage we approximate the technical meaning of *lûªḥ* in Cant 8:9. Although all the translations and commentaries consulted render *lûªḥ* either with 'board' or 'plank'—most construing it as a collective and thus using plural terms—we suggest that 'panel' is the most appropriate choice. Metal panels, of course, would afford maximum strength, when the frame would support them, and we know that they were so used. In one of his royal inscriptions, Nebuchadnezzar II boasts, "Door leaves of cedar wood with bronze plating, sills and pivots fashioned of copper, I erected in his gates."[39] Since fire always endangers a city's defenses, metal would also afford additional security against this threat.[40] But the installation of metal panels, however desirable, presumably was restricted in Palestine by considerations of availability, cost, and perhaps weight.

As we have already seen, according to the evidence in both Palestinian and Mesopotamian literature wood was the material most frequently used in the construction of doors, and of the various species actually cited cedar stands out most prominently. The evidence further supports the conclusion that in addition to its beauty cedar was selected because of its strength. Salonen gives relevant data found in annals ranging from Old Babylonian to Neo-Babylonian times which specifically mention cedar doors (*dalat erēni*). Wooden doors, whether or not of cedar, could naturally be beautiful in their own right. Nevertheless, we know that their beauty was occasionally enhanced by precious metals. References to *dalat ḫurāṣi/kaspi* ("a door plated with gold/silver") punctuate the period from Šamši-Adad I to Nebuchadnezzar and appear also in Hittite records.[41] Some doors were decorated with silver and gold 'stars' (*kakkabāni*), some with mountings of silver and gold; some with silver plating.[42] Throughout the biblical and extra-biblical texts describing cedar wood we must always allow for an interplay between the qualities of beauty and strength. Therefore, as previously suggested, the artistic and aesthetic dimensions inherent in the choice of *lûªḥ ʾārez* should not be overlooked. Nevertheless, protection is the issue at stake in our verse. It is, thus, the sturdiness of the material that must be emphasized and here again external evidence supports the picture given by Canticles.

In the Old Testament the cedar tree was revered for its majesty: Ezek 17:23 calls it "noble" (*ʾaddîr*); Ps 80:11 styles it "mighty" (*ʾēl*); and Cant 5:15 describes the lover's appearance as "choice (*bāḥûr*) as the cedars." These Israelite descriptions have close counterparts in Mesopotamian usage. When Nebuchadnezzar II claims that he made "an easy road for the (transport of the) cedars," he calls them "high, mighty, thick cedars."[43] But the cedar was renowned also for its strength and durability. A text from the time of Nabonidus refers to "strong cedars [GIŠ.ERIN.MEŠ *paglūti*], grown in the Amanus and the Lebanon."[44] It is these qualities which predominate in Cant 8:9b and help shape our interpretation of that verse.

Finally, in Neo-Assyrian texts which contain such descriptions as *daltu ša liʾāni* (*ša erê/kaspi*), "a door with panels (of bronze/silver)," we find an expresssion which is both philologically and conceptually analogous to the relation of *delet* to *lûªḥ* in Canticles.[45] When taken with the references to GIŠ.IG.MEŠ GIŠ.ERIN/*dalāti erēni* which occur in many texts such as those previously cited, the parallel could be seen as filled out completely.

36 Salonen would add the *dappu ša dalti*, which he identifies as "the horizontal cross bar of a door" (*Türen* [N 17]: 53). Although in Mishnaic Hebrew *dap* generally designates a board, plank, or sheet of parchment, it is used also of boards which form the frame of a wine press (M. Jastrow, *A Dictionary of the Targumim* [New York, 1926]: 317a).

37 *CAD* D, p. 54b.

38 That the same term can indicate both of these items is amply attested. GIŠ.IG.MEŠ/*dalāti* is frequently translated "door leaves" (*CAD* D, p. 52b), as is also the case in the Old Testament with *dᵉlātôt*. The description of the Temple as given in 1 Kgs 6:31-34 distinguishes between the doors (*dᵉlātôt*) and its leaves (*ṣᵉlāʿîm*), but Ezek 41:23-25, which is closely patterned after the former account, uses *delet* for both aspects (*RSV*: "The doors had two leaves apiece; two swinging leaves for each door").

39 GIŠ.IG.MEŠ GIŠ.EREN *ta-aḫ-lu-up-ti* UD.KA.BAR *as-ku-up-pu u nu-ku-še-e bi-ti-iq erê e-ma* KA$_2$-*ša*$_2$ *e-er-te-et-ti* (Salonen, *Türen* [N 17]: 33).

40 Note also the relation of door to gate in this representative text: "the enemy will set fire to the door of my city gate and enter the city" (*nakru ana* GIŠ.IG *abullija išāta inaddıma ana libbi āli* TU-*ba* [*CAD* D, p. 53b]).

41 Salonen, *Türen* (N 17): 39.

42 Cf. 1 Kgs 6:31–35. Here either the panels (*dᵉlātôt*) or the leaves (*ṣᵉlāʿîm*) of the cypress doors at the entrance to the *dᵉbîr* as well as to the *hêkāl* were decorated with carved figures which were then overlaid with gold. The Chronicler's briefer description says flatly that the inners doors to the nave were gold (2 Chr 4:22).

43 GIŠ.ERIN.MEŠ *dannūti šiḫūti paglūti* (*CAD* E, p. 274).

44 *Ibid.*

45 For a detailed study of the relations between *leʾu* and *delet* in the context of writing tablets and scroll columns, see my forthcoming article, "*Delet* and *Mᵉgillāh*: A Fresh Approach to Jeremiah XXXVI."

CONCLUSION

Pertinent data have been marshalled for addressing some questions about the nature as well as the function of the 'door' that divides every exegesis of v. 9. In contrast to the solid wall to be crowned with silver ornamentation, the door which permits passage must be secured. To prevent it from being opened, it is fortified with panels which are fittingly beautiful but impenetrable.

After reviewing the history of exegesis on this disputed passage, Pope cuts through to the core of the debate and with his usual clear insight calls the matter moot. "Whether the damsel as a door is open or closed, it is the relative's concern to keep her closed until the proper time for opening."[46] True, indeed. And this concern of the brothers, voiced in the impassioned language of vv. 8–9, is quite understandable. Viewed from their own position they chose well, for cedar panels are known to have been widely used for reinforcing the strength of a structure while also enhancing its beauty.

But both their concern and their efforts proved unnecessary. As the subject herself asserts (v. 10) in words equally impassioned, the door was not opened until he came who was worthy. Neither the defense measures threatened by the family nor the assault techniques suspected of the suitors could have prevailed.[47] Love alone can keep the door closed or open it joyfully, thus establishing *šālôm* for all concerned.

The door in Cant 8:9 is not a barrier to love but its proper portal. The spirit pervading this "most sublime song" is that of *amor* and the many beautiful ways in which it is expressed.[48] Seen in that spirit *delet*, far from being synonymous with *ḥômā*^{h}, is its logical opposite. It is itself the sublime 'door to love.'

---

46 Pope, *Song of Songs* (N 1): 680.

47 As is shown by the sampling of translations given above, *nāṣŭr ʿālêhā* can be so read as to support either the 'defensive' or the 'offensive' interpretation.

48 I suggest that the difficult clause *k*^{e}*môṣ*^{e}*ʿēt šālôm* is intentionally ambiguous and that, as is the case throughout Canticles, it thereby serves to remind the reader that language which is so easily and naturally used of human love also undeniably evokes the imagery of divine love.

"LIVE COALS HEAPED ON THE HEAD"

STANISLAV SEGERT

The contributions to this volume honoring the eminent interpreter of Song of Songs have to deal with love and death.[1] The following considerations of the imagery and the sense of Proverbs 25:21-22 comply with this requirement in a rather loose manner. The love, if this term can be applied at all, is directed toward an enemy; the death appears in an observation on the treatment of a person dying of rabies, which is being added to the possible analogies to this saying from the ancient and modern Near East.

The Hebrew advice on how to treat the enemy (Prov 25: 21-22) is quoted by the apostle Paul (Romans 12:20) in a context which gives to it greater importance than does its placement among other Solomonic proverbs collected by the men of Hezekiah. This New Testament use of the ancient proverb has attracted considerable attention from biblical scholars. Among the relatively recent studies, two major articles, by Krister Stendahl[2] and by William Klassen,[3] both presented first at scholarly meetings in 1961,[4] are devoted primarily to the meaning and function of this proverbial saying in the New Testament. Two articles dealing mostly with the Old Testament wording, by Mitchell Dahood[5] and Léonard Ramaroson,[6] even mention the New Testament quotation in their titles.[7]

These four articles also contain ample references to previous interpretations, which the present writer gratefully used, and to which he refers for further details. Other comparative material is listed in the commentaries to Proverbs by B. Gemser,[8] R. B. Y. Scott[9] and William McKane,[10] as well as in the comparative study by Theodor H. Gaster[11] and in the Theological Dictionaries to the Old[12] and New Testament.[13] The interpretation of both the Hebrew original and its Greek translation quoted in the New Testament is still considered difficult.[14] A survey of previous interpretations will be presented here and a few new observations added. A possible parallel is a custom of Rwala Bedouins, recorded by Alois Musil. Another is contained in a Babylonian text found at the excavation of Terqa conducted by Giorgio Buccellati, a text mentioning the pouring of hot asphalt on the head of a culprit. More parallels to the Hebrew proverbs are given from the Babylonian "Counsels of Wisdom."

The following attempt to classify some interpretations of Prov 25:21-22 put forward or quoted in recent literature uses as a basis the traditional understanding of the Septuagint, adopted in the Epistle to the Romans. First, explanations omitting or changing the wording will be singled out, then, those which claim for some words a meaning substantially different from the traditional. Many differences between interpretations, agreeing on the traditional sense of words and constructions, are determined by different ancient Babylonian and Egyptian or modern Arabic parallels used as model or analogy.

While a simple understanding of the Hebrew words and constructions does not appear difficult, as the agreement of ancient and most modern translations may indicate, a

1 Cf. Marvin H. Pope, *Song of Songs* (AB 7c; Garden City: Doubleday, 1977): x: "the mysterious bond of Love and Death."

2 Krister Stendahl, "Hate, Non-retaliation and Love: 1QS x, 17-20 and Rom. 12:19-21," *Harvard Theological Review* 55 (1962): 343-55.

3 William Klassen, "Coals of Fire: Sign of Repentance or Revenge?" *New Testament Studies* 9 (1962): 337-50.

4 Stendahl (N 2): 355, n. 26.

5 Mitchell J. Dahood, "Two Pauline Quotations from the Old Testament," *Catholic Biblical Quarterly* 17 (1955): 19-24.

6 Léonard Ramaroson, " 'Charbons ardents': 'sur la tête' ou 'pour le feu'? (Pr 25,22a–Rm 12,20b)," *Biblica* 51 (1970): 230-34.

7 The article by J. Banak, "Tak bowiem czyniac, węgle żarzące zgromazdzisz na jego głowę (Rz 12,20)," is known to me only from the reference in the *Elenchus Bibliographicus Biblicus* 55 (1974): no. 4370.

8 B. Gemser, *Sprüche Salomos* (Handbuch zum Alten Testament I 16; Tübingen: Mohr, 1937).

9 R. B. Y. Scott, *Proverbs, Ecclesiastes* (AB 18; Garden City: Doubleday, 1965).

10 William McKane, *Proverbs: A New Approach* (The Old Testament Library; Philadelphia: Westminster, 1970).

11 Theodor H. Gaster, *Myth, Legend, and Custom in the Old Testament* (New York: Harper & Row, 1969, rpt. 1975).

12 H. F. Fuhs, "gḥl," in *Theological Dictionary of the Old Testament* (G. Johannes Botterweck and Helmer Ringgren, eds.; Grand Rapids: Eerdmans, 1975): 2.461-65.

13 Friedrich Lang, in *Theological Dictionary of the New Testament* (Gerhard Kittel, Gerhard Friedrich, eds.; Grand Rapids: Eerdmans, 1964–1976): 6.928-52; 7.1094-96.

14 Klassen (N 3): 337: "crux interpretum"; Stendahl (N 2): 346; Edwin Cyril Blackman, in *The Interpreter's One-Volume Commentary on the Bible* (Charles M. Laymon, ed.; Nashville: Abingdon, 1971): 790: "*Burning coals* has never been fully explained."

consensus on the meaning of the imagery of the "coals of fire" has not yet been reached. Since antiquity, at least two substantially different, if not opposite, interpretations have appeared. Various references to ancient and recent practices of similar kind have not yielded a reliable basis for interpretation. This explains why many exegetes skip this stage of interpretation in favor of a more spiritual, but less substantiated, explanation.

The words considered difficult, *ʿal rōʾšô* "upon his head," were deleted by Gustav Bickell[15] and by T. K. Cheyne.[16] The "coals of fire" are considered to be the substance of hatred which the addressed person has to take away. A similar understanding was reached later by Mitchell Dahood without omitting these words.[17]

A slight change of the Hebrew text was proposed by Léonard Ramaroson.[18] He reads instead of *ʿl rʾšw* "upon his head," *ʿly ʾšw,* i.e., *ʿălê ʾiššô* "on/for his fire." The entire colon thus receives quite a different meaning: "if you bring embers for his fire"; this would be a form of help to a needy person, parallel to that of feeding and giving drink.

No change in the Hebrew text but a different understanding of the word *rōʾš* was proposed by Sebastián Bartina:[19] not "head" but "venom,"[20] a meaning attested in Deut 32:33 and 20:16 for venom of snakes. Live embers have to be put upon a snake bite to destroy the effectiveness of the venom.[21]

An interpretation of the preposition *ʿal* indicating opposite direction was put forward by Mitchell Dahood.[22] It yields the translation "thus you will remove coals of fire from his head." Such an understanding of the preposition requires a corresponding interpretation of the governing verb *ḥ-t-y*;[23] Dahood supports his translation by analogies from biblical[24] and later Hebrew.[25]

For *ʿal* having the directional sense "from" rather than its usual meaning, "upon," parallels in older inscriptions are available. The sentence *ʾḥz . ʾt . nbh . ʿl . yśrʾl* in the inscription of king Mešaʿ of Moab[26] was understood as "take Nebo from Israel" by Vojtěch Šanda[27] as early as 1912. Also *ʿl* in the old Phoenician inscription of king Aḥirom of Byblos[28] is translated as "from": *wnḥt . tbrḥ . ʿl . gbl* "and may peace flee from Byblos."[29]

It is remarkable that all textual emendations and lexical interpretations mentioned above point in one direction: toward the interpretation requiring improvement or help for the enemy.

The two major interpretations that have survived from the patristic period until the present are presented by Mitchell Dahood.[30] According to one of them, represented by Augustine and Jerome, "coals of fire" refer to the "burning pangs of shame," which may produce remorse and contrition. But according to Origen and Chrysostom, the enemy who after being fed remains inimical, will be subjected to more serious punishment.

Among the interpretations presented or quoted recently, the line of Augustine seems to prevail.[31] Some of these interpreters find new supporting evidence from the ancient and modern Near East. The imagery of fire in a smelting furnace, as applied by Adam Clarke in 1957 and by J. E. Yonge in 1885,[32] does not agree with that of a head, or with the common use of the Hebrew word for "coals." A "head"—or *keph*—as a metaphor for hot coals on top of the fuel pile is used by Arabs, according to the observation of F. Ruffenach.[33] The real head of a

15 Gustav Bickell, "Kritische Bearbeitung der Proverbien," *Wiener Zeitschrift für die Kunde des Morgenlandes* 5 (1891): 283-84. Quoted from Dahood (N 5): 20-21.

16 T. K. Cheyne, *Jewish Religious Life After the Exile* (New York: Putnams, 1908): 142. Quoted by Dahood (N 5): 21, and by Klassen (N 3): 342.

17 Dahood (N 5): 21-22, see below.

18 Ramaroson (N 6): 234, "si tu apportes toi-même des braises pour son feu."

19 Sebastián Bartina, "Carbones encendidos, ¿sobre la cabeza o sobre el veneno? (Prov. 25, 21-22; Rom. 12,20)," *Estudios Biblicos* 31 (1972): 201-203.

20 Cf. Koehler-Baumgartner, *Lexicon*, 2d ed., 866a.

21 Bartina (N 19): 200, "porque brasas tú estarás poniendo sobre su veneno."

22 Dahood (N 5): 12-22.

23 For relations of prepositions to verbs cf. Dennis G. Pardee, "The Preposition in Ugaritic," *Ugarit-Forschungen* 7 (1975): 329-78; 8 (1976): 215-322 (see p. 316); "Attestations in Ugaritic Verb/Preposition Combinations in Later Dialects," 9 (1977): 205-31.

24 Psalm 52:7; Isaiah 30:14. Supported also by the Greek Septuagint translation.

25 Cf. also W. Baumgartner, *Hebräisches und aramäisches Lexikon*, 3rd ed., 347a.

26 H. Donner and W. Röllig, *KAI*², 181:14, cf. n. 27.

27 V(ojtěch) Šanda, *Starosemitské nápisy* (Praha: Kotrba, 1912): 203: "Jdi a odejmi Nebo Israelským!" ["Go and take Nebo from the Israelites!"]. Also W. F. Albright, *ANET*², 320; Kurt Galling, Textbuch zur Geschichte Israels (2nd. ed.; Tübingen: Mohr, 1968): 52; Stanislav Segert, "Die Sprache der moabitischen Königsinschrift," *ArOr* 29 (1961): 228; for other translations cf. Mark Lidzbarski, *Handbuch der nordsemitischen Epigraphik* (Weimar: Felber, 1898): 340, "über" (lat. *super*); G. A. Cooke, *A Text-Book of North-Semitic Inscriptions* (Oxford: Clarendon, 1903): 3, "Take Nebo against Israel"; H. Donner and W. Röllig, *KAI*², p. 169, "gegen Israel," but cf. 176.

28 *KAI* 1:2.

29 Franz Rosenthal, *ANET*², 504, "may peace flee from Byblos"; H. Donner and W. Röllig, *KAI*²: "und der Friede soll weichen von Byblos," with reference to the ambivalence in *KAI* 181:14, cf. 4.

30 Dahood (N 5): 19-20.

31 Cf. Klassen (N 3): 338, n. 1; 339, n. 4; 340, nn. 1 and 7.

32 Cf. Klassen (N 3): 338, n. 4 and 339, n. 1.

33 Cf. Klassen (N 3): 340, n. 3.

person is mentioned in the explanation provided by A. T. Fryer.[34] In Palestine the wealthy people, sharing their burning embers for culinary purposes with the poor, had their servants carry the embers on trays on their heads.

A similar reference to a tray of burning coals carried on the head was presented by the Egyptologist Siegfried Morenz[35] and widely accepted.[36] In a demotic text from the third century B.C. this gesture, together with the carrying of a forked staff in the hand, served allegedly as a sign of repentance on the part of a person who had stolen a book.

A biblical parallel to this custom or its interpretation can be adduced: a humiliated person throwing ashes upon his head (2 Sam 13:14).[37] An Egyptian model for Prov 25:21-22 is considered probable because of the possible Egyptian provenience of the immediately following proverb 25:23. The northern wind bringing rain can be explained by the climatic conditions in Egypt, whereas in Palestine the rain is brought by the wind from the west.[38] Some interpreters prefer the Palestinian origin of Prov 25:23, since the wind can be understood as north-western.[39] Wording very similar to that of Prov 25:21-22 points rather to Babylonia[40] than to Egypt. The proverbs related to Egyptian Wisdom are contained mostly in the preceding collection, Prov 22:17–24:22, and seem to be rare among the proverbs of Solomon collected by the men of Hezekiah (25:1–29:27).

It may be admitted that an Egyptian text from the third century B.C. might refer to a much older ritual.[41] However, different interpretations of this demotic magical text have been presented. Its first editor (1900), F. L. Griffith,[42] understood the gesture as a punishment by beating and burning while G. Maspéro (1911) saw in it a preliminary ritual for evocation and expulsion of spirits.[43]

The living coal (*riṣpā*), which one of the Seraphim took by tongs from the altar to purify the lips of the prophet Isaiah (6:6-7), was also adduced as a parallel to live coals in Prov 25:22.[44]

In his detailed and original, though not widely cited, treatment of the Old Testament quotations in the New Testament, Eduard Böhl[45] mentioned thermotherapeutic procedures in the Near East, especially in the Arab countries, according to the travel reports by G. Kuipers, C. Niebuhr and Thévenot. A more recent report from an Arab country was given by Alois Musil:[46] "If a mad dog, *čalb mṛalūṯ*, bites a man, *ji-ˁaẓẓ*, sulphur is applied to the wound, which is then burned with a red-hot nail. After forty days the injured person usually is stricken with rabies. Then they fetter him and throw hot ashes on his head until he dies."[47]

The heaping of hot ashes on the head of a person who was doomed to die may be understood either as an attempt to alleviate his pain—similar to the thermotherapeutic procedures mentioned above—or as another means, in addition to the fetters, to restrain a person stricken by rabies from transmitting the fatal disease to another person by biting. The use of hot coals or ashes for healing may be well applied to the interpretation of the biblical proverb: The enemy has to be healed from his enmity by benefits provided to him. Another possible application of

34 Cf. Klassen (N 3): 339, n. 3.

35 Siegfried Morenz, "Feurige Kohlen auf dem Haupt," *Theologische Literaturzeitung* 78 (1953): 187-92. A reference to the same Egyptian text as possibly relating to Romans 12:20 was made in 1901 by Ernst von Dobschütz; cf. Klassen (N 3): 343, n. 5. The most recent translation is available in Miriam Lichtheim, *Ancient Egyptian Literature: A Book of Readings*, Volume III: *The Late Period* (Berkeley–Los Angeles–London: University of California Press, 1980): 127-38: "Setne Khamwas and Nareferkaptah (Setne II)," cf. p. 136. Dr. Lichtheim understands this as an act of repentance (Los Angeles, March 20, 1980).

36 Klassen (N 3): 343-44; Gerhard von Rad, *Wisdom in Israel* (Nashville: Abingdon, 1972): 133, n. 25; Scott (N 9): 156; McKane (N 10): 592; Gaster (N 11): 2.805, 867, n. 1; Ramaroson (N 6): 231, n. 4; Fuhs (N 12): 2.464, n. 15; O. Michel (1955) quoted by Klassen (N 3): 481, n. 1; Stendahl (N 2): 347, n. 1; Joseph A. Fitzmyer, *The Jerome Bible Commentary* (Englewood Cliffs: Prentice-Hall, 1968): 2.326a.

37 Klassen (N 3): 344.

38 Cf. the quotations presented by McKane (N 10): 583; cf. also Gaster (N 11): 687, n. 4.

39 Scott (N 9): 156.

40 Cf. below p. 162 and nn. 49, 53, 55-57.

41 Cf. Klassen (N 3): 343, n. 6.

42 F. L. Griffith, *Stories of the High Priests of Memphis* (Oxford, 1900), quoted from Klassen (N 3): 343, n. 5.

43 Quoted by Ramaroson (N 6): 231, n. 4.

44 Cf. Ramaroson (N 6): 231; he gives no reference to his source.

45 Edward Böhl, *Die alttestamentlichen Citate im Neuen Testament* (Wien: Braumüller, 1878): 202-203. Cf. Ramaroson (N 6): 231, n. 3. G. Kuipers in a note to "Ritter d'Arvieux Reise nach dem Lager des grossen Emir," 365, explains the proverb—advising to do favor to someone, but in such a way that it burns him—by an observation of d'Arvieux: "The Arabs place on a hurting head a stockinglike cloth and then put fire upon it; the slowly carbonizing cloth heats the head and removes the pain." According to the final remarks, an enemy keeps the memory of a charitable act longer than a friend does.

46 Alois Musil, *The Manners and Customs of the Rwala Bedouins* (New York: American Geographical Society, 1928): 669.

47 Musil (N 46): 326, "The Poet, Bitten by a Mad Dog and Abandoned by His Kin, Laments a Friend." After "the poet, a member of the Dahâmše tribe, had been bitten by a mad dog, his relatives dragged him to a water hole, gave him salt, flour, and dried dates to last him forty days and threatened him with death should he leave the place and come near them before the forty days had expired. About that time the rabies was supposed to declare itself."

the Rwala custom: The enemy has to be constrained from exerting his hate by deeds of friendship. For the heaping of live coals on the head as punishment no parallels from the modern Near East are quoted, only those from the ancient Near East. The Egyptian custom mentioned above was interpreted by the first editor of the tale, F. L. Griffith, as punishment by burning.[48]

Technically different, but functionally meant as punishment, was the pouring of hot asphalt on the head of a culprit in ancient Mesopotamia and Eastern Syria. The punishment required by middle Assyrian laws for a harlot who was seen veiled was to pour pitch on her head.[49] This pouring of hot asphalt on the head is quoted as a parallel to heaping hot coals on the head by some commentators on Proverbs.[50] The pouring of asphalt on the head is mentioned also in Old Babylonian texts from the Ḫana period (about 1550-1350 B.C.).[51]

Another instance of this punishment from the Middle Euphrates area was found in an Akkadian tablet unearthed from the ruins of the ancient city of Terqa (now Tell Ašʿara in Northeastern Syria) during the excavation conducted by Giorgio Buccellati in 1977, and published by Olivier Rouault.[52] According to a contract for the sale of a piece of land, also from the Ḫana period, the person who would claim the field has to pay 10 minas of silver, and "hot asphalt will be poured upon his head."[53]

Hot asphalt poured on the head means clearly a severe punishment. In this function it can be adduced as an analogy to hot coals on the head. While asphalt had to be used in Mesopotamia and adjacent countries, in Palestine it was not available and could be replaced by charcoals.

The wording of Prov 25:21-22 is even closer to Babylonian models than this imagery. Some similarities of this proverb to some sayings contained among the "Counsels of Wisdom," collected probably in the Kassite period (about 1500-1200 B.C.)[54] have already been adduced by commentators,[55] but more parallels can be listed.

A simple juxtaposition shows that most of Prov 25:21-22 can be duplicated from the Babylonian "Counsels of Wisdom":[56]

	Proverbs 25		*Counsels of Wisdom*
21a	if your enemy is hungry,	45a	if your ill-wisher is . . .
21b	give him bread to eat;	45b	nurture him
		61a	give food to eat,
21c	and if he is thirsty,		
21d	give him water to drink;	61b	beer to drink
22a	for you will heap coals of fire on his head,		
22b	and the LORD will reward you. (RSV)	64	. . . (Šamaš), who will repay him with favor.

The Babylonian analogy of asphalt poured on the head as punishment may be used to fill the missing correspondence to Prov 25:22a. The entire proverb is clearly related rather to Babylonian than to Egyptian wisdom tradition.

The heaping of live coals on the head is seldom understood as punishment by Old Testament interpreters.[57] They stress rather the religious requirement to help an enemy, beyond utilitarian and opportunistic practice. The interpretation as punishment is attested clearly, however, in the Jewish and Christian tradition of the postbiblical period.

Rabbi Berachiah (ca. A.D. 340) makes this meaning of the biblical proverb clear by using a comparison to a baker standing before the oven door:[58] "his enemy came, he took coals of fire from it and heaped them upon his head" (*wəḥātā geḥālīm wə-nātan ʿal rōʾšô*)." "The coals of fire and the bread both come from the (same) oven, similarly God caused fire to fall from heaven on the Sodomites and manna to fall from heaven on the Israelites."[59]

A similar interpretation appears in the pseudepigraphical Fourth Book of Esra, in its last part called also Sixth

48 Quoted by Ramaroson (N 6): 231, n. 4.

49 Middle Assyrian Laws, Tablet A, 40, tr. Th. J. Meek, *ANET*³, 183a.

50 Gemser (N 8): 72.

51 Wolfram von Soden, *Akkadisches Handwörterbuch* (Wiesbaden: Harrassowitz, 1965-): 1.443a, s.v. *kapārum* II.

52 Olivier Rouault, *Terqa Preliminary Reports*, No. 7: Les documents épigraphiques de la troisième saison (Syro-Mesopotamian Studies 2/7; Malibu: Undena, 1979): 3-6, pl. II-III. The information concerning the Terqa text was kindly provided by my colleague Prof. Giorgio Buccellati.

53 A.ESÍR.⟨È.A⟩ *e*[*m*]-*m*[*u-um*] S[A]G.DU-*su i*-[*k*]*a*!-*p*[*a-ar*] "de l'asphalte c[h]au[d] sera ré[p]an[du] sur sa t[ê]te," ibid., 7,2, rev. 2, pages 3 and 6.

54 For English translation of selected sayings cf. Robert H. Pfeiffer, *ANET*², 426-27; the complete Akkadian text and translation is contained in W. G. Lambert, *Babylonian Wisdom Literature* (Oxford: Clarendon, 1960, rpt. 1975): 96-107. The lines are here indicated according to this complete edition.

55 McKane (N 10): 591-92, quotes lines 41-42; Robert Dentan refers to the same in *The Interpreter's One-Volume Commentary on the Bible* (Nashville: Abingdon, 1971): 316b, following the translation of Pfeiffer (N 55).

56 Lambert, *Babylonian Wisdom Literature* (N 55): line 45 cf. also 314, where a pertinent Ugaritic parallel (2 Aqht:V:19-20) to 61-62 is quoted.

57 Cf. H. Frankenberg, *Die Sprüche* (1890): 142, quoted by Dahood (N 5): 19, n. 3, and by Klassen (N 3): 343, n. 3; Bernard Weiss (1899), and Albinus Škrinjar (1938): suffering of self-hatred, both quoted by Klassen, 338, nn. 2 and 3.

58 Quoted from Lang (N 13): 7.1095, n. 5; Midraš Tanḥuma, *bšlh* 20 (Buber, p. 33b).

59 Cf. Klassen (N 3): 344-45, who refers to the German translation by Paul Billerbeck, *Kommentar zum Neuen Testament aus Talmud und Midrasch*, 2nd. ed., 3.301ff.

Book of Esra,[60] preserved only in a secondary Latin translation, in an addition probably composed by Christians during the persecutions in the third century A.D.:[61] ". . .for coals of fire will burn on the head of him who says, 'I have not sinned before God and his glory!' " (16:54).[62]

This Christian use of the imagery of coals of fire may be related to the quotation from Proverbs by Paul in his Epistle to Romans 12:20 which follows exactly the wording of the Septuagint. Just before this quotation (Romans 12:19) Paul refers to the wrath of God who alone will vindicate and repay, quoting Deut 32:35.

Coals of fire apparently signified punishment in the Old Testament proverb, according to its Babylonian background, and also in the saying of Rabbi Berachiah preserved in Midrash Tanḥuma, and in the Sixth Book of Esra. This understanding stresses the sovereignty of God as judge who will repay both the evil-doer and the innocent. In the later Christian tradition, this line of interpretation is represented by Origen and Chrysostom.[63]

It does not seem necessary to suppose that Paul's understanding of this proverb and its imagery was basically different from that of its original meaning in the Hebrew Bible.[64] The last part of the Hebrew proverb (25:22b) was not quoted in the Epistle to Romans, since the same idea of god as supreme judge was already expressed more forcefully just before (12:19), with reference to Deuteronomy (32:35).

This understanding leads Christians to conquer evil through good (Romans 12:21). The Qumran Essenes likewise warned not to return evil;[65] nonetheless they had to keep up eternal hatred towards the men of perdition.[66]

The interpretation of "coals of fire" as "pangs of shame," represented in antiquity by Augustine and Jerome,[67] does not seem to express adequately the sense of the proverb as quoted by Paul, but this interpretation, moderating and weakening the power and impact of the image, was apparently attractive for many interpreters.[68]

According to an authoritative handbook for translators, the sense is perhaps best taken as "for by doing this you will make him ashamed."[69] But in only a few translations is the metaphor—in accordance with this recommendation—changed into a non-metaphor. Moffatt's translation "for in this way you will make him feel a burning sense of shame" gives, according to C. H. Dodd,[70] Paul's understanding adequately. *Good News Bible*[71] consistently replaces the metaphor both in Prov 25:22 and Romans 12:20: "you will make him burn with shame."[72] The word "shame" is introduced even into 2 Esdras 16:53 in this translation: ". . .are only bringing fiery shame upon themselves."[73] The non-metaphoric rendering appears in the New Czech ecumenical translation.[74]

A few other remarks relating to ancient and modern translations of the Hebrew proverb may be added.

The addition in the Septaugint, *anthrakas pyros* "coals of fire,"[75] is based on the Hebrew qualification by the attribute *gaḥălē ʾēš* which appears in other passages of the Hebrew Bible.[76] Even without the genitival attribute *ʾēš* "of fire" *geḥālīm* usually means "live coals."[77] It appears in contrast to *peḥām* meaning simply "charcoal," without indicating if burning.[78] In Prov 26:21 this pair is paralleled by *ʾēš* "fire" contrasting with *ʿēṣīm* "wood."

60 Cf. H. Duensing, "The Fifth and Sixth Book of Esra," *New Testament Apocrypha* (Philadelphia: Westminster, 1965): 2.689-703.

61 English translation by David Hill, from Duensing (N 60): 701. Latin original "carbones ignis conburet super caput eius," *Biblia sacra iuxta vulgatam versionem* (Robertus Weber, ed.; Stuttgart: Württembergische Bibelanstalt, 1969): 2.1973. Cf. also 16:69, 78.

62 The Latin wording differs from Prov 25:22: "prunam congregabis super caput eius."

63 Cf. Fitzmyer (N 36): 2. 291-331, cf. 326: Klassen (N 3): 347; Stendahl (N 2): 346.

64 Cf. Fitzmyer (N 36): 326; against Klassen (N 3): 347-48, who admits that Paul did not know the Egyptian ritual.

65 1QS X:17-20 (Manual of Discipline); cf. Stendahl (N 2): 343; Klassen (N 3): 345.

66 1QS IX:21-22; cf. also Psalm 139:21-22; cf. Stendahl (N 2): 344.

67 Cf. above p. 160.

68 Cf. above p. 160 and n. 31.

69 Barclay M. Newman and Eugene A. Nida, *A Translator's Handbook on Paul's Letter to the Romans* (Helps for Translators XIV; London: United Bible Societies, 1973): 243.

70 Dahood (N 5): 20, n. 6.

71 *Good News Bible with Deuterocanonicals/Apocrypha: The Bible in Today's English Version* (New York: American Bible Society, 1978).

72 But cf. *Good News for Modern Man: The New Testament in Today's English Version* (2nd ed.; New York: American Bible Society, 1966): "you will heap burning coals on his head."

73 (Latin 16:54); *Good News for Modern Man*, "Some Additional Books," 56.

74 *Nový Zákon: Překlad s poznámkami. Skutky apoštolské, Epištoly, Kniha Zjevení* (Praha: Kalich, 1978): 90: "tím ho zahanbíš a přivedeš k lítosti" ["by this you will shame him and bring him to repentance"], with footnote giving a literal rendering of the Greek original.

75 Cf. also Prov. 6:28; Isa. 47:14.

76 E.g. Lev. 16:12; Psalm 18:13 and 14; Ezek. 1:13.

77 Walter Baumgartner, *Hebräisches und aramäisches Lexikon*^{3}, 180b, while Ludwig Koehler, *Lexicon*^{2}, 179a, differentiated between **gaḥal* (*gaḥḥal*?) "burning charcoals," pl. constr. *gaḥălê-* and **gəḥāl* (**gaḥḥāl*) "charcoals," pl. abs. and suff. *gəḥāl-*. Cf. Fuhs (N 12): 461-65.

78 Cf. Koehler, *Lexicon*^{2}, 758a.

Even though the words *ʿal rōʾšô* are considered difficult[79] they are translated as "upon his head" or similarly in nearly all translations. If the metaphor of burning coals is replaced by the non-metaphor,[80] this change affects also the rendering of "his head" which is replaced by "you." A similar replacement appears in the *Good News Bible* translation of 2 Esdras 16:53 (Latin 54)[81] even if the metaphor of fire is retained: "bringing fiery shame upon themselves." Such interpretation and translation can be supported by similar use of Hebrew *rōʾš* "head" in Esth 9:25.[82]

79 Cf. above, n. 18.

80 Cf. above, p. 163 and n. 72 for both Prov 25:22 and Rom 12:20.

81 Cf. above, n. 74.

82 Cf. *BDB*, 911a, s.v. *rōʾš* 8. Cf. also *Good News Bible* (N 72): 552, "Haman suffered the fate."

NOTES ON LOVE AND DEATH IN PROVERBS

DANIEL C. SNELL

The pursuit of a theme within the Book of Proverbs is likely to appear less integrated and coherent than examinations of other corpora from the ancient world because Proverbs is itself a conglomerate. But the themes of love and death appear in two aspects that are important for the understanding of the composition and rhetoric of the book.

I. Love and Death

The verses in Proverbs that mention both love and death are only two in number:[1]

8:36 וחטאי חמס נפשו כל־משנאי אהבו מות
And he who misses me does violence to himself; all who hate me love death.

18:21 מות וחיים ביד־לשון ואהביה יאכל פריה
Death and life are in the control of the tongue, and he who loves it will eat its fruit.

Proverbs 18:21, which is from the collection attributed to Solomon and therefore potentially older than 8:36, argues that one who is interested in his art of expression will reap the benefits. To say this the verse uses a slightly humorous expression with "tongue," *b*^{e}*yad,* "in the hand of," that is, "in the control of." And the eating image is meant to recall the physical existence of the tongue in the mouth. The eloquence goes forth from the tongue but its benefits return and go past the tongue.

The context of the verse may define more precisely what is meant, at least by the final proverb-compiler. Proverbs 18:21 is preceded by statements on eloquence and especially eloquence connected with legal proceedings. There is an important exception to the thrust of this section; 18:22 seems completely irrelevant to the context. But an overview of the section may show that it is present for a reason, and in an unexpected way links 18:21 to 8:36. The subject may begin in 18:16:

18:16 The gift of a man makes room for him, and it brings him before great ones.
:17 The first in his lawsuit seems(?) right; his fellow comes and examines him.
:18 The lot stops strifes and makes distinctions (*yafrīd*) among important people.
:19 An offended (*nifšāʿ*) brother is more than a powerful city (?), and disputes are like the bolt of a tower.[2]
:20 From the fruit of the mouth of a man his belly is satisfied; he is satisfied with the produce of his lips.
:21 Death and life are in the control of the tongue, and he who loves it will eat its fruit.[3]
:22 He finds a woman: he finds a good thing, and gets favor from the Lord.
:23 A poor man may speak ingratiations, but a rich man will answer strong words.
:24 There are friends to spend time with, but there is a lover who sticks closer than a brother.[4]
19:1 Better is a poor man who goes in his integrity than one crooked of lips who is a fool.

---

1 Translations unless otherwise noted are my own; they tend to be over-literal and wooden because I want to reflect differences of expression in Hebrew. On 18:21 see note 3 below.

2 On this verse compare C. Toy, *Proverbs* (ICC; Edinburgh: T. & T. Clark, 1899): 363, "It is difficult, if not impossible, to construe the Heb. text"; R. B. Y. Scott, *Proverbs and Ecclesiastes* (Garden City: Doubleday, 1965): 113, "A brother offended is harder [to be won] than a strong city, and his antagonism is like the bar of a castle," reading *m*^{e}*dōnāw* for *midyānīm*; and W. McKane, *Proverbs* (Philadelphia: Westminster, 1975): 239 and 520, "An aggrieved brother *is more inaccessible* than a fortified city, and quarrels are like the bars of a palace." My resolution of the problems accords with those of Scott and McKane. But perhaps the offended brother is one who is involved in a dispute about land, if one can rely on the cognate noun *pešaʿ* in Exodus 22:8. Compare for *pešaʿ* in Proverbs as "dispute" the parallelism in 10:12: "Hate arouses strifes, and all disputes (*p*^{e}*šāʿīm*) love covers up," and 29:22: "A man of anger starts strife, and a man of wrath is great (in) dispute (*pāšaʿ*)." But parallelism cannot always be the final guide to a word's meaning; see note 12 below.

3 W. A. van der Weiden, *Le livre des proverbes* (Rome: Biblical Institute Press, 1970): 128, suggests that since the subject of the second half is clearly plural, the verb may be read as a plural written defectively, *yōʾk*^{e}*lū* for MT's *yōʾkal.* Of the parallels he adduces, however, 3:21's *yāluzū* for *yālūzū* seems not analogous since the long vowel is internal, and 3:3's *yaʿazbukā* for *yaʿazbūkā* has a suffix, also making the long vowel internal. I prefer with other commentators to delete the *yod* that makes *ʾōhăbeyhā* plural if only because the other verses around 21 are in the singular.

4 I accept the obvious emendation of *ʾīš* to *yēš* by analogy to the second half of the verse. With the commentators I accept an emendation of *hitrōʿē*^{aʿ} to *hitrāʿōt,* making "crushing" into "being friendly."

The discussion then goes elsewhere, on to foolishness, though poor and rich appear again in 19:4 (with *prd*, reminding one of 18:18) and 19:6, 7.

The other verse on love and death, 8:36, has a more obvious context in the speech of the personified Wisdom. This is the last verse in this important chapter, and the next begins the description of Wisdom's house and further invitation. What precedes gives 8:36 a context of some interest. The section probably begins with Wisdom's address in 8:32:

> 8:32 And now, boys, listen to me; happy are those who keep my ways.
> :33 Hear correction and get wise, and don't neglect it.
> :34 Happy is the man who listens to me, to watch at my doors day by day, to guard the posts of my gates.
> :35 For he who finds me finds life, and gets favor from the Lord.
> :36 And he who misses me does violence to himself; all who hate me love death.

It seems ironic to say that anyone loves death; no one reasonably would hurt himself, but in ignorance people daily do that, the verses argue. The odd thing about the context of 8:36 is that it echoes that of 18:21 in that the verses about finding a woman and getting the Lord's favor appear with variation in both places. The resemblance between the two is so close as to make them virtually the same, though technically they are of the sort that constitute a half-repeated proverb, one in which half the verse is exactly repeated and the other half not. In Hebrew they read:

8:35 כי מצאי מצאי[5] חיים ויפק רצון מיהוה

18:22 מצא אשה מצא טוב ויפק רצון מיהוה

Other verses, Proverbs 16:20, 17:20, and 19:8, speak of finding good, and 31:10 speaks of finding a woman, but none other uses the repeated verb *mṣʾ*.[6]

This is not the place to discuss the several possibilities for the meaning of repetition of verses in Proverbs, but it may be possible to come to a conclusion about the relation of these two verses.[7] The inclusion of 18:22 seems, as we saw, rather forced, or at least partakes of an extension of meaning that is not an obvious one. In chapter 8 the verse seems to follow naturally in its context.

One might assume that the late composer of chapter 8 borrowed 8:35 from the presumably earlier Solomonic collection. But to assume so would overlook the natures of both chapters 8 and 18. A survey of repeated verses indicates that besides the case of 8:35 and 18:22 chapter 8 has only one repeated verse, 8:11, which is essentially the same as 3:15; 3:15 is part also of the discourse on Wisdom, and, if not from the same hand as chapter 8, is from a rather late composer. But chapter 18 is studded with verses repeated elsewhere, including 18:4a = 20:5a (imprecisely repeated), 18:8 = 26:22 (precisely repeated), 18:9b = 28:24b, 18:11a = 10:15a, 18:12 = 16:18a = 15:33b, 18:15a = 15:14a, 18:20a = 12:14a = 13:2a (all half-repeated). None of the other repetitions in the chapter relates to passages in chapters 1-9. One hypothesis to explain the make-up of chapter 18 is that someone was interested in collecting there saws from several places.

A full evaluation of the phenomenon of chapter 18, which may or may not be a unit in itself, must await the detailed consideration of the contexts of all the repeated verses in Proverbs. But this much seems likely now: 8:35 and 18:22 bind their contexts to each other. And it may be possible to suggest an editor's thought process in inserting 18:22 in its present place. He gives sayings about disputes at law, including one concerning perhaps disputes within the family (19). Then he adds one from elsewhere (20a = 12:14a = 13:2a) about the eloquent arguer's enjoyment of his gain. But disputes at law are not only about property but also about death and life; being eloquent allows one to enjoy the positive benefits of eloquence (21). And how does one find life and get the favor of the Lord? Through Wisdom, that quintessentially good woman (18:22, relying on 8:35). A poor man will not be able to pay for her but must get her through kind words, and a rich person may abuse him (23).

But 18:22 is now more general than getting Wisdom and advises that a marriage is a good thing.[8] Why it was changed, if it was changed, may elude us, and the reconstruction of an editor's thoughts as he worked to create an admittedly diffuse context remains hypothetical. From this instance alone one does not gain a coherent picture, of course, of the progress of inner-Proverbs development or much insight into the class ethic or situation in life of these bits and pieces. The intentions of the editors remain opaque. And yet it may be that the linking of love and death, which is striking and provocative for another biblical writer and for us, was striking for the composer of chapter 18 also.

5 With BH I would delete the extra *yod*.

6 12:2a rephrases the second half of 8:35 and 18:22, but does not clearly deal with a similar subject: "A good man gets favor from the Lord, but a man of evil plans he condemns." Outside the Book of Proverbs there is no instance of the double use of *mṣʾ* in the same clause. Compare however Section II below.

7 P. Skehan, "A Single Editor for the Whole Book of Proverbs," *Studies in Israelite Poetry and Wisdom* (CBQ Monograph Series 1, 1971): 15-26, reprinted in *Studies in Ancient Israelite Wisdom* (J. Crenshaw, ed.; New York: Ktav, 1976): 329-40, is the only modern scholar to have considered the problem of repetition systematically.

8 This is an old sentiment in the ancient Near East; compare W. G. Lambert, "Celibacy in the World's Oldest Proverbs," *BASOR* 169 (1963): 63f., for an example attested in the Fara, Old Babylonian, and Neo-Assyrian periods.

II. Love and Love

Above we saw that repetition of the verb *mṣ*ʾ "find" allowed proverbialists to equate two things not clearly commensurate in normal language: Wisdom and life, a woman and good. It is well-known that the definition of the proverb eludes even students of sayings in modern languages, and yet many languages have expressions that seem to the native speaker somehow proverbial.[9] Sometimes that proverbialness seems to have to do with pith, and certainly, as a recent observer has written, pith counts; but one cannot be sure that something pithy necessarily would be considered proverbial-sounding by the native speaker. Still, if a form of expression is repeated within a collection of saws like the Book of Proverbs, one could begin to imagine that this form is one, at least, which is proverbial. I would argue that the double verb form may be one such, that is, a form of utterance in which the same verb is used twice in the same clause, as in 8:35; closely related are cases in which the same verb appears in two clauses that are logically connected, as in 18:22. It happens that this form appears in some verses within the Book of Proverbs with the verb "to love":

> 8:17 I [Wisdom] love those who love me (אני אהביה אהב), and those who seek me will find me.
>
> 12:1 He who loves correction loves knowledge (אהב מוסר אהב דעת), and he who hates correction is a boor.
>
> 17:19 He who loves sin loves dispute (אהב פשע אהב מצה); he who exalts his gate is asking for destruction.

The form also appears with the verb "to keep":

> 19:16 He who keeps a command keeps his life (שמר מצוה שמר נפשו); he who despises his ways will die.

This idea seems to be expanded in

> 21:23 He who keeps his mouth and tongue keeps his life from troubles (שמר פיו ולשונו שמר מצרות נפשו).

Oddly there are also two verses that convey the idea of "keeping" by using two different verbs, *nṣr* and *šmr*:

> 13:3 He who keeps his mouth keeps his life (נצר פיו שמר נפשו); he who opens wide his lips has ruin.
>
> 16:17 The highway of the righteous is to turn from evil; he who keeps his life keeps his way (שמר נפשו נצר דרכו).

There is at present no special reason to see these as secondary or primary; they obviously accomplish the same end as the "purer" form with a single verbal root.

Two other verses show the double verb form:

> 22:23 For the Lord will prosecute their [poor people's, from 22:22] suit, and he robs those who rob them of life (וקבע את־קבעיהם נפש).
>
> 27:16 He who treasures her [a woman of strife, from 27:15] treasures wind (צפניה צפן־רוח), and he'll call his right hand oil (?).[10]

Proverbs 22:23 is part of the section loosely translated from the Egyptian instruction, but it has no parallel in the Egyptian.[11] The existence of these latter instances with verbs that are not very common presumably shows that the form was at some time a productive one which was not limited merely to a couple of common verbs.

Another verse, 3:34, may be related to the double verb form, though it does not have two verbs in the relevant clause:

> 3:34 With regard to scoffers he [the Lord, in 3:33] scoffs (אם־ללצים הוא־יליץ), but to meek people he gives favor.

"Scoffers" is merely an adjective, but the use of its cognate verb shows that here it may have the force of a participle.

Two verses use an infinitive to express a similar sort of cause and effect relation as in the examples above:

> 18:3 In the coming of a wicked man contempt also comes (בבוא־רשע בא גם־בוז), and with dishonor disgrace.
>
> 29:16 In the increasing of bad men sin increases (ברבות רשעים ירבה־פשע), but the righteous will look upon their downfall.[12]

9 A. Taylor, *The Proverb* (Cambridge, MA: Harvard, 1931): 3f.

10 Again because of singular verbs one may emend the plural participle to the singular. The second half of the verse eludes explanation; see the commentaries.

11 So after J. Pritchard, *Ancient Near Eastern Texts* (3rd ed.; Princeton: Princeton Univ., 1969): 424 n. 46, quoting D. C. Simpson. But C. Kayatz, *Studien zu Proverbien 1–9* (WMANT 22; Neukirchen: Neukirchener, 1966): 101-102, noted that such a "reziproke Formel" is used with the same sense as in the Prov 8:17 referring to several Egyptian gods and suggested that the expression was borrowed from Egyptian. E. Drioton, "Maximes relatives à l'amour pour les dieux," *Studia biblica et orientalia* 3 (1959): 57-68, found the expression, normally in the form "(Divine name) loves one who loves him" on New Kingdom scarabs, and he interpreted the scarabs as expressions of a popular piety. Scarabs from controlled archaeological contexts date from about 950 to 660 B.C.E., though the legends may be related to the cliché "with a loving heart" dating from the 18th Dynasty, about 1558 to 1303 B.C.E., pp. 67-68.

12 The obviously related verse 29:2, "In the increasing of righteous men the people rejoices, but in the governing of a bad one a people groans," is taken by *RSV* following B. Gemser to

Logically related though not formally related to the above examples is the verse 11:2:

> 11:2 Pride comes, and calumny comes (בא - זדון ויבא קלון), but wisdom is with modest men.

The use of the same verb twice, though not in the same clause, appears again to bind logically the two events described, as in 18:22, and to underline the eudaemonistic outlook on the way the world works.[13]

But is this form a form? It is not in the sense of a fully definable and ultimately localizable bit of literature. But if, as Gene Tucker has written, "Formulas actually are short genres,"[14] then perhaps these examples embody a formula, a shorthand way of expressing an identity. We will never know whether it felt pithy and proverbial to the ancient Hebrews. We cannot avoid the sense that it feels pithy and proverbial to us.

Inevitably it will be asked whether the isolation of proverbial clichés like this can help us attack the old question of wisdom influence. I would personally avoid positing any wisdom influence stemming from wisdom schools until we find out something about schools.[15] But there is no reason that proverbial ways of speaking should not be found elsewhere. As noted above, it happens that the repeated verb form does not occur outside Proverbs with the verb *mṣʾ* "to find"; neither does the form appear with *ʾhb* "to love."[16] But it does appear with other verbs, notably in the retributive formula in Genesis 9:6, most recently studied by E. M. Good:

> He who spills the blood of the man
> by the man his blood will be spilt.[17]

Is this then wisdom? It is, like other instances of the double verb form, constructed so as to emphasize the simple justice it describes.[18] Perhaps when we know more about what the clichés of proverbial speech were we will be able to say a bit more about the use of these clichés outside the books that emphasize what is wise.

Proverbs sometimes seems like the book of the poet J. V. Cunningham which one critic did not like. Cunningham responds, first paraphrasing the critic's characterization of his book:

> The trivial, vulgar, and exalted jostle
> Each other in a way to make the apostle
> of culture and right feeling shudder faintly.
> It is a shudder that affects the saintly.
> It is a shudder by which I am faulted.
> I like the trivial, vulgar, and exalted.[19]

And so do I. And so, I have it on good authority, does the one whom we honor here.

---

show that *rbh* in both verses means "govern." But *RSV* translates the syntactically similar 28:28 "When the wicked rise, men hide themselves, but when they perish, the righteous increase." It would seem safer to translate *rbh* in its occurrences in Proverbs as "increase" and not to rely over much on meanings of parallel words. See the discussion by McKane (N 2): 639.

13 Also perhaps related may be the obscure 26:10, where *śōkēr* "he who hires" is repeated, but the text is corrupt; see Toy (N 2): 475f. Possibly related to the form in a general way is 9:12, "If you get wise, you get wise for yourself, and if you scoff, you alone will bear it." Here, though, the point is not to draw analogies but merely to specify who gets the benefit or punishment.

Another example is Prov 10:9a "He who walks in blamelessness walks securely (הולך בתם ילך בטח), but he who makes crooked his ways will be found out", and, less clearly, 11:25b, "A soul (worthy) of blessing will be fattened, and one who waters will also be watered (ומרוה גם־הוא יורא)", if one is willing to emend the final verb to a form from רוה.

14 *Form Criticism of the Old Testament* (Philadelphia: Fortress, 1973): 14. My use of the word "formula" is not related to the technical definition proposed by W. R. Watters, *Formula Criticism and the Poetry of the Old Testament* (BZAW 138; Berlin and New York: de Gruyter, 1976): esp. 150, "a formula is a repeated word pair or phrase in one or more lines of poetry."

15 On the problem of the lack of evidence for schools see R. N. Whybray, *The Intellectual Tradition in the Old Testament* (BZAW 135; Berlin and New York: de Gruyter, 1974): esp. 33-43. For the difficulties involved in seeking wisdom influence see J. Crenshaw, "Method in Determining Wisdom Influence Upon 'Historical Literature,' " *JBL* 88 (1969): 129-42, reprinted in his *Studies in Ancient Israelite Wisdom* (N 7): 481-94.

16 But its inverse occurs in Psalm 97:10a, which, following the MT, reads, "Hate evil, lovers of the Lord . . ." though *RSV* emends to "The Lord loves those who hate evil . . . ." Similar is Psalm 11:5b: ". . . and his [the Lord's] soul hates the lover of violence."

Another case, Psalm 18:26, noted by Toy [N 2]: 81), uses cognate adjectives like Proverbs 3:34: "With the loyal you show loyalty; with the blameless man you show blamelessness." None of these psalms is usually claimed as a "wisdom psalm"; on that term see R. Murphy, "A Consideration of the Classification 'Wisdom Psalms,' " *VTS* 9 (1962): 156-67, reprinted in J. Crenshaw, *Studies in Ancient Israelite Wisdom* (N 7): 456-67.

17 "The Unfilled Sea: Style and Meaning in Ecclesiastes 1:2-11," *Israelite Wisdom* (J. Gammie, et al., eds.; S. Terrien Anniv. Vol.; Missoula: Scholars, 1978): 59-73, esp. 59-61.

18 Another case related to the double verb form may be Exodus 33:19b: ". . . and I will be gracious to whom I will be gracious and will show mercy on whom I will show mercy."

Other possible examples, all in speeches by God, are the blessing in Gen 12:8a, and the curses in Lev 26:23-24, 27-28, 40-41, and Hosea 4:6; in these curses, however, the similar verbs are in separate clauses.

19 J. V. Cunningham, from "On Doctor Drink," *The Exclusions of a Rhyme* (Denver: Alan Swallow, 1960): 95, reprinted with the permission of The Ohio University Press, Athens.

WHAT IS MAN THAT YOU HAVE BEEN MINDFUL OF HIM? (ON PSALM 8:4–5)*

JEFFREY H. TIGAY

One of the most evocative passages in Psalms—a book which I had the privilege of studying with Professor Pope more than a decade ago—is Ps. 8:4-5:

כי אראה שמיך מעשי אצבעותיך
ירח וכוכבים אשר כוננתה:
מה־אנוש כי תזכרנו
ובן־אדם כי תפקדנו:

When I behold your heavens, the works of your fingers,
the moon and stars that you set in place:
what is man that you have been mindful of him,
mortal man that you have taken note of him . . . ?[1]

Through centuries of repetition these verses have come to seem self-understood, as has their connection to each other. But the logic of that connection, variously expressed in modern translations by commas, semicolons, colons, and hyphens, is less than obvious. Some translators and exegetes have tried to make the connection more explicit. Saadia, in his translation, introduced a transitional אקול, "I say," at the beginning of verse 5,[2] just as Moffatt introduced the verse with "I say."[3] Commentators similarly supplied such transitional phrases as אני תמה בלבי, "I wonder in my mind" (Rashi),[4] or, "nun fällt es ihm [i.e., the psalmist] aufs Herz" (Gunkel).[5] Contemplating the heavens thus prompts the psalmist to wonder why God has shown such regard for man. But what is it about the heavens and about man that prompts such a question? The Targum[6] rendered v. 5: מה בר נשא מטול תדכר עובדוי, "What is man that you are mindful of his works?" The additional עובדוי echoes v. 4's עובדי אצבעתך (= MT מעשי אצבעותיך), suggesting that a contrast between God's works and man's prompts the speculation. Most treatments of the psalm have contrasted God's works with man himself, stressing the grandeur of the heavens and the lowliness of man. Saadia,[7] in avoiding the anthropomorphism of "the works of your fingers," rendered עמלך אלבאהר, "your brilliant (i.e., dazzling, splendid) works." Meiri[8] paraphrased: כשאני רואה שמיך וגו׳ אני מכיר שפלותי, "When I behold your heavens, etc. I recognize my lowliness . . . ," while Ibn Ezra[9] explains: מה אנוש כי תזכרנו דרך בזוי והטעם . . . אחר שיש לך בריאות גדולות ונכבדות מהאדם איך שמת לב לתת כבוד " 'What is man that you have been mindful of him' is deprecatory, and the reasoning is: Since you have creations greater and more glorious than man, how did you take thought to give him honor?" Modern commentators similarly speak of the vastness and splendor of the heavens, many adding that these testify to the majesty and greatness of their Maker. Thus Kirkpatrick paraphrases vv. 4–5: "The contemplation of the heavens in all their splendour forces the Psalmist to wonder that God should choose so insignificant a thing as man for the object of His special regard."[10]

But is it man's insignificance and lowliness which are expressed in the question "What is man that you have been mindful of him . . . ?" In slightly varying forms

---

* It is a great pleasure to take part in this tribute to Professor Pope and to express thereby my gratitude for all that I owe him, both intellectually and personally.

1 Translation based on *The Book of Psalms* (Philadelphia: Jewish Publication Society of America, 1972): 8 (henceforth: *NJV*). In v. 4, the singular מַעֲשֵׂה is the reading of most of the current masoretic Bibles (e.g., מקראות גדולות, Letteris, Cassuto, Koren, Snaith), whereas Leningrad Codex B19, printed in BH[3] and BHS and the Dothan edition, reads מַעֲשֵׂי; cf. Targum.

2 Y. Kafiḥ, תהלים עם תרגום ופירוש הגאון רבינו סעדיה בן יוסף פיומי זצ״ל (Jerusalem, 1966): 64.

3 James Moffatt, *A New Translation of the Bible* (New York and London: Harper, 1950): 609.

4 I. Maarsen, *Parshandatha. The Commentary of Rashi on the Prophets and Hagiographs, Part III. Psalms* (Jerusalem, 1936; reprint, Jerusalem: Makor, 1972): 8; Kimḥi's comment is similar; see A. Darom, ר׳ דוד קמחי (רד״ק). הפירוש השלם על תהלים (Jerusalem: Mosad Harav Kook, 1971): 26 top.

5 H. Gunkel, *Die Psalmen* (fünfte Auflage; Göttingen: Vandenhoeck & Ruprecht, 1968): 28

6 Quoted from מקראות גדולות (New York: Pardes, 1951): 5a. The reading in P. de Lagarde, *Hagiographa Chaldaice* (Leipzig: Teubner, 1873): 4 is the same.

7 Saadia (N 2).

8 Y. Hakohen, פירוש לספר תהלים. חברו רבי מנחם ב״ר שלמה המאירי (Jerusalem, 1960): 28.

9 In מקראות גדולות *ad loc.*

10 A. F. Kirkpatrick, *The Book of Psalms* (Cambridge Bible; Cambridge: Cambridge University, 1957): 39, cf. 35–36. Similarly Gunkel (N 5): 28; C. A. and E. G. Briggs, *A Critical and Exegetical Commentary on the Book of Psalms* 1 (ICC: Edinburgh: T. & T. Clark, 1952): 63–64; E. J. Kissane, *The Book of Psalms* (Dublin: Browne and Nolan, 1964): 34; H.-J. Kraus, *Psalmen. I. Teilband*[3] (BKAT XV/1; Neukirchen-Vluyn: Neukirchener Verlag des Erziehungsvereins, 1966): 69; H. P. Chajes, ספר תהלים (in series תורה נביאים וכתובים עם פירוש מדעי, ed. Abraham Kahana; reprint, Jerusalem:

"What is man" became a topos in the Hebrew Bible and apocryphal / pseudepigraphical literature,[11] and it expressed not man's insignificance but, as a rule, his mortality and transitoriness:[12]

ה׳ מה־אדם ותדעהו בן־אנוש ותחשבהו:
אדם להבל דמה ימיו כצל עובר:

O Lord, what is man that you should care about him,
mortal man, that you should think of him?
Man is like a breath;
his days are like a passing shadow.
(Ps 144:3–4)[13]

. . . לא לעלם אחנה חדל ממיי כי־הבל ימי:
מה־אנוש כי תגדלנו וכי תשית אליו לבך:

. . . I shall not live forever.
Let me alone, for my days are a breath.
What is man, that you should rear him,
that you should pay any mind to him?
(Job 7:16–17)[14]

τί ἄνθρωπος καὶ τί ἡ χρῆσις αὐτοῦ;
τί τὸ ἀγαθὸν αὐτοῦ καὶ τί τὸ κακὸν αὐτοῦ;
ἀριθμὸς ἡμερῶν ἀνθρώπου
πολλὰ ἔτη ἑκατόν·
ὡς σταγὼν ὕδατος ἀπὸ θαλάσσης καὶ ψῆφος ἄμμου,
οὕτως ὀλίγα ἔτη ἐν ἡμέρᾳ αἰῶνος.

What is man, of what worth is he?
the good, the evil in him, what are these?
The sum of a man's days is great
if it reaches a hundred years:
Like a drop of sea water, like a grain of sand,
so few are these years among the days of eternity.
(Ecclus 18:6–8)[15]

That Ps 8:5 expresses man's transitoriness is confirmed by the contrasting theme of permanence in the preceding verse, for that is what the heavenly bodies symbolize. Recent studies by Greenfield and Paul[16] have shown that throughout ancient literature the heavens, moon, and stars, as well as the sun, served as similes for length of days, permanence and eternity. These similes appear in Sumerian, Akkadian, Ugaritic, Phoenician and Punic, Aramaic, Egyptian and Latin, as well as Hebrew literature.[17] From the Bible itself one may cite such usages as לעד // כימי שמים, "forever" // "like the days of the heavens" (Ps 89:30); . . . למען ירבו ימיכם וימי בניכם כימי השמים על הארץ, "That your days and the days of your children may be multiplied as the days of the heavens above the earth" (Deut 11:21); כירח יכון עולם, "It shall be established forever, as the moon" (Ps 89:38). Similar usages in other literature are cited by Greenfield and Paul. There is no unambiguous use of the stars in this sense in the Bible,[18] but the Pyrgi inscription speaks of *šnt km hkkbm* . . . , "years like the stars."[19]

The logic connecting verses 4 and 5 is therefore: when the poet contemplates the heavens and their host, he is reminded of their permanence and then of man's transitoriness,[20] and he wonders that the Lord has taken note of so transitory a creature, going to the extent of making him nearly divine, adorning him with "glory and majesty,"[21] and making him ruler over all God's creatures.

In reading the psalm closely one can detect a possible implication that the psalmist would have expected God to assign such rule (תמשילהו) to the heavens, moon, and stars, becaused of their permanence, rather than to a transitory creature like man. Would this constitute an echo of Gen 1:16 and 18 (cf. Ps 136:9)? Those verses state that the sun and moon are to rule (לממשלת, למשל)[22] the day and night. Conceivably the psalmist was aware of

Makor, 1970): 14–15; B. D. Eerdmans, *The Hebrew Book of Psalms* (OTS 4; Leiden: Brill, 1947): 117; B. S. Childs, *Biblical Theology in Crisis* (Philadelphia: Westminster, 1970): 153; I. L. Seeligmann in VTS 1 (1953): 156.

11 Seeligmann (N 10): 156.

12 The exception is 4 Ezra 8:34–35, which refers to man's sinfulness and his need for mercy. A different motif beginning "what is man" appears in Job 15:14, with differently phrased parallels in 4:17 and 25:4.

13 Translation from *NJV*, 146.

14 I have intentionally translated the verse more literally than did Prof. Pope (*Job*[3] [AB 15; Garden City, NY: Doubleday, 1973]: 58) in order to highlight the similarity with Ps 8:5 and 144:3.

15 Translation from *The New American Bible* (New York: P. J. Kenedy, 1970): 964.

16 J. C. Greenfield, "Scripture and Inscription: The Literary and Rhetorical Element in Some Early Phoenician Inscriptions" in *Near Eastern Studies in Honor of William Foxwell Albright* (H. Goedicke, ed.; Baltimore: Johns Hopkins, 1971): 266–68; S. M. Paul, "Psalm 72:5—A Traditional Blessing for the Long Life of the King," *JNES* 31 (1972): 351–55. Note also F. M. Cross, *Canaanite Myth and Hebrew Epic* (Cambridge, MA: Harvard University, 1973): 18, n. 33.

17 For an example in Greek see M. Weinfeld, "Covenant Terminology in the Ancient Near East and Its Influence on the West," *JAOS* 93 (1973): 198–99, n. 109.

18 In Dan 12:3b the simile of stars refers primarily to shining, like the parallel firmament in v 12a, but perhaps it also partakes of the eternity expressed in the concluding phrase לעלם ועד.

19 *KAI* 277:10.

20 The logic was perceived by A. Weiser, *The Psalms* (Old Testament Library; Philadelphia: Westminster, 1952): 143.

21 For הוד והדר as the divine and royal radiance see M. Weinfeld, "The Creator God in Genesis 1 and in Second Isaiah," *Tarbiz* 37 (1968): 131–32 (Hebrew).

22 Ps 136:8–9 construe ממשלת as a noun (meaning "ruler") as shown by the plural ממשלות in v. 9; see M. J. Dahood, *Psalms III* (AB 17a; Garden City, NY: Doubleday, 1970): 266.

that concept—perhaps even of those verses or others like them—and was for that reason prompted to wonder why the "authority" of the heavens, moon, and stars was not more extensive, covering the living creatures as well. This would reflect a sense of the falsity of astrology or of heavenly-astral-lunar cults. The account of the creation of the luminaries in Gen 1:14–19 has sometimes been taken as a polemic against such cults,[23] but it would be going too far to see such a polemic in the psalm. Polemic is very difficult to demonstrate unless it is explicit,[24] and it would seem in the present case to overload a lyrical psalm. The poet's contemplation of the nighttime[25] sky has moved him to exclamation and wonder,[26] not to argument.[27]

23 *S. D. Luzzatto's Commentary to the Pentateuch* (P. Schlesinger, ed.; Tel Aviv: Dvir, 1965): 11–12; U. M. D. Cassuto, *Commentary on the Book of Genesis* Part I (I. Abrahams, trans.; Jerusalem: Magnes, 1961): 43.

24 Note Kaufmann's refutation of Cassuto's polemic interpretation of Gen 1:14–19: Y. Kaufman, מכבשונה של היצירה המקראית (Tel Aviv: Dvir, 1966): 232.

25 Most commentators have reasoned from the mention of moon and stars and the absence of the sun that the psalmist was looking at the sky at night; see, for example, Kimḥi (N 4): 25; Briggs and Briggs (N 10): 61 top; Kissane (N 10): 34; Kraus (N 10): 66. Indeed, were the psalm not based on a visual experience there would be no obvious reason for the omission of the sun, which would surely have been mentioned were the psalmist simply reflecting in the abstract. Some scholars, on the other hand, emend שמיך to שמש; see Gunkel (N 5): 30 (emendation rejected); Kissane (N 9): 34; H. L. Ginsberg, "Some Emendations in Psalms," *HUCA* 23 (1950–51) : 98.

26 Note the threefold repetition of מה, in the first, middle, and last verses of the psalm (excluding the title).

27 For an Akkadian lyric prayer inspired by contemplation of the nighttime sky see *ANET* 390–91 and A. L. Oppenheim, "A New Prayer to 'the Gods of the Night,' " in *Analecta Biblica* 12/III (1959): 282–301.

IN DEFIANCE OF DEATH: ZECHARIAH'S SYMBOLIC UNIVERSE

PAUL D. HANSON

Death scarcely could have been further from the minds of the Deuteronomistic commentators as they reported on their *David redivivus,* Josiah: "Before him there was no king like him, who turned to the Lord with all his heart and with all his soul and with all his might, according to all the laws of Moses; nor did any like him arise after him" (2 Kgs 23:25). On the basis of their orthodox theology, it was as easy to extrapolate the destruction of the Northern Kingdom from the sin of Jeroboam as it was to predict national prosperity and security for Judah because of the covenant fidelity of this Davidide. Therefore, no harsher contradiction to their theological construction could have been encountered than the chain of disasters extending from 609 to 587 B.C.E.: the senseless death of Josiah in a battle from which he had nothing to gain; a series of selfish, weak successors to the Davidic throne; the first exile in 596; the second a decade later; and finally the destruction of the central symbol of the royal cult, the Jerusalem temple.

How could the propitious early years of Josiah's reign and their culmination in the reform of 622 issue forth in such calamitous defeats as these? How could a pattern of happenings signifying life lead instead to death, death of the king, death of the cult, death of the nation? The theology of the Deuteronomistic School was sorely challenged, and its underlying retributive doctrine became vulnerable to attack from several different perspectives. The result was the growth of a number of distinct theological explanations of the nation's suffering. Careful study of the biblical literature of the period reveals the contours of several traditions, each with its ideal of how the nation could be reconstituted so as to live again in covenant fidelity with God.

In this article we shall examine a prophetic witness to one of the traditions which developed in the exilic and post-exilic periods. In Zechariah 1–8, we discover visions and oracles which arose out of the efforts of a prophet to reconstitute order out of the chaos of the late seventh and early sixth centuries. The *Gestalt* which emerges can be described as a symbolic universe, for through the selection of familiar symbols and their utilization in an overreaching linguistic structure the prophet painted a picture of the new community which God was already raising up from the ruins of national calamity. The result was a daring claim that God had not forsaken his people. Defiantly and with holy zeal Zechariah announced God's word: though world events seemed to indicate so, death was not God's last pronouncement on the Jewish community.

Our examination of Zechariah's symbolic universe entails several stages.[1] Accordingly we shall proceed as follows: I) sketch the literary stratification of Zechariah 1–8 in the effort to distinguish between different levels of tradition within a corpus which passed through several stages of growth; II) seek to establish the historical setting of the core of Zechariah material in these chapters and to describe the community situation which pertained at that time; III) delineate the community ideal underlying this core; IV) study how that ideal was translated into a program of restoration by means of a series of seven symbolical visions and a group of divine pronouncements; V) identify the theological tradition out of which this community ideal grew; VI) contrast it with other ideals current at that time; VII) consider theological implications.

I. Levels of Tradition in Zechariah 1–8

Because the present book of Zechariah is the result of a growth process which was over a century in duration, it is necessary to identify levels of tradition before addressing the questions of setting and meaning. We shall exclude chapters 9–11 and 12–14 from consideration, for they represent two separate booklets, which along with Malachi, were attached to the minor prophets at a late date. What follows consists of a summary of the present writer's previous research, since detailed analysis of each level would extend beyond the limits of this paper.

A. A Series of Seven Nocturnal Visions, Elaborated by Prophetic Logia

The core of Zechariah 1–8 is found in a series of visions, which at an early point were elaborated by divine sayings which seem to come from Zechariah himself. Whether they were added to the visions by the prophet or by followers is impossible to determine. Besides these elaborations, we shall simply list in brackets additions which likely were added at a later time, which will not concern us here.

The seven visions, in their original collection (which because of their collective symmetry and thematic unity, may have been the product of a single visionary experience), were introduced by 1:7a, which would have

1 The material which follows was presented to the "Consultation on Post-exilic Theology" at the annual meeting of the Society of Biblical Literature in New York on November 15, 1979.

been followed immediately by 1:8 in a form resembling Ezekiel 1:1. 1:7b was added at a later date (by the final editor whom we shall call "the Chronicler") to bring this introduction into conformity with the introductory form found in Hag 1:1; 2:1, 10, 20; Zech 1:1 and 7:1 (a third person form resembling Ezek 1:2).

1. 1:8-15 is the first vision. It betrays the tripartite structure characteristic of these visions: description of the spectacle, the seer's inquiry after its meaning, the interpretation. As in visions 3, 5, and 7, the interpretation contained within the context of the vision itself is amplified by a divine word in vv. 14-15, which was, however, an original part of the unit, necessary because the interpretation was incomplete without it. This original unit was elaborated by another divine word, in v. 16, a word, while likely from Zechariah's own sayings, not original to this context. [Later addition: v. 17.]

2. 2:1-4. This vision contains two symbols, and thus the description-inquiry-interpretation occurs twice.

3. 2:5-9. Here the interpretation was again amplified by a divine word in vv. 8b-9. That original unit was subsequently elaborated by two divine pronouncements using imperatives followed by motive clauses introduced by *kî hinnî*. The first, in vv. 10-13, is a summons to flee, the second, in vv. 14 and 15b, is a summons to rejoice. They represent two stages in a holy war scenario, and elaborate the original divine word in vv. 8b-9 effectively. They likely come from original Zechariah material. [Later additions: v. 15a, v. 16 (cf. 1:17), v. 17.]

4. 4:1-6α. 10b-14. The fourth vision contains a double inquiry and interpretation. Central both in position and significance, it also received the most elaboration. An entire vision was placed before it in chapter 3 to elaborate on the theme of one of the "sons of oil" of 4:14, even as two divine sayings, vv. 6aα-7 and vv. 8-10a, were inserted into the fourth vision to elaborate on the theme of the other anointed one. The vision in chapter 3 is distinctly different in form from the seven others, and hence is to be judged as originating separately. Like the two divine sayings, though, it gives every appearance of belonging to authentic Zechariah tradition.

5. 5:1-4, within which the interpretation is amplified by the divine word in v. 4.

6. 5:5-11. Here the description-inquiry-interpretation is repeated thrice, in keeping with the enlarged repertoire of symbolism in this vision.

7. 6:1-8. The interpretation is amplified by a divine word in v. 8.

B. Other Zechariah Materials

We shall not analyze the remaining parts of Zechariah 1–8 in detail, since the seven nocturnal visions and the prophetic logia acompanying them will provide sufficient material for our inquiry. We should note, however, that an original Zechariah unit, closely related in theme and setting to the seven visions and the Joshua vision in chapter 3, is preserved in 6:9-15. In 1:1-6 and chapters 7 and 8, various Zechariah materials, elaborated by later additions, have been gathered and formed into a framework around the visions. These sections, replete with complex literary and historical questions, cannot be studied here.

C. Final Redaction

We see evidence of a final redaction by a "Chronicler" in a series of chronological introductions here and in Haggai: Hag 1:1; 2:1; 2:10 and 2:20; Zech 1:1, 7b; 7:1.[2]

II. Historical Setting and Community Situation

A. Historical Setting

What we have taken to be the original introduction to the seven nocturnal visions in 1:7a gives us this date for the visions: Second year of Darius, eleventh month, twenty-fourth day, i.e., February 519.[3] This date is very plausible for the following reasons: 1) Late in November, 521, Darius defeated the last of his opponents, the two rival claimants to the Babylonian throne. This inaugurated a period in which the Persian Empire was securely in the hands of Darius, the picture given to us in the first vision and in keeping with the message of the others; 2) Haggai's oracles are dated August, September, and December, 520. His message is aimed at getting the temple-building underway. This dating is corroborated by Ezra 4:24 and 5:1. It is entirely reasonable to assume that Zechariah's visions were made public in the period right after Haggai's initial attempts, and that they were timed to add support to the temple-rebuilding efforts of Zerubbabel (and Jeshua).[4]

As for the Zechariah materials which were added to amplify the message of the visions, the following may be surmised: 1) 1:16 seems to be the conclusion of an oracle delivered by Zechariah at the time of Haggai's activity, for it is a divine promise in support of the rebuilding of the temple (cf. Hag. 1:8, 13; 2:4-5); 2) 2:10-13 and 14, 15b reflect a Babylonian setting, and would have been pronounced by Zechariah before his group returned from Babylon, and indeed, as a part of the effort to motivate such a return. It could be conjectured that the time in question was that of the rebellious eruptions occurring in the Persian Empire after the death of Cambyses in 522. The revolt of Gaumata, and the fires of revolution which swept over Elam, Babylon, Media, Parthia, Hyrcania, and Armenia must have appeared to a devout Jew as the shaking of Yahweh's hand over the nations, an altogether appropriate setting for a summons to flee from Babylon

2 Cf. P. Ackroyd, "Studies in the Book of Haggai," *JJS* 2 (1951): 163–76 and *JJS* 3 (1952): 1–13, and *idem*., "The Book of Haggai and Zechariah I–VIII," *JJS* 3 (1952): 151–56.

3 Darius' first year: 4/13/521–4/13/520.
Darius' second year: 4/12/520–4/13/519.

4 On the relation of the date in 1:7a to the visions, see further Ch. Jeremias, *Die Nachtgesichte des Sacharja* (Göttingen: Vandenhoeck & Ruprecht, 1977): 15–36.

directed at the daughter of Zion. Later that period of unrest would have been interpreted by Zechariah as an adumbration of Yahweh's final theophany when he would appear to the daughter of Zion as "a wall of fire," and his *kābôd* would take up dwelling in her midst (2:9). Thus the earlier saying would have seemed appropriate as an amplification of the third vision at a time when the Empire was at rest, and God's people eagerly awaited the decisive theophany; 3) We do not know precisely when Jeshua was anointed High Priest. Chapter 3 would have originated in connection with that ceremony, and it proved to be an entirely appropriate addition to the central vision in chapter 4; 4) The divine word in 4:6aβ-7 would have been delivered by Zechariah at the time of the (re)laying of the cornerstone of the temple, i.e., roughly in September of 520. The same applies to 4:8-10a (compare 4:10a with Hag 2:3-9). Even as chapter 3 was brought into juxtaposition with chapter 4 so as to elaborate on the authority of Jeshua, so too the earlier sayings in 4:6aβ-7 and 4:8-10a were added to enhance the position of the other key authority figure of the fourth vision, Zerubbabel; 5) 6:9-14 has been worked and reworked in relation to the changing positions of the Prince and High Priest. But in its original form it contained a divine word directed at establishing the authority of Zerubbabel and Jeshua in a manner similar to the fourth vision and its elaborations in chapter 3 and 4:6aβ-7 and 8-10a. Since it focuses on Zerubabbel's role in rebuilding the temple, it likely stems, in its original form, from a divine pronouncement made by Zechariah in the latter half of 520; 6) 6:15 is now out of context. It may have been the climax of the seventh vision. Or it may have been a concluding section of another Zechariah word, since lost. It reflects the pro-*golah* bias of Zechariah, and would have stemmed from the early period of rebuilding when controversy raged over the question how inclusive participation was to be.

B. Community Situation

We receive only a glimpse of the prophet in the period immediately preceding the return of his group from exile. But 2:10-13 and 14, 15b suggest that he was scanning the stage of history for signs of Yahweh's intervention to fulfill his promises to the exilic community. The bulk of the Zechariah material, however, derives from the period after his *golah* group had returned to the land. Lingering in their memory were the brilliant promises of Second Isaiah, which tied the return to the glories of a new era of salvation. But the record created doubts: at some time previous an attempt had been made to rebuild the temple under the leadership of Sheshbazzar, but it had come to naught. Hag 1:2-11 describes the times in terms of drought and economic reversal. Zech 4:10a corroborates this description of the late 520's. It is a time of "small things." Where were those glorious acts of Yahweh which Second Isaiah promised would accompany the return? Why were they delayed? Why were opponents able to frustrate the efforts of the returnees to rebuild Yahweh's house and restore their community? What were the Zadokite leaders and their followers to do with the charges of the opposition that the failure of the eschaton to materialize was due to corruption in the nation's leadership?[5]

We are able to recognize a community situation in which the harsh challenge to community identity inflicted by 587 has been exacerbated by the failure of Second Isaiah's message to find fulfillment, and by the accusations of disenfranchised opponents and affronted Samaritans. Certain followers of Second Isaiah are claiming that God's people has experienced "darkness" instead of "light" because of an apostate Zadokite leadership class: the temple which it seeks to rebuild is defiled by its impurity.

The hour called desperately for a clarification of the community ideal of the Zadokite-led *golah* group, and for a grounding of that ideal in the authoritative traditions of the past. Haggai contributed an impassioned plea for renewed dedication to the rebuilding program. But it fell to Zechariah to paint that ideal in the arresting imagery of a symbolic universe.

III. Zechariah's Community Ideal

We shall sketch briefly the community ideal as delineated in the core of Zechariah 1-8; 1) *bat-ṣiyyôn* (i.e., exclusively the returned *golah*-group [6:15]) is a community belonging to the "Lord of the Whole Earth" (4:14; 1:8-15; 2:1-4; 6:1-8); 2) It is a community which is heir to the ancient promises of Abraham (e.g., Gen 17:1-8), promises expressed in terms of a covenant bringing with it faithful leaders (4:14; 6:13), as well as a land of prosperity (3:9) and abundant human and animal offspring (2:8); 3) In keeping with the Abrahamic covenant (Gen 17:1), the covenant obligates the people to be a holy people (3:9; 5:1-4 and 5-11); 4) This holiness is a necessary condition for Yahweh's dwelling within her and protecting her (2:9, 10-15); 5) As a holy people of Yahweh, her land is centered around Yahweh's temple (1:16; 4:6aβ-7 and 8-10a; 6:12-13); 6) Yahweh's representatives on earth are the two anointed ones, the Prince and the High Priest (chapter 3; 4:14; 4:6aβ-10a; 6:9-14).

IV. The Seven Visions as Symbolic Expression of Zechariah's Community Ideal

In a remarkably skillful manner the series of seven visions is structured into a symbolic portrayal of the sacral universe which is the basis of Zechariah's community ideal. As such it constitutes a *hieros logos* of the temple and its gathered community comparable to Gen 28:10-22 and 2 Samuel 7, to which also the Gudea

5 Isa 56:9–57:13; 65; 66:1–17. Cf. P. D. Hanson, *The Dawn of Apocalyptic* (Philadelphia: Fortress, 1979²): 32–208.

and Nabonidus Inscriptions might be compared. As a *hieros logos,* it offers divine authorization for the temple and its organization of leadership coming from the Lord of the Whole Earth who resides in the Divine Council.

The structure of the series of seven visions reflects the architecture of the temple and its surrounding precincts. At the center is the menorah (fourth vision), at its extremities the courtyard which blends into the cosmic gates of the heavenly court (first and seventh visions). To one side is the world of earthly kingdoms which are a part of Yahweh's domain (second vision) and the holy city (third vision). To the other side is the community protected from the defiled (fifth vision) and purified of evil (sixth vision). Thereby portrayed is a symbolic universe generating tremendous centrifugal force (*yṣʾ* occurs fourteen times, compared with *ʿmd* four times). It teems with all of the functions of the temple. In order, the visions portray this sacred center as: 1) place of audience before the divine council; 2) seat of judgment on the nations; 3) source of protection of the community of Zion; 4) residence of Yahweh, seat of government, locus of authority; 5) place of origin of the curses of the covenant; 6) place of atonement and purification; 7) center of the universal divine kingdom.[6]

The authority of this symbolic universe, however, does not derive merely from its representing an earthly cult place. Rather, the archetypal thinking expressed in the Priestly account of the tabernacle (cf. *tabnît* in Exod 25:9 and 40), and deriving from the archetype/copy relation between cosmic and mundane temple in ancient Near Eastern mythopoeic thought, expresses itself powerfully in the seven visions (as well as in the Jeshua vision of chapter 3). The greatest significance of the temple portrayed in the vision and which the people are to build is that it is the reflection of the heavenly temple within which Yahweh resides amidst his holy attendants. This is the reason why lines blur between temple courtyard and cosmic gates in vision one, between earthly and heavenly antagonists in vision two, between hamlets and divine walls in vision three, between human and divine court attendants in the Jeshua vision, between menorah and a supermundane scroll in vision five, between community sin and angelic beings in vision six, between earthly kingdoms and heavenly chariots in vision seven.

This archetype/copy relationship at the base of the symbolic universe in these visions provides the theological foundation for Zechariah's message. People are deceived who look merely at earthly happenings and conditions, for they are mere reflections. That "all the earth remains at rest" is therefore deceptive, in and of itself. But in the visions the prophet has been made privy to the prototype from which all reflections derive, to the temple courtyard wherein are gathered the divine beings who execute the commands of the one true Lord of all the Earth. On the mundane surface of things all may appear securely within the power of the Persian Emperor, but in the heavenly court a remarkable scenario is unfolding.

We now view the symbols seen by the seer, and, with the aid of the interpreting angel, penetrate the veil to glimpse the heavenly court of the Almighty.

The sweep of the visions is cosmic in embrace: at each end the seer observes the divine patrols, with steeds hoofing impatiently as they await orders to patrol the earth. At the center the seer encounters Yahweh face-to-face as the menorah unveils the eyes which watch over all. This is a graphic portrayal of the temple as *omphalos mundi*, where the *pānîm* of Yahweh is encountered in the divine theophany, and where the *kābôd* dwells in splendor symbolized by precious metals and fire. This center, portrayed by the menorah of the middle vision which, with its seven shining lamps represents the seven "eyes of Yahweh which range through the whole earth," already embraces the entire cosmic reality symbolized by all seven visions. And as the center Reality which embraces all, the menorah representing the Presence of Yahweh is static, at rest. But from it derives the restless motion which moves out in ever broadening waves till the extremities of the gates of heaven and the far north are reached in the first and seventh visions respectively.

We have seen how the nocturnal visions are structured in such a way that the symbolic universe they portray is upheld and embraced by the center, the temple of Yahweh. There are set the eyes of Yahweh which watch over the whole world, and there the divine attendants stand at attention. In tension with this static form, however, is a dramatic movement which unfolds in a rectilinear fashion through the visions, from the first through the seventh. This movement indicates that the transcendent Reality which maintains the formal structures of the universe is also the Reality which guides the events of history in a meaningful progression toward a goal. Let us now trace that movement.

Vision one occurs at the outer gates of the heavenly court. The seer sees the equestrian patrols who have just returned from their mission, under the orders of Yahweh. Their report is, "We have patrolled the earth, and behold, all the earth remains at rest" (1:11). As the human community knows only too well, nothing is happening to suggest a turn of events; all is securely in the hands of the Persian overlords. As intercessor of the people, the angel expresses their concern: "How long?" And the reference to the "seventy years of indignation" suggests that a denouement should be imminent. The scene moves towards the inner court, and the veil is parted as the voice of Yahweh is heard, the voice of the one directing the events of history, and his words are "gracious and comforting." Amplifying this assuring description is a direct word of Yahweh through the angel to the seer: "I am exceedingly jealous for Jerusalem and Zion. And I am very angry with the nations that are at ease; for while I was angry but a little, they furthered the disaster." Yahweh has not given up his covenant with Jerusalem and

6 Cf. K. Seybold, *Bilder zum Tempelbau. Die Visionen des Prophetes Sacharja* (SB 70; Stuttgart: KBW, 1974): 99.

Zion, that is, the exilic community. They were punished because of Yahweh's anger, to be sure, but this was but "a little," that is, limited in intensity and duration. The nations at ease, the very powers who maintain the earth in the state of rest witnessed by the patrols, have overstepped their commission of executing Yahweh's judgment. Therefore, a turning point is imminent. The anger formerly directed against Jerusalem and utilizing the nations as a rod of punishment has now been redirected against the nations. Moreover, in contrast to the "little" (*meᶜaṭ*) anger against Jerusalem, the anger against the nations is "great" (*gādôl*)! The word of explication in v. 16, deriving from another point in Zechariah's career, draws out the concrete implication of this great turn of events already underway in heaven and, according to divine assurance, to be witnessed on earth in the near future. The vision is thus a clear warning not to let appearances deceive, but to trust in the Lord's plan.

After this clear statement that the initiative is Yahweh's, vision two, through the symbols of the "horns" and the "smiths," announces that Yahweh has already commissioned agents to remove all (four = totality) earthly kingdoms which have scattered the nation. The result will be freedom of God's people from external threats. The institutional milieu of this vision is holy war.

Under the symbol of the man with the measuring line, the third vision pictures a nation reestablished under the covenant blessings of Yahweh, with increase of progeny and prosperity, and with the Warrior God of exodus tradition protecting her as a wall of fire and dwelling within her in the theophanic nimbus of the *kābôd*.

The action of the first three visions thus has secured the land for the people of God, and has already promised Yahweh's indwelling. This preparation and promise leads to the fourth vision, which in the directional movement of the drama as in the structural form of the symbolic universe is the critical center of the visions. The focus is on the symbol of the menorah, standing splendidly at the center of the center, at the heart of the temple, with its seven lamps and two olive trees. This leads to a two-fold interpretation: "These seven are the eyes of Yahweh which range through the whole earth." Here dwells the universal Lord in whose service stand the patrols seen in vision one, and again to be encountered in vision seven. And closely tied to this Lord are the "two branches," symbolizing "the two anointed who stand by the Lord of the whole earth." Here too the prototypological thinking of a mythopoeic world view glimmers through, according to which the heavenly temple/earthly temple polarity is matched by the corresponding pair of heavenly ruler/earthly ruler. The residence of the deity is also the administrative center of those who represent Yahweh on earth, who thereby "stand by the Lord of the whole earth." Thus the temple program and the diarchical administrative structure are given the most powerful theological authorization possible by being grounded in the central reality of Zechariah's symbolical universe. Appropriately, the Jeshua vision of chapter three and the two divine words relating to Zerubbabel in 4:6aβ-10a add weight to this authorization, as does the passage in 6:9-14. The hints left in the text of the complicated history of transmission through which these passages passed betrays how precarious was the innovation of a diarchy in the post-exilic community.

The covenant life of blessing in the land and the indwelling of Yahweh prepare for the next concern, ritual purity. Yahweh cannot live in the context of defilement; neither can the blessings of the covenant be enjoyed amidst sinfulness. Vision five, under the symbol of the gigantic flying scroll, portrays the elimination of those elements in the land which, by perpetrating evil, threaten the viability of the entire community (because of the Hebrew view of corporate contamination). And vision six expands on this concern with the dramatic banishment of Lady Wickedness to Shinar (Babylon), where an anti-temple is built for her.

The seventh vision draws on a symbol of holy war, the multi-colored chariotry, to proclaim that the crucial divine action is already underway in heaven, and soon to be experienced on earth. Critical is the north country, that region so awesome for the Jews in their mythology and history alike. There Yahweh's "Spirit has been set at rest," a cryptic phrase which must refer to some important aspect of the divine war which will reverse the fortunes of Israel in relation to the kingdoms of this earth.

Here, then, we see the dramatic movement portrayed by the visions, as both external and internal obstacles are removed, making way for the reestablishment of Israel's holy center on Zion, where Yahweh will again take up his dwelling and where Yahweh's anointed will rule over a sanctified and secured people.

Now we take special note of the significance of the two structural patterns which we have observed in the nocturnal visions. The former, in which the entire cosmos is embraced from the motionless center of the temple, is the pattern at home in the world view of myth. Its orientation is spatial; it is a view emphasizing formal structures which are static and eternal. Upon them rest the foundations of the universe. It is crucial that those structures be maintained, lest all reality collapse into chaos. According to this view, the importance of temple and properly anointed rulers cannot be overemphasized. The latter pattern, which traces chronological movement through historical events along a purposeful continuum directed towards a goal, is the one we associate with Israel's central contribution to religious thought. It is the movement from promise to fulfillment found in the patriarchal narratives, in exodus tradition and in prophetic Yahwism. We recognize that the drama which unfolds in the seven visions also moves from the promises implicit in the covenant toward a denouement in which God's purposes with his people will be accomplished. It is a dramatic view which sees divine assembly and earthly temple not as the center of motionless reality, but of activity aimed at judgment, salvation and purification.

Zechariah is not the first biblical witness to the tension

between mythopoeic and historical worldviews. Such tension is found already in early Yahwistic poetry; it permeates Israel's hymnody, and is not absent in the classical prophets. But this tension emerges with a new intensity in the post-exilic period, and the increased weight given to the mythopoeic pattern is a sure sign of the emergence of apocalyptic eschatology.

V. Theological Tradition out of which Zechariah's Community Ideal Grew

Mention should first be made of the fact that Zechariah clearly stands within the same theological tradition as Haggai. Though differences are not lacking, both envision God's people (= the *golah*) gathered around the temple, protected by Yahweh from external threats, led by a sanctified prince and high priest, and safeguarding the indwelling of Yahweh's *kābôd* by a life of ritual purity and careful separation from defilement. (Hag 2:11b–14).

Behind this, it is clear that the theological tradition within which Zechariah stands traces back to the temple-centered theology of the Priestly writers, a tradition which also found powerful expression in Ezekiel. Zechariah's model is the Solomonic temple, and he seeks to establish a line of connection with the tradition which he regards as normative, which thus can serve to renew the spiritual identity of the people and serve as the basis for restoring the community as a People of God. In describing the community situation of Zechariah's time in II.B. above, we indicated that the trauma of 587, the failure of Second Isaiah's glorious promises to materialize with the return from exile, and the criticism of opponents, called for a clarification of the community ideal of the Zadokite-led *golah* group, and for a grounding of that ideal in the authoritative traditions of the past. It was by building upon the powerful Priestly traditions that Zechariah was able to establish an authoritative foundation under his message.

Here, for reasons of space, our evidence must be sketchy. We can note that the visions of Zechariah set forth a program of restoration which recapitulates the original establishment of the cult at Sinai, as recorded by P. For P, that cult is the central reality of Israel's life, indeed, the goal of all history. Careful descriptions of what was required for a sanctuary, and careful regulating of cult personnel was the first order of business. After this, the crucial event was Yahweh's coming to be with Israel as the *kābôd* which appeared over the Tabernacle (Exod 40:34–35). Essential to life was the holy structure at the very center of the community, and important as well was the maintaining of ritual purity as a necessary condition for Yahweh's remaining at the people's disposal. Hence, the laws regulating purity; for Israel was to be a "kingdom of priests and a holy nation" (Exod 19:6).

We have seen how the centrality of the temple and the holiness of the people are of central importance to Zechariah as well. Indeed the fifth and sixth visions closely resemble priestly accounts such as Leviticus 14 and 16 respectively. Rites of purification and laws regulating procedure in the event of defilement are of intense concern, for sin and impurity would defile the place where Yahweh tabernacled among the people, and would lead to Yahweh's withdrawal. That, of course, spelled doom, as Israel would be cut off from her source.

The Book of Ezekiel, developing within the same Zadokite-priestly tradition, describes the outcome of the defilement of the people. In the visions of chapters 8-11, Ezekiel witnesses the abominations which polluted God's sanctuary, and led to the destruction of temple and city. On the level of divine reality, this event is described as the withdrawal of Yahweh's *kābôd* from the temple (9:3; 10:18; 11:22–25). Though removed from the temple, however, Yahweh's *kābôd* does not abandon the people. It goes eastward, and appears to Ezekiel by the river Chebar. Which is to say that according to the tradition developed by Ezekiel, the *golah* is the carrier of God's plan for restoration.

Ezekiel proceeds to sketch the blueprint for restoration which will enable the return of people and *kābôd yahweh* to Zion, and indeed he sees that return in a vision (43:1-5), even as he had earlier witnessed its withdrawal. Zechariah inherited that blueprint, and on that basis and on the basis of the Solomonic temple behind it were constructed his symbolic universe and community ideal.

Two texts from within the priestly-Zadokite tradition illustrate the position of Zechariah's prophecy within the overall history of that theological tradition. Lev 26:3–46 was added to the Holiness Code after 587. It enumerates both the conditions of covenantal blessing (vv. 3–13) and of curse (vv. 14–33). The disobedience of the people led to the latter, and hence, the description in verses 16–33 of all that Israel had suffered. But Yahweh promises that if the people confess their sin (*ʿăwonām* = Zech 5:6), Yahweh will remember his covenant (vv. 40–45). Zechariah comes out of the same tradition, addresses the same conditions, and offers the same answer, though more vividly than the author of Lev 26:3–46.

Secondly, Ezekiel 38–39 reflects the same tradition at the same period as Zechariah. After the vivid vision of the valley of dry bones and the sign act of the repaired staff, Proto-Ezekiel promised the restoration of the land under the Davidic prince in 37:24–28: "I will make a covenant of peace with them . . . an everlasting covenant . . . I will bless them and multiply them, and will set my sanctuary in the midst of them for evermore." The logical progression occurs in Ezekiel 40–48, where the plan of restoration is portrayed. But someone saw fit to insert the harsh pictures of judgment and deliverance of Ezekiel 38–39, which interupt the smooth progression from promise to fulfillment. That someone was close in time and spirit to the community of Zechariah. The return had not inaugurated the era of salvation. Further trial awaited the *golah*. Fierce foes lay in wait to attack "the quiet people who dwell securely, all of them dwelling without walls" (38:11, cf. Zech. 2:8!). But the final message of these terrifying chapters is one of hope: Yahweh will turn against the foes of Israel, and "restore the fortunes of Jacob; and have mercy upon the whole house of Israel; and I will be jealous for my holy name" (39:25). Once again they will dwell securely in the land, this time in faithfulness to Yahweh (39:26–29). Compared to Zechariah we here find the same community ideal, the same response to a bleak community situation, the same reply to those questioning why Yahweh had not fulfilled his promises: Do not be deceived by appearances. The seers (Zechariah and the author of Ezekiel 38–39) see through the veil to what is happening in heaven. "I am exceedingly jealous for Jerusalem and for Zion. And I am very angry with the nations that are at ease; for while I was angry but a little they furthered the disaster" (Zech 1:14–15). Just wait, the fortunes of the nations will soon reverse, and the hand of Yahweh will be exposed to all, in judgment to the nations and in salvation to his people.

VI. Other Community Ideals of the Period

Not all agreed with Zechariah and the exilic/post-exilic authors of Leviticus 26 and Ezekiel 38–39. One oppositions group was treated in the present writer's *The Dawn of Apocalyptic.*[7] Further study must be devoted to the school of Jeremiah, to the exilic additions of the Deuteronomistic School (with its *šēm* theology), to wisdom writings, and to other prophetic voices like Joel and Malachi.

7 Pp. 32–208 and 280–401.

VII. Theological Implications

Rectilinear schemes for constructing biblical theologies do not provide a framework within which divergent theological traditions can be adequately interpreted and evaluated. They tend to ignore even the tensions residing within a single theological tradition, such as the tension between mythic and historical world views noted above (IV, end) in Zechariah. A more promising approach may be a dialectical one, which recognizes the unfolding of theological traditions in the Bible within polarities which are faithful witnesses to the fulness of biblical revelation only if taken in their tension-filled totality.[8]

8 In *Dynamic Transcendence* (Philadelphia: Fortress, 1978), the present writer has described one polarity which is found in the biblical traditions of the exilic and early post-exilic period, which can be designated a visionary / pragmatic polarity. Another polarity, involving tension between form and reform perspectives, characterizes the age of kings and prophets in Israel. It is described in the book, *In Many and Various Ways: The Diversity of Scripture* (Philadelphia: Fortress, 1981).

HOLINESS AND DEATH IN THE REDACTION OF NUMBERS 16:1–20:13

THOMAS W. MANN

Studies from a variety of phenomenological and anthropological approaches have revealed the close connection in many religious symbol-systems between holiness and death. Long ago Rudolf Otto described the absolute dread and terror with which primitive religious consciousness faced the *mysterium tremendum*, a basic aspect of which was the "absolute unapproachability" of the divine "Wholly Other."[1] More recently, Mary Douglas has explored related themes in a study suggestively titled *Purity and Danger,*[2] a title which could stand as an analogue for our phrase "holiness and death." About the same time, Paul Ricoeur issued his profound study, *The Symbolism of Evil,* part of which investigated the dynamics of "defilement," the subjective aspect of which was connected with "the intuition of primordial fatality," an intuition which Ricoeur identified as the root of primitive religious consciousness.[3] All of these studies, of course, have drawn on the Old Testament as part of their source material. Accordingly, before we turn to the examination of a particular literary unit in which the themes of holiness and death are prominent (Num 16:1–20:13), it will be helpful to review several of the passages which often enter into the discussion. Such a review will serve to introduce some of the language and conceptuality which is peculiar to our topic.

In Isaiah 6 the connection between the holiness of Yahweh and the subjective aspect of defilement is revealed in the prophet's agonizing reaction to "the Holy One of Israel." While the seraphim proclaim the trisagion—"Holy, holy, holy is Yahweh of hosts"—Isaiah is overwhelmed by the fact that he has *seen* (*rʾh*) Yahweh of hosts, and his experience propels him into a confession of his "uncleanness" (*ṭmʾ*). It is precisely this state of defilement in the face of the Holy which threatens the prophet's life, and only a burning coal from the incense altar can remove his guilt or atone for his sin.[4] While a visual dimension dominates this encounter with the Holy (*rʾh*, vv. 1 and 5),[5] and is no doubt related to the belief that one cannot see God and live,[6] elsewhere the connection between holiness and death also has to do with spatial and tactile configurations. Two examples from Exodus are instructive. In the call of Moses when Moses turns to see (*rʾh*) the burning bush more closely, there is a real sense of danger expressed in the divine prohibition, "Do not come near (*qrb*); take off your shoes, for the place on which you are standing is holy ground" (Exod 3:5). Even more striking are the associations between holiness and death in various materials attached to the account of the Sinai theophany (Exodus 19): the people are to be "consecrated" (*qdš* Piel) before the appearance of Yahweh, and this is associated with the cleansing of garments (vv. 10, 14); anyone who touches (*ngʿ*) the mountain is to be executed, and the prohibition is expressed by an apodictic formula (*kol-hannōgēaʿ bāhār môt yûmāt*, v. 12); the execution must be done by stoning or shooting with arrows, so that no one touches (*ngʿ*) the guilty party; as with Isaiah and Moses (3:3-4a), even an unrestrained attempt to see (*rʾh*) Yahweh will lead to the death of many, v. 21. Even more germane to our interests in this paper, much of the remaining narrative (through chapter 24) concerns those who may and may not "approach" (*ngš*) the divinity. In 19:22-24, Yahweh warns that the priests who approach must consecrate themselves (*qdš*, Hith.), lest Yahweh break out upon them, yet in the end only Moses and Aaron are allowed to ascend the mountain. Similar language is used in the sequel to the theophany in 20:18-23. The people do not want Yahweh to speak to them directly, "lest we die." While the people stand "at a distance," Moses "approaches" (*ngš*) the awesome divine presence. Although with some ambiguity, the same issue of "approachability" is involved in 24:1-2, 9-11. Here Moses and others are to ascend the mountain and worship Yahweh "at a distance," but Moses alone will be allowed to "approach" (*ngš*) Yahweh. On the other hand, in vv. 9-11, Aaron, Nadab, Abihu, and the seventy elders all are allowed to "see" (*rʾh* and *ḥzh*) the God of Israel, and the text emphasizes the astounding fact that this happened without divine punishment (v. 11a). Similar associations between holiness and death are connected with the well known incidents involving the ark in 1 and 2 Samuel 6. In the former, Yahweh deals a fatal blow (*nkh*) to a number of men who look (*rʾh*) into the ark, and the townspeople recognize that no one can stand before Yahweh, "this

1 R. Otto, *The Idea of the Holy* (New York: Oxford, 1958).

2 Mary Douglas, *Purity and Danger* (London: Routledge & Kegan Paul, 1966).

3 Paul Ricoeur, *The Symbolism of Evil* (Boston: Beacon Press, 1967). See especially chap. 1; the quotation is from p. 30.

4 On the relation between the altar of incense and atonement, cf. below, n. 27, regarding Num 17:11-12.

5 Even so, the tactile dimension discussed below is present here as well, particularly in v 7 (*ngʿ*).

6 Exod 19:21; 33:20; Judg 6:22-23; 13:22.

holy God" (vv. 19-20); in the latter, the unfortunate Uzzah is struck dead (*nkh*) because he recklessly (albeit conscientiously) grabbed hold (*ʾḥz*) of the sacred palladium.

These few examples are enough to introduce the theme of holiness and death. In them one can see the danger which is intrinsic to holiness, a danger which represents a threat to the life of anyone who would approach (*qrb* and *ngš*) the divinity recklessly and without proper authorization. Furthermore, it is not surprising that most of the above examples are in some fashion connected with the cult. The narrative of the Sinai theophany has been influenced by cultic language at a number of points,[7] and the ark is obviously a cultic object. These observations about the phenomenology of holiness and death, particularly within the sacerdotal realm, could be illustrated further in a number of places in the Old Testament, but that is not the purpose of this paper. Rather, I want to show how the relationship between holiness and death has been utilized in the redactional crystallization of Numbers 16:1 to 20:13. In short, I shall argue that one can, and indeed should, read this complex body of material as an integral narrative, that the basic narrative thread is formed by the themes of holiness and death, and that, in its final form, this narrative unit, is properly understood as a complement to that contained in chapters 11-14.

Before we look at the text in its present form, we need at least to sketch some of the literary problems which confront the interpreter. Looking at the material in Numbers 16:1–20:13 first from a broad perspective, it is not at all obvious that this is the proper delimitation of a unit as a perusal of various commentaries will demonstrate. J. Marsh appears to arrange the material according to the Priestly itinerary, yielding the units: "Sojourn in Paran (13:1–19:22)" and "March from Kadesh to Moab (20:1–22:1)," and Marsh adds that the latter section "resumes the chronological narrative form last used in chs. 13-14."[8] With this, M. Noth would at first seem to agree, for he suggests that chap. 20 is "the beginning of another narrative section," but in the body of his commentary Noth has arranged the material somewhat differently: chap. III, 16:1–20:13, and chap. IV, 20:14–36:13.[9] He also observes that chap. 19 "introduces a ritual of distinct character, without there being any obvious reason why it should stand at this precise point."[10] Yet another organization, overlapping that of Marsh and Noth, has been propounded by B. Anderson, for whom the two middle units of Numbers are "The Sojourn at Kadesh-barnea (10:11–20:13)" and "The Journey from Kadesh via Transjordan (20:14–27:23)."[11] Still another system is employed by J. J. Owens, who subsumes the material under "The Murmurings in the Wilderness of Paran (13:1–21:35)," and, more specifically, "Struggle for Authority (16:1–18:32)," followed by two other sub-units, chaps. 19 and 20.[12] Even more broadly, A. Goldberg includes all of chaps. 11–20 within a unit entitled "The Rebellion," the end of which is broken down into the sub-units 16:1-35; 17:1-26; 17:27–18:28; and 20:1-29 (chap. 19 is skipped)[13] [throughout this paper, we shall follow the Masoretic division of chapter and verse]. In short, where one literary unit begins and another ends within the middle portion of Numbers, and what criteria one uses to make the divisions, are clearly debatable issues.

Even more complex than the designation of redactional units is the division of various literary strata according to the methods of source criticism. Although a detailed literary analysis of this material is beyond the scope and purpose of this paper, it is important to highlight the composite nature of the text in order to appreciate more fully its redactional integrity. There is a general consensus that chap. 16 contains a story belonging to J and at least two strata deriving from the Priestly school. While there are, of course, considerable differences in detail among various commentators, J. Liver has provided a helpful summary of the consensus:[14]

J(E) 1b, 2a, 12-15, 25-26, 27b-32a, 33-34
P_1 1a, 2b-7a, 18-24, 27a, 32b, 35
P_2 7b-11, 16-17

In general, the J stratum would have reported the rebellion of Dathan and Abiram against Moses' leadership (probably excluding Aaron), and their cataclysmic death. P_1 was added to J, telling of the rebellion involving Korah, 250 leaders, and ultimately the whole congregation (3a), and including an ordeal using censers. The

7 The cleansing (*kbs*) of garments is especially notable, since this clearly has to do with the concepts of "purity and danger" (Douglas), and since *kbs* is almost exclusively used for ritual purification (e.g., Lev 15:1-12; Num 19:7, 8, 10, 19, 21).

8 *Numbers, IB* 2, 140-41, 237.

9 *Numbers* (Philadelphia: Westminster, 1968): 3 and vii-viii.

10 *Ibid.,* 7.

11 Anderson's outline is found in the appendix to his translation of Noth's *A History of Pentateuchal Traditions* (Englewood Cliffs: Prentice-Hall, 1972): 273-74.

12 *Numbers* (The Broadman Bible Commentary 2; Nashville: Broadman, 1970): 80-81. Owens's one-sentence categorization of chaps. 16–18 is noteworthy: "These chapters are also instructions concerning approach to the tent of meeting" (p. 127).

13 *Das Buch Numeri* (Die Welt der Bibel; Kleinkommentare zur Heiligen Schrift 11; Düsseldorf: Patmos, 1970): 5-6.

14 J. Liver, "Korah, Dathan, and Abiram," in *Scripta Hierosolymitana 8* (C. Rabin, ed.; Jerusalem: Magnes, 1961) 193. For other studies see S. Lehming, "Versuch zu Num 16," *ZAW* 74 (1962): 291-321; A. H. J. Gunneweg, *Leviten und Priester* (Göttingen: Vandenhoeck & Ruprecht, 1965): 171-88; Noth, *Numbers,* 118-31; G. Coats, *Rebellion in the Wilderness* (Nashville: Abingdon, 1968): 156-84; V. Fritz, *Israel in der Wüste* (Marburger theologische Studien 7; Marburg: N. G. Elwert, 1970): 24-26, 86-89.

composite narrative of J and P_1 was then surcharged by P_2, which sharpened the opposition between Levites (Korah) and priests (Aaron). As an adjustment to this outline, some would suggest that the Korah of P_1 was a layperson, and only in P_2 were he and his followers made into Levites. Yet another alternative—and a more attractive one—is to excise Korah and the Levites altogether from P_1, which then would represent a rebellion only of the 250 leaders as representatives of the whole congregation (P_1 would then be: 2-4, 6abα, 7a, 18, 19b-22, 35).[15] In either case, neither P_1 nor P_2 should be understood as an originally independent narrative strand, but should be seen as supplements to the J narrative (both require the bulk of vv. 25-34 as the [initial!] denouement). Most scholars seem to understand the essential narrative to conclude at the end of chap. 16, with the rest (chaps. 17–19) being only clumsily attached appendices, and the story in 20:1-13 a separate incident.[16]

With this brief accounting of the complex stratification of chap. 16, we may turn to a review of 16:1–20:13, now more with an eye for the ways in which the disparate materials have been connected. While there has been some dislocation in 16:1-2, the narrative gets under way with the Priestly stratum in 1a, 2-7a. Here Korah and his band of 250 leaders raise the issue which dominates much of the following material. They claim that *all the congregation* is holy, and that Moses and Aaron are unduly "exalting" themselves.[17] Moses responds by proposing a test involving censers: the one whom Yahweh will "cause to approach" him (*qrb* Hiphil) is the one whom Yahweh has chosen (*bḥr*)—he alone is "the holy one" (*haqqādôš*; v 5).[18] This material, of course, has been combined with the beginning of the Dathan and Abiram story of J (v. 1b), but also has been expanded by P_2 in vv. 7b-11.[19] The latter, on close reading, betrays a rather different concern: it is not the status of the whole congregation over against Moses and Aaron, but the role of the Levites vis-à-vis the priesthood (*kehunnāh*, v. 10), which means, as v. 11 points out, vis-à-vis Aaron.[20]

At this point, the J story resumes in vv. 12-15. Although in isolation this material is quite distinctive,[21] it is not difficult to see how naturally it was combined with P_1, for here too there is a rebellion against Mosaic authority.[22] Verses 16-18 seem intended to resume the contest proposed in 2-7a between Korah and company and Aaron,[23] yet immediately vv. 19-22 have the whole congregation involved, and not merely as witnesses to the imminent contest, but (vv. 20-22) also as the guilty party doomed to destruction. Apparently vv. 23-24 are then intended immediately to resolve the threat of annihilation of the whole congregation by anticipating the separation

15 This is the solution of Gunneweg, *Leviten und Priester* (N 14): 176-79. One of the most attractive features of this view is that it would explain the emphasis on "all the congregation, every one of them" (16:3a), which one would not expect if Korah (=Levites) were making a claim only for themselves (of course, this problem is removed if Korah is a layperson, but along with Gunneweg [175], this seems most unlikely). Gunneweg (183) also points to 17:6 as a continuation of the "whole people" stratum. One of the major problems with excluding Korah/Levites from P_1 comes when one tries to ascertain what historical background such a supplement might reflect. When would the priesthood have been challenged by a large group of representatives of the people with respect to their "holy" status? One might suspect a date relatively early in the monarchical period, but Gunneweg (179) argues that the controversy was provoked by the increasing powers claimed by the high priest in the post-exilic period. His view of the *Tendenz* of P_1 is also highly subtle and at times difficult to grasp. He argues that "it is not the priesthood (*Priestertum*) itself which is in question and challenged by the laity; rather it concerns the absolute special privilege (*Sonderstellung*) of the priestly office (*Priesteramt*; 179)." Also problematic is the role of the incense ritual as a test. Gunneweg (187) argues that P_1 is not concerned with the question of "whether lay people could perform priestly functions." This at least ignores the interpretation given in the later stratum 17:5. On the other hand, one wonders if a test involving the manipulation of incense does not, by its very nature, imply a controversy limited to clerical circles.

16 As somewhat of an exception, Gunneweg ([N 14]: 183) pays more attention to 17:1-5 as a continuation of his P_2, and 17:6-15 as part of his P_1. See below, n. 27.

17 The relatively rare use of the Hithpael of *nśʾ* suggests that a pretension of royal prerogative is concerned (cf. 24:7; 1 Kgs 1:5 2 Chr 32:23: Ezek 17:14; 29:15 [Prov 30:32 and Dan 11:14?]). Otherwise, see Num 23:24; 1 Chr 29:11. Royal pretension is also indicated by the Hithpael of *śrr* in v 13, with which cf. Exod 2:14. The complaint, especially in the Yahwistic stratum, stands near the end of a long line of questions concerning Moses' legitimation.

18 This absolute form of the noun with article is found only twice elsewhere, both times referring to Yahweh (1 Sam 6:20; Isa 5:16). In the light of 7aβ, v 5 seems to be expansive, adding the key term *hiqrîb*. Cf. Gunneweg (N 14): 176, 178.

19 On the other hand, v 7b may belong to the preceding, and perhaps was intended to form a bracket with the *rab lākem* of v 3; still another alternative is to include v 7b with a "levite stratum."

20 Of course, one of the elements in vv 8-11 which conflicts with the preceding is the fact that here (vv 9-10) the Levites have already been "brought near" to Yahweh, whereas the test of v 4 suggests that this status is yet to be determined.

21 In vv 12-15 there is no reference to Aaron, priests, or Levites, nor any use of the key words *qrb* and *qdš* which dominate the preceding material. The motif of death in the wilderness (v 13), is, of course, a stock element within the wilderness stories (cf. Exod 14:11-12; 16:3; 17:3; Num 14:2; 20:4-5; 21:5), on which see Coats, *Rebellion*, (N 14): 29-43, and, more recently, B. Childs, *The Book of Exodus* (Philadelphia: Westminster, 1974): 254-64.

22 The reference to an "offering" in v 15 remains obscure, and some scholars suspect it to be a harmonizing gloss. On the other hand, Gunneweg [N 14]: 172) follows the suggestion of others that this is an indication of a controversy over the legitimacy of cultic personnel even in J. He sets the text within an historical situation of a general decline of the amphictyony, when a centralized "Mosaic" cult was opposed by a group in favor of decentralization. The problem, of course, is that vv 12bβ-14 give no indication of such a background.

23 Note the parallels between vv 16 and 7a, 17 and 6.

called for subsequently in v. 26.[24] At any rate, the sequel to the Dathan and Abiram story of J can easily be isolated in vv. 25-34, even though it clearly has been fused with the Korah episode by the introduction of the latter (vv. 27a; 32b). Somewhat awkwardly, v. 35 then adds that the 250 leaders met a separate but equally gruesome death.[25]

At the end of chap. 16 the casual reader might think that we have reached the denouement of the narrative, since all of the rebels have died. But the major issue clearly has not been resolved: whom has Yahweh chosen as the holy one(s) who may come near (*qrb*) to the divine presence? Or in other words, what has become of the censer contest which Moses proposed in vv. 5-7? Of course, 17:1-5 is an attempt to draw a moral (and an etiology) from the preceding narrative. The censers (made into plates for the altar) are to become a "sign" (*ʾôt*) and a "reminder" (*zikkārôn*), "so that no unauthorized person (*ʾîš zār*), who is not of the ancestry of Aaron, may draw near (*qrb*) to offer incense before Yahweh, lest he become as Korah and his company . . ." (v 5). But this is an inadequate resolution to the contest, since Aaron wins only by default (he is the only protagonist left alive!), and not by explicit choice, nor is there any reference to the Levites in vv. 1-5.

Now in vv. 6-15 the whole congregation, which had literally withdrawn into the background in 16:27, again comes to the front. Suddenly their sympathy with the rebels (only implied heretofore) becomes overt when they "murmur" (*lyn*) against Moses and Aaron, charging them with murder. While there are some suspicious connections with previous material,[26] in the present context it is the people's murmuring which causes a plague. Aaron and his censer play a prominent role here, but this is at best only indirectly connected with the previous contest, and is primarily concerned with Aaron's role in effecting atonement:[27] it is he who stands "between the dead and the living," bringing an end to the plague. Yet no sooner is this accomplished than the focus shifts again. In 17:16-26 there is a contest which is reminiscent of 16:3-7a, but, although Aaron here is finally "chosen" (*bḥr*, v. 5), the differences outweigh the similarities. The contest involves tribal staffs rather than priestly censers, and instead of distinguishing between Aaron and the Levites, this episode distinguishes between Aaron (as representative of the tribe of Levi) and all the other tribes. To add to the confusion, the references to the people's murmurings (vv. 20, 25) remind us of the previous episode of plague (v. 6), and the "sign" at the end (v. 25) reminds us of the moral drawn in 17:3.

Despite what has already become an extremely tortuous narrative thread, 17:27-28 presents another new turn. In fact, as we shall emphasize later, the addition of these verses represents a pivotal point within 16:1–20:13. Vv. 27-28 seem totally unaware of vv. 16-26, would perhaps be more fitting immediately after the emergency procedure in vv. 6-15, and, at any rate, now serve as a transition to chap. 18. As for chap. 18, it too is hardly an originally unified account. Significantly, the bulk of the material is a divine speech addressed to Aaron alone, which is quite unusual.[28] Moreover, most of the material (especially vv. 8-21, 23b-32a) has no direct bearing on the preceding narrative, but represents legislation dealing with the priestly and Levitical shares of tithes, legislation which could have been located almost anywhere in Leviticus or Numbers. Nevertheless, this extraneous material obviously has been linked with the preceding narrative by vv. 1-7, 22-23a, and possibly v. 32b (note again the use of *qrb* and *mwt*). These verses are intended as an elaboration and specification of the explicit advancement of Aaron (and sons; i.e., priests) in 17:16-26, and the subordination of the Levites which has been at least implicit from the beginning of chap. 16. These verses are also an answer to the people's question at the end of chap. 17: "Are we all to perish?"—that is, all who "come near" (*qrb*) to the tabernacle. Here the holiness of Yahweh is seen—especially in the context of the preceding narrative (earthquake, fire, plague)—as an almost uncontrollable and immediate threat to the entire community. To this 18:1-7 offers a solution: approach (*qrb*) to Yahweh will be regulated according to concentric circles of authority, moving from the congregation as a whole, to the Levites, to the priests. Only the priests can "approach"—"any unauthorized person (*hazzār*) who approaches shall be put to death" (v. 7). This resolution to the problem raised as far back as the beginning of chap.

24 Noth (*Numbers* [N 9]: 126) has understandably complained about the inordinate complexity of vv 16-24. Especially problematic are the spatial discrepancies between vv 19a and 24-25. Gunneweg [N 14]: 178, n. 1) also has trouble with vv 19-24.

25 This despite the implication in v 32b that the 250 were included along with Korah.

26 E.g., is v 7 to be seen as originally connected with 16:19, and v 10 with 16:21?

27 This use of the censer to effect atonement is unique (unless something similar is meant in Isa 6:6-7). Even in Lev 16:12-13 (which, along with vv 1-2, is an addition), the function of the incense is not involved with atonement, but with protecting the priest from Yahweh's invisible presence. Cf. Exod 30:1-10 where the final verse also indicates that it is the blood manipulation which effects atonement. On the uniqueness of Num 17:11-12, see also M. Haran, "The Uses of Incense in the Ancient Israelite Ritual," *VT* 10 (1960): 122. See also below, n. 61. We would thus have to disagree with Gunneweg [N 14]: 183) who sees 17:6-15 as a continuation of P_1 and the positive side of the test: "That which, in the hands of those who were not 'holy,' led to ruin, now through the mediation of the uniquely 'hallowing' Aaron achieves the people's atonement." Thus the uniquely privileged position of Aaron is legitimated. But even though Aaron clearly achieves a prominent position here, as opposed to 16:31-35, the plague incident does not seem originally to have been constructed as the sequel to the censer test (it should also be noted that 16:28-30 introduces a completely separate test).

28 Note vv 1, 8, and 20. Elsewhere Yahweh speaks to Aaron alone only at Exod 4:27 (by necessity) and Lev 10:8 (see below).

16 is two-fold: it legitimates the privileged position of the priests (Aaron and sons) over against the Levites (Korah and company) and, at the same time, it protects the people as a whole from the wrath of a holy God (v. 5; cf. 17:11b).[29] In a very real sense, then, 18:1-7, 22-23a institutionalize the liturgy of atonement which was an emergency procedure in 17:6-15—the priests will stand in between holiness and death on behalf of the whole congregation.

Finally, a few words need to be said about chaps. 19 and 20:1-13. It is obvious that chap. 19 is a self-contained unit of legislation dealing with the means of removing defilement caused by contact with a corpse. This material, like much of chap. 18, could be located almost anywhere that cultic legislation is appropriate. It is also probable, however, that chap. 19 has gone through some development before reaching its present form. In particular, it is remarkable how the material moves from the specific to the general, and from the clergy to the laity. Thus the chapter opens with a typical divine address to Moses and Aaron, with instructions for Eleazar the (high?) priest (vv. 3-4); but this subtly shifts to simply "the priest" in vv. 6-7, and finally moves to general terms such as "the one who burns the heifer" or "a person who is clean" (vv. 8-9, 18-19, etc.). In fact, there is no mention of cultic officials after v. 7. Thus it would appear that, while vv. 11-22 presuppose vv. 1-10, the latter have been adapted to include the priest in the crucial preparation of the potion. In fact, one suspects that the specific inclusion of Eleazar in 19:3-4 may be related to the material in 17:1-5, where he is also prominent. This may also provide a clue for the reason behind the insertion of chap. 19 in its present position. Since the priests emerge in chaps. 16–18 as the "inner circle" who prevent the congregation from encroaching on the realm of the holy and thus from inviting death, what better place to insert legislation in which the priests are the manufacturers of a substance which counteracts the effects of contact with the dead? This is particularly the case if, as some claim, death is the ultimate form of defilement and thus the extreme opposite to holiness.[30]

We turn at last to 20:1-13, which contains two units: a brief itinerary and chronological notice attached to a report of Miriam's death (v 1), and the incident of water from the rock in vv 2-13. While Noth would see a basic Priestly account here, modified by a later Priestly redactor on the basis of Exod 17:1-7, most commentators opt for a unified Priestly narrative.[31] Neither case affects the question which interests us: In what ways, if any, is this material connected with chaps. 16–19? What strikes us at first sight, of course, is the disjunctiveness in relation to the preceding, not only because the Kadesh incident does not originally belong with chaps. 16–18 (and certainly not with 19), but also because the notice in v 1a clearly separates this incident from the preceding in terms of space and time (that chaps. 16-18 are basically *without* such a location does not affect the disjunction).[32] In fact, the location at Kadesh points to the most obvious connection, namely the catchwords based on the root *qdš*. Not only is the root used in the toponym, but more significantly it also provides the vocabulary for the climax of the incident, as well as a concluding editorial comment. Moses and Aaron are denied entrance into the land because they did not "sanctify" Yahweh (*qdš*, Hiphil),[33] and the narrator, in reviewing the incident, characterizes it as one in which Yahweh "showed himself holy (*qdš*, Niphal) among them." In short, however disparate their origins, the fact that both the Kadesh incident and the Korah incident are concerned with the relationship between Israel's leaders and Yahweh's holiness, makes the two appropriate components within one narrative framework.

Other stylistic features suggest a literary relationship with material in chap. 17. While the use of the rod in the Kadesh incident is no doubt an original part of the tradition (cf. Exod 17:1-7), the fact that it is taken *millipnê yhwh* (v. 9) is reminiscent of 17:25 where Aaron's rod is placed *lipnê hāʿēdût*. It is also interesting that the latter verse refers to "the rebels" (*bĕnê-mĕrî*), just as in 20:10 Moses castigates the people as "rebels" (*hammōrîm*).[34] While these connections with the preceding narrative may well be coincidental, such is definitely not the case with the opening part of the people's complaint against Moses (v 3b): "Would that we had died the death (*gāwaʿnû bigwaʿ*) of our fellows before Yahweh." On the surface, this retrospective reference could be to almost any incident beginning at least as far back as Num 11:1-3. However, the phrase "before

29 Noth (*Numbers* [N 9]: 134) suggests that 18:5, although intended to follow upon 16:1-35, is an awkward addition, since "in that section there was no question of any violation of the holiness of the altar having occurred. . . ." However, 18:5 is probably a reference to 17:6-15 where the people assemble against Moses and Aaron. Such a connection is also indicated by the use of the word *qeṣep*, which occurs elsewhere in the Pentateuch only at 17:11 and 1:53 (on the latter, see below); the verb *qṣp* is used at 16:22, and, with divine subject in the Pentateuch, is limited to Lev 10:6; Deut 1:34; 9:7-8, 22 (the latter three in the Hiphil).

30 See E. Feldman, *Biblical and Post-Biblical Defilement and Mourning: Law as Theology* (Library of Jewish Law and Ethics; New York: Yeshiva University/KTAV, 1977): esp. 13-30; and J. Soler, "The Dietary Prohibitions of the Hebrews," *New York Review of Books,* vol. 26, no. 10 (June 14, 1979): p. 27.

31 Noth, *Numbers* (N 9): 144; Coats, Rebellion (N 14): 73 (he excludes only 1aβ); the conclusion of Fritz (*Israel in der Wüste* [N 14]: 29) is the same as that of Coats.

32 The most likely setting would be Kadesh, in the light of 13:26. This would be another reason for excluding 20:1aβ; but vv 14 and 22 would have to be reckoned with as well.

33 For the differences between this view of Moses' denial and that of the Deuteronomic school, see my article, "Theological Reflections on the Denial of Moses," *JBL* 98 (1979): 481-94.

34 Otherwise P uses the root *mrh* only as a verb and only with respect to Moses' offense (20:24; 27:14).

Yahweh" often connotes a cultic setting, which would be most fitting for the story in chaps. 16–17.[35] Even more telling is the use of the rare word *gwʿ*. Except for 20:29, its only other use in the Pentateuch outside of Genesis is in Num 17:27-28:[36] "And the people of Israel said to Moses, 'Behold, we die (*gwʿ*), we are undone, we are all undone. Every one who comes near (*qrb*), who comes near to the tabernacle of Yahweh, will die (*mwt*). Are we all to die (*gwʿ*)?' " As we have seen, these verses provide the transition which makes the material in chap. 18 (and, by juxtaposition, ultimately chap. 19) part of the narrative of chaps. 16–17. It was quite likely the same redactor who used 20:3b to make an explicit connection between chaps. 16–17 and the Kadesh incident as well.[37] Thus if the theme of holiness provides a connection with the preceding narrative, so does the theme of death—and not simply the people's *fear* of death expressed in vv 3-4, but even more so the *sentence* of death *outside the land* which comes to Moses and Aaron.

We may now summarize our review of the various interlocking pieces of Num 16:1–20:13. To begin with, it should be clear that the themes of holiness and death appear throughout this material, not only by way of the specific roots *qdš* and *mwt*, but also in passages where these words themselves do not occur.[38] There are also other words whose high frequency in this material creates the effect of a continual focus (e.g., *qrb* and *qhl*).[39] The presence of key words is hardly the only force which binds this material together, however, especially when one notes that their recurrence is often due to coincidence rather than to a discernible redactional plan. Rather, the lexical redundancy only enhances what is otherwise accomplished simply by narrative consecution. Despite obvious signs of ubiquitous redactional insertions, with the resultant inconsistencies, the material of chaps. 16–17 retains a remarkable thematic unity and sequential direction, especially when one remembers that, in the final version, the action takes place over a period of four days and three nights (16:5, 7, 16; 17:6, 23). The redactor's task of shaping the material into a unified narrative reached the critical stage only at the end of chap. 17. Because of the implicit distinction between priests and Levites gained from chap. 16, this was deemed an appropriate place to insert 18:8-22, 23b-32. Whether 17:27-28 belongs to the same redactor as 18:1-7, 22-23a is difficult to determine. The latter material is already linked to the preceding by the key words *qrb* and *mwt*, as well as by the reference in 18:5 to 17:11b. At any rate, 17:27-28 skillfully picks up on the role of the people as a whole which has played in and out of chaps. 16–17 (the transition in 17:6 is especially comparable),[40] and thus emphasizes the *mediatorial* role of priests and Levites vis-à-vis the theme of holiness and death which follows. As we have seen, 17:27-28 is almost certainly to be attributed to the same redactor as 20:3b, a redactor who thereby saw fit to tie together not only chaps. 16–17 with 18, but also with 20:1-13. Whether or not chap. 19 is an even later insertion between 18 and 20 is impossible to determine, but we have seen that its position is not inappropriate, especially in the light of 17:27-28—through the mediation of the priests, the people have access to the means of avoiding ostracism (v 20; = death?) despite having become defiled by the dead. In short, there are solid internal grounds for viewing 16:1–20:13 in its present form as a distinct redactional unit. The task which remains is to determine if this conclusion can be sustained after an examination of the surrounding material, and, if so, how the unit 16:1–20:13 is to be interpreted in the light of its literary context.

Before we turn to an examination of the wider literary context of Num 16:1–20:13, however, a few words should be said concerning the traditio-historical issues involved. The central question would seem to be this: at what time and under what sociological conditions did performance of an incense ritual become a criterion of priestly prerogative? To investigate this question thoroughly would involve us in problems far more complex than those already entailed in the literary analysis, and thus a brief survey here must suffice. Even the way in which the central question is posed above presents problems. For example, outside of the unit under discussion, frequently it is not clear when verbal or nominal forms of *qṭr* refer to incense offerings or to sacrificial burning.[41] Similarly, one may have to draw a distinction between a ceremony

35 Cf. also Lev 10:2 and the restrospective reference in Lev 1:1.

36 Aside from Gen 6:17 and 7:21, the use in Num 20:29 follows the pattern in the death notices of patriarchal figures (Gen 25:8, 17; 35:29; 49:33). Outside the Pentateuch, the word is used several times in Job, and a few elsewhere.

37 It is worth noting that v 4 is more fitting as a "complaint" (*ryb*) following 3a than is the cry of despair in 3b.

38 E.g., 17:1-5, where neither appears, or chap. 19, where *qdš* does not appear, but "holiness" is manifestly a governing issue.

39 For *qrb*, see 16:5, 9-10; 17:5, 28; 18:3-4, 7, 22; for *qhl* as a noun referring to the congregation, see 16:3, 33; 17:12; 19:20; 20:4, 6, 10, 12 (elsewhere in Numbers only 10:7; 14:5; 15:15; in Exodus and Leviticus, only 8 times). The use of the verb *qhl* in the hostile sense of Num 16:3, 19; 17:7 and 20:2 occurs elsewhere in the Pentateuch only at Exod 32:1.

40 Here again we would have to disagree with Noth (Numbers [N 9]: 133) who asserts that 17:27-28 "is not entirely suitable, for there had never been any mention in ch.16-17 of the Israelites having come too near the 'tabernacle of Yahweh' (17:13 [=Heb. 17:28])." While one may agree that it is "a loose connection," 17:27-28 seems to interpret 17:6-15. See above, n. 29, and below, n. 61.

41 For the former, e.g., Exod 30:7, for the latter, 1 Sam 2:16, Numerous instances involving parallelism seem to demand the meaning associated with animal sacrifice, rather than incense (*contra* most English versions), as already Deut 33:10b. For another example see Hos 4:13 and the translation and commentary by H. W. Wolff, *Hosea* (Philadelphia: Fortress, 1974): 86. On the general ambiguity of *qṭr*, see A. Cody, *A History of Old Testament Priesthood* (AnBib 35; Rome: Pontifical Biblical Institute, 1969): 119, n. 29. See also M. Haran, "The Uses of Incense" (N 27): 116-17.

involving the incense altar (e.g., Exodus 30), and one involving censers.[42] It has often been suggested on the basis of both literary and archaeological evidence that the use of incense altars in Israel was a relatively late development (*ca.* 7th century),[43] but the discovery of the Arad sanctuary incense altar now allows for a date as early as the united monarchy.[44] On the other hand, explicit references to the use of "censers" (*mḥth*) in contexts other than lists of cultic appurtenances are extremely rare, and provide little help in dating literary material.[45]

Given the ambiguity of the data concerning incense rituals, and adding to that the thorny problems in tracing the development of priestly and Levitical traditions, it is surprising that candidates for the historical background of Numbers 16–18 have been suggested from the early monarchical to the late post-exilic periods.[46] One way to address the problem would be to look for incidents of controversy surrounding the use of incense. Most immediately, Lev 10:1-7 comes to mind, but its relationship to Numbers 16 is too close to permit its use as a basis for interpreting the latter.[47] Another such incident might be that of Jeroboam's cultic installations (1 Kgs 12:25–13:7), but there again it is not clear that *l^ehaqṭîr* (12:33; 13:1-2) refers to incense rather than burnt sacrifice, and the polemic is aimed against *non-Levitical* priests (12:31; cf. 2 Chr 13:8-12). Similarly, while the incident of Uzziah's offering incense is less ambiguous (2 Chr 26:16-21, especially v 19),[48] still the opposition is between king and (Aaronide) priests, rather than priests and Levites (v 18).[49] If this angle is unproductive, another might be to investigate places in which priests and/or Levites are referred to as "chosen" (*bḥr*, as in Num 16:5-7; 17:20; or *bdl*, as in Num 16:9). While there are a number of such occurrences—most involving a similar form of cultic "job description" (*bḥr*: 1 Sam 2:28; Deut 18:5; 1 Chr 15:2; 2 Chr 29:11; Ps 105:26, without the form]; and *bdl*: Num 8:14 [without the form]; Deut 10:8 1 Chr 23:13)—only three also use the root *qṭr*, and here again without making clear whether it refers to incense or sacrificial offerings (1 Sam 2:28; 1 Chr 23:13; 2 Chr 29:11). Even if *qṭr* does refer to incense here, we are further confounded by the possibility of references from at least the early monarchical to the post-exilic period.

Despite the problems outlined above, most commentators opt for a post-exilic background to the incense dispute in Numbers 16. It is an argument from silence, but support for such a conclusion might come from the fact that the book of Ezekiel uses the root *qṭr* only three times (8:11; 16:18 parallel 23:41), all clearly referring to incense, but in no case associated with the distinction between priests and Levites, which is so sharply drawn in that book (44:9-27). From this one might conclude that the performance of incense rituals became a priestly criterion only after the Exile. At any rate, Gese, for example, places the background for Numbers 16 in the fifth century, involving the subordination of the Korahite singers.[50] Gunneweg points to the same period, but is more cautious about defining the precise group, and he rightly notes that Numbers 16–18 does not reflect a complete degradation of the Levites.[51] This we have seen above in the way in which the Levites, although denied the priestly incense rite, nevertheless serve vis-à-vis the priests as a secondary barrier, preventing the encroachment of lay people into the holy precincts, and therefore preventing their death.

Since the major purpose of this study is to delineate the interplay between holiness and death in the final redaction of Num 16:1–20:13, it would lead us astray to delve any further into the traditio-historical background of the present text. We may turn, therefore, to the question of the material surrounding this unit, i.e., does an examination of the context of 16:1–20:13 support the conclusion, already reached on internal grounds, that it *is* a distinct unit? There should be no question about the beginning of the unit. Even if we eliminate chap. 15 as

42 See Haran, "The Uses of Incense" (N 27): 127-28.

43 For examples, see W. A. L. Elmslie, *1 and 2 Chronicles* (*IB* 3; Nashville: Abingdon, 1954): 514-15; N. Glueck, "Incense Altars," in *Translating and Understanding the Old Testament* (H. Frank and W. Reed eds.; Nashville: Abingdon, 1970): 328.

44 Y. Aharoni, "Temples, Semitic," *IDBSup,* 875, and, already, H. F. Beck, "Incense," *IDB* 2, 698, and K. Galling, "Incense Altar," *IDB* 2, 699. According to Aharoni, the Arad ostraca mention the priestly family of Korah, among others.

45 Outside of such lists (e.g., Exod 25:38; 27:3; Num 4:9, 14, etc.), the word is used in narrative material only at Lev 10:1 (16:12); Num 16:6, 17-18; 17:2-4.

46 For the early dating, see Liver, "Korah, Dathan, and Abiram" (N 14): 210; for the later dating, see below. Although Cody (*OT Priesthood* [N 41]: 168-74) seems to decide for a post-exilic date also, his analysis of the ups and downs of Levitical fortunes could be used to argue for various dates beginning at least as early as the 8th century (see pp. 129-34).

47 In fact, some would argue that Numbers 16-17 formed the basis for Lev 10:1-7 (so K. Elliger, *Leviticus* [Handbuch zum Alten Testament 4; Tübingen: J. C. B. Mohr, 1966]: 133). Perhaps more cautiously, Coats (*Rebellion* [N 14]: 260) concludes that there are some significant differences between the two stories, and that where the agreement is greatest, both are probably relying on a common tradition. For some of the literary connections, see further below.

48 Note the explicit reference to the censer. The Hebrew word is used elsewhere only at Ezek 8:11.

49 It is also worth noting that, in both stories (Jeroboam and Uzziah), the kings are struck with leprosy.

50 H. Gese, "Zur Geschichte der Kultsänger am zweiten Tempel," in *Abraham unser Vater: Juden und Christen im Gespräch über die Bibel* (Leiden: Brill, 1963): 232-33. For more recent discussion along these lines, see D. L. Petersen, *Late Israelite Prophecy: Studies in Deutero-Prophetic Literature and in Chronicles 1* (SBLMS: 23; Missoula: Scholars Press, 1977): 62 and 81.

51 Gunneweg (N 14): 180-81.

intrusive,[52] there is no apparent connection between chap. 16 and chaps. 11–14. While the latter also tell of rebellions against Moses' authority, and the "spy narrative" ends with an emphasis on the death of the wilderness generation (see further below), the peculiar connection between *holiness* and death is nowhere to be found,[53] much less any controversy surrounding the priestly office. In fact, except for some important correlations with parts of chaps. 1–8, to which we shall return, the beginning of chap. 16 is abrupt and altogether puzzling. In particular, the charge against Moses and Aaron in v 3 (which introduces a major theme dominating the rest of the unit—holiness vis-à-vis leaders and people), seems to be completely without precedent in the book of Numbers.[54] The closest associations lie in the brief account of the death of Nadab and Abihu recorded in Lev 10:1-3, and the sequel in vv 4-20.[55] In vv 1-3 alone we find the key words *qdš, qrb,* and *mwt,* as well as an unauthorized liturgical act involving censers. Moreover, the way in which the originally terse story in vv 1-3 has been expanded to incorporate various priestly regulations within the narrative framework (vv 4-20) is strikingly similar to the redactional process in Numbers 16–19.[56] There are even several distinctive lexical commonalities.[57] Nevertheless, we should at least observe that Lev 10:1-3 could not serve as the immediate literary antecedent for Num 16:3 without its own difficulties.[58]

As we have already indicated, there is also material related to both Leviticus 10 and Numbers 16–18 in Numbers 1–8. This is not surprising, since all of this material is related in some way to the Priestly school. More particularly, the interest in the Levites which is so prevalent in chaps. 16–18 also abounds in chaps. 1–8, although concentrated in chaps. 3 and 8. In fact, as D. Kellermann has written, "Simply from the relatively large number of verses within Numbers 1–10 which have to do with the Levites, one can see how much interest was invested in this theme."[59] It should also not be surprising, therefore, that there are other thematic parallels, as well as lexical associations, between these two blocks of material. So, for example, the key root *qdš*, prominent in chaps. 16–18 and 20, is also prevalent in chaps. 1–8, but almost totally absent in the intervening material.[60] However, to focus on this general level, both in terms of texts and in terms of language and themes, is to miss the way in which chaps. 16–18 are related to specific literary *strata* within the introductory chapters (and within Leviticus). By and large, those passages related by language and theme are the following:

Lev 10:1-9
16:1-2, 12-13
Num 1:47-54
3:1-4, 5-10, 38
4:15aβ-20
(8:19aβb)[61]

A few examples of the correspondence may be cited in support of this concatenation (occurrences in the above passages and chaps. 16–18 are italicized):

1. the designation of the sanctuary as "the ta-bernacle/tent of the testimony" (*mškn/ʾhl hʿdt*): the former, only at Exod 38:21; *Num 1:50, 53;* 10:11; the latter, only at Num 9:15; *17:(19), 22-23 (25); 18:2;* 2 Chr 24:6 (for entire OT).
2. the warning in cultic legislation, "lest they (etc.) die" (*mwt,* various aspects): Exod 28:35, 43; 30:20-21;

52 According to Noth (*Numbers* [N 14]: 114), chap. 15 "ought to be considered one of the very latest sections of the Pentateuch . . . ." It is worth noting, however, that v 2 (cf. v 18) provides a note of irony in juxtaposition to chaps. 13-14.

53 In chaps 11-15 the root *qdš* is found only twice (11:18; 15:40). See further below, n. 60.

54 The only immediate possibility would be 15:40 ("be holy"), reminiscent of the Holiness Code (e.g., Lev 19:2).

55 See above, n. 47.

56 Verse 4-7 may belong originally to vv 1-3. Note the warning "lest you die" in vv 7 and 9, and that of Yahweh's wrath (*qṣp*) in v 6 (cf. Num 18:5). Similar connecting devices occur in vv 12 and 16 ("the sons who are left"). Verse 6 constitutes a narrative etiology for the legislation in 21:10-12.

57 Compare *haśśᵉrēpāh* in 10:6 and Num 17:2(4); *ʾēš yṣʾ* in (9:24); 10:2 and Num 16:35; and, of course, the occurrences of "censer," 10:1; 16:12; Num 16:6, 17, 18; 17:2-4 (elsewhere only in descriptions of the Tabernacle/Temple appurtenances, e.g., Exod 25:38; Num 4:9, 14; 2 Kgs 25:15, etc.).

58 For one thing, the story of Nadab and Abihu centers in illegitimate *fire* (*ʾēš zārāh*), whereas the story beginning in Numbers 16 centers in illegitimate *officiants* (*ʾîš zar,* 17:5).

59 D. Kellermann, *Die Priesterschrift von Numeri 1:1 bis 10:10, literar-kritisch und traditions-geschichtlich untersucht* (BZAW, 10; Berlin: Walter de Gruyter, 1970): 149. The title of the biblical book notwithstanding, references to Levites are extremely rare in Leviticus, as well as Exodus.

60 Within chaps. 1–20, the adjective occurs at 5:17; 6:5, 8; 15:40; and 16:3, 5, 7; as a verb, the root occurs at 6:11; 7:1; 8:17; 11:18; and 17:2, 3; 20:12-14. The statistics for *qōdeš* (="sanctuary" or "holy thing[s]") are also intriguing. The former occurs 23 times in chaps. 1–8, none in 9–17 and 19–27, but 4 times in chap. 18 (vv 3, 5, [10], 16). The latter occurs 9 times in chaps. 1–5:10, none in 5:11–chap. 17 or chaps. 19–27, but 5 times in chap. 18 (vv 8-9, 17, 19, 32). Again within chaps. 19–20, the other term for sanctuary (*mqdš*) occurs only at 3:38; 10:21; and 18:1; 19:20.

61 We may agree with Noth (*Numbers* [N 9]: 69) that this is "a very strange definition of the Levites' duties. Elsewhere, 'making atonement' is a priestly task, not a Levitical one . . . ." However, we cannot agree when he adds, "that 'atonement' should then be necessary if the Israelites come too near the sanctuary (it remains quite obscure what in actual fact is meant by this) is an idea which never materialized." Kellermann ([N 59]: 119) also agrees with the first statement, but rightly refers to the protective role of the Levites in 1:53. We should also point out that 8:19 makes sense in the light of 17:11, 28; 18:4, 22-23. See above, n. 40.

Lev 8:35; *10:6-7, 9; 16-2, 13;* 22:9; *Num 4:15, 19-20; 17:25; 18:3, 22, 32* (in Pentateuch).[62]

3. the concurrence of references to death (*mwt*) in the previous entry is even more striking when we narrow the focus to concurrence with the root *qrb*:[63] Lev *16:1;* (22:3);*Num 1:51; 3:10, 38 (17:5), 28; 18:3, 7, 22* (entire OT; cf. with *ngš*, only *Num 4:19;* the references in parentheses do not contain *mwt* but clearly warn of death). Four of these contain the identical formula, *hazzār hāqqārēb yûmāt* (*Num 1:51; 3:10, 38; 18:7*), which may be compared to *17:5* (*lōʾ-yiqrab ʾîš zār*), and *18:4* (*wᵉzār lōʾ-yiqrab*).[64] Two of the occurrences set the Levites over against the laity (*Num 1:51; 18:4;* cf. also vv *22-23*), whereas the others set the priests against both laity and Levites (*3:10, 38;* [*17:5*]; *18:3, 7*).
4. the word *mḥth* ("censer") occurs (aside from cultic inventories, e.g., Exod 25:38; 2 Kgs 25:15, etc.) only at *Lev 10:1; 16:12; Num 16:6, 17-18; 17:2–4.*

When we take into consideration the thematic and lexical correspondences cited above, we cannot but conclude that there is a direct literary relationship between the designated strata in chaps. 1–4 (8) and 16–18. While it would be premature and hazardous to posit a single redactional hand at work in all of these (the various inconsistencies make this all but impossible), all of the material certainly bears a peculiar ideological stamp. The relationship also seems to be confirmed in terms of internal relative dating—i.e., just as the thematic and lexical correspondences within chaps. 16–18 are often concentrated in later additions not only to J but also to P_1, so the passages in chaps. 1, 3, and 4 cited above also are generally relegated to the latest strata.[65]

In sum: one or more redactors of chaps. 16–18 seem at least to have been aware of, if not also responsible for, portions of chaps. 1–10, especially chaps. 1, 3, and 4. Quite clearly the major incentive for the additions in the latter chapters had to do, in the main, with the legitimation of later priestly authority over against the Levites, a legitimation anchored in legislation delivered to Moses at Sinai. At the same time, one can see how the additions to the opening chapters of the book serve a *narrative* role as well, in that they foreshadow the controversy which erupts in chap. 16 regarding holiness, cultic access (*qrb*), and death. Or perhaps it would be more appropriate to look at the literary relationship retrospectively: the *story* (plus integrated interpretations!) now contained in chaps. 16–18 constitutes a narrative paradigm of the *legislation* contained in parts of chaps. 1–10. This is all the more significant when we note that chaps. 1–10 themselves do not contain any such narrative legitimation, especially for the distinction between priests and Levites. That is, within these chapters there is no "historical" answer available for the question, "Why did Yahweh ordain the priests to a position superior to the Levites?"

Before we turn to even wider connections between 16:1–20:13 and the preceding chapters of Numbers, we need to confirm our conclusion that 20:13 does, in fact, constitute the end of a redactional unit. As we have seen above, it is in determining the conclusion of the unit that most commentators disagree, whether they see the story which begins in chap. 16 as part of a unit which begins at 10:11, 11:1, or 13:1. While most interpreters opt for a new beginning either at 20:1 or 20:14, there are those who would include all of chap. 20 and even chap. 21 along with the preceding material. It is not difficult to see how such divergent readings could arise. Those who want to argue for a basic thematic continuity between chaps. 16ff. and 20:14ff. have good reason to do so. Even though there is a geographical and temporal shift at 20:1, and clearly a new turn taken at 20:14, the end of chap. 20 (vv 22-29) recounts the death of Aaron, which is explicitly connected with the incident in 20:1-13.[66] Moreover, the incident of the brazen serpent in 21:4-9 fits hand-in-hand with earlier occasions of rebellion against Moses.[67]

On the other hand, those who want to draw the redactional unit to a close at 20:13 also can marshal weighty evidence. From a literary-critical perspective, it is at 20:14 that JE material resumes after a long hiatus (since 16:34), and continues to play an increasingly dominant role in the following chapters (through 25:5). In terms of thematic development, 20:14 also represents, quite literally, a new departure, for it is here that Israel begins that "passage" through the nations which will constitute the primary focus through chap. 25.[68] In my judgment, this last point is the most significant, and decisively turns the argument in favor of a close at 20:13, even though the caesura there is by no means marked by

---

62 Also in Deut 18:16 (cf. Exod 20:19 and see above pp. 181-82) and 20:5-7, the latter not cultic regulations comparable to those in the Tetrateuch.

63 Otherwise the use of *qrb* by itself as a technical term for priestly service is limited to Exod 40:32; Lev 9:7-8; 21:17-18 (cf. v 21, *ngš*, and v 23, *bwʾ* and *ngš*); Ezek 40:32, 46; 44:15-16; 45:4. For the apparently nontechnical usage, see Exod 12:48; 16:9; Lev 9:5. The use of *qrb* here under discussion refers only to the Qal conjugation; the Hiphil has a much wider usage.

64 Here again there is both a similarity and a difference with Lev 10:1-3, for the latter concerns *ʾēš zārāh* (cf. Exod 30:9 *qᵉṭōret zārāh*).

65 See, *ad loc.*, the studies by Noth (*Numbers* [N 9] and Kellermann (N 59). On the relationship between much of chap. 4 of Numbers and the story of Korah, see also Gunneweg (N 14): 180.

66 Note especially 20:24, it is also worth mentioning that the parallels in 27:14 and Deut 32:51 contain the key word *qdš*, as in Num 20:12. See my article, "Denial of Moses" (N 33): 483-85.

67 Note especially the motif in v 5a and its counterpart in Exod 14:11-12; 16:3; 17:3; Num 14:2; 16:13; 20:4, on which see Coats, *Rebellion* (N 14): *passim*.

68 This theme is appropriately introduced by the key word *ʿbr*, 20:19, 21; 21:22-23 (cf. Deut 29:15; Josh 24:17; Judg 11:20).

editorial flourish. At any rate, one should not fail to observe the interlocking effect of the juxtaposition of the two units at this point, caused by the fact that 20:22-29 and 21:4-9 are more retrospective, while 20:14-21 and 21:1-3 are obviously prospective. The juncture can be schematized accordingly:

11:1–20:13 ← 20:22-29 ← 21:4-9
20:14-21 → 21:1-3 → 21:10–25:18

Thus I would argue that the redactional units of Numbers should be understood as follows:

1:1–10:36	Marching Orders and Departure from Sinai
11:1–20:13	Rebellion in the Camp
11:1–14:45	Prophetic Controversies and the Fate of the Wilderness Generation
15:1–41	Legislative Interlude[69]
16:1–20:13	Priestly Controversies and the Fate of Moses and Aaron
20:14–25:18	Passage Through the Nations
26:1–36:13	The Inheritors of the Land

Looked at internally, one can easily see that 16:1–20:13 ends in a bitter irony, and one which is directly connected to the interplay of holiness and death. The challenge of the rebels to Moses and Aaron ("everyone is holy—why do you exalt yourselves?"), at first leads to the death of the rebels and to the exaltation of the leaders (along with *their* party, the priests). But in the end, the controversies lead to the humiliation of Moses and Aaron, and to a divine verdict of death outside the land of promise, a verdict which is seen as necessary because the holy ones (16:5, 7) failed to sanctify *the* Holy One (20:12-13). The irony is all the more salient when we compare this unit with the preceding one (11:1–14:45 [chap. 15]). As already adumbrated in the outline above, the initial unit of "rebellion in the camp" turns, not on controversies involving leadership and priesthood, but on disputes regarding leadership and *prophecy* (cf. 11:26-30 and especially 12:6-8). Seen in this light, the complaint in 12:2 ("Has Yahweh indeed spoken only through Moses? Has he not spoken through us also?") is the precise thematic counterpart to that in 16:3. Moreover, whereas the initial unit issues in a verdict of death outside the land for the whole *people* (except Caleb and Joshua, chaps. 13–14), the final unit issues in a verdict of death outside the land for the *leaders.* The contrast is highlighted by a glance at the motif of "trust" (*ʾmn*). Whereas in the first unit it is Moses who is "entrusted with all Yahweh's house" (12:7), and it is the people who refuse to trust in Yahweh (14:11), in the final unit it is Moses and Aaron who do not trust in Yahweh (20:12).[70] Thus the theme of holiness and death, which constitutes a distinct thread uniting 16:1–20:13, ultimately links this unit with the preceding in the form of an ironic contrast.

To summarize: despite obvious indications of various literary hands at work in Num 16:1–20:13, the material in its present shape should be understood as a discrete unit within the book. The individual redactional touches which point most clearly to a continuous reading of this material occur in 17:27-28 and 20:3, but the unit as a whole is cemented by the recurring references (either by specific words or by general understanding) to holiness and death. From a wider perspective, the narrative involving holiness and death is related to a previous incident reported in Lev 10:1-3, but also to legislation lodged in distinctive redactional layers of Numbers 1–10. In effect, 16:1–19:22 can be seen as a narrative explanation—an extended etiology—of those portions of chaps. 1–10, even though the latter, of course, do not prepare us for the dramatic reversal which takes place in 20:1-13. This last incident, the verdict of death against Moses and Aaron, constitutes the counterpart to the end of the first unit of "the rebellion in the camp" (chaps. 13–14), where it is the people who are doomed to die outside the land. Thus the redactional process at work in Num 16:1–20:13 entailed a skillful and sensitive shaping of the material utilizing the interplay of the themes of holiness and death. Here at least is one instance in which the redactor's interest clearly went beyond the literary fusion of separate accounts within a relatively constricted pericope, and even beyond any sociological polemic which the redactor wished to enjoin—here the redactor is at work in the construction of larger narrative units, already with an eye for the way in which such units fit together to form something like a "book."

69 On chap. 15, see Noth (*Numbers* [N 9]: 114) who suggests that this is some of the latest material in the Pentateuch. (The redactor gives himself away in vv 22-23!) The introductory formula in vv 2 and 18 (which has a long and complicated history) may be intentionally ironic here next to chap. 14. Perhaps v 40 (*qᵉdōšîm*) is also intended to link chap. 15 with chap. 16, but this remains speculative.

70 The contrast is probably deliberate on the part of the P redactor; see my "Denial of Moses" (N 33): 483-84.

PSALM 106: YAHWEH'S SUCCORING LOVE SAVES FROM THE DEATH OF A BROKEN COVENANT*

NEIL H. RICHARDSON

Introduction

Psalm 106, historical in nature, is a recital of Israel's ingratitude, with an emphasis upon the incredible tension between the rebellion of a covenant people and Yahweh's compassion. It stresses what Yahweh has done—his acts of *ḥesed*—and how Israel responded: the classic dialectic between God and humanity. Such a recital, rather than being itself a lament, is better regarded as an inducement to lament,[1] leading to covenant renewal[2] through confession of sin.

Most recent commentators divide Psalm 106 into three parts: vv 1–5/6; 6/7–46; 47–48.[3] As far as v 6 is concerned, it is best viewed as introductory to what follows: a recitation of the sins to which the verse alludes.

Part II, vv 6–46, consists of nine strophes of unequal length. The words הושיענו יהוה אלהינו "save us, Yahweh, our God" (v 47) begin a new unit. It is generally recognized that v 48 does not belong to this psalm but was originally written as a conclusion to Book IV of the Psalter; hence it will not be considered in this study.

The method of this essay will be to consider the psalm part by part and strophe by strophe in four divisions: translation, textual notes, structural notes[4] and exegetical notes, leading to a brief conclusion in which date, authorship and provenance will be suggested. Space does not permit an exhaustive treatment but some new directions may be intimated for future study of the psalm and others like it.

Part I

הַלְלוּיָה	1.0	Hallelujah!				
הודו ליהוה כִּי־טוֹב	1.1	Give thanks to Yahweh, for he is good.	a	b	c	
כִּי לְעוֹלָם חַסְדּוֹ	1.2	Indeed eternal is his power to liberate.		d	e	
מִי יְמַלֵּל גְּבוּרוֹת יהוה	2.3	Who can recount the mighty acts of Yahweh,	a^1		e^1	b
יַשְׁמִיעַ כָּל־תְּהִלָּתוֹ:	2.4	Proclaim his every praiseworthy deed?[a]	a^2		e^2	
אַשְׁרֵי שֹׁמְרֵי מִשְׁפָּט	3.1	Happy are they who are attentive to justice,	a	b	c	
עֹשֵׂי[b] צְדָקָה בְכָל־עֵת:	3.2	Who do[b] what is right at all times.	a^1		c^1	d
זָכְרֵנִי יהוה בִּרְצוֹן עַמֶּךָ	4.1	Remember me,[c] O Yahweh, when favoring your people;	a	b	c	d
פָּקְדֵנִי בִּישׁוּעָתֶךָ:	4.2	Take care of me[c] with your saving power	a^1	e		
לִרְאוֹת בְּטוֹבַת בְּחִירֶיךָ	5.1	That I may see the prosperity of your chosen,	a	b	c	
לִשְׂמֹחַ בְּשִׂמְחַת גּוֹיֶךָ	5.2	Rejoice in the joy of your nation,	a^1	b^1	c^1	
לְהִתְהַלֵּל עִם־נַחֲלָתֶךָ:	5.3	Take pride in your heirs.	a^2		c^2	

* It is a great privilege to dedicate this essay to Marvin Pope whose friendship I have cherished, from whom I have learned much, and with whom, on several occasions, I have had the pleasure of discussing the incident at Baal Peor and its numerous and varied ramifications. It is also offered in loving memory of Helen. The paper has benefited from the editorial corrections and skillful typing of C. Faith Richardson, the perceptive reading of my Teaching Assistant, Deborah R. Kennedy, the assistance of John T. Greene in translating some German material, and a lively discussion at a colloquy of my Old Testament colleagues in the Boston Theological Institute. The defects that remain are my responsibility alone.

1 Cf. W. I. Wolverton, "Sermons in the Psalms," *Canadian Journal of Theology* 10 (1964): 166–76 (n.b. 174).

2 Cf. L. E. Toombs, "The Psalms" in *The Interpreter's One-Volume Commentary on the Bible* (C. M. Laymon, ed.; Nashville: Abingdon, 1971): 292.

3 So C. A. and E. G. Briggs, *A Critical and Exegetical Commentary on the Book of Psalms* 2 (ICC; New York: Charles Scribner's Sons, 1907): 348, 353 (vv 44–47 are dealt with as one strophe); M. Dahood, *Psalms III. 101–150* (AB 17A; Garden City: Doubleday, 1970): 67; D. Kidner, *Psalms 73–150. A Commentary on Books III–IV of the Psalms* (London: Inter-varsity, 1975): 378, 381 (vv 40–46 are treated as a unit); E. J. Kissane, *The Book of Psalms. Translated from a Critically Revised Hebrew Text* (Westminster: Newman, 1954): 169, 173 (vv 40–47 are treated as a unit); H.-J. Kraus, *Psalmen* 2 (2nd ed.; BKAT; Neukirchen, 1962): 727; A. Weiser, *The Psalms. A Commentary* (Old Testament Library; Philadelphia: Westminster, 1962): 680–82.

4 This discussion will concern the shape of Psalm 106 in its various parts together with prosodic considerations, in particular strophic structures and the associated problems of metrical analysis.

Textual Notes

a. The LXX, Jerome and Pesh. assume תהלתיו for MT תהלתו, perhaps under the influence of Exod 15:11. While parallelism might support such a reading, MT is possible and has been retained.

b. Read עשי for the MT עשה following several ancient versions. Clearly a plural form is needed.

c. Several Greek versions assume זכרנו and פקדנו for MT זכרני and פקדני. While some modern commentators adopt the plural readings, they also commonly fail to deal with the resulting exegetical problem (viz., Kraus, Weiser).

Structural Notes[5]

Part I falls into two subdivisions: vv 1–3 and vv 4–5. Following "hallelujah,"[6] vv 1–2 constitute a double bicolon. Lines 1.1, 2.3 and 2.4 exhibit a repetitive pattern: הודו // ימלל // ישמיע; likewise 1.2, 2.3 and 2.4: חסדי // גבורות // תהלתו. In this way a tight literary unit was created. Verse 3 consists of a bicolon, the repetitive pattern being exhibited by the presence of the complementary words שמרו // עשי and משפט // צדקה.

Verse 4 also consists of a bicolon, the repetitive pattern being exhibited by זכרני // פקדני. The syllable count is 11:9. For some reason the first line was overbalanced, perhaps for melodic or rhythmic reasons or for the sake of emphasis. Verse 5 is a tricolon, the repetitive patterns appearing in the following complementary terms: לראות // לשמח // להתהלל, טובת // שמחת and בחיריך // גויך // נחלתך. We should also note the repetition of the infinitives at the beginning of each line: לראות, לשמח and להתהלל, as well as the rhyming device *-ka* at the end of each line.

Part I exhibits the following patterns in respect to length of lines:

Syllable count[7]	Vocable count[7]	Stress count[8]
7:6:9:7	21:17:25:18	3:3:3:3
7:8	19:20	3:3
11:9	29:22	4:2
9:8:10	25:21:24	3:3:2

Thus this strophe is marked by a striking unevenness in the length of lines. On the other hand, there is a skillful use of complementary words, forms and sounds.

Exegetical Notes

In a hymnic *introitus* (vv 1, 2) the community is called to a mood of thankful praise. Yahweh is to be recognized as the one who is able to do for his chosen people whatever they need.

In translating *ḥesed* "power to liberate" I have followed the conclusion of K. D. Sakenfeld who states: *ḥesed* "normally provides deliverance from dire straits .... God's *ḥesed* is delivering, protecting power ...."[9] The parallelism further supports such a view of *ḥesed* as primarily an action word.

Following the *introitus* proper there is a beatitude (v 3) exhorting the community to strive for righteousness. As W. Janzen has shown,[10] the pronouncement of blessing anticipates the favors that God will shower upon those who are pious. Hence "happy are they who are attentive to justice" means that the future righteous will be happy, will be blessed by Yahweh because they are righteous.

Part I closes with a beautiful prayer (vv 4, 5) that God may look upon his chosen people with favor. Thus they will joyously experience future prosperity. The retention of the singular form of the MT permits us to sense not only the personal nature of the prayer but "relates the one to the many, refusing to lose the individual in the crowd."[11]

5 Here we shall be guided mainly by the work of David Noel Freedman: "Archaic Forms in Early Hebrew Poetry," *ZAW* 72 (1960): 101–07; "Prolegomenon" in G. B. Gray, *The Forms of Hebrew Poetry* (New York: KTAV, 1972): vii–lvi; "Strophe and Meter in Exodus 15" in *A Light Unto My Path. Old Testament Studies in Honor of Jacob Myers* (H. N. Bream, R. D. Hein, C. A. Moore, eds.; Gettysburg Theological Studies 4; Philadelphia: Temple University, 1974): 163–203; "Pottery, Poetry, and Prophecy: An Essay on Biblical Poetry," *JBL* 96 (1977): 5–26. Prose particles such as the object marker את (9 occurrences), the article ה (1 occurrence) and conjunctive ו have not been eliminated since it is difficult to determine when they became a part of poetic language or were added to already existing poems. (In contrast see P. D. Hanson, *The Dawn of Apocalyptic* [Philadelphia: Fortress, 1975]: 49.)

6 The word actually serves as a cultic exclamation and stands outside the psalm proper.

7 For explanation of these methods of counting see Freedman, "Exodus 15" (N 5) and "Archaic Forms" (N 5).

8 I prefer this terminology to the use of "meter."

9 K. D. Sakenfeld, *The Meaning of Hesed* (sic) *in the Hebrew Bible: A New Inquiry* (HSM 17; Missoula: Scholars, 1978): 234, 237.

10 W. Janzen, "ʾAšrê in the Old Testament," *HTR* 58 (1965): 215–16.

11 Kidner (N 3): 378.

Part II—Strophe 1

חָטָאנוּ עִם־אֲבוֹתֵינוּ	6.1	We have sinned as our ancestors did;	a	b	
הֶעֱוִינוּ הִרְשָׁעְנוּ׃	6.2	We have acted in wicked and evil ways.	a^1	a^2	
אֲבוֹתֵינוּ בְמִצְרַיִם [וַיַּמְרְדוּ][a]	7.1	Our ancestors in Egypt [rebelled];[a]	a	b	c
לֹא־הִשְׂכִּילוּ נִפְלְאוֹתֶיךָ	7.2	They did not comprehend your marvelous acts,		d	e
לֹא זָכְרוּ אֶת־רֹב חֲסָדֶיךָ	7.3	Did not remember your many deliverances.		d^1	e^1
וַיַּמְרוּ עלים[b] בְּיַם־סוּף	7.4	They defied the Most High[b] at the Reed Sea.	c^1	f	b^1
וַיּוֹשִׁיעֵם לְמַעַן שְׁמוֹ	8.1	But he saved them for the sake of his reputation,	a	b	
לְהוֹדִיעַ אֶת־גְּבוּרָתוֹ׃	8.2	In order to demonstrate his mighty act	c	d	
וַיִּגְעַר בְּיַם־סוּף וַיֶּחֱרָב	9.3	He rebuked the Reed Sea and it dried up.	e	f	g
וַיּוֹלִיכֵם בַּתְּהֹמוֹת כַּמִּדְבָּר׃	9.4	He led them through the Abyss as through a desert.	h	f^1	g^1
וַיּוֹשִׁיעֵם מִיַּד שׂוֹנֵא	10.5	He saved them from the power of the foe,	a	i	j
וַיִּגְאָלֵם מִיַּד אוֹיֵב׃	10.6	Redeemed them from the power of the enemy.	a^1	i	j^1
וַיְכַסּוּ־מַיִם צָרֵיהֶם	11.7	Waters covered their adversaries:	k	f^2	j^2
אֶחָד מֵהֶם לֹא נוֹתָר׃	11.8	Not one of them survived.	l	m	n
וַיַּאֲמִינוּ בִדְבָרָיו	12.1	Then they believed his words,	a	b	
יָשִׁירוּ תְּהִלָּתוֹ׃	12.2	Sang[c] his praise.	a^1	c	

Textual Notes

a. It has been correctly observed that "the last part of the first line appears to have been lost."[12] Following this assumption we may view the verse as a double bicola in which case we would look for a verb complementary or synonymous with וימרו (מרה). Hence וימרדו (מרד) has been supplied as a purely conjectural emendation. At the same time it is clear that MT makes good sense, as in most translations. The exegetical problem is not seriously affected either way.

b. For MT על־ים the LXX reads ἀναβαίνοντες presupposing Hebrew עלים. Many commentators emend MT to עליון. This is unnecessary since a form עלים will produce the same sense. The final *m* may be viewed as enclitic and the form construed as *ʿēlî-ma*. The exegetical consequences of this reconstruction will be noted below.

c. Some MSS of LXX, Jerome and Pesh. presuppose וישירו for MT ישירו. However it should be noted that the prefix form of the verb occurs six times to express past (or frequentative) action.[13]

Structural Notes

The first strophe consists of vv 6–12, even though v 6 is introductory to the whole of Part II. Verse 6 is a bicolon. The repetitive pattern is unusual in that חטאנו of the first colon is paralleled by *two* verbs in the colon: העוינו and הרשענו.

Verse 7 is best viewed as a double bicolon. We have already observed that something has been lost out of the first colon and suggested supplying וימרדו. Adopting this reading we see that 7.1 and 7.4 exhibit a repetitive pattern: וימרדו // וימרו and מצרים // ים־סוף; while in 7.2 and 7.3 we have השכילו // זכרו and נפלאותיך // חסדיך. In addition we see a partial chiasmus in that 7.1 ends with the verb while the complementary term begins 7.4

In vv 8–11 there is a tetrad of bicola in which the first two cola exhibit no repetitive pattern while in the remainder of the tetrad the repetitive patterns are very intricate. The word ויושיעם in 8.1 is repeated in 10.5 and has a synonym in ויגאלם in 10.6. The phrase ים־סוף (9.3) has its complements in תהמות (9.4) and מים (11.7). The word שונא (10.5) has its synonyms in אויב (10.6) and צריהם (11.7) while יד is repeated in 10.5 and 10.6. Finally, we note the correspondence in meaning between ויחרב "it dried up" in 9.3 and מדבר "desert" in 9.4. Alliteration may also be noted: 8.1, 9.4 and 10.5 begin *wayyŏ-* while 9.3 and 10.6 begin *wayyig-*, followed in 9.3 by *-ʿar* and in 10.6 by *-ʾāl*.

Verse 12 is a bicolon concluding the strophe. The two cola are only loosely related, although it is possible to see a complementary relationship between ויאמינו (12.1) and ישירו (12.2).[14]

The strophe exhibits the following line lengths:

Syllable count	Vocable count	Stress count
8:7	22:19	2:2
10:9:10:9	28:25:25:24	3:3:4:4
8:8:10:10:8:8:8:7	23:21:26:29:24:23:20:19	3:2:3:3:3:3:3:4
8:7	22:17	2:2

The pattern is very remarkable: the strophe begins and ends with bicola in each of which the syllable count is identical, the first bicolon being followed by a double bicolon and that in turn by a tetrad or bicola in which the deviation in lengths of lines follows a markedly consistent pattern. This is in noted constrast to the rather erratic pattern of vv 1–5.

---

12 Sakenfeld (N 9): 208.

13 Cf. D. A. Robertson, *Linguistic Evidence in Dating Early Hebrew Poetry* (SBLDS 3; Missoula: SBL, 1972): 47–49, 51.

14 R. G. Boling, " 'Synonymous' Parallelism in the Psalms," *JSS* 5 (1960): 239.

Exegetical Notes

In Strophe 1 traditions of the escape from the Egyptian army at the Reed Sea are drawn upon freely and eclectically. Some of these are recorded in Exodus 14 and 15, but the lack of word correspondences belies a theory of literary dependence.[15] The rebellion of the Israelites is traced back to the period of their residence in Egypt. This reflects the same point of view as that expressed in Ezek 23:2, 3 where it is stated that "young girls played the whore in Egypt," thereby making clear Ezekiel's view that Egypt had indeed been "the place of the most impious immorality and sin of God's people with powers other than God's own sovereign power."[16] This undoubtedly indicates a view that relationship with Egypt was corruptive, as first noted by Isaiah but also stressed by Jeremiah and Ezekiel.

So it was *in Egypt* that rebellion began, because there Israel failed to call to mind all of God's acts of *ḥesed*. *Ḥesed* stands in parallelism with נפלאות "marvelous acts" and may thus be properly translated "deliverance."[17] Thus the affirmation was made that God had acted in wondrous ways on Israel's behalf *even before* the Exodus. The psalm may well reflect traditions concerning the patriarchs and the many times God's interventions had preserved the Israelite's ancestors.

If the reading *ᶜly-m* "Most High" in v 7 is correct, we have a term that is essentially early (i.e., pre-exilic) and northern. It appears in Ugaritic as an epithet of Baal; in the Hebrew Bible, of Yahweh. It is also seen in the name יחועלי (Samaria ostracon No. 55). It is an alternative to עליון since both rarely appear in the same poem. The word על / עלי as a divine epithet may be noted in Gen 49:2b; Deut 33:12; 1 Sam 2:10; 2 Sam 23:1; Pss 7:9; 13:6; 16:5, 6; 18:42 (omitted from 2 Sam 22:42); 32:5; 55:23; 57 :3; 62:8; 68:35.[18] Of these passages for which a date and provenance can be established with any degree of certainty, the majority are not later than the eighth century. Exegetically, the significance of this reading is that it is made explicit that it was God whom they defied. The MT merely assumes this and at the same time presents a reading that is difficult.

With the word תהמות "Abyss" (v 9) a mythological note is introduced. When God, viz., the Most High, "rebuked the Reed Sea" and dried up the Abyss, we have the motif of a struggle with primeval cosmic forces. This in turn gives added meaning to "waters" in 11.7. Thus the historical event of liberation was enlarged by incorporating into it elements of the creation myth where God defeated תהום[19] in the creation of light (Gen 1:2, 3). In Isa 51:9–11 we also find the joining of mythic and historical material where "the battle of Yahweh (Baal) against Yamm is recalled to add a cosmic dimension to the Second Exodus announced by the prophet."[20]

Part II—Strophe 2

מִהֲרוּ שָׁכְחוּ מַעֲשָׂיו	13.1	Quickly they forgot his deeds,	a	b	c
לֹא חִכּוּ לַעֲצָתוֹ׃	13.2	Did not wait for his counsel.		b^1	c^1
וַיִּתְאַוּוּ תַאֲוָה בַּמִּדְבָּר	14.1	They were filled with craving in the desert;	a	b	c
וַיְנַסּוּ־אֵל בִּישִׁימוֹן׃	14.2	They put God to the test in the wilderness.	d	e	c^1
וַיִּתֶּן לָהֶם שֶׁאֱלָתָם	15.3	He gave them their request;	f	g	h
וַיְשַׁלַּח רָזוֹן בְּנַפְשָׁם׃	15.4	He cast out leanness[a] from their throat.	i	j	k

Textual Note

a. For MT רזון the LXX reads πλησμονὴν (satiety, surfeit, abundance); the Pesh. and Vulg. attest to the same sense. Hence the text has been emended to רוון (√רוה) by Kissane, or מזון by Briggs. However, רזון can be seen to make perfect sense here (see below) and an emendation is not necesary.

Structural Notes

Strophe 2 consists of vv 13-15. Verse 13 is a bicolon related by the complementary terms שכחו // חכו and מעשיו // עצתו. The syllable count is 9:7, reflecting an unbalanced bicolon which is, of course, a legitimate

15 Cf. Weiser (N 3): 681.

16 W. Zimmerli, *Ezekiel 1* (Hermeneia; Philadelphia: Fortress, 1979): 489.

17 See Sakenfeld (N 9).

18 For studies of על / עלי see the following: M. Dahood, "The Divine Name of ᶜELĪ in the Psalms," *Theological Studies* 14 (1953): 452–57; Dahood *Psalms I* (AB 16), *Psalms II* (AB 17), *Psalms III*, pass.; Freedman, "Divine Names and Titles in Early Hebrew Poetry" in *Magnalia Dei. The Mighty Acts of God; Essays on the Bible and Archaeology in Memory of G. Ernest Wright* (F. M. Cross, W. E. Lemke and P. D. Miller, Jr., eds.; Garden City: Doubleday, 1976): 55–107; M. Pope, "Baal-Hadad" in *Götter und Mythen im Vorderen Orient* (*Wörterbuch der Mythologie* 1; Stuttgart: Ernest Klett, 1965): 253–64 (n.b. 254, 255); H. N. Richardson, "The Last Words of David: Some Notes on II Samuel 23:1–7," *JBL* 90 (1971): 257–66 (n.b. 260, 261).

19 The different spellings—תהום, תהמות, etc.—need not detain us. In Ug. we regularly find *thmt* comparable to Babylonian *tʾmt*, i.e., both with final *-t*. Hence Hebrew תהום may be a back formation creating a singular from a supposed plural.

20 Hanson (N 5): 127.

variation from the usual balanced one. Verse 14 and 15 constitute a double bicolon based primarily upon thought patterns rather than word correspondences. However, in 14.1 and 14.2 we do see the complementary terms ישימון // מרבר.

Strophe 2 exhibits the following pattern:

Syllable count	Vocable count	Stress count
9:7	21:17	3:3
10:8:9:9	25:22:22:23	3:3:3:3

Exegetical Notes

Strophe 2 alludes to Num 11:4–9, 31, 32 (JE) in which a certain group of Israelite discontents (האספסף) led the whole company to a strong craving for more substantial food than was available in the desert. Here the verbal correspondence is very clear: Num 11:4—התאוו תאוה; Ps 106:14—ויתאוו תאוה. To the basic statement in Numbers an interpretation is added: this was a testing of God; in this way Israel's sinfulness was enhanced. But God "gave them their request"; this probably alludes to the manna and quails of the account in Numbers.

Line 15.4 remains a *crux interpretum*, the most difficult one in the psalm. The readings of the ancient versions are no help. The translators of the LXX either had an entirely different text or they were guessing at the meaning since πλησμονὴν was commonly used to translate some form of שלח although we find the semantic equivalent in Ugaritic in such collocations as *ṭrb b* "drove (Baal) from"; *grš b* "drive out from"; *yṣʾ b* "go forth from." Although M. Dahood is correct in insisting that 15.3 and 15.4 are synonymous in thought, he probably is not quite accurate in stating that ב means "from."[21] The following statement by D. Pardee is more exact and provides the solution to our *crux*: "... I have concluded that it is wiser to describe the general Ugaritic prepositional system in terms of position than to describe it in terms of direction. If this is correct, *b* does not mean 'in,' 'from,' and 'into,' but 'position within the confines of,' and direction 'to' or 'from,' or lack of direction, are provided by verb, context or idiomatic usage."[22] The same is no doubt true for Hebrew. In line 15.4 the sense of "from" inheres in the verb while the preposition ב indicates the location of the "leanness"; hence we might understand the line—"he cast out leanness which was in their throat from their throat." In God's giving them the food they requested his attitude was positive and life saving.

Part II—Strophe 3

וַיְקַנְאוּ לְמֹשֶׁה בַּמַּחֲנֶה	16.1	In the camp they envied Moses,	a	b	c				
לְאַהֲרֹן קְדוֹשׁ יהוה׃	16.2	Aaron, the holy one of Yahweh.			c^1	d	e		
תִּפְתַּח־אֶרֶץ וַתִּבְלַע דָּתָן	17.1	The earth opened and swallowed Dathan;	a	b	c	d			
וַתְּכַס עַל־עֲדַת אֲבִירָם׃	17.2	It covered Abiram's gang.		c^1	e	d^1			
וַתִּבְעַר־אֵשׁ בַּעֲדָתָם	18.3	Fire raged among the gang;	f	g	e				
לֶהָבָה תְּלַהֵט רְשָׁעִים׃	18.4	Flames devoured the wicked.		g^1	c^2	h			

Structural Notes

Strophe 3 consists of vv 16–18. Verse 16 is a bicolon, משה and אהרן being in parallelism. In addition we note that the verb ויקנאו (16.1) serves both lines as another way of relating them. Verses 17 and 18 constitute a double bicolon. Through the use of complementary terms, synonyms and repetition, a compact unit has been created. The words דתך (17.1) and אבירם are complementary. The verbs ותבלע (17.1), ותכם (17.2) and תלהט (18.4) are synonymous / complementary as are also the nouns אשׁ (18.3) and להבה (18.4). The word עד appears in 17.2 and 18.3.

The pattern of the strophe is as follows:

Syllable count	Vocable count	Stress count
11:8	26:21	3:3
8:9:8:9	23:23:20:22	4:4:3:3

Exegetical Notes

Strophe 3 very briefly summarizes incidents recorded in Numbers 16. "Envied" (קנא) is obviously an *interpretation* by which a motive is provided for the words of Num 16:3. Then the text moves quickly to the account of the earth's swallowing up Dathan and Abiram, their families and all their possessions (Num 16:31–33). But it is a short account and one is led to question whether an original version has been abbreviated or whether Numbers gives an expanded one. The account in Numbers where the fire consumes 250 persons gathered around Korah was further conflated by telling of the fire that destroyed Abiram's gang. The omission in the psalm of any reference to Korah may very well suggest that the psalm is best viewed as not dependent upon Numbers as it has come down to us. As M. Noth observed,[23] Num 16:1–35 reflects three literary sources. Of the three, the two involving Korah should most probably be attributed to the Priestly (P) material. Psalm 106 may then be said to predate the inclusion of the Korah traditions in Numbers.

21 Dahood, *Psalms III* (N 3): 71.

22 D. Pardee, "The Preposition in Ugaritic," *Ugarit-Forschungen* 8 (1976): 289.

23 M. Noth, *Numbers. A Commentary* (Old Testament Library; Philadelphia: Westminster, 1968): 120–21.

Part II—Strophe 4

יַעֲשׂוּ־עֵגֶל בְּחֹרֵב	19.1	They made[a] a calf at Horeb;	a	b	c		
וַיִּשְׁתַּחֲווּ לְמַסֵּכָה׃	19.2	They worshipped an idol.	d	e			
וַיָּמִירוּ אֶת־כְּבוֹדָם	20.3	They exchanged their Glory		f	g		
בְּתַבְנִית שׁוֹר אֹכֵל עֵשֶׂב׃	20.4	For an image of a grass-eating steer.	e^1	b^1	h	i	
שָׁכְחוּ אֵל מוֹשִׁיעָם	21.1	They forgot God, their Savior,	a	b	c		
עֹשֶׂה גְדֹלוֹת בְּמִצְרָיִם׃	21.2	Who did great deeds in Egypt,		b^1	d		e
נִפְלָאוֹת בְּאֶרֶץ חָם	22.3	Marvelous acts in the land of Ham,			d^1	f	e^1
נוֹרָאוֹת עַל־יַם־סוּף׃	22.4	Awesome things at the Reed Sea.			d^2		e^2
וַיֹּאמֶר לְהַשְׁמִידָם	23.1	Then he thought to destroy them	a		b		
לוּלֵי מֹשֶׁה בְחִירוֹ	23.2	Were it not for Moses, his chosen:	c	d			
עָמַד בַּפֶּרֶץ לְפָנָיו	23.3	He stood in the breach before him	e	f	g		
לְהָשִׁיב חֲמָתוֹ מֵהַשְׁחִית׃	23.4	To turn away his destructive wrath.	h	i	b^1		

Textual Note

a. The LXX assumes ויעשו for MT יעשו. See note *c* on v 12.2

Structural Notes

Strophe 4 consists of three double bicola. The first one (vv 19–20) is marked by the use of complementary, explanatory, synonymous and antithetical terms. In 19.1 עגל is synonymous with שור in 20.4. The word מסכה is explanatory of עגל while כבוד in 20.3 is antithetical to all the following: עגל, מסכה, and the phrase בתבנית שור אכל עשב in 20.4. Finally, מסכה is synonymous with תבנית. Thus we find a very remarkable compactness.

The second double bicola (vv 21, 22)—actually a colon which introduces the unit followed by a tricolon—represents a new pattern. Line 21.1 is related to 21.2: אל // עשה גדלות. The three cola, 21.2, 22.3 and 22.4, have two synonymous / complementary terms in each: גדלות // נפלאות // נוראות; מצרים // ארץ חם // ים־סוף.

The third double bicola (v 23), while not exhibiting clear repetitive patterns, is a single unit on the basis of thought. Especially striking is the repetition of the idea of destruction in להשמידם (23.1) and חמתו מהשחית (23.4), emphasized by the alliteration השמיד—השחית.

The count for Strophe 4:

Syllable count	Vocable count	Stress count
7:9:8:8	18:21:21:22	3:2:3:4
7:8:6:6	20:22:17:19	3:3:3:3
7:7:7:9	19:18:19:25	2:3:3:3

For the first time we have *breve* syllable counts in contrast to the consistent *longum* of the preceding cola.[24]

Exegetical Notes

Strophe 4 reflects the account of the making of the golden calf in Exod 31:18–32:35 (J;E) except that in the psalm the mountain is identified as Horeb as in Deut 9:8–12. The religious leaders of Israel, not the least the Elohist, constantly had to contend with the sin of idolatry. Calf / bull worship was central to the Canaanite cult. In the Ugaritic texts both El and Baal are described as "Bull."[25] When Jeroboam I established cult centers at Bethel (and Dan) with the Bull as central (1 Kgs 12) he was no doubt catering to strong Canaanite elements in northern society. Exodus 32:1–6 is best understood as a cultic aetiology explaining the construction and cultic veneration of the calf-image at Bethel.[26] "In this way the Elohist tradition unmistakably registers condemnation of Jeroboam's cult and priesthood, relating it to the primal apostacy of Israel at Sinai."[27] With this view Hosea concurred (Hos 8:5–6; 10:5–6). That it actually happened in the period of the wilderness wandering is the view expressed in the psalm although Jeroboam's sin may also be reflected.

Certainly in this psalm bull worship is viewed as "primal apostacy" so that the idol was more than "a mere focus for worship for the true God. It was an exchange."[28] This is further emphasized by the statement: "they forgot God, their Savior," etc. (vv 21, 22); and once again the congregation is reminded of God's past "marvelous acts" (נפלאות; cf. v 7.2).

But God can also destroy: here is an intimation of how exasperated God can become. In Exod 32:11–14 is recorded Moses' speech in which he pleads for Israel with the result that Yahweh relents from destroying the nation. Thus a special point is made (v 23) of Moses' intervention which enhanced his figure.

24 For the use of the terms *breve* and *longum* see F. M. Cross, "The Song of the Sea and Canaanite Myth," *Journal for Theology and the Church* (New York: Harper Torchbooks, 1968): 4–5, note 12, Hanson (N 5): 47–48.

25 Cf. M. Pope, *El in the Ugaritic Texts* (VTSup 4; Leiden: Brill, 1955): 35–41.

26 W. Beyerlin, *Origins and History of the Oldest Sinaitic Traditions* (Oxford: Basil Blackwell, 1965): 128.

27 A. W. Jenks, *The Elohist and North Israelite Traditions* (SBLMS 22; Missoula: Scholars, 1977): 51.

28 Kidner (N 3): 380.

Part II—Strophe 5

וַיִּמְאֲסוּ בְּאֶרֶץ חֶמְדָּה	24.1	They despised the desirable land,	a	b	c
לֹא־הֶאֱמִינוּ לִדְבָרוֹ:	24.2	Believed not his word.	a^1	d	
וַיֵּרָגְנוּ בְאָהֳלֵיהֶם	25.1	They murmured in their tents.	a	b	
לֹא שָׁמְעוּ בְּקוֹל יהוה:	25.2	They did not obey Yahweh.	a^1	c	d
וַיִּשָּׂא יָדוֹ לָהֶם	26.1	He raised his hand against them	a	b	c
לְהַפִּיל אוֹתָם בַּמִּדְבָּר:	26.2	To strike them down in the desert,	d	e	f
וּלְהָפִיץ[a] זַרְעָם בַּגּוֹיִם	27.3	To disperse[a] their descendants among the nations,	d^1	g	h
וּלְזָרוֹתָם בָּאֲרָצוֹת:	27.4	To scatter them throughout the lands.	d^2		h^1

Textual Note

a. Read ולהפיץ for MT ולהפיל following the Pesh. Cf. Ezek 20:23. Weiser and Kraus adopt this reading, which makes better sense. The error is one of dittography from להפיל of v 26. The exegetical consequences of the change will be noted below.

Structural Note

Strophe 5 is made up of two bicola and a double bicola. The first bicolon (v 24) displays a very loose connection between the two parts but לא האמינו (24.2) may be said to be in either complementary or explanatory relationship to וימאסו (24.1). The second bicolon (v 25) likewise shows only the slightest relationship between two parts. Again one might view לא שמעו as in some sense complementary to וירגנו. While vv 24, 25 seem to be treated best as two bicola, they are related stylistically since each of the two second bicola begins with לא. In addition it should be noted that the pronominal suffix ו on לדברו (24.2) is proleptic to יהוה (25.4), a device which also serves to bring the two bicola closer.

The double bicolon (vv 26, 27) is the same form as that in Strophe 4, i.e., an introductory colon followed by a tricolon. Here, however, the relationship between the first colon and the succeeding cola is even closer in that the verb of 26.1 is followed by infinitives at the beginning of each of the following three cola. In the tricolas we find להפיל (26.2) in complementary relationship to ולהפיע[29] (27.3) and ולזרותם (27.4), as are also גוים (27.3) and ארצות (27.4), while ולזרותם (27.4) are in synonymous relationship.

The count for the strophe is as follows:

Syllable count	Vocable count	Stress count
8:8	22:21	3:2
9:8	23:23	2:4
7:8:8:8	17:23:22:21	3:3:3:2

Exegetical Notes

The antecedents of Strophe 5 must be recognized from "they murmured in their tents" (וירגנו באהליהם, v 25.1) which also occurs in Deut 1:27: "you murmured in your tents" (ותרגנו באהליכם); this phrase appears nowhere else in the Hebrew Bible. The context in Deuteronomy is the sending out of the spies to Canaan and their return with an encouraging report; it is paralleled by an account in Numbers 13, 14. The people murmured among themselves and refused to obey Yahweh. This was to result in virtual death for they were to be struck down, dispersed and scattered among the nations.

Given the reading adopted here, the parallel between Ps 106:26 and Ezek 20:23 is very striking: "I raised my hand against them in the desert to disperse them among the nations, to scatter them throughout the lands" (Ezek 20:23: גַּם־אֲנִי נָשָׂאתִי אֶת־יָדִי לָהֶם בַּמִּדְבָּר לְהָפִיץ אֹתָם בַּגּוֹיִם וּלְזָרוֹת אוֹתָם בָּאֲרָצוֹת; Ps 106:26.1, 27,3, 4: . . . וישא ידו להם ולהפיץ זרעם בגוים ולזרותם בארצות). The same thought appears in Lev 26:33 but there only the verb זרה appears followed by גוים rather than ארצות as in the other texts. By making reference to the scattering the psalm moves from the wilderness period to the future history of Israel.

That the Babylonian exile is meant is by no means certain. The affinities with the language of Deuteronomy and Ezekiel suggest a pre-exilic date. The previous strophe was ultimately concerned with the sin of the Northern Kingdom; hence the scattering mentioned in 27.4 might very well represent the fate of the people of the Northern Kingdom following the fall of Samaria.

Part II—Strophe 6

וַיִּצָּמְדוּ לְבַעַל פְּעוֹר	28.1	They united themselves with Baal-Peor.	a	b	c
וַיֹּאכְלוּ זִבְחֵי מֵתִים:	28.2	They ate sacrifices offered to the dead.	d	e	f
וַיַּכְעִיסוּ בְּמַעַלְלֵיהֶם	29.1	They angered (him)[a] by their deeds.	a	b	
וַתִּפְרָץ־בָּם מַגֵּפָה:	29.2	A plague broke out among them.	c	d	
וַיַּעֲמֹד פִּינְחָס וַיְפַלֵּל	30.3	Then Phinehas appeared to execute judgment—	e	f	g
וַתֵּעָצַר הַמַּגֵּפָה:	30.4	The plague was stopped.	h	d	
וַתֵּחָשֶׁב לוֹ לִצְדָקָה	31.1	It was surely reckoned to him as righteousness	a	b	c
לְדֹר וָדֹר עַד־עוֹלָם:	31.2	From generation to generation, eternally.	d	d	d^1

29 See textual note above.

Textual Note

a. Some versions of LXX, Jerome, Pesh. and Targ. read the equivalent of ויכעיסוהו for MT ויכעיסו. Given the interrelatedness of these versions, the evidence for the suffix *-hû* is not as strong as it might seem at first glance. Hebrew frequently omits the pronoun object.[30]

Structural Notes

Strophe 6 consists of a bicolon (v 28), a double bicolon (vv 29, 30) and a bicolon (v 31). However, the cola are very loosely related, the only real repetitive pattern to be noted is in the use of מגפה (29.2 and 30.4). The analysis of v 28 as a bicolon views 28.2 as explanatory of 28.1. The colon in v 31 may be said scarcely to lend itself to poetic analysis; it is virtually a single sentence: the thought proceeds in consecutive fashion with no attempt at repetitive patterns. This style is true throughout Hebrew poetry from earliest times, e.g., Exod 15:1.[31] Hence we view it as poetry; the virtually equal lengths of the two cola, no different from other sections, further warrant treating it as poetical.

The count for Strophe 6 is as follows:

Syllable count	Vocable count	Stress count
9:8	23:22	3:3
9:7:10:8	23:18:25:20	2:2:3:2
8:7	21:19	3:3

Thus it exhibits greater variety of form and line lengths than any other strophe in the psalm.

Exegetical Notes

This strophe refers to the activities at Baal-Peor related in Num 25:1-8 (J[1-5]; P[6-8]).[32] Aside from the abbreviated nature of the account, the striking and unique feature of the psalm is the reference to "sacrifices offered to the dead" (זבחי מתים; v 28.2). This is paralleled by the more neutral expression "sacrifices offered to their god" (זבחי אלהיהן) in Num 25:2. The statement in the psalm, to be taken seriously as reflecting an authentic tradition,[33] reveals that these were indeed funeral feasts. That weal and woe derive from the departed is the belief that lies at the heart of funerary practices, viz., the disposal and continued concern for and communion with the dead. Sacrifices to the dead consisted of communal meals around the burial place; blessing, health, prosperity and fertility were believed to be the reward of fidelity in these matters.

Among the terms for the dead throughout the Northwest Semitic sphere were "Rephaim" (Ug. *rpʾm*; Heb. רפאים). These Rephaim are the deceased, the denizens of the netherworld. The people of Ugarit regarded them as divine beings. Rephaim were conjured up at lavish sacrificial meals.

It is also clear that necrolatry was accompanied by ritual sexual intercourse. "If necrolatry consists of offerings by the living of those things which cause the dead to be made happy, then the sequence of sacrifice, food and drink, and ritual intercourse would represent the gamut of those things necessary to put the restless spirits at ease."[34] There is growing evidence "that funeral feasts in the ancient Near East were love feasts celebrated with wine, women and song."[35]

This combination of necrolatry and sacral sexual intercourse was called a *marzeaḥ* (Ug. *mrzḥ*; Heb. מרזח) in Rabbinic Judaism.[36] It is of particular interest that on the sixth century A.D. mosaic map in the church at Medeba, the locale of Baal-Peor is designated as "Betomarsea, also Maiumas" (βητομαρσεα ἡ κ[αὶ] μαιουμας). Clearly the Greek "Betomarsea" is a transliteration of Heb. בית מרזח: *marzeaḥ*-house. "Maiumas" refers to a licentious festival that was so extreme that the Romans banned it! This accords well with the picture we see in the two biblical references to the *marzeaḥ*: Jer 16:6–9 and Amos 6:4–7. In Jeremiah בית מרזח designates "a place in which banquets were held in both mourning and revelry for the dead, with drunkenness and sacral sexual intercourse. The mention of ivory beds, feasting, music and song, wine bibbing, and perfume oil in Amos 6:4–7 and of mourning and lamentation, eating and drinking, the sound of exultation and joy, and the sounds of groom and bride in Jer 16:6–9 are all features of the

30 A. B. Davidson, *Hebrew Syntax* (Edinburgh: T. & T. Clark, 1894): 106.

31 See Freedman "Exodus 15" (N 5): 175.

32 The presence of "Phinehas" marks vv 6–8 as P material but not necessarily exilic or post-exilic. The dependence of Priestly material on earlier (epic: JE) traditions is widely recognized. (Cf. Cross, *Canaanite Myth and Hebrew Epic* [Cambridge: Harvard University, 1973]): 324; M. Haran, "Studies in the Account of Levitical Cities," *JBL* 80 [1961]: 156.

33 The absence in Numbers of a reference to sacrifices to the dead is best viewed as an act of suppression. That the psalm's statement is more authentic is based on the principle of *lectio difficilior* which, of course, is not to be restricted to textual criticism.

34 G. E. Mendenhall, *The Tenth Generation* (Baltimore: Johns Hopkins, 1973): 111.

35 M. Pope, *Song of Songs* (AB 7c; Garden City: Doubleday, 1977): 228. For a contrary view see J. M. Sasson, "On M. H. Pope's Song of Songs [AB 7c]," *Maarav* 1 [1979]: 177–96 (n.b. 188–90).

36 On *marzeaḥ* the following will be useful: E. Y. Kutscher, *Millīn ve-Toledotehen* (Jerusalem: Kiryath, 1965): 4–7; J. T. Milik, *Dedicaces faites part des dieux (Palmyre, Katra, Tyr) et des thiases sémitiques â l'époque romain* (Recherches d'épigraphie proche-Orientale 1. Institute français d'archéologie de Beyrouth. Bibliothèque archéologique et historique XCII; Paris, 1972); B. Porten, "The Marzēaḥ Association" in *Archives from Elephantine* (Berkeley: University of California, 1968): 179–86; M. Pope, "A Divine Banquet at Ugarit" in *The Use of the Old Testament in the New and Other Essays. Studies in Honor of William Franklin Stinespring* (J. M. Efird, ed.; Durham: Duke University, 1972): 170–203; Pope, *Song of Songs* (N 35): 210–29.

funeral feast in the *marzeaḥ* (-house), or the drinking house."[37]

This, then, sums up briefly what is reflected in this strophe where a fuller account of the activity at Baal-Peor has been preserved, one which illuminates with greater fidelity what actually took place. This in turn may serve to enhance our understanding of the remark in Hos 9:10 that at Baal-Peor the Israelites consecrated (נזר) themselves to shame (בשת).[38]

Part II—Strophe 7

וַיַּקְצִיפוּ עַל־מֵי מְרִיבָה	32.1	They provoked (him)[a] to anger at the waters of Meribah.	a	b	c
וַיֵּרַע לְמֹשֶׁה בַּעֲבוּרָם׃	32.2	Thus Moses suffered on their account.	d	e	f
כִּי־הִמְרוּ אֶת־רוּחוֹ	33.3	Yea, they embittered his spirit	g	h	
וַיְבַטֵּא בִּשְׂפָתָיו׃	33.4	So that he made rash statements.	i	j	

Textual Note

a. Some MSS of LXX and Pesh. read ויקרציפוהו for MT ויקציפו. See note *c* on v 12.2.

Structural Notes

Strophe 7 consists of a single double bicolon whose members are again only loosely related. It is viewed as a unit more by the thought content than by any repetitive pattern, the subject of the cola (32.3–33.4) being Moses. It might be possible to consider these lines as forming a tricolon, but we do not so view them. The count is as follows:

Syllable count	Vocable count	Stress count
9:10:6:7	25:25:18:19	3:3:3:2

Thus it is seen that in overall form this strophe differs strikingly from all others in Psalm 106: it is shorter, lacks clear repetitive patterns and the length of lines is more erratic.

Exegetical Notes

Strophe 7 alludes to the incident in which Moses obtained water from a rock as recorded in Exod 17:1–7 and Num 20:5–13. However, the differences in the three passages lead to the conclusion that the psalm reflects the tradition in a different form from that in the other two accounts. In Exodus the place bears two names: Massah and Meribah (17:1); the psalmist mentions only the second, as in Num 20:13. In Numbers both Moses and Aaron are involved in contrast to the Exodus account; the psalmist mentions only Moses. Finally, we should note Deut 32:51 which explains that Moses (and Aaron) will not enter the Promised Land because it was at Meribah that Moses (and Aaron) failed to sanctify Yahweh.

Two aspects of the relationship between Ps 106:32–33 and the other passages suggest that the psalm is earlier that the Priestly (P) account. Aaron appears along with Moses only in Priestly sources.[39] Deut 32:51 reflects Num 20:12 and it is particularly noteworthy that both employ the same verb: "sanctify" (Hiph. of קדש). In turn this verb is absent from both Exod 17:1–7 and Strophe 7 of the psalm. Both the account in Numbers and the passage in Deuteronomy are the work of Priestly writers;[40] since the language and viewpoint of the psalm show little affinity with those passages, it may be concluded that the psalm is earlier than P.

Part II—Strophe 8

לֹא־הִשְׁמִידוּ אֶת־הָעַמִּים	34.1	They did not exterminate the nations	a	b			
[אֲשֶׁר אָמַר יהוה לָהֶם][a]		[as Yahweh had said to them].[a]					
וַיִּתְעָרְבוּ בַגּוֹיִם	35.2	They mingled with the peoples;	a^1	b^1			
וַיִּלְמְדוּ מַעֲשֵׂיהֶם׃	35.3	They learned their ways.	a^2		c		
וַיַּעַבְדוּ אֶת־עֲצַבֵּיהֶם	36.1	They served their idols;	a	b			
וַיִּהְיוּ לָהֶם לְמוֹקֵשׁ׃	36.2	They became a snare to them.	c	d	e		
[וַיִּזְבְּחוּ אֶת־בְּנֵיהֶם וְאֶת־בְּנוֹתֵיהֶם לַשֵּׁדִים׃][b]	37	[They sacrificed their sons and daughters to demons.][b]					
וַיִּשְׁפְּכוּ דָם נָקִי	38.1	They shed innocent blood—	a	b	c		
דַּם־בְּנֵיהֶם וּבְנוֹתֵיהֶם	38.2	The blood of their sons and daughters—		b	d	e	
[אֲשֶׁר זִבְּחוּ לַעֲצַבֵּי כְנָעַן][c]		[which they sacrificed to the idols of Canaan][c]					
וַתֶּחֱנַף הָאָרֶץ בַּדָּמִים׃	38.3	So that the land was profaned with blood.	f	g	b		
וַיִּטְמְאוּ בְמַעֲשֵׂיהֶם	39.1	They became unclean through their deeds;	a	b			
וַיִּזְנוּ בְּמַעַלְלֵיהֶם׃	39.2	They committed harlotries by their actions.	a^1	b^1			

37 Pope, *Song of Songs* (N 35): 216.

38 Cf. H. W. Wolff, *Hosea* (Hermeneia; Philadelphia: Fortress, 1974): 165.

39 Cross, *Canaanite Myth* (N 32): 197, note 16.

40 Noth, *Numbers* (N 23): 146–47; G. von Rad, *Deuteronomy. A Commentary* (Old Testament Library; Philadelphia: Westminster, 1966): 201.

Textual Notes

a. The phrase אשר אמר יהוה להם "as Yahweh had said to them" is best viewed as an editorial expansion. The word אשר is now recognized as not having a proper place in poetry[41] and often functions to introduce an editorial comment.

b. Verse 37 is viewed as an explanatory gloss on verse 38.

c. The phrase אשר זבחו לעצבי כנען "which they sacrificed to the idols of Canaan" is best viewed as an editorial expansion between 38.2 and 38.3 for the reason given in note *a*.

Structural Notes

Strophe 8 consists of two tricola and two bicola alternating, beginning with a tricolon.[42] Verse 37 is obviously prose and breaks the pattern just noted, leading us to conclude that it is best viewed as a gloss written to explain 38.2.

The first tricolon of Strophe 8 exhibits both synonymous and complementary repetitions. The words עמים and גוים are synonymous while the verbs לא־השמידו, יתערבו and ילמדו may be said to be complementary.

The first bicolon (v 36) exhibits very little by way of repetitive patterns. The two cola are related by virtue of thought, although ויהיו . . . למוקש might be said to be complementary to ויעבדו.

The second tricolon (v 38) exhibits a very striking use of דם, especially in its placement in the cola. In 38.1 it ends the line. In addition, in the third instance, the plural form has been used to intensify the meaning.

In the second bicolon (v 39) synonymous terms מעשיהם and מעלליהם appear, while ויטמאו and ויזנו are complementary.

The count for Strophe 8 is as follows:

Syllable count	Vocable count	Stress count
8:8:8	23:20:20	2:2:2
9:8	23:22	2:3
7:8:9	19:22:23	3:2:3
9:8	21:20	2:2

While the text is not to be emended *metri causa*, one cannot but observe that the pattern thus exhibited certainly lends support to the emendations which have been suggested on other grounds.

Exegetical Notes

Strophe 8, as Kidner points out,[43] "has common ground with Deuteronomy 32:15–18." In his form-critical study of Deuteronomy 32, G. E. Wright characterized these verses as an "indictment."[44] This is precisely the role the strophe plays in Psalm 106. Israel is indicted for actions by which covenant is broken.

Israel had been expected to separate itself from the world around it, refusing especially to worship foreign gods (Deut 13; 17:2–7). Instead "they did not exterminate the nations" but "mingled with" them, "learned their ways" and "served their idols" (vv 34.1–36.1; cf. Judg 3:5, 6). Verse 34.1 is an allusion to holy war ideology. This is expressed by the Hiph. of the verb שמד which appears also in Deut 9:3 in the passage (9:1–6) which G. E. Wright characterized as important in expressing the ideology and law of holy war.[45]

Special reference is made to harlotries (זנה), "a theme which is a dominant motif in Hosea's oracles."[46] In Hosea, as in Deut 32, 1 Kings 18 and Ps 106:34–39, the covenant is a broken one.[47] Thus the strophe reflects close affinites in thought and language with both Hosea and Deuteronomy, but ultimately northern in their geographical orientation.

Viewing two phrases and an entire verse as editorial expansions disturbs the canonical shape of the psalm. Following 34.1 there is the repetition of the idea that the extermination of the nations was Yahweh's command, a characteristic expression found in Deut 20:17, Josh 10:40, 11:12, 15. In these passages the verb is צוה "command" while here it is אמר "say," leading to the conclusion that the gloss is independent of Deuteronomic formulation.

Verse 37 may have been dependent on Deut 32:17: "they sacrificed to the Shaddayim." The key word is שדים "Shaddayim" which occurs only in Deuteronomy and Psalm 106. On the basis of the occurrence of *šdyn* in the Deir ʿAllā text in parallelism with *ʾlhn*[48] "ʾIlahin" Hackett has suggested that שדים in the MT should be repointed as שַׁדַּיִם, the plural of שַׁדַּי in a preexilic orthography."[49] The intent of the gloss was to explicate the manner in which the Israelites shed their children's blood.

A second level gloss on v 38 appears in the phrase "which they sacrificed to the idols of Canaan." Here the gloss (probably not made by the one who added v 37)

41 Freedman, "Poetry, Pottery, and Prophecy" (N 5): 6.

42 This view is based in part upon emendations, justification for which see above.

43 Kidner (N 3): 381.

44 G. E. Wright, "The Lawsuit of God: A Form Critical Study of Deuteronomy 32" in *Israel's Prophetic Heritage. Essays in Honor of James Muilenburg* (B. W. Anderson and W. Harrelson, eds.; New York: Harper, 1962): 26–67.

45 G. E. Wright, "Deuteronomy" in *IB* 2, 390.

46 J. L. Mays, *Hosea. A Commentary* (Old Testament Library; Philadelphia: Westminster, 1969): 25.

47 Cf. Jenks (N 27): 114.

48 Cf. *Aramaic Texts from Deir ʿAlla* (J. Hoftijzer and G. von der Kooij, et al., eds.; Leiden: E. J. Brill, 1976): Combination 18 and 275-76, 307.

49 See the Ph.D. thesis of Jo Ann Carlton (Hackett), "Studies in the Plaster Text from Tell Deir ʿAllā" ([Harvard, 1980]: 192-97), for a discussion of the presence of *šdyn* in the Deir ʿAllā texts and its implications for an understanding of Hebrew שַׁדַּי.

associates the activities of the Israelites to the Canaanite cult.

Thus the canonical shape of the psalm at Strophe 8 is very strong in its condemnation of the Israelites for offering their children as sacrifices to both Shaddayim and Canaanite gods. Such practices are reflected in 2 Kgs 16:3, during the reign of Ahaz. Israel was also warned against human sacrifices to Molech in Lev 18:21.

Part II—Strophe 9

וַיִּחַר־אַף יהוה בְּעַמּוֹ	40.1	Then Yahweh became angry with his people;	a	b	c	d	
וַיְתָעֵב אֶת־נַחֲלָתוֹ׃	40.2	He loathed his heirs.	a^1			d^1	
וַיִּתְּנֵם בְּיַד־גּוֹיִם	41.1	He put them under the power of the nations—	a	b	c		
וַיִּמְשְׁלוּ בָהֶם שֹׂנְאֵיהֶם׃	41.2	Their foes ruled over them,	d	e	f		
וַיִּלְחָצוּם אוֹיְבֵיהֶם	42.3	Their enemies oppressed them—	d^1		f^1		
וַיִּכָּנְעוּ תַּחַת יָדָם׃	42.4	They were humbled under their power.			f^2	g	b
פְּעָמִים רַבּוֹת יַצִּילֵם	43.1	Many times he rescued (them)[a]	a	b	c		
וְהֵמָּה יַמְרוּ בַעֲצָתָם	43.2	But they defied him with their deliberation;	d	e	f		
וַיָּמֹכּוּ בַּעֲוֹנָם׃	43.3	They were in poor straits because of their sin.		g	h		
וַיַּרְא בַּצַּר לָהֶם	44.1	Yet he[b] looked upon their distress	a	b	c		
בְּשָׁמְעוֹ אֶת־רִנָּתָם׃	44.2	When he heard their moaning.	a^1	b^1			
וַיִּזְכֹּר לָהֶם בְּרִיתוֹ	45.1	He remembered his covenant for their sake	a	b	c		
וַיִּנָּחֵם כְּרֹב חֲסָדָיו׃[c]	45.2	And relented as in his many past deliverances.[c]	d	e	c^1		
[וַיִּתֵּן אוֹתָם לְרַחֲמִים לִפְנֵי כָּל־שׁוֹבֵיהֶם׃][d]	46	[Thus he aroused compassion for them among all their captors.][d]					

Textual Notes

a. LXX, Pesh. and Targ. assume ימרוהו for MT ימרו. See note on 29.1.

b. Certain MSS of Alexandrinus and Lucian assume יהוה after וירא. This is a very tempting emendation which would provide an attractive syllable count.

c. Qere חסדיו is preferable to Kethib חסדו.

d. A post-exilic gloss or editorial expansion.

Structural Notes

Strophe 9 is varied in its makeup, consisting of a bicolon (v 40), a double bicolon (vv 41, 42), a tricolon (v 43), two bicola (vv 44, 45) and a prose gloss. The first bicolon is marked by its complementary and / or explanatory terms. The word ויתעב carries the thought of ויחר־אף one step further. The word נחלתו (40.2) further identifies עמו (40.1). The double bicolon is another example of the type found in Strophes 4 and 5, i.e., a single colon followed by a tricolon. The first colon expresses what Yahweh did while the tricolon states how the nations acted. Cola 41.2, 42.3, 42.4 contain complementary words וימשלו, וילחצום and ויכנעו. Finally, we note that the unit is held together by יד which forms an *inclusio* between 41.1 and 42.4.

The tricolon exhibits no repetitive word patterns but the thought relationships are rather interesting: 43.2 is the opposite of 43.1 while 43.3 states the consequences of the action expressed in 43.2. The next bicolon (v 44) is marked by two examples of complementary terms in each colon: וירא // בשמעו and בצר // רנתם. The bicolon in v 45 reflects no clear repetitive patterns although in some sense בריתו and חסדיו are complementary.[50] In thought, however, 45.2 is consequential to 45.1.

Verse 46 is to be viewed as a prose gloss. It lacks completely any kind of repetitive patterns, word or thought. In addition, if one attempts to determine lengths of possible cola, one is confronted with a 9:6 syllable count; while this is not impossible, it does argue against seeing here a poetic bicola.

The count for Strophe 9 is as follows:

Syllable count	Vocable count	Stress count
9:9	22:22	3:2
8:10:8:8	21:25:22:20	2:3:2:3
8:9:8	22:22:18	3:3:2
6:8	16:19	3:2
8:9	21:23	3:3

Exegetical Notes

Strophe 9 continues the thought of Strophe 8 by expressing the sentence or penalty in response to the indictment. Here we are most sharply reminded of the Deuteronomic framework of the individual narratives of the judges. In that framework, as in Stophe 9, is expressed the recurring cycle of apostasy, a cry for help, liberation and renewal.

Special emphasis is placed upon the covenant as the reason for Yahweh's repeated liberations. This is the Mosaic / Sinaitic rather than the Davidic / Royal covenant, since the Sinai experience is basic to the early part of the psalm while the latter is conspicuous by its absence. There is expressed the conviction that Yahweh's succoring love which liberated Israel from Egypt would be shown in acts of *ḥesed* by which Israel would be continually freed and by which covenant would be continually reestablished. But this constancy does not exclude punishment;

50 See Boling (N 14): 231.

rather, punishment is used to restore the covenant that Israel has broken.[51]

Verse 46, while not viewed as part of the original composition, is a part of the canonical psalm and, therefore, requires comment. This verse makes clear the effect which Yahweh's actions had on Israel's captors; they were compassionate in allowing Israel to go free because they had seen Yahweh's compassion.

Part III

הוֹשִׁיעֵנוּ יהוה אֱלֹהֵינוּ	47.1	Save us, Yahweh, our God,	a b c
וְקַבְּצֵנוּ מִן־הַגּוֹיִם	47.2	And gather us from the nations	a^1 d e
לְהוֹדוֹת לְשֵׁם קָדְשֶׁךָ׃	47.3	That we may give thanks to your holy name,	f g h
לְהִשְׁתַּבֵּחַ בִּתְהִלָּתֶךָ׃	47.4	Glory in praising you.	f^1 i

Structural Notes

Part III consists only of v 47. Here we have a double bicolon marked by complementary terms in each of the two bicola: הושיענו//וקבצנו (47.1, 47.2) and להשתבח//להדות (47.3, 47.4). The syllable count is 10:9:8:9, vocable count 27:23:21:22, stress count 3:2:3:2.

Exegetical Notes

Part III is a prayer petitioning Yahweh to restore the nation so that it may once again praise and glorify God's name. While it is true, as A. Weiser points out,[52] that the people alluded to in this verse could be those who had suffered the calamity of the Northern Kingdom's destruction, it is more likely that the setting is the period of the Babylonian exile. This does not necessarily mean, however, that the words were written in Babylonia. They may have been composed anywhere outside Judah or, given the sense of national solidarity, in Judah on behalf of all the people of Yahweh scattered throughout the world.

Conclusion

What we have discovered regarding the structure of Psalm 106 is that a variety of repetitive devices was utilized. The majority of these would have to be identified as complementary rather than either synonymous or antithetical parallelism. There are very few examples either of *chiasmus* or *inclusio*.

In respect to lengths of cola it is clear that there is a marked preference for eight syllables. It should be noted that only three cola may be characterized as *breve*, taking seven as the dividing point. Basing our observation on such studies as those of M. D. Coogan, D. N. Freedman, P. D. Hanson and D. K. Stuart,[53] we note that the earliest poetry, e.g., Exodus 15 or Judges 5, tend to employ more short cola, i.e., *breve*, than does Psalm 106. However, beginning about the eighth century, cola became longer so that, e.g., in Amos, the tendency is to have cola of eight syllables.

On the other hand, post-exilic poetry as seen, e.g., in Isaiah 50–56, while employing short cola, evidences a much greater lack of consistency than is to be observed in Part II of Psalm 106. While this may be a limited criterion, to the extent that it has any validity at all, it points to a pre-exilic rather than to a post-exilic date for this part of the psalm. Moreover, the picture in Part II differs markedly from that in Part I where, although the average number of syllables per cola is almost identical (8.272), the lack of consistency is to be noted. The range is from six to eleven syllables with only two cola having eight—more in keeping with post-exilic poetry. However, the amount of material is too small to form a definite conclusion other than that Part I probably comes from a different hand than Part II.

From the standpoint of the morphology of verb forms the best we can say is that the language of the poem resembles standard poetry. Six prefix forms without *w-* refer to past events, including two (v 43) that should be taken as frequentives, a characteristic of early poetry; but, due to the overall picture, we should probably view them as archaisms.[54]

In terms of thought it can hardly be denied that "the Ps shows the general influence of Dt."[55] In 19.1 the psalmist refers to the sacred mountain as Horeb as in Deuteronomy 9. The murmuring motif, a major theme of the wilderness wandering (25.1), is found in Deuteronomy 1, but also in Exod 15:24 (J?), 16:2 (P), 17:3 (JE?); Num 11:1 (JE?); etc. However, in all passages the verb is לון except in Psalm 106 and Deut 1:27. Thus, while the motif is old, the exact expression of it occurs only in Deuteronomy and the psalm. Finally, both Strophes 8 and 9 have been shown to have close affinities with Deuteronomic thought.

51 Cf. W. Eichrodt, *Theology of the Old Testament* (Old Testament Library; Philadelphia: Westminster, 1961): I, 233; II, 475.

52 Weiser (N 3): 682.

53 M. D. Coogan, "A Structural and Literary Analysis of the Song of Deborah," *CBQ* 40 (1978): 143–66; Freedman, "Exodus 15" (N 5): 163–203; Hanson (N 5): pass.; D. K. Stuart, *Studies in Early Hebrew Meter* (HSM 13; Missoula: Scholars, 1976): pass.

54 Cf. Robertson (N 13): 47–49, 51.

55 R. E. Murphy, *Psalms* (Englewood Cliffs: Prentice-Hall, 1968): 1.595.

In Strophe 1 we noted a correspondence with the thought of Ezekiel; the time must certainly be pre-exilic.[56] The parallel between 26.1, 27.3, 4 and Ezek 20:23 is also very striking. The absence of Aaron from Strophe 7 points to sometime before the Priestly material early in the exile.

From these prosodic and thought affinities one is inclined to attribute Part II of Psalm 106 to a Deuteronomic school in Judah sometime just prior to the fall of Jerusalem in 586 B.C. It is clear that such a "school" was active from the reign of Josiah until well into the exile.[57] It may well be that this part of the psalm was composed in the period between 597 and 586 for use in the temple in Jerusalem.

On the basis of language affinities there is no compelling reason against viewing vv 1–5 as having been written in the same period as Part II. But the style argues for a different hand and I would, therefore, suggest a later Deuteronomist. No conclusion can be drawn regarding v 47, but I am inclined to identify it with the author of Part I.

The psalm expresses confidence in Yahweh's power and willingness to preserve the covenant people. Strophe 9 strikes an element of hope which is largely absent from the latest Deuteronomic material, but there is no hope for the revival of the Davidic state. These elements, when seen together, point to that period in the life of the nation between the first and second falls of Jerusalem.

---

56 Cf. Zimmerli (N 16): 483.

57 Cross, *Canaanite Myth* (N 32): 274–89.

LOVE'S ROOTS: ON THE REDACTION OF GENESIS 30:14–24

JACK M. SASSON

In his massive commentary to the *Canticles*, the scholar to whom these pages are affectionately dedicated annotated v. 14 of the Song's chapter 7 with much arcane lore connected with the mandrake [*Mandragora officinarum*][1] We need not multiply the ancient testimonies in order to conclude that the mandrake [Hebrew: *dûday* (pl. *dûdāʾîm*)] was sought primarily for its aphrodisiacal qualities; nor need we debate its erotic and curative powers in light of modern pharmaceutical knowledge. Rather, the biblical passage which contains the only other mention of mandrake, Gen 30:14-24, will retain our attention. By means of textual, but primarily literary, and folkloristic analyses, we aim to show that the episode commonly labelled "Reuben's mandrakes" is of signal importance not only because it permits us to highlight an important moment in the "biography" of Jacob, but because it also allows us insight into the purpose and method of the Genesis redactor(s), as (t)he(y) selected, shaped, and ordered inherited traditions that were concerned with patriarchs and eponymous ancestors.[2] In order not to overload the annotations for this paper, information commonly available in the commentaries is recalled only when it supplements, emphasizes, or contradicts specific or generally accepted opinions.[3]

The Text [Gen 30:14–24]

*14*Once, when Reuben[a] went out during the wheat harvest,[b] found mandrakes[c] in the fields, and fetched them to his mother Leah, Rachel said to Leah: "Give me some[d] of your son's mandrakes." *15*"So, taking away my husband is not enough for you, you would even take my son's mandrakes?" she reacted. "Very well," replied Rachel, "he shall sleep with you in return for your son's mandrakes."

*16*As Jacob was returning from the field at evening time, Leah went out to meet him saying: "You are to sleep with me tonight, for I have secured you with my son's mandrakes."

That night he slept with her, *17*and God fulfilled her wish. When she conceived and bore a fifth son to Jacob, *18*she said: "God has provided me with means to obtain an engagement, just as[e] I provided my maidservant to my husband." She therefore named the child Issachar.[f]

*19*Conceiving again, Leah bore a sixth son to Jacob, *20*and stated: "since God has endowed me with a worthy gift,[g] this time my husband will surely honor me,[h] for I bore him six sons." She therefore named him Zebulun.

*21*Subsequently, she bore a daughter and named her Dinah.[i] *22*Meanwhile, God, paying attention[j] to Rachel, fulfilled her wish by making her fertile. *23*She then conceived, bore a son, and said: "God has removed my disgrace." She therefore named him Joseph,[k] adding: "May God supply me with another son."

1. Textual Comments

a. As it will be shown, the choice of Reuben as the gatherer of mandrakes is not because "[he was] the only child old enough to follow the reapers in the fields" (Skinner, 388; note also Driver, 275: ". . . a child of seven or eight; Jacob, 597: ". . . who could not have been more than four to five years old at that time"). In such narratives, the age of a child is stated only if something particularly unusual is associated with his/her deeds. It might not be accidental, however, that the Leah section of this episode (vv. 14/21) emphasizes the word for "son," *bēn*, whence is derived the simplest etymology for the name "Reuben" [but cf. the grammatically impossible derivation of Gen 29:32], repeating it seven times.

b. The mention of the wheat harvest need not be taken as highlighting an agricultural background, which would supposedly show that "the episode is out of place in its present nomadic setting" (Skinner, 388), but only to establish a time factor, since both the wheat and the fruit of the mandrake ripen in late spring.

c. Interesting remarks regarding the Mesopotamian Etana legend's "plant of birth" and its relation to Reuben's mandrakes are made by E. I. Gordon, *JCS* 21 (1967): 80, n. 27. For Akkadian allusions to the mandrake, see W. von Soden, *Akkadisches Handwörterbuch* p.863 (sub *pillû*). Additions to Pope's own bibliographical collection on mandrakes can be had by referring to R. C. Campbell *A Dictionary of Assyrian*

1 Marvin H. Pope, *Song of Songs* (AB 7c; New York, 1977): 647-50.

2 To avoid cumbersome English, we shall henceforth speak of the singular, readactor, without implying that not more than one person was involved in the task.

3 Those mentioned in our paper are: Driver = S. R. Driver, *The Book of Genesis* (Westminster Commentaries, 12th ed.; London, 1926); Gunkel = H. Gunkel, *Genesis* (Göttinger Handkommentar zum Alten Testament, 2nd ed.; Göttingen, 1969); Jacob = B. Jacob, *Das Erste Buch der Tora: Genesis* (KTAV reprint of the 1934 edition; New York, 1974); Skinner = J. Skinner, *Genesis* (International Critical Commentary, 2nd ed.; Edinburgh, 1956).

Botany, 217-19; to the *Encyclopedia Judaica* 11.870 (s.v.) and to the Genesis commentaries.

d. middûdāʾēy benēk, "*some* of your son's mandrakes," implies that Leah might have partaken of the remainders.

e. ʾašer is understood here as equivalent to *kaʾašer*; cf. *BDB* 83 (8,e). Others render "because," reinforcing the notion that *ʾašer-nātattî šipḥātî leʾîšî* is a redactional addition to E (Skinner, 389, notes to 18aβ). But the etymology for Issachar requires a connection between *śekārî* and *ʾîšî,* now spread out between the two clauses.

f. The variation in writing and punctuating the name [ben Asher: *yiśśā(ś)kār* (with a quiescent second *śin*); ben Naphtali: *yiśśākār/yiššākār*] has given rise to a number of etymologies. Verse 18 stoutly connects with *ʾîš śākār,* "a hireling," while the spelling might suggest **yeš śākār,* "a loan/reward is at stake." Both are obviously folk etymologies to explain a name whose "real" meaning was apparently lost to time, but we do have evidence that a number of Hebrew personal names exhibit an *ʾ/y* alternation in initial position (e.g., *yišay/ʾišay; yesarʾēlāh/ʾasarʾēlāh*; on this phenomenon, see C. Isbell, "A Note on Amos 1:1," *JNES* 36 (1977): 213-14). Albright, *JAOS* 74 (1954): 227, is followed by many scholars who analyze as an Š-stem verbal form **yašaśkir* and render something like "May (God) grant favor." The root *śkr,* "to hire," occurs in Ugaritic; cf. Gordon's *Ugaritic Textbook*, 19:2415.

g. The root *zbd* occurs in Hebrew only here. Its meaning has been posited mainly through Syriac. Some have suggested that it is merely a dialectal variant for *zbl* (e.g. Skinner).

h. Diverse renderings have been proposed. They are conveniently collected in M. Held's "The Root *ZBL/SBL* in Akkadian, Ugaritic and Biblical Hebrew," *JAOS* 68 (1968 = *Essays in Memory of E. A. Speiser*): 90-92. Our rendering matches his "This time my husband will exalt/elevate me." Further on *zbl* is found in J. Gamberoni's entry for *TWAT* 2.531-34.

i. Jacob (599) rightly points out that the mention of Dinah's birth allows Leah's own children to reach the optimal number 7.

j. This translation for *zākar ʾet* PN tries to avoid the negative connotation implicit in the usual rendering "remember," a connotation which could not have been intended by the Hebrew. On the usage, see H. Eising, *TWAT* 2.578-81 (sub *zākar*, II, 3).

k. On the various attempts to find ancient Near Eastern equivalents to this name, see R. de Vaux, *The Early Traditions of Israel*, 314 n. 87.

2. Literary Considerations

As a literary genre, the biography is not unknown to the Old Testament.[4] In consonance with tenets which became better known to us through the works of Aristotle's peripatetic students, e.g., Theophrastus, Heraclides Ponticus, and Aristoxenus of Tarentum (ca. 4th century B.C.), legendary materials, polemics against foreign nations, genealogical asides, scandals, etc., were woven into the accounts concerning a heroic character who was often chosen because of his prototypical personality.[5] Through a recounting of his deeds—and even of those associated with him—the "biographer" was able not only to reflect upon the moral quality of a man who helped shape his nation's destiny, but also to underscore the manner by which the nation's destiny was fulfilled and actualized, in microscopic fashion, by an ancestor's activities. It is not of immediate concern to us whether, in light of recent research, a more specialized label, such as "historical biography," "fictional biography," or even "biographical fiction" ought to be attached to some of the accounts concerning the biblical examples; we need only note at this stage that, in addition to countless biographical "torsos," the OT contains at least three examples of full-fledged "biographies," those of Jacob, Moses, and David, and one example, that of Samson, of a particular manifestation of the genre.

A full-fledged dramatic biography would feature the following: 1. An interest in the birth and death of the hero that goes beyond mere biographical notices; 2. A certitude that the historical realities, important to the biographer's own generation, were shaped by events associated with the subject of the account; 3. An awareness that the heroic character is not static, but one which develops and deepens as recollections of his deeds are mounted upon the biographical canvas; and 4. A tendency to undergird a narrative and reduce the episodic nature of the accounts by often allowing the secondary characters to repeat paradigmatic patterns established by the chief protagonist's own activities.

The biography of Jacob spans chapters 29:19–50:21 of Genesis, and is clearly blocked out by two narratives, both featuring dim-eyed patriarchs giving blessings and birthrights to the younger of two brothers (Jacob/Esau; Ephraim/ Manasseh), and strikingly recalling parallel themes and vocabulary. Within this biography are placed

---

4 Skinner, xx-xxix, speaks of the "biography" of Jacob, Abraham, and Joseph without, however, establishing criteria for usage of the term. We shall try to show, below, that the term can be applied only to a limited number of narratives in the Old Testament.

We hope to return to this topic on a much wider and deeper basis in a future monograph.

5 Much has been written on this topic in the recent past; cf. Arnaldo Momigliano's text of his Jackson lectures at Harvard, *The Development of Greek Biography* (Cambridge, MA, 1971) and his *Second Thoughts on Greek Biography* (Mededelingen der Koninklijke Nederlandse Akademie van Wetenschappen, Afd. Letterkunde, Nieuwe reeks: deel 34, Mo. 7; Amsterdam, 1971). Still a source of much information and written in an elegant style is D. R. Stuart's *Epochs of Greek and Roman Biography* (Berkeley, 1928). The subject has hardly been touched, at least in a comprehensible manner, by ancient Near Eastern and biblical scholarship. See now J. Blenkinsopp's rambling attempt in *JSOT* 20(1981): 27–46.

accounts which either tie it to past generations (26:1-33) or future ones (38; 50:1-21). A biographical "torso," concerned solely with a circumscribed number of years in the life of Joseph, occupies 39–41. The circumstances that led Jacob—and thus Israel—into Egypt are made the subject of other chapters (37, 42–48) and are to be judged as equally concerned with the activities of Jacob and his sons as those of Joseph. Two biographical notices regarding Joseph's life are placed outside the "torso" devoted to his youthful deeds (39–41). The second of these is concerned with his death and burial, given mostly to satisfy genealogical and chronological requirements (50:22-26), and links Jacob's biography to that of Moses (Exod 1ff.). The first, attesting to the unusual nature of Joseph's birth, occurs in the episode under consideration.

The mandrake episode feeds upon an account of the strife between two sisters, married to the same husband. This motif is not unconventional, even to the Old Testament.[6] In order to sustain interest in a narrative that would otherwise be scarcely dramatic, the presentation of birth etiologies is interrupted by a highly charged dialogue between Rachel, the preferred wife, and Jacob (30:1-3). This permits the audience to share in the anxiety of women whose sense of well-being and fulfillment depended upon the production of (male) children. The mandrake episode, however, entertains a more complex agenda by recalling a direct confrontation, unique to the whole patriarchal narratives, between the two sisters. This is followed by a terse statement which Leah makes to Jacob.

As sketched by the narrator, the characters involved in the drama fit into pre-determined stock roles, assigned by biblical conventions whenever such themes are developed (cf. Abraham and the Sarah/Hagar episodes). The hero (Jacob) whose attention is desperately sought, is passive and is willing to abide by whatever decision is presented by the antagonists. The supplicant (Rachel) is polite and eager to accept her rival's offer. Center stage is assigned to the aggrieved (Leah) who does not allow the occasion to pass without hurling choice invectives at her lifelong nemesis. From the audience's perspective—but *not*, as we shall see, from that of the redactor—Reuben's role is important only as that of a catalyst for the confrontation; he says nothing. A presence, however, hovers over this section of the narrative and exerts a deterministic influence, that of Rachel's unborn child, Joseph.

From a literary perspective, as distinguished from a narratological or redactional one, the time sequence is imprecise and retroactively open-ended. The episode could be moved back and forth without affecting the presentation, development, or impact of the account. This feature is quite consonant with biblical narrative tenets where precise temporal settings are established only when specific characteristics associated with the main protagonist are thereby highlighted.

3. Folkloristic Considerations

The mandrake episode will allow us to focus on the manner in which two of the four features of full-fledged biographies, listed above as numbers 2 and 4, operate with regard to Jacob's life history.

In a wide ranging article, "The Youngest Son or Where Does Genesis 38 Belong," J. Goldin takes up a theme that is shared by Near Eastern and biblical literatures, one in which the younger/youngest son eclipses the older/oldest.[7] On the life and fortunes of Reuben, Goldin has this to say: "[Reuben] may not be the smartest person in the world, [but] he is basically one of the most decent characters in Genesis .... Reuben is no Ishmael, no Esau, not an unworthy successor to Jacob the Patriarch."[8] To account for the loss of his primal position, Goldin, however, can only cite the well-known incident in which, before his father's death, Reuben slept with Bilhah, Rachel's maidservant and Jacob's handmaid. Thus, Reuben earned for himself his father's damning testament (Gen 49:3-4). "So much for that nice boy who brought his mother mandrakes," adds Goldin.[9]

We ought to recall, however, the manner in which Jacob's biography opens with two acts by which Esau is supplanted by his younger twin. In the first, Jacob and Esau have a *direct* confrontation at the end of which the birthright (*bekōrāh*) becomes Jacob's (26:27-34). In the second, in which the blessing of the favored (*berākāh*) is grasped by Jacob, it is through the schemings of Rebekah that the goal is achieved. We note here that, in this second episode, there is no direct meeting between Esau and Jacob, and that the bestower of blessings, Isaac, is unwittingly used for Rebekah's purposes. These transfers of rights and privileges usually reserved for the elders, are the result of acts of trickery successfully negotiated by a hero who, moreover, retains the sympathy of narrator and audience despite the underhanded manner in which he obtains his goal. I have elsewhere written on this motif that is so generally prevalent in Genesis, particularly in Jacob's biography.[10] By selecting and allocating episodes which detail its presence throughout the Jacob saga (e.g., Laban's trickeries; Jacob's responses; Rachel's absconding with the idols; Jacob's sons conniving to rid themselves of the Schechemites; of Joseph; Joseph's own cat-and-mouse games with his brothers, etc.), the narrator was able to fulfill one of the four tenets of our

6 B. O. Long, *The Problem of Etiological Narrative in the Old Testament* (Beihefte zur Zeitschrift für die alttestamentliche Wissenschaft, No. 108; Berlin, 1968): 311-34.

7 *JBL* 96 (1977): 27-44; cf. pp. 30ff. and note 22 on p. 30. On the rights and privileges of the first-born, see J. Milgrom in the *IDB, Supplement,* 337-38.

8 *JBL* 96 (1977): 37.

9 *Ibid.*, 41.

10 J. M. Sasson, *Ruth, A New Translation; with a Philological Commentary and a Formalist-Folklorist Interpretation* (The Johns Hopkins Near Eastern Studies; Baltimore, 1979): 231-32.

biographical requirements (see above) and thus succeeded in bracing his life-history with repeated underpinnings.

In the case of Reuben, we are dealing with the reverse of what happened to Jacob. Here the matter is not one in which the younger/youngest succeeded in obtaining the birthright and blessing not normally due him, but one in which the oldest *loses* those rights and privileges. We are therefore not given accounts that clearly delineate how Joseph and Benjamin obtained them through direct or indirect acts of trickery, but ones in which, again directly and indirectly, Reuben forfeits their bounties. His dalliance with Bilhah, registered in Gen 35:22, was a *direct act of confrontation* with his father; and this only earned him, if not the loss of the choicest blessing (*berākāh*), certainly the unwelcome curse of his father. Note that this event is in opposite presentation to the one in which Jacob gained his own *berākāh*. The mandrake episode, I believe, offers an explanation for the manner in which Reuben lost his birthright, the *bekōrāh*, and this is also made in a presentation that reverses the one by which Jacob obtained the birthright from his twin, Esau.

Reuben fetches mandrakes for his mother. His role is minimal beyond that. But Rachel, desperate for sons from her own womb, approaches her sister. Leah finds in this situation an excellent opportunity to renew her birth-givings. It is not necessary for our purpose to detail whether the characters, the narrator or his audience—or even medieval Rabbis and contemporary scholarship—believed that mandrakes had effective fertilizing powers.[11] But what we ought to take into account is that by means of the mandrakes, Leah sought to trick her sister in order to find more favor with Jacob. But in doing so, she was only partially successful. She did manage to bear two more sons and a daughter; but she also gave Rachel the opportunity to conceive Joseph and then Benjamin. With the birth of these two—last among Jacob's sons, but first from his beloved Rachel—a reversal of the pattern, which had obtained in the accounts concerning Jacob's appropriation of Esau's birthright, is again at stake. Reuben unwittingly and innocently becomes the victim, as Jacob's affection is drawn from the "first fruit of strength" to the last ones.

The manner in which the mandrake episode fulfills the second of our biographical propositions, by which events associated with a protagonist's life predict or help shape the historical realities as known to the biographer, remains to be discussed. Far from being "so curtailed as to be shorn of its original significance,"[12] our brief narrative adequately fulfills its purpose. By selecting a tradition which accounts for Reuben's loss of the birthright in favor of Rachel's sons, and by allocating it at the earliest moments of tribal geneses, the redactor—i.e., Jacob's biographer—makes an important prediction concerning the evolution of Hebrew kingship. Reuben's tribe, which might rightfully have produced Israel's first kings, is supplanted by Benjamin's. The last's descendant, Saul, will be God's first anointed king. The manner in which Judah and Joseph (Ephraim) will share in ruling the promised land, is also entertained in the Jacob saga. But this will await his narratives which recount the sack of Schechem, and those which give Judah and Joseph prominent roles in the entry into Egypt.

4. The Role of the Redactor

Our episode was located by the redactor roughly midway between the accounts of Jacob's flight to Upper Syria and his return to the promised land. This centering becomes more dramatic when Jacob's birth and death narratives are added to the tabulation of verses: 130 and 127 verses flank the mandrake episode.[13] With respect to the accounts (chapters 25–49) which span the entire block of narratives regarding Jacob—including the ones concerned primarily with Joseph—our episode is also centrally placed. In locating it in this slot, the redactor may have paid heed to the following considerations: *a. contextual.* By ending with Joseph's birth, and by picking up the narrative of Jacob's struggles with Laban at precisely that moment ["As Rachel bore Joseph, Jacob said to Laban: 'Give me leave to go towards my own area and land' " (v. 25)], the redactor resorted to a well-known technique by which the entire birth narrative is highlighted by making it seem independent of, and only marginally important to, the course of actions which took Jacob out of Harran. Beginning with the introduction of Reuben into the mandrake sodden wheatfields, however, the section succeeds in breaking a pattern which had monotonously unraveled succeeding births and established name etymologies. Reinvigorated by a folkloristic detail, the narrative pursues its course until the birth of Joseph. *b. genealogical.* Except for that of Benjamin, reported in Gen 35:18 but already foreshadowed in this episode, the births of Jacob's children are set within Gen 29:31–30:24. But it is worth noticing that in its final redacted shape, the narrative has given Joseph special attention by having him as Jacob's 12th child (count includes Dinah), and by placing him as the 7th son born to Jacob after Rachel took up the challenge of her sister and entered Bilhah into the fray (Gen 30:1ff.).

Our treatment of the mandrake episode has been concerned neither with establishing the origin of the traditions behind Gen 30:14-24, nor with detailing their permutations as they were transmitted through time and space. It has focused, instead, on the role played by the redactor in selecting this tradition, doubtless from among many which recalled the acts of Jacob and of his sons,

11 The *Testament of Issachar* clearly recognizes the power of the mandrake to bring about fertility. See further, J. Feliks in the *Encyclopedia Judaica* 11.870.

12 Skinner, 388.

13 This estimate, of course, depends on a division into verses which did not obtain until the common era.

and in assigning it to its present slot. That role, we have tried to indicate, was not static or passive. For even if critical scholarship has determined that two separate strands, commonly labelled J and E,[14] were available to him, it is nevertheless the redactor who infused life into a narrative which, if isolated, was likely to have proved of interest solely to collectors of arcane motifs. But in locating it in its present position, the redactor established for it a purpose which transcended the merits of its contents and the quality of its style. In this respect, the redactor proved himself to be as creative as the originators of this tradition. Moreover, in framing it within its present confines, the redactor forced attention away from the immediate unfoldings of birth narratives, and invited those who shared his interest in Israel's past to appreciate the manner in which the present and the more recent past have already been coded within the distant activities of heroic patriarch and eponymous ancestors. In this respect, the redactor, even when obviously didactic in his goals, managed to make a philosophical (for him, read: theological) statement: that the humblest of accidents (Reuben finding mandrakes), the most mundane of human interactions (two women agonizing over their husband's favor), ought to be considered as adumbrative of more significant events. Concomitantly, he would suggest, one would only have to explore past traditions and explore their mysteries, to be guided accurately in charting the future.

On closer inspection, therefore, the redactor compares favorably with most other ancient historiographers who collected traditions and juxtaposed them in such a way as to give them meaning beyond their immediate contents. In stringing out the various episodes concerned with Jacob and his sons, the redactor can be singled out for his biographical skills. In the task that he laid out for himself, in his ideals and vision for his nation's welfare, he does not differ much from those of other generations and cultures who likewise sought to entertain similar agenda. Witness the oft-quoted program outlined by Thomas Fuller, English divine and shrewd biographer, as he introduced his *History of the Worthies of England* (1662):

> Know then, I propound five ends to myself in this Book: first, to gain some glory to God; secondly, to preserve the memories of the dead; thirdly, to present examples for the living; fourthly, to entertain the reader with delight, and lastly (which I am not ashamed to publicly profess), to procure some honest profit to myself.

14 The most concentrated discussion about source division for this episode is to be found in the following: S. Lehming, "Zur Erzählung von der Geburt der Jakobssöhne," *Vetus Testamentum* 13 (1963): 74-81; Gunkel, 329-36; Jacob, 997-1000 (Anhang: Quellenscheidung). Generally speaking, the sources regarded as behind the mandrake episode are assigned to J and E, with "redactional intrusions," e.g., at v. 18. The etymological "doublets" are respectively allocated to J and E, even if, in most cases, the Hebrew etymology cuts across the two strands. See now, also, G. G. Nicol in *Journal of Theological Study* 31 (1980): 536–39; G. Brim in *Tarbiz* 48 (1978): 1–8.

The episode has received its share of absurd interpretations, the largest selection of which is collected in H. W. Hogg's article in the 1903 *Encyclopedia Biblica* 4.4088-4091.

For Rabbinical elaborations, one might look at the handy compendium of Kasher's *Encyclopedia of Biblical Interpretation,* s.v. An interesting article on Rabbinic elaborations regarding Gen 30:15 is D. Daube's "The Night of Death," *Harvard Theological Review* 61 (1968): 629-32.

THE DEATH OF THE KING OF TYRE: THE EDITORIAL HISTORY OF EZEKIEL 28

ROBERT R. WILSON

Marvin Pope has devoted much of his scholarly career to studying the Ugaritic mythological texts and has been a pioneer in using Ugaritic to interpret the Hebrew Bible. In his monumental commentaries on Job and Song of Songs and in a host of shorter studies, he has provided models for the judicious use of Ugaritic in translating the Bible and has elucidated many obscure passages by pointing to their Northwest Semitic mythological background. One of his early contributions in this area was included in his comprehensive study of the Canaanite god El. After constructing a convincing argument for the thesis that El was viewed at Ugarit as a former divine ruler who had been deposed by his younger rival Baal and exiled to an underworld abode, Pope made the intriguing suggestion that this myth of El's downfall is reflected in Ezekiel's enigmatic oracles against the king of Tyre (Ezekiel 28).[1] Although Pope's suggestion helped to solve some of the problems connected with this passage, many difficulties still remain. It therefore seems appropriate to reexamine Ezekiel's words on the death of the king of Tyre and to offer the results of this study as a tribute to Marvin Pope, who through the years has been an esteemed teacher, a congenial colleague, and a treasured friend.

I

Ezekiel's oracles against the king of Tyre (Ezek 28:1-19) are riddled with problems that have defied even the best scholarly solutions. In addition to containing obscure words and possible textual corruptions that make even the translation of the Hebrew text difficult and uncertain, the oracles themselves do not seem to be unified in form or content. This apparent lack of unity enormously increases the chapter's opaqueness and suggests to most modern critics that the oracles in their present form are the product of a long and complex editorial history. For this reason many scholars perform radical surgery on the text in order to recover its original form before they attempt any sort of interpretation.

On form-critical grounds, Ezek 28:1-19 is usually divided into two major units.[2] The first unit (Ezek 28:1-10) is an announcement of judgment against the prince of Tyre. After the standard introductory formulas giving instructions to the prophet (vv 1-2a), the oracle states the reasons for the judgment in a causal clause beginning in v 2b. The announceent of the judgment itself begins in v 7. It is introduced in the normal fashion by *lākēn*, and its conclusion is marked by a variant of the traditional *nəʾum*-formula (v 10). The second major unit (Ezek 28:11-19) also opens with a standard introductory formula and an address to the prophet (vv 11-12a), but in this case the oracle takes the form of a dirge (*qînāh*), which the prophet is to deliver over the king of Tyre. The dirge itself contains the reasons for the king's downfall and ends with an announcement of judgment unmarked by further formulas.

This division of Ezek 28:1-19 into two major units is reinforced by the fact that each of the formally distinct units deals with a slightly different subject. The first unit (vv 1-10) is directed against the *prince* (*nāgîd*) of Tyre, who is appropriately described as dwelling in the midst of the seas (v 2). He is accused of elevating himself to divine status by claiming to be a god (or by claiming to be the Canaanite high god El [vv 2, 6, 9]), and because of this proud boast the ruler will be killed by foreigners and brought down to the underworld (*šaḥat* [vv 7-10]).[3] Throughout the unit the ruler seems to be a symbolic figure, and as a result the oracle refers not only to the death of the prince of Tyre himself but also to the fate of the people of Tyre, who are doomed to be captured and destroyed because of their pride. In contrast, the second unit (vv 11-19) deals with the *king (melek)* of Tyre (v 12), who does not claim to be a deity but who in fact at one time did dwell in Eden, which is identified both as the garden of God and as the mountain of God (vv 13-14).

1 Marvin H. Pope, *El in the Ugaritic Texts* (Leiden: E. J. Brill, 1955): 97-103.

2 For representative form-critical treatments of Ezek 28:1-19, see Walther Zimmerli, *Ezechiel* (BKAT 13; Neukirchen-Vluyn: Neukirchener Verlag, 1969): 664-88; Walther Eichrodt, *Ezekiel* (Old Testament Library; London: SCM, 1970): 390-95; Georg Fohrer, *Ezechiel* (HAT 1/3; Tübingen: J. C. B. Mohr, 1955): 159-64; Jörg Garscha, *Studien zum Ezechielbuch* (Bern: Herbert Lang, 1974): 160-64; and Frank Hossfeld, *Untersuchungen zu Komposition und Theologie des Ezechielbuches* (Forschung zur Bibel 20; Würzburg: Echter Verlag, 1977): 153-83.

3 For a discussion of the word *šaḥat* as a designation for the netherworld, see Marvin H. Pope, "The Word *šaḥat* in Job 9:31," *JBL* 83 (1964): 269-78. Cf. Moshe Held, "Pits and Pitfalls in Akkadian and Biblical Hebrew," *JANES* 5 (1973): 173-90; and Marvin H. Pope, "A Little Soul-Searching," *Maarav* 1 (1978): 25-31.

Because of the king's sin, which the text describes in several ways, he was cast out of the garden (or down from the mountain), then burned and perhaps relegated to the underworld (vv 16-19). Throughout most of the unit the king seems to represent an individual, although at points he may be a symbol for the Tyrian people (vv 16, 18a, 19).[4]

Although form and tradition critics usually agree on the general sense of Ezek 28:1-10 and 28:11-19, they also agree that the units contain a number of later editorial additions which must be eliminated before coherent interpretations can be obtained. In the first unit, vv 3-5 are usually considered a later insertion.[5] These verses, which deal with the wisdom of the prince, seem to be unrelated to the surrounding material describing the ruler's pride. They are loosely integrated into the following announcement of judgment by means of the word *lākēn* and by means of the awkward causal clause in v 6, which in fact simply summarizes the indictment of v 2 without making any reference to wisdom. Even more editorial reworking is usually seen in the second unit. The list of gems included in v 13 is clearly drawn from the description of the stones set in the breastplate of the Israelite high priest (Exod 28:17-20; 39:10-13) and is normally considered simply an elaboration of an original vague reference to precious stones.[6] The notion that trade is the source of the king's sin (vv 16, 18a) seems to be intrusive, and some critics consider these references to be additions influenced by similar expressions in Ezek 27:9, 12-25, 27, 33, 34.[7] The accusation that the king defiled his sanctuaries (v 18) is a strange charge to bring against a pagan king, the legitimacy of whose sanctuaries neither Yahweh nor the Israelite writer would have recognized. This accusation, along with the related image of the divine judgmental fire (v 18), is therefore also occasionally excised as an addition.[8] Finally, the references to the wisdom of the king (vv 12, 17) are usually thought to be the work of the same editor responsible for the wisdom insertion in vv 3-5.[9]

It is important to note that this sort of form-critical and redaction-critical analysis of Ezek 28:1-19 still leaves two major problems unsolved. First, the excision of the editorial additions does not result in a completely comprehensible text. Several obscure images and phrases still remain. Thus, for example, even when the later expansions are removed from Ezek 28:11-19, the remaining material is unclear because of curious but crucial expressions such as *ḥôtēm tāknît* (v 12) and *ʾabnê-ʾēš* (vv 14, 16) and because of residual uncertainties concerning the role of the cherub (vv 14, 16). Second, the removal of supposed editorial additions does not shed any light on the factors that motivated the editors' work in the first place. Unless one wishes to believe that the editors were totally unconcerned about the overall meaning of the text, one must assume that they intended their work to clarify or modify the text in a comprehensible way.

Because of the problems which are left unsolved by purely literary approaches to Ezekiel 28, many scholars have attempted to demonstrate the chapter's overall cohesion by placing it against a mythological background. By examining the mythological dimensions of the text, they hope to clarify the meaning of obscure passages and bring some unity to the text as a whole, or at least to its major parts. This comparative approach has been most fruitful when it has been applied to Ezek 28:11-19. Modern scholars have seen a number of mythological motifs in this unit and have usually argued that behind the passage lies an old Mesopotamian or Canaanite myth describing a primal royal figure who, along with a guardian cherub, lived in a wondrously fertile gem-studded garden located on a cosmic mountain. The idyllic existence of this first man was finally disrupted when he

4 Kalman Yaron, "The Dirge over the King of Tyre," *ASTI* 3 (1964): 45-49. For attempts to treat Ezek 28:1-19 as a single literary unit, see Rudolf Smend, *Der Prophet Ezechiel* (Kurzgefasstes exegetisches Handbuch zum Alten Testament 8, 2d ed.; Leipzig: S. Hirzel, 1880): 218; J. H. Kroeze, "The Tyre-Passages in the Book of Ezekiel," in *Studies on the Book of Ezekiel* (Pretoria: Die Oud Testamentiese Werkgemeenskap in Suid-Afrika, 1961): 20-23; and Hossfeld (N 2): 153-83.

5 Almost all critical scholars agree on this point. For representative arguments, see Ernst Haag, *Der Mensch am Anfang* (Trierer Theologische Studien 24; Trier: Paulinus-Verlag, 1970): 78; John W. Wevers, *Ezekiel* (The New Century Bible, New Series; London: Nelson, 1969): 216-17; Anthony J. Williams, "The Mythological Background of Ezekiel 28:12-19?" *BTB* 6 (1976): 56; Garscha (N 2): 161; and Zimmerli (N 2): 669-70.

6 Richard Kraetzschmar, *Das Buch Ezechiel* (HKAT; Göttingen: Vandenhoeck & Ruprecht, 1900): 216; Hedwig Jahnow, *Das Hebräische Leichenlied* (BZAW 36; Giessen: Alfred Töpelmann, 1923): 221, 226; G.A. Cooke, *A Critical and Exegetical Commentary on the Book of Ezekiel* (ICC; Edinburgh: T. & T. Clark, 1936): 316-17; Keith W. Carley, *The Book of the Prophet Ezekiel* (The Cambridge Bible Commentary on the New English Bible; Cambridge: Cambridge University, 1974): 191; Garscha (N 2): 162; Williams (N 5): 56; Zimmerli (N 2): 673; Eichrodt (N 2): 389; Wevers (N 5): 216-17. For representative arguments in favor of the originality of the list, see Geo Widengren, *The Ascension of the Apostle and the Heavenly Book* (Uppsala Universitetsårsskrift 1950. 7, Uppsala: A. B. Lundequistska Bokhandeln, 1950): 95; Julien Weill, "Les mots *tuppêkā ûnəqābêkā* dans la complainte d'Ezéchiel sur le roi de Tyr," *REJ* 42 (1901): 9; and Yaron (N 4): 35-38.

7 G. A. Cooke, "The Paradise Story of Ezekiel XXVIII," in *Old Testament Essays* (London: Charles Griffin, 1927): 37; Zimmerli (N 2): 686-87; Wevers (N 5): 216; Garscha (N 2): 161.

8 Zimmerli (N 2): 687-88; Wevers (N 5): 219.

9 Zimmerli (N 2): 672, 686; Garscha (N 2): 161; Wevers (N 5): 216-17; Williams (N 5): 56.

sought divinity or committed some other sin and as a result was banished from the garden and hurled down from the mountain. According to this form of the argument, remnants of the original myth can still be seen not only in Ezekiel 28 but also in Genesis 2-3 and Isa 14:12-20.[10] A more fully developed version of this position has tried to connect the old myth explicitly with Tyre, or at least with Phoenicia, and some scholars have even identified the Tyrian god Melqart with the royal figure described in the biblical text.[11]

Although this particular application of the comparative mythological approach does have the advantage of explaining the undeniable mythological allusions in Ezek 28:11-19 and even manages to lend cohesion to the passage by supplying plausible interpretations of such enigmatic features as the seal, the gems, and the cherub, the overall result is not fully satisfying because it is based solely on reconstructed evidence. Neither Genesis 2-3 nor Isa 14:12-20 contains a fully developed myth similar to the one alleged to lie behind Ezekiel 28, and neither is such a myth attested in extant Canaanite or Mesopotamian sources. Although scattered mythological motifs in Ezekiel 28 do appear in extrabiblical literature, no complete myth has yet been found. Any use of hypothetical myths as an aid to biblical interpretation must necessarily remain tentative.[12]

On somewhat firmer ground is the argument advanced by Marvin Pope, who interprets Ezekiel 28 against the background of the El myths embedded in the Ugaritic texts. According to Pope's plausible theory, El was originally both the titular and actual head of the Ugaritic pantheon and lived in a splendid dwelling on the mountain of assembly, Mount Zaphon. However, he was deposed by the young storm god, Baal, a relative newcomer to the pantheon, who took over El's position, along with his abode and his wives, and banished the aging god to an infernal dwelling "at the springs of the (two) rivers, in the midst of the channels of the (two) deeps" (*mbk nhrm qrb apq thmtm*) (2.3[129].4; 6.1.34[49.1.6]; 3[ᶜNT.VI].5.14; 4[51].4.22; 5[67].6.01*; 17[2AQHT].6.48).[13] From his underworld residence El tried vainly to regain his former power, even employing Prince Sea to fight against the usurper. However, Baal was finally victorious, and El remained an underworld deity.[14]

After carefully establishing this Canaanite version of the myth of the deposed god, Pope applies it to Ezekiel 28. According to Pope, Ezek 28:1-10 must be read on two levels. On one level the unit refers to the prince of Tyre, whose proud claim to divinity leads to his downfall. However, on a deeper level the unit reflects elements of the El myth. The deposed god, whose name is explicitly mentioned in v 2 ("I am El"), dwells in an infernal abode in the midst of the seas (vv 2, 8) after having been deposed by Baal. The fate of the old god, who was noted for his wisdom (cf. vv 3-5), foreshadows the fate of the prince of Tyre, who claims to be a god (*ʾēl*) and who will soon be deposed and relegated to the underworld. The actual account of El's fall is reflected in Ezek 28:11-19. Although he once lived on the cosmic mountain in a dwelling constructed by a fiery fusion of precious metals and gems, he was cast down from the mountain and consigned to the underworld.[15]

Pope's interpretation has the virtue of being based on

10 For examples of mythological interpretations of Ezekiel 28, see Geo Widengren, *Sakrales Königtum im Alten Testament und im Judentum* (Stuttgart: Kohlhammer, 1955): 26-33, "Early Hebrew Myths and their Interpretation," in *Myth, Ritual, and Kingship* (ed. S. H. Hooke; Oxford: Clarendon, 1958): 165-76; Hermann Gunkel, *Schöpfung und Chaos in Urzeit und Endzeit* (2d ed.; Göttingen: Vandenhoeck & Ruprecht, 1921): 148-49, *Genesis* (HKAT, 3d ed.; Göttingen: Vandenhoeck & Ruprecht, 1910): 34-40; Johannes Herrmann, *Ezechiel* (Kommentar zum Alten Testament; Leipzig: A. Deichert, 1924): 182-84; Th. C. Vriezen, *Onderzoek naar de Paradijsvoorstelling bij de oude semietische Volken* (Wageningen: H. Veenman & Zonen, 1937): 220-23; Julian Morgenstern, "The Mythological Background of Psalm 82," *HUCA* 14 (1939): 111-14; Herbert G. May, "The King in the Garden of Eden: A Study of Ezekiel 28:12-19," in *Israel's Prophetic Heritage: Essays in Honor of James Muilenburg* (New York: Harper, 1962): 166-76; D. Neiman, "Eden, the Garden of God," *Acta Antiqua Academiae Scientiarum Hungaricae* 17 (1969): 109-24; Albert Brock-Utne, *Der Gottesgarten* (Oslo: Jacob Dybwad, 1936): 107-20; Alfred Bertholet, *Hesekiel* (HAT 1/13; Tübingen: J. C. B. Mohr, 1936): 101-3; Cooke, *Ezekiel* (N 6): 315; Eichrodt (N 2): 392-95; and Fohrer (N 2): 162. There is still much debate about the relationship between the mythological backgrounds of Ezekiel 28, Genesis 2-3, and Isa 14:12-20. For a thorough discussion of the issues, see Williams (N 5): 49-61. Cf. U. Cassuto, *A Commentary on the Book of Genesis: From Adam to Noah* (Jerusalem: Magnes, 1961): 74-84.

11 A. A. Bevan, "The King of Tyre in Ezekiel XXVIII," *JTS* 4 (1903): 500-505; Cameron Mackay, "The King of Tyre," *The Church Quarterly Review* 117 (1933-1934): 239-58; Jan Dus, "Melek ṣōr-Melqart?" *ArOr* 26 (1958): 179-85; Roland de Vaux, "The Prophets of Baal on Mount Carmel," in his *The Bible and the Ancient Near East* (Garden City, NY: Doubleday, 1971): 242-51; Julian Morgenstern, "The King-God among the Western Semites and the Meaning of Epiphanes," *VT* 10 (1960): 152-55.

12 For a thorough critique of the mythological approach to Ezekiel 28, see John L. McKenzie, "Mythological Allusions in Ezek 28:12-18," *JBL* 75 (1956): 322-27.

13 For a justification of this translation and a thorough discussion of the nature and location of El's abode, see Pope, *El* (N 1): 61-81.

14 Pope, *El* (N 1): 82-97.

15 Pope, *El* (N 1): 97-103. Cf. the similar interpretation of Richard J. Clifford, *The Cosmic Mountain in Canaan and the Old Testament* (HSM 4; Cambridge: Harvard University, 1972): 168-73.

an actual myth, or at least on a myth that can plausibly be gleaned from the Ugaritic texts. In addition, the story of the fall of El does seem to fit the mythological allusions in Ezek 28:11-19, although motifs such as the seal and the guardian cherub are not attested at Ugarit and the figure in Ezek 28:11-19 seems more human than divine. Similarly, Ezek 28:1-10 gains a deeper level of meaning if the unit is read against the background of the El myth. The prince who dwells in his island fortress in the heart of the seas and who claims to be a god (*ʾēl* [v 2]) will suffer the same fate as the former high god El, who was deposed. The prince will be slain and go down to the underworld to dwell with El in his watery abode in the midst of the seas (v 8). However, even if one accepts Pope's thesis that the El myth lies behind Ezekiel 28, several problems still remain. First, although the two major subdivisions of the chapter (Ezek 28:1-10, 11-19) individually take on new meaning when they are seen against the background of the El myth, the subdivisions in their present editorial sequence do not actually follow the chain of events found in the reconstructed myth. The beginning of the myth—the story of El's preeminence, his fall from power, and his exile to the underworld—is reflected in the second subdivision (Ezek 28:11-19), not in the first as one might expect. At the same time, the first subdivision (Ezek 28:1-10) seems to reflect the conclusion of the myth. El has already fallen and dwells in the underworld, where he will soon be joined by the prince of Tyre. Thus, while the El myth may lie behind each of the two subdivisions of Ezekiel 28, the myth cannot be invoked to explain their present editorial sequence or to argue for the unity of the whole passage. Second, even when Ezekiel 28 is seen against the background of the El myth, the function of most of the apparent editorial additions remains obscure. For the most part they are not clarified by the myth, and the editor's reasons for adding them are unclear. Finally, many enigmatic features of the original text cannot be clarified simply by placing them against the background of the El myth.

II

The above survey of the various approaches to Ezekiel 28 suggests that no single approach has been able to solve all of the interpretive problems in the chapter. In particular, the problem of the function of the editorial additions remains a vexing one, and as a result important parts of the chapter's redactional history are still unclear. Neither the form-critical nor the comparative mythological approach has been able to deal successfully with this issue, and it is possible that no plausible solution can be found. The text of the chapter does seem corrupt at crucial points, and important mythological allusions may still lie hidden in obscure passages. However, perhaps some new light can be thrown on the problem by observing that many of the alleged editorial additions contain specifically Israelite allusions. Some of these allusions are clearer than others, but they all seem to point to an Israelite rather than to a Phoenician setting.

The best examples of "editorial additions" containing Israelite allusions are to be found in Ezek 28:11-19. The clearest case is the list of gems in v 13. The list does not simply contain a random enumeration of precious stones but is clearly based on the list of stones set in the breastplate of the Israelite high priest (Exod 28:17-20; 39:10-13). The MT of v 13 preserves nine of the twelve stones mentioned in Exodus and even retains the tripartite grouping found there, although in Ezekiel the order of the second group of breastplate stones is reversed and the third group is omitted entirely. However, in the LXX of Ezek 28:13 all twelve stones are mentioned in the same order in which they appear in Exodus. Furthermore, Ezek 28:13 does not portray the stones as a feature of the garden but explicitly says that they are worn by the royal figure (*kol-ʾeben yəqārāh məsûkātekā*), just as the jeweled breastplate is worn by the high priest.[16]

Although all commentators agree that the list in v 13 is based on the description of the high priest's breastplate, there is debate about the function of the list. Those who see it as an editorial addition usually argue that it simply serves to amplify the immediately preceding general reference to precious stones.[17] However, if this were the case one would expect a random list and not an explicit allusion to the high priest's breastplate. Taking a different tack, scholars expounding the mythological background of the passage argue that the stones are simply a feature of the garden or that jeweled breastplates were routinely worn by Phoenician kings.[18] However, the former position is contradicted by the text, which suggests that the stones were worn, while no solid evidence can be produced for the latter position. Therefore, it seems necessary to conclude that the list of stones, whether an editorial addition or part of the original text, is intended as an explicit reference to the priestly breastplate. If so, then the purpose of the list must be to identify the figure in the garden as the Israelite high priest. It is difficult to see how the members of Ezekiel's audience, some of whom came from priestly backgrounds, could have understood the list in any other way.

If one assumes that the function of the list of stones in v 13 is to identify the wearer of the gems as the Israelite high priest, then one may also assume that the author of the list wished Ezek 28:11-19 to be interpreted as a unit dealing with the priest rather than with the king of Tyre.

16 The precise meaning of *məsûkātekā* is unclear, but the word can plausibly be derived from *skk*, "to cover." For a discussion of the problem, see the contrasting views of H. J. van Dijk, *Ezekiel's Prophecy on Tyre* (BibOr 20; Rome: Pontifical Biblical Institute, 1968): 116-18; and Yaron (N 4): 36-38.

17 Jahnow (N 6): 221, 226; Kraetzschmar (N 6): 216; Cooke, *Ezekiel* (N 6): 316-17; Garscha (N 2): 162; Zimmerli (N 2): 673.

18 Weill (N 6): 9-13; Widengren, *Ascension* (N 6): 95; van Dijk (N 16): 117-18.

When the unit is understood in the way that the list's author suggests, then a coherent interpretation of the passage can be obtained, and some of its enigmatic references can be clarified. In v 12 the figure who is the subject of the dirge is described as *ḥôtēm tāknît*, a phrase which has successfully defied scholarly elucidation. Taking a cue from the LXX, most interpreters emend the otherwise unattested *ḥôtēm* to *ḥôtām* and understand the whole phrase to mean "perfect seal" or the like, although they are usually at a loss to explain the meaning of this characterization of the king.[19] On two other occasions *ḥôtām* is used to describe kings, and in both instances the rulers are compared to seal rings on Yahweh's hand (Jer 22:24; Hag 2:23). The comparison seems to imply that Yahweh uses kings to exercise his royal power just as an earthly official uses a seal to give authority to his commands. However, the notion that a human being can be an authentic representative of Yahweh's power can apply to priests as well as kings, for in the priestly establishment of Ezekiel's time the priest, particularly the high priest, was the authoritative interpreter of the divine will. In this connection it is interesting to note that although the word *ḥôtām* is relatively rare in the Hebrew Bible, it does appear a number of times in the description of the high priest's vestments, which are said to have been covered with stones engraved like seals (Exod 28:11, 21, 36; 39:6, 14, 30). Thus it would be possible to interpret the phrase *ḥôtām tāknît* as a description of a priest, a description which would fit well with the reference to the high priestly regalia in v 13.

Ezek 28:13 further describes the figure in question as one who dwelled in Eden, the garden of God. It is in this context that the figure wore the high priestly breastplate, so it is fair to assume that "garden of God" is here synonymous with the temple in which the high priest exercised his authority. This interpretation is supported by the following verse, where the garden is further characterized as "the holy mountain of God" (*har qōdeš ʾĕlōhîm* [v 14]). For Ezekiel's audience this characterization would immediately suggest the Jerusalem temple on Mount Zion, which is often called "the holy mountain" (Jer 31:23; Zech 8:3) or "my holy mountain" (Isa 11:9; 56:7; 57:13; 65:11, 25; 66:20; Ezek 20:40; Joel 4:17; Obad 16; Dan 9:20; Pss 2:6; 43:3; 48:2 and elsewhere). No other historical mountain would have been considered holy by an orthodox Yahwist of Ezekiel's time.[20]

If the "garden of God" and "the holy mountain of God" are to be identified with the Jerusalem temple, then the role of the cherub in the scenario becomes clearer. If one follows the majority of commentators in emending *ʾat* to *ʾet* at the beginning of v 14 on the basis of the LXX, then the verse can be translated, "with the {anointed} overshadowing cherub (*kərûb {mimšaḥ} hassôkēk*) I placed you; you were on the holy mountain of God; you walked in the midst of the firestones (*ʾabnê-ʾēš*)."[21] Although the cherub in this verse is usually identified with the cherub in the Garden of Eden (Gen 3:24), such an identification is unlikely. In Genesis more than one cherub is mentioned, and there is no indication that these beings lived in the garden along with the primal humans. Rather, the cherubim were placed at the entrance of the garden after the human pair had been expelled. The function of these celestial beings was to guard the path to the tree of life, not to protect the human inhabitants of the garden. Because of the difficulties raised by associating the cherub in Ezek 28:14 with the ones mentioned in Genesis, it is preferable to link the cherub with the Jerusalem temple, the one place in Israelite society where cherubim and humans were associated with each other. Two guardian cherubim flanked the ark in the holy of holies and overshadowed it with their wings (Exod 25:18-20; 37:9; 1 Kgs 8:7; 1 Chr 28:18).[22] According to priestly law, only the high priest was allowed to enter the holy of holies and then only on the Day of Atonement, so presumably he was the only human to have regular contact with these figures (Leviticus 16). However, these cherubim were not the only ones in the temple. Representations of cherubim were sewn into various cloth hangings in the temple and were carved on doors and walls (Exod 26:1, 31; 36:8, 35; 37:7; 1 Kgs 6:23, 25, 27, 28, 29, 32, 35; 7:29, 36; Ezek 41:18, 20, 25 and

19 For arguments in favor of the emendation and for a discussion of the whole phrase, see Yaron (N 4): 34-35; Wevers (N 5): 216; May (N 10): 169; Eichrodt (N 2): 392-93; and Zimmerli (N 2): 672. More radical emendations and interpretations have also been suggested, but to date no completely plausible translation of v 12 has been proposed. See, for example, the suggestions of Cooke (*Ezekiel* [N 6]: 315-16), Widengren (*Ascension* [N 6]: 95), van Dijk ([N 16]: 113-14), Kroeze ([N 4]: 21), Haag ([N 5]: 85), Hugo Gressmann (*Der Messias* [Göttingen: Vandenhoeck & Ruprecht, 1929]: 166-67), and Carl Heinrich Cornill (*Das Buch des Propheten Ezechiel* [Leipzig: J. C. Hinrichs, 1886]: 359-60).

20 For a discussion of cosmic-mountain symbolism in the Jerusalem temple, see Clifford (N 15): 177-81.

21 For a justification of the emendation and a discussion of the other translational difficulties in the verse, particularly the problematic *mimšaḥ*, see Zimmerli (N 2): 675; Yaron (N 4): 28-32; Kroeze (N 4): 23; May (N 10): 168; Haag (N 5): 89; Kraetzschmar (N 6): 217; Vriezen (N 10): 220; and Wevers (N 5): 217. Attempts to translate the MT as it stands have generally been unsatisfactory because of the problems of syntax and meaning raised by such translations. See, for example, Widengren, "Myths" (N 10): 166; Bertholet (N 10): 101; and van Dijk (N 16): 119.

22 Note that Ezek 28:14 follows Exod 25:20, 37:9, 1 Kgs 8:7, and 1 Chr 28:18 in using the root *skk* to describe the cherubim, a fact which strengthens the suggestion that Ezek 28:14 refers specifically to the temple cherubim rather than to the ones mentioned in Genesis. See the discussion of Zimmerli (N 2): 675; and Yaron (N 4): 31-32.

elsewhere). The fact that the temple cherubim are usually referred to in the plural does not argue against the interpretation suggested here, for Ezekiel elsewhere speaks of a single cherub when he describes his visions of the Jerusalem temple (Ezek 9:3; 10:2, 4, 7, 14). It is therefore appropriate to interpret Ezek 28:14 as a reference to the high priest being placed with the cherub in the temple, and the temple setting may also explain the enigmatic firestones (*ʾabnê-ʾēš*) mentioned in the same verse. In the context of the temple, these firestones may be the coals of fire (*gaḥălê-ʾēš*) which are found on the altar and which represent the glowing fire of Yahweh's presence (Ezek 10:2; Lev 16:12; cf. Ezek 1:13; 2 Sam 22:13; Ps 18:13, 14).[23]

If the interpretation given thus far to Ezek 28:11-19 is legitimate, then the remainder of the section is not incoherent, as many critics have claimed. Rather, once it is assumed on the basis of vv 11-14 that the dirge deals with the high priest, then the rest of the unit is not only cohesive but reasonably comprehensible. After describing the installation of the high priest as Yahweh's representative in the temple (vv 12-14), the text goes on to state that the priest was perfect in all his activities until he sinned (v 15). This sin is most explicitly identified in v 18, where an "editorial addition" attributes the priest's downfall to the fact that he defiled his sanctuaries. Although this remark does not make much sense when seen in the context of an announcement of judgment against the king of Tyre, the indictment is perfectly appropriate if it is directed against the Israelite high priest. Ezekiel elsewhere condemns Israel for defiling its sanctuaries (Ezek 5:11; 23:38, 39; cf. 24:24; 25:3), and he explicitly speaks against the sanctuaries (*miqdāšîm*) of Jerusalem (Ezek 21:7). Because of this sin the priest was punished by being removed from the sanctuary. The agent of judgment was the overshadowing cherub, which from the midst of the firestones made the priest perish (v 16).[24] The priest is told, "I brought forth fire from your midst; it consumed you" (v 18). Both of these descriptions of judgment are difficult to understand if seen in the oracle against Tyre, and particularly the latter one is puzzling, for it seems to imply that the divine judgmental fire of Yahweh flashed forth from an altar in a foreign temple. However, when seen in an Israelite context, the descriptions of judgment are not problematic. In fact they are in perfect harmony with Ezekiel's earlier description of the beginning of Yahweh's judgment against Jerusalem and the temple. In Ezekiel 8-11 the prophet describes in horrifying detail the implementation of Yahweh's judgment against the city. The destruction begins in the temple itself with the slaughter of all those who do not grieve over the abominations committed in Jerusalem (Ezek 9:1-11). The judgment then enters a second phase, which is inaugurated by the appearance of the temple cherubim bearing Yahweh's throne (Ezek 10:1-5). A man clothed in linen is then commanded to take glowing coals from the altar beneath the throne. He does not actually take the coals himself, however. Instead, one of the throne-bearing cherubim stretches out a hand from under his wing, takes the coals, and gives them to the man clothed in linen, who then leaves the temple to scatter the coals over the city and begin the conflagration that will destroy it (Ezek 10:6-8). The sequence of events sketched here is precisely the same as the one described in Ezek 28:16, 18. The cherub from the temple executes God's judgment on the city—and by implication on the temple and on the priesthood as well—by burning Jerusalem with divine fire brought from the temple altar.

The Israelite allusions contained in Ezek 28:11-19 thus permit the unit to be read in an Israelite rather than a Tyrian context, and when this is done, a picture emerges which is fully in keeping with the theological views expressed elsewhere in Ezekiel. The Israelite priesthood, represented by the high priest and including some of Ezekiel's fellow exiles, enjoyed divine favor in the temple until the priests defiled the sanctuary. This sin led to divine judgment that took the form of the expulsion and exile of the priesthood and ultimately the destruction of the temple itself.

While the Israelite allusions in the "editorial additions" to Ezek 28:11-19 are fairly clear, the allusions in Ezek 28:1-10 are much less obvious. In this unit there is only one indisputable editorial addition, the comments on wisdom in vv 3-5. These comments are quite general in character and might be applied appropriately to rulers of any nationality. In the ancient Near East, wisdom was a quality which all good rulers were expected to possess, so there is nothing in these verses to suggest directly that their author had an Israelite king in mind. However, the wisdom insertion does have two noteworthy features. First, when vv 3-5 are read in isolation from their context, they are positive in tone. The fact of the addressee's great wisdom is simply stated, and no attempt is made to condemn it. Yet, when vv 3-5 are read in their present context, they acquire negative overtones by virtue of being associated with an oracle condemning the prince's proud claims to be divine (v 2). Although logical connections between v 2 and vv 3-5 are never explicitly stated, the very location of the wisdom insertion implies

23 The firestones, which are not mentioned elsewhere, have been variously interpreted as stars, jewels, lightning (cf. Ug. *abn brq*), glowing fused bricks, and (with emendation) deities. For a discussion of the various possibilities, see Zimmerli (N 2): 685-86 and the literature cited there. The connection between the firestones and the coals of the temple altar was made on other grounds by Jahnow ([N 6]: 227).

24 Following the LXX of Ezek 28:16, which takes the cherub as the subject of the verb "to perish," one should read *wəʾibbadkā* for the anomalous *wāʾabbedkā* of the MT and translate "the overshadowing cherub made you perish from the midst of the firestones." See the discussion of Zimmerli (N 2): 676; Cooke, *Ezekiel* (N 6): 324; and A. B. Davidson, *The Book of the Prophet Ezekiel* (Cambridge Bible; Cambridge: Cambridge University, 1893): 207.

that somehow the prince's wisdom, in addition to his pride, is responsible for his imminent destruction. Second, the insertion in vv 3-5 clearly links the prince's wisdom with trade (v 5) and with the accumulation of vast wealth (vv 3-4). Such a linkage would of course be appropriate in a description of a ruler of Tyre, for the riches and power of Tyre were based on extensive foreign trade. However, Israelite tradition associates wisdom, trade, and wealth in particular with one historical period, the reign of Solomon. 1 Kings 10 preserves an elaborate account of Solomon's proverbial wisdom (vv 1-10), and the text connects his wisdom directly with his extensive trading relationships and with his vast wealth (vv 11-29).[25]

If in fact the editor responsible for Ezek 28:3-5 had Solomon in mind when he wrote and inserted these verses in the oracle against the ruler of Tyre, then the editor clearly did not share the positive evaluation of Solomon's activities now found in 1 Kings 10. Negative views of Solomon's reign are also attested elsewhere in Israelite tradition and are particularly prominent in Deuteronomic sources. The bearers of the Deuteronomic traditions interpreted the secession of the Northern Kingdom as a divine judgment on Solomon's religious policies and on the imperial form of monarchy associated with them (1 Kgs 11:31-40). Solomon's apostasy was particularly reprehensible because the Deuteronomists believed that Yahweh himself had appointed Solomon ruler (*nāgîd*) over Israel (1 Kgs 1:35). The relatively unusual title *nāgîd* was apparently used in early Israelite tradition to indicate that a ruler was designated directly by Yahweh (2 Sam 6:21; 7:8; 1 Kgs 1:35; 14:7; 16:2).[26] In return for this divine designation, the ruler was expected to obey Yahweh's will, and the Deuteronomists believed that great care should be taken to insure that Israelite rulers always remained subservient to Yahweh's commands (Deut 17:14-20). The editor who inserted the oblique allusions to Solomon in Ezek 28:3-5 may have shared this Deuteronomic perspective. If so, then the purpose of the insertion was presumably to remind Israelite readers that even their own rulers were not immune to the pride that led the Tyrian prince to strive for divinity. Jerusalemite kings apparently did at least claim to be sons of Yahweh, even if they did not claim to be divine themselves (cf. Psalms 2, 110), and it may be that the editor wished to warn his readers not to tolerate such royal pretensions. If this was the editor's intent, then he may have also been responsible for using the title *nāgîd* in Ezek 28:2 to describe the ruler of Tyre. Only here is this title used of a foreign ruler. Elsewhere it is applied to native Israelites, and, as noted above, in monarchical contexts the title indicates that the ruler is divinely appointed. He has no claim to divinity but remains a human being under the control of the God who appointed him.

III

In the light of the above discussion of the Israelite allusions in the "editorial additions" to Ezekiel 28, it is now possible to return to the question of the structural unity of the chapter and to reassess traditional scholarly views on its editorial history. Although there seem to be no grounds for opposing the standard form-critical view that Ezek 28:1-19 is composed of two originally separate oracles (Ezek 28:1-10, 11-19), there are reasons to believe that the two oracles once had different functions and settings. The clue to these differences can be seen in the distinct ways in which the "editorial additions" are integrated into their contexts. In Ezek 28:11-19 the so-called editorial additions seem to be an integral part of the overall unit and are capable of being interpreted coherently once it is assumed that the unit intends to describe the Israelite high priest rather than the king of Tyre. Seen in this light, most of the "editorial additions" need not be considered additions at all but can be interpreted as part of the original text. When the unit is considered as a whole, its contents are consistent with the theological views expressed elsewhere in Ezekiel. It is therefore tempting to speculate that the original version of Ezek 28:1-19 was delivered by the prophet to the exiles in the period before the fall of the city, precisely the period in which the text itself places the anti-Tyrian oracles (Ezek 26:1). The original form of the unit was presumably not much different from its present form. The prophet delivered a dirge which was ostensibly concerned with the king of Tyre but which in fact was so laced with allusions to the Israelite high priest that the real thrust of the dirge could not possibly have been missed by Ezekiel's audience, which consisted of upper-class bureaucrats and priests taken into captivity during the first deportation. Such oblique oracles are found elsewhere in Ezekiel, and the prophet seems to have delighted in clothing his divine message in concrete but obscure images which even his original audience could not always understand. A classic example of this sort of oblique oracle is found in Ezekiel 17, where the prophet develops a detailed and sometimes enigmatic tale involving two eagles and a cedar from Lebanon. Here too the image of the cedar seems to point to a Phoenician

25 The traditions preserved in 1 Kings 10 are difficult to date. R. B. Y. Scott ("Solomon and the Beginnings of Wisdom in Israel," in *Wisdom in Israel and in the Ancient Near East* [VTSup 3; ed. M. Noth and D. Winton Thomas; Leiden: E. J. Brill, 1960]: 262-79) has argued that the attribution of great wisdom to Solomon cannot be earlier than the time of Hezekiah, while Albrecht Alt ("Die Weisheit Salomos," *TLZ* 76 [1951]: 139-44) feels that Solomon may have been famous for his wisdom during his own lifetime. In either case, traditions about Solomon's great wisdom would have been current in Ezekiel's time and would presumably have been well known to his audience.

26 For a history of the use of the title *nāgîd*, see Wolfgang Richter, "Die *nāgîd*-Formel," *BZ* n.s. 9 (1965): 71-84.

setting, for Hiram of Tyre was Israel's chief supplier of Lebanese cedar (1 Kgs 5:7-18), but in fact the oracle is clearly concerned with Israel.[27] Oblique oracles of a similar type are preserved in Ezekiel 16, 20, and 23, and in connection with them the prophet himself admits that his words were not always comprehensible (Ezek 21:5; cf. 33:32). In fact the very complexity and obscurity of Ezekiel's oracles may be invoked to account for the present position of Ezek 28:11-19. It is quite possible that the real point of the dirge was lost when it was removed from its original setting, with the result that later transmitters failed to see the double meaning of the unit, interpreted it literally as a dirge against the king of Tyre, and then attached it to a genuine anti-Tyrian oracle (Ezek 28:1-10). Once this move took place, further editorial changes may have been made in order to integrate the unit into its new context, and because of these changes the original point of the unit became less clear.

In contrast to the situation in Ezek 28:11-19, the wisdom insertion in Ezek 28:3-5 seems only loosely related to its context and may be a genuine editorial addition. If so, then the original oracle (vv 1-2, 7-10) was presumably precisely what it claims to be: a judgment oracle against the Tyrian prince because of his pride and his claim to be divine. The wisdom insertion somewhat changes the focus of the oracle and may be a late attempt to make the oracle more relevant to an Israelite audience. In this case Ezek 28:1-10 would be an example of a prophetic oracle being reshaped to fit a new social context.

27 The strong connection between Tyre and the building and operation of the temple may have also influenced Ezekiel's choice of images in Ezek 28:11-19.

THE DEATH OF MOSES: AN EXERCISE IN MIDRASHIC TRANSPOSITION

JUDAH GOLDIN

How the contemporaries of Moses, or perhaps better, how the contemporaries of the author of the last chapter of Deuteronomy felt about Moses' death-sentence, is not recorded. Scripture does say (Deut 34:8), "And the Israelites bewailed Moses in the steppes of Moab for thirty days"—a detail to which we shall return. But this is not singular. Aaron's death too, earlier (Num 20:29), was bewailed for thirty days by all the house of Israel. (See further n. 38.)

On the other hand, what was superlative about Moses is explicitly announced. Though he lived 120 years, his eyes remained undimmed and his vigor unabated; the spirit of wisdom filled Joshua because Moses had laid his hands upon him. "Never again did there arise in Israel a prophet like Moses—whom the Lord singled out, face to face, for the various signs and portents that the Lord sent him to display" in Egypt and before all Israel. Nevertheless, Moses had to die and be buried (Deut 34:5-6), in the land of Moab, just before the Israelites entered the Promised Land. Before dying he was allowed to gaze at the various regions of the land[1] from a distance, but under no circumstance was he permitted to cross over. אראה is granted but not אעברה נא.[2] As we have said, he had to die.

For the exclusion from the land and death penalty, Scripture offered two reasons,[3] probably derived from two distinct traditions or literary sources. According to one tradition or source, Num 20:2-13 (alluded to also in Deut 32:48-52; but see also Ps 106:32), it was because instead of commanding the rock to produce water, "Moses raised his hand and struck the rock twice with his rod" (Num 20:11). This was tantamount to not trusting God enough (Numbers) or to breaking faith with Him (Deuteronomy).[4] Still another explanation is offered in Deut 1:37 (also in 3:26 and apparently 4:21 too): When the spies delivered their evil report of the land, God grew incensed with that whole ungrateful generation, and swore that with the exception of Caleb and Joshua (and the younger generation) none would enter the land. "Because of you," Moses says, "the Lord was incensed with me too"; or as he put it again, "Now the Lord was angry with me *on your account* and swore that I should not cross the Jordan and enter the good land that the Lord your God is giving you as a heritage" (Deut 4:21). In other words, in this explanation Moses himself appears to be blameless; he is simply swept along by the penalty imposed on his contemporaries.[5]

Nothing in this summary is unknown to students of Scripture. Nor very likely the following: We must presume that the reasons given for Moses' death-sentence must have appeared sufficient, more or less—or, more rather than less—to the biblical narrators. The reasons they offer are not challenged, and presumably the narrators are satisfied with the contents of their accounts. Only one appeal against that sentence is heard, the appeal by Moses—by the very victim, the interested party—and all he does is plead, "Let me, I pray, cross over and see the good land on the other side of the Jordan, that good hill country, and the Lebanon" (Deut 3:25). The charges, if charges there be, are not denied or contradicted: either striking the rock, or, one must die along with one's own (sinful) generation; the appeal is a petition after the invocation of God's omnipotence (Deut 3:24), as though one were asking for special favor. Hence we will have to say that in the framework of Scripture, the death-sentence is legitimate, even to Moses.[6] God's decisions are just.

In the end, the same is true of the Midrash, but not without expression first of many protestations, all illustrating on the one hand how profoundly disturbing the

1 See the nice observation of S. E. Loewenstamm in "Mot Moshe," *Tarbiz* 27 (1958): 147, n. 7. Note how in *Sifre Deut.* 357, ed. L. Finkelstein, pp. 425-27, geographical terms are given a historical interpretation, to emphasize Moses' prophetic powers. On the lore of death and mountains, see T. H. Gaster, *Myth, Legend, and Custom in the Old Testament* (New York, 1969): 234f. However, Moses was buried in the valley (Deut 34:6).

2 Cf. Deut 3:25; 34:4.

3 Nevertheless, see Loewenstamm (N 1): 146.

4 On these and additional verses regarding the waters of Meribah, cf. Loewenstamm (N 1): 142ff. On the *ḥillul ha-Shem* "(as it were)," cf. *Midrash ha-Gadol,* Num., ed. S. Fisch, II, 125 and n. 32. Note also III Armenian account, 120. Thanks to Professor Michael E. Stone, I was able to get a copy of his "Three Armenian Accounts of the Death of Moses" (in G. W. E. Nickelsburg, Jr., *Studies on the Testament of Moses* [Cambridge, MA, 1973]: 118–21). All references to Armenian accounts are to the Stone paper.

5 Note the complaint made by Moses in *Tanḥuma wa-Etḥanan* 1 (ed. Buber 2, 4b–5a). See also *Midrash ha-Gadol,* Deut., ed. Fisch, 82 and n. to line 10; also 64, lines 18ff.

6 Note also Deut 4:22. In Deuteronomy 34, there's not a word out of Moses. On proper presentation of petition, see *B. Berakot* 32a, bottom. Cf. also *Sifre Deut.*, 343, p. 394.

fate of Moses was to later generations,[7] and on the other hand how God's sentence might be defended. The latter was not always successful but remains instructive nonetheless.

First, however, the view quoted in a tannaitic midrash[8] that Moses did not really die: ויש אומרים לא מת משה אלא עומד ומשרת למעלה.[9] Although he does not accept this view, Josephus is already familiar with it: "But he (i.e., Moses) has written of himself in the sacred books that he died, for fear lest they should venture to say that by reason of his surpassing virtue he had gone back to the Deity."[10] Before him Philo too seems to have known of this.[11] The view, therefore, seems to have been current for some time (though I can't say how far back). And after all, why not? If Enoch[12] and Elijah (2 Kgs 2:1, 11) could escape death, why not Moses?

It is not a serious problem that it is distinctly stated Moses died (Deut 34:5; Josh 1:2). On a number of occasions the Midrash does not hesitate to go its independent way, ignoring the biblical plain-spoken statement. Let me give just one example. Forty years, Scripture tells us, the Israelites had to spend in the wilderness because they accepted the defeatist report of the scouts sent in advance to the Promised Land: "You shall bear your punishment for forty years, corresponding to the number of days—forty days—that you scouted[13] the land: a year for each day. Thus you shall know what it means to thwart Me" (Num 14:34). The forty years, therefore, are a punishment, measure for measure and then some.

Despite this, there is a view in the Mekilta[14] that at the very outset, at the exodus from Egypt, God had resolved not to lead the Israelites directly into their land because He feared that on their arrival they might rush immediately to the labors required by their newly acquired fields, and thus neglect to study Torah. That is why He kept them going round and round in the wilderness for forty years: for here their needs were taken care of, they could study without distraction of livelihood worries, and the Torah would be thoroughly incorporated in themselves.

Regardless of the Book of Numbers, then, the forty years, according to this (and still another)[15] interpretation in the Mekilta, were no punishment for adopting the negative report of the land, but on the contrary an ideal opportunity provided in order to achieve mastery of the Torah. Similarly, the verse in Deuteronomy may say "So Moses the servant of the Lord died there," the verse at the beginning of Joshua (1:2) may quote God as saying "My servant Moses is dead," but that will not prevent some people from believing that Moses did not die, that in his role of "servant of the Lord" he still ministers on high (to the Lord). The reference to death may be no more than what Philo may have had in mind when he wrote,[16] ". . . the time came when he had to make his pilgrimage from earth to heaven, and leave this mortal life for immortality" and so forth.

It does not necessarily follow that this view is merely and from the first one more attempt to come to God's defense against what seems a spectacular unfairness, injustice. Ascensions are not unheard of.[17] Interestingly, however, the view that Moses did not die is not included in that lore assembled, for example, by the *Midrash*

7 Cf. also *Memar Marqah* (J. Macdonald, ed. and trans.; Berlin, 1963): 5:1ff. (trans., 193ff.).

Attempts at "explanation" never cease, even whimsical speculation. Here is I. B. Singer in an interview (*New York Times*, Magazine Section, 3 December 1978, pp. 40, 44), "from the point of view of religion. When Moses gave the Torah, he believed it was possible to create a nation of spiritual people . . . . This never became a reality. I would say that the reason why, according to legend, Moses wasn't allowed to cross the Jordan was because what he wanted to create and what followed in the years after the revelation on Mount Sinai were two different things altogether."

8 *Sifre Deut.* 357, p. 428; *Midrash Tannaim*, 224; see also Finkelstein's references to *B. Soṭah, Sefer Ḥasidim,* and *Yalquṭ ha-Makiri*. Cf. Philostratus, *Apollonius of Tyana*, VIII, 2, end (Loeb Classics, II, 277), that Socrates did not die "though the Athenians thought he did."

9 Or as *B. Soṭah* reads, עומד ומשמש (already noted by Freimann in *Sefer Ḥasidim*, p. 313) and without the word למעלה.

10 *Antiquities*, IV, 326 (Loeb Classics, IV, 633).

11 Philo, *Sacrifices of Abel and Cain*, 8 (LC, II, 99, bottom) and L. Ginzberg, *Legends of the Jews*, VI, 162, top.

12 See H. St. John Thackeray's note *d* in LC, Josephus, *Antiquities*, IV, 633. (Is Elijah in chariot and whirlwind an attempt to make up for the death of Moses?)

13 See R. Ishmael in *Sifre Zuta*, ed. H. S. Horovitz, 279; *Midrash ha-Gadol*, Num., 324, n. 62.

14 *Be-Shallaḥ* 1, ed. J. Z. Lauterbach, I, 171; *Mekilta R. Simeon*, ed. Epstein-Melamed, 45. Cf. Ginzberg, *Legends*, VI, 2, n. 8.

15 *Be-Shallaḥ*, *ibid.*, 171f.; *Mekilta R. Simeon*, 45.

16 *II Moses*, 288 (LC, VI, 593). See I. Lévy, *La Légende de Pythagore* (Paris, 1927): 151f. On the resurrection of Moses as witness to the divinity of Christ, see III Armenian account, 121.

17 Cf. *Interpreter's Dictionary of the Bible*, s.v., "Ascension"; "Moses, Assumption of"; "Isaiah, Ascension of." E. Rohde, *Psyche* (New York, 1966): 2.538 and 568, n. 109. See now also L. Nemoy in *Essays on the Occasion of the Seventieth Anniversary of the Dropsie University* (Philadelphia, 1979): 361–64, and nn. 1–2. Perhaps this too should be noted: *Sifre Deut.* 338 and 357 (pp. 387, 425) emphasize that Moses was summoned to *ascend* (noun: *aliyyah*) the mountain; hence his death is not to be regarded as punishment. (Contrast this with *Gen. R.* 85:3, 1034, where *yeridah*, "descent," is spoken of.)

For *Gedullat Moshe*, cf. Ginzberg, *Legends*, V, 416ff., nn. 117, 118. See I. Lévy (N 16): 154ff.

Petirat Mosheh,[18] where the exchanges between Moses and God are the direct result of the feeling that Moses is being treated unjustly, in that he had to *die* (see below n. 23, and p. 222): it is, we must remember, a midrash of *petirat* Moses, of Moses' *death.* It is in these exchanges primarily that complaint and efforts at clarification rise to the surface: Moses' complaint articulating what obviously human readers or auditors of the Moses story in midrashic-talmudic times feel, God's retort articulating what human readers of the story imagine to be God's self-justification. The dialogues are at the same time protest and theodicy.

There are times when God has no answer except repetition of a biblical verse. For example: Moses pleads, "After all the toils I endured, You tell me to die?" To which God replies in the words of Deut 3:26b, "Enough! Never speak to Me of this matter again."[19] Hardly an answer; it is no surprise that Moses is not silenced.

Then there are what may be called belabored defenses. For example,[20] Moses says, "All Your other creatures You are prepared to forgive once, twice, and thrice; I have been guilty of only one iniquity, yet You refuse to forgive me." To which God replies, "Not of one but of six iniquities you were guilty, though I never before told you about them"—and He lists the biblical verses which contain traces of sin. This defense by inventory hardly does justice to God, for if our prophet indeed merits immortality, the punishment does not fit the crimes, even if there were those six instances.

One exchange of plea and denial must have grown out of academic experience. Moses pleads:[21] "Since my death is intended to make it possible for Joshua to succeed, let him begin at once to be the master and I will be his disciple." At that Moses starts to serve Joshua: "Moses began to do for Joshua what Joshua had previously done for him." But when he entered the Tent of Meeting and the cloud descended and separated Joshua from Moses, when Joshua was admitted into the (holy) interior and Moses was left outside, then Moses cried out, "Better a hundred deaths than one experience of envy." The master cannot endure being replaced by his disciple. Here it is Moses who begs to die; God does not deprive him of this!

Another exchange immediately relevant to midrashic-talmudic centuries is preserved in *Deut. R.* 2:8 (see also *Mid. Tan.,* 178; cf. 19): here the issue is entry into the land. "You allowed Joseph's bones to be carried into the land," Moses says to God, "why not mine?" And the Lord replies, "Joseph never denied his origins, in Egypt he admitted he was a Hebrew (Gen 40:15; cf. 39:14): but when you were identified as an Egyptian by the daughters of the priest of Midian (Exod 2:19), you heard but held your peace." Moses become the model of Jews seeking to pass as non-Jews! Jewish hellenizers and all their descendants down through the ages. The moral was clear to all—even Moses could not escape punishment for that. But what is noteworthy is this, that in his defense of God the homilist does not flinch from attributing such behavior to Moses.[21a]

Nor should this be overlooked: When the galgallim and seraphim on high[22] observed that even toward Moses, God would not show partiality, they exclaimed in praise of Him (ברוך כבוד ה׳ ממקומו) who is scrupulously fair and plays no favorites. Not God's injustice but His meticulous

18 In *Bet ha-Midrasch,* ed. A. Jellinek, I, 115–29 (I *Petirat Moshe*); VI, 71–78 (II *Petirat Moshe*). See also *Batei Midrashot,* ed. Wertheimer (Jerusalem, 1950); 1.286–87. Additional material in J. D. Eisenstein, *Ozar Midrashim,* (New York, 1915): 368ff. Also Z. M. Rabinowitz, *Ginzê Midrash* (Tel-Aviv, 1976): 222–24 (*Midrash Mishle* 14, ed. Buber, 39a–b); *Abot de-Rabbi Natan* (ed. S. Schechter—hereinafter ARN), 49ff., 156f. Cf. *Mekilta,* Amalek 2, II, 149ff. and parallels. See *Deut. R.* and the two Tanḥumas on *Wa-Etḥanan* and *Zot ha-Berakah.* For poetry on the Death of Moses theme, see L. J. Weinberger, in *HUCA* 37 (1966): 1–11 and additional references, 1f. (Hebrew); *idem.* on the theme of searching for Moses, in *Tarbiz,* 38 (1968–69): 285–93. On the theme of Moses' wealth and the significance of the criticism thereof, cf. M. Beer in *Tarbiz* 43 (1973–74): 70–87.

In I *Petirat Moshe* (121 and 122f.; cf. Eisenstein, *Ozar,* II, 377a, 378b) there are two poems: the first, 13 lines of essentially 3 words to a line (but not throughout), being God's promise to Moses of the splendor that awaits him; the second (a doxology recited by Joshua, *ha-midrash she-darash Yehoshua!*—as introduction to a homily?) approximately 33 lines of essentially 4 words to a line (not always). Cf. Zunz-Albeck, *Ha-Derashot,* 67 and 316, n. 116. Are these poems meant to be imitations of the style of Merkabah hymns? Cf. G. G. Scholem, *Jewish Gnosticism, Merkabah Mysticism, and Talmudic Tradition* (New York, 1960): 21ff.

19 I *Petirat Moshe,* 116; see also line 2 from bottom of the page.

20 *Ibid.* 117. Note also 119, top, for the charge that Moses on his own, without permission, slew the Egyptian! Cf. *Assumption of Moses,* ed. R. H. Charles (London, 1897): 106. Contrast this with ARNA, ch. 20, p. 72. Or Moses "cornered" by God: I *Petirat Moshe,* 120, top. And on the retort by Moses, cf. *Gen. R.* 49:9, 511.

21 I *Petirat Moshe,* 116; see also 124, 127. This is contrary to the cliché quoted by *Leqaḥ Ṭob* on Deut 34:9. The relationship between Moses and Joshua is conceived of as the relationship between a *ḥakam* and his *talmid.* What a disciple does for his master, 123. Cf. *Deut. R.* 9:9, 117c.

21a That in periods of persecution there was no objection to disguising oneself in order to escape identification as a Jew (see *Gen. R.* 82:5, 984ff., two disciples of R. Joshua), hardly affects our midrashic passage (yet, note the taunts of the apostate *stratiotes* in the *Gen. R.* anecdote!).

22 I *Petirat Moshe,* 121. In *Deut. R.* 11:8, 120a, "the galgallim of the Merkabah and the seraphim of flame (*lehabah*)." See also *Midrash ha-Gadol,* Deut., 65, lines 17–20. Cf. *Sifre Deut.* 29, p. 46.

justice is witnessed here. Let there be no more talk of injustice. God has to take into account the reactions of more than men.

There are however retorts where the human conception of justice is made secondary to a fundamental principle of monotheism. For example,[23] in one exchange God reassures Moses that he is in fact blameless, but that he must nevertheless die because he is a descendant of Adam, i.e., death is the fate of all human beings (no reference to Enoch and Elijah here!); or, put alternatively, "You have sipped from the cup of Adam"; or, even more acutely, "If you remain alive, people will be misled by you, they will make you into a god and will worship you."[24] There is danger of apotheosis here, in other words, that like the cult of emperor (?) or hero worship there will develop a cult of Moses worship.[25] The very remarkable achievements of Moses from Egypt on, are themselves the cause of his undoing, to underscore that even Moses is not a divine being—though he spent time with angels on high (God "made him equal in glory to the holy ones": Ecclus 45:2; cf. ARN, 157) and did not taste food or drink for forty days and nights.[26] Moses may outweigh all the works of creation;[27] though his days come to an end, his light never will.[28] But all men die; Moses is a man, although with extraordinary virtues; hence he must die.[29]

(Yet if Scripture says of Moses that at the age of 120 his eyes remained undimmed and his vigor unabated; if when God asks Moses, "Are you better than ancient worthies," or "Did not your parents and all your ancestors die," Moses rejects comparison between himself and them [I *Petirat Moshe* 118f.; II *Petirat Moshe* 71ff.]—evidently for the homilist there *is* something more-than-human to this *ish Elohim* who is superior to Adam, Noah, the Patriarchs.)

There are a number of still other exchanges,[30] assembled conveniently (with some repetition) in the *Midrash Petirat Moseh* I and II,[31] all emphasizing that in debate with God (for his own benefit), Moses cannot prevail. (This is not unexpected!) The protests put in the mouth of Moses reveal to us a moral disquietude of sensitive readers of the Moses stories in midrashic-talmudic times; God's various retorts reveal how in those days men tried to justify His ways: for His ways must be just. Protest and retort brought together create a complex religio-intellectual involvement with the ethical and theological (there's something Kierkegaardian about this): is this how the righteous is rewarded, the one trusted throughout Your household? What *is* a just reward? Shall the righteous be rewarded even if that may undermine a principle without which the purity of the faith cannot survive? "How can a man be just before God? . . . Behold, He snatches away; who can hinder Him? Who will say to Him, 'What doest Thou?' "

And parenthetically I would like to add: Whether or

---

23 ARNB, p. 51. Loewenstamm, 147, rightly underscores that in this passage not entry into the land is being discussed, but death. Indeed, death and exclusion from the land are referred to as two separate penalties (for the sin at Meribah, not entering into the land; but why *die*?). Note that in ARNA, 48–50, also, death is the subject and that Moses requests a death like his brother Aaron's. See also Ginzberg, *Legends*, VI, 148, n. 888. Cf. ARN, 156.

This too deserves to be noted, that (approximately) in I *Petirat Moshe*, first appear Moses' appeals not to die (116f.), then (117, 120, top, 123ff.) specifically his appeals to be permitted to enter the land, one way or another. This arrangement seems to be deliberate: if Moses can't persuade God to let him live on, then perhaps he might get from Him the permission to enter the land; sometimes there is an overlapping of the appeals for continued life and for admission into the land (e.g., 120, 125f., 127)—possibly the result of the homilist's healthy instinct, that if Moses is admitted into the land, the transition to immortality would follow (consummation of all one has projected is the privilege of those who live forever). Nor is Moses indifferent to the fact that neither his own sons nor Aaron's will succeed him (121, bottom). Contrast Philo, *On the Virtues*, 66f. (LC, VIII, 203); *Sifre Num.* 141, p. 187, *Sifre Zuta*, 322, top.

Let no one imagine that the reason Moses wanted to enter the Holy Land was his desire to enjoy its delicious fruits. He wished to carry out the commands having to do with the land (II *Petirat Moshe*, VI, 74)!

24 I *Petirat Moshe*, 116, 118. On the cup of Adam, see also *Deut. R.*, ed. S. Lieberman, 125 (and n. 2). Drinking from the same cup = sharing same fate: *Sifre Deut.* 349, p. 407. Cf. Prov 1:13.

25 Cf. J. Goldin in *Mordecai M. Kaplan Jubilee Volume* (New York, 1953): 278ff. See also the quotation from Josephus, above (n. 10). And see also III Armenian account, 120, bottom paragraph! Cf. the Nilsson quotation, below p. 224 and n. 47.

26 Exod 34:28. Deut 9:9. According to III Armenian account, 121, Moses fasted three forty-day periods, "corresponding to the number of his years."

27 II *Petirat Moshe*, VI, 71ff.

28 I *Petirat Moshe*, 121.

29 Cf. *Deut. R.*, ed. Lieberman, 130. As he gave up his ghost, according to II Armenian account, 119, he exclaimed, "Oh for the heavenly things that are sweeter than honeycomb." For the theme of the righteous refusing to die, see also, e.g., *The Testament of Abraham* (tr. by M. E. Stone, Society of Biblical Literature, 1972). Cf. L. Ginzberg in *Jewish Encyclopedia* (New York, 1901); 1.93–96.

30 One even draws on the Osiris motif: I *Petirat Moshe*, 124, bottom. Cf. E. R. Goodenough, *Jewish Symbols in the Greco-Roman Period*, II (Bollingen, 1953): 197. For another excruciating appeal, cf. ARN, 156, and S. Lieberman in *Louis Ginzberg Jubilee Volume* (Hebrew; New York, 1945): 254; *idem, Shkiin* (Jerusalem, 1970): 39f., n. 4 and p. 101 (to p. 40).

31 See above, n. 18. Were the *Petirat Moshe Midrashim* drawn up in order to put a stop to dangerous speculation, in order to demonstrate that Moses was given every opportunity to argue his case? However, see the last paragraph of this paper.

not so intended by the haggadic interpreters, the problem exemplified by the pleas of Moses and their rejection, recalls the outcry in other contexts of grief: זו תורה וזו שכרה, So this is the reward for devotion to the Torah! Here is how *Deut. R.* 11:10, 120a, puts it: "So this is the compensation for forty years of service (שילום עבודה של מ' שנה) in which I toiled to make them a holy and faithful nation?" And here is I *Petirat Moshe,* 121: "Where is my reward for the forty years (היכן שכרי של מ' שנה) I wore myself out for Your sons and in their behalf went to great pains," etc. It's almost as though the Moses story, unique as it surely is, is treated as a forecast of what to expect in the centuries to come: a life-time of loyalty without commensurate reward in this world. The problem, growing out of Israel's experience, may have suggested to the midrashic-talmudic homilist how to interpret the biblical Moses story.

Since if the purity of the faith fails to survive, it is futile to ask about the justice of rewards or punishments—and Moses, after all, is pleading only for what he feels he deserves—something like a compromise must be attempted. Note incidentally that no Job-like, God-out-of-the-storm, answer is resorted to, i.e., the Lord is just but *we* can't understand His ways, just as we can't understand much else: though this may be implied occasionally: but no overwhelming theophany—though in the end God does appear to take his soul. Hence, after Moses finally realizes that there is no one in the whole universe, animate or inanimate, who can help him and that he cannot persuade God to revoke His sentence, and discovers that his intellectual strength has vanished, he asks to die—but he does not want to die as all men die, he wants to die at God's own hand, not at Samael's, the chief of the satans,[32] not by the hand of the angel of death. This is indeed granted to him: the angel of death is powerless in the presence of Moses. Finally God and the archangels Michael and Gabriel, and the angel Zagzagel put him to his final rest.[33] The treatment of Moses at death would therefore seem to be exceptional. Moses has had at least and at last one wish of his granted in regard to his death, his uniqueness is thereby dramatically confirmed.[34]

But is it really? Has God then yielded to Moses' importunings? It is true that no one knows where he is buried (Deut 34:6),[35] that his soul is reluctant to quit his clean and pure and holy body which was never subject to the affliction of flies or of leprosy,[36] that beneficent angels attend him at his death. Yet even in making concessions, the Midrash Masters feel that they must exercise restraint. The reason no one knows where Moses is buried, says *Leqaḥ Ṭob* on Deut 34:6, is a precaution, lest his sepulcher become a shrine of idolatrous worship. Besides, Aaron's burial-place also disappeared from sight.[37] For thirty days the children of Israel mourned for Moses, the same period of mourning as for Aaron (as we have noted)—but not so, for Moses only the males of Israel, בני ישראל, mourned, while for Aaron *all* the house of Israel, כל בית ישראל, mourned (because Aaron went about making peace, while Moses did not refrain from reproving them).[38] It was by God's kiss that Moses died.[39] But Aaron too, and Miriam, and the Patriarchs,[40] and all the righteous so met their deaths.[41] And maybe even that comment[42] on "Never again did there arise in Israel a prophet like Moses," that "one such did arise among the gentiles," is also partially intended to keep the praise of Moses within bounds.

What is the point? Along with reverence ("Moses our master, the greatest of great scholars, the father of the

32 I *Petirat Moshe,* 125. From the fire of gehenna he was created and to the fire of gehenna he will return (*ibid.,* 128). Cf. Jude 9.

33 I *Petirat Moshe,* 128f. Zagzagel was Moses' teacher (*Ibid.,* 127). Cf. Ginzberg, *Legends,* V, 417. According to III Armenian account, 120, Michael buried him.

34 I *Peirat Moshe,* 119, line 5 from bottom. According to *Ps.-Philo* 19:16 ([M. R. James, ed. and trans.; New York, 1971]: 132), on the day Moses died the hymn of the angels was not recited. This never happened with any other human being, before or since.

35 Note also *Assumption of Moses* 11:8, and Charles' note, p. 46, s.v., "All the world . . ." Cf. III Armenian account, 120.

36 I *Petirat Moshe,* 129, and Ginzberg, *Legends,* VI, 161, n. 948. Is the reference to flies associated with the thought in Abot 5:5? (Nevertheless, cf. S. Lieberman, *Hellenism in Jewish Palestine* [New York, 1962]: 174ff.) Is the reference to leprosy reminiscent of what happened to his sister (Num 12:9), that Moses never gossiped? On leprosy, see also Eleh Ezkerah in *Bet ha-Midrasch,* II, 66.

37 *Midrash Petirat Aharon* in Jellinek, *Bet ha-Midrasch,* I, 95, top. Lest Israel think he is alive and therefore a god: *ibid.*

38 ARNA, p. 49; see also ARNB, p. 51. At Aaron's death also, angels mourned, ARNB, p. 51; as for Moses, see also ARNB, p. 52, end of ch. 25. Cf. I *Petirat Moshe,* 128f. Further, as A. B. Ehrlich points out (*Mikra Ki-Pheshuto* [New York, 1969]: 1.383), the captive woman was also given a month's time to lament her father and mother (Deut 21: 10–14). On thirty-day mourning for Moses, cf. also III Armenian account, 121 top. On thirty-day mourning, see one view in P. Nazir 1:3 and Maimonides, *Code,* Book of Judges, Mourning 6:1 and Radbaz and *Leḥem Mishneh ad loc.*

39 I *Petirat Moshe,* 129. Cf. Ginzberg, *Legends,* VI, 161, n. 950.

40 Cf. Ginzberg, *Legends,* VI, 112, n. 639.

41 Cf. *Midrash Tannaim,* 225; *M. Soṭah* 1:9, end (cf. reading in ed. Lowe).

42 *Sifre Deut.* 357, p. 430. Balaam's wisdom superior to Moses': *Seder Eliyahu R.* (ed. Friedmann), 142. See also ARNA, p. 41, on the (relative) meekness of Moses! The soul of Moses is of course put in safekeeping under the Throne of Glory, but the same is true of the souls of all the righteous (ARNA, p. 50).

prophets")[43] went a deep religio-intellectual fear of Moses—at least on the part of thoughtful students and teachers of Scripture—I don't think that is putting it too strongly, in the light of these and still other available references, for no other biblical personality so succeeded in shortening the distance between God and man as he did. For this reason his humanity must be repeatedly underlined, even (above all?) when he gets what he asked for. Even the manner of Moses' death does not release him from the limits of the human condition: the extraordinary honors paid him are paid to other outstanding personalities as well. The give-and-take between Moses and God is not suppressed: hear the response of the Lord! The death of Moses before Israel's entrance into the Promised Land did not—at least in midrashic-talmudic times and circles—entirely cease to be an embarrassment[44] or a perplexity, because of the gross unfairness it represented; on the other hand, considerations regarded as higher, or profounder, than the miscarriage of justice (by human standards) had to triumph particularly in a world where in the popular mind the nature and treatment of the gods were sometimes indistinguishable from that of men. "When . . . we think," says Epictetus, "that the gods stand in the way of [our own interests], we revile even them, cast their statues to the ground, and burn their temples, as Alexander ordered the temples of Asclepius to be burned when his loved one (Hephaestion) died."[45] On a more cultivated level possibly, but still flowing too easily from God to man and back again, we hear Apollonius of Tyana,[46] when the Emperor asks him, "Why is it that men call you a god?" reply, "Because every man that is thought to be good, is honored by the title of god," ὅτι πᾶς ἄνθρωπος ἀγαθὸς νομιζόμενος θεοῦ ἐπωνυμίᾳ τιμᾶται.

Of course this is not to say that the Midrash on the death of Moses is a direct counter-attack on Apollonius or Epictetus. But the Midrash is aware of a world where, as Martin Nilsson once put it, a time came when "The ancient gods were tottering. . . . Men began to worship personages in authority." Even that ambiguous characterization, *ish ha-Elohim, anthrōpos tou theou* (or, *anthrōpos theou*), as the Greek Bible translates with admirable literalness, is evidently not without its risks, for the Targum insists that it means "prophet of the Lord," not just man of God or divine man, whatever that might mean.[47] It was a natural question; should such a one die? At one point Moses defended himself thus, "Did You not put me to the test when the golden calf was made and I destroyed it? Why is it necessary for me to die?"[48] Moses doesn't seem to understand that not *his* motives are suspect but the impulse and attitude of his people to him. Therefore he must die, with honors as all the righteous die but not in a unique manner. Moses himself had proclaimed "that the Lord alone is God, there is none beside Him" (Deut 4:35, II *Petirat Moshe,* VI, 78); consequently *His* sovereign will shall be done (though it might fill Him too with inexpressible grief!).[49]

Are we to say then that for the Midrash there is nothing unique about Moses? The conclusion of the *Midrash Petirat Moshe*[50] suggests otherwise, seems indeed prepared to have God adopt some of the appeals made earlier by Moses and at that time dismissed by Him.[51] Once Moses has made his peace with the death-sentence and his soul is taken from him, God begins to weep, the

43 ARNA, p. 3 (and despite this forgets what God commanded him to say when he lost his temper). Cf. S. Abramson in *Leshonenu* 41 (1977): 159.

44 Is this also why God weeps (and the angels too) when Moses finally dies? (I *Petirat Moshe*, 129.) That even God can do nothing about it? See below, notes 52–53.

45 Epictetus, II, 22:17 (LC, I, 397). Cf. R. Aqiba in *Mekilta*, Ba-Ḥodesh 10 (II, 277, lines 10–12). Cf. F. de Coulanges, *The Ancient City* (Garden City, NY, n.d.); 152.

46 8:5, LC, II, 281; cf. 3:18 (LC, I, 269).

47 M. P. Nilsson, *A History of Greek Religion* (2nd ed.; New York, 1964): 285; and note how he goes on (286ff.) to review the historical development—which is almost a confirmation of what the late Harold Rosenberg once observed (*The New Yorker*, 14 April 1975, p. 77), "In the absence of a supernatural order, men are impelled to seek the aid of supernatural powers. If religion is the opium of the people, the fading of religion turns people toward opium."

In the second century, to describe someone as *theios* probably did not mean too much; on the other hand, neither was it altogether meaningless. And, as A. D. Nock said, "The words a man uses do in religion also use him" (*Essays on Religion and the Ancient World* [Oxford, 1972]: 1.61). To one of an entirely different commitment—on the sidelines, as it were, of the official or popular religions—to witness the easygoing and loose use of terms or conduct that ought to express reverence but doesn't, was bound to serve as warning, beware of this happening in our own midst. I'm tempted to say that one reason Jews and Christians refused to take pagan worship seriously is that not infrequently they beheld pagans themselves adopting an indifferent or flippant attitude towards gods and sanctuaries (Nock, *op. cit.*, 59).

On *ish ha-Elohim* (Deut 33:1; cf. Josh 14:6; Ps 90:1; Ezra 3:2) cf. *Sifre Deut.* 342, p. 393 and ARNB, pp. 95f.; and the very listings may suggest (at least in part) that the Rabbis are eager to point out that even as regards this expression, Moses is not unique. Cf. Ginzberg, *Legends*, VI, 166, n. 965. As for the biblical *ish ha-Elohim*, see now J. A. Holstein in *HUCA* 48 (1977): 69–81, esp. 74f.

As to the recurring Greek and targumic renderings of *ish ha-Elohim*, cf. these versions of the biblical verses cited by *Sifre Deut.*, *ibid.*, and all others listed in Mandelkern's *Concordance.*

48 I *Petirat Moshe*, 118.

49 See also, for example, *Midrash Eleh Ezkerah* in *Bet ha-Midrasch*, II, 67. On dualism reflected by the "original" *Assumption of Moses*, see Loewenstamm (N 1): 155–57.

50 I and II; they are not identical, but they are in agreement.

51 Cf., e.g., I *Petirat Moshe*, 117.

Midrash informs us; and not only God but heaven and earth and all the orders of Creation, all with appropriate biblical verses of lament. At this point Metatron[52] attempts to comfort God; he says to the Lord, "Master of the universe, while he was alive Moses was Yours, and now that he's dead he's still Yours," that is, he's still at Your service;[53] why weep then?

But God responds: "It's not for Moses only that I mourn[54] but for Moses and Israel. For (Israel) angered Me many times, and in their behalf he would offer up prayer and placate Me. He said of Me, 'that the Lord alone is God in heaven above and on the earth below (there is no other, *ʿod*)' (Deut 4:39). I in turn therefore bear witness[55] that "never again (*ʿod*) did there arise in Israel a prophet like Moses whom the Lord singled out face to face' (Deut 34:10)."

For the Midrash even Metatron misses the point. Moses is indeed still in God's service. But what was unique in the life of Moses was his role as Israel's advocate on frequent critical occasions before a God given to anger, and his teaching Israel[56] that only the Lord is God, none else.[57] Now Israel's intercessor is gone, the great teacher, *safra rabba,* is taken away. The death of Moses is so great a loss (to God and Israel), even the Almighty, by whose decree the man Moses dies, cannot hold back his tears. Moses had to die, but not because he deserved to die: no longer any mention of Waters of Meribah, of belonging to a faithless generation.

The death is not punitive. It is even regrettable. This, the divine regret,[58] is the specific midrashic addition to the biblical account. In Scripture the sentence on Moses is pronounced with majestic severity. "And die on the mountain that you are about to ascend" (Deut 32:50). "Go up to the summit of Pisgah and gaze about . . . for you shall not go across yonder Jordan" (Deut 3:27). In the Midrash, on the other hand, what is heard is not only God's verdict but God's grief. A transposition has taken place—as often in haggadic midrash,—especially on tragic occasions—from the heavenly to the paternal. The petitions of Moses and their denial are still audible, but now there is also the mourning Voice of the Lord for His favorite:

בכה עליו הקב'ה והתחיל לקונן עליו . . .
מי יקום לי עם מרעים
מי יתיצב לי עם פועלי און

"The Holy One, blessed be He, wept over him and began to keen, Who will rise up before Me[59] when men are evil, who will stand up before Me in behalf of wrongdoers?" (Ps 94:16).

We owe this insight of course (as we owe the earlier dialogues between Moses and God) to the homilist, who felt that, although Scripture said nothing about it, over the death of Moses God could not be less distressed than Israel. It is perhaps the only way that he, the homilist, and his audience could be persuaded anew that "The Rock! His deeds are perfect . . . all His ways are just; a faithful God, never false" (Deut 32:4).[60]

---

52 I *Petirat Moshe,* 129, and other midrashim (in *Ginzė Midrash,* 223: Michael). On Metatron, cf. G. Scholem, *Major Trends in Jewish Mysticism* (New York, 1961): 67-70; *idem, Gnosticism,* ch. 7; idem, *Kabbalah* (New York, 1974): 377-81. (Is Metatron deliberately introduced here to emphasize that no second deity exists?)

53 On the expression *shel-lak* "was/is Yours," cf. *Tg. Onqelos* for Num 8:14b.

54 Text, *Mitnaḥem* (and so too in *Deut. R.,* ed. Lieberman, 42), as euphemism. Should one understand: "for *God* and Israel?"

The exchange between Metatron and God does not occur in II *Petirat Moshe.* In the *Tanḥuma midrashim, wa-Ethanan* (also *Deut. R.,* ed. Lieberman, 41f.), it does appear along with an explanatory parable in God's reply.

55 II *Petirat Moshe,* 78 *meqalles* ("praise, hail"). Cf. *Deut. R.* 11:5, 119b.

56 Note how this thought is expressed (paraphrased?) in *Ginzė Midrash,* 224.

57 It may be that the play on the verses with the word *ʿod* is intended only as a peroration on an auspicious note. These verses do not follow the exchange between Metatron and God in *Tanḥuma midrashim,* etc. Is the emphasis, regardless of the appearance God adopts on different occasions (*Pesiqta Kahana,* ed. B. Mandelbaum, 223f.), it is always He and none but He? Or simply, only God is God, not Moses?

58 Plus the long give-and-take, of course. For examples of divine regret in Scripture, cf., e.g., Gen 6:6f., or Amos 7 (several times). In our Midrash, the notion of regret is not an outgrowth of disappointment with Moses, but the contrary: he deserves better!

59 Such is the midrashic interpretation. Who (in the future) will rise up before Me as advocate for those who have done wrong.

60 Dr. Judith S. Neaman has graciously called my attention to a woodcut from the Cologne Bible showing the burial of Moses, reproduced on p. 199 of Gustav Davidson, *A Dictionary of Angels* (New York, 1967), from James Strachan, *Pictures from a Mediaeval Bible* (Boston, 1961): 63, fig. 49: on left, God in the act of interring Moses; in center and on right two assisting angels, presumably Michael and Gabriel ("or Zagzagel"). Moses' hands are crossed (but not across his chest: I *Petirat Moshe,* 129, line 5). Another illustration from the *Leon Bible* (12th century, Spain) in *Encyclopaedia Judaica* (Jerusalem, 1972): 5. 1426. And I am especially grateful to Professor Roland M. Frye for bringing to my attention the paper "Moses Shown the Promised Land," by A. Heimann, in the *Journal of the Warburg and Courtauld Institutes* 34 (1971): 321-24; plates 52-53.

THE CULT OF THE DEAD IN CORINTH

CHARLES A. KENNEDY

Reflecting on his career in comparative anthropology, James Frazer acknowledged the frustration shared by all field observers of behavior: "Customs often live on for ages after the circumstances and modes of thought which gave rise to them have disappeared, and in their new environment new motives are invented to explain them . . . Sometimes people give no explanation of their customs, sometimes (much oftener than not) a wrong one."[1]

A funeral director once assured the author that the laurel wreath insert on a stamped aluminum grave marker "didn't mean anything." Since the deceased had not belonged to any fraternal order having a special emblem, the laurel wreath was used to fill up the space. The incident was a confirmation of Frazer's observation, especially in matters relating to death and burial in contemporary society. There is a continuity in our funeral rituals and traditions extending back to the ancient Near East, although most of us, like that funeral director, are either unaware of this continuity or have invented new explanations for the old symbols.

Marvin Pope has demonstrated that Frazer's remark is also true of texts. Texts, too, often live on for ages after the circumstances and mode of thought which gave rise to them have disappeared, and later generations invent new interpretations to suit their own times. Pope's commentary on the Song of Songs attempted to peel away the layers of metaphorical and symbolic exegesis from the text and to recover the original context of the love poems. The Wagnerian dimension of his efforts is an appropriate setting for his *Liebestod* conclusions. This essay in Pope's honor attempts to test his hypothesis about the substructure of funeral practices in the Bible as they occur in the New Testament.

The Apostle's Creed affirms Jesus "crucified, dead and buried," yet little has been done to investigate the impact of that assertion at a very pragmatic level on the population of the Roman world. The Gospel narratives give few details about the funeral rites for Jesus, a circumstance that could be ascribed to the constraints of time. But even when time does not seem to be a factor, the text is equally brief, e.g., the funerals of Ananias and Sapphira in Acts 5:5ff. Only in the case of Stephen is it said, They "made great lamentation over him" (Acts 8:2). There is a minimum of ritual reported, in part because it served no purpose in furthering the narrative, but also for the more likely reason that everyone "knows" what happens at a funeral.

It is this common knowledge about funeral customs that obviates their inclusion in our texts. Since everyone knows what takes place, there is no reason to report it. Sociologists of religion have distinguished between the Great Tradition and the little tradition.[2] The former is the realm of the scholars, theologians and scriptures. The latter is the area of the common people and their practices in the name of their religion. Often there is a great difference between the ways these two view the same religious heritage. One need only think of Santa Claus and the Easter Bunny. While Death may fall within the purview of the Great Tradition, funerals are a function of the little tradition. Only in religions where the Great Tradition impinges directly on the lives of the faithful, as for example in Orthodox Judaism, do we find manuals prepared for the conduct of funerals, including such matters as the proper preparation of the body for burial and the requirements for a gravesite.[3] Most religions are content to provide a suitable or prescribed liturgy for the occasion, but leave the pragmatic details to be determined by local custom or even the individual wishes of the family.[4]

That one must die sooner or later is known to all. The question is what change death will bring. It is clear that for the ancients death was considered as a change of status more than as cessation of life.[5] Tewfik Canaan

---

1 James G. Frazer, *Garnered Sheaves* (London: Macmillan and Co., Ltd., 1931): 18.

2 Robert Redfield, *The Little Community and Peasant Society and Culture* (Chicago: University of Chicago Press, 1960).

3 Maurice Lamm, *The Jewish Way of Death and Mourning* (New York: Jonathan David Publishers, 1969).

4 In BT, *Shab.* 153a the Galileans said that the mourners should perform in front of the bier; the Judeans said behind the bier. But they do not differ, as each spoke in accordance with the usage of his own locality. St. Augustine applied the same principle to the report of Jesus' burial in John 19:40. " The evangelist, I think, was not without a purpose in so framing his words, 'as the manner of the Jews is to bury;' for in this way, unless I am mistaken, he has admonished us that in duties of this kind, which are observed to the dead, the customs of every nation ought to be preserved." *Hom. evang. joh. Tract.* CXX, 4 (*NPNF* VII, 435).

5 E. Rohde in speaking of the Greek psychology of death notes, "It is plain that no impassable gulf was fixed between life

reported the Arabic proverb, "But for the living, the dead would have died long ago." The dead had changed status by leaving the company of the living, but they were still "alive" in a very real sense and therefore had to be fed and clothed. An inscription from Phrygia reads:[6]

> Mother, not even there with the infernal deities (*katachthoniois daimosin*) should you be without a share of the gifts it is meet we should give you. Therefore have I, Nichomachus, and your daughter Dione erected this tomb (*tumbon*) and pillar (*stēlēn*) for your sake (*charin*).

Without the amenities the dead would have a miserable existence and be quite justified in doing whatever possible to convince the living to provide them with the necessities of death. Hence ghosts and haunts.

The first requirement for the dead was the provision of a suitable interment. The need for a proper burial has been recognized in Scripture since Abraham was obliged to purchase a tomb for Sarah, "to bury the dead from out of my sight." It is also apparent that in Israel as elsewhere in the ancient world it was thought necessary to provide periodically for the well-being of the deceased after the funeral. Although the later tradition rejected the practice associated with the cult of the dead, the biblical witness is clear that both the populace and the rulers continued to consult mediums and to place food offerings on graves. Isa. 65:4 complains that there were those who were spending the night in tombs "eating swine's flesh and drinking the broth of abominable things," certainly a reference to memorial meals associated with the cult of the dead. As the religion of Israel was transformed into Judaism, the concern for regulating funerals appeared again and again. Excessive eating and drinking seemed to be the chief problems; and implicit in this is the general matter of overspending on funerals.[7] In the Talmud (*Keth.* 8b) it is stated that the wine drunk in the house of mourners should be limited to ten cups (of unspecified size): three before the meal to open the small bowels; three during the meal to dissolve the food in the bowels; and four after the meal: one for "him who feedeth," one for the blessing of the land, one for the rebuilder of Jerusalem and one for "him who is good and does good." An additional four cups were allowed by some authorities: one for the officers of the town, one for the leader of the town, one for the Temple and finally one for Rabbi Gamaliel who wished to cut back on the lavishness of funerals!

While much has been written on the cult of the dead in the ancient Near East and in Israel, little attention has been paid to its appearance in the early Christian church. The catacombs of Rome give vivid evidence of its development in the late second and third centuries, but there has been a gap in our knowledge about the practices of Christians in the century and a half following the death of Jesus. Styger[8] posed the question nearly a half century ago: where were the Christians buried before the catacombs were established under Pope Zephyrinus in the early third century? He could give no answer, except to assume that since the Christians were from the lower classes of society, they would most likely be buried in common pit graves or in other unmarked graves now lost to us.

As our understanding of the social dynamics of the Roman world has increased it has become clearer that Christianity had to thread its way through an elaborate social structure before becoming the religion of the Empire.[9] In order to accomplish this the Christian Gospel had to be made appealing to gentiles apart from its Jewish setting. In practical terms this meant that to the degree that the Gospel was separated from its Jewish roots, Roman customs and practices would be adapted to replace that which had been lost. Here again the paradigm of the Great Tradition and little tradition is helpful. The Gospel as preached became part of the Great Tradition; the behavior of Christian converts formed the little tradition. Insofar as the little tradition did not subvert or contradict the proclamation of the Gospel, it could be tolerated. But if a situation arose that set the local practices against the Great Tradition, the authority of the latter would be forced to intervene. Funeral customs afforded this kind of circumstance, and what Paul heard from Corinth prompted him to compose the prompt and decisive reply found in 1 Corinthians 8–10.

The subject of "food offered to idols" (1 Cor. 8:1 *et seq.*) has been treated in some detail in two studies and one dissertation in recent years.[10] In each of these presentations the arguments proceed from the same presupposition, namely that the word *eidōlothuton* is, as

---

and death. It almost seems as though life went on quite uninterupted by death." *Psyche. The Cult of Souls and Belief in Immortality Among the Greeks* 1 (New York: Harper and Row Torchbooks, 1966): 167–68.

6 *A.P* 7.333. It should be noted that the dead are called "demons" without any signification of evil as the English term denotes.

7 Funeral expenses could be so great as to bankrupt families. A contract to purchase one-sixth interest in a Roman tomb at Palmyra stipulated the cost to be ca. 120 denarii in A.D. 171, a sum of money insufficient to support an adult for a whole year. T. Frank, ed., *An Economic Survey of Ancient Rome* 4 (Baltimore: Johns Hopkins, 1938): 174–75.

8 P. Styger, *Die Römischen Katakomben* (Berlin, 1933): 319.

9 R. MacMullen, *Roman Social Relations 50 BC to AD 284.* (New Haven and London: Yale University, 1974); W. Meeks, "The Social World of Pauline Christianity" in *ANRW* II/27 (forthcoming); J. Gager, *Kingdom and Community. The Social World of Early Christianity* (Englewood Cliffs, N.J.: Prentice Hall, 1975).

10 C. K. Barrett, "Things Sacrificed to Idols" in *NTS* 11 (1964): 138–53; A. Ehrhardt, "The Sunday Joint of the Christian Housewife" in *Framework of the New Testament*

it were, self-explanatory. The two elements of the word, "idol" and "sacrifice" combine to form the compound "meat / food / things offered to idols." The "idols" are taken to mean the statues of the Greek gods, therefore the sacrifices must be the victims slaughtered at their temples. Such meat, so the argument goes, is not to be eaten by Christians (1 Cor. 10:14; cf. Acts 15:29). Commentators have then assumed that virtually all meat sold in the market was in some sense dedicated to a pagan god and therefore under the ban for Christians. How was a Corinthian Christian to know which meats in the butcher shop had been ritually slaughtered at a temple altar and which had not? If Paul's injunction to avoid such meat was carried out to the letter (a most un-Pauline principle), Ehrhardt worried that "most Christian housewives, especially the poorer ones, would find it almost impossible to return hospitality to their husband's business friends."[11]

All of these assumptions seem to be inventions of the exegetes to help explain the use of the term "idol" in the troublesome word *eidōlothuton*. As the word moved from Greek to Latin it was transliterated, not translated, becoming *idolothyton*,[12] possibly indicating that the original word was a technical term and therefore not easily translatable. The English "food offered to idols" is yet another form of transliteration, reproducing the original parts, but not the sense of the whole.

As a solution to this problem I propose a new translation of the word that will provide a key to understanding the structure and meaning of Paul's concern for the issue in 1 Cor 8-10. It is my contention that Paul is addressing himself to one of the most pervasive problems faced by Christians anywhere at any time, the proper rites to be accorded to their dead. *Eidōlothuton* should be translated as "memorial meals for the dead." Confirmation for this can be found in Greek and Hebrew usage, some of which has been cited in previous discussions, but the implications of which have not always been realized.

Büchsel in his *TDNT* article states that *eidōlothuton* "is obviously a Jewish term for *hierothuton* or the rare *theothuton*. It denotes that meat which derives from heathen sacrifices, though without the intolerable implication of the sanctity of what is offered to heathen gods, or to the divinity of these gods."[13] *Eidōlothuton* first appears in 4 Macc 5:2 when Antiochus decrees that Jews shall be forced to eat swine's flesh and "meat offered to idols." The term reappears in the Apostolic Decree (Acts 15:29, but not in the "preliminary draft" mentioned in v. 20). To complicate our understanding of *eidōlothuton* even further, the word *heirothuton* occurs in 1 Cor 10:28. This has led exegetes to equate the two words. Paul and his Christian correspondent in Corinth use the word *eidōlothuton*, whereas 1 Cor 10:28 quotes an informant assumed to be gentile.[14] It is then further assumed that it would be only natural for a gentile to use the word *hierothuton* rather than *eidōlothuton*. Conzelmann goes so far as to call the latter "a Jewish term, constructed with a polemical edge against the Greek *hierothuton*," but he stays with the translation of "meat sacrificed to idols."[15]

The translation of *eidōlothuton* in this manner has gained its status from repetition rather than from rigorous linguistic analysis. The two elements of the word have been treated almost exclusively from the context of the LXX and the NT. The evidence from secular Greek usage and from the Hebrew sources has been overlooked or unrecognized. A fresh look at these other sources can provide a better translation of this puzzling term.

We begin with the element *eidōlo-*. *Eidōlon* in the sense of "idol" is rare in secular Greek. The common meaning of the term is "image," "likeness," or a range of meanings we today would associate with a photograph. It is the representation of a real person. Herodotus[16] reports that Croessus sent an image to the shrine at Delphi as an offering. It was a golden figure, three cubits high, modelled, it was said, after a woman who served in his royal bakery. It was an *eidōlon* of her. Eusebius recounts the gruesome end of Maximin, who had persecuted the Christians. Beaten in battle, Maximin tried to escape the field and the wrath of God by disguising himself in the rags of a slave. But God's fiery dart found him and consumed his whole body, "so that all trace of the original lineaments of his body was lost and nothing remained of him but dry bones and a skeleton-like appearance (*kataskeleteumenōn eidōlōn*)."[17] Note that here the *eidōlon* is an actual corpse, but only "a shadow of his former self."

This connection with the dead leads to the second association of the word *eidōlon*: the shade or shadow of a person in the sense of the Latin *umbra*, the unsubstantial form and shape of one who had died.[18] Homer twice describes Hades "where dwell the unheeding dead, the

Stories (Cambridge: Harvard University, 1964): 276–90; W. T. Sawyer, *The Problem of Meat Sacrificed to Idols in the Corinthian Church* (unpublished dissertation, Southern Baptist Theological Seminary, 1968).

11 Ehrhardt, "Christian Housewife" (N 10): 280.

12 Tert., *de spect.*, 13; Council of Elvira, Canon 40.

13 "Eidōlothuton," *TDNT* 2, 378.

14 H. Conzelmann, *First Corinthians* (Philadelphia: Fortress, 1975): 177, n. 21, following Lietzmann, *An Die Korinther* (4th ed.; Tübingen: J. C. B. Mohr, 1979): *ad loc.*

15 Conzelmann, *First Corinthians* (N 14): 139.

16 Histories, I, 5.

17 *Life of Constantine* I, 58.

18 Pausanius reports this story about Actaeon. "A ghost (*eidōlon*), they say, carrying a rock (emend.: was running about and ravaging) was ravaging the land. When the Orchomenians inquired at Delphi, the god bade them discover the remains of Actaeon and bury them in the earth. He also bade them make a bronze likeness (*eikōn*) of the ghost and fasten it to a rock with

phantoms of men outworn (*eidōla kamontōn*)."[19] It is the image, the *eidōlon*, that can be represented plastically in portraits and busts such as the funeral portraits and masks which formed an important part of the cult of the dead in the ancient world.[20] Lucretius[21] speaks of men as consisting of three parts: the body (*sōma*), the spirit (*psychē*) and the *eidōlon*, "certain similitudes pallid in wondrous wise." It is only this third part that reaches the regions of Acheron, for the body decomposes in the grave and the spirit rises to the stars. Fulgentius (6th century, A.D.) repeated a tradition from Diophantus of Sparta that the origin of idols went back to Syrophanes of Egypt, who lost his son "by a bitter blow of Fate." "In the grip of grief which always endeavors to relieve its need, he set up an effigy of his son in his household; but when he sought a cure thereby for his grief, he found it rather a renewal of sorrow .... This is called an idol, that is *idos dolu*, which in Latin we call appearance of grief."[22] Even with allowances for Fulgentius' fractured Greek, it is important to note that "idol" had its primary association with an image of a deceased member of the family.

The element *-thuton* also needs a closer look. It is often translated as "sacrifice," but this term itself has a wide range of meanings. In Homer it was used of making any offering to the gods and was not restricted to the sense of slaughtering animals, which was properly called *sphazein*.[23] Nock cautioned against insisting on the word "sacrifices," for as early as Herodotus VIII, 99, it had come to mean "dinner party."[24] The close connection between dining and sacrificing can be seen in Odysseus' command to Telemachus, "Take you and quickly sacrifice that we may dine."[25] Here the object is a meal, although incidentally, sacrifice to the gods is implied.

The combination of *eidōlo-* and *thuton* should then be understood to mean "meal for the image of the deceased" or more simply "a funerary meal / offering," "a memorial meal for the dead." Confirmation for this translation can be found in the OT and rabbinic phrase *zibḥē mētîm*, "sacrifices of the dead" in Psalm 106:28. Dahood[26] better translates it "banquets of the dead." He correctly equates this phrase with the *zibḥē ʾĕlōhēhen* of Num 25:2, the idolatrous meals introduced to the Israelites by the Moabite women. These meals were apparently funeral banquets in honor of their ancestors. The dead are described as gods in 1 Sam 28:13 and Isa 8:19, two situations where men wish to know about the future and seek out the dead for answers. In a text from Ugarit, Anat addresses her deceased brother Baal with these words: "Your comrades are the gods, the dead your comrades."[27] Since Baal was already a god in life, the change of status brought about by his death put him in a new company of gods, the dead.

The real problem at Corinth is Christian participation in the pagan funeral rites for members of the family or for friends. It is not a matter of finding kosher meat in the market place,[28] since Paul himself dismisses that concern by his remark in 1 Cor 10:25; "You may eat anything sold in the market without raising questions of conscience." Funeral meals on the other hand involve a host of social and theological problems about which the Law of Moses and the teachings of Jesus have nothing constructive to say.[29] It is this perpetual problem of dealing with the care and feeding of the dead that Paul addresses in 1 Cor 8–10, and not the eating of meats that were slaughtered in pagan temples or offered to pagan gods in the sense of the Olympians such as Zeus or Apollo.

Funerals in the Graeco-Roman world were conducted *kata nomous*, according to custom or tradition.[30] Rituals and procedures were carefully detailed to insure the proper burial for the deceased and the purification of the family from the contamination of death. Funeral banquets were prescribed on certain days immediately following the death and on anniversaries of the burial in subsequent

iron. I myself have seen this image (*agalma*) thus fastened. They also sacrifice every year to Actaeon as to a hero." Paus. 9.38, 5 (Loeb ed. IV, 342).

19 Homer, *Od.* 11.476; 24.14.

20 Rachel's theft of the household gods, *tĕrāphîm* (Gen 31:19), shows the critical importance of possessing these images of the ancestors. Cf. C. H. Gordon, "Biblical Customs and the Nuzu Tablets," *BA* 3 (1940): 1–12. The LXX calls them *eidōla*.

21 *De Rerum natura* I, 122, quoting from Ennius.

22 *Myth.* 1.1.15; ET *Fulgentius the Mythographer* (L. G. Whitbread, trans.; Ohio State University, 1971): 48.

23 J. C. Lawson, *Modern Greek Folklore and Ancient Greek Religion* (Cambridge: Harvard University, 1910): 335–36.

24 A. D. Nock, "The Cult of Heroes" in *HTR* 37 (1944): 151.

25 Homer, *Od.* 25.215.

26 M. Dahood, *Psalms III* (AB 174; Garden City, NY: Doubleday, 1970): p. 73.

27 *UT* 6.6(62).46: *ʿdk ilm hn mtm ʿdk*. Marvin H. Pope, "Notes on the Rephaim Texts from Ugarit" in *Ancient Near Eastern Studies in Memory of J. J. Finklestein* (New Haven: Connecticut Academy of Arts and Sciences, 1977): 172.

28 *Contra* A. Ehrhardt; see note 10.

29 John Chrysostom comments on the prohibitions listed in the Apostolic Decree (Acts 15:29): "These things the New Testament did not enjoin: we nowhere find that Christ discoursed about these matters; but these things they take from the Law." (*Hom. on Acts*, XXXIII). Chrysostom refers to Gen 9:5 and interprets the ban on "blood" and "things strangled" to mean homicide, a moralistic approach adopted in the west as well. Cf. Augustine, *Speculum* (*PL* 34:994).

30 For a general survey see J. M. C. Toynbee, *Death and Burial in the Roman World* (Ithaca: Cornell University, 1971). A concise description of the funeral itself is found in D. P. Harmon, "The Family Festivals of Rome" in *ANRW* II / 16.2, pp. 1592–1603, esp. 1600–1603.

Fig. 1 Roman Patrician with the Death-masks of his ancestors. Rome, Museo Barberini. (Goldscheider, L., *Roman Portraits* [New York: Oxford Univ. Press, 1940]: 6, fig. 1)

years. One of the sacrifices specified by Cicero[31] was the slaughter of a pig at the gravesite and a sow as expiation to Ceres or to Tellus and Ceres. The *parentatio*, an annual rite, honored the dead as one of the *divi parentum* or *di parentes*.

An important element in the funeral rites was the image of the deceased.[32] Wax masks were made and incorporated into effigies that might be displayed in public. In other instances painted portraits were made and exhibited. For the rich there were sculpted portrait busts. Images of the ancestors would be carried in the funeral procession (Fig. 1). Where masks were available, members of the family would be invited to wear them, and whenever possible the build of the deceased would be matched with the build of the mourner. A further note of surrealism was added by having the maskers wear the clothes of the deceased they were impersonating.

The degree to which the Romans were concerned about the care and feeding of the dead can best be illustrated by an inscription from Langres, France, in which Sextus Julius Frontinus (d. 103 A.D.) provides for a funerary endowment in anticipation of his needs after death.[33]

> I desire that the memorial chapel (*cella*) which I have built be completed precisely according to the pattern which I have given, to wit: there is to be a parlor (*exedra*) in that place, in which is to be placed a seated marble statue [of myself] . . . or else a bronze one . . . not less than five feet high. Under the parlor there is to be a couch and two benches of imported stone at the two sides. Let there be a coverlet which is to be spread on those days on which the chapel is opened, and two blankets and pillows, two pairs of dinner clothes and woolen robes, and two tunics. . . .
>
> The edifice and gardens and lake are to be tended under the supervision of my freedmen Philadelphius and Verus, and a sum is to be provided for restoration and repair . . ., and it is to be attended by three landscape gardeners and their apprentices . . . and each of the three shall receive annually sixty measures of wheat and twenty denarii for clothing. . . .
>
> But all my freedmen and freedwomen whom I manumitted either while alive or by this testament are to get together a donation of a sesterce apiece annually. And Aquila my grandson and his heir shall appoint annually money from which each is to prepare food and drink for himself, which is to be consecrated before the memorial chapel . . . and there they are to consume it. And they are to remain there until they consume it all. . . .
>
> After my death these named curators are to perform the sacred rites on the aforementioned altar on the *kalends* of April, May, June, July, August and October.

31 *De leg.* 2.22: *nec tamen eorum ante sepulchrum est, quam iusta facta et porcus caesus est*; about the sow he says *quaeque in porca contracta iura sint.*

32 A. N. Zadoks-Jitta, *Ancestral Portraiture in Rome* (Amsterdam: N. V. Noordhollandsche Uitgevers mij Amsterdam, 1932); H. T. Rowell, "The Forum and the Funeral *Imagines* of Augustus" in *Memoirs of the American Academy in Rome* 17 (1940): 131–43; E. Beth, *Ahnenbild und Familiengeschichte bei Römern und Griechen* (München: C. H. Bech'sche, 1935).

33 *C.I.L.* XIII, 5708. I am indebted to my colleague, T. O. MacAdoo, for this new translation.

Fig. 2 Artist's Reconstruction of the Street of Tombs and Herculaneum Gate, Pompeii. (Gell, W. and Gandy, J. P., *Pompeiiana* [4 vols.; London, 1817-1832]: Pl. 19)

In this testament all the elements for the cult of the dead are enumerated. The tomb with surrounding grounds for a garden in which food can be grown, the provision for caretakers and administrators, the obligations (and rewards) for the family and freedmen clients, a dining room provided and the times stated at which the memorial meals are to be eaten in the presence of the statue of the benefactor.

In 1 Cor 8:10 Paul speaks of the situation in which a "weak" brother sees a "stronger" brother dining in "an idol's temple." Both Goldstein[34] and Smith[35] have developed the idea that what Paul has in mind are the temple dining rooms which have been discovered at several sites in Greece. Ehrhardt goes so far as to compare these facilities with restaurants. "It has to be realized that it was the temples of the ancient world which had to supply the need for restaurants, particularly in the Greek cities. If a Christian husband for some reason or other wanted to go out for dinner he had, unless he lived in one of the big cities, no other choice."[36]

But there are two problems with this kind of reasoning. The temple dining rooms were not public rooms in any sense that would merit the name "restaurant." They were designed to accommodate private parties that wished to participate in ceremonial meals, a circumstance that 1 Cor 10:21 militates against. Christians could not eat at the table of demons and at the table of the Lord.

A second reason for rejecting the interpretation of the "idol's temple" as the dining room associated with certain Greek temples is that the examples cited date from 300 B.C. and earlier. There is no direct connection between these facilities and the circumstances at Corinth in the first century, A.D. By that time the city was a Roman colonial capital populated by Italian freedmen and their descendents in accordance with the charter issued by Julius Caesar in 46 B.C.

A much stronger case can be made for identifying the site of the dinner mentioned in 1 Cor 8:10 with a tomb triclinium. As the testamentary inscription from France illustrates most vividly, Roman tombs could be quite elaborate. Minimally the tomb marked off a plot of land that was consecrated for the burial of the dead. The size

34 M. S. Goldstein, *The Setting of the Ritual Meal in Greek Sanctuaries: 600–300 B. C.* (unpublished dissertation, University of California at Berkeley, 1978).

35 Dennis E. Smith, "The Egyptian Cults at Corinth" in *HTR* 70 (1977): 201–31.

36 Ehrhardt, "Christian Housewife" (N 10): 279.

Fig. 3 Tomb Triclinium of Gnaeus Vibrius Saturninus on the Street of Tombs, Pompeii. (Gell and Gandy, *Pompeiiana*, Pl. 4)

of the plot and the opulence of the structures varied with the wealth and ambition of the owners.[37] The best place to see how these tombs functioned is on the Street of the Tombs at Pompeii. (Fig. 2) While all of the tombs are intended to house or commemorate burials, this was only one of the reasons to erect a tomb monument. The periodic celebrations and memorial meals required a place to assemble, such as an *exedra*. Where possible a garden was included in which flowers and food could be raised to help support the endowment.[38] For the less affluent, the memorial meal would be more like a picnic; the wealthy could afford a complete dining room with adjacent kitchen. (Fig. 3) The tomb triclinium shown here is only a few steps off the street. Passers-by could look through the doorway and catch glimpses of the diners within. For some, if not most of the diners, it was desirable to be seen at these affairs. Members of the family would gain in their reputations for filial piety, while friends would like to be seen in the company of such devoted and hospitable people.

A memorial chapel (*cella*) like the one mentioned in the inscription from Langres was restored in the Joanneum Museum in Graz. (Fig. 4) It demonstrates very well the complaint voiced by Clement of Alexandria:[39]

> Tombs are objects of reverence in just the same way as temples are: in fact, pyramids, mausoleums and labyrinths are as it were temples (*naoi*) of dead men, just as the temples are tombs of the gods.

In this very nice turn of phrases, Clement manages to criticize the cult of the dead and the pagan gods at the same time. If men set up shrines (i.e., tombs) to dead men, they tacitly admit that the gods venerated in shrines (i.e., temples) are just as dead.

This connection between the tomb built by a family and a temple dedicated to a god is the key to understanding what Paul is talking about in 1 Cor 8–10. The confusion among exegetes has been caused by reading only the

37 Trimalchio's maudlin performance in the *Satyricon* in which he entertains his dinner guests with a description of his tomb comes immediately to mind. Petronius did not have to do much to turn reality into satire, as recent authors have also discovered, e.g., Jessica Mitford, *The American Way of Death* (New York: Simon and Schuster, 1963) and Evelyn Waugh, *The Loved One* (Boston: Little, Brown, 1948).

38 W. F. Jashemski, *The Gardens of Pompeii* (New Rochelle, N.Y.: Caratzas Bros., 1979): 141–53.

39 *Prot.* IV, 44 (Loeb ed. p. 112; *PG* 8.141). Cf. Pausanius 2.25.7 where a pyramid was erected as a *mnēma* for fallen warriors.

Fig. 4 Reconstructed Roman Grave Chapel. Graz, Austria, Landesmuseum Joanneum. (Schober, A., *Die Römischen Grabsteine von Noricum und Pannonien* [Wien, 1923]: 195, fig. 203)

second meaning, shrine as temple of a pagan god, and ignoring the first, shrine as tomb. Gentile Corinthians would consider their dead ancestors to be among the gods and therefore the tombs were properly called temples and could be the place where an image ("idol") might be enshrined.[40] The food brought to the shrine for the well-being of the ancestral gods and the gratification of the living would be the "offerings for the images," *eidōlothuton*.[41]

Two passages in the patristic literature support this interpretation of *eidōlothuton*. Origen and Tertullian use the term in apologetic contexts and each finds it necessary to explain the meaning of the word to his respective audience, the one Greek-, the other Latin-speaking. Whereas Paul was dealing with the question of eating under varying social circumstances, the apologists were attempting to interpret a word which had become a technical term among Christians in the Roman world.

In his criticism of Christianity Celsus asserted that Christians should eat *hierothuton*, "holy sacrifices," without feeling that they were in any way compromising their faith.

> God is the god of all alike; He is good, He stands in need of nothing, and He is without jealousy. What, then, is there to hinder those who are most devoted to His service from taking part in public feasts? . . . If these idols are nothing, what harm will there be in taking part in the feast? On the other hand, if they are demons, it is certain that they too are God's creatures, and that we must believe in them, sacrifice to them according to the laws, and pray to them that they may be propitious.[42]

It is usually assumed that what these people were eating was "food offered to idols," based in part on what Origen says in response, but probably also based on the use of *hierothuton* in 1 Cor 10:28, where commentators are virtually unanimous in taking *hierothuton* to be the "accepted Greek usage" for the "Jewish [-Christian] pejorative word" *eidōlothuton*.

But if *hierothuton* was a sacrifice or food offering that

40 "Around all matters of religion (*eusebeias*) and theology (*theōn*), there rages violent controversy. For while the majority declare that gods exist, some deny their existence . . . . And of those who maintain the existence of gods, some believe in the ancestral gods (*tous patrious nomizousi theous*), others in such as are constructed in the Dogmatic systems—as Aristotle asserted that God is incorporeal and 'the limit of heaven' the Stoics . . . ." Sextus Empiricus, *Outlines of Pyrrhonism* III, 218 (Loeb ed. I, 470–73).

41 Tyndale translated it "thinges offred unto ymages," which provoked Thomas More to accuse Tyndale of a deliberate perversion of the text. For More *images* referred to representations of Christ, the Virgin and the saints, while *idols* were "euyll ymages & deuelyshe," and if idols are images then devils are angels. *Confutation of Tyndale's Answer* 2 (New Haven and London: Yale University, 1973): 174–75. The argument continued through the sixteenth century. In 1583 William Fulke wrote *A Defense of the sincere and true translation of the holy Scriptures into the English tongue, against the manifold cavils, frivolous quarrels and impudent slanders of Gregory Martin, one of the readers of Popish divinity in the traitorous Seminary of Rheims* (Cambridge: Cambridge University, 1843; rep. New York: Johnson Reprint Corp., 1968). Fulkes insisted that *idol*, *idolater* and *idolatry* "be rather Greekish than English words; which though they be used with many Englishmen, yet they are not understood by all" as are *images, worshippers of images* and *worshipping of images* (p. 179). Martin had complained that the choice of the word *image* was maliciously done "to make the reader think that St. Paul speaketh here not only of pagan idolaters, but also of catholic Christians that reverently kneel in prayer before the cross, the holy rood, the images of our Saviour Christ and his saints" (Fulke, p. 187). The issue was resolved on the side of the "catholics" in the King James Version by retaining *idol* for *eidōlon* and using *image* to translate *eikōn*, a decision made on theological, not linguistic grounds.

42 Origen, *c. Celsus*, VII, 21.

formed part of a pagan cult (understood as a ritual performed in honor of a Olympian god or one of the lesser godlings), it is difficult to see how any Christian could rationalize a position that would allow participation in such rites. The scriptural [OT] tradition alone should have been sufficient to preclude such thoughts, not to mention Paul's outright condemnation of the practice (1 Cor 5:11).

In his response to Celsus, Origen seeks to set the record straight. Celsus may wish for his part to refer to the shared meals that some Christians eat with their pagan neighbors as *hierothuton*, "holy sacrifice." If one wishes to be proper (*alētheian*) about it, however, Origen insists that these meals should rather be called *eidōlothuton*, or better yet, *daimoniothuton*. It is our contention that what Origen is saying needs to be understood as follows: "These so-called sacred meals Celsus speaks of are really meals offered to the images of ancestors and dead relatives, which is a polite way of saying it is food for ghosts." This interpretation assumes that the word *daimōn* cannot be limited to the English meaning of "demon" or "devil," but must be taken in the sense of the Greek word, the spirit of a dead person. Origen is not, in other words, talking about Christian participation in a pagan ritual at some temple. He is rather concerned about their involvement in funeral rites and memorial meals, which in the society of his day was a far greater threat to morality than we might imagine.[43]

Tertullian clearly puts the matter of *eidōlothuton* in the context of funeral games and tombs. Participation in spectacles is inconsistent with the Christian's profession of faith, which includes a renunciation of idols. Then Tertullian picks up Paul's argument and proceeds from there:

> "Not that an idol is anything," says the Apostle, "but what they do, they do in honor of demons," who plant themselves in the consecrated images of whatever they are, dead men, or as they think, gods. So on that account, since both kinds of idols stand on the same footing (dead men and gods are one and the same thing), we abstain from both kinds of idolatry. Temples or tombs, we abominate both equally; we know neither sort of altar; we adore neither sort of image (*effigiem*), we pay no sacrifice, we pay no funeral rite (*parentum*).[44]

For Tertullian an image of a god and an image of a man (such as a portrait of a family member) are equally reprehensible and Christians should have nothing to do with either. As we have noted above, the matter of participation in the pagan cults of the gods could not have been a matter for discussion among Christians: idolatry in this sense is clearly condemned. But idolatry in the second sense, the veneration of portraits of family members, is not covered in the biblical injunctions specifically. The Roman custom of family portraits has no counterpart in Jewish culture. Roman memorial meals for the dead are similarly missing from "normative" Jewish texts. But as the rabbinic materials show, meals for the family were common at the conclusion of the funeral. The conversion of Gentiles would exacerbate the problem, since the absence of specific rules against the practice of funeral meals could be construed as permission to continue the usage. Tertullian returns to Paul for support.

> We do not eat of what is offered in sacrificial or funeral rite (*de sacrificio et parentato*), because "we cannot eat of the Lord's supper (*cenam dei*) and the supper of demons." If, then, we try to keep our gullet and belly free from defilement, how much more our nobler parts, our ears and eyes, do we guard from the pleasures of "idol sacrifice" or sacrifice to the dead (*idolothytis et necrothytis*), pleasures which are satisfied not [just] in the gut, but which spread to the Spirit itself and the Soul, whose purity much more relates to God than that of the guts.[45]

The Christian is prevented from participation in the funeral meals because such food is offered to "demons," i.e., the dead. Lest there be any question about the meaning of *idolothytis* in the minds of his North African audience, Tertullian coins a Latinized Greek synonym "*necrothytis*" whose meaning is transparent: "offerings to or for the dead." He also follows the lead of Paul in arguing that the problem with eating the memorial meals is not simply a matter of dietary scruples. The act of eating in the circumstances of funeral banquets or memorial meals involves the acknowledgment of the existence of the spirits of the dead in whose honor the food is offered. The Christian is forbidden to participate in this "idolatry" of a Roman funeral, not only because it involves the decorating of images of the deceased, but also because of the sacramental aspect of the sharing of food with the dead. The similarities and contrasts with the Lord's Supper are immediately evident, and therein lies

43 Bulwer-Lytton, *Last Days of Pompeii*, ch. VII, provides a properly titilating description in this dialogue in which Nydia warns Apaecides of the danger threatening his sister Ione at such a dinner:

> "Thou knowest the banquets of the dead, stranger—it pleases thee, perhaps, to share them—would it please thee to have thy sister a partaker? Would it please thee that Arbaces was her host?"
>
> "O gods, he dare not! Girl, if thou mockest me, tremble! I will tear thee limb from limb!"
>
> "I speak the truth; and while I speak Ione is in the halls of Arbaces—for the first time his guest. Thou knowest if there be peril in that first time!"
>
> "If this be true, what—what can be done to save her?"

44 *De spect.* 13. See J. Danielou, *The Origins of Latin Christianity* (Philadelphia: Westminster, 1977): 412–14 and J. H. Waszink, "Pompa Diaboli" in *VC* 1 (1947): 13–41.

45 Ibid.

the danger for the Christians. If the Church ritual shares bread and wine "to show the Lord's death till he comes," why would it not be proper for Christians to share food and drink with their neighbors in honor of mutual friends who have died? The spread of Christianity entailed a change in the social life of the Empire and nowhere are social customs more conservative than with those that relate to funerals. For the neophyte Christian to abstain from attending funerals meant a radical separation from the social network within which he lived. As Williams puts it:

> The quietest and nicest Christians tactfully stepped away on such occasions; if they came they did not inquire about "meats offered to idols"; they did not parade their consciences. But since they did not, in the last resort, wish to pour out libations to the household gods of their friends, they were all driven gradually—or suddenly—to drop dinner-parties. To any ordinary Roman it was all very odd and rather beastly.[46]

46 C. Williams, *Descent of the Dove* (New York: Living Age Books, 1956): 19. William's remarks are addressed to the matter of the Genius of the Emperor and the household gods, but it must be remembered that the household gods included the deceased members of the family.

THE DEATH OF ABŪ ṬĀLIB

FRED MCGRAW DONNER

I

The death of the Prophet Muḥammad's uncle, Abū Ṭālib, in ca. A.D. 620 became the subject of considerable controversy among the early purveyors of historical and religious traditions in the Islamic world. On the one hand, as the chief of the clan of Hāshim among the Quraysh, Abū Ṭālib had defended Muḥammad and his earliest followers against the attacks of the rest of the Quraysh, who were outraged by Muḥammad's new religious ideas, and had thereby done signal service in the cause of Islam at a critical time in its early history. On the other hand, it seems to have been generally accepted that Abū Ṭālib himself never embraced Islam, but died a pagan, which implied that he would, like all pagans, be consigned on judgment day to everlasting punishment in the fires of hell.

The irony of Abū Ṭālib's apparent fate—that this stalwart defender of Muḥammad and of Islam in its earliest, most vulnerable days, should nonetheless suffer the extreme penalty after death—is not without a certain intrinsic interest, and may well have piqued the curiosity of the justice-conscious early Islamic community for that reason alone. But the main reason for the debate over Abū Ṭālib's death and fate was that they became matters of some importance in the religious and political polemic that developed between the Abbasids and the Shia after the Abbasids' accession to power in A.H. 132 / A.D. 749.[1]

In seizing power, the Abbasids had capitalized on widespread opposition to the ruling Umayyad dynasty, which they overthrew and virtually annihilated; and they justified their actions not only on the grounds that the Umayyads had been godless and oppressive rulers, but also on the principle that they—the Abbasids—were more closely related to the Prophet than the Umayyads were. The Abbasids, after all, belonged to the B. Hāshim, the Prophet's clan, whereas the B. Umayya constituted a different clan of the Quraysh altogether. It was therefore possible for the Abbasids to present one of their number as being the very one intended by the phrase *al-riḍā min āli Muḥammad*, "the one pleasing [to God] from the family of Muḥammad," in whose ambiguous name the revolution against the Umayyads had been raised.

The Shia posed a problem for the Abbasids, however. Much of the wave of opposition to the Umayyads that the Abbasids had succeeded in riding to power had been generated by the Shia; and the ʿAlids and other descendants of Abū Ṭālib, whose claims to leadership the Shia supported, had, by their peculiar combination of religious zeal and political miscalculation, managed to supply a goodly number of martyrs to the struggle against the Umayyads. At the same time, prominent members of the Abbasid house had been on rather cozy terms with the Umayyads during many of these decades of strife, and had only joined the opposition at a late date. In short, the descendants of Abū Ṭālib had far more impressive martyrological and "revolutionary" credentials than did the Abbasids. The descendants of Abū Ṭālib, furthermore, were every bit as closely related to Muḥammad as were the descendants of al-ʿAbbās, both men having been paternal uncles of the Prophet (see Figure 1). It was therefore fruitless for the Abbasids merely to raise the fact of their ancestry and relationship to Muḥammad when grappling with the ideological challenge posed by the Ṭālibids. They also had to find other, more effective, arguments to counter the Shiite claim that the ʿAlids were more entitled to rule than others in the B. Hāshim because ʿAlī b. Abī Ṭālib had been on such intimate terms with the Prophet, had been one of the earliest converts to Islam, had been favored with the hand of the Prophet's daughter Fāṭima in marriage, and so on—whereas al-ʿAbbās had only embraced Islam late, probably in the year before the conquest of Mecca by Muḥammad in A.H. 8/A.D. 630.

The ideological threat that the Ṭālibids, and especially the ʿAlids, represented must thus have been perfectly clear to the Abbasids from the moment of their accession, and it was certainly underscored in their minds by the outbreak of a number of Shiite rebellions in the opening decades of their rule. It was made yet more pointed by the elaboration of a systematic Shiite doctrine of the imamate, with its assertion of a single line of divinely guided spiritual leaders, or imams, descended from ʿAlī b. Abī Ṭālib and his wife Fāṭima. This theory, drawing on older Gnostic ideas of charismatic leadership, appears to have taken full form in the intellectual circle surrounding Jaʿfar "al-Ṣādiq" b. Muḥammad b. ʿAlī b. al-Ḥusayn b. ʿAlī b. Abī Ṭālib (d. A.H. 148/A.D. 765), who became the sixth imam in the series.[2] For the Abbasids, such a

1 For an earlier study of this theme, see Theodor Nöldeke, "Zur tendenziösen Gestaltung der Urgeschichte des Islam's," *ZDMG* 52 (1898): 27–28. The following abbreviations have been employed in these pages to render the technical terms in *isnāds*: —s— = *samiʿtu ʿan*; —h— = *ḥaddatha-nī*, *ḥaddatha-nā*; < = *ʿan*.

2 On the development of the Shiite theory of the imamate,

concept was especially dangerous because its seductive logic deprived them of any right to rule at all, since according to it the imamate had been transferred by explicit designation (*naṣṣ*) from the Prophet to ᶜAlī and then on to specific descendants of ᶜAlī, who were alone imbued with the divine guidance and special knowledge that was requisite to rule the Islamic community legitimately and justly.

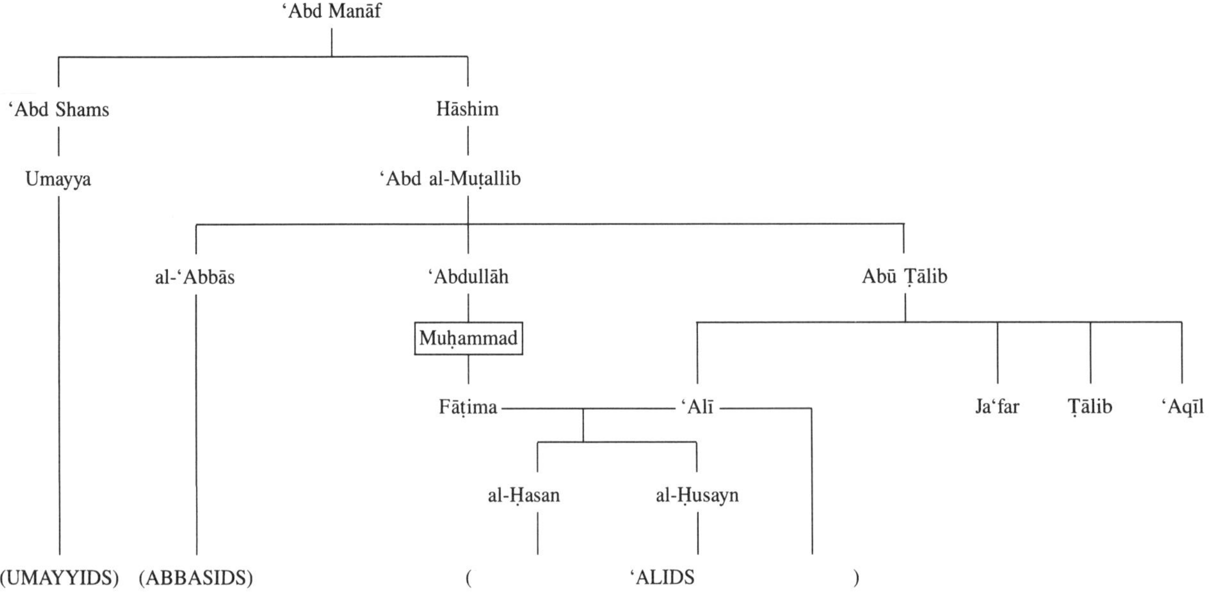

II

One line of attack pursued by the Abbasids or their apologists in their efforts to undermine the claims raised by the Shia was to emphasize the fact that Abū Ṭālib had died a pagan, thus placing him in a bad light in comparison with their own ancestor al-ᶜAbbās. They tried, in short, by discrediting Abū Ṭālib to discredit the whole lot of his descendants. This policy was evidently already in place by A.H. 145/A.D. 762, for during the rebellion of Muḥammad b. ᶜAbdullāh b. al-Ḥasan in Medina in that year the caliph al-Manṣūr wrote to the rebel, "The Apostle was sent [by God], and he had four paternal uncles. Two believed in him, one of whom was my father [i.e., ancestor], and two refused to believe in him, one of whom was your father."[3] Traditions such as the following one, transmitted by the historian al-Madāʾinī (d. A.H. 225/A.D. 840), underscored Abū Ṭālib's failure to become a Muslim: one of two men comparing pious wishes says, "I wish that Abū Ṭālib had embraced Islam, for the Apostle of God would have been delighted at that. But he was an unbeliever."[4] Such accounts, which stressed the Prophet's disappointment with his uncle, were doubtless sought out and widely circulated by the Abbasids and their backers.[5]

On the other hand, there circulated some traditions that attempted to demonstrate that Abū Ṭālib had inwardly accepted Islam, and that Muḥammad had recognized this fact. In some accounts, for example, Abū Ṭālib relates that Muḥammad had explained his mission to him. God had instructed him, he was told, to treat his relatives kindly, to worship God alone, and not to worship anything beside Him—"and," Abū Ṭālib concludes, "Muḥammad was veracious and trustworthy (*ṣadūq amīn*)."[6] According to another tradition, when Abū Ṭālib fell ill, Muḥammad fed him a bunch of grapes from his

see *Encyclopaedia of Islam*, 2nd edition, "Hishām b. al-Ḥakam" (W. Madelung); also Marshall G. S. Hodgson, "How did the Early Shīᶜa become Sectarian?" *JAOS* 75 (1955): 1–13.

3 Ibn Ḥajar al-ᶜAsqalānī, *al-Iṣāba fī tamyīz al-ṣaḥāba* (4 vols.; Cairo, A.H. 1328): 4.118 (hereinafter cited as *Iṣāba*).

4 Ibn Qutayba, *ᶜUyūn al-akhbār* (4 vols.; Cairo, 1963): 1.263.

5 We should note, however, that the account itself—even though serving a polemical purpose—may be old; successful polemic requires not so much the fabrication of new material, as the careful selection (and repression) of existing material to convey the desired message.

6 *Iṣāba* 4.116 middle (Isḥāq b. ᶜĪsā al-Hāshimī < his father—s—al-Muhājir, *mawlā* of B. Nufayl—s—Abū Rāfiᶜ—s—Abū Ṭālib); *Iṣāba* 4.118–19 Aḥmad b. al-Ḥasan "Dubays"—h—Muḥammad b. Ismāᶜīl b. Ibrāhīm al-ᶜAlawī—h—uncle of Abū l-Ḥusayn b. Muḥammad—his father Mūsā b. Jaᶜfar < his father < ᶜAlī b. al-Ḥusayn < al-Ḥusayn b. ᶜAlī; *Iṣāba* 4.119 (. . . Jaᶜfar b. ᶜAbd al-Wāḥad al-qāss—q—Muḥammad b. ᶜAbbād < Isḥāq b. ᶜĪsā < Muhājir, *mawlā* of B. Nawfal—s—Abū Rāfiᶜ—s—Abū Ṭālib).

garden,[7] which Abū Bakr later said God had forbidden to unbelievers.[8] The implication of such traditions is clearly that Abū Ṭālib—whatever his outward actions—had privately accepted the correctness of Muḥammad's teachings, and that Muḥammad had recognized his inner conversion.

Another way of salvaging Abū Ṭālib's reputation was to emphasize his positive service to Islam. One of the milder of such traditions, attributed to the historian al-Wāqidī (d. A.H. 207 / A.D. 843), focuses on how Abū Ṭālib and the clans of Hāshim and al-Muṭallib, under his leadership, protected Muḥammad from persecution by the rest of Quraysh. When the Quraysh came to see that they could not coerce Abū Ṭālib into handing Muḥammad over to them, they ended their boycott of the two clans after three years. The account then notes that the boycott ended in the tenth year of Muḥammad's prophetic career, and was followed shortly thereafter by Abū Ṭālib's death. But no further remarks on Abū Ṭālib's death, except for some differing opinions on dating it, are provided.[9]

Such efforts to stress Abū Ṭālib's meritorious past were counter-balanced by other traditions in circulation. According to one, traced in its *isnād* back to ᶜAlī himself, Abū Ṭālib, upon learning of ᶜAlī's conversion to Islam, turned his son out with the brusque command, "Go live with your cousin" (scil. Muḥammad).[10] The effect, of course, was to call into question the notion that Abū Ṭālib had been favorably disposed to Islam at all. Far more numerous, however, were accounts that demonstrated that Abū Ṭālib was destined to suffer perdition regardless of his service in defending Muḥammad and the first Muslims. The many *ḥadīth*s in this category generally relate to the question of Muḥammad's attempts to intercede for his uncle by praying for him after his death. A typical representative from this group of accounts goes as follows: people used to say that Abū Ṭālib had supported Muḥammad and aided him, so how did the Prophet help him? Muḥammad, learning of this, replied, "God favored him [in this way]; he used to be in the depths of hell, but He took him out for my sake and placed him in a shallow bank of fire; he has two sandals of fire, which cause his brains to boil."[11] Another common variant has Muḥammad declare, "Perhaps my intercession will help [Abū Ṭālib] on judgment day and make for him a shoal of fire reaching [only] to his heels, from which his brains will boil."[12] Such traditions could leave little doubt about Abū Ṭālib's ultimate fate.

The question of Abū Ṭālib's fate was also debated within the context of accounts of his burial. There exists a sizeable number of traditions describing how Muḥammad ordered ᶜAlī to wind and bury his father's corpse, but the details vary considerably, and with them the tone and implications of the accounts. In the simplest of them, the Prophet directs ᶜAlī to wind and bury the body, but ᶜAlī objects that his father had died a polytheist. Muḥammad therefore repeats his instructions and ᶜAlī, seeing his insistence, then complies.[13] Like other accounts examined above, this one appears to suggest that Abū Ṭālib was recognized by Muḥammad as having been a Muslim, even though his conversion was not common knowledge—even his own son is shown to be ignorant of his "inner" conversion. Indeed, in one variant, ᶜAlī informs Muḥammad of his father's death by announcing, "Your uncle, the erring old man, has died."[14] His strongly disapproving tone makes the contrast between his own expectations and Muḥammad's treatment of Abū Ṭālib's corpse much more dramatic, and highlights the Prophet's favorable treatment of his uncle.

Indeed, not even Abū Ṭālib's wife, Fāṭima bint Asad b. Hāshim, could escape being drawn—posthumously—into the debate over Abū Ṭālib's death. All accounts agree that she embraced Islam, and this fact alone may have been sufficient in some circles to cast a favorable reflection on her son, ᶜAlī, and the later religious and political claims of the ᶜAlids. But, once again, the details provided in these accounts often bolster a certain tendentious viewpoint. According to one account, for example, the Prophet wound Fāṭima's corpse in his own shirt, and then lay down beside her in her grave before she was buried. His companions asked him about this, as they had never seen him do so for anyone else; to which Muḥammad replied, "No one after Abū Ṭālib was more devoted to me than she was. I dressed her in my shirt that she might be clothed in the vestments of paradise, and I lay down with her so that [lying in the grave] might be easier for her."[15] In its roundabout way, the tradition thus emphasizes Abū Ṭālib's support for Muḥammad, and

7 *unqūd min jannati-hi*. The other meaning of *al-janna*, "paradise," is clearly hinted at in the account.

8 al-Balādhurī, *Ansāb al-ashrāf* (ed. Muḥammad Bāqir al-Maḥmūdī; Beirut, 1974): 34 (h—ᶜAmr b. Muḥammad—h—Abū Muᶜāwiya < al-Aᶜmash < Abū Ṣāliḥ). (Hereinafter cited as *Ansāb*.) Cf. *Iṣāba* 4.116 top.

9 al-Balādhurī, *Ansāb al-ashrāf* 1 (ed. Muḥammad Ḥamīdullāh; Cairo, 1959): 236 (account no. 560, from al-Wāqidī).

10 *Iṣāba* 4.116 (ᶜAbdullāh b. Ḍamīra < his father < ᶜAlī).

11 *Ansāb* (Maḥmūdī): 29, 30.

12 Aḥmad b. Ḥanbal, *Musnad* (6 vols.; Cairo, A.H. 1313): 3.8–9, 50, 55; cf. also *Iṣāba* 4.119; *Musnad* 1.206, 207, 210; al-Bukhārī, *Ṣaḥīḥ* (2 vols.; Cairo, A.H. 1309): 2.209; Ibn ᶜAbd Rabbihi, *al-ᶜIqd al-farīd* (8 vols. in 4; Cairo, 1953): 6.159.

13 Aḥmad b. Ḥanbal, *Musnad* 1.97 (. . . Muḥammad b. Jaᶜfar—h—Shuᶜba Abū Isḥāq—s—Nājiya b. Kaᶜb—h—ᶜAlī); cf. 1.103, 129–30, 131.

14 Aḥmad Ibn Ḥanbal, *Musnad* 1.131.

15 *innahu lam yakun aḥadun baᶜda Abī Ṭālibin abirra bī minhā*. Abū l-Faraj al-Iṣfahānī, *Maqātil al-Ṭālibiyīn* (ed. Aḥmad Ṣaqr; Cairo, 1949): 8–9 (al-ᶜAbbās b. ᶜAlī b. al-ᶜAbbās al-Nasāʾī—h—ᶜAbdullāh b. Muḥammad b. Ayyūb—h—al-Ḥasan b. Bishr—h—Saᶜdān b. al-Walīd Bayyāᶜ al-Sāburī < ᶜAṭāʾ < Ibn ᶜAbbās). Cf. the briefer account in *Ansāb* (Maḥmūdī): 35.

Muḥammad's fondness for his deceased uncle. In another account, on the other hand, Muḥammad approached Fāṭima bint Asad and asked her to embrace Islam. Fāṭima answered, "I know that you are true and good, but I would not like to die except in the religion of your uncle." Muḥammad replied, "Oh mother, I fear [hell-] fire for you." Fāṭima held her ground, however, so the Prophet left, saying "Verily, God's command (*ʾamr*) is a fate decreed." Only later, in her final illness, did Fāṭima bint Asad embrace Islam, and after her death the Apostle wrapped her in his shirt.[16] In contrast to the preceding account, this one clearly emphasizes Abū Ṭālib's death as a pagan, and makes it clear that Muḥammad assumed him to be in hellfire.

Some of those who desired to defend Abū Ṭālib's reputation went so far as to foster the notion that not only Abū Ṭālib, but also his ancestors, had been truly Muslims. One interesting account of this kind can be seen as a response to a series of traditions, to be examined below,[17] that emphasized that Abū Ṭālib had died "in the religion of ʿAbd al-Muṭallib," i.e., a pagan. According to this account, ʿAlī said that Abū Ṭālib had followed ʿAbd al-Muṭallib in all his affairs, and died still following his religion. Abū Ṭālib had requested ʿAlī to bury him in ʿAbd al-Muṭallib's grave, and the Prophet, informed of this, acquiesced and instructed ʿAlī to wash and wind the body properly before burial. After ʿAlī had done so, he opened ʿAbd al-Muṭallib's grave, and found his body facing the *qibla*. The narrator notes that neither ʿAlī nor any of his ancestors worshipped anything but God up to their deaths.[18] By thus making ʿAbd al-Muṭallib and his forebears into believers, the account clearly aims to dispel any misgivings about Abū Ṭālib's death "in the religion of ʿAbd al-Muṭallib."

Even such exercises in historical reinterpretation must seem modest in comparison with the efforts of some of the ideological extremists among the Shia; for in such circles the notion of divine incarnation and the transmigration of the spirit were applied to ʿAlī and his family—ancestors as well as descendants—so as to transcend entirely the "petty" question of whether or not Abū Ṭālib had made an open confession of his belief in God before dying. According to one sect, which followed the extremist leader Abū l-Khaṭṭāb Muḥammad b. Abī Zaynab al-Asadī (d. ca. A.D. 755 or 762),[19] God was a light that entered the bodies of the various designated trustees (*awṣiyāʾ*) and occupied them. The light that was God had been in ʿAbd al-Muṭallib, and then went to Abū Ṭālib, who became God and sent Muḥammad as his apostle; when Abū Ṭālib died, the spirit (*rūḥ*) went on to settle in Muḥammad, who became God, and ʿAlī became his apostle; and so on down to Jaʿfar al-Ṣādiq and from him to Abū l-Khaṭṭāb himself.[20] Such views were, of course, shared only by a small number even among the Shia; for most, the question of Abū Ṭālib's death was doubtless still one to be understood in more straightforward terms.

The Qurʾān was also brought into the service of those who desired to elucidate Abū Ṭālib's fate, as certain verses were said to have been revealed in connection with him. One such verse was *sūra* 6 (*al-Anʿām*) v 26, "And they forbid [others] from it, and they keep away from it; and they ruin none but their own souls while they perceive not,"[21] which was considered by some to refer to the efforts of Quraysh to prevent Abū Ṭālib from embracing Islam on his deathbed (on which see the discussion below). The impact of the verse, taken in this context, is implicitly to absolve Abū Ṭālib of his failure to convert, while simultaneously putting full blame—and the promise of punishment—on those members of Quraysh who intimidated him.

Many of the Qurʾānic references said to relate to Abū Ṭālib, however, deal with the question of Muḥammad's intercession for him, and tend to work to his detriment rather than in his favor like the preceding example. A case in point is an account that states that the Prophet, after Abū Ṭālib's death, used to pray to God to forgive him until Qurʾān 9 (*al-Barāʾa*) v. 113 was revealed: "It is not for the Prophet and those who believe to ask forgiveness for the polytheists, even though they should be near relatives, after it has become clear to them that they are companions of the flaming fire." Certainly linking Abū Ṭālib to this particular verse made the implication about his fate vividly clear. Only somewhat less compromising to his reputation, perhaps, is the linkage of Abū Ṭālib to the revelation of Qurʾān 28 (*al-Qaṣaṣ*) v 56: "Surely thou canst not guide whom thou lovest, but Allāh guides whom He pleases; and He knows best those who walk aright."[22] Other verses of the Qurʾān, too, could sometimes be used very effectively by authors who apparently wished to undercut Abū Ṭālib's reputation. Ibn Qutayba, in his *ʿUyūn al-akhbār*, for instance, mentions (with no *isnād*) that Muḥammad tried to get Abū Ṭālib to make on his deathbed the basic

16 *Ansāb* (Maḥmūdī): 35–36.

17 See section III below, nos. 3, 5, 6, 7.

18 *Iṣāba* 4.118 (. . . Abū Bishr al-Mutaqaddim < Abū Burda al-Sulamī < al-Ḥasan b. Māshāʾallāh < his father < ʿAlī b. Muḥammad b. Mutīm—s—his father—s—ʿAlī).

19 On Abū l-Khaṭṭāb, see *Encyclopaedia of Islam*, 2nd edition, "Abū l-Khaṭṭāb al-Asadī" (B. Lewis).

20 al-Nawbakhtī, *Firaq al-shīʿa* (ed. Hellmut Ritter; Istanbul, 1931 = *Bibliotheca Islamica* 4): 39–41. On the idea of transmigration and God's spirit as light, see U. Rubin, "Pre-existence and light. Aspects of the concept of Nūr Muḥammad," *Israel Oriental Studies* 5 (1975): 62–119.

21 E.g., *Ansāb* (Maḥmūdī): 26 (Ibn Saʿd < al-Wāqidī < Sufyān al-Thawrī < Ḥabīb b. Abī Thābit < Yaḥyā b. Juʿda < Ibn ʿAbbās). In this and following Qurʾānic passages, I follow the translation of Muḥammad ʿAlī (5th edition, Lahore, 1963).

22 E.g., *Ansāb* (Maḥmūdī): 27–28 (Ibn Saʿd < al-Wāqidī < Sufyān al-Thawrī < Yazīd b. Abī Yazīd < ʿAbdullāh b. al-Ḥārith b. Nawfal).

statement of belief in one God, and follows it with a resounding reference to Qur᾽ān 4 (*al-Nisā᾽*), v 18: "And repentance is not for those who go on doing evil deeds, until when death comes to one of them, he says: Now I repent; nor (for) those who die while they are disbelievers. For such We have prepared a painful chatisement."[23]

III

The most vexing problem for the historian, of course, is to establish what actually happened at Abū Ṭālib's death, a task that is complicated by the polemical content of many accounts. The accounts described in the preceding section all display a fairly obvious polemical utility (even if some of them may not, originally, have been recorded or transmitted with polemical intent). Other accounts, of a polemically "neutral" character, also existed, of course, such as one that notes simply that Abū Ṭālib died at age eighty, ten years after Muḥammad's teaching began, and was buried in the cemetery at al-Ḥajūn.[24] But by far the most complex accounts dealing with the question of Abū Ṭālib's fate are those that purport to describe the actual circumstances surrounding Abū Ṭālib's death. Many of them are what can be called *synthetic accounts*, that is, composite accounts constructed from a number of shorter elements that originally existed as independent "simple" accounts. In some cases, the underlying components out of which a synthetic account was built are still extant; more frequently, they must be retrieved by a process of "deconstructing" the synthetic accounts of which they now form a part, which can only be successfully done by comparison of similar accounts. Ideally, such a process will enable the investigator to determine which parts of a synthetic account represent older, perhaps historically reliable, material, which parts are somewhat later or may have obvious polemical intent, and which parts represent idiosyncratic formulations or elaborations introduced by the transmitter who constructed the synthetic account. In practice, of course, the analysis of synthetic traditions is complicated by factors such as the incomplete preservation of accounts on a certain theme or the fact that some such traditions appear to be constructed out of elements that themselves represent earlier, less extensive, attempts to synthesize existing material. Despite these shortcomings, however, the method does enable us to delve a bit more deeply into these accounts in such a way as to help us distinguish earlier from later material.

23 Ibn Qutayba, *ᶜUyūn al-akhbār* (4 vols.; Cairo: Wizārat al-thaqāfa wa-l-irshād al-qawmī, 1963): 1.6. Ibn Qutayba further reinforces this negative image of Abū Ṭālib by other means elsewhere in his work; cf. 2.49 top.

24 E.g., *Ansāb* (Maḥmūdī): 29 (*qālū*). On al-Ḥajūn, see Yāqūt, *Muᶜjam al-buldān*, s.v.; it was a mountain above Mecca where the cemeteries of its inhabitants were.

A close comparison of the accounts of Abū Ṭālib's death will enable us to isolate some of the earlier components that went into these synthetic accounts. As the analysis below of fourteen synthetic traditions will show, the most important component accounts appear to have been the following, which we list here briefly for convenience of reference:

a Statement locating events at Abū Ṭālib's deathbed, or notice of his death
b Description of a gathering of leaders of Quraysh at Abū Ṭālib's house to discuss the question of Muḥammad's activities
c Muḥammad requests Abū Ṭālib to make the statement "There is no God but God," but Abū Ṭālib refuses because Quraysh would mock him
d Muḥammad requests Abū Ṭālib to make the statement "There is no God but God," but Abū Ṭālib is dissuaded by Abū Jahl and ᶜAbdullāh b. Abī Umayya
e Muḥammad asks the Quraysh to make the statement "There is no God but God," saying that it would give them dominion over Arabs and non-Arabs; Quraysh reply with paraphrase of Qur᾽ān 38, vv 1–8
f Muḥammad asks forgiveness for Abū Ṭālib until God revealed Qur᾽ān 9, v 113
g Gloss to Qur᾽ān 28 v 56, barring intercession for unbelievers
h Gloss to Qur᾽ān 6 v 26, "They forbid others from it. . . ."

Further analysis of the details of each of these component elements will follow the analysis of synthetic traditions, to which we now turn.

* * *

1. h–Muḥammad b. Bashshār—h—Yaḥyā b. Saᶜīd < Yazīd b. Kaysān—h—Abū Ḥāzim al-Ashjaᶜī < Abū Hurayra (al-Tirmidhī, *Ṣaḥīḥ* [13 vols.; Cairo: Maṭbaᶜat al-Ṣāwī]: 12.63 = commentary to Qur᾽ān 28: 56).

This account opens with a description of Muḥammad's effort to convert Abū Ṭālib. Abū Ṭālib refuses because he fears that Quraysh would revile him. It concludes with the remark that God revealed Qur᾽ān 28, v 56, "Surely thou canst not guide whom thou lovest, but Allāh guides whom he pleases. . . ." It is noteworthy that there is nothing that places this account explicitly in the context of Abū Ṭālib's death. The account appears to be a composite of elements c and g.

2. h—Bakr b. al-Haytham—h—Hishām b. Yūsuf < Maᶜmar < al-Zuhrī < Saᶜīd b. al-Musayyib (Bal. *Ansāb* [ed. Maḥmūdī; Beirut: al-Mu᾽assasa al-᾽aᶜlamī, 1974]: 25–26).

During Abū Ṭālib's final illness, Muḥammad tries to get Abū Ṭālib to declare his belief in God, but he refuses out of fear that the Quraysh would mock him after his death, saying he had embraced Islam out of fear of death after having repudiated it in good health. Abū Ṭālib then calls together the B. Hāshim and orders them to follow the Prophet and to assist him and defend him from injury. The account then notes that Qur᾽ān 6, v 26 was sent down concerning Abū Ṭālib: "And they forbid [others] from it. . . ." The Prophet, after Abū Ṭālib's death, asks God's forgiveness for him until Qurʾān 9 v 113 was revealed, barring intercession.

The basic components of this account are elements a, c, f, and h, which set the context at Abū Ṭālib's death, describe one variant of the "*shahāda* episode," and provide the background explanations for the two Qurʾānic verses. However, the account also includes other information, which does not occur in other accounts about Abū Ṭālib's death, notably Abū Ṭālib's exhortation to the B. Hāshim to support and aid Muḥammad. Whether this material represents another early account that has not survived elsewhere, or is an elaboration introduced by the collator who made up the synthesis, cannot be ascertained. It is noteworthy, however, that this material, which is favorable to Abū Ṭālib in that it strengthens his image as defender of the Prophet and Islam, occurs in the only synthetic account where Qurʾān 6 v 26—which is also favorable to Abū Ṭālib—is mentioned. It is therefore possible, though far from certain, that these two pieces of material made up another original early account.

3. no *isnād* (Bal. *Ansāb* [ed. Maḥmūdī]: 24).

This interesting account begins with the observation that Abū Ṭālib agreed to defend Muḥammad until his death. When the end came, Muḥammad attempted to get his uncle to state the *shahāda*, but Abū Ṭālib replied, "O nephew, I know you say only the truth, but I would hate to contravene the religion of ʿAbd al-Muṭallib, and [would hate] for the women of Quraysh to say that I was afraid at the time of death and [therefore] broke with his practice," so he died a pagan. ʿAlī was informed of his father's death, but hesitated to bury him because he had been an unbeliever. The account concludes with Muḥammad instructing ʿAlī to bury him and perform a major ablution, noting that when Muḥammad watched Abū Ṭālib's funeral he said, "I have treated you, as a relative, with kindness" (*waṣaltu-ka al-raḥim*).

In addition to the elements a and c, this account includes considerable material derived from accounts usually separate from those describing Abū Ṭālib's death—notably information about Abū Ṭālib's burial and details drawn from accounts attempting to verify Abū Ṭālib's recognition of Muḥammad's and Islam's virtues. These accounts have been noted in the preceding pages; in particular, the opening observation that Abū Ṭālib had vowed to defend Muḥammad as long as he lived, his remark that he knew Muḥammad always to speak the truth, and Muḥammad's comment *waṣaltu-ka al-raḥim* can be seen to derive from them. Such information, although sometimes occurring independently as we have seen, is not linked to the "deathbed" context in any other account examined here.

4. ak—al-Wāqidī—h—Maʿmar b. Rāshid < al-Zuhrī < Saʿīd b. al-Musayyib < his father (Ibn Saʿd, *Ṭabaqāt* [9 vols.; ed. E. Sachau et al., Leiden : E. J. Brill, 1917–1940]: 1 / 1.77–78).

In this account the Prophet comes to Abū Ṭālib during his last illness, finding Abū Jahl and ʿAbdullāh b. Abī Umayya already with him. The Prophet asks his uncle to say "There is no God but God," but Abū Jahl and Ibn Abī Umayya ask Abū Ṭālib whether he had taken a dislike to the religion (*milla*) of ʿAbd al-Muṭallib, and the parties keep talking thus—Muḥammad urging Abū Ṭālib to make the *shahāda*, the two others pressing him about the religion of ʿAbd al-Muṭallib—until Abū Ṭālib utters as his last words that he remained in the religion of ʿAbd al-Muṭallib, and then dies. The Prophet declares that he would ask God's forgiveness for his uncle and did so until Qurʾān 9, v 113 was revealed. This account is a composite of elements a, d, and f.

5. h—Maḥmūd—h—ʿAbd al-Razzāq—ak—Maʿmar b. Rāshid < al-Zuhrī < Saʿīd b. al-Musayyib < his father (al-Bukhārī, *al-Ṣaḥīḥ* [Cairo, A.H. 1309]: 2.209; Ibn Ḥajar al-ʿAsqalānī, *al-Iṣāba fī tamyīz al-saḥāba* [4 vols.; Cairo: Maṭbaʿat al-saʿāda, A.H. 1328]: 4.116–17).

This account is virtually identical to the preceding one, except that the phrasing is slightly condensed in a few places. In addition, it ends with a revelation of both Qurʾān 9, v 113, and 28, v 56. It thus appears to be a composite of a, d, f, and g—perhaps formed by combining g with account no. 4 in a second phase of synthesis. Comparison of the *isnāds* of the two accounts indicates that the g material must have been added by ʿAbd al-Razzāq b. Hammām al-Ḥimyarī (d. A.H. 211 / A.D. 827) or by one of the later transmitters in the chain, in any case, not before the last third of the second / eighth century.

6. h—ʿAbdullāh—h—Ubayy—h—ʿAbd al-Razzāq—h—Maʿmar b. Rāshid < al-Zuhrī < Saʿīd b. al-Musayyib < his father (Aḥmad b. Ḥanbal, *Musnad* [6 vols.; Cairo, A.H. 1313]: 5.433).

Virtually identical to preceding account.

7. h—Ibn Saʿd < al-Wāqidī < Maʿmar b. Rāshid < al-Zuhrī < Saʿīd b. al-Musayyib < his father (Bal. *Ansāb* [ed. Maḥmūdī]: 35).

This account is identical to accounts 4–6 above from its beginning up to the point at which Abū Jahl and ʿAbdullāh b. Abī Umayya ask Abū Ṭālib if he had taken a dislike to the religion (here *dīn*) of ʿAbd al-Muṭallib. The account then ends by stating that Abū Ṭālib said nothing in reply to this question. No mention is made of Qurʾān 9 v 113 or 28 v 56.

Since the *isnāds* for all these accounts (4–7) share the same early links, we are faced with two possibilities for explaining the discrepancies among them; either the longer versions (accounts 4–6) represent the older form(s) of the account, from which no. 7 was derived by dropping the ending from the older account (including the Qurʾānic references) and adding the comment that Abū Ṭālib died without saying anything, or account no. 7 is the older version, from which the longer version (account

4–6) was formed changing Abū Ṭālib's words of response and adding the Qurʾānic glosses.

8. h—Maḥmūd b. Ghaylān and ʿAbd b. Ḥumayd al-Maʿnī—h—Abū Aḥmad—h—Sufyān < al-Aʿmash < Yaḥyā b. ʿUmāra < Saʿīd b. Jubayr < Ibn ʿAbbās (al-Tirmidhī, *Ṣaḥīḥ* [13 vols.; Cairo, 1931–1934]: 12.109–10; Aḥmad ibn Ḥanbal, *Musnad*, [see no. 6]: 1.227–28).

According to this account, a group of Quraysh came to Abū Ṭālib after he fell ill, and Muḥammad arrived while the Quraysh chiefs were there. Abū Jahl stood up as if to block the Prophet from nearing Abū Ṭālib, and complained to the latter about Muḥammad's activities, so Abū Ṭālib asked Muḥammad what he wanted of his tribe. Muḥammad replied, "I want them [to say] one word, by which the bedouin (*al-ʿarab*) will be subject to them and the non-Arabs (*al-ʿajam*) will offer tribute (*jizya*)." When they asked what that word might be, Muḥammad told them "There is no God but God." The Quraysh responded, "One God? We never heard of this in the former religion—this must be some innovation" (a paraphrase of part of Qurʾān 38, vv 1–8). The account concludes by noting that Qurʾān 38, vv 1–8 was therefore revealed about them.

The account appears to be a fusion of elements a, b, and e, dealing with the gathering of Quraysh in Abū Ṭālib's house, and a specific formulation of the *shahāda* episode serving as the occasion for the revelation of Qurʾān 38, vv 1–8. All this is placed in the context of Abū Ṭālib's final illness. The presentation of the b material, however, does not fit very well into this context, for it seems ludicrous to suggest that Abū Ṭālib, who had for three years been undergoing with his tribe a boycott by other clans of Quraysh over Muḥammad's religious teachings, should not know what the nature of the Quraysh's complaint against Muḥammad was. Nor does it seem very likely that the Quraysh would have waited until Abū Ṭālib was on his deathbed to bring their complaints before Abū Ṭālib. It seems probable, therefore, that an early account of a meeting between Quraysh and Abū Ṭālib in which the former complained about Muḥammad's activities—an episode that presumably occurred at about the time the Quraysh decided to institute their boycott of B. Hāshim and B. Muṭallib, roughly three years before Abū Ṭālib's death—has been transposed into the context of Abū Ṭālib's death for, perhaps, dramatic effect. Other aspects of the b material—notably Abū Jahl's deliberate effort to block Muḥammad's approach to Abū Ṭālib—also seem to be intended to heighten the dramatic character of the confrontation between Muḥammad and the Quraysh.

The e material, on the other hand, appears less dramatic in intent, being focused rather on providing an explanation for the revelation of Qurʾān 38, vv 1–8. The references to *ʿarab* and *ʿajam*,as well *jizya*, suggest that this material assumed its present form after the early conquest period, perhaps at a time when the legal debate over *jizya* was much in the air, presumably after the middle of the Umayyad period, i.e., around A.D. 700.

9. h—Abū Kurayb—h—Muʿāwiya b. Hishām < Sufyān < Yaḥyā b. ʿUmāra < Saʿīd b. Jubayr < Ibn ʿAbbās (al-Ṭabarī, *Tafsīr* [30 vols.; Būlāq, A.H. 1323–1329]: 23.79 lower).

This account is virtually identical to no. 8.

10. h—Ibn Wakīʿ—h—Yaḥyā b. Saʿīd < Sufyān < al-Aʿmash < Yaḥyā b. ʿUmāra < Saʿīd b. Jubayr < Ibn ʿAbbās (al-Ṭabarī, *Tafsīr* [see no. 9]: 23.79 lower).

Also virtually identical to nos. 8 and 9.

11. h—Abū Kurayb and Ibn Wakīʿ—h—Abū Usāma—h—al-Aʿmash—h—ʿAbbād < Saʿīd b. Jubayr < Ibn ʿAbbās (al-Ṭabarī, *Tafsīr* [see no. 9]: 23.79 middle).

This account resembles in most substantial respects the preceding three (accounts 8–10). In it, however, the chiefs of Quraysh complain to Abū Ṭālib about Muḥammad and ask him to summon the Prophet and to forbid him from cursing the Quraysh's gods. Abū Ṭālib summons Muḥammad, and it is for this reason that he comes to Abū Ṭālib's house. When he arrives, Abū Jahl notices that there is one free seat near Abū Ṭālib, so he sits in it himself to prevent the Prophet from doing so. After Muḥammad tells the assembly that he wants the Quraysh to say the *shahāda*, and that Arabs and non-Arabs will submit by it, the Quraysh chiefs get up in a disturbed state and, shaking the dust from their clothing, say "He has made the gods into one; indeed this is something strange" (a paraphrase of part of Qurʾān 38, vv 1–8). The account ends with the note that Qurʾān 38, vv 1–8 was revealed regarding this occasion.

12. h—Ibn Bashshār—h—ʿAbd al-Raḥmān—h—Sufyān < al-Aʿmash < Yaḥyā b. ʿUmāra < Saʿīd b. Jubayr (al-Ṭabarī, *Tafsīr* [see no. 9]: 23.79–80).

Virtually identical to no. 11, but lacking the notice about the Qurʾānic verses at the end.

13. h—ʿAbdullāh—h—Ubayy—h—Ḥammād b. Usāma—s—al-Aʿmash—h—ʿAbbād b. Jaʿfar < Saʿīd b. Jubayr < Ibn ʿAbbās (Aḥmad b. Ḥanbal, *Musnad* [see no. 6]: 1.362).

Virtually identical to no. 11.

14. q—Ibn Isḥāq—h—al-ʿAbbās b. ʿAbdullāh b. Maʿbad b. al-ʿAbbās < one of his family < Ibn ʿAbbās (Ibn Hishām, *Sīra* [2 vols.; ed. Ferdinand Wüstenfeld; Göttingen: Dieterich, 1858–1860]: 277–78).

ʿUtba and Shayba bb. Rabīʿa, Abū Jahl, Umayya b. Khalaf and Abū Sufyān came to Abū Ṭālib along with other notables of Quraysh, asking him to call Muḥammad so that an agreement could be reached whereby they would leave one another and their religion alone. When Muḥammad arrived, Abū Ṭālib told him that the Quraysh had gathered so that he and they could make mutual assurances (literally, "so they can give to you and take from you"). Muḥammad replied that he would give them one word which, if they say it, will let them rule the Arabs and dominate the non-Arabs. In response to their curiosity, he revealed that the intended words were "There is no God but God," and told them they should repudiate what they worshipped besides God. At this the Quraysh clapped and said, "Do you want to make all the gods into one? That is strange!" and, feeling that their efforts to reach an agreement with the Prophet were fruitless, they left. After their departure, Abū Ṭālib said to Muḥammad, "What you said wasn't so strange." Muḥammad, encouraged by these words to hope that his uncle might embrace Islam, pressed him to say the *shahāda*, telling him he would intercede on his behalf on the day of resurrection. But Abū Ṭālib refused on the grounds that the Quraysh would abuse Muḥammad and others after his death if he did so, that they would mock him, thinking that he had said it only from fear of death, and only to please Muḥammad.

When Abū Ṭālib was near death, the account continues, al-ᶜAbbās saw him moving his lips and went close to listen; then he informed Muḥammad that he had heard Abū Ṭālib saying the *shahāda*. Muḥammad replied that he had not heard it.

The account continues with the remark that Qurʾān 38, vv 1–6 was revealed concerning the people who had come to Muḥammad to reach an agreement with him but rejected the oneness of God. Then, it concludes, Abū Ṭālib died.

More clearly than any of the other accounts, this one is a patchwork of several older accounts. Elements a, b, c, e, and f make up the bulk of the report, but they are not very smoothly combined. The b material, describing the gathering of Quraysh at Abū Ṭālib's house to complain about Muḥammad's preaching, is given with no reference to Abū Ṭālib's death in the material itself, but is followed by other material that takes place in that context. In order to make the two episodes fit more logically together, Ibn Iṣḥāq (d. A.H. 151 / A.D. 768) therefore prefixed the b material with an introduction that placed the Quraysh gathering at the time of Abū Ṭālib's death. That this material was originally separate from the b material is evident from the fact that Ibn Iṣḥāq's introduction is followed by the *isnād* of the b material, clearly marking its original beginning.

The combination of elements b and e in this account resembles that in accounts 8–13, except that in those accounts it is merely stated that a group of Quraysh were present with Abū Ṭālib, whereas here a list of names is provided. It is worth noting that the short list is similar to one provided in an account by al-Wāqidī for a meeting between Abū Ṭālib and the Quraysh said to have taken place earlier in Abū Ṭālib's life.[25] In the present account, however, the name of Abū Sufyān has been added and the names of several other Quraysh leaders dropped. It is possible that this reflects manipulation with polemical intent dating to the Umayyad period.

Peculiar to this account is the juxtaposition of elements c and e; that is, Muḥammad is shown proposing the *shahāda* to both the Quraysh and to Abū Ṭālib. In all other accounts, we find only one or the other, and the presence of both seems to reflect the fact that this account was pieced together from earlier (perhaps already synthetic) traditions. We find, however, an interesting transition between the c and the e material; after the Quraysh declare Muḥammad's idea of one God to be something strange and leave the room, Abū Ṭālib is said to tell Muḥammad that he did not find the idea of one God strange. As noted above, this serves to introduce the c material, since Muḥammad is now encouraged to ask Abū Ṭālib to say the *shahāda*. But it does so in a manner that is very favorable to Abū Ṭālib's image, implying that he accepted inwardly the idea of one God. The fact that the e material given here serves as the background for the revelation of Qurʾān 38, vv. 1–6, which comes at the end of the account, also suggests that the intervening material—element c and the episode in which al-ᶜAbbās hears Abū Ṭālib murmuring the *shahāda*—was inserted in the midst of the e material, and made to fit by constructing the transition described above, which should therefore be considered relatively late.

The episode involving al-ᶜAbbās is a unique element in this account. As it places both Abū Ṭālib and al-ᶜAbbās in a favorable light it is tempting to see in it a vestige of pre-Abbasid polemic, when the B. Hāshim were attempting to establish their claim at the expense of the B. Umayya and the enmity between the Abbasids and the Ṭālibids had not yet arisen. It is more likely, however, that the episode is rather a polemical effort by Shiite apologists to demonstrate that even al-ᶜAbbās himself recognized that Abū Ṭālib had become a Muslim on his deathbed, and to explain why Muḥammad himself did not seem to utter many or any statements to the effect that Abū Ṭālib had converted—for Muḥammad, as the episode would have it, did not hear Abū Ṭālib's words.

This account thus contains numerous bits of evidence to show that it has been built up from earlier, simpler elements, and that in the process much material that was favorable to Abū Ṭālib was introduced. It is interesting that this account was included in Ibn Iṣḥāq's *Sīra* and in Ibn Hishām's recension of it—a book that took shape and was widely circulated in the Abbasid period.

* * *

Reviewing this lengthy examination of the synthetic traditions dealing with Abū Ṭālib's death, we can draw the following general conclusions:

1. One important element in several accounts describes a meeting between Abū Ṭālib and the Quraysh chiefs (referred to as element b in the foregoing analysis). As noted in the discussion of accounts 8 and 14, there is reason to think that this episode originally took place earlier in Abū Ṭālib's life, but that accounts of it were

25 *Ansāb* (Maḥmūdī): 31 (al-Wāqidī). Mentioned there are ᶜUtba and Shayba bb. Rabīᶜa, Ubayy b. Khalaf, Abū Jahl, al-ᶜĀṣ b. Wāʾil, Muṭᶜim and Ṭāᶜima bb. ᶜAdī, Munabbih and Nubayh bb. al-Ḥajjāj, and al-Akhnas b. Shariq al-Thaqafī.

transposed into synthetic accounts dealing with his death. In fact, separate accounts describing such an earlier meeting are extant.[26] The synthetic accounts describing this meeting go back to Ibn ᶜAbbās (d. ca. A.H. 69 / A.D. 688), usually via Saᶜīd b. Jubayr (d. A.H. 95 / A.D. 714), a prominent Qurʾān commentator and historian who was a student of Ibn ᶜAbbās.[27] In the case of account 14, however, the chain of transmission of this material from Ibn ᶜAbbās is different, passing via members of his family; it is hardly surprising, therefore, that the other material in this synthetic tradition is quite different from that in the accounts transmitted by Ibn Jubayr (accounts 8–13). One striking difference is that in account 14, the placement of the meeting in the context of Abū Ṭālib's death is only done by a late transmitter, Ibn Iṣḥāq, and it is clear that the original material deriving from Ibn ᶜAbbās did not mention Abū Ṭālib's deathbed. We can conclude that the synthesis of the deathbed scene and the story of Abū Ṭālib's meeting with Quraysh in accounts 8–13 was probably done by Ibn Jubayr. The separate accounts of Abū Ṭālib's meeting with Quraysh do not have full *isnāds*, so they cannot assist us in this regard.

2. The episode in which Muḥammad proposes the *shahāda* to Quraysh, and they respond with words paraphrasing Qurʾān 38, vv 1–8 (referred to above as e) is closely linked with the meeting between Abū Ṭālib and Quraysh (element b) in accounts 8–14. This suggests that the synthesis of these two elements was already effected by Ibn ᶜAbbās, probably as part of his Qurʾān commentary. On the other hand, the presence in this episode of material that seems to derive from the post-conquest period (see discussion of account 8) requires that we resist dating the episode, in its present form at least, too early. Again, it seems likely that this material was originally separate from the accounts of Abū Ṭālib's death, and later transposed into that context by Ibn Jubayr.

3. The episode in which Muḥammad asks his uncle Abū Ṭālib to state the *shahāda* occurs in two forms (referred to above as c and d). In one (element c), Abū Ṭālib refuses to state the *shahāda* for fear of the scorn of Quraysh; in the other, two prominent members of Quraysh are present and actively dissuade Abū Ṭālib from declaring the *shahāda* (element d). The first variant is transmitted by two completely different chains of authorities, one (account 1) going back via Yazīd b Kaysān and Salmān b. Abī Ḥāzim al-Ashjaᶜī (d. ca. A.H. 100 / A.D. 718) to Abū Hurayra (d. A.H. 58 / A.D. 678), and the other (account 2) via Maᶜmar b. Rāshid (d. A.H. 154 / A.D. 770) and al-Zuhrī (d. A.H. 124 / A.D. 742) to Saᶜīd b. al-Musayyib (d. A.H. 94 / A.D. 713).[28] It is worth noting that, in the former case (account 1), the episode is not placed in the context of Abū Ṭālib's death as it is in account 2. We are probably dealing once again, then, with material that has been transposed into this context by one of its transmitters.

The second variant (element d) is given in accounts 4–7 and is also transmitted via Maᶜmar b. Rāshid, al-Zuhrī, and ultimately Ibn al-Musayyib who is said to have obtained the material from his father.

It is impossible to determine with certainty which of these two variants is earlier or if both may be early. But the fact that the first variant is transmitted by at least two different chains of authorities, whereas the second is transmitted only by one of those two chains, suggests that the first variant may represent old material and the second a modification of that old material—that is, that the first form is the original account. Examination of the *isnāds*, however, forces us in this case to conclude that if we are in fact dealing with a modification or distortion of old material, the distortion must have been effected by *both* al-Wāqidī (d. A.H. 207 / A.D. 823 in Baghdād) and ᶜAbd al-Razzāq b. Ḥammām (d. A.H. 211 / A.D. 827 in the Yemen), which seems unlikely. If the distortion was introduced by an earlier transmitter, he must have passed on both the original and the distorted form of the account, which seems equally unlikely. It is therefore tempting to conclude—however tentatively—that both forms of this episode (that is, elements c and d) represent fairly old material, already in circulation in the early eighth century A.D.

4. It is possible, as noted above in the discussion of account 2, that an early gloss of Qurʾān 6, v 26 involving Abū Ṭālib's exhortation to the B. Hāshim once circulated as a separate body of material, but it has survived only combined with other material in a synthetic account.

5. The glosses to Qurʾān 9, v 113 and Qurʾān 28, v 56, which appear in synthetic traditions combined with other material, also occur independently and probably also represent fairly early accounts.

6. Much of the remaining material found in the various synthetic accounts must be handled with caution. While it is possible that in some cases this material may represent very early accounts that were only transmitted to and synthesized by one particular authority, it seems more likely that such material reflects later elaborations carried out with polemical or dramatic intent.

26 *Ansāb* (Maḥmūdī): 31 (al-Wāqidī); Ibn Hishām, *Sīra* (2 vols.; ed. Ferdinand Wüstenfeld; Göttingen; Dieterich, 1858–1860): 167. The latter is evidently a "dressed up" version, but probably is based in its essentials on simpler old accounts describing a meeting between the two parties.

27 On Ibn ᶜAbbās see Fuat Sezgin, *Geschichte des arabischen Schrifttums* (5 vols.; Leiden: E. J. Brill, 1967–1975): 1.25–28 (Hereinafter *GAS*). On Ibn Jubayr, see *GAS* 1.28–29.

28 On Salmān b. Abī Ḥāzim al-Ashjaᶜī, see *GAS* 1.index; on Abū Hurayra, see *Encyclopaedia of Islam*, 2nd. edition, "Abū Hurayra" (J. Robson). On Maᶜmar b. Rāshid, see *GAS* 1.290–91; on al-Zuhrī, *GAS* 1.280–83; on Saᶜīd b. al-Musayyib, *GAS* 1.276. The episode in which Abū Ṭālib refuses to say the *shahāda* out of fear of the scorn of Quraysh (element c) is also found in account 3 (no *isnād*), and in account 14. In the latter it may not belong to the material conveyed by the opening *isnād*, because it is separated from that material by the word *qāla*, which may indicate that it was originally independent.

REFLECTIONS ON LOVE IN PARADISE

FRANZ ROSENTHAL

There are two reasons for the appearance of the following brief remarks in this volume. One of them is my wish to be present and counted when a good old friend and long-time colleague is honored. The other is my feeling that Islam deserves to be heard in connection with the theme of love and death. Both love and death were fundamental concerns in Muslim intellectual activity. The ideas of Muslim thinkers and littérateurs on these subjects had, of course, changed perceptibly from those current in the ancient Near East as the result of the long history of the assimilation, in the region, of a variety of cultures, with the Hellenistic one being the most prominent and effective among them. Yet, significant echoes of the more remote Near Eastern past continue to be heard in Islam.[1]

"Love" became known in Muslim civilization as the primary and all-encompassing "moving" force. In the spiritual sense as well as the physical one, it provided the "motion" that was considered identical with all worldly existence, animate and inanimate. The experience of love was particularly necessary for human beings. "The heart of one who has never loved" was a hard, inhuman heart,[2] and a person who did not know love was no better than a donkey or a stone.[3] "Death" was the contrary of love. It marked the cessation of motion certain to come speedily to all individuals and to all human endeavor in this world. Love and death were felt by sensitive thinkers to be joined inseparably in the fabric of human life. Their views found expression in the pervasive discussion among poets and philosophers of the true significance of love and, even more importantly, in the speculations of mystics, on the basis of religious experience and philosophical contemplation, about the true significance of death.

Love, if it was true and deep, was considered destined to lead to sickness, insanity, or death. There are various stages of love, the last being most fittingly expressed by the metaphor of "killing" and "being killed."[4] And it was indeed no mere metaphor. The emotional strain of love and, in particular, the voluntary or involuntary denial of love fulfillment caused actual death through a prolonged period of wasting away or an unexpected, sudden collapse. There were those who ridiculed these notions,[5] but they were firmly anchored in the esthetic sensibilities of littérateurs. They became the unconscious attitude toward the meaning of love in many, if not most, individuals.

Death to the world while still in it is the ultimate expression of the mystic's unconditional love of the divine. From the philosopher's command to seek a voluntary death in order to achieve true life to the mystic's spiritual self-annihilation for the sake of ridding himself of the encumbrances of the material world and being ready for the full measure of divine love, it was only a short step but one that shaped the religious complexion of Islam. It could lead to abstruseness provoking self-mockery, as in these verses:

> I have died in my love, being identical with my beloved.
> My heart is distressed because of my separation.

---

1 Recent works on love in European languages are L. A. Giffen, *Theory of Profane Love among the Arabs: The Development of the Genre* (New York and London, 1971), and Joseph N. Bell, *Love Theory in Later Ḥanbalite Islam* (Albany, NY, 1979). The literature on death, especially the theological side of it, has not been studied extensively, but cf. Mohamed Abdesselem, *Le thème de la mort dans la poésie arabe des origines à la fin du III/IXe siècle* (Tunis, 1977).

For Muslim views on Paradise and love and sex in it, see, e.g., Ṣoubḥî El-Ṣaleḥ, *La vie future selon le Coran* (Paris, 1971). A modern interpretation is that of Abdelwahab Bouhdiba, *La sexualité en Islam* (Paris, 1975). See also A. J. Wensinck and C. Pellat, "Ḥûr," *Encyclopaedia of Islam*,[2] and the chapter on Islam by T. Nagel in *Tod und Jenseits im Glauben der Völker* (H.-J. Klimkeit, ed.; Wiesbaden, 1978): 130-144. The *ḥadîth* material is so commonly known and quoted in the sources that no detailed references are as a rule needed here. A thorough study of it in all its variety would be desirable, even if medieval scholars have done a splendid job of collecting it in many books.

2 Cf. an-Nuwayrî, *Nihâyah* (Cairo, 1342ff, undated reprint): VII, 41.

3 Cf. the relevant verses in Ibn Qayyim al-Jawzîyah, *Rawḍat al-muḥibbîn* (A. ʿUbayd, ed.; Cairo, 1375/1956): 176-78.

4 Cf., for instance, the often quoted verse on the three stages of love. Because it contains the rare word *timillâq*, it was also quoted by the lexicographers, see Ibn Manẓûr, *Lisân al-ʿArab, s. rad. m-l-q*.

5 When one of the Banû ʿÂmir was asked about his tribesman Majnûn who was consumed by his love for Laylâ, he said that only weak-hearted Yemenites died of love; see Ibn al-Jawzî, *Dhamm al-hawâ* (Muṣṭafâ ʿAbd-al-Wâḥid and M. al-Ghazzâlî, eds.; Cairo, 1381/1962): 310. Cf. also Abû l-Faraj al-Iṣfahânî, *Kitâb al-Aghânî* (Bûlâq, 1285): I, 147 = *Agh.*[3] I, 369.

> I am removed from myself. Thus, whenever I gather myself
> I am because of my ecstasy in a state of annihilation from myself.
>
> O listener! Do you know what I am saying
> When, indeed, I myself do not know?[6]

But the seriousness and intensity of the mystical identification of love with death were not to be denied. The conviction that the entire universe, material and metaphysical, was united by the force of disembodied love and death of the self was alive in many and accepted as the ultimate wisdom by myriads of Muslims.

The large amount of discussion devoted to these ideas in Muslim literature is an indication of the hold they exercised over vast numbers of the believers. Because of their importance for the understanding of Islam, they have also found much attention in the modern scholarly literature in East and West. Their historical interest is matched by the importance of their inherent character as being fundamental for a better insight into general religious and psychological phenomena; this has added to their attraction for the modern student.

A more specifically Islamic aspect of the interaction of love and death developed as the result of Muslim religious views going back to the beginnings of Islam. It deals with man's fate after death in the realm beyond nature and is, therefore, not directly combinable with common human concerns, although it retains a full complement of sidelights on the human psyche and provides valuable information on the workings of the medieval Muslim mind and social attitudes. Life after death was a crucial dogma for traditional monotheism. It was as important as the belief in one God, perhaps even more so because of its great impact upon moral behavior on earth and the possibility to control it. Everything connected with the other world was an inexhaustible subject of speculation in Islam, elaborated according to the dictates of fancy and repeated over and over again in the literature; the inherited information was cited endlessly, but it was also often modified at will and enriched.

The problems of love and sex in Paradise constituted only a small part of this never-ending discussion. They involved, however, issues that were particularly sensitive for several reasons. First and foremost, there were unusually many Qurʾânic data that had to be taken into consideration. They were supplemented by traditions of the Prophet. At the beginning, these *ḥadîth*s were few in number. The correctness of their attribution to the Prophet can be neither proved nor disproved, but they definitely were ancient as well as generally accepted. Moreover, they were specific and full of details. Another factor was the unresolved relationship between love and sex. The understanding of this difficult problem was complicated by the prevailing, if debated, view of love as a separate, totally spiritual phenomenon. Furthermore, the emotional character of the subject naturally exercised an excessively strong hold on the imagination and came up against the conflict between frankness and prudery, which is present everywhere in Islam, in particular, in the religious attitudes toward sex inculcated in the masses.[7] The overarching fact, of course, was that human knowledge with respect to anything in the hereafter was limited to traditional statements not verifiable by reason or experience and thus open to all kinds of arbitrary assumptions and interpretations. Moreover, religion and society as established by Islam made open expressions of doubt impractical and dangerous.

The many references to Paradisiacal pleasures in the Qurʾân give prominence to beautiful maidens, *al-ḥûr al-ʿîn*, thus called after their attractively colored and shaped eyes. The descriptions of the huris in Paradise are in no way explicitly sexual in the sense that they were said to gratify coarse sexual desires of the blessed in Paradise.[8] The implication of sexuality is, however, unmistakable. Medieval Muslims had no doubt about it, even if it was at times difficult to reconcile them to the inappropriateness of assuming the existence in Paradise of something that was viewed as having the potential of danger for individuals and society. Sex life had its immoral aspects. If an individual indulged in them and remained unrepentant, he could be almost sure of forfeiting Paradise and being condemned to Hell. Naturally, sex does not play any role in the tortures of Hell because, whatever the morality of it, its profoundly pleasurable character was never in doubt. For this same reason, whatever its problematic aspects, it could not be ruled absent from Paradise.

Tradition confirms the sexual appeal of the huris and their willingness to make themselves attractive and pleasing to the blessed. They do so by assuming the ingratiating and submissive attitude that was considered ideal for women in this world in their relationship to the dominating male. Men were rewarded with sexual potency increased beyond mortal human capability to the degree unrestrained imagination would allow. On the other hand, anything considered on earth unpleasant in the physical functions of the human body has no place in Paradise. This includes all bodily excretions. They are

6 Cf. aṣ-Ṣafadî, *al-Ghayth al-musajjam fî sharḥ Lâmîyat al-ʿAjam* (Cairo, 1305): I, 106.

7 Cf. J. A. Bellamy, in *Society and the Sexes in Medieval Islam* (A. L. Marsot, ed.; Malibu, 1979, *Sixth Giorgio Levi Della Vida Biennial Conference*): 34. An editorial footnote in the edition of the *Nihâyah* of Ibn Kathîr, *al-Bidâyah wa-n-nihâyah* (ar-Riyâḍ, 1968): II, 292f., explains that the Prophet's answer to the question whether the people in Paradise would touch their wives was omitted from this edition because it contains coarse language which the Prophet would never have used. Ibn Kathîr is criticized for having mentioned it, see also, II, 286. (Cf. Murtaḍâ az-Zabîdî, *Itḥâf as-sâdah* [Cairo, 1311, undated reprint]: X, 545f.)

8 Cf. El-Ṣaleḥ, *La vie future* (N 1): 64.

non-existent in Paradise. The desire to produce children may be alive among the blessed, but those children are born without the discomforts of pregnancy, and instantaneously as desired. There will be children only if one wants them. Expectedly, the contrary opinion is also represented. No birth will be given to children in Paradise.[9] It may be noted that this discussion appears to consider only the desire of men for children; women were not asked. Incidentally, the position of infants and small children in Paradise was another troublesome question for theologicans who were well aware how important an answer was for sorrowful parents; whatever solutions were suggested, none of them squared with what was considered bliss for the adults who were admitted to Paradise. A concession to popular sentiment is, however, occasionally made. Thus, it was said that Muslim infants who had died before their parents would bring them water to quench their terrible thirst on the Day of Resurrection and enter Paradise with them when they did.[10]

Paradise is pleasure conceived most easily in human terms, but it is also pure spirituality in no way defiled by sensuality. How to combine the contradiction was by and large left unexplained and probably was overlooked by many. Rare thinkers came to the wise conclusion that the situation in Paradise cannot be understood and conveyed in human terms. Like everything concerning the metaphysical realm, the "how" of love and sex in Paradise was an unanswerable question that should not be asked. Things that are desired or feared may not turn out to be as good or as bad as one expects, but with respect to the other world the contrary is the case; everything there is bigger and better than described because of the spirituality attaching to Paradisiacal delights.[11] And it was contended in connection with Qur᾿ân 2:25 that the identity of the attractions of Paradise with those known on earth had merely psychological significance in that human beings like only what is familiar to them and dislike anything unfamiliar.[12] This would seem to be a hint that the reality of Paradise was by no means exhausted by the available descriptions.

Critical thinkers of the lively and daring tenth century felt that the constant and effortless eating, drinking, and cohabiting in Paradise, unaccompanied by the physical and emotional upsets that give spice and variety to these functions in earthly life, would produce boredom and thus be anything but pleasure. It was recognized as a commonplace paradox that man desires what he does not have and is bored with anything that is easily available.[13] Abû Ḥayyân at-Tawḥîdî was bothered by this unhappy consequence of views generally held about Paradise. He was, however, afraid to take the responsibility for giving expression to a thought that ran contrary to popular as well as official belief. Therefore, he chose a rather obscure speculative theologian, "a doubter of all prophecies" as he is characterized elsewhere by the same at-Tawḥîdî,[14] and had him raise the question dramatically: "How remarkable is the situation of people in Paradise! They stay there with nothing to do[15] except eating and drinking and cohabiting. Does this not make them depressed? Are they not bored? Do they not feel dull? Do they not consider themselves superior to such a vile state which is similar to that of dumb animals? Do they not become indignant? Are they not disgusted?" At-Tawḥîdî's reply is given in the name of Abû Sulaymân al-Manṭiqî as-Sijistânî, his revered teacher, whom he often puts forward as spokesman for his own ideas. In this particular case, the appearance of Abû Sulaymân is clearly an added precaution on at-Tawḥîdî's part which enabled him to avoid expressing unorthodox views about the other world as his own. Abû Sulaymân posits the intellect (reason: *al-ʿaql*) as the dominant force controlling life after death in Paradise. The intellect does not know any boredom or malaise. It is never bored with its activity, with the object of its intellection, and feels one with it. This is the way, he states, the intellect behaves in this world. All the more so can the intellect be expected to function in this manner in the other world, its true home, the realm of pure existence. This construction is clearly a spin-off from neo-Platonic philosophy. It was hardly acceptable to religious Muslims as an explanation for something as fundamental as life in Paradise—and, we may add, while it may explain the absence of boredom in the other world, it hardly explains the need for any presence there of eating, drinking, and cohabiting. At-Tawḥîdî adds still another precaution. In a highly apologetic vein, he concludes that the problem is a difficult one, even an impossible one, to solve in human terms.[16] The entire discussion is a good example of the extreme delicacy with which rationalists such as they were had to approach metaphysical problems, especially

9 Cf. Ibn Kathîr, *Nihâyah* (N 7): II, 291ff.; ash-Shaʿrânî, *Mukhtaṣar Tadhkirat al-Qurṭubî* (Cairo-Aleppo, 1395/1975): 136. The *Tadhkirah* itself was not available to me. Cf. also Ibn Taymîyah, *al-Fatâwî al-kubrâ* (Cairo, 1966): II, 209.

10 Cf. Abû Ṭâlib al-Makkî, *Qût al-qulûb* (Cairo, 1310): II, 242.

11 Cf. Ibn Abî l-Ḥadîd, *Sharḥ Nahj al-balâghah* (Beirut, 1963): II, 761.

12 Cf. az-Zamakhsharî, *Kashshâf* (Bûlâq, 1318-19): I, 202.

13 Cf. at-Tawḥîdî and Miskawayh, *al-Hawâmil wa-sh-shawâmil* (A. Amîn and as-Sayyid A. Ṣaqr, eds.; Cairo 1370/1951): 172f.

14 *Kitâb al-Imtâʿ wa-l-mu᾿ânasah* (A. Amîn and A. az-Zayn, eds.; Cairo, 1939-44): I, 141. Attacks on prophecy were identical with the denial of life after death.

15 "They have no work (*ʿamal*)." "Work" is a human being's most important means toward self-fulfillment and salvation.

16 At-Tawḥîdî, *Muqâbasât* (M. T. Ḥusayn, ed.; Baghdâd, 1970): 159-61, no. 35. The passage from at-Tawḥîdî is referred to by El-Ṣaleḥ, *La vie future* (N 1): 133. For the philosophical view of the problem of Paradise, cf., for instance, *Rasâ᾿il Ikhwân aṣ-ṣafâ᾿* (Cairo, 1347/1928): III, 77f.

if, as in this case, they were likely to touch deep emotions.

If pure spirituality, or pure rationality, rules in Paradise, "love," as differentiated from sex, might be expected to be triumphant there, for the ideal of worldly love was depicted as realized only if it was truly spiritual and devoid of contamination by active sexuality. There is, however, little to be found about love in this sense in Paradise. A tradition of the Prophet describes the huris as receiving the blessed who are destined to be their husbands, when they arrive in Paradise, lovingly (*mutaḥabbibât*), but theirs is also an attitude pervaded by sexual sensuality (*mutaʿashshiqât*);[17] they desire (*yashtahîna*) their husbands passionately (*ʿawâshiq*),[18] and it is passionate love (*ʿishq*) that impels them to hurry toward them to welcome them.[19] The Qurʾânic use of a *hapax legomenon* of somewhat doubtful interpretation (*ʿuruban* Qurʾân 56:37/36) is principally responsible for endowing the huris with warm feelings of love, though not of an entirely spiritual kind.

In fact, loneliness, in the form of not needing, or not having, as on earth the support of others in order to be able to function, is seen as playing a large part in life after death. Men will be summoned to the Last Judgement in droves, but then each one of them will be left to answer for himself. Nobody he was familiar with on earth will be there to stand up for him, and comparatively little is said about the various possibilities of intercession that might ease his lot. People will be admitted to Paradise, or driven to Hell, in large groups, but again human contacts as they were common on earth fade into insignificance. Even if indications to the contrary can be found in the traditions[20] and even if there existed a strong undercurrent in favor of seeing in Paradise merely a continuation of conditions on earth, the blessed are pretty much left to themselves, with the company of huris but with little need for emotions such as love. A famous *ḥadîth* says, in a variety of slightly different formulations, that "a man will be with those whom he loves." On occasion, "on the Day of Resurrection" is expressly added to it. Even without the addition, it is clear from the contexts in which the *ḥadîth* is reported that the statement refers to a situation expected to arise on the day of awe. The contexts also make it quite clear that the object of that love is the Prophet and God, and the love mentioned is manifested by the eager performance of the religious duties of Islam. Such love expressed on earth will assure an individual's protection by God and His Prophet in his hour of greatest need. The statement seems, however, also to have been taken by itself to refer to togetherness with a person's loved ones at the Resurrection whenever they were people whom he had loved in God on earth. Each one in the group is nevertheless judged according to his own merit, and it is left unspecified who might be included in the group of loved ones.[21] It could be friends, relatives, or wives. However this may be, the *ḥadîth* is dominated by the idea of religious love, a love in God and for God, which is transferred from earth to Paradise with the individual who had practiced it while he was alive. Paradise is indeed the ideal place for true love in that it opens up the opportunity to love God exclusively in the way every human being should love Him. If people love each other truly, they do so in God, a recurring expression to signify unselfish proper relations between human beings also on earth. But it is, of course, a love very different from the spiritual love of the writers on erotic themes.

The very position of the subject of love in Paradise in the famous Muslim treatises on the theory of love is revealing in this connection. Originally, love in Paradise was of no concern to the writers of those works. The *Dhamm al-hawâ* of Ibn al-Jawzî, for example—even

17 Cf. Ibn Qayyim al-Jawzîyah, *Rawḍah* (N 3): 240, 243.

18 Cf. ʿAbdallâh b. al-Mubârak, *Kitâb az-Zuhd wa-r-raqâ'iq* (Ḥabîb-ar-Raḥmân al-Aʿẓamî, ed.; Nasik, India, no year [1971 ?]): 553.

19 Cf. al-Muḥâsibî, *Kitâb al-Tawahhum* (A. J. Arberry, ed.; Cairo, 1937): 42.

20 According to a tradition, old friends meet sociably in Paradise and reminisce about the good old days on earth when they prayed and obtained God's forgiveness, cf. Murtaḍâ az-Zabîdî, *Itḥâf as-sâdah* (N 7): X, 549.

21 Cf. Ibn Ḥajar's commentary on al-Bukhârî, entitled *Fatḥ al-Bârî* (Cairo, 1378-83/1959-63): XIII, 176-79. According to Ibn Ḥajar, Abû Nuʿaym al-Iṣfahânî appears to have written a monograph on the subject, entitled *Kitâb al-Muḥibbîn maʿ al-maḥbûbîn*. Cf. also ʿAbdallâh b. al-Mubârak, *Kitâb az-Zuhd* (N 18): 360f., and at-Tirmidhî, *al-Jâmiʿ aṣ-ṣaḥîḥ* (with the commentary of Ibn al-ʿArabî, *ʿÂriḍat al-aḥwadhî*) (Cairo, 1350/1931ff.): XIII, 56, IX, 232, and the modern commentary by al-Mahârakfûrî, *Tuḥfat al-aḥwadhî* (Cairo, 1382-84/1963-65): IX, 518; VII, 60f.

ʿAlî will enter Paradise with his entire family and staff, including, of course, his wife, the Prophet's daughter Fâṭimah, cf. Muḥammad b. Abî l-Qâsim aṭ-Ṭabarî, *Bishârat al-Muṣṭafâ li-Shîʿat al-Murtaḍâ* (2nd ed.; an-Najaf, 1383/1963): 159, 173.

In the elegy on a brother of his, Ismâʿîl b. Yasâr, whose life spanned the second half of the seventh and the first half of the eighth centuries, stated that he would not meet him again "till the Day of Resurrection" (lit., "gathering" *ilâ l-ḥashr*), cf. *Kitâb al-Aghânî* (N 5): IIV, 126 = *Agh.*[3] IV, 426. The same idea occurs in the elegy of Isḥâq al-Mawṣilî upon his deceased father, cf. *Agh.* V, 47 = *Agh.*[3] V, 257. However, the expression *ilâ l-ḥashr* was used already in the seventh century in the sense of "for all eternity," as in a poem by Anas b. Zunaym who threatens that he would leave Ḥârithah b. Badr *ilâ l-ḥashr* if he does not give up drinking wine, cf. *Agh.* XXI, 33 = *Agh.*[3] VIII, 406. And in a satirical poem directed against the eighth-century poet Marwân b. Abî Ḥafṣah, meanness is said to be encamped at his house *ilâ l-ḥashr*, cf. *Agh.* IX, 47 = *Agh.*[3] X, 93. Cf. also *Agh.* XVIII, 7 (Abû Nuwâs). Cf., further, al-Qâlî, *Amâlî* (Cairo, 1373): II, 71, line 18. Cf. also, for instance, Ibn Qutaybah, *ʿUyûn* (Cairo, 1963-64, reprint): III, 59, 61; IV, 137.

though it was written long after the early period when secular thought was less intertwined with religious thought than later on—totally disregards love in Paradise. Ibn al-Jawzî's professed purpose in writing his work, which was to argue for the blameworthiness of love and passion, may account for this fact. A man of his outlook would see no blameworthy fault whatever in the religious promise of love and sexual pleasure in the other world. However, his disregard of otherworldly love continued an accepted literary tradition. By contrast, the Ḥanbalite jurist Ibn Qayyim al-Jawzîyah, more than a century and a half after Ibn al-Jawzî, included a section on the subject in his *Rawḍat al-muḥibbîn*.[22] He placed it appropriately after the theoretical discussion of love and before the large section devoted to the description of love which may be harmful if it disregards established laws and which is right and good if it is governed by pious abstinence and asceticism and centers around the love of God. Ibn Qayyim al-Jawzîyah pursues legal and moral aims and views love and sex as matters strictly to be controlled by Muslim religious conventions. Thus, the promise of erotic pleasure in Paradise, as a substitute for failures and shortcomings with respect to love and sex on earth, has its definite place in his work. But it is no longer the tradition of love theory that he continues. Significantly, his argument gives no indication of the existence after death of spiritual love as conceived by secular thinkers.

Passionate worldly love might be described in poetic hyperbole as eternal and only temporarily suspended by death. The poetess Faḍl was greatly in love with the well-known ninth-century poet, Saʿîd b. Ḥumayd. Being very sick, she reproached him with not caring for her and rather wishing she were dead and he were rid of her. Gallantly he reassured her of his love in moving verses:

> May you not die before me, but let us both stay alive!
> I do not want to see the day you die.
>
> Rather let us both live in passion and hope, while God
> Cuts down to size those who spread malicious gossip about us,
>
> Until at last, when the Merciful One decides that we must die
> And we have to face the inescapable,
>
> We shall die together, like two willow branches withered
> After they had been, for a while, fresh and green.
>
> Then let there be peace upon us in our resting places,
> Until we stand before the scales of our Maker.
>
> If we achieve Paradise, it will hold both of us, if such
> Is His will. Or, if He wills, He will throw us into the Fire.
>
> When it burns hot, kisses will cool us both,
> And the coolness of sucking (saliva) will arouse us in pangs of love,
>
> So that at last all those who are there eternally will say:
> Would that we altogether had been lovers![23]

Verses by another poet, Ibn ʿAbdal, addressed to a songstress with whom he was in love referred to the possibility that if he were to see her in the hottest spot of Hell, its fire would seem to him to cool.[24] Beautiful as these verses are, especially those of Saʿîd b. Ḥumayd, they concern the extraordinary and rare passion a particularly sensitive person may have for a lover, but they tell us little about the usual attitudes toward conjugal love.

What happens to ordinary human relations of love and affection that existed on earth once death has done its cruel work of separation? Does Paradise support the idea of an undying love between husband and wife? Does it afford the opportunity to resume broken ties and see one's beloved ones again? This, I believe,is the real test for the existence or non-existence of a meaningful interaction between social life as lived on earth and as envisioned for Paradise.

A very old *ḥadîth*[25]—one that, among other things, also suggests the absence of some bodily excretions in Paradise—speaks of *zawjatân* "two wives" as a portion

22 Above (N 3). Ibn Qayyim al-Jawzîyah also wrote a large monograph on life after death which deals in some detail with sexual pleasure in Paradise, *Ḥâdî al-arwâḥ ilâ bilâd al-afrâḥ*, which has been printed repeatedly. The text used here was printed in Cairo, 1381/1962.

23 Cf. *Agh.* XVII, 7. In our context, the last three verses are the ones that are most important. They are, however, not found in *Agh.* but in aṣ-Ṣafadî, *Wâfî* (B. Radtke, ed.; *Bibliotheca Islamica* 6:15 Wiesbaden, 1979): XV, 214f. This is strange since aṣ-Ṣafadî obviously quotes from *Agh.* Possibly, the text in the old edition of *Agh.*, which is the only one available to me, is defective. Cf. also aṣ-Ṣafadî, *Ghayth* (N 6): II, 93, where reference is made further to verses ascribed to ʿUmar b. Abî Rabîʿah (P. Schwarz, ed.): II, 244.

24 Cf. *Agh.* II, 153 = *Agh.*[3] II, 414.

In a verse by al-Aḥwaṣ, love is spoken of as lasting to the day on which the hearts are tested, cf. his *Dîwân* (ʿÂdil S. Jamâl and Shawqî Ḍayf, eds.; Cairo, 1390/1970): 118. Again in poetry it is stated that eternal love may continue in the grave and beyond the grave until the Day of Resurrection and new life in either Paradise or Hell, cf. Hans Wehr (ed.), *Das Buch der wunderbaren Erzählungen und seltsamen Geschichten* (*Bibliotheca Islamica* 18 [Wiesbaden, 1956]): 259, 264. In both cases the idea expressed is the eternality of love. An eventual reunion and the resumption of earthly bonds are not really considered, though they may be implied.

25 It appears also in the old *Ṣaḥîfah* of Hammâm b. Munabbih (M. Hamidullah, ed.; in *Majallat al-Majmaʿ al-ʿIlmî al-ʿArabî bi-Dimashq*, 1372-3/1953): XXVIII, 445, but its antiquity does not depend on whether the *Ṣaḥîfah* has, or has not, come down to us in its original form.

of the bliss that awaits every man admitted to Paradise. They are of the most dainty beauty, so that "the marrow of their leg(bone)s can be seen through the flesh." The presence of "two wives" would appear to upset the numerical balance between the sexes in Paradise, as was frequently observed by Muslim scholars. Moreover, it contradicted a *ḥadîth* stating that women are very much in the minority in Paradise, and another one, which was even more popular, saying that women are numerically preponderant in Hell because of their likely failure to acquire sufficient religious merit in this world. The surplus of women over men was pronounced one of the signs (*ashrâṭ*) heralding the coming of the Hour, which, however, did not mean anything for the eventual situation in Paradise. If the "two wives" were huris—and the Qur'ân 44:54, 52:20 speaks indeed of "marrying"[26] the blessed in Paradise to huris—, they would not have to conform to ordinary human expectations as to the distribution of the sexes. Counting the huris, there would anyhow be many more females than males in the other world. Whether the "two wives" were human beings or huris was, in fact, widely debated. To a scholar like Ibn Ḥajar, reaching a decision on this point seemed beyond human capability. It was assumed by some that they were human beings. They were considered additional to the number of huris allotted to the blessed. The lengthy "Tradition of the Trumpet" (*ḥadîth aṣ-ṣûr*) speaks of seventy-two huris in addition to two human wives.[27] But the number of huris for each man alternated between the conservative seventy-two and five hundred as the maximum. More extravagant *ḥadîth*s speak of 4,000 virgins and 8,000 no longer virginal women, or of a paltry one hundred virgins, without specifying their terrestrial or Paradisiacal origin. The dual in "two wives" gave rise, furthermore, to attempts to explain it as a figurative allusion to other duals used in connection with the description of Paradise (so that it did not have to be taken literally) or just as an indication of unspecific plurality. Another possibility which seemed to many to contain the germs for a solution of the dilemma was that "two" was intended merely as a minimum figure. Interestingly, the figure of seventy-two huris was also described as being in addition to "(a man's) wives from this world."[28]

The gap existing between wives on earth and huris in Paradise is made clear by the statement that the huris assigned to future inhabitants of Paradise watch and censure their misbehaving wives on earth and tell them that their marriage is only temporary, while they, the huris, will belong to their husbands for eternity.[29] This statement is clearly meant to warn women to be good to their husbands, but its principal lesson would seem to be that wives from this world have no claim to their husbands in Paradise. On the other hand, it may be noted that, in spite of the delightfulness of the huris, we encounter a tradition to the effect that human women are much superior to them because of the religious merit they have a chance of accumulating in life, although, as we have already seen, pessimists were of the opinion that they did not make use of that opportunity in any large numbers. The *ḥadîth* also has a hortatory purpose and was not meant to pass a definite comparative judgement. It may, however, be considered as a hint that there was an occasional awareness, even among the credulous, of the inanity, with respect to human relationships, of the traditional speculations on Paradisiacal love and sex.

The continuity between life in this world and life in the other world was further interrupted by the widely accepted traditional pronouncement that the age during which human life on earth was seen as imperfect, that is, childhood and old age, was not to be perpetuated in Paradise.[30] Old women were not to be found there, according to a practical joke played by the Prophet himself on an old woman who became distressed when he told her that old women were not allowed in Paradise. She was consoled when he explained that she would find herself rejuvenated.[31] Everybody lived in Paradise in youthful beauty and at an unchanging age of thirty or thirty-three years.[32] Moreover, since so much value was placed on virginity, women in Paradise would be virginal and be returned each time after coitus to their virginal state. All this clearly made it difficult to see in Paradise a direct continuation of marital happiness as experienced on earth.

It seems doubtful whether much weight should be attached to the seemingly offhand remark just cited that a man will meet "his wives from this world" in Paradise, but it may, in fact, reflect a suppressed majority sentiment that hoped for the resumption of earthly relations in the

26 *Wa-zawwajnâhum bi-ḥûr ʿîn*. Cf. Ibn Qayyim al-Jawzîyah, *Ḥâdî al-arwâḥ* (N 22): 175. *Zawwaja* is explained as "joining" (*qarannâhum*).

27 The *ḥadîth aṣ-ṣûr* is discussed at length by Ibn Kathîr, *Nihâyah* I, 245ff. According to Ibn Qayyim al-Jawzîyah, *Ḥâdî al-arwâḥ* (N 22): 182, already al-Walîd b. Muslim (d. 195/810) wrote a monograph on it.

28 The preceding information reproduces what Ibn Ḥajar, *Fatḥ* (N 21): VII, 133, has to say on the subject. Cf. also Ibn Qayyim al-Jawzîyah, *Ḥâdî al-arwâḥ* (N 22): 107, 185, etc.

29 Cf. ash-Shaʿrânî, *Mukhtaṣar* (N 9): 136. Cf. also the *ḥadîth* found in Ibn Mâjah and Ibn Ḥanbal (see A. J. Wensinck and others, *Concordance et indices de la tradition musulmane* [Leiden, 1936-69]): II, 116a15: "Whenever a woman harms her husband, his huri wife says, Don't harm him, damn you! He is with you just as a guest and about to leave you soon and come to us."

30 See above (N 10), which, however, does not necessarily contradict this since there was so much vacillation as to what to do with infants in Paradise; the idea of just having them become adults there does not seem to have been entertained, or at least was not common.

31 Cf., for instance, F. Rosenthal, *Humor in Early Islam* (Leiden, 1956): 5f.

32 Cf. Ibn Qayyim al-Jawzîyah, *Ḥâdî al-arwâḥ* (N 22): 131; El-Ṣaleḥ, *La vie future* (N 1): 38.

hereafter. There is a small number of stories telling of the hope expressed for some remembrance of former marital bliss in Paradise. Probably the most famous story of this kind is that of Hind bint Asmâʾ b. Khârijah. Her first husband was ʿUbaydallâh b. Ziyâd b. Abîhi. She was with him on the day he was killed in battle (10 al-Muḥarram 67/6 August 686). She could not bear his loss. One day she expressed her feelings in these words: "I am looking forward to the Day of Resurrection, so that I might see the face of ʿUbaydallâh b. Ziyâd."[33] Soon thereafter, she entered upon a successful marrying career, counting among her husbands Bishr b. Marwān and the governor al-Ḥajjâj. Another version of the same story is in the form of a comparison between her three husbands. Hind is assumed to have said that Bishr b. Marwân was most attentive to women and that al-Ḥajjâj was most respectful, but "I wish that the Resurrection were here now, so that I might see ʿUbaydallâh b. Ziyâd and find comfort in talking to him and looking at him."[34] The first version goes back to the historian al-Madâʾinî who died in the early decades of the ninth century.[35] The story, or at least the remark quoted, may be historical. If it is not, it was certainly current within a century of the time when it is supposed to have originated. It does not exemplify a love that defies the awesome perils of the Judgment.[36] It exemplifies above all the common belief that a woman's love is strongest for her first husband and lover of her youth.

Fully in the realm of fiction is the story of a certain Umm ʿUqbah who had vowed that she would never marry again after the death of her husband Ghassân. She soon realized that "he who is dead is gone (*man mâta fa-qad fâta*)," and remarried. On the wedding night, she saw her late husband in a dream. He reproached her for what she had done, and she was so upset that she committed suicide. While she was still faithful to her vow, she had spoken the verses:

> I shall remember Ghassân, though he is far away,
> And think of him till we meet again when we are resurrected.[37]

Poetry is also involved in the story about a Kûfan named Abû sh-Shaʿthâʾ and the songstress Danânîr who belonged to a friend of his. Abû sh-Shaʿthâʾ confided to her that he was greatly smitten with her. Whether it was merely amorous banter with a man reputed to be chaste and having a sense of humor or a pointed reproach of thoughts of love in an old man, we cannot be sure. At any rate, she told him in verses that he should fast and pray. Then his appointed place after death would be Paradise where she would meet him as a grown youth in his prime endowed with all good qualities.[38] The Day of Resurrection, even the promise of the pleasures offered by the huris,[39] was often considered to be more of a deterrent to worldly passion than a potential boon to lovers. A man very much in love with his wife reflected one night that such passion as he felt was unbecoming and would constitute a burden for him when he approached the Resurrection with it in his heart. He prayed to God to restore his heart to a more becoming state—with the result that his wife soon fell ill and died a few days later.[40]

The Pyramus-and-Thisbe tragedy of errors, which was well known to Muslim writers on love, was also transposed into a religious setting featuring the hope for life after death. A Muslim who had fallen in love with a Christian woman converted to Christianity at the point of death, so as to be guaranteed to meet her in the other world. The woman was also very sick. Not having been informed that her lover had died, she on her part converted to Islam in order to be able to meet her lover in Paradise, and she died right thereafter.[41] A joke in which Paradise plays a role tells of a beautiful wife of an ugly husband. Looking into the mirror, she exclaimed that they both were vouchsafed Paradise, he because he had gratefully supported her, and she because she had patiently endured being married to such an ugly man; after all, Paradise belongs to both the patient and the grateful.[42] Nothing, one can see, is said here about the couple being together again in Paradise in their former marital state. One rather gets the impression that this would be a calamity that could not happen in the glorious hereafter.

---

33 *Kitâb al-Aghânî* XVIII, 129. Cf. ʿUrwah b. Ḥizâm, in al-Qâlî, *Amâlî*: III, 159, line 21.

34 Cf. Ibn Kathîr, *Kitâb al-Bidâyah* (Cairo, 1351-8): VIII, 285.

35 Al-Madâʾinî's treatise on women who were married several times (*murdifât*) is preserved and published, but it deals with the Qurashites among them. His bibliography contains other titles that might have been the source of the *Kitâb al-Aghânî*.

36 As stated by A. Mez, *Die Renaissance des Islâms* (Heidelberg, 1922): 310. Mez says that the story is told "everywhere," but he indicates only the insignificant reference in at-Tîfâshî, *Tuḥfat al-ʿarûs* (Cairo, 1301): 162.

37 Ibn al-Jawzî, *Dhamm al-hawâ* (N 5): 571. Cf. also al-Qâlî, *Amâlî*: III, 202-4.

38 Cf. *Agh.*, XII, 114f. = *Agh.*³, XIII, 345 (where Abû sh-Shaʿthâʾ is described as *ʿafîf mazzâḥ*), and Ibn al-Jawzî, *Dhamm al-hawâ* (N 5): 274f. (where he is called a *shaykh*). From the chain of transmitters indicated in *Agh.*, it would seem that the proximate written source was a work by az-Zubayr b. Bakkâr.

39 For instance, Ibn al-Jawzî, *Dhamm al-hawâ* (N 5): 85: Seeing a young man stealing glances at a passing woman, Dhû n-Nûn al-Miṣrî recited verses to the effect that he should leave alone women made of water and clay and turn his passion toward the huris, that is, he should think about attaining Paradise.

40 Ibn al-Jawzî, *Dhamm al-hawâ* (N 5): 79.

41 Ibn al-Jawzî, *Dhamm al-hawâ* (N 5): 459.

42 Ar-Râghib al-Iṣfahânî, *Muḥâḍarât al-udabâʾ* (Bûlâq, 1286-7): II, 125. The man figuring in the anecdote appears to be the famous Khârijite poet ʿImrân b. Ḥiṭṭân. Cf. an-Nuwayrî, *Ilmâm* (A. S. Atiya, ed.; Hyderabad, 1393/1973): VI, 248.

What these stories have in common is that they are set in the days of old; that they seem to have originated in the early years of Islam and had a long history of transmission; that they do not pay much attention to all the elaborate religious mythology that grew up around Resurrection and Paradise; and that they reflect the fact that women in Islam, especially those of the upper classes, often were married in succession to several, sometimes prominent men.[43] In addition to illustrating the strong affection supposed to be felt by a woman for her first love, Hind's story also contains, it seems, an evaluation of ᶜUbaydallâh as a human being which, positive as it was, may have been welcome to his supporters. But it does not really indicate that she expects, or would wish to expect, to continue marital relations with him in Paradise.

However, the feeling that marital relationships of this world should be continued in the other world has found yet another expression in traditional religious speculation, the setting again being the multiplicity of marriages not uncommon among Muslim women. The *ḥadîth* ponders the problem which of her husbands a woman should join in Paradise. The solution most commonly proferred is that she choose the one with the best character. An alternative suggestion was made to the effect that it would be the one who on earth had been her first husband whose bride she became as a virgin. It was also said that she would belong automatically to the last of her husbands; this served as a warning against remarriage.[44]

These traditions, it may be noted, show some concern for the situation of women in Paradise. They seem to attempt to secure some rights for them there, although this may be more apparent than real. Nearly all the fantasies about Paradise are meant for men. They did not have to make a choice among those of their wives whom they would like to encounter again in Paradise. Perhaps, the *ḥadîth* of the two wives (from earth) should have given rise to speculations on this subject, but to all appearances it did not do so.

The foregoing excerpts from a vast corpus of materials containing Muslims views on love and sex after death permit a few general observations. One must keep in mind, however, that the vagueness of the subject has given rise to unusual fluidity in its treatment, and there was no real agreement among medieval scholars upon many points of detail.

It is not surprising that the interests of women were almost totally disregarded in the traditional picture of Paradise. This is a clear extension of the attitude predominant on earth. Life after death reflects life on earth also in other respects, as is only natural since it was impossible to get away from human experience and human terminology when thinking about Paradise (present-day speculations on extraterrestrial life and the entire literary genre of science fiction are witness to this fact). To intellectuals, it was at times acceptable to profess agnosticism, to admit only that life in Paradise was much better than life in this world but incomprehensible to our imagination and inexpressible in human terms. Ordinary people, like true believers, saw the delights of Paradise in human terms, unaware of the contradictions this tended to lead to. An unconscious desire to hold on to what they were accustomed to and familiar with contributed to this attitude.

Factors inherent in the historical development of Muslim religion and civilization precluded the transfer of some of the refinements of erotic theory to Paradise. The literature on love was essentially divorced from religious beliefs and traditions. It was the creation of literary men and had its roots outside Islam, though not entirely outside pre-Islamic Arabia. Further, love, in the sense of pure friendship, was a standard topic in medieval Islam even beyond the confines of books on love and poetry. It held, however, not much meaning for Paradise where all inhabitants were seen as enjoying self-sufficient bliss—something that Muslims, except for a minority among Ṣûfis, considered unsuitable for human beings.

Conjugal love beyond death was given little consideration. The view of marriage as a contract may have contributed to this attitude; in Paradise, there was no need for business and legal dealings. The peerless Qur'ânic huris were fierce competition for human wives who were as imperfect as everything in this world must needs be by its very nature. Yet, it would seem that the theologians and intellectuals did not reckon with human nature. The hope for a continuation of marital relationships in Paradise may have been much more alive in the majority of people than the written sources lead us to believe. Death was viewed basically as an inevitable end and a radically new beginning. Human love in its fullness reached out to it and succumbed to it, but it constituted an effective barrier to all that was undesirable as well as the little that was desirable in this world. It was seen as leaving only an uncertain chance for the relationships that human beings had enjoyed on earth. Paradise, it must be concluded, was not developed into a helpful model for viewing the role of love and death in human society.

43 For the frequency of remarriage among women in general, cf. S. D. Goitein, *A Mediterranean Society* (Berkeley-Los Angeles-London, 1978): III, 274.

44 Cf. Ibn Qayyim al-Jawzîyah, *Ḥâdî al-arwâḥ* (N 22): 182, and *Rawḍah* (N 3): 240; ash-Shaᶜrânî, *Mukhtaṣar* (N 9): 135.

BIBLIOGRAPHY OF MARVIN H. POPE

Books

El in the Ugaritic Texts. Supplements to Vetus Testamentum II: Leiden: E. J. Brill, 1955.

The Book of Job: A New Translation, with Introduction and Notes. Anchor Bible. Garden City, New York: Doubleday, 1963. Second edition, 1965. Third edition, 1973.

The Song of Songs: A New Translation with Introduction and Commentary. Anchor Bible. Garden City, New York: Doubleday, 1977.

Articles and Abstracts

"A Note on Ugaritic *ndd-ydd*." *JCS* I (1947): 337–341.

"Ugaritic Enclitic *-m*." *JCS* 5 (1951): 123–128.

"Isaiah 34 in Relation to 35, 40–66." *JBL* 81 (1952): 235–243.

"Pleonastic *wāw* before Nouns in Ugaritic and Hebrew." *JAOS* 73 (1953): 95–98.

"The Word *šaḥaṯ* in Job 9:31." *JBL* 83 (1964): 269–278.

"Marginalia to M. Dahood's Ugaritic-Hebrew Philology." *JBL* 85 (1966): 455–466.

"The Goddesses Anat and Kali." *Proceedings of the 26th International Congress of Orientalists, New Delhi* (1968): 51.

"The Saltire of Atargatis Reconsidered." In *Near Eastern Archaeology in the Twentieth Century: Essays in Honor of Nelson Glueck*, edited by J. A. Sanders, 178–196. Garden City, New York: Doubleday, 1970.

"A Mare in the Chariotry of Pharaoh." *BASOR* 200 (1970): 56–61.

"A Description of Baal." *UF* 3 (1971): 117–130 (with J. Tigay).

"The Scene on the Drinking Mug from Ugarit." In *Near Eastern Studies in Honor of William Foxwell Albright*, edited by H. Goedicke, 393–405. Garden City, New York: Doubleday, 1971.

"A Divine Banquet at Ugarit." In *The Use of the Old Testament in the New and Other Essays: Studies in Honor of William F. Stinespring*, edited by J. M. Efrid, 170–203. Durham, North Carolina: Duke University Press, 1972.

"Of Locusts and Locust Eggs." *JBL* 93 (1974): 293.

"Notes on the Rephaim Texts from Ugarit." In *Essays on the Ancient Near East in Memory of Jacob Joel Finkelstein*, edited by M. J. Ellis, 163–182. *Memoirs of the Connecticut Academy of Arts and Sciences* 19, 1977.

"Mid Rock and Scrub. A Ugaritic Parallel to Exodus 7:19." In *Biblical and Near Eastern Studies: Essays in Honor of W. S. Lasor*, edited by Gary Tuttle, 146–150. Grand Rapids, Michigan: Eerdmans, 1978.

"A Little Soul-Searching," *Maarav* 1 (1978): 25–31.

"Ups and Downs in El's Amours," *UF* 11 (Festschrift fur Claude F. A. Schaeffer; 1979): 701–708.

"Le Marziḥ à Ugarit et ailleurs." *Les Annales Archéologiques Arabes Syriennes, Revue d'Archéologie et d'Histoire* 29–30 (1979–80): 141–143.

"Response to Sasson on the Sublime Song." *Maarav* 2 (1980): 207–214.

"An Arabic Cognate for Ugaritic BRLT." *UF* 13 (1981): 305–306.

"The Cult of the Dead at Ugarit." In *Ugarit in Retrospect. Fifty Years of Ugarit and Ugaritic*, edited by Gordon Douglas Young, 159–179. Winona Lake, Indiana: Eisenbraun, 1981.

Introduction and Comments to "Divine Names and Epithets in the Ugaritic Texts," by Alan Cooper. In *Ras Shamra Parallels*, III, 1981: 333–469.

"Millar Burrows 1889–1980. In Memoriam." *Biblical Archaeologist* 4 (1981): 116–121.

"Some Early West Semitic Prayer Formulae." *Tantur Yearbook 1978–79* (date of publication 1981): 89–96.

"The Timing of the Snagging of the Ram, Genesis 22:13." *Biblical Archaeologist* 49 (1986): 114–117.

Articles in Dictionaries and Encyclopedias

H. W. Haussig, ed. *Wörterbuch der Mythologie* I:1. Stuttgart: Ernst Klett, 1965:

'Anat, 235–241

Aqhat Legende, 241–244

Arṣy, 244

Atirat, 246–249

‘Aṯtar, 249–250

‘Aṯtart, 250–252

Baal-Hadad, 253–264

Baal-Zyklus, 264–269 (with W. Rollig)

Dagan, 276–278

Die Dichtung SS, 278–279

El, 279–283

‘Eljon, 283–284

Gapn und Ugar, 284–285

Horon, 288–289 (with W. Rollig)

Ilš, 289

Jamm, 289–291

Jaṭpan, 291

Jw, 291–292

Keret Legende, 292–295

Koṯar, Kotarot, 295–297

Mot, 300–302

Nikkal, 302–303

Nikkal Gedicht, 303

Pidrai, 303–304 (with W. Rollig)

Qdš-w-Amrr, 304

Rephaim-Texte, 304–305

Rešep, 305–306 (with W. Rollig)

Šaḥr und Šalim, 306–307

Šapš, 308–309

Ṭlj, 312

G. A. Buttrick, ed. *The Interpreter's Dictionary of the Bible*. Nashville: Abingdon, 1962; Supplementary Volume, 1976:

Accursed, I:25

‘Am Ha'arez, I:106–107

Congregation, Assembly, I:669–670

Devoted, I:838–839

Excommunication, II:183–185

Fertility Cults, II:265

Godless, II:436

Godly, II:436

Hasidim, II:528–529

Homosexuality, Sup:415–417

Job, Book of, II:911–925

Mot, Sup:607–608

Number, Numbering, Numbers, III:561–567

Oaths, III:575–577

Proselyte, III:921–931

Rainbow, Sup:725–726

Rechab, Rechabites, IV:14–16

Seven, Seventh, Seventy, IV:285–295

Totemism, IV:674–675

Twelve, IV:719

Way, IV:817–818

Encyclopedia Judaica

Adam, II:234–235

Anath, II:925–927

Baal Worship, IV:7–12

Eve, VI:979–980

Book Reviews

The Gilgamesh Epic and the Old Testament Parallels, by A. Heidel. *Journal of Bible and Religion* XVI (1948): 191.

Who Crucified Jesus?, by S. Zeitlin. *Jewish Social Studies* 10 (1948): 400–402.

The Goddess Anath (Hebrew), by U. Cassuto. *JCS* 6 (1952): 133–136.

Marriage and Family Life in Ugaritic Literature, by A. van Selms. *JBL* 74 (1955): 293–294.

The Linguistic and Literary Form of the Book of Ruth, by J. M. Myers. *JBL* 75 (1956): 84–95.

Apocryphal Scrolls Belonging to the Hebrew University, by E. L. Sukenik, *JBL* 75 (1956): 87–88.

La Sainte Bible, traduite en français sous la direction de l'École Biblique de Jerusalem. *JBL* 79 (1960): 172–173.

Old Testament Dissertations, 1928–1958, by M. J. Buss. *JBL* 79 (1960): 195.

Guide to the Bible (revised edition of Robert and Tricot, Initiation Biblique), translated by Edward P. Arbez and Martin R. P. McGuire. *JBL* 80 (1961): 186–187.

How the Hebrew Language Grew, by E. Horowitz. *JBL* 80 (1961): 196–197.

Textus: Annual of the Hebrew University Bible Project, Vol. I, edited by C. Ragin. *JBL* 80 (1961): 197–198.

Sacra Pagina (Miscellanea Biblica Congressus Internationalis de re Biblica). *JBL* 80 (1961): 201–202.

New Directions in Biblical Thought, edited by Martin E. Marty. *JBL* 80 (1961): 206.

Biblical Archaeology, by G. E. Wright. *JBL* 80 (1961): 207.

The Bible and the Ancient Near East, edited by G. E. Wright. *JBL* 80 (1961): 272–275.

Seventh Day Adventist Bible Dictionary, by S. H. Horn. *JBL* 80 (1961): 287–288.

Il Semitico di Nord Ovest, by G. Garbini. *JBL* 80 (1961): 290–291.

Ancient Israel, by R. de Vaux. *The Yale Review* (Summer 1962): 620–622.

Le Palais Royal d'Ugarit II (Mission de Ras Shamra VII), by C. Virolleaud. *American Journal of Archaeology* 65 (1961): 198–199.

Essays on the Dead Sea Scrolls: In Memory of E. L. Sukenik, edited by C. Rabin. *JBL* 81 (1962): 102–103.

Hebrew Union College Annual, Vol. 32 (Morgenstern Jubilee Volume). *JBL* 81 (1962): 194–197.

maqqél shâqédh: Hommage à Wilhelm Vischer. JBL 81 (1962): 213.

Die Texte vom Toten Meer, by Johann Maier. *JBL* 81 (1962): 214.

Adam to Daniel: An Illustrated Guide to the Bible and Its Background, edited by G. Cornfeld. *JBL* 81 (1962): 319–320.

An Introductory Hebrew Grammar, by A. B. Davidson. Revised by J. Mauchline. *JBL* 81 (1962): 434–435.

Linguistica Semitica: Presente e Futuro, by G. Levi Della Vida. *JBL* 81 (1962): 436–437.

Grammar of Palestinian Jewish Aramaic, by W. B. Stevenson. *JBL* 81 (1962): 438.

Our Living Bible, by M. Avi-Yonah and E. G. Kraeling. *International Journal of Religious Education* (October 1963): 47.

Studies and Essays in Honor of Abraham A. Neumann, edited by Meir Ben Horin, Bernard D. Weinryb, and Solomon Zeitlin. *JBL* 82 (1963): 142–143.

Aramäische Chrestomathie, by J. J. Koopmans. *JBL* 82 (1963): 143.

Mythologies of the Ancient World, edited by S. N. Kramer. *JBL* 82 (1963): 226–227.

The New Bible Dictionary, edited by J. D. Douglas. *JBL* 82 (1963): 243.

In the Time of Harvest: Essays in Honor of Abba Hillel Silver, edited by D. J. Silver. *JBL* 82 (1963): 326–328.

Hebrew Union College Annual, Vol. 33, edited by Elias L. Epstein. *JBL* 82 (1963): 355–356.

The Scroll of the War of the Sons of Light Against the Sons of Darkness, edited by Yigael Yadin. *JBL* 82 (1963): 359–360.

The Documentary Hypothesis, by U. Cassuto. *JBL* 82 (1963): 360.

Aramaic Bible Versions: Comprehensive Selections and Glossary, edited by M. H. Goshen-Gottstein. *JBL* 82 (1963): 360–361.

A Commentary on the Book of Genesis I, from Adam to Noah, by U. Cassuto. *JBL* 82 (1963): 365.

The Ras Shamra Discoveries and the Old Testament, by Arvid S. Kapelrud. *JBL* 83 (1964): 33.

Einleitung in das Alte Testament, by Otto Eissfeldt. 3rd ed. *JBL* 83 (1964): 44.

Before the Bible: The Common Background of Greek and Hebrew Civilizations, by Cyrus H. Gordon. *JBL* 83 (1964): 72–76.

The Work of Père Lagrange, by Père F. M. Braun, O.P. Translated by Richard T. A. Murphy. *JBL* 83 (1964): 97–98.

Men of God: Studies in Old Testament History and Prophecy, by H. H. Rowley. *JBL* 83 (1964): 225.

The Art of Warfare in Biblical Lands in the Light of Archaeological Study, by Yigael Yadin. Translated by M. Perlmann. *JBL* 83 (1964): 226.

Hebrew and Semitic Studies, Presented to Godfrey Rolles Driver, edited by D. Winton Thomas and W. D. Hardy. *JBL* 83 (1964): 313–315.

Hebrew Union College Annual, Vol. 34, edited by Elias L. Epstein. *JBL* 83 (1964): 328–329.

Promise and Fulfillment: Essays Presented to Professor S. H. Hooke in Celebration of His Ninetieth Birthday, edited by F. F. Bruce. *JBL* 83 (1964): 334.

From Moses to Qumran, by H. H. Rowley. *JBL* 83 (1964): 337–338.

The Seed of Wisdom: Essays in Honor of T. J. Meek, edited by W. S. McCullough. *JBL* 83 (1964): 444–445.

Ras Shamra and the Bible, by C. F. Pfeiffer. *Interpretation* 19 (1965): 74–75.

History, Archaeology, and Christian Humanism, by W. F. Albright. *JBL* 84 (1965): 180–181.

The Legacy of Canaan, by J. Gray. *JSS* 11 (1966): 228–241.

Oriental and Biblical Studies, Collected Writings of E. A. Speiser, edited by J. J. Finkelstein and M. Greenberg. *JBL* 87 (1968): 477.

Studies in Divine Kingship in the Ancient Near East, by Ivan Engnell. *JBL* 87 (1968): 486–487.

Archives from Elephantine, by Bezalel Porten. *JBL* 89 (1970): 92–94.

Die Religion Altsyriens, Altarabiens und der Mandäer, by Harmut Gese, M. Höfner, and Kurt Rudolph. *UF* 3 (1971): 375–376.

Northwest Semitic Grammar and Job, by A. C. M. Blommerde. *Biblica* 52 (1971): 146–151.

Biblischer Kommentar-Altes Testament XVI/I *Hiob* 1.Teilband (Hiob 1-19), by Friedrich Horst. *JBL* 90 (1971): 222–223.

A Matter of Life and Death, by B. Margalit. *UF* 13 (1981): 316–321.

Rank Among the Canaanite Gods, by Conrad L'Heureux. *BASOR* 251 (1983): 67–79.